Hopi Ruin Legends

Kiqötutuwutsi

Hopi Ruin Legends
Kiqötutuwutsi

Narrated by Michael Lomatuway'ma,

Lorena Lomatuway'ma,

and Sidney Namingha, Jr.

Collected, translated,

and edited by

Ekkehart Malotki

Published for Northern Arizona University
by the University of Nebraska Press, Lincoln and London

© 1993 by Northern Arizona University
Manufactured in the United States of America

The paper in this book meets the minimum requirements of American
National Standard for Information Sciences—Permanence of Paper for
Printed Library Materials, ANSI Z39.48–1984.

#27430034
Library of Congress Cataloging-in-Publication Data
Lomatuway'ma, Michael.
Hopi ruin legends / by Michael Lomatuway'ma, Lorena Lomatuway'ma, and
Sidney Namingha; edited by Ekkehart Malotki; foreword by Ivan Sidney.
p. cm.
Includes bibliographical references.
ISBN 0-8032-2905-4 (cloth: alk. paper)
1. Hopi Indians—Legends. 2. Hopi Indians—Antiquities. I. Lomatu-
way'ma, Lorena, 1933–   . II. Namingha, Sidney, 1935–1983. III. Malotki,
Ekkehart. IV. Title.
E99.H7L65 1993
398.2'089974—dc20
93–358 CIP

Contents

Foreword

As a Hopi, I firmly believe that our oral history should be recorded for the benefit of today's young people, as well as for those of future generations. Further, it is my conviction that cultural traditions can only be accurately passed on in the language of those from whom they are received. Sadly, this is frequently not the case.

Fortunately, however, this *is* the case with Dr. Ekkehart Malotki, whom I have known for several years. An expert in the Hopi language, he has devoted virtually the past 20 years of his life to gathering Hopi stories in the vernacular, in the sincere belief that they should be preserved for the future. These stories, recorded directly from Hopi storytellers, in the Hopi language, and frequently published in bilingual Hopi/English form, as is this collection, are therefore not only given back to the Hopis for their own use, but are also made accessible to scholarly and general readers alike in the world at large. I am happy, therefore, to recommend this collection of ruin legends compiled by Dr. Malotki.

Ivan Sidney

Special Assistant for Native
American Programs
Office of the President
Northern Arizona University

Hopi Tribal Chairman 1981-1989

Preface

Myths, legends, tales, and other kinds of oral narratives are a significant part of the vast expanse of expressive folk culture. Summarily referred to as oral literature, they must be regarded as true examples of "verbal art" (Bascom 1955). Unfortunately, the performance of this verbal art has experienced a dramatic decline. Worldwide, whole bodies of oral literature are vanishing into oblivion.

One of the bitter ironies of Western culture is that it began to appreciate the special qualities of oral literature at the very time when such orality was beginning to vanish. Persons who spoke only European languages were either oblivious about other languages or made it a policy to suppress them, thereby eradicating rich and ancient cultural traditions. Few cultures have been able to resist this onslaught.

This deplorable development also holds for the Hopi Indians of Northern Arizona. As Terrance Honventewa observed in 1984 at the Third Annual Hopi Mental Health Conference, "Today, that precious and expressive language is in danger of extinction ... Many contemporary tribal members speak little or no Hopi at all. Therefore much of the folklore, religion and other cultural treasures are already being lost."[1] Along the same vein, Emory Sekaquaptewa reports[2] that in an informal survey of high school students conducted by the Hopi Health Department in 1986, when the new Hopi High School was opened at First Mesa, 85 percent of respondents claimed to be unable to speak or understand Hopi.

With the disuse of the Hopi language, functional storytelling, which requires a narrator and an audience in a face-to-face encounter, suffered equally and is nearly extinct in Hopi society.

All the ruin legends presented in this volume were collected from what I call "story rememberers." They differ from the large body of Hopi oral literature in that they revolve around some actual historic event. Overall more fictitious than factual, the legends provide explanations for the demise of villages that now lie in ruin. In spite of their mythic trimmings, which do not make them "history" in the modern sense of the word, these destruction legends are culturally important. In the absence of authentic historical records they shed light not only on the Hopi past, but also on the Hopi psyche. For this reason, Courlander considers them more significant than scientific findings. "Apart from the excavations and conclusions of anthropologists, the oral tradition ... is a more revealing instrument in some ways than the archaeologist's shovel. For out of the oral tradition, we get insights about values and motivations that are not visible in potsherds" (1971: 15).

Due to the mixture of mythic, legendary, and historic events that distinguish the narratives of this collection, I will classify them as "mytho-historical" in nature. The qualifier mytho- is not intended to designate these legends as sacred or venerable. Nor is it supposed to conjure up such associations as "false" or "fantastic." It is chosen with the sole purpose of reminding the reader that the historical accounts compiled here are distinctly laden with actors and agents from preliterate Hopi mythology, all of whom are endowed with greater-than-human faculties: gods and goddesses, culture heroes and evil sorcerers, terrifying spirits, animals capable of speech, and others.

To Hopi audiences, the events portrayed in these narratives once constituted true, factual history, regardless of whether they were perceived as rational-possible or irrational-impossible. They served the Hopis to reinforce the bonds of ethnic and cultural identity and to create a sense of continuity. Vecsey has factored out some of the most salient functions that pertain to the role of mythology in society and individual life. His perceptive observations also apply to the mytho-historical narratives presented here. According to him, they "tend to anchor the present generations in a meaningful, significant past, functioning as eternal and ideal models for human behavior and goals. They can teach moral lessons to children and adults alike, communicating cultural messages and representing the community's philosophical positions to its own members through a revered vehicle of tradition." They "can bind a community in a knot of belief and common consciousness, glorifying ancestors and heroes of the recent and distant past, imaginary and historical, who can serve as paradigms for conduct. They can authorize institutions or call for their alteration, marking off a culture as an accepted way of life. They can contemplate unsatisfactory compromises in social life, provide safe outlets for deviant desires, and serve as ideological weapons by one portion of the population against another" (1988: 24).

In the light of the above observations this book constitutes what might be called an "oral history primer." The following ancient villages, each briefly characterized by its unique historical fate, are contained in the primer: 1. Sikyatki: Destroyed by Hopis from Qöö-tsaptuvela at the request of its own village chief to terminate intra-village animosities resulting from an unjustified life-and-death race demanded by the sorcerer faction in the community. 2. Hisatsongoo-pavi: Destroyed by an earthquake triggered by the Water Serpent gods residing in the local village spring when implored to flatten the land for greater planting convenience. 3. Pivanhonkyapi: Destroyed by fire at the request of the village chief to cleanse the community of its evil ways brought on by a gambling craze. 4. Huk'ovi: Abandoned due to an act of sorcery perpetrated by a Hopi girl against neighboring Pivanhonkyapi. 5. Qa'ötaqtipu: Destroyed when a fire, initiated by its chief to avenge a crime committed by neighboring Matsonpi, consumes Qa'ötaqtipu instead. 6. Hovi'itstuyqa: Destroyed by enemy raiders when persuaded to do so by a man from Tupats'ovi who loses his wife through adultery committed by a man from Hovi'itstuyqa. 7. Awat'ovi: Destroyed in 1700 by a contingent of Hopi warriors from Oraibi, Mishongnovi, and Walpi at the request of its leader when Awat'ovi's residents, twenty years after the Pueblo Revolt of 1680, readmit Spanish missionaries, thereby creating a state of *koyaanisqatsi,* or "social chaos," among the town's population.

For reasons of linguistic preservation as well as cultural authenticity and sensitivity, the seven narratives, which were recorded in the Hopi vernacular, are presented bilingually. They constitute original, unexpurgated Hopi source materials published here for the first time. They owe their existence to the remarkable memory of several story rememberers of Third and Second Mesa who were sincerely committed to seeing this portion of their cultural heritage preserved for posterity. Concerned about the accelerating loss of their native language and culture, they also volunteered the ethnographic information contained in the introductory chapters accompanying the tales. These introductory chapters provide general background information, analytic comments, and other pertinent observations designed to complement the reading of the legendary accounts. They are not, however, exhaustive interpretations of the legends. In addition to the extensive treatment of the topics of *powaqa,* "witchcraft," *koyaanisqatsi,* "social chaos," and *Paalölöqangw,* the "Water Serpent," in three of these chapters, further insights can be gleaned from the bilingual Glossary.

Unfortunately, three of the four contributors to this book are already deceased. My greatest gratitude belongs to the late Michael Lomatuway'ma, my friend and research assistant of many years. In the early and mid-eighties, when I amassed the bulk of my Hopi oral literature corpus, he contributed extensively to this work. While, initially, I transcribed all of the field recordings, Michael, during the time when he was employed at Northern Arizona University, became so skilled in writing his native language that he frequently wrote the stories directly on the computer. Four of the seven legends preserved in this book are his. They relate to the end of Huk'ovi, Pivanhonkya-pi, Sikyatki, and Awat'ovi.

Spontaneous storytelling recorded in the field inevitably contains "flaws" such as repetitions, omissions, unfinished sentences, and grammatical inconsistencies. To make the stories more readable, Michael edited the Hopi texts of the seven legends. He aligned episodes recalled by the narrator after completing the story. He replaced occasional lapses into English by the storyteller with the corresponding Hopi words. On occasion, he also inserted story details familiar to him which had been omitted by the storyteller. "The End of Hovi'its-tuyqa," originally told in the Second Mesa dialect of Shungopavi, was adjusted by him in all phonological, morphological, and lexical aspects to the Third Mesa dialect, to make it conform linguistically to the idiom of all the other Hopi text materials contained in this book. Expertly versed in his native language and culture, Michael undertook all of these editorial tasks with great ease.

The English renderings of the legends as well as of the ethnographic passages in the introductory sections are all mine. They attempt to capture a middle course between too close and too free a translation. Michael's wife, Lorena Lomatuway'ma, was of great help during the lengthy translation process undertaken several years after Michael's untimely death in 1987. I consulted her in all instances where I had translation difficulties. But for any errors or other shortcomings in the final English versions I alone am accountable.

Lorena, initiate of the Maraw society at Hotevilla, also told "The Downfall of Qa'ötaqtipu." In addition, many of the ethnographic details in the introductory segments and the Glossary are hers. Both her sweeping command of her native language as well as her intimate knowledge of Hopi culture eminently qualified her to assist me in preparing this volume. These qualifications, meanwhile, have also made her one of the most valuable contributors to the comprehensive Hopi Dictionary Project, on which I have been working with my colleague Emory Sekaquaptewa and others at the University of Arizona since 1986. Her enthusiastic sharing of linguistic and cultural insights to this book is acknowledged with great gratitude.

I am equally indebted to her late brother Sidney Namingha, Jr., who remembered the fate of Hisatsongoopavi, or "Ancient Shungo-pavi." He was greatly respected as a song poet, both in his native Hotevilla and in Shungopavi, where he was married, and it was his recollection of the song sung by Pavayoykyasi also which was incorporated into the "The Destruction of Awat'ovi."

The events leading up to the demise of Hovi'itstuyqa, finally, were narrated by a man from Second Mesa, who preferred to have his name withheld. He was endowed with a near-encyclopedic familiarity with Hopi culture, and his death was a great loss not only for Hopi scholarship but for the Hopi community at large.

The book owes its existence to a number of people. For unfailing encouragement and moral support to complete the lengthy manuscript and pursue its publication my foremost thanks must go to Eugene M. Hughes, president of Northern Arizona University, and Henry Hooper, associate vice-president for Academic Affairs, Research and Graduate Studies. Karl Webb, dean of the College of Arts and Science, Nicholas Meyerhofer, chair of the Department of Modern Languages, Ronald W. Langacker, professor of linguistics at the University of California, San Diego, and Kenneth C. Hill, editor-in-chief and dir   ʿ ʿ ʿ Hopi Dictionary Project at the University of Arizona, wer   ndorsement of the manuscript. The latter als   of one of the Hopi possessive suffixes as -'ı   been my practice in my earlier publications   the special assistant for Native American Pr   esident, also strongly advocated publication   of preserving both cultural heritage and th   ne of them deserves my sincere gratitude.

As alw   greatly profited from the writing skills of my   Diego. He provided an editorial facelift for   aluable editing suggestions were also thankfully accepted   fani Salkeld of San Diego for the English story versions and from Charles O. Rand and Claudette Piper for the introductory materials to the legends.

Finally, for the preparation of the camera-ready typescript, I need to thank Louella Holter, associate editor at the NAU Ralph M. Bilby Research Center. Her care and skill in completing this task was most impressive. The professional assistance of Robyn O'Reilly and Dan Boone with the graphic designs was equally appreciated.

E.M.

Endnotes

1. *Report of the 3rd Annual Hopi Mental Health Conference. "Prophecy in Motion."* Kykotsmovi: Hopi Health Department, pp. 67 and 68.
2. Personal communication, August 1991.

Hisatsongoopavi: Devastation by Earthquake

This is the first published account of the legendary demise of Hisat-songoopavi, or "Old Shungopavi."[1] Originally, the village was simply named Songoopavi, "Sand grass spring place," after the adjacent spring, Songoopa. By attaching the epithet *hisat*, "old, ancient," to the placename, the narrator merely points to the fact that the ancestral village site on the eastern foothills of the mesa is not identical with the location of the present-day village of Shungopavi on top of one of the spurs of Second Mesa. Modern Shungopavi is one of the most populous Hopi communities and remains a stronghold of Hopi culture. No other Hopi village can boast an annual ceremonial cycle more intact. No other Hopi village replenishes its religious societies by inducting new initiates to the same degree.[2]

Historical as well as archaeological evidence indicates that the residents of Hisatsongoopavi moved to the top of the mesa in the late 17th century. Following the Pueblo Revolt of 1680 against the Spanish yoke, during which the people of Shungopavi razed the mission San Bartolomé and killed its resident priest Fray José de Trujillo, "the Pueblos began to quarrel among themselves. The Apaches and other semi-nomads, noting the Pueblo dissensions and withdrawal of Spanish arms, spread fresh devastation over the land. No wonder then that the people of [Old] Shungopavi soon abandoned their mission village and built the one they occupy today high up on the mesa edge" (Holterman 1955: 35). Potsherds retrieved from the middens adjacent to the ancient mission are archaeological proof that during the period between 1629 and 1680, Old Shungopavi was clustered around the mission (Hargrave 1930: 2).

While many of the Hopi potsherds from this time show distinct Spanish influence, others represent genuine Spanish Majolica ware. Among the sherds identified by Montgomery as foreign imports, "one came from Valencia, four from Puebla, and two from China" (Holterman 1955: 33).

From a study of sherds and other archaeological remains collected in the foothills of Second Mesa, Hargrave posits the existence of two additional Old Shungopavis prior to 17th-century Mission Shungopavi: 13th and 14th-century Shungopavi and 15th and 16th-century Shungopavi (1930: 3). He determines that the original habitation site was established "before 1250 A.D. and occupied until the early part of the 15th century," when the natives relocated closer to the spring Songoopa (1930: 1). They were residing here when the Spanish arrived in Tusayan, the Spanish appellation for Hopiland. Whether Pedro de Tovar, who commanded a Spanish contingent from the Coronado Expedition at Zuni, also visited Shungopavi after reaching Awat'ovi in 1540, is not recorded. The first documented Spanish sojourn at the pueblo took place on April 22 and 23, 1583, when the party of Antonio de Espejo arrived (Hammond and Rey 1929: 101).

In 1896, when Fewkes attempted a first archaeological exploration of the ruins of Old Shungopavi, the remaining walls of the mission served as a sheep corral. After Fewkes excavated the extensive graveyards for two days, Nacihiptewa [Nasiheptiwa], the Shungopavi village leader, entreated him to halt the digging "on the ground that such work would blow away rain clouds and thus deprive them of rain for their farms. He likewise stated that disturbing the graves would incense Masauuh [Maasaw], the god of death, and kill the little children" (1896: 536). Fewkes yielded to the request and abandoned the project, convinced that "the necropolis of Old Cuñopavi [was] one of the richest in scientific treasures in Tusayan, and [would] some day yield to the student a wealth of material destined to throw a flood of light on Tusayan cults and customs in prehistoric and early historic times" (1896: 536). The artifacts removed during the two-day dig are housed today in the Field Columbian Museum in Chicago.

The mythic narrative recorded here features the deific *Paalölö-qangwt*, or "Water Serpents," as the agents responsible for the ruin of Old Shungopavi. Endowed with supernatural powers, they are represented as anthropomorphized beast-gods who freely communicate with the village people. The legend thus contains elements typically associated with prehuman mythical times when all living beings, including the gods, freely intermingled.[3] Luckert has coined the term "prehuman flux" for this state of affairs (1975: 133). As powerful controllers of *paahu*, i.e., all contained bodies of water such as springs, pools, lakes, rivers, and the oceans, the Water Serpents are dreaded as well as revered by the Hopis, as is evident from the following folk-statement.

Text 1

Paalölöqangw pi pay paangaqw ki'ytangwuniiqe oovi paniqw pan maatsiwa. Pam yaw kuuyit nanayö'ngwu. Oovi haqam paatingwu. Oovi kuuyi Paalölö-qangwuy naayö'i'at. Noq i' Hopi pay put hiita as mamqaskyangw pu' pay piw put kyaptsi'yta. Pay piw Paalölöqangwt paayupa ki'yyungwa, pu' piw patuphava.

The Water Serpent is so named because he lives in springs. He vomits up the water. As a result of this action a spring forms. So the water is the Serpent's vomit. This creature is both feared and respected by the Hopi. The Serpents are also at home in rivers and lakes.

While likened in his appearance to the rattlesnake, the mighty Serpent has no analogue in the real world. Portrayed with bulging eyes, dentate mouth, a cephalic projection, and greenish skin, the god is cast as a monster reminiscent of the dragon in the lore of European sagas and fairy tales.

Text 2

I' Paalölöqangw it paatuwaqatsit himu'yta. Pam pay as it tsuu'at ankyangw pam pas hoskyanii-kyangw pay hihin mokingpu. Pu' pam qötö'ykyangw pu' piw posvölö'ykyangw pu' a'ni tama'yta. Pu' pam suukoopaveq aala'ytaqw pam aakwayngya-voqwat ngölöwta. Pankyangw pu' pam imuy Tsuutsu'tuy amuntaqat nakwa'ykyangw pu' piw aakwayngyavoq kwasrut pootakni'yta. Pankyangw pu' pam pay pas sotsavatsa ngönta.

The Water Serpent is the master of the oceans. He is similar to a rattlesnake but is of gigantic pro-portions and greenish hue. His head is round with protruding eyes, and his mouth is studded with teeth. On top of his head he sports a horn which is bent back-wards. In addition, his head is crested with a bunch of ocher-stained feathers, similar to those worn by members of the Snake society, and a fan of eagle tail feathers. Around his neck hangs a necklace made entirely of sea shells.

This combination of different attributes from various animals (mammalian horn, avian feathers, reptilian body) makes for a hybrid, composite creature, thereby emphasizing the greater-than-human powers of the Serpent deity. Overall, the deity represents one of the most powerful embodiments of fertility and fecundity in Hopi reli-gious imagery. The vegetal fertility association of wells, the abode of the god, is obvious. Furthermore, the horn as an excrescence from the god's head is a widely-diffused symbol of male sexual potency.[4] Finally, there is the phallic icon of the snake itself as a potent emblem of genital energy which fertilizes fields in the form of rain and thus produces life-sustaining crops.[5]

Curiously enough, it is the monster's furry skin which, in the eyes of the Hopi, gives the god the rather innocent-looking appearance of a cat.

Text 3

Pay pi pangqaqwangwuniqw pay yaw pam Paalölöqangw it moosat pas su'an soniwngwu.

They say the Water Serpent looks exactly like a cat. Just like a cat he has ears and whiskers. In

Pan it moosat an naqvu'y-
kyangw pu' piw pay an sowits-
mi'ytangwu. Pu' pam kya pi piw
moosat an pöhö'ytangwu. Noq
pu' ima put tuwa'ynumyaqam
pangqaqwangwuniqw yaw pam
sikyangpuwa pepeq Hotvelpeq
qatuqw oovi yaw pam sikyamo-
sa pepeq qatungwu.

addition, he has wooly fur like a
cat. Those who have seen a
Water Serpent claim that a yellow Serpent lives in Hotevilla.
For this reason yellow cats are at
home there.

The Hopi belief that all springs are inhabited by Water Serpents,
that is, receive their life-sustaining flow from the presence of the god
Paalölöqangw, has two implications. First, new springs can be created
by burying in the ground a *paa'u'uypi*, or "water planting instrument," containing a Paalölöqangw specimen. An instance of such an
act of spring generation occurs in the present tale when the shaman
from Walpi removes one of the Serpents from Songoopa Well and
transfers it to a new location near his home village. Conversely,
withdrawal of the animal from its abode leads to the extinction of the
spring. This belief is confirmed in the following anecdote which
describes the theft of a Paalölöqangw and the ensuing consequences.

Text 4

Orayvit hisat pay as kya pi
paahu'yyungwa, nönganvat,
Orayviy tatkyaqöyve, tutskwave,
Masqötvasvehaqam. Pu' pay kya
pi hisat hak Songoopangaqw
taaqa navotqe pu' pay awniiqe
pu' put paahut heeva. Niiqe pu'
pay tuwaaqe pu' wikoro'y-
kyangw awi'. Niiqe pu' pangqw
pam put Paalölöqangwhoyat
wikoroy aqw panat pu' naalös
angqw aqw kuuya. Pantit pu'
pam pangqw put yawmakyangw
pu' pam Songoopave put
kwiipa, atkyave. Tutskwave
hangwat pu' aqw put wikorot
pana. Pu' aapiy pantaqw pu' kya

Long ago, the Oraibi people had
a spring. I guess, a flowing
spring. It was down on the plain
on the southeastern flank of the
mesa at a place called Masqötvasa. One day, a man from Shungopavi found out about the
spring and went to the place in
search of it. He had a canteen
with him when he found it.
Upon placing a little Water Serpent into the vessel, he scooped
water into it four times. Thereupon, he took it home and transplanted it to a location below the
[present] village of Shungopavi.
After digging a hole in the earth,

pi pay pam aw popta. Noq pu' pay ep palmok'iwta. Pu' pam ep tsöqavötoyna. Pu' pay ep paati. Niiqe pu' pam pan put tungwa, Songoopavi. Paapiy pu' puma tuwat put paahu'yyungwa, Songoopavit.

Pu' aapiy pay pantaqw lööq yaasangwuy aw pay yaw pep Masqötvasve paahu tööqö. Pu' yaw pep Songoopave taaqa tuutuyti. Niiqe pay pam paahut ööyiwta kya pi. Niiqe pam yaw wukovoyniwtaqe pavan yaw pam wukovono'yta. Pu' aapiy pay tuutuykyangw mokhaykyaltiqe pu' yaw pam paas mowati. Pu' put poosi'at yaw piw angqw yamakto. Pu' yaw sikwi'at, toko'at Paalölöqangwuy puukyayat an sonilti. Pay kya pi Paalölöqangwuy pam na'pala. Yan pam yaw son pi qa sisvit pu' mooki.

he put the canteen inside. From that day on, he went there to check on it. Soon the area was saturated with moisture. So the man built a dike, behind which the water collected. He named the spring Songoopa, and from that time on the villagers of [Old] Shungopavi drew their water from it.

Two years later, the water hole at Masqötvasa dried up. And now the Shungopavi man fell ill. I guess he was full with the water from the spring, for he was all bloated up and had a big belly. By the time he was near his death, his entire body was wet with moisture. Now his eyes started bulging out and the flesh of his body took on the appearance of the Serpent's skin. I suppose the man had contracted the disease of Paalölöqangw. In this way he was punished for his theft and died.[6]

Because of his fundamental linkage with water, Paalölöqangw is implored for rain by the Hopis. This is achieved by tying ingredients of his furry skin into prayer sticks made for the god's supplication.

Text 5

Hak yaw haqam paave Paalölöqangwuy tuwe' qa mamqast awnen ang mawpangwu. Pu' yaw hakiy aw pöhö'at huurtiqw pu' yaw hak put angqw kimangwu. Pu' yaw put enang paahototangwu. Noq pay yaw pas kur hintiqw qa yokvangwu.

If a person comes across a Water Serpent at a spring, he will step up to him and rub his body, if he has the courage. The furry skin that adheres to his hand he then takes home. There it is used in fashioning pahos. As a rule, the rains come then.

The reptile's aquatic connection also explains why he is held as one of the totems of the Piikyas, "Small Maize," and Patki, "Parted Water," clans.

Text 6

I' Paalölöqangw pi a'ni himuningwu. Oovi pay piw hak put
aw naawaknangwu, yokvaniqat
ooviyo. Pay ima Piikyasngyam
pu' Patkingyam put enang naatoyla'yyungwa.

The Water Serpent is a powerful deity. That's why people pray to him for rain. Members of the Piikyas and Patki clans have him as a totem.

The Horned Serpent god of the Hopi pantheon readily brings to mind Quetzalcoatl, the famous Plumed Serpent[7] of the ancient Mexicans of Teotihuacan. The question that immediately arises at this point is whether the Hopi Paalölöqangw cult possibly represents a distant echo of any of the Middle American serpent religions. As far as Quetzalcoatl is concerned, Tyler suggests that "at most the two gods were distantly related by belonging to the general family of snake gods" (1964: 244). I tend to agree. Quetzalcoatl, a culture hero and bringer of civilization and learning, at one time became the most important religious personage in Precolumbian Mexico. His cult, which was embraced by the Toltec ruler Topiltzin in the Tula of the 10th century, was a beneficent one which did not demand "to be fed frequently on the warm blood and still-beating hearts of human sacrificial victims" (Leonard 1967: 59).

The Hopi Paalölöqangw, on the other hand, is notoriously associated with human sacrifice.[8] Nor can he claim the aura of a culture hero. It is the god's overt connection with human sacrifice, however, which makes him a plausible candidate for an offspring of a Maya-type Water Serpent. Luckert believes that Middle American Serpent religion reached the Hopi Indians "in at least two distinct waves ... The first wave is still pulsating in the Snake dances of the Snake-clan tradition; the second wave has survived in the Feathered- or Horned-Water ceremonies of the Water and Maize clans" (1976: 150). The Maya serpent cult was practiced, as Luckert shows, not only at the tops of the pyramids, but also at the famous cenote at Chichen Itzá, whose waters rose and fell with the Water Serpent's breathing and blowing (1976: 146). In addition to the thousands of sacrificial offerings which include ceramics, jewelry, jade ornaments, copal incense, masks, bells and other objects of gold and copper, the treasure-level of the sinkhole has yielded many human skeletons. While Edward Thompson, who excavated the well for nearly seven years (1904-1911), reported (in Willard 1926: 114) "upward of ninety" detached skeletons, "the remains of possibly a thousand victims" were more recently uncovered in the archaeological exploration of "Expeditions Unlimited" (Ediger 1971: 276). The skeletal materials were both male and female and seem to have comprised all age groups. The widely-held assumption that only virgin maidens were sacrificed in the cenote must therefore be considered inaccurate.[9]

When Luckert referred to a connection between the Hopi Paalölöqangw ceremonies and the Mayan Serpent cult, this legend featuring the sacrifice of a beautiful virgin girl to the Serpent gods in the village well was still unrecorded and unpublished (1976: 156-66). In my view, it further supports his theory about the Middle American origin of or influence on the Hopi cult.[10]

In addition to being the nurturing god of all the springs and pools across the land, the Hopi Paalölöqangw also has a dark side. He is believed to be the bringer of floods as well as the producer of earthquakes and landslides. In the present story, the sacrifice of the virgin girl is carried out to halt the destructive earth tremors triggered by the Serpent.[11] Curtin has recorded a folk episode from a Hopi Indian which, from all indications, features a witchcraft plot against the village of Shungopavi (1971: 89-101). The scheme involving an earthquake is set in motion through a sorceress who provokes the Water Serpent by immersing herself in the local village spring. In the Patki legend of Palatkwapi, a combination of flooding and shaking of the earth subsides with the immolation of a little boy and girl (Nequatewa 1967: 85, Parsons 1926: 185).[12] Text 7 illustrates the appeasement of such a flood-earthquake combination for the village of Oraibi.

Text 7

Pu' yaw i' paatsikiw kya pi pay hisat piw pephaqam Orayve paniwtiqw pu' yaw i' tutskwa tayayaykuqw pu' yaw puma put qe'tapnayaniqe pu' puma yaw put hakiy kikmongwit maanayat, pay pas wukomanat, kya pi puma taviya. Niiqe pu' yaw

Long ago, I guess, there was a flood somewhere at Oraibi accompanied by an earthquake. In order to stop the disaster, the people decided to sacrifice the grown daughter of the village leader. For this purpose, they dressed her in the finest clothes.

puma put taviyaniqe pu' yaw puma put pas lomayuwsinaya. Poli'innayat pu' yaw put kwasaatoynaya pu' piw atö'öt usiitoynaya. Yan yaw puma put yuwsinayaqe puma put pas soosok hiita puuvuhut, pas qa yuuyaavut, yuwsinaya. Paasat pu' puma yaw it paahot tumaltotaqe pu' puma put it yungyaput aw intotaqe pu' yaw put na'at put kimakyangw pu' yaw put maanay pangso paamiq suutawanasave yaw wiiki. Noq pu' puma aqw pituqw pu' pam put tiy aw pangqawu puma hapi put panayaqw pu' pam qe'tiniqat. Pu' pam maana pay paas nakwhaqe pay yaw oovi qa hin naawaknakyangw pu' pay yaw piw qa pas tsawiniwkyangw pangsoq put nay amum. Niiqe pu' puma pep paahut qalaveq aqw wunuptuqw pu' paasat yaw put paahut suusunasangaqw yaw pam Paalölöqangw yayma.

Noq hisatniqw pu' yaw pam pas angqw wuupa wunuptuqw paasat pu' yaw put maanat na'at put aw pangqawu, "Ta'ay, um aqw pakiniy," yaw pam put aw kitat pu' yaw pam put tiy put paho'init tsöpaatoynaqw pu' yaw pam oovi put tsöpkyangw pu' pangsoq paki. Noq pu' yaw pam naat pu' pangsoq pakiqw paasat pay yaw pam pep paahu walalaykukyangw pu' paasat pay qöniniykukyangw pu' pay put enang pakima.

Having done up her hair in butterfly whorls, they put a black woolen dress on her and placed a cape around her shoulders. Everything was new, nothing had been previously worn. Next, they fashioned prayer sticks which were placed on a wicker plaque. Thereupon, the girl's father took his daughter to the spring at noontime. Upon arrival there, he explained to her, if she were to be offered to the spring, both the flood and earthquake would stop. The girl agreed, without any protestations or sign of fear. As soon as the two stood at the edge of the spring, the Water Serpent emerged right in the center of the spring.

As the Serpent stood there at his full height, the father said to his daughter, "All right, go in now." With that, he placed the tray with the prayer sticks into her hands. Whereupon, she entered the spring. The moment she stepped in, the water began sloshing and whirling in spirals. The Serpent then vanished into the depths with the girl.

Yantiqw paasat pu' yaw pam kikmongwi pangqw pay ahoy mima. Noq pay yaw antsa naat qa pas nawutstiqw pay yaw pam tutskwa tayayataqe yaw qe'ti. Noq pu' yaw pay aapiy pay yaw puma yeese. Noq paasat pu' pay yaw pam paahu piw pep tööqökiwma. Haqaapiy pu' yaw pam pay pas soosoy tööqö.

Noq paasat pu' yaw puma Paalölöqangwt pay aapiyyaqw pay yaw oovi paapu pepeq qa himu pam pakiwtangwu. Puma yaw hapi qa antoti put maanat panayaqe. Noq oovi puma yaw naap qa'antipuy akw haqamiya. Noq paniqw oovi pay yaw pam pu' pepeq qa nööngantaqat pay yan pi it piw lavaytangwu. Put ep yaw puma hovarya put maanat panayaqe.

Now the village leader returned home again. True enough, it was not long before the earth stopped shaking. The people were now able to live again. Soon the flood waters receded, until all the water had dried up.

Soon thereafter, the Water Serpents too departed. There were none left in the spring. By accepting the sacrifice of the girl, they had committed a wrong. They left because of their own transgression. For this reason people say the water is no longer flowing there. It was the Serpents that had sinned by taking the girl under.

Apart from legendary sources, hardly anything is known about the practice and function of human sacrifice in prehistoric Hopi society. Fred Kabotie, in an interpretation of a Mimbres pottery design, intimates that in the past, under extreme conditions of drought and famine, a human life was considered a legitimate sacrifice to obligate the rain gods to send their life-sustaining moisture (1982: 75-76). According to him, this one-time custom is still reflected in the act of feeding *hooma*, "sacred cornmeal," a substitute for the human offering, to the kachina gods when they arrive at a Hopi village to stage a rain dance. "Drought has been one of the worst foes of the pueblo people since unknown time. Long duration of dry weather brings disaster to people of the Southwest. When Earth Mother is dried up for lack of water, famine takes its toll of men, women, and children. When the Rain Deities, the holders and keepers of one of the sources of life, fail to respond to prayers, it is felt that to obtain rain from them is worth more than any worldly possession, even more than human life.

"In the pantheon of the Kachinas of the Zuni and the Hopi peoples there is a certain class of Kachinas who, by their potent power to make rain, require a human sacrifice. The offering to the Rain Deities is interpreted in terms of the white corn meal."

In this respect, the Hopi purpose of the human offering closely resembled that of the Mayan cenote ritual. As Tozzer has shown, the latter "was primarily a rite for rain" (1957: 214). Thus, the human sacrifice functioned as the ultimate intercession for rain, i.e., life-sustaining moisture.

A second important function of the human sacrifice, as can be gathered from Hopi oral traditions, seems to have been that of placating the fury of the water gods.[13] Furthermore, as the two following Hopi folk statements reveal, the act of human sacrifice could be used also as an incentive for the water god to do the very opposite, i.e., to unleash his devastating powers. Once again, this scenario seems to be limited, as occurs so often in Hopi oral literature, to the socially aberrant manifestation of *koyaanisqatsi*,[14] a way of life which is marked by corruption and turmoil. This state of affairs always calls for the most drastic remedy in Hopi mythology. The evildoers responsible for *koyaanisqatsi* must be eradicated.

Text 8

Ephaqam pi haqamwat pay kikmongwi timuy amumi puutsemokye' pu' amungem hinkiwakwlawngwu. Pu' pay kur hin unangwyamuy taalawnanik pu' pay ephaqam hiitawat tiy hom'oyngwu. Pu' put oovi pu' Paalölöqangw tutskwat tayayaykinangwu. Pu' ephaqam pay yooyoktive' pas qa qe'tingwu. Pu' paasat paahu kitpik tutskwava oopokqw pu' paatsikngwu. Pay yan it piw lavaytangwu.

Once in a while, a village leader somewhere becomes so disgusted with his children [the villagers], that he has to draw up a scheme against them. In order to purify their hearts, he usually resorts to sacrificing one of his own children. In return, the Water Serpent will shake the earth [causing an earthquake]. At other times, it will start raining without cessation. As the water fills the land, the village gets flooded. This is what people say.

Text 9

Ephaqam pi pay kikmongwi timuy qa unangwtalyaqw

Occasionally, a village chief, upon realizing that his children

amungem hiita nukustunat-
yawte' pu' sen tiy maanat pu'
sen tiyot ti'yte' pumuy hom'oyngwu. Hiitawat engem nakwa-
kwuste' pu' put engem intangwu. Pu' pantaqat pam put
paami wiikye' pu' aw pangqawngwu aqw pakiniqat. Pantiqw
pu' enang qöniniykungwu.
Pantiqw pu' pay Paalölöqangw
put panangwu.

[the villagers] are out of their
senses, will plot something to
their detriment. As a rule, he
then sacrifices either his son or
daughter. After making prayer
feathers for either one of them,
he places the offerings in a tray.
Upon taking the victim to the
spring, he tells it to enter the
water. As soon as the victim has
done so, the water starts whirling around. Then the Water
Serpent pulls the victim under.

Destructive forces of an apocalyptic magnitude are expected to
come to pass on the doomsday of the Hopi world. Again, the purification of evil Hopikind is carried out by the Water Serpents who are
released by the avenging Pöqangw Brothers. Text 10 assigns the
cleansing powers of devastation to one Serpent, Text 11 to two.[15]

Text 10

Pay pi peetuy Hopiituy navoti-
'amniqw i' Paalölöqangw antsa
it paatuwaqatsit ep ki'yta. Pu'
yaw ima Pöqangwhoyat put
atsveq tsokiwta. Pu' puma yuk
Hopiituy aw tunatyawyung-
ngwu. Kur antsa Hopiit hisat pas
qa unangwtalawvayaniniqw pu'
antsa yaw puma Pöqangwhoyat
put pan aa'awnani. "Ta'ay," pu'
puma yaw kitani, "pay kya antsa
aw pituni. Kur pi yan ima itaatim qa unangwtalawvayaqw ura
um it antsa tutskwat namtökna-
ni." Pu' yaw pay i' Kookyangwso'wuuti sonqa piw navoti'ytani.
Pu' puma paasa'niiqam antsa
navoti'yyungwe' pu', "Ta'ay,"
yaw kitotani, "pay antsa kya pi

The tradition of some Hopis has
it that the Water Serpent inhabits
the oceans and that the two Pöqangw Brothers straddle him.[16]
All three of them keep watchful
eyes on the Hopi. It is said that if
the Hopi ever reach the point of
utter disintegration, the brothers
will issue certain instructions to
the Serpent. "All right," they will
say, "that is enough! You were
instructed to turn this land over
if ever these our children did not
come to their senses." Since Old
Spider Woman will also share
this knowledge, all four of them
will say, "Well then, it looks as if
they're not going to heed our
warnings. If they will not listen,

qa itamumi tuuqayyungwni. Pay
pi qa nanapta. Pay pi nam tur aw
pituniy," yaw kitotani. Pu' yaw
puma Pöqangwhoyat paahot
yawtani, naama. Pu' yaw puma
put qöhiknat pu' yaw puma put
tuuvani. Pu' yaw aw pangqawni,
"Ta'ay," yaw kitani, "pu' umniy," yaw kitaqw pu' yaw pam
pi a'ni öqalaniiqe pu' yaw poniniykuqw pu' yaw i' tutskwa soosoy namtökni. Paayumiq yaw
pam it tutskwat soosok namtök-
nani.

then let it commence." Pöqangwhoya and Palöngawhoya, holding pahos in their hands, will
break these now and cast them
aside. Then they will direct the
Water Serpent, "Come, it is your
turn." Following this order, the
Serpent who possesses enormous strength will start to
writhe, causing the entire world
to turn over,[17] and the land to be
flung into the sea.

Text 11

Ima yaw Paalölöqangwt nan'i-
kyaqe tuuwaqalpaqe itamungem
tutskwat ngu'yta, kwiningyaqe
pu' tatkyaqe. Pu' yaw pumuy
amutsveq ima Pöqangwhoyat
tsokiwta. Naat yaw pas sinom
tuuwaqalmoqhaqami qa
unangwtalawvayaqw pep pu'
yaw puma Pöqangwhoyat
pumuy maatapni. Pu' yaw puma
poniniykuni. Pantiqw pu' yaw i'
tutskwa soosoy tayayaykuni.
Paasat pu' yaw pas qa hakiy
qatsi'atniwtini, kitotangwu.
Pumuy poniniykuqw pu' yaw
paahu walalaykuni. Pu' tutskwa
tayayatani. Pu' yaw pam pas
soosokmuy enang namtökni.

Two Water Serpents are holding
the world in balance for us, one
along the northwest side, the
other along the southeast. On top
of them sit the Pöqangw Brothers. If by the end of this world
the people have not desisted in
their evil ways, the brothers will
let loose the Snakes. They will
then stir, as a result of which,
chaos and pandemonium will
reign. Owing to the Serpent's
movement, the waters of the
ocean will start to boil, and the
entire land will be shaken by
earthquakes. The earth will then
turn over, taking with it all
mortals.

To avoid the god's wrath in the form of dreaded earthquakes,
prayer sticks are constantly fashioned for him.

Text 12

I' Hopi Paalölöqangwuy engem
pay it paahot piw tumaltangwu,
pam hapi put qa hinwat itsivu-
toynaniqe oovi, qa hinwat qövis-
toynaniqe oovi. Pam hapi pante'
pam yaw poniniykuqw pu' yaw
i' tutskwa tayayaykuni.

The Hopi make pahos for the
Water Serpent lest he become
angry or irritated in any manner.
Were this to happen, the Snake
would cause earth tremors by
moving his body.

As might be expected, a number of stringent *maqastutavo*, or
"taboos," regulate Hopi conduct at springs. Contamination of the
precious water source must be avoided. Hence, playing by or in a
spring, including bathing and swimming, are strictly forbidden.

Text 13

I' piw maqastutavo tsaatsakwmuy amungem. Tsaatsakw-
muy kuy'ayatote' pu' amumi
pangqaqwangwu, "Uma qa
paave hohonaqyani. Uma qa
paahut aqw hohonaqyani, taq
pep Paalölöqangw ki'yta. Taq
umuy put paahuyat itsehe'to-
taqw songqa umuy haqawat
panani." Hisat yaw paniwtiqw
oovi. It itam pumuy meewanto-
ta. Pu' hak pep pantsakye' pu'
piw hak Paalölöqangwuy
na'pale' soosoy pöstingwu.

The following taboo is addressed
to children. When children are
asked to get water, people say to
them, "Don't horse around at the
spring. Don't play in the water.
Because the Water Serpent lives
there. If you soil his water, he is
bound to pull one of you under."
Because this has happened in the
past, we forbid our children to
do these things. A child that does
not obey, contracts the disease of
the Serpents and swells all over
his body.

Text 14

I' piw maqastutavo. Piw hak
haqam paahut nööngantaqat qa
aqw pakingwu, taq hak aqw
pakye' pep naavahome' Paalölöqangwuy na'pale' pöstingwu.

It is also a taboo to enter a flowing spring. If someone does so
and takes a bath, he gets infected
with the disease of the Water
Serpent and swells up.

Text 15

Hak paangaqw qa motolhik-
ngwu, taq Paalölöqangw hakiy
huutukngwu.

One does not drink from a
spring directly with the mouth
[rather than using one's cupped
hands], or one gets sucked in by
the Water Serpent.

Text 16

Hak nönganvamiq momore'
hapi put paahut öyngwu. Okiw
put öyqa pi wukovontingwu.
Noq hisat put tiyooyat put
paahut öyqw put tutuykimi
wikyaqe pu' aqw hötayat pu'
piw angqw tsoykinayaqw pay
piw antingwu. Piw hiisavo akw
kwangwahintit pu' pay piw
ahoy wukovon'iwmangwu. Pay
kya pi qa suus put angqw pan
tsoykinaya. Noq pay pam pas qa
qalaptuqe pankyangw pay paas
laaki. Pu' lakmoki. Oovi himuwa
akw okiw lakmokngwu. Panti-
ngwuniqw oovi put tuumewan-
totangwu.

Whoever swims in a flowing
spring fills up with water. This
happened to a little boy once. He
was taken to the hospital, and
they opened him up and drained
the liquid from him. However,
he got full of water again. For a
while he was all right, but then
his stomach started bloating
again. The boy was drained
several times, but his condition
did not improve. In the end, he
became completely dehydrated.
This is what typically happens
[to a transgressor of this taboo].
For this reason, people are
warned not to swim in a spring.

Of all the taboos, the ones with the most dire consequences are
those which prohibit behavior that might tempt the Serpent sexually.
Thus, a strict dress code is supposed to prevent a woman from expos-
ing her genitals to the god.[18] Any kind of flirting or love-making in or
near a source of water is equally intolerable.

Text 17

Hak nönganvami kuyte' hak
kwasay qas'aatsami tsuruknat
pu' aqw pakingwuqat pangqaqwangwu. Pu' pay piw taapaloy
huur naamokyaatat pankyangw
angqw kuukuyngwu.

They say that a woman who
goes to a flowing spring for
water must tuck her dress between her thighs prior to entering the spring. Or, she can wrap
herself tightly into her shawl
before she scoops out the water.

Text 18

Hak yaw hakiy paaveq tsopqw yaw hakiy engem nö'yiltiqa lölöqangwuy tiitangwu.

A female who has intercourse at the spring bears a snake to the one who impregnates her.

Text 19

Hak haqam maanat aw pite' qa paave put amumningwu. Hakim qa naami ma'ytangwu. Hak pep maanat aw hintsanqw pam nö'yilte' put paahut ööye' pu' nu'an wukovontiqw pu' pam tsiikyaqw putakw mokngwu.

When a boy meets a girl, he must not be together with her at the spring. They are not to touch each other when there. For after the girl engages in intercourse and gets pregnant, she becomes filled with water. As a result, her stomach is tremendously bloated. Eventually it bursts, and the girl dies.

Text 20

Yaw hak hakiy aw qa nuvöhintingwu, paave. Taq hak yaw pantiqw Paalölöqangw hakiy kwangwa'yngwu. Pam Paalölö-qangw hapi yaw pas paas sinmuy ang taytangwu. Pam hapi yaw pep pas sinmuy pangqw paangaqw pakiwkyangw pumuy sinmuy amumi paas tunatyaw-tangwuniiqe oovi yaw pam hii-tuywatuy hintiqw navotngwu. Himuwa maanat aqw maa-kwutsqw paasat pay Paalölö-qangw put kya pi hintsanngwu, tsopngwu. Pay pi songyawnen pi oovi kya pi aw hikwsungwu sonpiqeniqw pu' pay pam paasat kya pay pantingwu, put paahut öyngwu. Hakiy aw pam hikw-suqw pay hak Paalölöqangwuy nö'yiltingwuqat kitotangwu.

One does not flirt with a person at the spring. The person who engages in such an activity makes himself desirable to the Water Serpent. The Serpent care-fully watches a person's behav-ior. Living in the spring, he sees what two people do. Thus, when a boy reaches under a girl's dress to feel her up, it is the Serpent that subsequently copulates with the girl. It is as if he breathed on her, whereupon she gets satu-rated with the water. A female so breathed upon gets impregnated by the Serpent.

In addition to presiding over the waters of the earth, Paalölö-qangw is also attributed powers of fecundity. Stephen characterizes him as one who "nourishes the germs, supplies sap to those of vegetation, and life blood to those of animals" (1940: 102). This fertility aspect of the god is acted out by the Hopi in a number of puppet dramas. In these dramatizations, the god is portrayed not by a mask but by an effigy which is manipulated like a marionette. Ceremonial Paalölöqangw performances are staged in a variety of forms. The *Kuy-sip-lölöqangw*, or "Water-vessel-snake," features single serpent marionettes rising from waters jars. Other, more elaborate dramatizations are described as *Paalölöqangwt timu'yyungqam*, "the Water Serpents who have offspring," and *Paalölöqangwt naanaywaqam*, "the Water Serpents who are fighting." The manifold aspects of these theatrical exhibitions have been reported in great detail by Fewkes and Stephen (1893) and Fewkes (1903) for First Mesa, and by Geertz (1987: 217-52)[19] for Third Mesa. Tyler suggests that the fertility mimetically invoked in these Serpent dramas "seems to be that of the earth" (1964: 246). The Hopis believe that the performing Serpents are actually alive, as may be gathered from Text 19.

Text 21

Pu' Hopi piw oovi put wuni-manangwu. Suukyawa pay kuysivut angqw yaymakngwu. Pam pay suyukiwta. Noq pu' i'wa naalöqmuy Lölöqangwu'y-taqa pas hiihinta. Niikyangw pay pi pas taayungqamuy an hintsatskyangwuqat kitotangwu. Pam naat piw Powamuyat pas an yukiltingwu. Pam naat piw pas Powamuyat antakyangw pu' piw sinotukwa. Ep ima Leelent piw pumuy amumumyangwu.

The Hopi also make the Water Serpent dance. In one performance, the Serpent emerges from a water jar. This performance is very simple. Another version, in which four Serpents are present, is more complex. They say that the Serpents behave as if alive. This latter dramatization follows exactly the pattern of the Powamuy ceremony and requires a great many participants. Members of the Flute society are also involved in this rite.

Text 22 shows that, once again, owing to the strong sexual symbolism associated with the Snakes, a pregnant woman is not supposed to watch any of these puppet dramas.

Text 22

Hak pi oovi nö'yiwte' piw Paalölöqangwtuy qa tiimaytongwu. Pu' hak nö'yiwkyangw tiimaytoq pu' yaw tsay put na'palngwu. Noq pay pi nö'i hiita suna'palngwuniqw oovi. Noq pay pi songqa antsa'. Pay lööpwatuy pay pi hakimuy aw meewantotangwu, hak pumuy qa hiituywatuy tiimaytongwu, Kuysiplölöqangwuynit pu' pay Paalölöqangwuy.

When a woman is pregnant, she is not supposed to go see the Paalölöqangw performances. If she does, her child will get affected by the Serpent's power. As is well known, a fetus readily contracts disease. There's no doubt that this is true. Hence, women are barred from watching both types of puppet rituals, the one of the "Water Vessel Snake" and the one involving several Serpents.

Although the present myth casts the Water Serpents in the role of destructive agents, it is ultimately the villagers themselves, however, who set the scenario of destruction in motion. In their hubris to change the lay of the land, they invoke powers they cannot control. As a result, the entire community suffers the punishment of the gods. To be sure, only the evil instigators of the scheme perish in the disaster, but the story also contains a prophetic warning for the present community of Shungopavi: If the ceremonies are not carried out properly, the fate of the village will be sealed when it is swallowed by the earth to the accompaniment of new cataclysmic earthquakes.

Endnotes

1. In the spelling of village sites presently inhabited on the Hopi reservation I follow the conventional, if "distorted," orthographic practice. Thus, for example, Shungopavi will be used instead of Songoopavi, which would conform with the standardized writing system now available for the Hopi language. All uninhabited ruin sites, on the other hand, will be rendered in phonemically correct spelling. In accordance with this approach, Hopi place names occurring in quoted passages will be accompanied by their appropriate spellings in square brackets.

2. At Shungopavi, the Popwamuyt, Leelent, Tsuutsu't, Mamrawt, and Lalkont, i.e., the Powamuy, Flute, Snake, Maraw, and Lakon society members conduct initiations on a regular basis. The theft of

the altar pieces representing the goddess Taalawtumsi in 1978, however, has brought a halt to the quintessential Manhood initiation rites of the Wuwtsimt, Taatawkyam, Kwaakwant, and Aa'alt, i.e.; members of the Wuwtsim, Singer, Agave, and Horn societies (Shannon 1983: 33).

3. In a story recorded by Stephen, a youth destined to be the first chief and father of the Hopi is endowed with a variety of secrets and skills by the gods (1929: 55). Paalölöqangw, the Horned Water Serpent deity, entrusts him with the faculties of "where and how to dig for water."

4. According to Anne Ross, in Celtic iconography, the deity Cernunnos, "The Horned One," was accompanied by a horned serpent, "his most consistent cult animal. The relationship between the serpent and sexuality is widely diffused; to endow the beast with the horns of a potent ram would be to create a highly apotropaic and fecund symbol" (in Rawson 1973: 84).

5. Snakes, due to their skin-shedding ability, almost universally are linked with the power of healing, rejuvenation, and immortality. That the Hopis shared a similar belief is demonstrated in a folktale entitled "The Man Who Was Buried Alive." In this story the protagonist witnesses how one snake revives another, dead one, by means of magic herbs. The man then applies the same remedy to his deceased wife, with equally life-restoring results. He later becomes a famous medicine-man, bringing people back to life just like the Greek savior-healer god Asklepios (Roman Aesculapius) (Gimbutas 1989: 136).

6. For similar episodes, see Geertz (1987: 428) and Titiev (1944: 425-431).

7. "Plumed" or "Feathered Serpent" as a rendition for the Aztec term Quetzalcoatl is actually a misnomer. A more accurate translation would be "quetzal snake," for the name is composed of the Nahuatl elements *quetzalli*, a reference to the blue-green plumage of the exotic tropical bird, and *coatl*, a generic designation for "snake." In Maya, the concept of Quetzalcoatl appears rendered as Kukulcan.

8. Hopi mythology also contains Middle American memories of human sacrifices to the sun. Thus, in one episode of a hitherto unpublished version of the Hopi emergence myth which I recorded, Old Spider Woman suggests the use of fat, from a ritually slain girl, to keep the newly-created sun spinning properly in the sky. The Aztec belief that life flows from death and that people were created to

nourish the sun and earth with their blood and hearts is encountered here with the twist that fat rather than blood of the sacrificial victim assures the motion, i.e., the life, of the sun (González Torres 1985: 132). Unlike the Mexican sun cult, however, which demanded the ongoing practice of human sacrifice, Hopi mythology guarantees the continual rotation of the sun by the natural death of mortals, not by the unnatural death of human sacrificial victims. The key passage from the episode illustrating this scenario is cited in full below:

Pu' yaw puma oovi put maanat ngu'ayaqe pu' yaw puma put naap niinaya. Niinayaqw pu' yaw pam Kookyangwso'-wuuti put wihuyat hin tuhisay akw put taawat hintsanqw pu' yaw pam antsa piw riyayay-kukyangw pu' piw ahoy suyan taalawva. Paasat pu' yaw pam antsa qa qe'tiqe pu' yaw ooveti.

Pu' paasat yaw i' Koo-kyangwso'wuuti pangqawu, "Ta'a," yaw kita, "pay sonqa yantani. Kur i' hapi sonqa it Hopit wihuyat akw yan riyaya-tamantani. Nen umungem tal-ni'ytaniy," yaw pam kita. "Noq oovi himuwa Hopi mokqw pu' yaw pam taawa pay naap put wihuyat angqw naawihutoyne' pu' putakw riyayatamantani. Yaniqw oovi yaw pam taawa soosokmuy wihuyamuy tung-laytangwuniqw pay yaw oovi Hopit mokqw pu' pam put wihuyat akw pu' talni'ytaman-tani."

Niiqe pu' yaw puma oovi put hu'wanayaqe pu' yaw put so'wuutit aw pangqaqwa, "Kur antsa'ay, pay pi antsa pantaniy,"

So they grabbed the girl and killed her with their own hands. Old Spider Woman, in her skill-ful way, somehow applied the girl's fat to the sun. As a result, the sun began to spin again and it became daylight once more. This time, the sun did not stop its motion and reached a point high in the sky.

Thereupon Old Spider Woman said, "All right, it will have to be this way now. The fat of the Hopi will ensure that the sun keeps spinning. Then it will shine its light for you. Therefore, whenever a Hopi dies, the sun will grease itself from the fat of the deceased. In this fashion it will maintain its rotation. This is the reason the sun desires the fat of everybody. Thus, as long as a Hopi dies, the sun will provide its light from the dead person's fat."

The people declared their agreement and said to the old woman, "Very well, it will indeed be this way now. We'll inform all the Hopi who are here about this. And truly, when

yaw kitota. "Noq pay antsa itam soosokmuy Hopiituy yepyaqamuy navotnayani. Pay antsa himuwa yan mookye' pay toko'at qa haqamimantani. Pay put wihu'at it taawat riyakni'ytamantaniqw oovi pay himuwa Hopi sonqa mokmantani. Noq oovi pay himuwa haqaminiqw pay uma pas qa pas hin akw qa haalaymantani. Pay pi pam itamungem taawat riyakni'ytamantaniqe oovi haqamimantani," yaw pam mongwi pumuy sinmuy amumi kita.

Yaniqw oovi yaw Hopi pay sonqa mokngwu, putakw taawa warikiwtaniqw oovi. Yan put puma yukuya atkyaqw nöngakqamyaniqw oovi itam Hopiit taawa'yyungwa.

someone dies, his body will not disappear. Its grease will keep the sun turning, and for this reason a person will have to end his life. So don't be sad when someone passes away, for through his death he keeps the sun spinning for us," the leader explained to his people.

This is why a Hopi must die. For it is because of his death that the sun can travel. This is how things were decided after the people emerged from the underworld. And this is the reason we Hopi have the sun.

9. The fact that many of the skeletal remains retrieved from the well by "Expeditions Unlimited" belonged to children suggested to the members of the team "that the Mayas were not the intellectual pacifists they were once made out to be and that under Toltec domination they developed a child-slaughtering cult to rival the bloodthirst of most other native inhabitants of the Americas" (Ediger 1971: 276).

10. There is ample archaeological evidence for a Precolumbian Horned Serpent cult in the Southwest. This prehistoric evidence, in the form of petroglyphic and pictographic iconography, is especially widespread in Arizona and New Mexico. For an imposing array of horned snake figures from north central New Mexico, see Renaud (1938: Plates 17 and 18). The most remarkable serpent pertroglyph among these, which is found at a site east of the ruins of Pueblo Blanco, is eighteen feet long and two feet wide.

The Horned Serpent is not limited to the Hopi. He occurs in many of the Pueblo cultures of the Southwest. Thus, he is Kolowisi to the Zunis, and known as Avanyu to the Tewa Indians. In Keres mythology, he is Tsitsshrue or Gatoya, and the Jémez call him Wanakyu-dy'a (Parsons 1939: 184).

11. Colton and Nequatewa report that the spring, Songoopa, which gave the name to the village of Shungopavi, "went dry in the 1870s at the time of a landslide which caused a local earthquake" (1932: 54). This local event may well have served as a powerful reinforcement of the Hopi belief in the Water Serpent's connection with earthquakes and landslides.

12. Parsons reports that the flood and child sacrifice myth of the Patki clan is also "told at Zuni, and ... derives from Pima-Papago" (1939: 970). Underhill provides ethnographic information on a Papago shrine "where it is said that four children were sacrificed in ancient times to stop a flood" (1979: 141-146).

13. Interestingly enough, Scholes and Adams also mention "relief from hurricanes" as a reason for human sacrifice in the cenote (in Tozzer 1957: 202).

14. For a detailed discussion of the parameters of this ancient Hopi concept, see the introductory remarks to "The Destruction of Pivanhonkyapi."

15. In a folktale recorded by Wallis, which alludes to the same context, Paalölöqangw is portrayed as one that "has two heads facing different ways in almost opposite directions" (1936: 12). This may explain the dichotomy in the two versions which I recorded, featuring either one or two Serpents on the "last day."

16. Rawson points out that "in some versions of ancient pre-Classical Mediterranean myth, Okeanos, the immense belt of water said to encircle and bind the world together, was conceived as a vast serpent with human head and horns. This is clearly a transposition onto the cosmic scale of our inner image of the liquid psyche, source of all vitality and fertility" (1973: 51).

17. Nequatewa alludes to the same scenario. "Through pools of water and lakes the great Serpents are watching the doings of all people, waiting for the time to come to turn this body of land over and cause earthquake, when the people do wrong, go fighting among themselves. But the two Pukong-ho-yat [Pöqangwhoyat] (the little war gods) who have compassion and sympathy for us all are holding them down so the earthquake may not come to wipe life off this earth" (1936: 124).

18. Nequatewa implies that even accidental exposure must be avoided. "Every pool of water or lake, to them [i.e., the Water Ser-

pents] are like skylights in our houses. Through these waters they are always looking upward. Therefore, a Hopi never dares to step across a pool of water. The women are especially cautious because of this idea as they do not protect themselves like the men" (1936: 124).

19. Geertz's summary stands out in that the Hopi source materials are fully cited in the vernacular (1987: 295-303).

Hisatsongoopavi Kiiqöti

Aliksa'i. Yaw Songoopave yeesiwkyangw yaw pep pu' pam kitsoki
pan maatsiwqw pay yaw qa pepe'. Naat pay yaw atkyaq pas hisat-
kitsokiveq yaw yeesiwa. Noq yaw put kitsokit aakwiningqöyve pay
hihin oove yaw i' paahu Songoopa piw yan maatsiwa. Noq pep yaw
a'ni paahu nöönganta.

Noq yaw ima Songoopave kitsokivewat momngwit ki'yyungqam
yaw sutsep it hiita aw wuuwantotangwu. Pas yaw pang pumuy
amuuhaykye' qa haqe' atkyamiq pumuy tutskwa'am nukngwa. Kur
yaw puma haqe' it hiita akw nayesni'yyungwniqey uylalwani. Pay
yaw as aqw taatöqniikyangw pu' piw teevenge tutskwaniikyangw

Hisatsongoopavi: Devastation by Earthquake

Aliksa'i. People were living at Shungopavi, but not in the village presently known by this name. Rather, they were living in the ancient village below this location. Northwest of and a little bit above this community a spring was situated whose name was Songoopa. It was flowing with an abundance of water.

The leaders residing in the village of Shungopavi, however, were facing one problem that constantly occupied their thoughts. The sloping land in their vicinity was no good for farming. There was no place to plant the crops with which they could sustain themselves. To be sure, there was land to the southeast and the southwest, but it was

pay yaw pam pas kiingaqw pangsoq haq'a. Pu' yaw puma taataqt
tootim ephaqam pangsoqyaqw yaw soq ima tuwqam ephaqam pangso kiimiye' pay yaw puma soq imuy peetuy sinmuy tsamyangwu-
niqw yaw oovi puma momngwit as haqe' haykye' paasatotaniqey
naanawakna. Niiqe yaw puma put aw wuuwantotangwu.

Noq yaw pep paave piw yeesiwa. Noq pepwat yaw kur ima pas
hiitu yeese. Pepwat yaw ima Paalölöqangwt pay tuwat naap yeese.
Noq pay yaw haqam paahuniqw pay yaw puma pas son pep qa
yesngwu. Noq yaw puma Lölöqangwt pangqe' haqe' paahuniqw
puma yaw put pangqw nanayö'yaqw pan yaw pam paahu haqamwat
nööngantangwu. Noq yan yaw puma tuwat tuuhihikwnaya. Puma
yaw tuwat put paahut hin haqam nöngaknayaniqey tuwi'yyungwa.
Noq oovi yaw pumuy amutsviy pam pep paahu a'ni nöönganta. Noq
pu' yaw ima Songoopave momngwit yaw as pep paave ki'yyungqamuy amumi ö'qalyani. Puma yaw as pep paave put hihin wuuyaqto-
taqw pu' yaw pam paahu pang atkyamiq wukomunvaniqat yan yaw
puma sutsep as tunatyawyungwa.

Noq pay yaw as mootiniqw pay yaw puma qa soosoyam naanakwha. Noq yaw ima peetu pas a'ni ö'qalt qa tuutuqayyaqe pay
yaw oovi mimuywatuy amumi tuutuyqawvaqe pu' yaw pay pumuy
angwutota. Noq pu' yaw oovi puma Songoopavit nawis'ew put aw
suntiqw pu' yaw i' kikmongwiniqw pu' ima wimmomngwit hiita
pavan ang tangawtaqam yaw it kikmongwit kiiyat aw natsvalaya.
Niiqe pu' yaw puma it aw yan wuuwankyaakyangw pu' yaw pangqaqwa pay yaw pantaniqat. "Pay itam aw pay pitsinayaqw pay qa
wuuyavotiqw itamungem ang aqw paasat yukuyaqw pu' itam pang
uylalwamantaniy," yaw puma kitotaqe yaw oovi it aw sunti.

"Kur antsa'ay. Itam oovi hiita yukuwisniy," yaw hak pas kikmongwi kitaqw pu' yaw puma oovi pangqw kiingaqw nönga. Pu'
yaw puma hiihiita nakwakwustiwngwuy e'nang yankyaakyangw pu'
yaw aqw ahoy ökiwkyaakyangw pu' yaw puma pahotutkilalwa,
pahotumala'yvaya. Noq yaw kur puma peetu Songoopavit pay piw
a'ni hiitu. Niiqe puma yaw oovi pumuy Paalölöqangwtuy hintaqat
paahot akw put paahut nööngantoynayaqw put yaw puma tuwi'y-
yungqe puma yaw oovi put paahot su'an yukuutota. Pu' yaw puma
hisatniqw yukuyaqe pu' yaw puma put paho'iniy aw tsootsonglalwa.
Pu' yaw hak hin tunatyawte' pan yaw hak put paho'init aw hooyin-
tangwu. Paas yaw puma put tunatyay aw hooyintota. Noq pavan
yaw pam paaho pep wuko'iniwta. Nakwakwusi yaw niitilti.

too remote from the village. On several occasions when the men and young boys went there, enemies approached their village and took some of the people captive. For this reason, the leaders wanted to create some farmlands nearby. This was the problem they frequently pondered.

At the spring itself there was life, too. Apparently, some very powerful beings had made their home there. These beings were Water Serpents that had their own way of life. Wherever a spring exists, these creatures can be found. It is due to the Serpents disgorging water that a well springs up from the ground. In this way they supply water for all other living things. They possess the knowledge of providing moisture at any location. And because they were responsible for the flow of the spring there, the leaders of Shungopavi tried to persuade the Serpents to do something for them. They were hoping that the Serpents would enlarge the spring to the point where large masses of water would spill down the slopes in that area.

At first not all of the leaders were in favor of this request. But some of the more obstinate ones persisted and changed the minds of the others. When at long last the Shungopavis all agreed, the village chief and the heads of the different ceremonial societies met at the home of the village chief. With all of them now sharing the same intentions, they were determined to carry out their goal. "Let us begin at once so it won't be too long before the Serpents make the fields for us on which we can plant." The leaders were unanimous in this decision.

"Very well," the village chief said, "let's go fetch some of the necessary things." With that, everybody left the chief's house. Upon returning with the materials required to fashion prayer feathers, they first cut the prayer sticks and then proceeded to actually make the paho. Apparently, some of these Shungopavi leaders were endowed with great powers, for they were familiar with the very type of prayer feathers used by the Water Serpents to produce the flow of the water. Thus, they created exact duplicates of those used by the Serpents. This task completed, the leaders ritually smoked over the trayful of prayer feathers. Whatever wish a person had, he released by blowing the inhaled smoke on the feathers. The men literally blew their desires on them. Finally, before them was a great mound of prayer sticks and prayer feathers.

Paasat pu' yaw puma hakiy heevi'yyungwa. Niikyangw pam yaw hak sonqa lenwimkyani. Pay yaw son hak pumuy tumalayamuy amungem paami qa kimakyangw pu' pumuy tunatyayamuy enang aw tuu'awmani. Pu' yaw puma put hakiy amungem aw kimaniqat tutwa. Pu' yaw pam hak nakwhaqe pu' pumuy hu'wana, "Ta'ay, pay pi nu' umungem put aw kimaniy," yaw pam kita. "Noq pay nu' hakiy sungwa'ymaniqey pay tuwa'ytay," yaw pam pumuy amumi kita.

"Kur antsa'ay, pay antsa son hak qa umumniy," yaw puma put aw kitota.

Paasat pu' yaw puma awniqam pitkunay, kwatskyavut kwisto. Pu' yaw puma put kwusumakyangw pu' yaw ahoy epeq pituuqe pu' yaw yuwsiy oyat pu' put hiita yewasmokvaqey put yuwsi. Noq pu' yaw puma momngwit pumuy amungem oomawnakwat yukuyaqw pu' yaw puma put nakwatat pu' paasat pumuy paho'iniyamuy kwusut paasat pu' yaw puma pangqw yama.

Niiqe pu' yaw puma aw Songoopami paamiwatniiqe pu' yaw aw pituqw paasat pu' yaw pam suukyawa aqw paki. Noq pay yaw pam kur paasat naala aqw pakininiqw pu' yaw mi'wa sungwa'at pay pephaqam put nuutayta. Noq pam yaw hak aqw pakiiqa yaw kur imuy Leelentuy amungem pangsoq paamiq momorngwuniqw paniqw yaw puma oovi kur put ayatota. Niiqe pu' yaw pam haqe' aqw pakingwuniiqey pay put tuwi'ytaqe pu' yaw pam oovi pang aqw pakito. Pu' yaw pam piw put hiita taawit tawkyangw pangsoq pakito. Pu' yaw pam pangso kiiyamuy hötsiwayamuy aw pituuqe pu' yaw pam pang put paho'init tsöpkyangw aqw paki.

Noq pu' yaw pam antsa aqw pakiqw piw yaw antsa hakim pepeq yeese. Niiqe pay yaw puma hakim pep yesqam yaw kur antsa lölö-qangwtya. Niiqe puma yaw tuwat pephaqam kur wukoyese, kyaasta yaw puma pephaqam. Noq pu' yaw puma pay as itamun sinomnii-kyangw pumawat yaw tuwat pöhö'yyungqat puukya'yyungwa. Pu' yaw pam puukya'am tuletayamuy ang hayiyita. Noq pu' yaw pam aqw pakiiqe pu' yaw pangqawu, "Hin kwakwhat inam yeesey?" yaw pam kita.

Noq pu' yaw pam Lölöqangwtuy mongwi'am pay yaw as piw itamun taaqaniikyangw pam yaw tuwat suuqömvi. Pu' yaw pam put aw pangqawu, "Pay kwakwhatay," yaw kita. "Ta'ay, qatu'uy. Um hak waynumay," yaw kita.

"Owiy, pay antsa ima yep tatkyaqöyve ki'yyungqam umumi taqa'nangwtoti. Uma yaw as pumuy amungem yang yukiq atkyamiq

Next, a person had to be found for the special mission. Everyone knew that the person in question would need to be a member of the Flute society. He would take the prayer items to the spring and, at the same time, inform the Serpents of the men's desires. Presently the leaders found the right person. He consented to their wishes and said, "All right, I'll take your things there for you. I already have someone in mind who can accompany me."

"Yes, indeed, someone should go with you," they agreed.

The two who were to go on the mission now went to fetch their kilts, the type which has no embroidery. Upon their return, they took off the clothes they were wearing and put on the costumes they had brought. Next, they tied into their hair a plume, symbolizing a cloud, which had also been prepared by the leaders. Then they gathered up the tray of prayer feathers and went out.

They proceeded to Songoopa Spring and, upon their arrival, one of the men entered the spring. Evidently, he was expected to enter it alone, because his companion waited outside the water. The man entering the spring was the one who swims in it during the Flute ceremony. For this reason the leaders had appointed him to carry out this task. He was familiar with the path into the water, and he now went in along this route. He was chanting a song as he did so. When he reached the entrance of the Serpents' home, he made his way in with the tray of feathers in his arms.

Sure enough, after entering he noticed that there were people living inside, Serpent people. Their number was enormous. The place was heavily populated. These Serpent people possessed the same human form as we, but in addition they had scaly skins which were hanging on a beam attached to the ceiling by ropes. By way of greeting, the Flute member from Shungopavi said, "How are my fathers living?"

The Serpent chief was a man just like us, but quite dark complexioned. "We live in peace," he replied. "Well, be seated, stranger."

"Yes, we who live southeast of here have come to seek your help. We want you to level the slope that runs along here for us. If you topple the cliff at the top, the earth will become level and we can plant on that ground. That's our plan, thus all these prayer feathers were made for you, and we were sent to deliver them," the man explained.

it atvelawtaqat sun tutskwatotani. Yangqw yaw uma oongaqw it tuupelat saapuknayaqw pu' yaw pam aqw tutskwatiqw pang hapi yaw itam uylalwaniqat yanhaqam puma aw wuuwuyaqe oovi it yaasa' umungem pahotumalat yukuyat pu' pew itamuy ayatotay," yaw pam pumuy amumi kita.

Pu' yaw pam mongwi'am ep yanta. "Haw'owi?" yaw kita. "Kur pangqw put tavi'iy," yaw pam put aw kita.

Pu' yaw pam pep saaqat aqlap wunuwtaqe pu' yaw pam angqw aw nakwsu. Pu' yaw pam Paalölöqangwtuy mongwi'am put paho'iniyat kwusuna. Pu' yaw pam paasat put hihin talpumi yawmaqe pu' yaw aw tayta. Pu' yaw pam paas put paho'init aw yorikt pu' yaw pangqawu, "Ta'ay, kur antsa'ay," yaw pam kita. Paasat pu' yaw pam mongwi'am put natpipo tavit paasat pu' yaw pam put aw tsootsonglawu. Paasat pu' yaw pam oovi paas yukut pu' yaw pangqawu, "Ta'ay, pay pi itam tuwantotaniy," yaw pam mongwi'am kita.

Paasat pu' yaw pam put paho'init ep kwusut pu' yaw pam aqw kwiniwiq pumuy pongyayamuy aqwniiqe pu' pangqe put paahot tsöqömnaqe paas yaw pam put pongyat yuwsina. Noq pay pi yaw naap himu son aw hisat qa puuhutingwuniqw yaw pam pangqe pongya'iwtaqa paas sakwi'iwtaqw oovi pam yaw put ömaataqe yaw tsuya. Putakw yaw puma put aw puuhutota. Noq yaw antsa ima peetu put yukuyaqam kur yaw antsa a'ni hiituniqw yaw oovi pam pepeq pu' pongya'iwtaqat it mootiwatniiqat su'an yukiwyungwa. Niiqe pu' yaw pam oovi put pangqe pongyaatat pu' yaw pam put inpiyat aw ahoy tavi. Paasat pu' yaw pam mongwi'am put pas suyan hu'wana. Pay yaw puma pumuy tunatyayamuy aw antsatsnani.

Noq pu' yaw pam pangso ayatiwqa pangsoq paamiq pakitokyangw yaw naat piw pas hiita taawit akw pangsoq paamiq pakitongwu. Noq yaw pam aqw pakitoqe pam yaw kur haqamwat hiita qa su'an tungwaaqe pam yaw oovi as yamaknikyangw yaw kur hin yamakni. Pay as yaw pam put su'an tawme' pay yaw pam as son ahoy qa yamakni. Pu' yaw pam hak amum awniiqa as put yamakniqat aw maqaptsi'yta. Noq pay yaw pam pas qa yama. Nuwu pay hapi yaw nawutsti. Pu' yaw pam pay pangqw qa ahoy yamakqw pu' yaw pam ahoy kiimi pan tuu'awma. Niikyangw pu' yaw pam kur piw imuy peetuy Sakwalelentuy tsamto. Noq pu' yaw pam pep kiive ahoy pitukyangw yan tuu'awvaqw pu' yaw puma put amum ahoyyaqe pu' yaw puma pep paave tsovalti. Paasat pu' yaw puma as hiita akw put horoknayangwuniiqey put yaw puma paasat as aqw leelenyakyangw pu' piw taatawlalwa. Noq pay yaw pam pas qa yama.

The Serpent chief just sat there. "Is that so?" he replied. "Hand them over to me," he instructed the Flute man.

Until then, the Flute man had been standing next to the entrance ladder. He now approached the Serpent chief, who took the tray, carried it to a spot where the light was better and looked it over. After carefully inspecting the gifts he said, "Good, very well." Whereupon, he placed the tray at his feet and smoked over it. When done with this rite, he proclaimed, "All right, we'll give it a try."

With that, he picked up the tray and proceeded to the northwest of the abode where the Serpents' altar was located. This he adorned by inserting the pahos in it. Since things need to be renewed at some point in time, and the pieces on the altar were quite dilapidated, he was elated that they had received these prayer items. And so the Serpents refurbished their altar there. Sure enough, some of the men who had participated in producing the pahos had been endowed with great powers, for the new altar offerings were exact replicas of the old ones. When all were set out along the altar, the chief handed the Flute member back his tray. Then he gave his word that what the people of Shungopavi desired would become a reality.

The Flute man, who had been assigned this task, had been required to chant a certain song upon entering the spring. But, apparently, at some point within the song he had made an error and had not recited the correct words, because now he was unable to leave. Had he sung the song accurately, he would have been able to do so. Meanwhile, the man who had escorted him, was awaiting his return to the surface. But he failed to appear. Quite a bit of time had already passed, so when the Flute man did not emerge from the spring, his escort returned to the village to inform the others. He also went to fetch a few members of the Blue Flute society. After reporting this turn of events at the village, he and the Blue Flute initiates headed back to the spring, where they gathered, playing their flutes and chanting various songs in order to retrieve the missing man. But they did not succeed.

Noq pu' yaw pam pepeq Lölöqangwmongwi put paahot naat pu' ömaataqey put yaw pongyayamuy angqe yuwsina. Noq pu' paasat yaw ima hakim pepeq tuwat pay pas pavan momngwit pangsoq pumuy pongyayamuy aqw piw tuwat qeni'yyungqam yaw pangsoq yesva. Pay pi yaw puma pumuy hu'wanayaqe yaw oovi aqw yesvaqe pu' yaw pavasiwtivayaniqe pu' yaw puma oovi aw pitsinaya. Noq pu' yaw puma pepeq pavasiwyaqw pu' yaw mimawat Lölöqangwt pepeq poniniykuya. Pu' yaw pam paahu pep amutsve walalayku. Pu' yaw pay pam tutskwa paasat piw tayayayku. Panmakyangw pu' pay yaw pam nuwu a'nita. Pu' yaw pam pang tuupela aqwhaqami yantaqa pay yaw haqe'wat kwana. Pantikyangw pu' yaw pam pay atkyamiq siro. Noq paasat pay yaw naat suskya owa haqaqw posngwu. Pu' yaw paasat i' tutskwa pas a'ni tayayaykuqw pu' yaw puma Leelent pay paasat tsaatsawnaqe pu' yaw pay paasat pangqw kiimi ahoy watqa. Pay yaw puma put hakiy taaqat pas qa ahoy horoknaya. Pay yaw kur puma Lölöqangwt put naami sinototaniqe oovi put paasat pay naap qa horoknaya. Pay yaw puma put taaqat mooti pangsoq pakiiqat pay kwayya. Pay yaw pam kur paalölö-qangwniwti.

Noq pu' yaw puma Lölöqangwt pepeq piw pavan poninitotaqw pu' yaw pay pam tutskwa tayayayku. Pu' yaw pay antsa pam pang tuupela hopqöymiq sapupuyku. Pu' kiive yaw pumuy Songoopavi-tuy kii'am tayayaykuqe pu' yaw pay sapuputa. Pu' naat yaw pam pangsoq atkyamiq qa pas hin hintaniqey antiqw pay yaw pam tayayataqe nuwu a'nita. Pu' yaw pam tuupela pangqe sapuputa. Panmakyangw pu' yaw pay pam tatkyaqöymiqwat tuyqa haqe'wat piw kwana. Pantikyangw pu' pay yaw pamwa pangsoqwatniiqa tuupela piw sapupuyku.

Pu' yaw pam tuupela saapukye' pas yaw pam suupantaqa atkyamiq yeevangwu. Noq qa hin yaw pam pangsoq hopqöymiq tutskwa'iwma. Pay yaw himuwa tuupela saapukye' pay yaw pas pantaqa pangsoq mumamaykungwu. Noq qa pan hapi yaw as ima peetu tunatyawkyaakyangw yaw pan naanakwha. Pu' hapi yaw puma pep Songoopave sinom qa nakwhani'yyungwa. Noq pu' yaw pep kiive ima sinom yaw tsaatsawnaqe pu' yaw pangqw watkita. Pas pi yaw puma pavan hin qatsi'yyungwa.

Noq yaw ima haqawat yangqw atkyangaqw Songoopangaqw sinom yaw kur Musangnumi pumuy aa'awnaya, pay yaw pumuy mongwimat naap pumuy kiiyamuy ep pan naanawaknaqw oovi pam tutskwa tayayataqw pu' pam tuupela sapuputa. Noq pu' yaw puma

By now, the head of the Serpents had decked the altar with the prayer items he had received. Then all those of high rank who had a place at the altar stepped up to it and sat down next to it. Since they had given their word to help the villagers, they now began to pray for this undertaking. While the priests were performing the ritual, the other Serpents began writhing. As a result, the water in the spring above them started to slosh about, and the ground began to shake. The quake grew in intensity. Soon a portion of the cliff top looming above developed a crack. Finally, it crashed down. At this time, only individual boulders were tumbling down. The Blue Flute society members had not gotten the man to emerge from the spring. As the ground trembled more and more violently, they panicked and fled back to the village. They had, of course, not succeeded in getting the man back out of the spring. It was the intention of the Serpents to make him one of theirs. Therefore, they had purposely restrained him. So the Shungopavis had lost the first man that had entered the spring. Apparently, he had been transformed into a Water Serpent.

The Serpents, meanwhile, were wriggling a bit more, and the earth shook with even greater intensity. The cliff walls along the northeast side now really began cascading down. At the village of Shungopavi, too, the homes of the people started to shake and to collapse. The slopes near the spring still had not formed the desired fields, yet the earth was rocking violently. The cliffs on this side just kept crashing down. While all this was going on, the point along the southeast side of the mesa developed a fissure, which eventually led to that whole cliff sliding downward, too.

Whenever a cliff came tumbling down, the entire mass would land in one huge piece at the bottom. In no way was the ground towards the east side becoming level. Each rock pillar came rolling down in its entirety. This had not been the intention of those in favor of this undertaking. The people of Shungopavi themselves could not stand the earth tremors anymore. They were so frightened by now that they began to abandon the village. Everything was chaos and pandemonium.

Some of the Shungopavis sent word of the disaster to the people of Mishongnovi. They informed them that their own village leaders had initiated this occurrence and that, as a result, the earth was quaking and the cliff walls were breaking away from the mesa. The

pep haqam kiive put pasiwnayaqey naat yaw pep tangawtaqw yaw
hak pumuy amumi supki. Noq pam yaw kur imuy Musangnuvituy
kikmongwi'am paasat pep pakiiqe pu' yaw pumuy a'ni qööqöya. "Ya
uma hintiqw put panhaqam tunatuytotay?" Noq pay yaw pam kur as
pumuy hintsanikyangw yaw pumuy pan a'ni qööqöya.
Noq naat paasat yaw pantsaki, soosoy yaw tutskwa tayayata. Pu'
yaw himuwa tuupela haqe'wat kwanakye' pu' yaw saapukngwu.
Noq son yaw as pantaniqw yaw puma pep Songoopave tsaatsawnaqe
pu' yaw hakiy Walmiq ayatotaqw pu' yaw pam oovi put hakiy
pangsoq wikto. Noq pam yaw hak poosi'ytaqa pepeq pas a'niniiqa
ki'ytaqw put yaw pam hak wikto. Pepeq pu' yaw pam it poosi'ytaqat
pas payiwat wiktamaqw pangqw pu' yaw pam put pangso Songoopami kiimiwat wiiki. Niiqe pu' yaw pam Walngaqw poosi'ytaqat
pangso haqami puma Songoopapmomngwit put pasiwnayaqw
pangso yaw pam put wiiki.
   Pu' yaw pam ep pituuqe pu' yaw amumi pakiqw naat yaw puma
pep pongyay aw ngöyakiwta. Paasat pu' yaw pam ruupiy horoknaqe
pu' yaw pam putakw amuupa taytaqw pay yaw kur puma pas
pumasaya, nuunukpantsa'a. "Is ohi uma'ay," yaw kita. "Uma hapi
yep itamuy sopkyawatuy sinmuy amungem qa antotiy. Soosokmuy
itamuy uma haqami hintsatsnaniqey kur uma tunatyawyungway.
Uma hintiqw it yanhaqam pasiwnayay? Uma nuunukpantsa'ay,"
yaw kita. "So'on uma it yantsatskyanikyangoy. Uma tuwi'yvevewtsi-
muy, uma Songoopavit kwiikwivituy," yaw kita. "Pas uma yep hiita
ep pavan hintotiniqey tunatyawyungway. Uma hiita aw pas pootayaniqey naanawaknay. Uma hapi as navoti'yyungwa son uma it yantaqat naanawaknanikyangoy. Pay hapi i' yep tuuwaqatsi hin yukiltiqe
pay hapi as pantaniy. Pam hapi as qa itaamu put alönglawniqat'ay.
Noq uma peetu as pay it yantaqat piw navoti'ykyaakyangw hintiqw
uma imuywatuy amumi yan ö'qalyaqw'öy?" yaw pam pumuy
amumi kita. "Ta'ay, nam huvam mooti'ywisa'ay," yaw kita amumi.
"Umuy suutaq'ewyaqw paasat pu' aw aniwtiniy."
   Pu' yaw haqe' kwanakpuniqw pu' yaw pam pumuy pangso
tsamqw pi ason yaw kur puma son aqw yungniqey naanakwhani.
"Ta'ay, haqawa maanay kuwaatiniy. Son i' qa yante'sa qe'tini. Ta'ay,
noq it hapi uma yan pasiwnayaqe uma hapi pas qa antoti. Niiqe uma
hapi oovi nawus son hakiy umungaqwniiqat qa kwayyani. Noq pam
hak maana hapi son nawus i' hak naat pu' puhuwungwiwtaqa, pas
qa hovariwtaqa, pas naat qa puukukpu maanani. Noq oovi uma it
yantaqat qa lomahintaqat qe'tapnayani. Uma hapi oovi iits put hakiy

schemers of this were still in the house where everything had begun, when a man rushed inside. Apparently, he was the chief of the Mishongnovis. "Why did you plan such a thing?" he exclaimed harshly. There was really nothing that he could do to them, yet he still scolded them.

All this time the catastrophe continued. The entire earth kept on trembling. Whenever a cliff cracked, it would crash down. Things could not go on in this manner. The people of Shungopavi were scared, so they sent a messenger to the village of Walpi. There he was to fetch a shaman who had distinguished himself at his trade. The messenger informed the medicine man that he was needed immediately, and brought him back to Shungopavi. He escorted him to the location where the Shungopavi leaders hatched all of their plans.

When the shaman arrived, he went in to the men and found them still huddled around their altar. Immediately he took out his crystal and peered through it at the chiefs. He saw that every one of them was evil. "What a wretched bunch you are!" he exclaimed. "You've committed a wrong against the people. You seem bent on destroying everyone. Why on earth did you plan such a thing? Every one of you is bad. You had no business doing this. You think you know it all. Really, you Shungopavis are full of vanity," he chastised them. "It was your desire to do a great feat and to experiment with something. You ought to know that you are not to do these things. This world is supposed to stay the way it was created. It does not behoove us to alter it in any way. Some of you must have known this. So why did you persuade the others to go along with you?" he scolded them. "All right, come with me," he commanded them. "If you are willing to do so, the situation can be remedied."

With that, he led them to a place where the earth was cracked and ordered them to step inside. The priests, however, refused. "All right, I want someone to sacrifice his daughter then. Otherwise this disaster won't subside. By coming up with this scheme you committed a great wrong. Therefore, one of you will have to make a sacrifice. The girl to be sacrificed must be one who has just reached adolescence. She must be pure and still be a virgin. You must bring the evil process you started to an end. Hurry and seek out this girl right away. I want you to get the most beautiful one you have."

haqami hepyani. Niikyangw nu' pas piw hakiy susnukngwat maanat umumi tuuvinglawu."

Paasat pu' yaw puma peetu pangso kiimiyaqe pu' yaw as okiw hakiy pang hepnumya. Noq pay yaw paasat pep kiive qa pas wuuhaqniiqamyaqw yaw puma oovi hakiy pantaqat qa iits tutwa. Peetu yaw pay kur pangqw naanan'i'voq watqa. Pas yaw nawutsnayaqw pu' yaw puma pep kiive haqam naat kiihu wunuuqat tutwaqe pu' yaw puma oovi pangso yungya. Noq pep yaw kur ima hakim naawuutim ki'ykyangw piw yaw puma hakiy naat pay pu' puhuwungwiwtaqat maanat ti'ytaqw piw yaw pam hak lomamana. Pavan yaw pam hak sikyavu.

Pu' yaw puma put hakiy maanat tutwaqe pu' yaw put wikyaniqw okiw yaw as yumat qa naawakna puma put wikyaniniqw. Noq pu' yaw puma pumuy amumi pangqaqwa, "Pay son itam nawus it pumuy amumi qa no'ayaqw pam pep paave sun yukuni. Pay hapi itam qa pantote' pay itam sonqa soosoyam haqamiyaniy," yan yaw puma pumuy amumi lavaytoti.

Pu' yaw put maanat yumat yaw as okiw tiy kyaakyawnakyangw pay yaw pas nawustaqw pu' yaw puma suutaq'ewtaqw pu' yaw put yu'at oovi put aw poli'inna. Paas yaw pam put poli'innakyangw tukwapngöntoynakyangw pu' piw lomayuwsina, atö'öt usiitoyna.

Niiqe pu' yaw puma oovi put haqam tsotsvalyaqey pep wikvayaqw pu' yaw pam poosi'ytaqa aw pangqawu, "Ta'ay, pay pi sonqa umniy," yaw pam kita. "Pay sonqa umni. Pay itam nawus hakiy untaqat amumi sisviyani. Nuwu hapi tuupela a'ni kwanamiwmay," yaw kita.

Noq naat yaw pam pep kiihu kitsoki'am sapuputa. Pay yaw pam paasat qa suukw pay niina. Yaw tuupela hiitawat aw saapukye' pu' yaw niinangwu. Pu' peetu yaw pangqw aqw oomiq yayvantakyangw pu' kwiniwiqwat watkita.

Paasat pu' yaw puma pisoq pep put paahot put maanat enang ahoy naahoyngwayaniqey yaw piw tumala'yvaya. Pas yaw puma piw an wukoyukuyaqe wuko'intotat pu' yaw piw aw tsootsongya. Noq paasat pay yaw pam pep Songoopave paahu pas nuwu a'ni walalata. Paasat pu' yaw puma tsotsongyukuya. Noq yaw pam i' pangqw Walngaqw hak poosi'ytaqa yaw amumi tunatyawtaqe pu' pumuy yukuyaqw paasat pu' yaw pam pangqawu, "Ta'ay, pew umuutumalay taviya'ay. Pay itam payni." Paasat pu' yaw hak pep put tsöpaatoyna. "Tuma'iy," yaw pam put maanat aw kita.

So a few of the leaders ran into the village looking for such a girl. Since not many people had remained, they had a difficult time finding someone who fit the shaman's description. People had fled in every direction. Finally, they came across a house that was still standing and went inside. It was inhabited by a couple who, by coincidence, had a daughter with the characteristics they were looking for: the girl was adolescent, very beautiful, and her skin was quite light.

The men were going to take her, but her parents did not want to give her up. So the priests explained, "We must give her to the Serpents. That's the only way the spring will calm down. Otherwise, we will all perish."

The girl's parents really treasured their child, but in the end they consented to give her up. Her mother fixed her hair in the fashion that becomes a young unmarried girl. Then she put a strand of beautiful beads about her neck and dressed her attractively, putting a maiden's cape around her shoulders.

When the men brought her to the meeting place, the shaman said to her, "All right, it will have to be you. You'll have to be the one. We must bribe the Serpents with a girl of your qualities. The cliff walls are splitting off more and more."

The houses within the village continued to collapse. The quake had already claimed a number of lives. Each time a cliff came crashing down on a person, it crushed him to death. People by now were clambering to the mesa top and fleeing northward.

Immediately the leaders fell to fashioning more prayer feathers which they would exchange, along with the girl, for their lives. Once again they made a large quantity, which they heaped on a tray and ritually smoked over. Meanwhile, the sloshing of the water at the spring was becoming ever more violent. Finally, the smoking was completed. The shaman from Walpi kept a watchful eye on the men, and when they were done with their task, he said to them, "All right, hand the pahos over to me. We'll be leaving now." Someone placed them in his outstretched arms. "Let's go," he urged the young woman.

Pangqw pu' yaw pam put kiingaqw horoknakyangw pu' yaw put maanat aw paami wikkyangw. Pu' yaw puma angqw tatkyaqw aw pitutoq pas pi yaw pam paahu soosoy pep oove walalata. Pay yaw ephaqam angqw pam wunuptungwu. Pantsakqw pu' yaw pam put maanat aw pangqawu, "Ta'ay, pay um qa tsawiniwtat um inungk aqw pakitoniy," yaw aw kita. "Pay itam pas sutuki'ymani."

Paasat pu' yaw puma aw pas paami pituqw pu' yaw pam aqw pakito. Pu' yaw pam maana paasat put angk aqw'a. Paasat pu' yaw puma epeq pakiqw pu' yaw pam qa sööwunit pu' yaw pam pumuy Paalölöqangwtuy mongwiyamuy aw pangqawu, "Is ohiy," yaw kita, "ya uma hintiqw imuy nuunukpantuy momngwituy it yantaqat hu'wanayay? Nuwu hapi pay i' yang soosoy hoopoq itaakitsokiy akw enang pitutoy. Uma qe'totini. Uma pangqw ayo' watqaniy," yaw pam pumuy amumi kita. "Son uma yep sinot oyi'ykyaakyangw imuy nuunukpantuy hu'wanayaniy. Pay uma as hisatngahaqaqw pan navoti'yyungwa ima sinom umumi hin naanawaknaqw son hapi as uma pumuy unangwyamuyyaniy. Qa pan i' umumi tutavoy. Uma tis pas hakimuy," yaw kita. "Uma hapi yang aasupoq paanawit yeesey," yaw pam aw kita, put mongwit awi'. "Noq yep nu' oovi it kwusivay. Pay ason uma naap yep pan wuuwantote' paasat pi pay uma pantotini, qa pumuy nuunukpantuy tunatyayamuy uma epyay," yaw kita. "Uma as it yantaqat navoti'ykyaakyangw hintiqw uma pumuy tumalayamuy tunatyayamuy ömaatotay?" yaw kita. "Yepee'."

Paasat pu' yaw pam put paho'init piw aw tavi. Noq pu' yaw pam put kwusunat paasat pu' yaw pam piw put aw yan taynumlawqw pu' yaw pam poosi'ytaqa put aw pangqawu, "Um hapi itwat qa nakwhe' pu' um hapi pay yep sulawtiniy," yaw aw kita. "I' yep paahu hapi pay tööqökni. Qa hak itakw mongvasniqat yan kya pi uma naanawaknaqe oovi uma pumuy hu'wanaya. Noq oovi um itwat nuy kwusunaniy," yaw kita. "Pu' it maanat uma hapi piwyani. Yep nu' it paniqw wikvay. Uma hapi yep qatsit simoknaya. Noq puma umumi pan naanawaknaqe oovi puma hapi nawus naap naangaqw hakiy maanat pas qa hovariwtaqat umumi no'aye' pas pansa ahoy qatsiy tuutuyqawvani," yan yaw pam put aw lavayti.

Paasat pu' yaw pam Lölöqangwtuy mongwi'am pangqawu, "Ta'ay," yaw kita. "Ta'a. Pay nu' itwat paho'initniy," yaw aw kita.

"Owiy, um putwatni. Mitwat um angqe ayo' oyaniy. Pamwa hapi pay nukpanvewat yukiltiy," yaw pam put aw kita. "Noq oovi uma pangqw as yesqam ayo' watqaniy," yaw pam pumuy amumi kita. Paasat pu' yaw puma nawus pangqw ayo' watkita.

After ushering the girl outside, he led her to the spring. As the two were approaching it from the southeast, they could see the waves on top of the water. Every so often they simply rose up. As this was happening, he said to the girl, "Don't be afraid. Just follow me. We'll walk right in."

When they had reached the spring, the shaman made his way into the water, and the girl stepped in right behind him. Once inside, he addressed the Serpent chief without delay. "How terrible!" he exclaimed. "Why did you grant the desires of those evil priests? This quake is now approaching our village to the northeast. I want you to stop it. Get away from that altar," he ordered them. "You cannot grant the desires of the evil leaders while having all the people entrusted to your care. You've known from way, way back that you must not fulfill just any old wish. That was not what you were instructed to do, especially since you are powerful beings. Your sort lives within the springs all over the land," he said to the Serpent chief. "Now, I've come bearing these offerings. If you want this to happen on your own initiative, fine. But you shouldn't do things by the will of those who are evil," the shaman continued. "You knew about this all along. So why did you meet their wishes and accept pahos from them?" "Here!" With that, he handed the chief the trayful of prayer feathers.

The Serpent chief took the gift from the shaman and carefully looked it over. "If you do not accept this offering, you will die," the shaman warned. "The water here will simply dry up. I take it you don't want anyone to benefit from this spring anymore, for you yielded to these evil desires. So I urge you to take this gift from me. You can also have this girl I brought with me. You have disrupted life here, but because it was their desire, they must offer to you a girl who is still pure. This is the only way they will save their lives," he explained to them.

The Serpent chief replied, "Very well, I'll accept these prayer offerings."

"That's right, take them. Remove the others from the altar, for those were made with evil intentions," the shaman instructed him. "So you who are seated there by the altar move aside," he commanded. The Serpents did as bidden and moved away from the sacred place.

Paasat pu' yaw puma ayo' watqaqw pu' yaw pam pangqe put pongyat angqe put mootiwat paahot ayo' qenitakyangw pu' paasat saqtsami putwat maspa. Pu' itwat pu' aqw pakiiqat put yaw pam paasat ang qeniyat ang tsöqömna. Tsöqömnat paasat pu' yaw pam poosi'ytaqa put aw pangqawu, "Ta'ay, yep i'iy," yaw kitaaqe pu' yaw pam put maanat aw hawnakyangw pu' yaw pam qöpqöt kwiningyaqw yaw put qatuptsina. "Yep umniy," yaw aw kita. "Ta'ay, pay um nawus yep imuy amumum qatuniy. Noq pay utsviy hapi ima Hopiit son soosoyam sulawtiniy. Noq pay ason ima nuunukpant haqamiyaqw pay i' pangso yukiltiniy. Pu' i' hapi pay suus yan yukiltiniy. Niikyangw ima yepyaqam pas hapi a'ni hiituniqw son i' oova hiniwmaqa it paahotsa akw qe'tiniqw oovi itam nawus ung taviyay. Noq pay um tuwat yephaqam uuqatsiy ö'qalniy. Noq um hapi pas qa hakiy antiqw pay oovi ima sinom son ung qa u'ni'yyungwe' pay son pew ungem hiita tumalay qa oo'oyayaniy. Niikyangw yaapiy hapi hakim paahut aqlap natkolawqw pam hapi songyawnen uumi hintsakmantani. Nen pu' i' wuuti put amum naatsoptaqa hapi qa it tiposhoyat nö'yiltit pam hapi nawus it paahut nö'yiltimantani. Pante' pay pam nawus putakw sulawtimantani," yaw pam poosi'ytaqa put maanat aw kita. "Niikyangw nu' ungwat wikniy," paasat pu' yaw pam pumuy Paalölöqangwtuy mongwiyamuy aw kita.

Noq pu' yaw pam tutskwa tayayataqe pangso qe'tiqw paapiy pu' yaw pam maana tuwat pep pumuy Paalölöqangwtuy amumum qatu.

Pangqw pu' yaw pam poosi'ytaqa pumuy Paalölöqangwtuy mongwiyamuy wikkyangw yama. Niiqe pu' pam hoopoq Walpiy ang kwiningqöyvaniikyangw paasat pu' aqw oomiqa'. Pu' yaw pam Wiphomiq pituuqe pepeq pu' yaw pam haqam put aw pan wuuwantaqey pangsoq pu' yaw pam put Paalölöqangwuy koromiq pana. "Ta'ay, yangqw um pakiwkyangw um yukiq atkyamiq itamungemwat paasat yukuni. Walapsinot um engem paasat yukuqw pang itam enang natwantotani. Itaatimuy itam hiita noonopnayaniqey hiita itam akw nayesni'yyungwniqey put itam pang puhuvasat ang natwanlalwaniy," yaw pam put aw kita. "Noq ason puma pep taavangvit, nuunukpant, ason himuwa hisat hintaqat aw pite' pay nawus qa yepmantaniy. Panwiskyaakyangw puma sulawtiniy," yaw kita. "Ason pay nu' hiita piw tuwat ungem itaatumalay angqw peqw uumi oyaqw pu' um put aw yankyangw pu' um yepeq itamungem it paahut horoknaqw akw itam Walapsinom mongvasyani. Noq um oovi yepeqwatniy," yaw pam put aw kita.

No sooner had they left the altar than the Serpent leader removed the present prayer sticks and feathers from the altar and discarded them below the last rung of the ladder. In their place he set up the ones he had just received. When the Serpent chief finished this task, the shaman said to him, "All right, now take this one," pointing to the girl, whom he had descend to the lower portion of the kiva. There he bade her have a seat northwest of the fire pit. "Sit here," he told her. "You will now remain here with the Serpents. It will be to your merit if not all the Hopis perish. As soon as the evil ones are gone, this episode will be over. This is the only time this will happen. The inhabitants of this spring are not ordinary beings. They are quite powerful, so what is going on above cannot be stopped by prayer feathers alone. For this reason, we had no other choice but to sacrifice you to them. Strive that your life be a long one. Because you have done what no one has done before, the people will remember you and bring their pahos to you. Also, you shall know this: from today and into the future, when two people are having intercourse in the vicinity of a spring, it will be as if the man is having sex with you. The woman will then become impregnated with water, instead of a child, and will die as a result," the shaman explained to the girl. "And you I am going to take along with me," he said, pointing to the leader of the Serpents.

The earthquake now ceased, and from that time on the girl resided there along with the Water Serpents.

Ushering the leader of the Serpents out, the shaman then emerged from the spring. He went in a northeasterly direction and from there north along the northwest side of Walpi. Upon reaching Wipho, he placed the Serpent inside a hole, which he had selected for this purpose. "All right, in this hole here I want you to create a field for us that slopes downward. Make a planting site where the people of Walpi can produce crops. On that new field we will plant and grow whatever we need to sustain our children and ourselves," he commanded him. "And those evil ones in the southwest, whenever they meet their fate, will no longer be on this earth. In this way they will all die," he proclaimed. "And after I have brought you our prayer items, you will use them to bring forth a spring from which the Walpi people can benefit. You will now reside here," he concluded.

"Kur antsa'ay," yaw kita. "Pay nu' antsa pantini. Antsa pi nu' qa antiy," yaw aw kita. "Kur antsa nu' nuunukpantuywatuy hu'wanaqe oovi nu' peep umungem qatsit nukushintsanay," yaw kita.

"Owiy, pantay. Niikyangw pay nu' son ungem imaqsoniy, itumalay angqw qa kimamantaniy," yaw pam put aw kita.

"Kur antsa'ay," yaw kita.

Yan pu' yaw pam poosi'ytaqa pepeq put engem kiituwt pu' yaw pam pangsoq put panat pu' yaw pam angqw aw walminiiqe pu' yaw pam pöhötngay horoknat pu' yaw pam tuwat tumala'yva. Pu' hin lolmat qatsit pam naawaknaqey pan tunatyawkyangw yaw pam put paahot tumala'yta. Yukuuqe pu' yaw pam put intat pu' put aw tsootsonglawkyangw pu' it lomatunatyay aw hooyinta. Paasat pu' yaw pam paas yukut pu' yaw pam put aqw kima. Aqw pituuqe pu' yaw aw pangqawu, "Yep'ey," yaw kita.

Pu' yaw pan put kwusuna. Pu' yaw pam put aw taatayt pu' yaw aw pangqawu, "Pantaniy," yaw kita. "Kur um antsa it lolmat qatsit tunatyawkyangw it aw tumaltay," yaw pam put aw kita.

"Owiy. Noq oovi um naap it itunatyay, uulavayiy um qa aw ante' pay um paasat sulawtiniy," yaw aw kita.

"Kur antsa'ay, pay nu' sonqa pantini," yaw pam kita.

Yantaqat akw pu' yaw pam oovi pep put taviqw pu' pam pepeqwat qatuptu. Aapiy pay yaw naat pu' suukya yaasangwvaqw pay yaw pangqw palkuyva. Pangqw pu' yaw pam paahu yamakkyangw paasat pu' yaw pangqw piw wuuyoqa muunangw tso'o. Noq antsa yaw pam as paas tutavot enang hinkyangw pam pepeq Songoopave taviwa. Niikyangw pu' pam qa antiqe pu' pangqwwat pangsoqniiqe pepeq pu' yaw pam pumuy Walapsinmuy amungem oovi put paahut horoknakyangw pu' pepeq pu' yaw pam su'an put yuku.

Paapiy pu' yaw ima Walapsinom oovi pepeq uylalwa, Wiphoveq. Naat oovi puma pepeq uylalwaqw pu' imawat momngwit yep Songoopave qa an yukuyaqam puma yaw pep sulaw'iwmakyangw haqaapiy pu' yaw puma soosoyam sulawti. Yan pu' pam atkyaveqwa Songoopavi kiiqöti. Paasat pu' yaw pangqw hakim hikiyom oomiq watqaqam pumasa yaw pep akwsingwa. Pu' yaw puma maanat yumat pay piw ayo' yama. Noq pepeq ooveq pu' yaw puma piw ahoy pay hikiyom hiisakwhoyat kitsoktotakyangw haqaapiy pu' yaw puma pep piw hihin aw hoyo.

Yantaqat akw yaw i' pu' kitsoki Songoopavi yan maatsiwqa pep tukiwta. Hisat yaw piw yantaqat aw pituqw paasat pu' yaw pam tukiwmakyangw pu' pam pangso yukiltini. Noq pay pi pangqaq-

"Very well," the Serpent replied. "I will certainly do that. I readily admit I did wrong. I granted the wishes of evil ones and, as a result, almost ruined all of your lives," he confessed.

"Yes, that's the way it is," said the shaman. "As I assured you, I will bring what prayer feathers and prayer things I have."

"Good enough," the Serpent chief answered.

In this manner the shaman found a home for the Serpent. Having placed him inside the hole, he returned to Walpi where he got out his feather box and set to work on the prayer items. While carrying out his task, he concentrated on the desire for life to be good. This done, he piled the prayer feathers on a tray and smoked over them. Once more, while emitting the smoke from his mouth, he instilled in them all his good intentions. When the entire ritual was finally concluded, he took the pahos to the Serpent. "Here, these are for you," he said, upon entering the Serpent's abode.

The Serpent accepted the offering. After looking it over, he said, "This is the way it should be. I can see you worked on this with the wish that life be good."

"That's right," the shaman replied. "But remember, if you do not fulfill my wishes now and go back on your words, you will no longer live."

"Don't worry, I will do what I promised."

And thus the Water Serpent came to live in this place. A year had barely passed when suddenly there appeared some moisture at the site. Soon water began to flow until, in the end, a large stream of water spewed forth. To be sure, the Serpent had first been placed at Songoopa Spring with instructions to produce water there. But because of his failure to properly adhere to these instructions, he was transferred to this site where he produced a spring for the inhabitants of Walpi; and this time, he did it in the correct manner.

From that day on the Walpi people were planting at Wipho. To this time they are still planting there. Meanwhile, those leaders at Shungopavi who had not succeeded with their plan began to die off until no one remained. This is how the destruction of the village of Old Shungopavi came about. Only those few who fled to the mesa top survived. Also among them were the parents of the girl who was sacrificed. The few survivors established a small settlement on top of the mesa, which in time increased in population.

wangwu, yaw pep Songoopaviy ep qa an hiita hintsakwisqw oovi pam Songoopavi yaw soosoy pep pakini. Yan it piw navoti'yyungqw pu' pi aw pitsiwiwta. Noq oovi pam tuupela pep pantsaki, sapuputa tumkyaqe, Songoopave. Pam hapi oovi pu' pay yaynilti. Naat pu' hayphaqam piw naat hopqöyveq suukya tuukwi saapu. Pu' Songoo- paviy ephaqam ima tsotsvalkit wunuptsini'yyungqw put yep tatkya tsöqavöningwuniqw pang pam piw kwanakiwtangwu. Pay naat pu' hayphaqam ura pephaqam tsöqavöt ep poro. Pu' i' paahu aqw yungingitaqe aqw tsoykiwma. Porokqe pu' pam haqami pi yungta. Pu' tsaatsayom hiihiita aqw maspilalwakyangw nawis'ew put aqw oopoknaya. Noq pay suyan naat pam Songoopavi soosoy pakiniqat i' yan navoti. Pay yuk pölö.

This chain of events accounts for the fault in the present community of Shungopavi. If ever these events should recur, this fault will split open and destroy the village. It is said that if the rituals are not being carried out properly, Shungopavi in its entirety will sink into the ground. The time for this prediction is now at hand. That's why the cliff walls are falling down along the mesa rim of Shungopavi. The process has already started. Only recently a rock pillar toppled over at the southeastern side. South of where the community meeting house was erected is a dried-up dam, along which the fault also runs. Not too long ago a cavity appeared in the dam. Water flowing in is draining into this hole. Where it is draining, no one knows. The children have been throwing all sorts of things into it and finally filled it up. Prophecy has it that all of Shungopavi will still disappear in the crack. And here the story ends.

2

The Downfall of Qa'ötaqtipu

The ruin of Qa'ötaqtipu is said to lie somewhere northeast of the Third Mesa village of Bacavi. None of the Hopis I consulted were able to pinpoint its location more accurately since they personally had never visited the site. One clue which seems to lend credence to its geographic placement in the vicinity of Bacavi is the fact that Matsonpi, about a mile northwest of Bacavi, is portrayed in the story as a neighboring settlement of Qa'ötaqtipu. Matsonpi's location, a little mound badly ravaged by pothunters, approximately three quarters of a mile north of the center of Hotevilla, just below the mesa spur on which Hotevilla is situated, is well known. Its name is humorously interpreted as "Hand-kissing place." This interpretation, based on the elements *ma*, "hand," and *tsoonanta*, "to kiss," is linguistically not tenable, however. Nor is a more serious attempt to inject meaning into the place name. By relating *ma*, "hand," to *maqtö*, "paw," and *tson* to *tsoona*, "to suck," the place name is said to recall the ancient Hopi custom of dipping a rabbit's foot into salt water and sucking on it during a meal.

Evidently, Qa'ötaqtipu, which translates as "Burnt Corn," could not have been the name originally assigned to the village by its founders. It probably came about when, at a later time, Hopis discovered some charred corn cobs there. This discovery may also have led to the assumption that the village was destroyed by fire and inspired the present mytho-historic account.

To my knowledge, neither Qa'ötaqtipu nor Matsonpi has ever been investigated archaeologically, or if they have, the results have not been published. From a cursory sampling of the ceramics scattered around the site, however, there can be no doubt that the village was abandoned long before the coming of the Spaniards in the 16th century. Since Matsonpi existed contemporaneously with Qa'ötaqtipu and received some of its survivors, one can assume that Qa'ötaqtipu was destroyed before the demise of Matsonpi.

The tale of the destruction of Qa'ötaqtipu, recorded here for the first time, is a typical product of Hopi narrative tradition. Designed to entertain, it contains the average mix of ancient customs, didactic lore, rivalry, violence, crime and punishment, and supernatural magic. Several of the legend's motifs are reminiscent of other destruction tales in this collection. Thus, when one of the two competitors in the life-and-death race unfairly resorts to extraordinary powers by changing into a dove, a similar episode in "The Demise of Sikyatki" comes to mind. The fire which, as an act of revenge, is to burn Matsonpi, is caused by the Yaayapontsas just as in the narrative describing the conflagration of Pivanhonkyapi. And while there the firestorm's threat to Oraibi is averted by the intercession of Old Spider Woman and her two grandsons, here the goddess alone comes to the rescue of the Matsonpis as the fire is about to consume their homes. The story line also contains an interesting twist in that Qa'ötaqtipu, and not Matsonpi, ultimately meets with disaster. It is Matsonpi which transforms the rivalry with Qa'ötaqtipu into a murderous affair, and which would thus appear to be more deserving of punishment.

Initially, the friendly challenges between the two villages by means of *wawarkatsinam*, or "Runner kachinas" end more or less without any resentment on the part of the losers. The somewhat harsh behavior of Matsonpi's Hömsona and Qa'ötaqtipu's Tsiitsik-lawqa balance each other out. However, when the Matsonpis challenge the Qa'ötaqtipus to a kickball race and lose, they react with a mixture of jealousy and envy, the symptomatic and almost predictable Hopi reaction in the given situation. This sentiment of jealousy, typically expressed by *qa naaniya*, "they are filled with jealousy," in the Hopi original, is one of the most detrimental emotions that governs the Hopi character. As noted in the introductory remarks to "The Abandonment of Huk'ovi," jealousy is readily attributed to the "bad Hopi" who may operate with witchcraft. Here, too, we immediately witness an escalation to this level of black magic, although the son of the Matsonpi chief is not referred to expressly as a *powaqa*, or "sorcerer." After the Matsonpis invite the Qa'ötaqtipus to the same kind of race for a second time, they reveal at the last moment that the ante has been upped. With death waiting for the loser, they clearly use supernatural means during the race to influence the outcome of the life-and-death competition in their favor.

When the Qa'ötaqtipu chief, justifiably, it would appear, plans revenge for the unprovoked killing of his nephew, the Matsonpi leader, full of remorse about the crime and concerned about the fate of his villagers, turns to Old Spider Woman for help. That this help is granted comes as a surprise. As a result, the firestorm designed to destroy Matsonpi skips over the village, only to turn on Qa'ötaqtipu itself and burn it to the ground.

Hin Qa'ötaqtipu Kiiqöti

Aliksa'i. Yaw yangqe Hopiikivaqe yeesiwkyangw pu' yaw pay piw
aqwhaqami kitsokinawit piw sinom yeese. Niiqe yaw yepeq
Matsonpeq piw peetu Hopiit yeskyaakyangw pu' yaw piw ayam
Qa'ötaqtipuy ep pu' piw peetu sinom yeese. Noq pay pi puma hisat
naat sutsep pangqe kitsokinawit nanap kikmongwi'yyungngwuniqw
yaw oovi imuy Matsonpituy kikmongwi'am yaw nööma'ytaqw
puma yaw lööqmuy timu'yta. Suukyawa yaw maananiqw pu' mi'wa
yaw tiyo. Noq pu' yaw ayamwat piw imuy Qa'ötaqtipuy ep ki'y-
yungqamuy mongwi'am piw yaw tuwat pan nööma'ytaqw pumawat
pay yaw panis suukw manti'yta. Niikyangw pamwa pep kikmongwi
yaw piw it hakiy tiyot tiw'aya'yta.

The Downfall of Qa'ötaqtipu

Aliksa'i. People were settled throughout Hopi land. There were villages far and wide. A few Hopis were also living at Matsonpi and over at Qa'ötaqtipu. Long ago, each community had its own leader. The chief of the Matsonpis was married and had two children, a girl and a boy. The headman of Qa'ötaqtipu also had a wife, but this couple had only a daughter. The chief's sister, however, had a boy. So the chief had a nephew.

Way back then these ancient people were always doing something or other. They organized all kinds of kachina dances, and when the kachinas arrived, they would entertain the villagers. As a rule, they staged the dances during the day. They also held social

Niiqe yaw puma hisatsinom pay tuwat hiihiita hisat hintsatskyangwu. Pay yaw puma tuwat hiihiituy tiilalwangwu. Pu' pay yaw piw ima katsinam pumuy amumi ökye' pay yaw puma piw pumuy tiitaptotangwu. Pu' yaw pay ephaqam haqamwat pay pas tiikive'yyungngwu. Niikyangw pay yaw puma piw tsetsletuy hintsatskyangwu. Noq yan yeskyaakyangw pay piw nanamuniwuy puuvut hintsatskyangwu, qööngöt wungpayangwu. Pay kya pi put pas akw enang yesngwu, namunwanyese. Pu' yaw pay piw ima katsinam ephaqam tuwat imuy tootimuy taataqtuy hongviyamuy aw pootayanik pu' yaw puma piw wawar'ökingwu. Kwitangöntaqa, Kwitanono'a, Tsilimoktaqa, Petosmoktaqa, pu' Nahoykwurukni'ytaqa pu' Tsi'rumtaqa, Saytaqa, Tasiipölölö, Tsilitosmoktaqa, Putskoomoktaqa, Hömsona, Aykatsina. Puuvuma pi hiitu wawarkatsinam kya pi yuyutyangwuniqw puuvumuy kya pi hiituy yuuyaangwu.

Noq pu' yaw hisat Ösömuyva naat yaw pay qa pas pangqe' kwaakwangqattiqw naat yaw ima taataqt tootim kivaqlöva yeese. Noq yaw yep Matsonpe yaw puma haqamwat kivapt nanawinya yaw as puma yuk Qa'ötaqtipuy aw imuy wawarkatsinmuy akw pangso yuutukwisni. Niiqe pu' yaw puma pay put aw suntiqe pu' yaw puma oovi ang kivanawit mimuywatuy aa'awnayaqw pu' yaw pay pumawat piw tuwat kwangwtotoyaqe pay yaw sonqa amumumyaniqey pumuy amumi pangqaqwa.

Paapiy pu' yaw puma oovi piw nanamunlalwangwuniiqe pay yaw puma su'aw tsange' taalat aqwhaqami pay pas a'nitotiqe pay yaw puma oovi ep qavongvaqw pay awyaniqey yaw it aw sunti. Noq pumuy yaw amungaqw yaw i' kikmongwit ti'at pas yaw pay as hiisavo pan wawart pay yaw pam pas a'ni höngiti. Pas yaw put tsaavo qa wiikiyangwu. Pu' yaw pam pay se'elhaq kiimi ahoy pituqw pu' yaw mimawat tuwat ökiwtangwu.

Niiqe pu' yaw oovi ep qavongvaqw pay yaw puma iits talavay nöönösat pu' yaw puma pay suup haqam soosoyam tsovaltiqe pu' yaw puma pay paasat yuuyahiwta. Niiqe pu' yaw puma pay iits yukuyaqe pu' yaw puma pay aw Qa'ötaqtipuy paasat hoytakyangw pay yaw puma qa pisoq'iwwisa. Niiqe pay yaw oovi paasat taawanasaproyakiwtaqw pu' yaw puma pepwat kitsokive ökiiqe pu' yaw puma aw kiimi pas yungqe pu' yaw puma aw pas kiisonmi yungya. Niiqe pay yaw puma pep a'ni hiinumya. Pu' yaw ima lööyöm Kooyemsit pumuy amumumniiqe puma yaw pumuy na'mangwuyamuy amungem iikwiwnuma. Noq pay yaw paasat ima sinom kur nanaptaqe yaw oovi angqe' put naa'awintota ima wawarkatsinam pep ökiiqat.

dances. And every once in a while they arranged for special kickball races. Races were definitely part of their lives. For example, if the kachinas wanted to test the running endurance of boys and men, they came to challenge them to races. These were Runner kachinas such as the Kwitangöntaqa, Kwitanono'a, Tsilimoktaqa, Petosmoktaqa, Nahoykwurukni'ytaqa and Tsi'rumtaqa. Also the Saytaqa, Tatsiipölölö, Tsilitosmoktaqa, Putskoomoktaqa, Hömsona and Aykatsina. These and other Runner kachinas used to participate in these challenge races.

In those days of old during the month of Ösömuya, when the weather was not really warm yet, boys and men used to spend much of their time in the kivas. One day, the members of a kiva were planning at Matsonpi to dress up as Runner kachinas and go to Qa'ötaqtipu to challenge its people to races. Since everybody agreed with the idea, they let the residents of the other kivas know. They, too, were looking forward to the event and promised to join in.

From that time on they all practiced running. By the end of the seventh day they were all in excellent shape, so they decided to go the next day. The son of the chief, who was part of the contingent, had only been practicing for a short while, but had became a formidable runner. No one ever surpassed him over a short distance. During practice runs, he usually was back at the village long before the other runners returned.

The following morning the runners breakfasted early. Thereupon they all assembled at one place and put on their kachina costumes. And since they were finished early, they took their time on the way to Qa'ötaqtipu. The sun was already past the midday mark when they reached their destination. Upon entering the village, they headed straight to the plaza. There they strutted around, striking commanding poses. Two Kooyemsi kachinas, who had accompanied the group, were hauling their presents around for them. When the villagers became aware of the Runner kachinas, news of their arrival spread quickly.

Noq pu' yaw paasat i' hak pay wuuyoq taaqa, pam yaw pep hapi katsinmongwi, pumuy amumi nakwsu. Hisat pas pamsa pumuy tumala'ytangwu. Pas pumuy aw mongwi. Pam yaw amumi nakwsuqe pu' yaw pumuy amumi pangqawu, "Ya uma hakim tuwat yakta?" yaw pam pumuy amumi kita.

Noq pay pi ima Kooyemsit pi yu'a'atangwuniiqe puma yaw paniqw oovi piw pumuy amumum waynuma. Pumuy wawarkatsinmuy amungem yu'a'ataniqe oovi. Niiqe puma yaw oovi paasat pu' put taaqat hu'wana. Noq pu' yaw pam taaqa pumuy piw amumi pangqawu, "Ta'ay, noq pay pi uma son paysoq yaktay. Oovi uma hintsaknumyaqey nuy put aa'awnayaniy," yaw pam pumuy amumi kita.

"Owiy, pi pay ima angqw imuy tootimuy taataqtuy amumi nanavö'wisa. Itam angqw yuyutwisa, sinmuy tayawnawisa. Pay paniqw itam ökiwiwta," yaw aw kita. "Noq oovi ima hohongvit pew haane' yep imuy amumum yuyutyani," yaw puma put aw kita.

"Kur antsa'ay," yaw pam kita. "Ta'ay, uma tootim taataqt qa naavevewnayat pew haane' antsa imuy na'mangwuyamuy oovi imuy amumum yuyutyaniy. Tsangaw kur ima put niiti'yvayay," yaw pam pep pumuy tsovaltiqamuy amumi kita.

Noq pay yaw as mootiniqw pay yaw qa hak aw hawniqey naawakna. Pas yaw hisatniqw pu' yaw haqawa mooti awniiqe pu' yaw hiitawat amum warikniqe yaw put namortaqe pu' yaw put aw maamasaqw pu' yaw puma oovi naama wari. Noq pay yaw pam katsina put qa wiikiqw pu' yaw pam suukyawa Kooyemsi pumuy na'mangwuyamuy aw tunatyawtaqa pu' yaw oovi put warikqat angqw peehut maqa. Paasat pu' yaw mimawat aw kiisonmi hantivaya. Pu' yaw puma pangso naakwustakyangw pu' yaw puma pep pumuy amumum yuyutya. Noq pu' yaw imuy katsinmuy amungaqwwat yaw pam himuwa hiitawat amum warikye' qa wiikiqw pu' yaw pam put pö'aaqa pu' yaw pumuy na'mangwuyamuy peehut aasatangwu. Noq yaw imuy katsinmuy amungaqw yaw i' Hömsona pas yaw kur a'ni hönginiiqe pay yaw pas hiitawat amum warikye' pay yaw pas sonqa put wiikingwu. Pu' yaw pam pay panis hiitawat angk pite' pay yaw pam paasat put höömiyat tsöqöt pu' yaw pay paasat put angqw tsaakiknangwu. Pay yaw pam qa suukw oovi pay pantsanqw pay yaw put maqastoti, put Hömsonat. Pay pi son höömiy qa kyaakyawnayangwu. Pay yaw put pas qa hak suusa pö'a. Noq pam yaw pangqw Matsonngaqw put kikmongwit ti'at yaw kur putakw, mit Hömsonat akwniiqa.

An elderly man who was the kachina chief came up to them. Long ago it was always him who took take care of the kachinas. That was his task. He said to the viewers by way of a greeting, "Are you walking about, strangers?"

Kooyemsi kachinas, of course, are in the habit of talking. For this reason they were along so that they could speak on behalf of the Runner kachinas. They answered in the affirmative. The Kachina chief continued, "Well, you must be about with a purpose. Tell me what the reason for your coming is."

"Yes," replied the two Kooyemsi, "these here came to compete with your boys and men. We came to run and provide some entertainment for your people at the same time. That's why we are here. So let your strong runners come down from the rooftops and race against them."

"Very well," he consented. "All right then," he shouted up to the boys and men, who had gathered meanwhile. "Have confidence in yourselves and come on down from the roofs. You can run against these kachinas for these prizes. I'm glad they brought a great load."

At first, no one was willing to come down. Finally, one volunteered. He selected a Runner kachina and, at a given signal, the two raced off. The kachina failed to catch up with him, so one of the Kooyemsi who was in charge of the presents, gave the runner a few. Now the others also started to descend to the plaza. They came up to the Runner kachinas and challenged them. Each time one of the kachinas ran with a villager and could not catch him, he lost and the villager was awarded some of the prizes. One of the kachinas was a Hömsona. He was an excellent runner, so good in fact that he caught all of his challengers. The moment he caught up with one, he grabbed him by his hair and cut a piece from it. When several of the Qa'ötaqtipu runners had suffered this fate, they became scared of the Hömsona. After all, they really treasured their hair. Not one of the Qa'ötaqtipu runners succeeded in beating him. The boy who was impersonating the Hömsona was of course the son of the Matsonpi chief.

Noq pay yaw puma pas pep wuuyavo yuyutyaqw pu' yaw pay pumuy katsinmuy na'mangwu'am sulawtiqw pu' yaw pay nawus pantaniqat pam suukyawa Kooyemsi pangqawu. Noq pu' yaw i' katsinmongwi pu' yaw pangqawu, "Kur antsa'ay, pay pi nawus antsa pantaniy. Pay niikyangw uma itamuy a'ni tayawnayay. Noq pay ason nuy umuy mooti yuwsinaqw pu' uma haalaykyaakyangw aqwhaqami umuukiy aqw ninmaniy," yaw pam pumuy amumi kitaaqe pu' yaw pam pumuy soosokmuy pahohuytaqw, hoomay angqw pumuy amuupa oyaqw, pu' yaw puma paasat aqwhaqami ahoy ninma.

Pu' yaw puma ahoy kiy ep ökiiqe pay yaw puma haalaytotiqey pangqaqwa. Pay yaw puma kwangwa'ewtotaqey naanami pangqaqwa. Himuwa yaw hin hiniwtapnaqey pay yaw tuwat put mimuywatuy amumi yu'a'atangwu. Yanhaqam yaw puma pep hintotiqe pu' yaw paapiy oovi piw yeese.

Noq pu' yaw pay aapiy lööshaqam yaasangwvaqw pu' yaw ima Qa'ötaqtipuy angqw pu' tuwat yaw pangso Matsonpiy aw nanavö'-wisniqey yaw yan tunatuytotaqe pu' yaw puma oovi paapiy pu' tuwat naahongvilalwaqe yaw oovi naaqavo haqami yuutukwisngwu. Noq pu' yaw pumuy amungaqw i' kikmongwit tiw'aya'at pas tuwat a'nitiqw pay yaw haqaapiy puma put amum yuutukqam put qa wiikiyangwu. Niiqe pu' yaw puma oovi pay put aw yankyaakyangw pu' yaw oovi hisat pangsoyaniqey tokiltota.

Paapiy pu' yaw puma oovi tuwat put tokilay ngöytotaqe pu' yaw tuwat put wiikiya. Paasat pu' yaw puma oovi tuwat yuuyaaqe pu' yaw tuwat oovi matsonmiqya. Niiqe puma yaw pay oovi pas suhopaqw pangso ökiwisqe yaw oovi töötökiy qa pevewwisqw pay yaw kur puma pep kiivit nanaptaqe pay yaw oovi angqe' naa'awta. Niiqe pay yaw pumawat oovi amuusavo kiisonmi naakwusta. Niiqe pay yaw puma oovi pep tsovawtaqw pu' yaw puma pangso yungwisa. Pu' yaw puma pangso yungqe pu' yaw puma pep töötöqlalwakyangw pu' piw a'ni hiinumya.

Paasat pu' yaw pam katsinmongwi pep pu' tuwat pumuy amumi nakwsuqe pu' yaw pumuy tuwat tuuvingta puma hintsaknumyaqat. Noq pu' yaw pam piw pumuy amungaqw i' Kooyemsi put paasat aa'awna puma yuyut'ökiiqatniqw pu' yaw pam taaqa oovi pumuy taataqtuy tootimuy pangso kiisonmi hanniqat amumi pangqawu.

Noq pu' yaw puma oovi tuwat aw hanqe pu' yaw oovi tuwat pep pumuy yuyut'ökiiqamuy amumum yuyutlalwa. Noq pay yaw puma as oovi tuwat pay hiitawat as pö'ayangwuniqw pas yaw qa hak suusa

After the races had gone on for a long time, the Kachinas' presents were depleted, whereupon one of the Kooyemsi indicated that this was the end. The kachina chief said, "Very well, this will be it. You really provided us with great delight. So let me say farewell to you in the proper way, and then you return to your homes with happy hearts." With that he distributed pahos and sacred cornmeal among them, whereupon the Runner kachinas departed.

Upon arriving back at Matsonpi, everybody expressed his happiness. They all agreed that they had had a good time. Everybody shared with his friends how he had fared in the races. This is what the Matsonpis did there, and then life went on for them again.

About two years later the menfolk of Qa'ötaqtipu in turn expressed their intention to go to Matsonpi and have a running competition with its people. So they too began to prepare for the event and get in shape. Day after day they went running somewhere. The nephew of the chief also took part and became very good. Those who accompanied him no longer succeeded in keeping up with him. So with him as an excellent runner, they set a date on which they intended to go to Matsonpi.

From that day on the Qa'ötaqtipus lived in anticipation of the event. Eventually, the time for their departure arrived. Everybody put on his kachina costume, and then they headed out to Matsonpi. Arriving directly from the northeast, they let their cries ring out as they were moving along. The Matsonpi villagers heard them and were sharing the news with each other. Ahead of the arriving visitors, they headed to the plaza. When all the villagers were assembled there, the Runner kachinas made their entry. As they entered, they kept uttering their characteristic cries, and strutted about in commanding poses.

The kachina chief walked up to them and asked them what they were doing. Again it was the Kooyemsi who declared that they had come to race with them, whereupon the kachina chief bade the men and boys to come down to the plaza from the roofs.

The menfolk complied and started to compete with the Runner kachinas. They won several races against them, but not once did anyone succeed in beating the Tuutsiitsiklawqa. Whenever he caught up with someone, he tore up the loser's clothes. He really dealt severely with each loser. This Runner kachina was, of course, the nephew of the Qa'ötaqtipu chief. He had dressed in the guise of the Tuutsiitsiklawqa.

it Tuutsiitsiklawqat pö'a. Pu' yaw pamwa pu' tuwat hiitawat angk
pite' pu' yaw tuwat pi pantingwuniiqe pu' yaw oovi hiitawat yuwsiyat aapa tsiitsiktangwu. Niikyangw pay yaw pam hiitawat pas
okiw pas qa atsat nu'an hintsanngwu. Noq pam yaw kur put kikmongwit tiw'aya'at put tuwat yuwsi.

Noq pu' yaw puma oovi tuwat pep pumuy amumum pay pas
lomawuyavo yuyutlalwaqw pu' yaw pay hisatniqw pumuy katsinmuy na'mangwu'am sulawtiqw pangso pu' yaw puma pay oovi
qe'toti. Noq pu' yaw paasat i' katsinmongwi piw tuwat pumuy
hoomay amuupa maqaqw paasat pu' yaw puma tuwat ninma.

Noq pu' yaw pumuy ninmaqw pu' yaw ima Matsonpe taataqt
tootim pay yaw kur hihin qa naaniya pam Tuutsiitsiklawqa pumuy
pantsanqw. Niiqe pu' yaw puma piw pay suyan pangqw Qa'ötaqtipuy angqw katsinamyaqw puma navoti'yyungqe pu' yaw puma oovi
pumuy amumi piw naat hin hepyaniqey yan yaw puma yukuya.
Niiqe pu' yaw puma paapiy piw oovi naahongvilalwa. Niiqe pu' yaw
puma pay hihin pas hongvitotiqe pu' yaw puma paasat pumuy
kiiyamuy aw tuu'awwisni hisat puma yuutukniqat. Noq paasat pu'
yaw oovi puma hakiywat pangso hoonayaqw pu' yaw oovi pep
Qa'ötaqtipuy ep tuu'awi pitu. Noq pu' yaw pam hak pangso ayatiwqa pu' yaw pumuy aa'awna yaw puma yaapiynen naalötok pu'
pangso matsonmiye' pu' yaw puma pep pumuy amumum wung-
payaniqat yan yaw pam pep tuu'awva.

Noq pu' yaw oovi pep i' tuu'awi pituqw pu' yaw pep pumuy
tsa'akmongwi'am yan tsa'lawu. Noq pu' yaw puma pep hohongvit
paapiy pu' piw yuyutyangwuniiqe pay yaw puma su'aw piw pumuy
Matsonpituy tokilayamuy aqwhaqami a'nitoti. Niiqe pu' yaw oovi
pumuy tokilayamuy aqw pituqw pay yaw puma piw awya.

Noq pu' yaw ima Matsonpit pi pay suyan pumuy pangqw nuu-
tayyungqe pu' yaw puma pay oovi aapiy pep Matsonpiy ahopqöyve
tsovawtaqw pu' yaw mimawat angqw hoopaqw pumuy amumi öki.

Noq pu' yaw puma pep suuvo tsovaltiqw pu' yaw puma Matsonpit pumuy aa'awnaya haqami puma yuutukniqat. Noq yaw
puma aqw suukwiniwiqyakyangw pu' yaw puma pepeq it pöövat aw
ökye' paasat pu' yaw puma pay teevengewatyakyangw pu' yaw
pepehaq i' suukya sunalahotskiniqw put yaw puma paasat qönikwis-
ni. Paasat pu' yaw puma pay ason angqw ahoy haqaqw yuutukqey
pangsoq ahoyyani.

Noq pay yaw mimawat naanakwhaqw pu' yaw oovi haqawa,
"Taa'!" kitaqw pu' yaw puma oovi yuutukkyangw pu' yaw puma

After the two sides had raced with each other for a good while, the kachinas finally ran out of gifts and stopped. The kachina chief bade them farewell by bestowing pahos and cornmeal on them, and then the Runner kachinas departed.

Upon their leaving for home, the men and boys at Matsonpi were a little upset that the Tuutsiitsiklawqa had treated them so harshly. And since they knew for sure that the kachinas were from Qa'ötaqtipu, they decided to test their running skills in a kickball race. They started getting into shape, and when they felt pretty good, they thought it was time to inform the Qa'ötaqtipus about the day of the race. This time they sent a messenger, and this is how the news arrived at Qa'ötaqtipu. The one who delivered the message explained that if the runners from Qa'ötaqtipu came over to Matsonpi in four days, they could compete with them in a kickball race.

As soon as the message had arrived, the Qa'ötaqtipu crier-chief broadcast it from the rooftop. All the good runners started practicing, and just by the deadline the Matsonpis had set they reached their top form. So they went over to Matsonpi.

The Matsonpis were clearly expecting them. They were all gathered on the northeast side of their village when the visitors arrived from that direction.

As soon as they were all assembled at one place, the Matsonpis described to them the course along which the race was going to take place. Running due northwest, they first would come to a wash. From there they would head southwest until they reached a single juniper tree, which was to be the turning point. Then they would return along the same course.

The Qa'ötaqtipus agreed, whereupon someone shouted, "Taa!" and the race was under way. Sure enough, they headed out in a northwesterly direction. Both groups were equally good and moving along, kicking their kicking stones at about the same pace. Soon they reached the wash, from where they continued in a southwesterly direction. Once again, the two groups were advancing at the same speed, kicking the stone nodule with the same skill. Whenever one group drew ahead, it did not take long before the other drew even and took the lead. In this fashion the rival groups kept passing each other.

antsa aqw kwiniwiqwatya. Noq pay yaw puma pas kur sunhaqam a'niyaqe pay yaw puma oovi pas sunhaqam aqw wungpaya. Pu' yaw antsa puma oovi pangsoq pövamiq ökikyangw pangqw pu' yaw puma aqw teevengeya. Paapiy pu' yaw puma pay piw pas sun hinwisa. Pay yaw puma kur piw pas sun a'ni wungpatuwi'yyungwa. Pay yaw oovi hiituwat as mooti'ywisqw pay yaw naat qa wuuyavotiqw pay yaw piw mimawat momiq nöngakngwu. Pay yaw puma pas pansa aqwhaqami naa'eepeqtiwisa.

Panwiskyaakyangw pu' yaw puma pangso teevenge put hotskit aqw ökiiqe puma yaw pepeq nanamtökyaqe pu' yaw puma piw pangqwwat ahoy kiimiq pay piw an hoyta. Niiqe pay yaw puma oovi as pas sungsaq aqw ökikyangw pay yaw ima Qa'ötaqtipuy angqwyaqam yaw hihin mooti aqw ökiiqe pay yaw puma oovi puma Matsonpit haqe' tuuwuuyaqw put mooti nöngakqe yaw oovi puma mootitota. Niiqe pu' yaw puma paasat soosoyam ahoy ökiiqe pu' yaw puma pep haqam suuvo tsovaltiqe pu' yaw pep naanami haalaylalwa.

Yantoti yaw puma pepnit pu' yaw puma pay pangqw paasat ahoy ninma. Niikyangw pay yaw puma imuy Matsonpituy amumi maamatsya pay yaw puma suyan piw qa naaniya pö'yyaqe. Noq pay yaw kur puma pumuy amumi su'an maamatsyaqw pay yaw oovi puma Qa'ötaqtipuy angqw wawarkatsinam panis ahoy ökit pay yaw puma piw naat pumuy amumi pootayaniqey yaw yan pasiwnayaqe pay yaw naat oovi aapiy qa wuuyavotiqw pay yaw piw pumuy Qa'ötaqtipuy angqwyaqamuy amungk tuu'awi pitu. Niikyangw paasat pu' yaw pay ima hakim pas nalt pu' naama warikni. Noq pay yaw i' hak pep put tuu'awvaqa pay yaw put qa enang pangqawu. Noq pay ima Qa'ötaqtipuy angqwyaqam pay yaw piw naanakwha. Niikyangw paasat pay yaw puma oovi pay pas hihin yaavo tokiltota.

Paapiy pu' yaw puma oovi piw yuutukwisngwu. Noq pu' yaw i' Qa'ötaqtipuy angqw tiyo, put kikmongwit tiw'aya'at, pay hintiqw piw pan wuuwaqe pam yaw oovi paapiy pay pas put qa matavi'yma. Pam yaw aasakis talavaynit pu' tapkiqw piw warikngwu. Pay yaw pam pangqw kiy angqw taatöq tuwat pang haqe' sun tutskwa'ytaqw pangsa wawari. Noq pu' yaw i'wa Matsonngaqw kikmongwit ti'at pu' tuwat pay pas pangso kiy kwiniwiqsa yaw tuwat wawari. Panmakyangw pu' yaw paasat piw pumuy Matsonpituy tokilayamuy aqw pituqw pu' yaw oovi ima Qa'ötaqtipuy angqw tootim taataqt pu' piw ahoy pangsoyaqw pu' yaw puma pay piw pep Matsonpiy ahopqöyve naanami piw öki.

Eventually, they reached the juniper tree in the southwest. They circled this, and moved back towards the village again. They did not arrive at the same time, however. The group from Qa'ötaqtipu was a little faster and the first to cross the line that the Matsonpis had drawn. When everybody was back, they assembled in one place and mutually expressed their gratitude.

This is how the men from Qa'ötaqtipu fared in the kickball race. As they returned home, however, it was clear to them that the Matsonpis were upset about losing the race. It was not hard to figure out what was on their minds. Sure enough, no sooner were the Runner kachinas from Qa'ötaqtipu back home than they had decided to challenge the Matsonpis anew. So it was not long before a new message from Matsonpis came to them. This time it was planned that only two runners would compete, but the messenger did not mention this detail. The men from Qa'ötaqtipu consented to the invitation, and a date was set for some time in the not too distant future.

Once again everybody went to practice running. For some reason the nephew of the chief from Qa'ötaqtipu suspected something and decided not to quit running. Every morning and evening he practiced. He usually ran from his house in a southeasterly direction to an area where the land was flat. The son of the Matsonpi chief, on the other hand, only ran to a point northwest of his house. Eventually, they reached the date which the Matsonpis had set for the race. Once again the menfolks from Qa'ötaqtipu set out. As before, the two groups met northeast of Matsonpi.

Noq pay yaw pumuy pep pas tsovaltiqw pu' yaw puma pangqw
Matsonngaqwyaqam pu' pumuy amumi pangqaqwa pay yaw puma
hakim panis lööyöm warikni. Puma Qa'ötaqtipuy angqw kikmongwit
tiw'aya'at Matsonngaqw kikmongwit tiyat amum warikni. Niikyangw pu' yaw puma pas yaw qatsiy oovini. Noq pay yaw pumuy
kikmongwi'am yaw kur pumuy amumum ep pituuqe pam yaw
paasat pay nawus pumuy hu'wana. "Haw'owi? Ya pu' pas pantaniy?
Is ohi antsa'ay. Noq pay pi itam umumum yuutukniqe naanakwhaqe
oovi paniqw yep ökiy. Noq pay pi itam son kya pi oovi nawus qa
naanakwhaniy," yaw pam pumuy amumi kita.

Paasat pu' yaw puma Matsonngaqwyaqam piw yaw pang haqe'
tuuwuuya. Nit pu' yaw puma piw haqam paas qölötota. Pangsoq
yaw mootitaqa yaw mitwat kwaptukniqat puma pangqaqwa. Pantotiqw pu' yaw paasat hak pang tuuwuhiwtaqat ep pu' yaw hak piw it
poyot tsööqökna. Putakw yaw ason haqawa mitwat kwaptukni.

Paasat pu' yaw puma hakim naama warikniqam pu' yaw paasat
neepeq wunuptu, i' yaw Matsonngaqw kikmongwit ti'atniqw pu'
yaw i' Qa'ötaqtipuy angqw kikmongwit tiw'aya'at. Niiqe paasat pu'
yaw hak piw, "Taa'!" kitaqw paasat pu' yaw puma piw wari. Niiqe
pay yaw puma piw paasat haqe' puma mootiwat wungpayaqw pay
yaw puma piw pangni. Niiqe pu' yaw puma oovi pay piw aqw
kwiniwiq wari. Pu' yaw puma oovi piw aqw kwiniwiq pövamiq pitut
pu' yaw puma paasat piw teevengewat. Noq paasat pay yaw as i'
Matsonngaqw tiyo mooti'yma. Noq pay yaw hiisavoniqw pay yaw
miwa put wiikiqe pu' yaw pay eepeqtakyangw pu' yaw put aw
pangqawu, "Pay nu' haak yaapiy hiisavo mooti'ymaniy," yaw pam
put aw kitat pu' yaw pam pay aqle' aqwhaqami warikma. Niiqe pu'
yaw pam panmakyangw pu' yaw pay paasat aqwhaqami tuuwayamaqw pu' yaw pay pam angkniiqa pay pephaqam huruuti. Huruutit
pu' yaw pay pam paasat qötsahöwiniwti. Pay yaw pam kur piw pay
a'ni himuniiqe pay yaw pam paasat kur putakwniqe yaw oovi pam-
niwti. Paasat pu' yaw oovi mi'wa pay aqwhaqaminiqw pu' yaw pam
höwi pangqw puuyaltikyangw pay yaw pam paasat pas a'ni'maqe
pay yaw oovi naat qa wuuyavotiqw pay yaw pam put mooti'ymaqat
atsva aqw puuyawmaqw pam yaw qa navota. Niiqe pu' yaw pam
pay qa pan mimuywatuy amumi naamaataknaniqe pu' yaw pam
oovi pay naat as qa pumuy amumiq pitukyangw pay oovi mooti put
Qa'ötaqtipuy angqw tiyot haq apyevetikyangw pu' piw haqam
qatuptu. Paasat pu' yaw pam piw pay ahoy hopiniwti. Paapiy pu'
yaw pam piw oovi pay pas naap höngiy akw pangsoq pituto. Niiqe

When everyone had assembled, the men from Matsonpi revealed to the others that only two would compete against each other. These would be the nephew of the Qa'ötaqtipu chief and son of the Matsonpi chief. At stake would be life or death. Since the Qa'ötaqtipu chief had accompanied his group, he was compelled to agree to the proposition. "Is that so? Is this how it's going to be now? That's too bad, indeed. But we agreed to run with you, that's why we came. So we'll have to go along with these rules, whether we want to or not." This is what he replied.

The Matsonpis once again drew a line in the sand. Then they dug a hole into which the winner was to sever the loser's head. Finally, one of them thrust a knife into the ground by the line. That was to be used for cutting off the loser's head.

Now the two boys chosen to run against each other stood side by side at the starting line. They were, of course, the son of the Matsonpi chief and the nephew of the Qa'ötaqtipu chief. Someone shouted, "Taa!" and the two dashed off. They embarked on the same course that had earlier been used for the kicking stone race. So once more they ran in a northeasterly direction. Upon reaching the wash, they headed southwest. At this point the Matsonpi boy was ahead, but soon the other one caught up with him. Passing him, he said, "I'll take the lead now for a while," and sped on. After some time he disappeared over the horizon. Now the one following him stopped in his tracks. Having arrested his run, he changed himself into a white dove. Evidently, he possessed greater than human powers and now was going to race in the guise of the bird. His competitor was far gone, but flying in the form of the dove, he was able to advance with tremendous speed. Soon he passed over his rival, without the latter being aware of it. Since he had no desire to show himself in this guise to the spectators, he landed before reaching them. He was far ahead of the boy from Qa'ötaqtipu. Then he changed back into his human shape. Under his own power he was now arriving. When he reached the finish line first, the people from Qa'ötaqtipu, poor things, became unhappy. Surely they would have to return home without the chief's nephew.

pay yaw oovi pam mooti epeq pituqw yaw ima kiyavaqvit okiw qa
haalaytoti, suyan pi yaw puma pay paasat put kikmongwit tiw'ayayat pangqw qa ahoy wikkyaakyangw ninmaniqey oovi.

Pay yaw pam mooti pepeq pituqw pay yaw oovi aapiy pas
lomawuyavotiqw pu' yaw pam tuwat amumi pituuqe pu' tuuwihit
angqe tso'omti. Yaw hiikwislawu. Noq pay yaw Matsongngaqw tiyo
pepeq put poyot yawkyangw put nuutayta. Pas yaw pam as qa yan
unangwti. Suyan pi yaw pam as put eepeqta. Pu' yaw piw pam as qa
suusa put wiiki. Noq pay yaw pam put piw qa ep hingqawlawu.
Naap hisat pi yaw puma pas soosoyam naangu'aatote' kya pas a'ni
naahintsatsnaniqw oovi. Pay pi yaw ason putsa niinayani. Pay yaw
pam yantiqe pu' yaw pay oovi qa hingqawu.

Paasat pu' yaw pam tiyo mooti epeq pituuqa put yaw aw pangqawu, "Ta'ay, pay um nawus qa hin naawaknat pewniy. Pay pi
nuwupi itam naanami yan yukuyay," yaw pam put aw kitaqw put
yaw pam oovi pay nawus qa hin naawaknat pu' pay put angk pangso
pep haqam puma paniqw qölötotaqw. Paasat put yaw pam Matsonngaqw tiyo mitwat pang tutskwava tsooralat pu' yaw pam put koo-
paveq höömiyat tsöqööqe pu' yaw put kwuuvalat pu' put kwaptuku.
Pavan yaw put ungwa'at pangsoq qölömiq peep oopo. Yanhaqam
yaw puma put Qa'ötaqtipuy angqw put kikmongwit tiw'ayayat
pephaqam ngastatoti. Paasat pu' yaw puma oovi pay pangqw qa
haalaymokiwkyaakyangw ninma.

Paapiy pu' yaw puma oovi piw pankyaakyangw as yeese. Noq
pay yaw yep Qa'ötaqtipuy ep pumuy kikmongwi'am pay yaw tuwat
son naat pantaniqat yan yaw tuwat tunayalti. Niiqe pu' yaw pam
oovi imuy Matsonpituy amungem hiita qa ankiwakw pasiwnaniqey
yaw yan wuuwa. Niiqe paapiy pu' yaw pam oovi pay tuwat pas
putsa wuuwankyangw piw tuwat qatu.

Niiqe pu' yaw pam oovi panmakyangw pu' yaw pam imuy
Yaayapontsamuy u'na. Puma yaw it uuwingwuynit pu' piw it huu-
kyangwuy himu'yyungqw pu' yaw pam pumuy amumi pan naawaknaqw pu' yaw puma imuy Matsonpituy amumi put engem naa'o'ya-
niqat yan yaw pam pumuy amumi ö'qalniqey yaw wuuwankyangw
pu' yaw pam oovi pumuy amungem paaholawu. Niiqe pu' yaw pam
paasat put hiisa' pangsoq pumuy amungem kimaniqey paasa'
yukuuqe pu' yaw pam oovi pangso pumuy kiiyamuy aqw put kima.
Niikyangw pay yaw pam pepeq pituuqe pay yaw pam qa pas pumuy
amumi yori. Pay yaw pam panis pumuy kiiyamuy iip put oyat pu'
yaw pam pep put amumi naawakna. Noq kur yaw puma put

A good length of time later the boy from Qa'ötaqtipu also completed the race. Breathing heavily, he jumped over the line, where the Matsonpi boy was waiting for him with a knife in his hand. He could not believe his eyes, for surely he had overtaken the Matsonpi boy. After that the other had never caught up with him. But he did not want to complain. After all, they might all get into a fight and kill each other. This way they would only kill him. This is what he thought, and therefore he did not say anything.

The winner from Matsonpi now said to him, "All right, you must come here to me without any fuss. There's nothing you can do about this. This is what we agreed upon." The boy did not resist and followed the other to the hole in the ground. The Matsonpi now forced him to lie down, grabbed him by the hair, pulled his head back, and cut it off. The blood gushed out so profusely that the hole was nearly full. This is how the group from Qa'ötaqtipu lost the nephew of its chief. Overcome with sadness, the men returned home.

From that time life went on again. But the chief in Qa'ötaqtipu had no intention of letting things remain the way they were. He was determined to plan something to the peril of the Matsonpis. From that time on he lived only with this thought on his mind.

As the days went by, he suddenly remembered the Yaayapontsas. They had power over fire and wind. If he prayed to them, they might take revenge on the Matsonpis for him. Having decided to seek them out, he made prayer sticks for them. When he had finished the amount he was going to take to them, he carried the pahos to their abode. Upon his arrival, he did not see the Yaayapontsas, however. So he left the pahos outside their house and then prayed to them. If they should consent to his wish, they should pick up those prayer sticks, he told them there.

nakwhanaye' puma yaw put tumalayat ömaatotaniqat yaw pam pep
pumuy amumi kita.
    Pantit pu' yaw pam pay paasat pangqw ahoy nima. Niiqe pay
yaw pas aapiy nalöstalqw pu' yaw pam piw pangsoq hin navotto.
Sen pi yaw puma put pahotmalayat ömaatota. Noq pu' yaw pam
epeq pituqw pay yaw pam qa hiita pep tuwa haqam pam as put
oyaaqey. Pay yaw pam oovi yan navota puma put pay nakwhanaya-
qat. Paasat pu' yaw pam oovi pay pangqaqw nima. Niikyangw pay
yaw pam pumuy qa pas tokiltoyna hisat puma pantotiniqat. Pay yaw
pam panis pumuy amumi pangqawu, pay yaw pam pumuy amuu-
peni. Hisat puma pantotiniqey aw wuuwaye' pay ason epyani. Niikyangw puma yaw it uuwingwuy akw pep pumuy haqami hintsatsnaniqat pay yaw pam itsa tungla'ytaqey yan yaw amumi naawakna.
    Noq pi ason pi yaw kur i' Matsonpe kikmongwi pu'sa putakw qa
haalayi. Pay yaw as pam navoti'yta puma pep suyan qa antotiqw put
tiyot paysoq qa naaniyaqey put ep put okiw niinaya. Niiqe pay pi
yaw pam pumuy piw qa ngas'ew meewaqe pay yaw oovi pam
songyawnen pumuy amumum put tiyot niina. Pu'sa yaw pam oovi
imuy Qa'ötaqtipuy angqw sinmuy ismaqas'iwta. Son pi yaw puma
put tiyot kwayyakyangw paysoq nakwhani'yyungwni. Pu'sa yaw
pam oovi put wuuwantangwu, hisat hapi puma pangqw pumuy
amumi put ep naa'o'yani.
    Haqaapiy pu' yaw pay pam pas wuwniwuy akw pas so'ontiqe
pu' yaw pam oovi pangqw kiy angqw hisat mihikqw nakwsu. Niiqe
pu' yaw pam pangqw pay teevengeniikyangw aw hihin kwiniwi.
Noq pephaqam yaw kur i' Kookyangwso'wuuti piw imuy mömuy
amum ki'ytaqw pangso yaw kur pam pumuy amumi taqa'nangwti.
Niiqe pu' yaw pam oovi pep pituuqe pu' yaw pam put so'wuutit aw
put tu'awi'yta hin puma pep hintotikyangw pu' put niinayaqat. Pu'
yaw pam put piw tuuvingta sen yaw pam son pangso pumuy
kiiyamuy awnen pu' yaw sen hin pep navotni, hin pi yaw puma
tuwat pumuy amungem wuuwantota. Noq pay yaw pam so'wuuti
navoti'yta pam pep pumuy kikmongwi'am pumuy amungem hin qa
ankiwakw pasiwnaqat. Pu' yaw qa pas aw pootat pay yaw pangqawu, "Owi," yaw kita, "pay antsa umungem qa ankiway pasiwti,"
yaw aw kita. "Puma uuwingwuy akw naa'o'yani," yaw aw kita.
    "Haw'owi?" yaw kita.
    "Owi," yaw Kookyangwso'wuuti kita.
    Paasat pu' yaw pam kikmongwi qa haalaytiqe pu' yaw pam oovi
put tuuvingta sen yaw pam son pumuy amungem aw hin yukuqw

With that he returned home. Four days later he went back to the Yaayapontsas to check if they had accepted his offerings. When he arrived, he could not find anything where he had deposited the pahos. He thereby knew that they had looked favorably on his wish. So he returned home. He had of course not set a date when they were to carry out the revenge. He had declared that that would be up to them. Whenever they would see fit to do it, they could do it. His express desire, however, had been that they punish the Matsonpi with fire.

The Matsonpi chief, meanwhile, was full of remorse about the terrible deed. He knew full well that they had committed a crime for killing that boy merely because they were jealous of his racing capability. By not even trying to intercede, it was as if he had killed the boy himself. Now, after the fact, he was leery of the people of Qa'ötaqtipu. He was afraid that they might retaliate. They had lost that boy and would not just sit still. All he could think of now was when they would strike in revenge.

As the days went by, he got completely worn out with worrying. So one dark night he set out from his house. He went southwest and then a little northwest. There, somewhere, Old Spider Woman was at home with her two grandchildren. It was then that he decided to seek their assistance. Upon his arrival he told the old woman under what circumstances they had caused the death of that boy. He asked her if she could not possibly go to Qa'ötaqtipu and find out what they were scheming. Old Spider Woman, however, already knew that the chief there had initiated something to the peril of the Matsonpis. There was no need for her to check. So she said, "Yes, a terrible disaster has been set in motion for you. They intend to avenge themselves with fire."

"Is that so?" the Matsonpi chief exclaimed.

"Yes," replied Old Spider Woman.

The Matsonpi chief became most unhappy and asked if she could now arrange something so that they would not be harmed. And since the old woman has all the people as her grandchildren; she said, "Don't worry, we'll help you. You won't burn to death." Right away

puma yaw qa hintotiniqat. Noq pay pi yaw pam so'wuuti pas soo-sokmuy mömu'ytaqe pay yaw oovi son pumuy amumi qa unangw-tapniqey yaw put aw pangqawu, "Pay itam son umumi qa unangw-tatveni. Pay son pas hisat pay uma yep uwikni," yaw kita. Niiqe pu' yaw pam oovi put aw tutapta puma hintotiniqat. "Ason pay hisat aw talöngvaniqw pay nu' son ung qa navotnani. Noq pu' um ason it tsa'akmongwiy ayataqw pu' pam pep tsa'lawqw pu' uma yukiq tuukwit hopqöymiwatyani, pay ason hihin töngvaqw pu'yani. Pay uma pepeq kiinawit huur tangalte' pay uma son hintotini." Pay yaw pam yan put aw tutaptaqw pu' yaw pam oovi pay paasat pangqw pay hihin suyan unangwa'ykyangw pu' nima.

Panmakyangw pu' yaw kur aw pitu. Niiqe pu' yaw oovi suuta-vangqw pu' yaw pumuy amumiq i' uuwingw wukovölangwpu amumiq hoyta. Noq paasat pu' yaw oovi i' Kookyangwso'wuuti pep put kikmongwit aa'awna pay pam angqw hoytaniqat. Niikyangw pay yaw naat pam qa pas pay pumuy amumiq pituni. Pay yaw naat pam pas löötokmi pu' son pangsoq qa pituni. Niikyangw naat yaw pam pumuy amumiq pan hoytimakyangw pam yaw naat suytsep-ngwat a'ni öqawi'ymani.

Yanhaqam yaw pam put navotnaqw pu' yaw pam kikmongwi paasat pu' tuwat paaholawu. Son pi yaw pam pas paysoq pumuy tusoq'ayatani. Son pi yaw pam nawus pumuy amungem hiita qa yukuni. Niiqe pu' yaw pam oovi pumuy amungem nakwakwusta. Noq pu' yaw i' so'wuuti piw it hiita lööqmuy taqvahot put aw enang tutaptaqw pu' yaw pam oovi put enang yuku. Put yaw pam soosok yukuuqe pu' yaw pam pumuy amungem put pangso kima. Noq pay yaw pam put pep pumuy amungem panvaqw pay yaw puma put tsutsyakya. Pay yaw haalaytoti. Paasat pu' yaw pam so'wuuti piw put aw pangqawu hin pam tsa'akmongwi'at ep qavongvaqw tsa'law-niqat. Ep qavongvaqw hapi pi yaw pam uuwingw pangsoq pumuy amumiq pituni. Paasat pu' yaw pam pumuy amumi put oyat pu' yan navot pu' yaw pam piw pangqaqw nima.

Qavongvaqw pu' yaw pay pam tsa'akmongwi su'its talavay pay pan tsa'lawu. Noq pu' yaw puma sinom yan nanaptaqe pu' yaw puma oovi pay paasat pangsoq hoopoqwatsa watkita. Niiqe pay yaw puma oovi paasat pangqe haqe' huur tangaltiqw pu' yaw pam Koo-kyangwso'wuuti pangso Matsonpiy taavangqöyminiiqe pu' yaw pam pep pay hihin tatkya mooti it taqvahot tsööqöknat pu' yaw pam put angqe pu' mooti hiisavathaqam wishöviy tootona. Paasat pu' yaw pam kwiniwiqwat nakwsuqe pu' yaw pam wishöviy pangsoq enang

she instructed him what to do. "I'll let you know when the day of the disaster comes. At that time I want you to have your crier chief announce to the people to come here to the northeast side of the butte around mid-morning. Tell them to hole up in the houses there. Then nothing will happen to them." These were Old Spider Woman's instructions. Thereupon the chief went home slightly relieved.

Finally, the day came. Directly from the southwest a fire ball was moving their way. Old Spider Woman now informed the chief at Matsonpi about this turn of events, adding that the danger was not immediate. The fire would not arrive before two days. But as it was moving toward them, it would constantly increase in strength.

Having been warned in this manner, the chief kept making prayer sticks. He knew he could not just ask Old Spider Woman and the two Pöqangw Brothers for help without any payment. Also, he was certain that she would not let them down. So he made prayer feathers for them. And since the old woman had also asked for two *taqvaho*, a special kind of prayer stick, he also fashioned those. When he was done, he took everything over to Old Spider Woman and her grandchildren. When he arrived with his offerings, the three expressed their joy about them. They were elated. Then the old woman explained how the crier-chief was to make his announcement the next day, for that day the fire was bound to reach them. Upon handing over his prayer items, and having been informed about the coming events, the chief left for home again.

The next day the crier-chief made his announcement first thing in the morning. As soon as the people heard the news, they ran off to the northeast, where they holed up. Meanwhile Old Spider Woman went to the southwest side of Matsonpi. There, a little to the southeast, she stuck the first *taqvaho* into the ground and spun a short piece of spider web around it. Then she hurried to a place in the northwest and, dragging her web along, planted the second *taqvaho* in the ground. Around this she wove her web too. Then she started weaving her web back and forth between the two stakes. After doing this several times, she was finished. She left everything the way it was and went home. This is how she helped the Matsonpis.

wiisilni'ymakyangw pu' yaw pam pep haqam piw mitwat paahot pu' piw tsööqökna. Pantit pu' yaw pam putwat piw angqe put wishöviy tootona. Paasat pu' yaw pam pephaqam pumuy amuutsava naanahoy put wishöviy laanativa. Niiqe pay yaw pam oovi qa suus pantit pu' yaw kur pam yukuuqe pu' yaw pam pay paasat oovi pep put pantaqat maatapt pu' yaw tuwat pangqaqw ahoy nima. Yanhaqam yaw pam tuwat pumuy pa'angwa.

Noq pay yaw oovi naat qa pas wuuyavotiqw pay yaw antsa pam wukovölangwpu uuwingw pep pitu. Niiqe pas pi yaw pam paasat antsa a'ni öqalat pep put wishövit laana'iwtaqat aqw pitukyangw pay yaw pam put qa angwuta. Pay yaw pam panis put aqw yeevakyangw pay yaw pam put atsvaqe a'ni öqalat tso'omtiqe yaw oovi pay pas Matsonpiy ahoophaqam pu' hisatniqw yeeva. Noq pay yaw puma pep Matsonpe sinom kur nanapta pam pumuy amutsva panmaqw. Pas pi yaw put angqw susmataq a'ni kokhalawva. Nit pay yaw pam uuwingw qa hiita taqtsokya.

Paasat pu' yaw pam pay pas pumuy ahoop yeevakyangw pu' yaw pam pay yuumosa aqw hoopoqwat piw mumamatima. Pu' hapi yaw pay paasat pepeq qa haqam himu put uutsi'ytaqw pay yaw pam pas oovi aqwhaqami panma. Pas pi yaw pam qa hiita hiita'yma.

Panmakyangw pu' yaw pam pay Qa'ötaqtipuy pas su'aqwniqw yaw qa hak nanvota. Pay yaw pas pam pumuy amumiq pitutoq pu' yaw kur hak navotqe pu' yaw mimuywatuy aa'awnaqw paasat pu' yaw unangwti. Paasat pu' yaw hak pay ngas'ew hiita neengem nitkya'ykyangw waayaniqey putsa aw pisoqtingwu. Pu' yaw peetu angqe' timuy oovi hepwawartinumya. Pavan yaw hin unangwa. Paasat pu' yaw himuwa hin hintsakkyangw pu' yaw pangqw pay naap haqamiwat waayangwu. Noq pu' yaw pumuy amuukwayngyap pu' pam uuwingw pumuy kitsokiyamuy aw pituuqe pu' yaw put pep soosok uwikna. Yan pay yaw pam pumuywat awniwtiqe pay yaw oovi pumuysa kiiyamuy uwiknat pay yaw Matsonpituysa qa hintsana. Pay yaw oovi puma songyawnen naap piw naanami nukpantoti. Yaayapontsatuy amumi uuwingwuy tuuvingtota akw Matsonpituy qöyaniqey.

Paasat pu' yaw puma pangqw sinom angqe' kitsokinawit okiw qatsihepnumya. Pay yaw puma pas soosokiva aatsavala. Peetu yaw pas hopoqkimiqhaqamiyaqw pu' yaw peetu yuk oraymiya. Pu' yaw peetu walmiqya, pu' Songoopami, pu' Huk'omi. Noq pu' yaw peetu pay yuk Matsonmi haypotota. Noq pay yaw puma pep pumuy piw qa amumi hinyungwt pay yaw puma pumuy pangsoyaqamuy

Not much later the big fire ball arrived. With great might it roared against the woven web, but failed to overcome it. As soon as the fire struck the web, it was hurled over it with great force, and some time later landed on the southeast side of Matsonpi. The people of Matsonpi could see how the flames jumped over them. The heat that radiated from them was terrible, but it set nothing on fire.

Upon falling back to the ground, the fire rolled straight on in a southeasterly direction. Since there was no barrier there to stop it, it simply continued on. Everything in its path fell prey to its flames.

Meanwhile the fire headed directly toward Qa'ötaqtipu, where no one was aware of it. Not before it was at their doorsteps did someone notice it. Immediately he alerted the others. Panic broke out. People did not know what to do first. With only a little bit of food in their arms, everyone ran for their lives. Some were dashing around in search of their children. It was an incredible scene. Somehow or other one person here, one there, managed to escape. Right behind them the fire storm reached their houses and engulfed everything in flames. Thus the revenge backfired. It fell back on the Qa'ötaqtipus and their village was burned. Matsonpi, on the other hand, was spared. The Qa'ötaqtipus had brought this disaster upon themselves through their own evil doings. After all, they had requested the Yaayapontsa to let the Matsonpis perish in a fire.

From village to village the Qa'ötaqtipu people, poor wretches, went looking for a place to live. They got scattered all over. Some moved all the way to the pueblos along the Rio Grande, whereas others sought refuge in Oraibi. Small contingents also went to Walpi, Shungopavi and Huk'ovi. A few even moved into the vicinity of Matsonpi. The people there bore no animosity toward them, and actually admitted them into their community. After all it was clearly they themselves who had committed a great wrong. Thus, some of the inhabitants of Qa'ötaqtipu settled there with the Matsonpis.

tangatota. Pay pi yaw suyan puma mooti qa antotiqe oovi. Noq pu'
yaw puma peetu oovi pay pep pumuy amumum yesva.

Paapiy pu' yaw puma as oovi pumuy amumum pep yesva. Niikyangw pay yaw puma tuwat pay hintaqat akw pep qa kwangwayese. Niiqe pay yaw puma hiisa'niiqam pangsoyaqam pay yaw oovi
pangqw aapiyyaniqey yaw kur yan naanami yukuya. Niiqe pu' yaw
oovi paasat pay himuwa naanap hisat timuy tsamkyangw pu' piw
haqamiwat kitsokimi piw qatsiheptongwu. Yan yaw pay puma piw
paasat angqe' kitsokinawit aatsavala. Angqe' yaw puma naakwii-
paya. Naat kya oovi pumuy sinomat angqe' nuutum yeese. Pay yuk
pölö.

From that day on, Matsonpis and Qa'ötaqtipus lived there together. But for some reason the Qa'ötaqtipus did not enjoy their life there. Therefore, all of those who had moved there decided to leave Matsonpi again. One here, one there they would round up their children and set out in search of a new start at another village. In this manner the Qa'ötaqtipus became scattered over many settlements and found new roots for themselves. Their descendants probably still live there with the others. And here the story ends.

3

Pivanhonkyapi: Destruction by Fire

The remains of the extinct Third Mesa village of Pivanhonkyapi lie some three and three-quarter miles northwest of Old Oraibi. Its location on a shelf some two hundred feet below the rim of a mesa which projects from Hotevilla is almost equidistant between the ruin of Huk'ovi to its east and Apoonivi, the highest point on the Hopi reservation, to its southwest.

The untranslatable name of the site, for which not even a folk-etymological interpretation exists among the Hopis, may, in its initial morpheme, relate to *pivani*, "weasel." However, there is no linguistic evidence for this semantic linkage. Like its neighbor Huk'ovi to the east, Pivanhonkyapi has never been excavated. On the basis of potsherd types, among them Jeddito Black-on-orange and Jeddito Black-on-white "that do not seem to have been in use after 1300 A.D.," Colton and Nequatewa speculate that the site was "occupied in the twelve hundreds" and abandoned before 1300 due to the great drought at the end of the 13th century (1932: 54).

Ethnographically, Pivanhonkyapi has become famous for the *saqtikive*, or "Ladder Dance," which was once staged there according to Hopi legend.[1] The ceremony involved an acrobatic dance act of kachina impersonators on top of implanted pine trees. Several of the deep holes into which the poles were inserted are still visible at the cliff edge.

The mytho-historical chain of events leading up to the annihilation of the village is quite simple. Bored with the monotony of their everyday activities, the residents of Pivanhonkyapi introduce the new board game of *totolospi*.[2] The game catches on quickly. Before long, it becomes such a craze that the entire community is affected. Individual as well as communal responsibilities are neglected. Bent exclusively on fun and good times, people embrace what is commonly termed *kwangwa'ewqatsi*, a "life style of pleasure." With gambling by both sexes soon leading to promiscuous sex, the uncontrollable situation reaches a climax when the village chief's wife, who is expected to be a model of virtue and decency, also succumbs to the game.

This chaotic state of affairs, marked by the total disintegration of all socially accepted standards and values, is referred to as *koyaanisqatsi* or "corrupt life," in Hopi. Composed of the elements *koyaanis-*, which cannot occur in isolation, and *qatsi*, "life/way of life," it represents the polar opposite of *suyanisqatsi*, which designates a "life of harmony and balance."

Since, in the eyes of the Hopi, *koyaanisqatsi* generally engulfs an entire community and constitutes a point of no return, only a new beginning can remedy the situation. To eradicate the evil and begin anew, *tabula rasa* must be created, which regularly implies the wholesale destruction of the corrupt community.

The socially untenable and unacceptable phenomenon of *koyaanisqatsi* is a frequent motif in Hopi oral literature. It figured as the prime factor in motivating the Hopi exodus from the underworld. Having gained wide currency as a result of Godfrey Reggio's movie,[3] the abstract-philosophical concept of *koyaanisqatsi* comprises a wide range of symptomatic ingredients. Most of these are spotlighted in a number of other Hopi terms which try to capture facets of its nature.

Thus, *nukusqatsi* declares *koyaanisqatsi* as a "bad life," *nukpanqatsi* as "evil life," and *qahopqatsi* as "uncivilized life." *Tuskyapqatsi* as well as synonymous *honaqqatsi*, "crazy life," decry the frenzy that is so characteristic of it. *Natsopqatsi*, "intercourse life," focuses on the sexual license it demonstrates. *Kwangwa'ewqatsi*, as was already mentioned above, emphasizes the pleasure principle. Both *nangwu'yqatsi*, "life of quarreling," and *qa naavaasqatsi*, "life of mutual disrespect," point to the overall disharmony and noncaring that distinguish this mode of living. As *powaqqatsi*, "life of sorcery," it focuses on the witchcraft practices and beliefs that are ever present during times of moral degeneration. *Naanaphin qatsi*, finally, says that "anything goes" in the haphazard order of this life style.

Nor is *koyaanisqatsi* semantically a closed, rigid expression, applicable only to the behavioral excesses of legendary times. On the contrary, its content is open-ended and flexible enough to absorb any new social aberration. Thus, when defined as *honaqqatsi*, "life of drunkenness," today, it refers to the problems of alcoholism and substance abuse that also confront modern Hopi society.

The following folk-statements are given as a sample of some of the ramifications of *koyaanisqatsi* in greater detail. To begin with, Text 23 presents an excerpt from a hitherto unpublished Hopi emergence myth in which the curse of *koyaanisqatsi* is described as an ever-escalating social disease.

Text 23

Aliksa'i. Yaw haqam atkya yeesiwa. Pay yaw hisathaqam pep yesngwuniiqe pay yaw pasi'nangway yesngwu, nukwangwyesngwu yaw puma. Pu' yaw siitala.

Noq pay yaw wukoyesngwuniiqe pay yaw kyaastati songqe. Pay yaw sinom oopokqe pay yaw naa'ingyaltoti. Pay yaw puma qa naakyaptsi'yyungwa. Qa hak yaw hiita pu' hakiy kyaptsi'yta. Pu' yaw puma lomaqatsit as navoti'yykyaakyangw pay yaw antsa hak hakiy aw hin

Aliksa'i. People were living somewhere down below. A long time ago they were living there, peacefully and free of troubles. It was paradise.

As they were living there in large numbers, they probably greatly increased in population. As the place became crowded, people tired of each other's company and showed no respect for one another any more. Neither things nor people were respected. They should have known what the good life is like,

nukuslavaytingwu. Yaw sutsep
puma hiihiita akw pay naanami
qa kwangwataywisa, pay yaw pi
hiihiita akw naanami nunukpan-
tiwisa.

Panmakyangw pu' pay yaw
pas nuwu qa unangwtalawvaya.
Yaw qa unangwtalawvayaqe qa
hak hakiy hiita'yta. Pu' yaw
puma momoyam kiy angqw
nöngamtiqe pu' yaw pumuy
kongmuy pu' timuy paysoq
maataptotaqe puma yaw kivamiq tiivangwuqamuy aqw yungqe pu' yaw pas qa ninmangwu.
Pu' yaw qa hiita noovalalwa, pu'
kiy qa qenilalwa. Pu' yaw taataqt
tootim piw amuntotiqe yaw
imuy mamantuy ngöynumya.
Pu' momoymuysa suusumiya,
piw taataqtuy. Yan yaw puma
piw naatsönlalwa. Naat yaw pu'
himuwa haqam hiitawat wuutit
amum qatuptut qavongvaqw
piw pay ayam sutsvewatningwu.
Pas yaw qa hakiy qatsi'at. Honaqqatsit yaw puma yeese. Nukusyese, naatsikiwta. Pay pas
suuput itam pu' yeese. Sun as
sinomniikyaakyangw qa hak
hakiy haalayi.

Pay yaw paavantaqat akw
puma panwiskyaakyangw pu'
paasat yaw puma pephaqam pas
qa unangwtalawvaya. Yaw it
nukusqatsit yesva. Pu' yaw pay
puma naanap hiita nukustunat-
yat akw pay yaw koyaanistoti.
Pu' yaw puma it koyaanisqatsit
aqw ökiqw pu' yaw ima mom-

but instead, they spoke disre-
spectfully to one another. In
many ways, they looked unfavorably upon each other. They
also mistreated each other.

Slowly, people were getting
out of control. No one had a
liking for his fellow man. The
women began to leave their
homes and abandon their husbands and children, only to join
the dancers in the kiva and not
to return home. They neither
cooked nor cleaned house. The
married men and the boys did
the same. They were chasing
around after the girls. While the
women each went with several
men, the men had several
women. In this fashion they were
committing adultery. A man had
just slept with a woman and already, the next day, he was con-
sorting with someone else.
Hence, life was in total disarray.
The people were living a life of
madness. Evil ways reigned, and
people were divided into factions. The same kind of life we're
also living today. We should be
united as one people, but no one
gets along with the other.

For all these reasons, the
people of the underworld did
not come to their senses. An evil
way of life had set in. Thus, with
all their bad intentions, they
became totally corrupt. Upon
reaching this state of *koyaanisqatsi*, the leaders got together

ngwit tsovaltiqe pu' yaw amungem wuuwantota hin as puma
hintote' haqami sen naalakni.

and pondered what they could
possibly do in order to move to
another location.

One reason frequently cited by the Hopi for the development of
koyaanisqatsi is the breakdown of the native religion, especially as it
crystallizes around the institution of the *wiimi* or "secret society."

Text 24

Pu' wiimiy yaw antsa piw qa
himutotiqe hiihiita wiimit qa
yungtiwisa hiita wiiwimkyam. It
paahot paapu qa yukuya. Pam
pay pas pan wuwni amuupa
sulawti.

It is said that because the initiates no longer respect their
religious societies, they do not
assemble any more. Prayer sticks
are no longer fashioned. The
knowledge of how to make them
is gone.

Instead of devoting their energies to their religious obligations,
people pursue the sweet life. As a result, men in particular neglect
their farming duties, which results in hunger and famine.

Text 25

I' hapi koyaanisqatsi hakimuy
yan nukushintsankqw pu' hakim
it wiimiy hiita qa aw tunatyaw-
yungwe' pu' putsa hakim aqw
ö'qalyangwu, put kwangwa-
'ewpit. Yanhaqam kur pi atkya
hiniwtiqw pu' puma wiimiy
qe'toti.

    Pam koyaanisqatsi paniw-
tiqw puma pay pas putsa kwangwa'ewpitsa tunatyawyungqe
ima taataqt qa hin pasvayaniqey
unangwa'yyungwa. Pu' qa uu-
'uyangwu. Pu' qa hiita höqya-
ngwuniiqe pay tsöngös'iwwisa.
Noq qa pantani hapi asniqw
hisat itamumi pangqaqwangwu,
itam it naa'u'nantoyni'ywisni.

When *koyaanisqatsi* corrupts
people, they no longer pay
attention to their religion. Instead, they keep drifting into a
life of greater pleasure. This is
what happened in the underworld when they abandoned
their religious societies.

    When *koyaanisqatsi* takes
place, people are only interested
in pleasure. The men don't have
the desire to cultivate their fields
and so don't plant any more. As
there is nothing to harvest, people begin to experience a famine.
This is not supposed to happen,
so long ago they used to tell us
that we should remind each
other of these things.

The pursuit of *kwangwa'ewpi*, "pleasure," often begins with gambling, as is the case in the present story; or with dancing for the sake of fun, as is explained in Text 26. Unchecked gambling and dancing, as soon as both sexes are involved, typically leads to sexual indulgence and immorality, as is pointed out in Text 27.

Text 26

Pu' yaw puma pepeq pay pas koyaanisqatsit aqw ökiiqe pu' yaw puma it tselet hintsaktivaya. Yaw tookyep pu' piw taalö' teevep tiivanlalwangwu. Pay yaw puma pas as kur qa tiivanikyaakyangw pay yaw puma pas paysoq kwangwa'ewlalwa.

When the people reached the state of *koyaanisqatsi*, they started dancing social dances. All night and day they kept dancing. This dancing served no other purpose than enjoyment.

Text 27

Antsa it yaw pas koyaanisqatsit aw pituqw pas qa unangwtalawvaya. Yaw pay kya pi pas putsa wuuwantota hak hakiy haqam tsopniqey putsa wuuwantotaqw pu' imuy yaw mamanhoymuy soosokmuy pukuminkyaakyangw pu' wuuwukwmuy momoymuy pay piw nuwu enang tsoptiwisa.

Haqam himuwa wuuti yaw okiw kwayngyavoniqw pu' yaw haqam taaqa aw pite', ngu'e', amum naayawve' pay yaw pep put piw tsopngwu. Pu' yaw himuwa wuuti kuytoq pu' put haqam piw ngu'aye' pu' piw pantotingwu ima tootim, taataqt.

After reaching the state of *koyaanisqatsi*, people don't return to their senses. The only thing on their minds is how they can indulge in sex. Deflowering all the unmarried women, they even sleep with the old women.

Thus, when a woman, poor thing, goes to relieve herself at the toilet and refuse area, a man will approach her, seize her and, after a brief struggle with her, rape her. When a woman goes after water, the same thing happens. Men, whether unmarried or married, grab the woman and rape her.

In spite of the teachings and warnings of the elders, Hopi society today is engulfed anew in *koyaanisqatsi*. This is painfully realized by many Hopi and sadly deplored, as may be gathered from the next two statements:

Text 28

Pu' pas koyaanisqatsit awsa
taakukqw pu' pep hapi i' soosoy
himu qa antangwu. Soosoy himu
neyngawtangwu, himu qatsi
nukushintangwu. Noq pay pi
Hopiit sutsep pangqaqwangwu,
"I' hapi nukushintsakpi, koyaanisqatsi. Hakimuy nukushinta-
qat aqw ökinangwu. Hakimuy
sowantangwu, hakimuy kiiqö-
tangwu." Pay kya pi hisat angqaqw i' yaniwma. Pu' as paniqw
itam pew sukw qatsit aw waa-
'oyiwa. Noq pay piw itam ahoy
an qatsini'ywisa. Piw angqw
ahoy koyaanisqatsi kwuupu.

When things tip over into the
state of *koyaanisqatsi*, everything
is wrong. All things are mixed
up, and life is bad. The Hopis
always say, "*Koyaanisqatsi* reigns
when things are done poorly and
improperly. This situation leads
people to bad ends. It devours
them and destroys them." This
has been going on since long
ago. That is why we were shel-
tered in this life here on earth.
But we're living the same life all
over again. Once more *koyaanisqatsi* has reared its ugly head.

Text 29

Noq pu' itam hapi pay songyawnen piw koyaanisqatsit yeese.
Itam qa naakyaptsi'yyungwa.
Itam a'ni itaa'unangway yeese.
Ima wuuwuyom hakimuy amu-
mi as hiita su'antaqat tutap-
tiwisqw hakim qa pumuy la-
vayiyamuyyanik hakim pumuy
amumi naanap hingqaqwangwu.

Today, we're more or less living
a life of *koyaanisqatsi* again. We
have no respect for each other
and live according to our own
inclinations. The old people have
been trying to open our eyes to
the right ways, but we don't feel
like going by their words and
talk back to them improperly.

A great deal of the blame for *koyaanisqatsi* is put on the introduction of alcohol and drugs by White society.

Text 30

Itam pay it koyaanisqatsit yeese
puu'u. Soosoyam hoonaq'iwyungwa. It hiita peqw Pahaanam
honaqkuyit o'yaqw pu' it hiihiita
ngahut puuvut akw soosoyam
hoonaq'iwwisa. Oovi itam

We're experiencing *koyaanisqatsi*
now. Everyone is drunk. Since
the Whites brought alcohol and
drugs, everybody has been going
crazy with these substances.
That's why we're returning to

koyaanisqatsit ahoy aqw ökiwis-
kyangw itam as hinye' sen qa
put ahoy aqw ökini.

koyaanisqatsi. Goodness knows
what we can do to avoid it.

Text 31

Noq pu' i' koyaanisqatsi, honaqqatsi pay piw suyan yep itamumi maatakiwta. Ima peetu
aasakis pahankimiye' puma
ephaqam mooti hoonaq'iwnum-
yat pu' piw ahoy ökingwu. Pu'
ima momoyam mamant pay pas
hikwyaniqey oovi pangqe' naa-
kuwa'iwnumyangwu. Pu' ima
taataqt pay pas pumuy oovi piw
pang pannumyangwu. Pu' puma
pang pannumyaqam naap hakiy
nöömayat koongyayat amum-
yangwu naamahin pam put
aangaqwviniqw. Pu' puma
kiivaqe timuy tatamtotat pu'
angqe' pannumyangwu. Pu'
peetu pankyaakyangw ahoy
ökye' pu' kiy ep hin qaqtsinaya-
ngwu. Pu' pay peetu put hiikot
akw so'iwma.

Today we're looking once more
at *koyaanisqatsi,* especially in the
form of life led by those under
the influence of alcohol. Some
people, each time they go to
town, roam around drunk there
before they return. Women and
girls who want to drink prosti-
tute themselves for drinks wherever they are. Therefore, the men
also hang around there for them.
They are together with just anybody's wife or husband, even if
they are clan-related. Having
abandoned their children back
home, they carry on like this.
Finally, when they return home,
they fight and cause disturb-
ances.

Although the Hopis recognize their own renewed entanglement
in the madness of *koyaanisqatsi,* they are equally aware of the worldwide manifestation of this phenomenon. In addition, a great deal of
the internal turmoil at Hopi is attributed to the White man's greed for
land, including its mineral resources; as well as life in the United
States armed forces which first acquainted the Hopi with the White
man's crazy way of life.

Text 32

Noq pu' pay ima peetu
wuuwuyoqam pangqaqwaqw
pay ima Pahaanam piw put
koyaanisqatsit tuwat yeese. Pu'

A few of the elders say that the
White man and the other Indians
are also living a life of *koyaanisqatsi.* There is always killing and

pay ima himusinom piw. Puma angqe' sutsep naaqöyantota. Pu' angqe' haaqe' piw naaqöyta. Himuwa haqam pas pavannen pu' ayo'wat hakiy tutskwat nawkitongwu. Pu' itam yepeqwat Pahanmuy amumum sutsep neepewya. Puma pew itaatutskway aw hiihiita nukngwat tuwa'ykyaakyangw itamuy put hin kwahanayaniqey pan tunatyawyungwa. Niiqe pu' pay puma it owakot oovi yepeq pay yaahantota. Puma hapi qa soosokmuy hu'waniyamuy akw pantsatskyaqw oovi itam Hopiit naanami putakw qa yan unangwa'yyungwa.

Pu' ima Pahaanam piw sutsep it tunipit tumala'yyungwa. Yaw itam put himu'yyungwe' yaw itam a'niyaqw son yaw himu itamumi hintsakni. Pu' puma yan lavaykyaakyangw itaatotimuy pangqw haqaqw sutsep wangwaylalwa solaawalalwaniqat oovi. Pu' puma susmooti pangsoyaqam pep it Pahaanat tuskyapqatsiyat tuwi'yvaya. Noq oovi pay i' soosoy yaayantaqa hakimuy yaw it koyaanisqatsit aqw ökinangwu.

rioting somewhere. Whenever someone feels strong enough, he comes to take somebody's land. We constantly disagree with the White man, because they see the treasures in our land and are bent on causing us to lose this land. Then they dig up the coal in it. They are doing this without the consent of all the Hopi, and so we Hopi are at each other's throats over this.

Furthermore, the Whites always manufacture weapons. They say if we have weapons we are mighty and nobody can harm us. Talking like this, they keep calling our young men to serve in the armed forces. Those who were the first to join them really became familiar with the crazy ways of the White man. All of these reasons have brought us to the state of *koyaanisqatsi*.

Once more, as in the previous world, the Hopis feel that the time is ripe to create *tabula rasa* and make a new beginning. According to one of their prophecies, they believe that an avenger will appear who will destroy the wicked and eradicate the current *koyaanisqatsi*. A chance for survival remains, however, only if the old religion is not abandoned.

Text 33

Noq pu' hapi itam koyaanisqatsit yeese. Paapu itam son yan yesni. Noq oovi itam pu' pay pas himu itamuy powataniqat sen qenitaniqat hiita nukpanat putsa itam maqaptsi'yyungwa. Pu' i' himu itamuy powataniqa itamumi pituqw songqa nanaptani. Pep pu' itamuy yaw soosokmuy sivintoynani. Pep pu' itam tsaykinumyani. Yaw qa hak hakiy aw unangwtapmantani. Pay yaw qa hakiy qatsi'atniwtini. Tutavo ura panta: Hisat i' himu itamuy powataniqa, itamuy haqami hintsanniqa, itamuy itaaqatsiy nawkiniqa pituqw itam put wiimit yaw qa sootapnaye' putakw itam ayo' nöngakni.

We're now experiencing *koyaanisqatsi*. We cannot continue to live like this any longer. For this reason, we are waiting for the one that will purify us or destroy the evil. When he comes, we're bound to notice it. He will deal out punishment to all of us, and we will be walking around crying. No one will aid anyone. It will be total chaos. However, it's been foretold that on the day the purifier comes, the one who will destroy us and take away our lives, those of us who have not abandoned our religion will survive.

The legendary events leading to the destruction of the village of Pivanhonkyapi were recorded previously in English by two other collectors of Hopi narratives, Voth and Courlander. While, overall, Voth's version (1905: 241-244) and the earlier one of the two recorded by Courlander (1970: 241-244) resemble mine, Courlander's second version (1971: 157-163) drastically deviates from it. Its entire first half contains an elaborate subplot with a strong witchcraft component. The wife of the village leader's son is abducted by a sorcerer whose evil intentions are foiled when Old Spider Woman, cast in the role of a shamaness, diagnoses the situation with the aid of a quartz crystal and pinpoints the secret location of the abductor. In addition to the general moral sickness prevailing at the village, the story refers to a "society of evil ones ... who take women to a place where they can abuse them whenever they want" (Courlander 1971: 161). Its focus within the overall concept of *koyaanisqatsi* thus rests on the aspect commonly summed up as *powaqqatsi*, "life of sorcery."

All four legends concur in the motif that, at the request of the village chiefs, the *Yaayapontsam*, or "Yaayapontsas," become the avenging agents due to the immoral and degenerate lifestyles prevailing among the residents of Pivanhonkyapi. They initiate the devastating firestorm which burns its way across the plain from Nuvatukya'ovi, the San Francisco Mountains some sixty miles to the southwest, until it engulfs the village.

Not much ethnographic data exists on the Yaayapontsas. Nequatewa exclusively speaks of a Yaapontsa in the singular and characterizes him as a "wind god" (1936: 103). Colton does the same: "He is thought of as a horrid-looking creature with shaggy hair, body painted with ashes, and wearing a breech clout. He is never impersonated and takes no part in any ceremony. He is troublesome and is not liked" (1959: 84).

The home of the Wind God, according to Nequatewa, is "at the foot of Sunset Crater in a great crack in the black rock, through which he is ever breathing" (1936: 104). This general location is also borne out in the legend recorded here, although the Pivanhonkyapi chief initially contacts the Yaayapontsas at a place northwest of Oraibi.[4]

Portrayed as repulsive-looking supernaturals, the Yaayapontsas are said to control both the fire and the wind, the latter especially in the form of the dust devil.[5] Courlander's 1970 version, which gives them control over water, storm, lightning, wind, and fire, is culturally not commensurate with the scheme of Hopi mythology (1970: 121). Courlander's depiction of the "Yayaponcha People" in his 1971 publication is equally irreconcilable with Hopi mythography. "The Yayaponchas were feared, for they were sorcerers with special powers over the forces of nature, and they were wild in appearance, having long, unkempt hair. The Yayaponchas could make the north wind blow, call down storms, and make the lightning strike. They could kill people and revive them, cause landslides by pointing their fingers at cliffs, and control fire" (1971: 160). My informants agreed on their unattractive appearance, but were unable to confirm that they control the north wind. The north wind is commonly known as *kwingyaw* and differs markedly from the dust devil activated by Yaapontsa. Nor are they capable of performing the magic feats attributed to them. The latter are typically ascribed to adherents of the *yaya'wimi*, or "magician society." The initial sound similarity between *Yaya't* and *Yaayapontsam*, which is also attested in the variant shape of *Yaayapontsat*, leads me to suspect that Courlander's narrator confused the two terms and mixed up the mytho-cultural baggage associated with them. This may also explain why the Yaayapontsas are characterized as "sorcerers" by him. Hopi *Yaya't*, "magicians," and *popwaqt*, "sorcerers," share certain similarities.

Endnotes

1. Colton and Nequatewa surmise that the now extinct Ladder Dance may have been "a spring ceremony held once every four years.... In form the ceremony was a Kachina dance.... The leader of the Kachinas was a man dressed as a maiden. Four days before the public ceremony, two youths who were to play a leading part in the ceremony made a pilgrimage of 60 miles to the San Francisco Peaks where they deposited pahos in a shrine and from where they brought two Douglas fir trees which they planted in holes cut in the rock at the mesa edge" (1932: 61).

According to the two authors, the dance, which in the dialect of Second Mesa is referred to as *saqti*, was once also performed at the ancient mother village of Shungopavi. About a hundred yards south of the spring Songoopa lies a gigantic boulder "on top of which can be observed three holes in a row, each hole being about a foot in diameter and between a foot and two feet deep," into which the dance poles were placed (1932: 54).

For additional information see also the Glossary.

2. For the rules of *totolospi* consult the Glossary.

3. The motion picture, which was Reggio's film debut, was premiered with its original music score by Philip Glass at Radio City Music Hall in 1982 under the auspices of the New York Film Festival. The nonverbal film, designed as an evocation of modern life in the terms of *koyaanisqatsi*, "life out of balance," has received acclaim and recognition at festivals and public performances throughout the world.

4. Voth, in a different tale featuring two representatives of the Yaayapontsas who come trading to Oraibi, locates the place as "about three-fourths of a mile north of Oraibi" (1905: 123-124). In an additional story recorded by me, their home is referred to as Yaapontsa.

5. While Colton seems to equate the Yaapontsa with the "Dust Devil," he is probably more appropriately identified as its controlling agent (1959: 84). Only rarely do Hopis refer to a dust devil as *yaapontsa*. Instead, they prefer to use the more established term *tuviphayangw*.

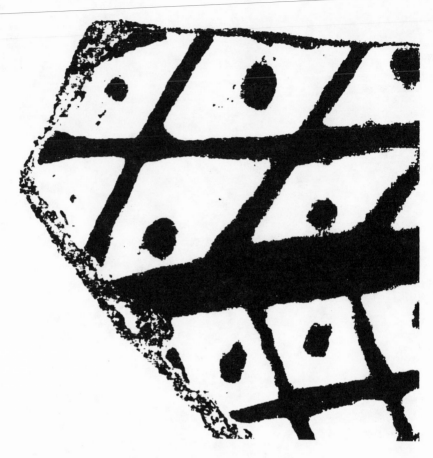

Hin Pivanhonkyapi Kiiqöti

Aliksa'i. Yaw Pivanhonkyape yeesiwa. Pep kya pi yaw pay naat pas hisathaqam piw sinom yesngwu. Pu' yaw Orayve piw pay angqe' yesngwuniikyangw pu' piw Huk'ove. Now yaw pangqw Pivanhonkyapiy angqw pay pangso nan'ivo haypo.

Noq yep Pivanhonkyape yaw ima sinom kitsoktotaqe pay yaw as mootiniqw kwangwayese, lomaqatsi'yyungwa, haalayyangwu. Noq pu' pay yaw ima tootim, taataqt pay piw sutsep kivanawit yeyese. Niiqe pay yaw puma pang tuwat pay hiihintsatskyangwuniiqe pay yaw haalayyangwu. Noq pay yaw haqaapiy pay puma pas puuvutsa hintsatskyangwuniiqe pay yaw puma soq yaavatotingwu. Niiqe pu' yaw i' hak kur it hiita navö'hiita haqaqw nasimokyaataqe pu' yaw

Pivanhonkyapi: Destruction by Fire

Aliksa'i. There was a settlement at Pivanhonkyapi. Long ago people really used to live there. Oraibi and Huk'ovi were also settled. It was only a short distance to these villages from Pivanhonkyapi.

After the founding of Pivanhonkyapi people lived at first in peace and tranquility. Life was good, and everyone was happy. The boys and men, of course, spent most of their days in the kivas. Engaging in all sorts of activities, they were basically content with their lot. Over time, however, they grew tired of doing the same old thing. Then, one day, one of them borrowed some kind of game somewhere. This game he was now busy teaching the others. As a result, they devoted their time to nothing but gambling. They were actually playing

pam pep pumuy kivaapa yesqamuy tutuwna. Niiqe puma yaw oovi
pang kivaapa pantsatskyangwu, pay nanavö'yangwu. Puma yaw
totolosyangwu. I' totolospi yaw pay pas hisat susmootihaqam pumuy
nanavö'pi'amningwu. Pay yaw puma pang kivaapa pantsatskyangwu, pay tootim, taataqt. Niikyangw pay yaw as puma taalö'sa
kivayese' pantsatskyangwu. Pu' pay mihikqw as qe'yangwu.
Pantsakkyaakyangw pu' pay puma put pas kwangwa'yyaqe yaw
qa ökingwu. Pay yaw puma mihikqw enangtota. Pu' pay nuwu
haqaapiy mihikqw pay yaw paapu sinom amumiq taayungngwu,
kukuyayangwu. Niiqe pay yaw as mootiniqw tootimsaya. Panwiskyaakyangw pay yaw nuwu mamant amumumtoti. Pay yaw puma
paasat pumuy tootimuy amumum pangqw oongaqw pangsoq
pumuy nanavö'yaqamuy tiitimayyangwu. Panwiskyaakyangw pu'
pay puma mamant pas aqw yungya pumuy aqw ngemnayaqw.
Paasat pu' yaw puma pumuy mamantuy tangatotaqe pu' pumuy
amumum pan nanavö'yangwu, pay pas neengawkyaakyangw
nanavö'yangwu. Pantsakkyaakyangw pu' pay yaw puma pas qa
ökingwu. Pas pi yaw taalö' teevepyangwu pu' mihikqw. Pas yaw
himuwa tsöngmokye' pu' kiy awnen pu' ep nöst pu' pay piw ahoy
awningwu.
    Pantaqw pu' pay yaw momoyam paasat nuutum tuwat aw sas-
qativaya. Puma pu' yaw tuwat nuutumtoti, momoyam kongmu'y-
kyaakyangw, timu'ykyaakyangw. Pay yaw himuwa noovatate'sa
yamakngwu. Pu' yaw himuwa timuy amungem panis noovatat,
nopnat, pu' pay paasat piw ahoy awningwu. Pangsosa yaw puma
sinom unangwa'yyungwa.
    Pu' yaw puma pepehaq kwangwa'ewlalwa, tootim, taataqt,
momoyam, mamant. Totolosye' yaw kwanokmantangwu. Haqaapiy
pay yaw puma pas qa naakyaptsitotaqw pu' yaw ima mamant,
momoyam qa naakyaakyawnaya. Pas pi yaw qa hak hakiy himu'at.
Naamahin yaw momoymuy kongmu'yyungqamuy amuupe haalayya. Pas yaw soosoyam nu'an tuskyap'iwyungwa.
    Haqaapiy pu' yaw pay it kikmongwit nööma'at nuutumti. Pay
yaw mootiniqw as paysoq aqw pay kuyvato. Aqw kuyvatoqe pu'
yaw angqw oongaqw aqw tayta. Noq pas pi yaw ima tootim, taataqt,
momoyam, mamant aqw qa yungqam yaw aqw homimita. Pumuy
yaw pam pangqw oongaqw amumum aqw kuyta. Noq antsa yaw
haalayya, kwangwa'ewlalwa.
    Pu' pay yaw hak put aqw ngemna aqw pakiniqat. Yaw hak aw
pangqawqw pay yaw pam qa nakwha. Niiqe pay yaw pam qa suus

totolospi, the first game to be played by the Hopi long ago. So this was going on in the kivas among the menfolk. At first, they only played *totolospi* during the day. At nightfall they usually stopped.

As the days went by, however, the players became addicted to the game and also played during the nights. In addition, people began to watch them at night in the kivas and peek in on them. At first only the young men came, but soon the unmarried women also joined them. Together with the young men they would watch the players through the hatch in the kiva roof. As time passed, the girls ventured inside because they were invited. Finally, the men simply took the girls inside. Both men and womenfolk were playing the board game of *totolospi* now. It was not long before the players quit returning home at the end of the day. Not only did they gamble all day, but also through the night. Whenever someone became hungry, he went home to have a bite to eat, whereupon he returned to the kiva.

Eventually, women who had husbands and children also started going. They too became involved with the game and would only leave to go cook. No sooner had these women made food for their children and fed them, than they ran back to the kiva to play *totolospi*. No other place was of interest to the people.

So the boys and men, women and girls were having a good time. The shouting and boisterous laughter never stopped. Everybody enjoyed himself. By now, women and girls would be playing against men and boys. Soon the game reached a point where the participants no longer showed any respect for each other. The unmarried women and young men completely abandoned themselves. No one belonged to anyone any more. It was total promiscuity. Everyone was in a state of craziness.

Before long, the wife of the village leader also came to participate. To begin with, she merely went to the kiva to peek in from the top. The roof was teeming with spectators, male and female, young and old, who had not entered the kiva. With these the wife of the village leader kept watching the players below. Sure enough, they were happy and were greatly enjoying themselves.

Then one of the players invited the village leader's wife to come inside the kiva. However, she declined. But since she went to the kiva several times, she was repeatedly asked inside. Finally, she succumbed to the temptation, entered the kiva, and sat down on the stone bench along the wall. She told herself she was only there to

aqwniqw pay yaw pi'ep himuwa put ngemnangwu. Noq pay yaw pam oovi as pas qa nakwhat pu' pay yaw pam uunati. Uunatiqe pu' yaw pam aqw pakiiqe pay tuuwingaqw qatuptu. Pay pi yaw pam panis tiimayniqey yaw wuuwaqe pu' yaw pam antsa pangqw tiimayi.

Hisatniqw pu' yaw puma kur put maamatsya pam hakniqw. Pu' yaw pay pam pumuy amumumniqat ngeemintota. Niiqe pay yaw pam as an piw mooti qa nakwhat pu' yaw pay piw uunati. Paasat pu' yaw pam pumuy amumum nanavö'qw pas yaw pam himu antsa kwangwa'ew. Pu' yaw pay kur pam kwangwa'ewlawqe pas qa tunatyaltiqw pay yaw nuwu taalawva. Pay yaw pam naat qa nimaqw pay yaw taalawva. Nuwu pay yaw töngva, taawanasapti. Pu' yaw pay piw tapkiwma. Pu' pay yaw pam pas qa nimaqw pay yaw piw ahoy mihi.

Noq yaw ep mihikqw pu' yaw hak angqaqw put kikmongwit nöömayat tungwanta. Noq yaw pam Talawaysi yan maatsiwa, pam mongwit nööma'at. Noq yaw hak angqaqw tungwantaqw nawis'ew yaw kur pam navotqe pu' yaw aqw yama. Noq yaw kur koongya'at-niiqe pu' yaw aw pangwawu, "Um itaakiy awnen itaatiy yooyong-naniy," yaw aw kita. "Um tookihaqaqw pu' teevep put qa suusa yooyongnaqw pam okiw tsöngmokiwtaqe qa o'okqw nu' kur hintsanni," yaw aw kita.

"Ta'a," yaw aw kita, "pay nu' awnen yooyongnani." Kitaqw pu' yaw puma oovi naama pangqw kiy aw'i.

Pu' yaw puma ep pituqw antsa yaw ti'at okiw a'ni pakmumuya. Paasat pu' yaw pam put yooyongna, tiy. Pavan pam yaw tsayhoya okiw tsöngmokiwtaqe pavan paysoq tsonasvevetikyangw öqöqöta. Pantsakkyangw pu' pas yaw pam nan'ivaqw put piihuyat angqw soosoktat pu' ööyi. Paasat pu' yaw i' wuuti koongyay aw pangqawu, "Ta'a, pay pi ööyi. Pay son pu' qa puwni," yaw aw kita.

"Ta'ay," yaw aw kita.

"Noq nu' pay ahoy piw awni," yaw pam koongyay aw kita.

Pay yaw pam koongya'at pas qa aw hingqawu. Paasat pu' pay yaw pam pangqw yamakt pu' piw ahoy kivami'. Pu' yaw pam piw ep pituuqe pu' yaw piw nuutuma. Pas pi yaw tuskyapqatsi. Pay yaw puma pas pangqw qa nöngakngwu.

Pu' yaw pam Talawaysi pay piw an qa pitu. Pu' yaw pam as piw an aqw oongaqw put tuuvinglawqw pay yaw pam pas qa yama. Pu' yaw pam mongwi nawus pas tiy aw wikkyango. Niiqe pu' yaw pam pas aqw pakiiqe pu' epeq aw pangqawu, "Um it yooyongnaniy," yaw

watch, and this is what she did.

As soon as the players recognized who she was they began urging her to join them. Again, she refused at first, but then she gave in and began playing with them. *Totolospi* really was a great deal of fun. Evidently she enjoyed herself so much that she was not even aware it had gotten daylight. Before long, the sun was high in the morning sky, but she did not return home. Soon it was noontime, then early evening, then night time, and still she had not gone home.

When it turned dark again, someone called the chief's wife from outside. Her name was Talawaysi. Finally, she heard her name being called and emerged from the kiva. It turned out to be her husband. He said to her, "Come to the house and breast-feed our child. Last night and all day today he has not suckled a single time, and the poor thing is hungry. He won't stop crying, and I don't know what to do."

"All right," his wife replied, "I'll go to him and let him suckle."

True enough, when the woman reached home, the poor baby was crying. So she breast-fed him. The little thing was starved and was gulping loudly as he avidly sucked. Soon he had depleted both of her breasts and was satiated. Thereupon the woman said to her husband, "All right, he's no longer hungry. He's bound to sleep now."

"Good," he replied.

"Well, I'll be going back to the kiva," the woman said.

Her husband remained silent, so the woman left the house and returned to the kiva. There, once more, she began to carry on with the players. It was absolute craziness. People did not bother to come out of the kiva any more.

Talawaysi too failed to go home just as before. Once again her husband kept pleading with her from above, but she did not leave. Finally, the village leader had no choice but to take the baby to her. Upon entering he said to her, "Here, nurse him."

aw kita.

Pu' yaw pam oovi put pepeq pas yooyongnaqw pu' yaw pam pangqw tiy wikkyangw ahoy nima. Paasat pu' pay yaw pam nöö-ma'at pas qa amum. Ep pu' yaw pam mongwi pas itsivuti. Qa haa-layti yaw pami'. "Is ohiy," yaw kita, "pas hapi as son yantani. Pay nu' as pi itimuy kyaakyawnaqw oovi pay son yantani. Pay pi nu' nawus son hin pumuy qa unangwtalawnani," yan yaw pam tunatyalti.

Pu' yaw pam ang wuuwantaqe haqami hakiy aw taqa'nangwti-niqey. Wuuwankyangw pu' yaw pam hakimuy tuwa, hakimuy amumi taqa'nangwtiniqey. Noq yaw Orayviy kwiningyahaqam yaw ima Yaayapontsam piw ki'yyungqw pumuy yaw pam tuwa. "Pay pi nu' kur pumuy amuminen ngas'ew pumuy amumi yep itaaqatsiy lalvayqw pay kya as puma inumi unangwtatveniy," yaw pam yan wuuwa. "Kur nu' pangsonen pumuy amumi na'okiwtani; hin pi lavaytotini."

Yan yaw pam wuuwaqw pu' yaw pam oovi ep mihikqw pumuy amungem nakwakwuslawu. Naalöqmuy yaw pam oovi nakwakwus-tat pu' yaw put sutalelwi. Pay yaw pam navoti'yta hiita puma tuwat akw mongvasyaqw. Niiqe pu' yaw pam oovi puuvut paas yukuutat pu' yaw pam put aw tsootsongt, naawaknat, paas puuvut mongvas-tit, pu' yaw pam wa'ökqe pu' yaw puuwi. Niikyangw pam yaw mooti put paahot paas mokyaatat pu' put haqami paas tavi.

Qavongvaqw pu' yaw pam hakiywat tumsiy aw put tiy wiiki. Haak engem tavi'ytaqw pam hapi pangso Yaayapontsamuy amumi-ni. Paasat pu' yaw pam put nakwakwusiy ömaatat pu' yaw pam kiy angqw yamakt pu' yaw pam taatöq tuuwimi. Niikyangw pu' yaw pam Huk'oviy kwiningye' waltsava yaw pam wuuvi. Oomiq wupqe pangqw pu' yaw pam pas as ayo' hoopo suwiptaniqey wuuwaqe pu' yaw pam pay oovi pangqe yuumosa tuuwik. Paasat pu' yaw pam oovi Mumurvat ang taavangqöyva aqw tuuwik. Pu' yaw pam Qö-ma'wat atpik yaw aqw taatöq. Pu' yaw Ngöyakwat angqeniikyangw pang pu' yaw Pöqangwhoymuy amuuhopkye'niikyangw pu' aqw Oraymiq kuyva. Kuyvat yaw pay qa oraymiqnit pay yaw pangqw hoopoq tupkye' yaw panmakyangw pephaqam yaw aw pösö'ytaqw pangsohaqami yaw pam hisatniqw pitu. Noq yaw pep kur ima hiitu Yaayapontsam yeese.

Noq pay yaw kur puma nanapta pam ep pituqw naat yaw pam oovi pu' kivats'omi wupqw yaw hak angqaqw put paki'a'awna. Noq pu' yaw pam oovi put pahomokiy mavoko'ykyangw yaw aqw paki. Pu' yaw pam epeq pakiiqe yaw pumuy pepeq yesqamuy amuupa

His wife complied and breast-fed him, whereupon he took the child back home. His wife did not accompany him, which made the village leader furious. His heart sank. "Impossible," he exclaimed. "Things cannot go on like this! I truly love the villagers, my children, but this must stop." He resolved to bring them back to their senses.

The village leader pondered the situation. Where could he go? Who could he ask for help? As he racked his brain, he thought of some people he could ask for assistance. These were the Yaayapontsas who made their home somewhere northwest of Oraibi. "I'll go to them," he said to himself, "and tell them about our life here. I'll give it a try, at least. Perhaps they'll help me," he thought. "I'll seek them out and beg them to have pity. Who knows what their response will be?"

This is what occurred to the village leader, so that same night he fashioned prayer feathers for the Yaayapontsas. Four in all he made, and daubed them with red ocher. He knew exactly what things were important to them. When he had finished the feathers, he smoked and prayed over them. Upon completion of the entire task, he went to bed and slept. Prior to that, however, he had carefully wrapped up the paho and stored them away.

The following day the village leader took his child to one of his clan's women. She would keep it for him while he was on his mission to the Yaayapontsas. Then he picked up his prayer feathers, exited from his house, and set out toward the ledge in the southeast. Northwest of Huk'ovi he climbed up through a gap. Once on top of the mesa, he decided to continue straight in a northeasterly direction, choosing a path right along the ledge. This ledge he followed all the way past Mumur Spring. Just below Qöma'wa he turned southeast. Going around Ngöyakwa, he stayed to the southeast of the Pöqangw place and finally came in view of Oraibi. Instead of going to the village though, he skirted the contours of the mesa edge in a northeasterly direction. There was a corner there, his destination. Before long, he arrived. This was the home of the Yaayapontsas.

The Yaayapontsas evidently were aware of his coming, for the minute he ascended to the roof of their abode, a voice bade him enter.

yorikqw is uti yaw hiitu a'ni sosniwa, Yaayapontsam. Pas yaw hiitu nuunuutsel'e'wayom. Pas yaw höömi'am ungwat akw yaw yanyungwa, pu' yaw pay ungwvukuwyungwa hiitu. Pu' yaw pam epeq pakiqw piw yaw pay put paas taviya. "Qatu'uy," yaw aw kitota, "um hak waynuma."

"Owiy," yaw pam amumi kita.

Pu' yaw puma pay paasat put tsootsongnaya. Pay pi hisat yaw hak haqam pakiqw pay yaw pas son hakiy qa tsootsongnayangwu. Niiqe pu' yaw puma oovi pantotiqe pumuy paas yukuyaqw paasat pu' yaw pumuy mongwi'am put tuuvingta, "Ta'ay, son pi um qa hiita oovi waynumay," yaw aw kita. "Pi qa hisat hak yangqaqw itaakiy papkiy," yaw pumuy mongwi'am aw kita.

"Hep owiy," yaw aw kita, "pay nu' yep Pivanhonkyape tuwat kikmongwiy," yaw aw kita. "Noq pas pep ima itim qa unangwtalyay," yaw aw kita. "Puma pay koyaanistotiqe pas qa hiita puma lomahintaqat paapu wuuwantota. Pay puma pas kwangwa'ewlalwaniqey, it hiita natkot, pay pas putsa wuuwantota. Pu' it hiita itam akw yesniqat pam pay amumi qa himu'uy. Pu' ima momoyam timu'yyungqam pay pas put oovi imuy timuy tatami'yyungway," yaw aw kita. "Noq inöma nuutumtiqe pay pu' pas nuutum qa pitungwuniqw oovi nu' pas itsivutiy. Niiqe nu' oovi hin as unangwayamuy taalawnaniqey put nu' oovi angqöy," yaw pam amumi kita. "Puma pay pas koyaanisqatsit aqw öki."

"Haw'owi? Is ohiy, antsaa'," yaw pam mongwi'am kita. Paysoq yaw pam ephaqam yooko'ta. Pay yaw pas oovi nawutstiqw pu' yaw pam put hu'wana, "Ta'ay," yaw aw kita, "pay pi antsa um pan naawaknaqw pay pi itam sonqe'yaniy," yaw aw kita. "Antsa um puutsemokqe pu' um as hin imuy uutimuy unangwyamuy taalawnaniqey wuuwanta. Noq itam uumi unangwtatveniy," yaw aw kita.

Paasat pu' yaw pam antsa pay nukwangwnavotqe paasat pu' yaw pam put nakwakwusit tumalay pumuy mongwiyamuy aw oya. Noq yaw antsa haalayti. Haalaytit pu' yaw aw pangqawu, "Ason um qaavo mihikqw pu' piw angqwniy. Niikyangw um imuy amumi yori. Itam kyaasta. Niiqe yaapiy pu' um oovi piw nakwakwuslawkyangw um tatam niitini. Um tatam imuy amuptsinani. Pay oovi um hapi put niite' um put qaavo mihikqw angqw kimakyangw piw angqwniqw paasat pu' nu' uumi hin piw tutaptaniy," yaw yan aw lavayti.

Paasat pu' yaw pay pam pan nukwangwnavotqe pu' pay pangqw oovi ahoy nima. Pay yaw pam piw kuukuy ang ahoyniikyangw pu' antsa piw ahoy kiy ep pitu. Pu' yaw pam oovi pituuqe

Clutching his bag of pahos, the village leader descended the ladder into their home. As he arrived down below and scanned the faces of the residents, he realized with a shock how frightful the Yaayapontsas looked. They were extremely ugly beings with blood spattered over their hair and faces. But, much to his surprise, they welcomed him. "Have a seat, stranger," they said to him.

"Yes, thank you," the chief replied.

The Yaayapontsa then offered him a pipe. This was a custom long ago, to offer a visitor a smoke. When the smoking ritual had ended, the headman of the Yaayapontsas spoke. "Well, you must be about for a reason," he said. "Nobody has called on us for a long time."

"Of course," the village leader replied. "I'm the chief at the village of Pivanhonkyapi. My children have lost all sense of proper living. They've become corrupt and no longer have anything good on their minds. All they can think of is how to amuse themselves, especially by way of having sex. Things we need for our survival, such as crops, no longer have any meaning to them. Even women with children are neglecting their offspring just to have fun. My wife, too, has joined the lot and no longer returns home. I'm seething with anger, and am seeking a remedy to cleanse their hearts. That's the reason for my coming," he said to them. "They've really reached *koyaanisqatsi*."

"Is that so? Truly, that's deplorable," the headman of the Yaayapontsas replied, just sitting there hunched over. A long time passed until he spoke again. "Very well," he said, "if this is your heartfelt desire, we can surely do something about it. I can see you are disgusted with the situation and are considering how to purge the hearts of your children. We will assist you in this undertaking," he promised.

When the chief from Pivanhonkyapi heard this favorable reply, he handed his prayer feathers to the leader of the Yaayapontsas who was elated with them. Thanking the chief, the leader said, "I want you to come back tomorrow night. You've seen all my people here. We are a great many. Make some more prayer feathers. Make so many that there are enough for all of us. As soon as you come back with them tomorrow night, I'll have further instructions for you."

Delighted with the good news, the Pivanhonkyapi chief started out for home. Walking back along his own tracks, he arrived at his house again. There he unfolded his bedroll, lay down, and quickly fell asleep.

pu' yaw neengem ang aapataqe pu' angqe wa'ökqe pay yaw suu-puwva.

Noq pu' yaw oovi qavongvaqw pam kikmongwi piw talavay nöst pu' yaw pam paasat piw nakwakwuslawu. Niiqe pam yaw oovi put pas niitiwtaqat yukut pu' yaw pam piw put sutat akw lelwi. Soosok yaw pam sutalelwit pu' yaw paasat piw aw naawakna. Pantit pu' yaw pam put haqami paas oya.

Noq ep mihikqw pu' yaw pam put nakwakwus'iniy ömaatat pu' yaw pam pangqw piw yama. Pangqw pu' yaw pam piw pumuy Yaayapontsamuy amumi ahoy. Niiqe pu' yaw pam pay piw kuukuy ang ahoy hinmakyangw pu' yaw piw ep pitu. Ep pituqw pu' yaw puma piw put paas taviyat pu' yaw piw paas tsootsongnaya. Pu' yaw puma tsotsongyukuqw pu' yaw pam kikmongwi put amuupa oya hiita amungem yukuuqey. "Ta'ay, nu' it umungem kivay," yaw pam mongwiyamuy aw kita.

"Is kwakwhay, antsaa'," pu' yaw pamwa put aw kita. "Pay ason ima uumi naakwustaqw pu' um pumuy ang huylawniy," yaw mongwi'am aw kitaqw paasat pu' yaw oovi himuwa aw nakwsuqw pu' yaw pam put tumalay angqw hiitawat maqanangwu. Noq yaw yaayapontsamniiqe yaw oovi wukovataqtöwyungwa. Noq pu' yaw himuwa put kwusune' pu' yaw aw haalaytingwu. Himuwa yaw pas kya pi qa atsat haalayte' pay yaw pam paasat mots'iniy aw soosom-ngwu, ephaqam yaw nakwalawngwu. Pantsakkyangw pu' yaw pam soosokmuy ang huyta. Pas yaw kur su'aw amuptsiwtaqat pam yuku. Pas pi yaw puma haalaytoti.

Paasat pu' yaw mongwi'am aw pangqawu, "Niikyangw pay pi itam lööpwat pas suyan tuwi'yyungwa. I' huukyangw, tuvipha-yangw, pam suukyawa," yaw kita. "Pu' i'wa piiwu, i' qööhi, uu-wingw, pam piw suukyawa. Noq oovi um piniy," yaw aw kita. "Hii-tawat um pangqawqw put itam akwyani," yaw pam put aw kita.

Paasat pu' yaw Pivanhonkyangaqw mongwi ephaqam yan-kyangw wuuwanta. Pas yaw pam put paas ang wuuwat pu' piw yaw nawutstiqw paasat pu' yaw pam pangqawu, "Pay uma it qööhit akw-yaniy," yaw aw kita.

"Kur antsa'ay," pu' yaw puma aw kitota. Yaw haalaytoti. "Um hapi tur yangqw pite' pu' um sinmuy aa'awnani. Pay pi as qa pas pi soosoyam panyungqw pay um soosokmuy sinmuy aa'awnani, yaapiy naalös taalat epeq hapi tiikiveniqat. Niikyangw um pangqawni pay um pas soosokmuy katsinmuy naawaknaqey. Noq pay hiisa'haqam pi ökini. Niikyangw paasat pu' um hapi itamuy piw enang wangway-

The following morning the chief ate breakfast, whereupon he resumed his task of making prayer feathers. When he had produced a large amount, he colored them red with ocher. That accomplished, he prayed over them. Then he carefully stashed them away.

That same evening he picked up the prayer items and once more departed to return to the Yaayapontsas. As before, he followed his tracks and soon arrived at his destination. As on the first occasion, he was well received and offered the welcoming smoke. When the smoking ritual was over, he distributed the prayer feathers he had fashioned among the Yaayapontsas. "Now then, these I brought for all of you," he said to their headman.

"Many thanks, indeed," the latter replied. "My people will come up to you and then you can pass them out." One after the other the Yaayapontsas stepped up to the chief from Pivanhonkyapi, and each one was given a prayer feather. The hair of the Yaayapontsas was entangled in big, wild tufts. As each one of them received his feather, he expressed his thanks. No doubt, they all felt happy. Immediately, each one tied his feather to his dishevelled hair, where it served as head decoration. Finally, all the prayer items had been handed out. The chief had made just enough for every one of them. All of the Yaayapontsas were full of joy.

Thereupon, their headman said, "There are two forces we control and have knowledge of. Wind, in particular the whirlwind, is one. The other is fire. It's up to you now. We will employ whichever one your prefer," he explained.

The leader from Pivanhonkyapi sat there, thinking. He carefully mulled over his decision. Finally, he said, "Use fire."

"Agreed," the Yaayapontsas responded. They were happy with his choice. "This is what we want you to do now," their leader advised him. "Upon your return you must inform your people, all of them, because they are all crazy, that there will be a dance in four days. Tell them that you want all kinds of kachinas to perform. You will soon find out how many will care to come. You must then also call for us," he added. "You can rely on us. We will be there. My

niy," yaw aw kita. "Noq pay itam sonqa awyaniy," yaw aw kita. "Pay
pi ima sonqa tapkiqw nuutungkhaqam pu' awyani. Pu' ima awye'
pay ason angqw Huk'oviy kwiningyaqw waltsangaqw pay maqaptsi'yyungwni. Pepeq maqaptsi'yyungqw pu' ason soosoyam yukuyaqw paasat pu' um' ason kits'omiq wuuve' pu' um' paasat pepeq
uupösaalay hapi wiiwilani. Ason um put wiiwilaqw pu' ima paasat
awyani. Yantotini hapi uma'ay," yan yaw pam tutapta.
    "Kur antsa'ay, pay son nu' qa pantini."
    Yanhaqam yaw pam antsa lomanavotqe pu' yaw pam pangqw
pay ahoy piw kiy awi'. Nimaaqe pu' pay yaw yuumosa Huk'omi'.
Noq pep pi yaw piw pam pumuy kikmongwiyamuy kwaatsi'yta. Pu'
yaw pam ep pituuqe pu' yaw kiiyat aw pakiqw yaw pam haalayti.
"Um piw waynumay," yaw aw kita. "Ta'ay, qatuu'." Noq naat yaw
puma pep yu'a'ataqw yaw pep Huk'ove tsa'akwmongwi piw ep pitu.
Pay pi yaw puma sutsep naami papki. Paasat pu' yaw pam pumuy
lööqmuy amumi piw yan lalvaya, hintiqw pam paasatniqwhaqam
waynumkyangw pu' piw haqamniiqey pu' pep hin navotqey. "Noq
oovi uma qaavo ason inuminiy," yaw pam pep pumuy ngemna kiy
awi. "Uma inuminiqw pu' itam piw as pas wuuwayaniy," yaw kita
pam pep pumuy amuminit pu' yaw pam pangqw yamakt pu' nima.
    Paasat pu' yaw pam pas Pivanhonkyami nima. Pep pu' yaw pam
pituqw is uti naat yaw kivaapehaq kwanonota. Paasat pu' yaw pam
piw tiy pangso yuyat aw yooyongnato. Noq pas pi as put nööma'at
lomawuuti. Noq pam yaw aw tiy yooyongnatoqe aqw pakiqw pas
pay yaw pam himu'u, mots'inta yaw pami', qa naami pi pam
hintsanngwuniiqe oovi. Pay yaw pas panyungqamsa epeqya, hiitu
pavataqtöm. Niiqe pay yaw put nööma'at panis put yooyongnaqw
pu' yaw pam piw put tiy wikkyangw angqw ahoy nimaaqe pu' pay
naap piw put puwna.
    Qavongvaqw pu' yaw ima Huk'ongaqw mongwit ep pitu. Pu'
yaw paasat pam hin wuuwantaqey yaw pumuy amumi put yu'a'ata.
"Yaapiy hapi naalös taalat epeq nu' oovi tiikive'ytani. Naanangktikive'yyungwni hapi itam," yaw pam amumi kita. "Noq ep hapi uma
piw angqwni. Pu' uma pep umuukiywat ep tuu'awvani. Pay nu' hapi
pangso piw katsinmuy enang tungla'yta," yaw kita amumi. "Uma ep
tuu'awvaqw pay pi naap hiisa'niiqam naanakwhe' paasa'niiqam
angqwyani," yaw pam kita amumi'.
    Noq pu' yaw puma oovi it pas paas hintaniqat pasiwnayaqw pu'
yaw puma pangqw nima, pangqw Huk'ongaqwwat mongnasu-
ngwam. Pivanhonkyape pu' yaw pam kikmongwi paasat kivanawit

people will arrive in the evening as the very last group. They will be waiting their turn at a place northwest of Huk'ovi, where the gap is. There they will be waiting until all the kachinas are done. At that time I want you to climb on your roof and wave your blanket about. At this signal we will come. This is how you will do this," he instructed him.

"Very well, I will certainly do that."

With this favorable response the Pivanhonkyapi chief started out back home. On the way he headed straight for Huk'ovi. The village chief there was his friend. Upon arriving at his house he entered. His friend was happy to see him. "What a surprise to see you about," he exclaimed. "Come, sit down." The two fell to talking and were still doing so when the crier chief of Huk'ovi also showed up. He and the village head frequently called upon each other. The Pivanhonkyapi chief now explained to them both why he was about at this hour of the day, where he had been, and how he had fared with the Yaayapontsa. "I would like you to come over to my place tomorrow," he invited the two. "If you do that, we can think about the whole thing some more," he said to them, whereupon he went out and headed for home.

He returned to Pivanhonkyapi. Upon his arrival he heard, much to his disgust, that the shouting and laughing in the kiva still had not abated. Once more he took the baby over to his mother to be breastfed. As it was, his wife was a beautiful woman. But as he entered the kiva with the baby, she looked awful. Her hair was all disheveled, because she had not made herself up. All of the participants in the game looked alike, with their hair wild and messy. No sooner had his wife suckled the child than her husband took it back home and put it to bed himself.

The following day the two men from Huk'ovi arrived. The Pivanhonkyapi chief now laid out his plan before them. "Four days from now I'll arrange for a plaza dance here," he explained. "We will have one kachina group dancing after another. I would also like you to join us that day. Let all the people at your village know that I want kachinas to come from Huk'ovi. Tell everybody that all those willing to dance may do so."

When the three had discussed every detail of the plan, the two chief partners from Huk'ovi went home. The Pivanhonkyapi chief in turn went from kiva to kiva informing the people about the forthcoming dance. Wherever he entered, he said to them, "From today on

pan tuu'awnuma yaw puma tiikive'yyungwniqat. Pu' yaw pam
haqam pakye' pu' yaw pumuy amumi pangqawu, "Uma hapi yaapiy
hiituy naawinyani. Pu' uma hiituy naawinye' uma pumuy tuwanti-
vayani. Yaapiy naalötok hapi itam naanangktikive'yyungwniy," yan
yaw pam hiituywatuy haqam kivaape aa'awnat pu' yaw piw sutsvo-
ningwu. Pu' yaw pam oovi soosovik pumuy navotnaqw paasat pu'
yaw puma pas tis oovi kwangwtapnaya. Pu' hapi yaw pas naap
kikmongwi pan naawaknaqw oovi yaw puma kwangwtapnayaqe
pay yaw puma paasat oovi yaw hiituyyaniqey nanawinya. Pu' yaw
puma paapiy put ngöyta.

Pu' yaw antsa panmakyangw pu' yaw tiikimi talöngva. Pu' tiikivet ep yaw qa hak nanavö'a. Pangso yaw puma pay hihin peveltoti.
Pay pi yaw puma suyan tiikivetniniqw navoti'yyungwa. Ep pu' yaw
oovi puma pay qa tuskyap'iwyungqe pay yaw oovi tiitimayya. Pu'
yaw antsa katsinam ep ökiwta. Pu' yaw hiituwat ökye', tiivat, pu'
ninmaqw pu' peetuwat tuwatyangwu. Niiqe puma oovi yaw pephaqam teevep tiikive'yyungwa.

Noq pay yaw tapkiwma. Tapkiwmaqw paasat yaw puma hiitu
supwat yaw tuwat paptuya. Niiqe puma yaw oovi suusyaqe taatöwat
naala. Pang pi yaw pep kitsokive susnuutungkyangwu.

Paasat pu' yaw pam kikmongwi oovi pangso kits'ominiiqe pu'
aqw wuuvi. Pantit pu' yaw pam pepeq pösaalay a'ni wiilanta. Pu'
yaw puma Yaayapontsam pay pangqw maqaptsi'yyungqe pu' pam
put pösaalay wiiwilaqw pu' yaw puma angqw taavangqöyngaqw
hant pangqw pu' yaw pumaya. Niiqe katsinam yaw naat oovi pang
tiivaqw pas yaw sinom hintiqw hoopoqhaqamisa taatatayaya.
Suupan yaw himu pangqaqwniiqat pan yaw puma hinyungwa. Noq
pay yaw kur pas antsa pangqw piw Pivanhonkyapiy hoopaqw yaw
hiitu maataqtoti. Noq naat yaw puma katsinam pang tatkye'yaqw
yaw pangqw hoopaqw hiitu leetsiwma. Noq pay yaw pas kur antsa
hiitu piw pangqwya. Pay yaw sinomsa aqw taykyaakyangw pu' yaw
naa'awinta, naatuvinglalwa hiitu pangqwyaqat. Noq pay yaw qa hak
navoti'yta.

Panwiskyaakyangw pu' yaw puma pumuy amumi haykyalaya.
Su'aw yaw oovi puma pep kiisonvewat katsinam tiitso'qw yaw puma
hiitu angqw hoopaqw amumiya. Niikyangw pay yaw kur puma
panis naalöyömya. Noq pay yaw pas qa hak tuwimu'yta hiitu pumayaqw. Qa hak yaw hisat pumuy hiituy pam sosniwqamuy amumi
hisat yori. Niikyangw yaw puma hiitu a'ni sosniwa, pala'vo'yyungwa hiitu, mots'inyungwa, qötsatsöqa'asi'yyungwa yawi'. Pankyaa-

I want you to think about what type of kachinas you care to imper-
sonate. Once you've made your decision, start practicing. Four days
from now we will have a dance, with one group dancing right after
another." After this announcement he continued on to the next kiva.
When everybody had heard the news, the merriment in the village
increased even more. After all, it was the express wish of the village
chief himself. There was great rejoicing, and the menfolk set to planning for the kachinas they were going to perform. Everyone was
eagerly awaiting the date set for the dance.

Soon it was the morning of the dance day. That day, no one was
playing *totolospi*. The people had calmed their gambling frenzy down
a little. After all, they knew that a dance was something special. So
that day they were not as crazy and came to see the dance. Indeed,
the kachinas were arriving. One group would arrive, dance, and then
withdraw, whereupon the next group had its turn. Throughout the
day they kept up this pattern.

By now it was getting to be early evening. Only one group of
kachinas was left. To finish their last dance they had moved to the
southeastern side of the plaza, where, traditionally, the final dance
sequence is staged.

Now the time had arrived for the village leader to climb on the
roof. This he did, whereupon he vigorously waved his blanket in the
air. The Yaayapontsas were waiting, and when they saw the blanket,
they began their descent on the southwest side of the mesa. The kachinas were still dancing when, for some reason, the spectators began
turning their heads in a northeasterly direction. Something seemed to
be nearing the village. True enough, from northeast of Pivanhonkyapi
some beings became visible. The kachinas were still stomping along
the southeastern edge of the plaza when these beings, whoever they
were, filed in from the northeast. There was no doubt, they were
some kind of beings. The people kept staring at them and passing
along the news. They were asking each other what kind of beings
were arriving, but no one had any idea.

Before long, the beings approached. Just as the kachinas terminated their performance in the plaza, the beings came up from the
northeast. There were four of them, in all, but none of the spectators
were familiar with them. No one in his life had ever seen these dread-
ful beings. They really looked horrible. Their eyes were blood-shot,
their hair was in disarray and their bodies were washed with white

kyangw pu' yaw hiita pay kanelsakwi'ewakw pitkunyungkyangw piw yaw soosoyam hiita tsöpyungwa. Niikyangw pu' yaw panhaqam töqwisa, "Aaw, aaw." Yanhaqam yaw puma kur tuwat töötöki'yyungwa. Noq put yaw hiita puma tsöpyungqw pam yaw it tuwvotat anhaqam soniwkyangw put yaw angqe qaqlavaqe hingsayhooya uwiwitota. Pantaqat yaw hiita soosoyam tsöpyungwa. Noq pu' yaw puma pumuy amumiq pas ökiqw pu' yaw puma pas suyan yoyrikyaqw pay yaw kur pam paho'ini. Paasat pu' yaw pam pep katsinmuy tumala'ytaqa pangqawu, "Naat kur hiitu piwyay," yaw kita. Pu' yaw pam amumi nakwsuqe pangqw pu' yaw pam pumuy paas tsaami'ymaqe pu' yaw pam pumuy kiisonmi tangata.

Pas yaw qa hak pumuy tuwimi'yta. Niiqe yaw puma as oovi naatuvinglalwa hiitu pumaniqw pay yaw pas qa hak navoti'yta hiitu pumayakyangw pu' piw haqaqw pumayaqw. Paasat pu' yaw puma oovi tuwat ang paas leetsilti. Leetsiltiqw pu' yaw pam nana'amqa pumuy ang homna. Pas yaw oovi pumuy homnaqw paasat pu' yaw puma tiivantivaya. Niiqe yanhaqam yaw puma taawi'yyungwa:

> Yeeholyee, yeeholyee holyeyeyeyeye
> Yeeholyee holye.
> Itam hapi taawat tiwungwnimatnikyango
> Oovi itam mumkiwuy akw umuy hiikyangwinmani yep'e.
> Oovi itam tiitiwayiwa.
> Hi'aa wi'aa wi'aa haa'a'a'a
> Hi'aa wi'aa wi'aa haa.
> Pay nuwupi yep'e
> Umuukiy pala'omawuy akwa' nöömiltiqw'ö.
> Haqami yang pamösisonaqa
> Naa'ikwilmuyiwni kiikiy nawita.
> Aa'ahaaha, ii'ihiihi'i.
> Yeeholyee, yeeholyee holyeyeyeyeye
> Yeeholyee holye.
> Hapi meh, hapi haw ingumu, haw inamu
> Soosok hiita oovi weetivayaqö'ö
> Qa soqvik yep qatsiyesnikyango
> Umuutimuy kwaayinmumuya.
> Hi'aa wi'aa wi'aa haa'a'a'a
> Hi'aa wi'aa wi'aa haa.

Yanhaqam yaw puma taawi'yyungwa.

mud. They each wore a tattered black woolen dress in the form of a kilt, and held something in their arms. "Aaw, aaw," were the cries they uttered as they approached. The thing they held in their hands resembled a shield. Along its edge tiny flames flickered. When the four beings finally reached the spectators, the latter were able to see them better. They noticed that the weird objects held prayer sticks. The father of the kachinas cried out, "Here is one more group." With that he walked toward the Yaayapontsas and, leading them along with great care brought them into the plaza.

None of the people of Pivanhonkyapi had any idea who the strangers were. The people kept asking each other who they might be, but no one knew what they represented or where they had come from. The four dancers took great care lining up, whereupon the father sprinkled sacred cornmeal on them. No sooner had he done this than the four began to dance. This is how their song went:

Yeeholyee, yeeholyee holyeyeyeyeye
Yeeholyee holye.
We for sure are the children of the sun.
Therefore we provide you here with heat.
For this reason we were asked to dance.
Hi'aa wi'aa wi'aa haa'a'a'a
Hi'aa wi'aa wi'aa haa.
It's inevitable here now
That your homes will be enshrouded in a red cloud.
Through thick smoke
People will be carrying each other throughout the village.
Aa'ahaaha, ii'ihiihi'i.
Yeeholyee, yeeholyee holyeyeyeyeye
Yeeholyee holye.
Look, my mothers, my fathers
Start doing all sorts of things.
They should live a good life.
Instead, you allow your children to perish.
Hi'aa wi'aa wi'aa haa'a'a'a
Hi'aa wi'aa wi'aa haa.

A handful of the onlookers, whose hearts were not as closed as most of the villagers of Pivanhonkyapi, quickly grasped the meaning of the song. It was foreboding something terrible. Those realizing what it was exclaimed, "We knew it, this was bound to happen, but

Noq pu' peetu ima tiitimayt pay qa pas pep Pivanhonkyape sinmuy amun unangwa'yyungqam pay yaw put taawit aw suumamats-
ya hiita lalvayqw. A'ni yaw pumuy taawi'am hiita lalvaya. Pu' yaw
puma nanaptaqam pangqaqwa, "Puye'emi," yaw kitota, "puye'em
sonqa yantiniqw pas itam yep qa nanvoti'ynumyay," yaw kitota, ima
pay naat qa pas nu'an hinyungqam. Niiqe yaw puma qa haalaytoti.
"Paniqw pi as itam pumuy sutsep meewantotaqw pas puma qa
tuutuqayyay," yaw puma kitota.

Pu' yaw puma oovi tuwat tiitso'qw paasat pu' yaw pam pumuy
amungem kukuynaqa yaw it Pivanhonkyape kikmongwit iniy maqa.
Paasat pu' yaw mooti'ymaqa tuwat Huk'oviy angqw kikmongwit
sukw maqa. Noq pu' yaw puma piw pangqw nan'ivaqw Huk'o-
ngaqwnit pu' piw Pivanhonkyapiy angqw tsa'akmongwiyamuy
nan'ik piw maqaya. Paasa'niiqamuy yaw puma pumuy pep put
huytota, pumuy naalöqmuy. Pantotiqw pu' yaw puma pumuy
yuwsinayaqw paasat pu' yaw puma pangqaqw ahoy ninma. Noq
paasat pu' yaw puma pangqw pay qa Orayviy aqwwat ahoyyat pay
yaw puma teevengewat aqw tuuwikyaqe yaw pangqawwisa, "Aaw,
aaw," kitiwisa. Panwiskyangw pu' yaw puma Apooniviy suutatkya-
qöymiq hawiwa'ytaqat aqw hankyangw pu' yaw puma paapiy pay
pas Nuvatukya'omi ninma kura'.

Pu' yaw ima sinom pay naat hihin suyanis'unangwa'yyungqam
qa haalaytoti. Pas yaw puma hiitu a'löngtniqw oovi yaw puma pay
pavan wuwni'yyungqam pumuy amumi wuuwantota. Qa hisat yaw
puma pumuy hiituy amumi yorikya. Pay pi yaw puma son paysoq
piw öki. Oovi pi yaw taawi'am a'ni hiita lalvaya.

Yanhaqam yaw puma pep hintoti. Pantotiqw paasat pu' yaw piw
talöngva. Talöngvaqw paasat pu' Huk'ongaqw yaw puma mongna-
sungwam piw ep pitu. Niiqe pu' yaw puma pep kikmongwit kiiyat
ep it piw yu'a'atota. Paasat pu' yaw i' Pivanhonkyapiy angqw mongwi pumuy tsa'akmongwituy yaw amumi pangqawu, "Put umuy
maqayaqat put uma yawkyangw Nuvatukya'ominiy," yaw amumi
kita. "Put uma pangso yawme' pep uma put pep it suswukotsmot
nan'ivaq hom'oyt pu' pay pangqw ahoyni," kita yaw amumi.

"Antsa kya pantaniy," yaw puma kita. Paasat pu' yaw puma oovi
put himuy yawkyangw pu' pangqw paasatniqwhaqam pay nakwsu,
Nuvatukya'omi'. Noq yaw ep tiikivet aapiy pay naat suus talöngvaqat ep yaw puma tsa'akmongwit put pangsohaqami yawma.

Noq pay yaw ep tapkimi pay yaw puma piw ahoy aw pitsinaya,
ima navö'hooyam, tuskyaphooyam. Pay yaw puma piw kivami tsots-

we here fail to understand it." This is what the ones said who were not completely crazy yet. Sadness came over them. "That's why we kept warning them all the time, but they simply did not listen."

When the dance ended, the group's song starter handed the village leader of Pivanhonkyapi his tray of prayer sticks. Next, the dancer in front gave one tray to the village chief of Huk'ovi. Thereupon, each of the two village criers received their flaming paho tray. These four men were the only ones to get this gift. Thereupon, the Yaayapontsas were bidden farewell, receiving cornmeal and prayer feathers from the kachina father. Then they departed. This time, however, they did not return toward Oraibi. Rather they went along the ledge in a southwesterly direction, uttering their cries, "Aaw, aaw." In due course they descended the path directly southeast of Apoonivi and then went all the way home to Nuvatukya'ovi, the San Francisco Mountains.

Those Pivanhonkyapis who were still somewhat clear-headed became quite depressed now. Those beings had really been different, hence those villagers who were endowed with wisdom and intelligence kept pondering their significance. They had never encountered beings of this kind. But one thing was clear: They had not come without a purpose. Their song contained an important message.

This is what the people of Pivanhonkyapi experienced there. Then it was the new daybreak. That morning the two chiefs from Huk'ovi reappeared. Together with the leader and crier chief from Pivanhonkyapi they discussed the whole matter. Finally, the Pivanhonkyapi leader said to the two crier chiefs, "Those pahos you received I want you to carry to Nuvatukya'ovi. Deposit them there on both sides of the highest peak and then come back again."

"It shall be like that," the two replied. With that, they seized their trays and set out towards Nuvatukya'ovi. They undertook their task on the first day after the dance.

That same day, by early evening, the gamblers and crazy ones started all over again. Once more each of them went to the kiva to continue playing *totolospi*. And since the day before they had all dressed early to go see the dance and had somewhat straightened out their hair, they still looked quite decent.

vala. Niiqe pay yaw kur puma ahoy aw pitsinayani. Noq yaw puma ep tavoknen iits pay timayyuyaakyangw pu' piw hihin naawusyaqe pay yaw oovi naat lomahiitu ahoy aw sasqaya.

Noq pu' yaw puma Nuvatukya'omi put yawmaqam yaw ahoy pitu. Pu' yaw pumuy pituqw pu' yaw puma oovi paas piw soosoyam tsootsongya. Tsootsongyat yukuyaqw yaw i' mongwi haalayti pumuy amumi. "Kwakwhay, uma pituy," yaw amumi kita. "Yantani. Ta'a, pu' pay itam yaapiy putsa aw maqaptsi'yyungwniy," yaw amumi kita. "Pay pi oovi tsangaw itam aw antotiqw pay pi uma umuukiy ahoy awnen pay maqaptsi'ytaniy," yaw amumi kita, pam mongwi.

Paasat pu' puma oovi hisatniqw pangqw yaw ahoy pangso', Huk'omi'. Noq ep mihikqw pay yaw Nuvatukya'ongaqw hihin kootala, angqe Nuvatukya'oviy oovaqe. Noq pay yaw qa hak put pep pantaqw navoti'yta. Pay yaw panis pumasa nan'ip kitsokive momngwitsa put navoti'yta himu pamniqw.

Pu' yaw löös taalawvakyangw pu' paasat piw mihi. Ep pu' pay yaw pas angqe uuwingw hihin pavan maatsiwta. Pu' ima peetu kivamiq kuuyungqam pay qa aqw yungye' pay yaw angqw oongaqw aqw nuutum pay kwanonotangwu. Amumiq yaw tutaptsoni'yyungwa. Noq ep yaw puma löös talqat ep mooti nanapta. Pas yaw suupan uwiwita, Nuvatukya'oviy angqe. Pu' yaw puma as pumuy pangsoq put aawintota pangqe uuwingw pantaqw. Noq pay yaw pas qa hak amumi tuqayvasta. Pas yaw qa nanapta. Paysoq yaw amumiq yorikyat pu' pay piw aapiytotangwu.

Nuwu pay yaw paayis taala. Ep pu' pay yaw pas kwiitsingw amumiq pitsiwiwta. Pay yaw pas hihin kwits'oopokiwta, Pivanhonkyape. Pu' paasat pam uuwingw yaw tis pay susmataq. Niikyangw yaw sumataq pumuy amumiq hoyoyota. Pu' yaw puma as piw pumuy aawintotaqw pay yaw kur puma pas son tuutuptsiwni. Pas pi yaw puma hintsatskyaqey putsa aw yuki'yyungqe qa ngas'ew yaw amumi tuqayvastota. Pu' yaw as puma amumiq pangqaqwa, "Kur huvam nöngakye' aqw naap yoyrikya'ay."

"Son pini. Paysoq pi uma itamuy qe'tapnayaniqe oovi panhaqam hingqaqwa," pay yaw haqawa yan lavaytiqw pay yaw puma qa hin tuutuptsiwa. Qa hin yaw puma pumuy amumi tuqayvastotani. Pu' yaw puma as okiw pumuy amumiq qa naatusi'yyungwa. Susmataq piw yaw kwiikwitsi. Qa ngas'ew yaw puma qe'totiniqey unangwtoti.

Nalöstalqat ep pu' yaw pay pas susmataq uuwingw angqw

By this time the two crier chiefs who had taken the paho trays to Nuvatukya'ovi were back home. All four of them now engaged in a ritual smoke and when that was over, the Pivanhonkyapi chief expressed his gratitude to them. "That's the way it's going to be. All right, from now on we'll be looking for whatever events will unfold," he said to them. "I'm glad we did the right thing. You can go back to your homes now and wait."

Some time later the two crier chiefs departed, one to Huk'ovi, the other to his house in Pivanhonkyapi. That same night, a light from a small fire could be seen shining from Nuvatukya'ovi, from the area around the mountain peaks. No one had any explanation for it. Only the two village leaders knew what it meant.

A new day broke, and then it was night again. By now, the fire was somewhat more visible. Some of those who were at the kiva, but had not entered in order to watch from the top, were yelling and laughing with the players and kept shouting instructions to them with great fervor. That second day the spectators first became aware of the fire. There seemed to be flames licking up into the sky in the vicinity of Nuvatukya'ovi. Every so often they mentioned the fire to the players down below, but no one listened to them. Not being able to hear what they were saying, they merely looked at them and then continued on.

Meanwhile, the fire kept burning, and its smoke began to reach the people of Pivanhonkyapi. There was actually some smoke hanging over the village. The flames were distinctly visible now and apparently advancing on the village. Again the watchers on top of the kiva tried to tell the players, but they would not believe it. They were concentrating so hard on what they were doing that they didn't even bother to listen. So the onlookers shouted down to them, "Come on out and see for yourselves."

"No. You're only saying that to make us stop," one of the players retorted. They simply refused to believe that this news was true. They would not listen. In vain the onlookers tried to catch the attention of those inside the kiva. The smoke was clearly wafting about, but they had no intention of quitting their *totolospi*.

On the fourth day the firestorm was definitely moving closer. The village was beginning to fill with smoke, and its smell was quite intense. Once more the onlookers attempted to warn the players that a fire was approaching. But they still did not believe it. Instead, the

hoyoyota. Pu' yaw pay kwiitsingw pas pep kiive oopokiwma. A'ni
yaw as kwitshovaqtu. Pu' yaw puma as pumuy pangsoq aawintota
angqw uuwingw pitutoq, angqw hoytaqw. Piw naat yaw puma qa
tuutuptsiwa. Tuwat yaw puma tootim, taataqt manantuy, momoymuy pepeq kwangwa'ewlalwa. Naamamavoqlalwa, naamutstota
yaw puma pepeq.

Nuwu hapi pay yaw amumiq pitutoq naat yaw pas qa hak pepeq
pakiwtaqa tuptsiwa. Nuwu yaw pay paapu pas amumiq haykyala.
Pay yaw pas paysoq Apooniviy taavangqwniqw paasat pu' yaw hak
nawis'ew kur nöstoqe yaw kivangaqw yamakqe paasat pu' yaw
navota. Pu' yaw pam ahoy aqwhaqami uukwikmaqe pu' yaw pepeq
pumuy aa'awna. Pas pi yaw pam hin unangwa'ykyangw hin hiikwis-
kyangw epeq pakiqw pas yaw paasat pu' puma put aw tuqayvastota.
Niikyangw pay yaw piw as peep qa nanapta. "Pay kur pas qa atsay,"
yaw amumi kita. "Pay pas yangqw pew pituto."

Pas yaw paasat pu' puma pangqw nöönganta. Paasat pay yaw
pas amumi pitu. Paasat pu' yaw puma pangqw nööngankyaakyangw
ang aatsavala. Hiita pi hak sonqa kyaakyawne' ngas'ew yaw put hak
kwusut pu' haqami waayangwu, hihin iitsyaqam. Pu' imuy qa iitsya-
qamuy amumi suptu. Pu' yaw sinom tsaykikyaakyangw watkita.
Hak hakiy kyaakyawne' ngas'ew yaw put ngu'ykyangw, iikwiwkyangw waayangwu. Pu' yaw peetu qa naatuwa'ynumya. Pu'sa yaw
puma angqe timuy oovi hepwawartinumya. Pay yaw as puma kur
pumuy kyaakyawnayakyangw pumuy tatami'yyungwa. Noq pay
yaw hak tiikivet qavongvaqw pay pumuy tsaatsakwmuy tsamkyangw Huk'omi pumuy waa'oya. Pas pi yaw qa hakiy qatsi'atniwti.
Pu' yaw peetu naat kiikiy ang tangawtaqw pay yaw pumuy
uuwingw enang paysoq wari. Yan yaw pam pep pumuy wuukoqöya,
uuwingw. Pay yaw pas hikiyom nönga. Pep pu' yaw hiituwat haqam
tuusö'ytaqat tuwa'yyungqe pu' yaw puma pangsoq as okiw timuy
iikwiwkyaakyangw watkita. Pu' yaw peetu pay kiikiy ang yuuyu-
pavaqe huur tangalti.

Noq yaw i' kikmongwi put Yaapontsat iniyat nawkiqe pu' yaw
pam put kiy ep yuupomiqhaqami pana. Pu' yaw pam pepehaq pakiwtaqw pu' yaw put angqw pam uuwingw iniwtaqa yaw öqawi'y-
ma. Pu' yaw oovi su'aw pam pepeq yuupaveq öqawtaqw yaw mi'wa
Nuvatukya'ongaqwniiqa yaw Pivanhonkyapimi pitu. Pu' yaw puma
naamaniikyangw pu' yaw pep put soosok uwikna. Pangqw pu' yaw
pam uuwingw hoytakyangw pu' yaw imuy tuusöva na'uyi'yyungqamuy amumi pituqw pay yaw puma kohalangwuy akw soosoyam

boys and men were enjoying the girls and women. They kept embracing and squeezing each other.

The firestorm was coming closer and closer, yet none of those in the kiva believed it. When the fire was just southwest of Apoonivi, one of the gamblers finally came out to eat. As he left the kiva he realized the truth. Quickly he dashed down the kiva ladder again and told the others. He was excited and almost out of breath as he entered. They listened to him, but were hardly able to make out his words. "It's really true," he yelled at them. "There's a fire coming in!"

Now the players came out. By this time the fire had arrived. Leaving the kiva, they scurried all over. Whatever someone treasured he tried to grab before he ran off, at least those who were among the early ones to emerge. Those who were tardy were caught by the fire. Crying, people were running in all directions. If someone was fond of a person, he held on to him and loading him on his back, sought to escape. Some failed to see each other in the confusion. Only now it occurred to them to run in search of their children. Instead of holding them dear they had neglected them. Fortunately, someone had rounded up the children the morning after the dance and taken them into shelters at Huk'ovi. It was a real nightmare. Some people were still in their houses when the fire engulfed them. A few managed to get away, but the majority was killed by the fire. Several knew of an overhang to which they ran with their children on their back. A few also holed up in remote corners of their homes.

Now the village chief took the flaming paho tray he had received from the Yaayapontsa and placed it in the back room of his house. Right away the fire on the tray grew stronger. Just as it was blazing full force, the fire that had been burning its way across from Nuvatukya'ovi reached the village of Pivanhonkyapi. The two fires now merged and set everything aflame. Racing along from the point where the two had merged, it spread to the people hiding under the overhang. All of those inside died from the intense heat. Thus, nearly the entire population of Pivanhonkyapi was burned to death in the fire.

so'a. Pay yaw puma pephaqam soosoyam taqtotiqe pay so'a.

Panmakyangw pu' yaw paasat pam uuwingw pangqw suu'oray-miqwat hoyoyoyku. Noq pu' yaw pep Orayve kikmongwi put uuwi-ngwuy tuwa pangqw su'amumiqwat hoyoyotaqö'. Paasat pu' pam qa haalaykyangw pangqawu, "Is ohiy," yaw kita, "sumataq hintani. Nu' pay itimuy kyaakyawnay," yaw kita. "Niiqe nu' oovi haqami hakiy son aw qa taqa'nangwtaniy," yaw kitaaqe pu' yaw pam paasat Pöqangwwawarpimi, Kookyangwso'wuutit kiiyat awi'.

Niiqe yaw pam ep pituuqe naat as yaw pu' aqw hingqawniniqw yaw hak angqaqw paki'a'awna. Pu' yaw pam oovi aqw pakiqw yaw Kookyangwso'wuuti epeq qatu. Pu' yaw pam put paas tavi. Noq yaw ima Pöqangwhoyat naatupkom tuwat angqe' naayawtinuma, naatats-kwekinnuma. Pu' yaw so'am as amumi itsivutiqw pay yaw puma pas qa navota. Pu' yaw piwniiqe paasat pay yaw pavan kyee'ewniqw paasat pu' yaw puma qe'ti. Paasat pu' yaw pam Orayngaqw kik-mongwi put so'wuutit aw tu'awi'yta hintiqw pam pangsoniqey. Yaw pam pumuy amumi taqa'nangwtiqe yaw amumi pangqawu, "Yangqw hapi qööhi hoyoyotaqw nu' hapi pay qa amum put pasiw-nay. Nu' hapi itimuy kyaakyawnaqe oovi'oy. Noq uma as sen tuwat inumi unangwtatveqw pay as kya itim qa uwikyaniy. Yan nu' as naawaknaqe oovi angqöy," yaw pam Kookyangwso'wuutit aw kita.

Noq pay yaw puma son aw qa unangwtatveniqat yaw pam aw pangqawu. "Pay itam son uumi qa unangwtatveni. Noq oovi qaavo um hapi pay iits talavay kuyvansat qatupte' it um hoohut lööqmuy yukuni," yaw aw kita. "Niikyangw um nguringyawuy masayat hapi akw homastsokyanani. Pay um panis pantit pu' um Orayviy taavang sukw tsööqöknani. Pu' um sukw hihin kwiningya Atsamaliy pay pephaqam um piw sukw tsööqöknani," yaw aw kita. "Um niikyangw pisoqtini. Son pam peqw qa suptuni," yaw aw kita.

Paasat pu' yaw pam antsa pan nukwangwnavotqe pu' yaw pam pangqw ahoy kiy aw nima, Oraymi. Pu' yaw pam ep pituuqe pu' yaw naawakna, tsootsonglawu. Paasat pu' yaw pam aapatat pu' wa'ökqe pay antsa suupuwva. Niiqe yaw antsa qavongvaqw pam pay yaw su'its kuyvansat qatuptuqe yuwsit pu' yaw put tutavoyat anti. Pu' yaw pam oovi put suyukut pu' pam pangqw haqami aw tutaptaqw pangso yawmaqe pu' pep yaw pam pep pumuy tsöö-qökna. Pay yaw naat oovi qa wuuyavotiqw pay yaw antsa angqaqw aw puma Pöqangwhoyat Kookyangwso'wuutit amum.

Pu' yaw aw ökiiqe pu' yaw aw pangqawu, "Ya um pay pitu?" yaw so'wuuti aw kita.

The fire now embarked on a course that led directly to Oraibi. The village leader of Oraibi spotted it as it headed straight for them. In despair he cried out, "Oh my, there is going to be a disaster. I love my children. I have to ask someone for help." With that he ran to Pöqangwwawarpi, the abode of Old Spider Woman.

Upon his arrival he was about to announce his coming when a voice bade him enter. When he was inside, he saw that Old Spider Woman was at home. She welcomed him. The two Pöqangw Brothers were fighting, throwing each other down all over the place. Their old grandmother got after them, but they did not listen. Once more she yelled at them, this time more forcefully, and now the two quit. Right away, the village leader of Oraibi informed the old woman why he had come. Imploring her and her grandchildren's assistance, he said, "There is a fire approaching, with whose planning I had nothing to do. I greatly love my children. Maybe with your help they will not be burned to death. This is my wish. That's why I came."

Old Spider Woman assured him of their help. "Don't worry, we'll come to your rescue. Early tomorrow morning, when it is the time to address the sun in prayer, you must get up and make two arrows. Fletch them with feathers of the red-shafted flicker. As soon as you're done, ram one into the ground southwest of Oraibi, the other a little northwest of Atsamali. Now hurry," Old Spider Woman urged him. "The fire is going to be here before long."

The Oraibi chief was happy about the favorable response and returned to his village. There he prayed and smoked for some time. Then he made his bed, lay down, and fell asleep at once. The following day he was up early, at the time when people go to greet the rising sun in prayer. He dressed and then did as instructed by Old Spider Woman. He quickly fashioned the arrows, whereupon he took them to the two locations Old Spider Woman had pointed out to him and stuck them in the ground. Before long the two Pöqangw Brothers and Old Spider Woman arrived.

"You've come?" the old woman greeted the chief.

"Yes, I just got here."

"Very well. Are the two arrows in place?"

"Owiy, nu' naat pu' pew pituy," yaw aw kita.

"Kur antsa'a. Noq um put hoohut tsööqökna?" yaw aw kita.

"Owiy, pay nu' tsööqöknay," yaw pam aw kita.

Pep pu' yaw pam Kookyangwso'wuuti put hoohuy nan'ivaq tsööqökput ang wishöviy naanahoy laanalawu. Pas yaw pam oovi put hurulanata. Paas yaw pam oovi put naalökye' natsva laanatat pu' yaw pam put aw sisiwku. Paasat pu' yaw pam pumuy Pöqangwna-tupkomuy amumi pangqawu, "Ta'a, uma tuwatni. Uma put aawi-lawngat mömtse' pu' uma put laana'iwput ang pavoyaqw pay pam sonqa owatini."

Yan yaw pam pumuy naatupkomuy amumi tutapta. Paasat pu' yaw puma put ngahut pang laana'iwtaqat ang pavoyannuma. Noq pay yaw antsa pam huur pang owati.

Paasat pu' yaw pam uuwingw hoyoyoykukyangw pu' yaw pas Orayviy taavang yaw wunuptu. Pantiqw pu' yaw pam Kookyangw-so'wuuti pangqawu, "Pay sonqa yantani. Pay pam uuwingw it aw pite' pay pam sonqa umuukiy atsvaqe ayoqwat tso'omtini. Pay son oovi qa yantani. Pay pam uuwingw it pu' son angwutani," yaw Kookyangwso'wuuti aw kita. Panhaqam yaw puma pep yukuyaqw pangqw pu' yaw puma naanahoyya, puma Pöqangwhoyat soy amum kiy awniqw pu' kikmongwi Oraymiwat.

Pantaqw pu' hapi yaw pangqw uuwingw kuyva. Pepeq yaw put pantaqat suupang yaw as pam uuwingw oovini ang pan uutaqw. Niiqe pay yaw panis pam put aqw pitut pay yaw qa kiihut angqe tso'omtit pay yaw ponilti. Poniltiqe pu' pay pang Orayviy kwiningye' pu' pay aqw hoopoqhaqami. Pangqw pu' yaw pam Paaqaviy tatkye'-niikyangw pu' yaw aapiy hoopoqhaqami. Pang yaw pam aqw wup-kyangw pu' yaw pam pas Palapsömiqhaqami tsootso'a. Paniqw yaw oovi pangqw Pivanhonkyapiy angqw pam Orayviy aqwwat owa naat taq'iwyungwa. Pu' Orayviy ang kwiningye' aqw Paaqaviy tatkya-qöyva Paqaptsokviy aqw hoopoq pösöyat aqw hopqöymiq naat pam ang piw panta.

Yanhaqam yaw pam kikmongwi pumuy unangwyamuy taalaw-na. I' hapi yaw pas qa atsat pep yaniwti. Yan hapi yaw oovi Pivan-honkyapi kiiqöti. Paapiy pay yaw qa hak pep qatu soosokmuy yaw pam uuwingw pep qöyaqw. Pay yuk pölö.

"Yes, I stuck them both in the ground," he replied.

With that, Old Spider Woman began to weave a web back and forth between the two inserted arrows. She spun the web really tight. Four layers in all she wove on top of each other and then she urinated on the web. Then she turned to the Pöqangw Brothers and said, "All right, it's your turn now. Chew this mirage medicine and spurt it on the web. It's bound to turn into solid rock then."

These were her instructions to the two brothers. The two did as bidden and spurted the medicine all over the spun webbing. Sure enough, it became as solid as rock.

By now the fire wall was moving in. Already it stood southwest of Oraibi. Thereupon Old Spider Woman explained, "This is how it's going to be now. When the fire comes upon this barrier, it will jump over your houses and land on the other side. That's the way it's going to be. The fire cannot overcome this wall." With this task accomplished, they all went their own way again. The Pöqangw Brothers went home with their grandmother, and the village leader returned to Oraibi.

At this moment the firestorm surged over the horizon. It was headed straight for the rocky barrier. The minute it reached it, it did not jump over the houses, but instead was deflected. Veering off its path, it ran along the northwest side of Oraibi and continued in a northeasterly direction. From there it burned along the southeast side of Bacavi, and then once more rolled in a northeasterly direction. There it climbed up the terrain and burned itself out somewhere near Palapsö. For this reason, the rocks between Pivanhonkyapi and Oraibi still look burned today. The same is true for the area spanning from a point northwest of Oraibi to the southeast side of Bacavi, and to the northeast corner of Paqaptsokvi.

This is how the village leader of Pivanhonkyapi purged the dark hearts of his people. These events truly took place. In this manner Pivanhonkyapi fell into ruin. No one lives there any more, for the fire killed all the villagers. And here the story ends.

4

The Demise of Sikyatki

The extensive prehistoric ruin of Sikyatki is located about two and a half miles northeast of Walpi, the southernmost of the three present villages on top of First Mesa. Fewkes's contention that the name of the site alludes "to the color of the sandstone of which the walls were built" and hence translates "Yellow House," is not consistent with Hopi linguistic rules of composition (1898: 632, 636). This explanation does not account for the *t* in the place name. Compounding the elements *sikyangpu*, "yellow," and *kiihu*, "house," whose respective combining forms are *sikya-* and *-ki*, yields *sikyaki*, not *sikyatki*.

Since *tuki*, "cut," typically occurs in its contracted shape of *-tki*[1] in compounds, a semantic reading of Sikyatki as "yellow cut" would be more reasonable. Of course, the adjective *sikya*, "bitter, sour," could equally well serve as modifier element, resulting in a meaning of "bitter/sour cut."[2]

The most likely interpretation, however, which is linguistically tenable, is that of "cut-off/divided valley." It is based on the word *sikya* which, as an independent noun, denotes "small valley, ravine." This interpretation seems to be confirmed also by Waters who explains the name as "Narrow Valley" (1963: 102).

While most of the crumbled masonry structures of the ancient pueblo have long since been covered by drifting sand, masses of distinctive Jeddito yellow ware[3] and its polychrome descendants still litter the site. These pottery types were produced by using an oxidizing firing atmosphere rather than a reducing one and are among the most beautiful ever made in the Southwest. In 1895, Fewkes, by invitation of the Secretary of the Smithsonian Institution, excavated portions of the ruin. As was customary at the time, most of the archaeological work was concentrated in the cemeteries. They yielded more than eight hundred pottery vessels, "of which over five hundred were decorated with beautifully colored designs" (Fewkes 1896: 159).[4]

This wealth of outstanding ceramics is one of the reasons Sikyatki has perhaps received more attention than any other prehistoric site in Northern Arizona. As Hargrave points out, "Objects of material culture, especially pottery, were in great demand by eastern museums at that time and the superior quality and exceptional beauty of color and form of this pottery created a sensation among collectors of all classes" (1937: 63).

Also, among the workmen hired by Fewkes was a resident of Walpi named Lesou, who took a fancy to the unearthed pottery and thereby set into motion an interesting chain of events. Lesou was married to Nampeyo, a potter from Hano, the Tewa village at the northeastern end of First Mesa. When he returned home with potsherds from the excavation and showed them to his wife, she became so enchanted with the artistic designs and aesthetically pleasing colors that she soon began to integrate them into her own work (Dittert and Plog 1980: 31). Among Nampeyo's most famous creations are the low, wide-shouldered jars whose beautifully proportioned shape was modeled on Sikyatki originals. In copying this inspirational pottery from Sikyatki, she provided a powerful impetus to the deteriorating and disappearing local pottery industry and ultimately initiated a renaissance of Hopi ceramic art that became a great economic boon to the entire community of First Mesa.

While Hopi legendary history contains conflicting claims as to whether Walpi or Sikyatki was founded first, Hargrave suggests that archaeological evidence in the form of pottery remains "prove them to have been founded at approximately the same time, namely about 1425 A.D." (1931: 3). Although crude Basketmaker III sherds have been reported from the vicinity of Sikyatki spring, evidence of the subsequent periods, archaeologically known as Pueblo I, II, and III are apparently absent. Sikyatki's beginning in the 15th century thus falls into the late prehistoric phase of Pueblo IV, which is allocated a time frame between 1300 A.D. and 1600 A.D.

Although modern research has yet to determine the exact date of Sikyatki's abandonment, the fact that no Spanish chroniclers mention its name is a strong indication that the village was deserted between 1500 A.D. and 1600 A.D., prior to the arrival of the Spaniards (Hargrave 1931: 5). As to the reasons behind its abandonment, convincing scientific data is scarce.

Hargrave believes that sufficient archaeological proof exists to support his theory that the Jeddito pueblos to the east of First Mesa were not Hopi and that Sikyatki was part of this Jeddito group (1935). In spite of sharing a nearly identical material culture with the other villages from the Hopi group, as is evident from similar pottery types, the two groups probably were affiliated with different linguistic stocks. Thus, the inhabitants of Sikyatki would have spoken a language different from those of the Hopi at Qöötsaptuvela. This linguistic difference may have been one of the reasons for the feuding that existed between the two villages, as reflected in several of the legendary accounts of the destruction of Sikyatki.

Additionally, Mindeleff mentions disputes over land use and planting privileges which apparently arose when a contingent of families from Walpi left Qöötsaptuvela on the northwestern flank of the mesa point and settled on the east side of the mesa, close to territory claimed by the Sikyatkis (1891: 24). Finally, Fewkes reports that the ill feelings between the two communities may have been aggravated due to disagreements over control of the water supply (1898: 634).

Whatever the real grounds for the abandonment of Sikyatki may have been, one would not expect to find them factually expressed in the oral narratives that were, nevertheless, inspired by them. Of the ten accounts already published, whether in the form of a lengthy narrative or an abbreviated plot capsule, seven feature the First Mesa villages of Walpi or Qöötsaptuvela in addition to Sikyatki. The same is true for my original Hopi version.

Qöötsaptuvela, which is regarded by the people of Walpi as their ancestral home, translates as "Ash Slope." Obviously, this designation does not conform to the customary pattern of Hopi place name nomenclature. People do not name a new settlement "Ash Slope." Rather, ashes and refuse typically mark a site once it gets abandoned. The name must have originated, therefore, after Qöötsaptuvela's residents left it and began to occupy the top of the mesa after 1700 A.D.

Serious inter-village hostilities with bloody atrocities committed by both sides are reported in Fewkes (1895: 576), Mindeleff (1891: 24-25), James (1917: 93), Curtis (1922: 189-190), Parsons (1926: 227-233), and Courlander (1982: 39-44). While the first three have Walpi and Sikyatki as the opposing factions, Curtis and Courlander have Qöötsaptuvela instead of Walpi. Bunzel's tale (in Parsons 1926: 227-233) mentions a village by the name of Polixti at strife with Sikyatki, Courlander (1982: 49-53) a village by the name of Muchovi. The versions collected by Voth (1905: 244-246), Waters (1963: 97-102), and myself basically portray intra-village conflicts of Sikyatki. However, while Walpi in Voth's account and Qöötsaptuvela in mine still participate in the drama of the destruction, though merely as avenging instruments at the request of the Sikyatki village chief, Waters's is the only account that makes no mention of another village. In Bunzel's account, Sikyatki, after causing the destruction of Polixti, is in turn destroyed by combined forces from Samumpavi [Shungopavi] and Oraibi. All three of Courlander's versions agree with Waters on the point that Sikyatki was not destroyed at all but was freely abandoned by its inhabitants when relations with their neighbors became intolerable.

Interestingly enough, the legend recorded here combines plot elements found both in Waters and Voth. Waters's tale, as mine, features a life-and-death race between two male rivals over a female.[5] However, while Waters's rivals belong to two distinct clans, Coyote and Swallow, in mine only the protagonist is assigned a specific clan association. The antagonist, whose clan status is not revealed, is endowed with the evil and trouble-causing powers of sorcery, as so often happens in Hopi oral literature. In both tales the "good" protagonist triumphs over the "bad" challenger, but while the defeated Swallow faction complies with the Coyote clan's bid to leave the village, the

sorcerers in my story refuse to do so. As the ensuing tensions between the two groups escalate and poison the social atmosphere of
the pueblo, the Sikyatki village leader decides to purge the evil by
destroying the entire community. This episode is mirrored in Voth
and, to some extent, also in Curtis. Once more, as is also the case in
the destruction legends of Pivanhonkyapi and Awat'ovi, society is at
the brink of *koyaanisqatsi*, "chaos and corruption," which render life
no longer worth living. Hence, the village chief's resort to the ultimate remedy in the form of total annihilation of the village.

Endnotes

1. The clan name Patki denotes "Cut-off Water," and the place
name Wupatki, "Long Cut" or "Long Valley."

2. Fewkes reports that, according to traditionalists at First Mesa,
Sikyatki took its name "from the color of the water of the neighboring
spring, which still preserves its yellowish appearance" (1895: 575).
While *sikya-*, indeed, is the combining form for "yellow," *-tki* has no
relation to any word referring to water in the Hopi lexicon. Hence,
this interpretation has no language-based backing whatsoever.

3. Hargrave speculates that the tales of gold and wealth which
lured the early Spanish *conquistadores* into the Southwest in search of
the fabled Seven Cities of Cibola may have been inspired by pottery
vessels of Jeddito Yellow ware and the tons of bright yellow potsherds that speckle the ground. "To natives without knowledge of
metal, gold would only refer to color" (1935:20).

4. For some excellent examples of this collection, now in the National Museum, see Fewkes (1898: 631-742).

5. One of Courlander's versions also contains a life-and-death
race, triggered however, by a rather trivial dispute over fuel-cutting
privileges (1982: 43). In the race itself, two birds, a swallow and a
chicken hawk, represent the rival factions.

Hin Sikyatki Kiiqöti

Aliksa'i. Yaw Sikyatkiveq yeesiwa. Pu' yaw pay pi aqwhaqami
kitsokinawit yeesiwa. Noq yaw pepeq Sikyatkiveq yaw ima hakim
naawuutim ki'ykyangw yaw hakiy lomamanat ti'yta. Niiqe yaw ima
kiisonviy kwiningyahaqaqw ki'yyungwa.

Noq pay pi yaw pam pas pan lomamananiqw yaw oovi ima tootim pangsoq homta. Niikyangw pay yaw qa Sikyatkingaqwsa puma
tootim pangsoq tutumaywisngwu. Pay yaw ima yangqw Awat'o-
ngaqw pu' piw Qöötsaptuvelngaqw tootim yaw piw pangsoq pantsatskya, tutumaywisngwu. Noq pay yaw pam maana pepeq kiy atsveq
tupatsveq yaw ngumantangwuniqw pangsoq yaw puma tootim
ökiwtangwu, tutumaywisqam. Noq yaw himuwa oovi tutumayte'

The Demise of Sikyatki

Aliksa'i. People were settled at Sikyatki. In addition, there were villages all across the land. In Sikyatki there lived a couple with a beautiful daughter. Their house was somewhere northwest of the plaza.

The girl was a great beauty, so naturally the young men were flocking to her place. Not only from Sikyatki did they come to woo her, but also from Awat'ovi and Qöötsaptuvela. The girl was in the habit of grinding corn in the upper story of the house, so it was here that the clandestine lovers were courting her at night. As a rule, a suitor would talk to the girl from outside the vent hole to her grinding chamber. Whenever the girl did not feel like talking to a suitor,

pay yaw haqaqw poksö'ytaqw pangqw yaw aw yu'a'atangwu. Noq pu' pay kya pi put qa aw yu'a'atanik pay yaw oovi hisatniqw hoonangwu. Put hoonaqw pu' pay yaw pam aapiyniqw pu' kya pi haqawa tuwatningwuy. Pay yaw puma oovi naanangk pangsoq pantsatskya. Pu' hisatniqw kya pi pam pay maangu'e' puwmokye' pu' yaw pay hiitawat hoonat pu' paasat pangsoq poksömiq yaw pam hiita akw uutangwu. Aqw yaw uutat pu' paasat pay puwtongwu. Noq pantsatskyalalwa yaw puma tootim tutumayt pangsoq'a.

Pantsakmakyangw pu' pay yaw pam paapu qa soosokmuy amumi yu'a'aykungwu. Haqaapiy pu' yaw pam pay imuy hakimuy lööqmuysa amumi unangwtapngwu. Noq pu' oovi kya pi mimawat pan nanaptaqe pu' yaw oovi pay paapu qa aqw sasqayangwu. Noq pu' pay oovi kya pi ima lööyöm tiyotsa pangqw Sikyatkingaqw paasat pangsoq sasqangwu. Noq yaw imuy tiyotuy angqw yaw hak suukya iswungwa. Panmakyangw pu' yaw pay pam kur it iswungwtiyot yaw pas naawakna. Niiqe pu' yaw oovi mi'wa hisat ep kya pi piw pituqw pu' pam put aw pangqawu, pay yaw paapu qa aqw sasqaniqat. Pay yaw pam mitwatniqey paasat pu' aw pangqawu. Pantaqw pu' yaw pam oovi put iswungwtiyot kiiyat aw tsaqamto. Yaw aw qömi'yma. Pu' yaw pam pep qömi'yvaqw pay yaw put yu'at sunakwha. Niiqe yaw haalayti. Paasat pu' yaw oovi puma put pangso kiy aw panayaqw pu' yaw pam oovi pep ngumanta. Pam pep ngumantaqw pu' yaw put tiyot taahamat sinomat pu' haqawat haqamwat kivaape mö'wiy engem mö'önghiita yuykuya, oovat, wukokwewat, tootsit. Noq yaw oovi pam iswungwtiyo paasat pep kwusi'yta.

Noq pay yaw mi'ma tiyo kur qa naani. Yaw put aw kwa'yqe pas yaw qa naani. Pu' yaw pam wuuwanta, "Hinte' nu' as put nawkini?" yaw yan wuuwa. Noq pay yaw pam tiyo piw kur powaqa. Niiqe pay pam qa naani iswungwtiyo maanat tuyqawvaqw. Noq pay yaw put sinomat piw pas soosoyam popwaqt. Pay yaw puma pas a'ni hiituniiqe pay hiitawat pas sonqa hintsatsnangwu. Popwaqt pi pay lööq unangwa'yyungngwu. Niiqe pay naap sinomuy akw yap'iwwisngwu. Pu' pay haqamiyaniqw qa naap pas öqalay akwyangwu. Pay hiita iisawuy, kwewut sen mongwut, angwusit awniwte' pay putakw yaktangwu. Noq imuy popwaqtuy pay piw kwitavit kitotangwu.

Noq pay yaw pam tiyoniqw pu' put sinomat yaw kur piw pas a'ni hiitu'u. Noq pu' yaw oovi pam powaqtiyo sukwat taahay aw lalvaya, pay as pam put iswungwtiyot maanat nawkiniqey. Noq sen son puma aw unangwtatveniqat kya pi yan yaw tuuvingta.

Noq yaw pam taaha'at pay powaqaniiqe pay sunakwha. Pay yaw

she would tell him to leave. After his departure a new one usually took his place. One after the other they were trying their luck. When the girl finally got tired and felt sleepy, she sent off whoever was still there and closed up the vent hole. Then she went to bed. In this fashion the young men kept wooing the girl there.

As time passed, she did not bother to talk to most of them any more. At one point, there were only two boys left whom she showed an interest in. When the others heard about this, they no longer sought her out. Now only these two boys, both from Sikyatki, kept calling on her. One of the boys was a member of the Coyote clan. In time, it was this boy that the girl fell in love with. Thus, when the other boy arrived again, she told him not to visit her any more. She let him know that she loved the other one. To show her interest in the Coyote Boy the girl, therefore, took a stack of piki with some *qömi* to his family's house. When she arrived with her gift, the boy's mother accepted it, which meant that she approved of the girl as a bride. The girl was filled with joy that she had been accepted into the house of the groom. There she ground corn now. While she was performing this customary grinding, some of the boy's uncles and other male relatives were readying the wedding garments for their new daughter-in-law. They were weaving the bridal robe and the large belt, and were making the wedding boots. Thus, Coyote Boy now had a bride at his home and all the required wedding prerequisites were being met.

The boy who had been rejected was jealous. After all, he had lost the girl. "How on earth can I take her away from him?" he kept wondering. This boy was a witch. He was very upset that Coyote Boy had won the girl. His relatives, too, were all witches who were powerful and great troublemakers. As is well known, sorcerers, or witches, have two hearts. By causing the death of their own relatives, they lengthen their own lives. And if they intend to travel somewhere, they do not do so by the strength of their own legs but in the guise of coyotes, wolves, owls and crows. These sorcerers are contemptuously known as Turds.

This boy's relatives were very powerful, commanding greater than human powers. So the witch confided in one of his uncles and told him that he intended to get Coyote Boy's bride for himself. He asked if he and his people would assist him in this endeavor.

The uncle, who was also a witch, agreed at once. After all, the only thing on his mind was how to harm a person. He assembled the

pam tuwat hakiy pas hintsanniqeysa wuuwantaqe oovi. Noq pu' yaw
pam taaha'at mimuywatuy sinomuy piw tuwat tsovalaqw pu' yaw
puma put yu'a'atota. Pep aw hin wuuwantotaqe pu' yaw pay antsa
put engem nawkiyaniqey pasiwnaya. Yan yaw puma pasiwnayaqw
pu' yaw oovi ep iswungwtiyo nöömay amum asniqat ep pu' yaw
powaqtiyot taaha'at haqam maana mö'öngqatqw pangso yawniiqe
pu' yaw pep pumuy amumi pangqawu, "Pay itam son naanakwhani
pam put amum asniniqw'öy. Pay naat hintani," yaw pam amumi
kita. "Naat ason ima tiyot naami tuwantani. Naat ima pas nanavö'ni.
Niikyangw puma hapi pas qatsiy oovini. Ason haqawa ang ayo'
yamakqa pam pu' paasat ason it amumtiniy," yaw pam amumi kita.

Noq pay kya pi puma pas popwaqtniqw pay yaw oovi mö'wi'y-
yungqam nawus qa rohomtotit pay yaw okiw nawus naanakwha.
Noq yaw puma naama warikni. Pu' haqe' hapi puma warikniqat paas
yaw pam pumuy amumi yuku. Noq pu' hisat hapi puma warikniqat
put enang kya pi piw amumi yuku. Yanti yaw pamnit pu' pangqw
yamakqe pu' haqami ahoy kiy aw'i. Pu' pam yaw kiy ep ahoy pituuqe pu' yaw put tiw'ayay aw pangqawu, "Ta'ay, pay nu' amumi
yuku. Pay uma hapi naama warikni. Niikyangw uma hapi pas umuuqatsiy oovini. Himuwa pö'aaqa paasat pu' ason mitwat pay maanatniy," kita yaw pam tiw'ayay awi. "Noq pay oovi nawus naanakw-
hay," yaw pam aw kita. "Niikyangw pay um qa hin wuuwantani.
Pay pi itam sonqa itaapowaqay akw pö'yyani."

Paapiy pu' yaw oovi puma hisat warikniqat put ngöytota. Paasat
pu' yaw oovi i' iswungwtiyo pay kya pi as qa haalaytikyangw pay
yaw nawusta. Pay pi yaw ima kwitavit a'ni hiituniqw pay hapi yaw
pam qa nakwhaqw son yaw naat puma qa piw hinwat qaqtsinaya-
niqw pay yaw oovi puma nawus soosoyam naanakwha. Pay yaw
hisnen pam su'an yukye' pay yaw as kya qa qatsiy kwayni. Pu' pay
yaw mimawat sinomat piw pan engem hutunvaasi'yyungwa.

Yantiqe pu' yaw pam paapiy oovi wawarlawngwu. Wawarlaw-
ngwuniiqe pay yaw oovi pas su'aw kya pi a'ni hongvitiqw puma aqw
ökiwisa. Noq pu' yaw i' powaqtiyo pi pay a'ni himuniiqe pay yaw
oovi pam qa hin tuwat naahongvilawniqey wuuwanta. Pay yaw pam
kwusi'ytaqa kya pi oovi naala pan wawari. Noq pu' yaw pay kur
aye'wat kitsokiva piw sinom nanapta. Yaw puma nanaptaqe pay yaw
pas son aw qe'yaniqey yaw kitota, aw tiimaywisniqey. Himuwa pi
yaw put maanatni. Paapiy pu' yaw oovi puma put ngöytota, hisat
hapi aw talöngvaniqat put'a. Noq pay yaw oovi pam iswungwtiyo
pas paapu a'ni hongvi'iwtaqw yaw aw talöngva. Pu' ep aw talöngva-

other relatives, who discussed the matter. Mulling everything over, they came up with a scheme to deprive the boy of the girl. The day on which Coyote Boy and his bride were supposed to wash their hair, the witch uncle went to the groom's house, where the girl stayed, and declared, "We won't tolerate it if the girl washes her hair with Coyote Boy. At least not before my nephew and he test each other. They will compete against each other for their lives. Whoever survives can marry the girl." This is what he said.

These sorcerers were extremely powerful, so the Coyote members who had the female-in-law did not resist. They had no choice but to comply with the witch's proposal. The plan was for the two rivals to run a race. The course along which they were to run had already been decided. The time of the race too had already been set. After delivering his message, the witch returned home again. There he said to his nephew, "All right, it's all been arranged with them. You'll race with each other, with life or death at stake. The winner will get the girl," he explained. "The Coyote clan people had no choice but to accept the conditions. You, of course, need not worry. We are bound to win with the help of our witchcraft powers."

The two groups were now anticipating the day of the competition. Coyote Boy was not happy about this turn of events, but resigned himself to his fate. Those Turds were very powerful, and if he did not agree with them, they would probably seek to get into a fight with the Coyote clan. For this reason, they all had to comply. If, through some stroke of luck, he should win, he would not lose his life. His relatives were fervently praying for things to turn out favorably for him.

From that day on Coyote Boy practiced running on a regular basis. Just by the time he got to be in good shape, the set date was approaching. The witch boy, who commanded greater than human might, did not even consider getting into shape. Thus, the boy who had the girl going through the wedding prerequisites at his house, was the only one to practice running. By this time word of the life-and-death race had spread to the other villages. The people there declared that they would definitely come to watch the event. Who knows, either of the two rivals might win the girl. And so people lived in anticipation of the day on which the race was going to take place. When the morning of the great event was at hand, Coyote Boy was in top running condition. At the crack of dawn the spectators were already arriving. They were gathering at the southeast side of

qat ep pay su'its yaw antsa tiitimayt ökiwta. Niiqe yaw ayo' Sikyatkiy aatatkyaqöymihaqami kya pi puma tsotsvala. Pas pi yaw ep qa an'ewakw tsovawta sinom. Mowawata yaw epe. Pu' yaw pay naat oovi taawa kya pi pu' yamakqw yaw pumawat pangqw Sikyatkingaqw tiyot pangso. Pu' puma yaw taahamuy piw wikkyangw. Pu' pay aapiy pumuy sinomat piw kya pi awyaqe pay son pi qa pumuy öqalawisqe oovi. Pu' yaw puma ep pituqw pas pi yaw sinom qa an'ewakw tsovawta.

Noq pu' yaw puma aw pituqw pu' pam powaqtiyot taaha'at pu' yaw pang haqe' tuutuwuuta. Naalök yaw ang nana'löngöt akw tuutuwuuta. Pantit pu' yaw pam nan'ivaqw poyot tsööqökna. Tsööqöknat pu' pangqawu, "Ta'ay, yangqw hapi uma warikniy," yaw pam amumi kita. "Niikyangw uma yangqw mooti taatöq Paayumiq warikkyangw pu' uma hoopoq paayumiq. Pepeq mooti pituuqa hapi pep naatoylay owat ep tapamvenani. Pu' ason mi'wa angk pepeq pite' paasat pu' tuwat mooti'ymaqat naatoylayat atpip pu' himuy peenaniy. Pangqw pu' uma kwiniwiqwatnen ason uma yukiq Wukopisisvayuy aqw pite' pu' pay uma pan piw epeq hintiniy. Pangqw pu' uma pay ahoy peqwwat, niikyangw pu' uma yepeq Kawestimay epeq pay piw antiniy. Yan hapi uma umuunatoylay tapamventimaqw itam nanaptamantani uma haqam pitumaqw'öy. Pu' uma pangqe hapi warikkyangw pu' uma ahoy peqwniy. Pu' yepeq mooti pituuqa pu' paasat ason poyot ep kwuse' pu' paasat mitwat haak nuutaytani. Ason mi'ma pituqw paasat pu' pay mootitaqa ason mitwat yepeq kwaptukniy," yaw yan pam pumuy amumi tutapta.

Noq pu' yaw oovi it iswungwtiyot taaha'at kya pi put tiw'ayay haqami pay sunalkomi langakna. Pam yaw put pangso langaknaqe pu' yaw aw pangqawu, "Ta'ay, pay pi um nawus sonqa amum warikniy," yaw aw kita. "Niikyangw pay um sonqa navoti'yta puma a'ni popwaqtuy. Noq pay naat pam piw son naapni. Pam son naapniqe oovi pas suutaq'eway. Noq itam pi pay as qa pas powaqat tuwi'ykyaakyangw pay itam son ung tatamtotani. Pay itam naat yepeq piw ungem hin wuuwankyaakyangw sonqe kivaape tsovaltiniy," yaw aw kita. "Noq pay oovi um amum warikni. Niikyangw pay um aw tunatyawmani. Hisatniqw hapi pam son naapniy," yaw pam aw kita.

Yaw aw kitaqw pangqw pu' yaw oovi pam ahoy pangso'o haqaqw puma warikniniqw. Pu' oovi puma pepeq neepeq wunuptu. Neepeq yaw puma wunuptuqw pu' yaw pam hak amungem pootoyla. Naalöq yaw oovi aqw pootoylaqw pu' yaw puma wari. Pu'

Sikyatki. A huge crowd was assembled by now. One could hear the hum of many voices. Just as the sun rose, the two boys from Sikyatki showed up. Each of them brought his uncles along. Many of their other relatives also came, in order to wish the runners well. By the time of their arrival, hundreds of spectators were already in place.

The uncle of the witch boy drew several lines in the sand. He drew four lines in all, each a different color. Next, he rammed two knives in the ground, one on each side of the lines. Having done that he said, "Well then, from this point I want you to run. Your first goal will be the Little Colorado southeast of here. Then you will continue to the Rio Grande in the northeast. Whoever gets there first, must carve his clan symbol on a rock. The one who comes in second, is to add his mark underneath the one in the lead. Next you will turn northwest until you reach the Big Colorado River. There you draw your clan symbols again. From the Colorado you are to run this way. Before you do so, however, you must also leave your clan mark at Kawestima. In doing so, we will know where you have been. This is your course. The one who comes in first will pick up his knife and wait for the loser. As soon as he arrives, the winner is to sever his head." This is how the witch instructed the two boys.

At this point, the uncle of the Coyote Boy pulled his nephew aside to a place where they were alone. There he said to him, "All right, you have to run with him now. There is no way out. You probably know that your opponents are witches. Therefore, that boy won't run the entire course on foot. If he had to do that, he would not have agreed to the race. We who have no knowledge of witchcraft, however, won't forsake you. We'll probably meet in the kiva to ponder a solution for you," he said. "So compete with him, but be on your guard. At one point he won't be racing on foot."

After these words from his uncle, Coyote Boy went back to the starting line. The two runners placed themselves side by side. As they stood there, someone started counting for them. He counted up to four, and then the two were off. Sure enough, they headed out in a southeasterly direction. The people all started speaking at the same time, then they were shouting. Some were for the Coyote Boy, others for his opponent. They were wishing them well and exhorting them.

yaw puma antsa taatöqwat mooti wari. Pu' yaw oovi puma warikqw
pas pi yaw sinom epeq mowawayku, pu' yaw piw a'ni töötöqya.
Peetu yaw iswungwtiyot engemya. Pu' peetu pay mitwat yaw
engemya. Pu' yaw puma pumuy a'ni öqalantota. A'ni yaw puma
öqalantotaqw puma aqwhaqami yaw warikiwta. Noq pay yaw antsa
i' iswungwtiyo pay haqaapiy mooti'yma. Pam pi pay wawarqe a'ni
hongvitiqe pay yaw oovi aapiy pay mooti'yma. Niiqe pay yaw oovi
puma haqami kya pi tuuwayamaqw pay yaw paasat sinom pumuy
qa tuwa'yyungwa. Pu' kya pi puma haqami tuuwayaqw pay yaw
puma tiitimayt qa hin niman'unangwa'yyungwa. Pay yaw pas
amumum hin nanaptaniqey pay yaw oovi pas pep nakwhani'y-
yungwa.

Pu' yaw pay pam iswungwtiyo pas yuumosa warikiwkyangw
pay yaw pas qa haqam yaw huruuti. Noq pay yaw puma oovi haqti.
Haqtiqw pu' yaw pam ahoy yorikqw pay yaw mi'wa qa haqam. Pay
yaw pam pas qa haqam. Pu' yaw pam iswungwtiyo ahoy as aqw
taynuma. Pay kya pi pam pep hiisavo huruutiqe as aqw taynumqw
pay yaw pas qa angqaqwniqw suusa maatsilti. Pu' yaw pam pay oovi
put qa pas nuutaytat pay aapiyta. Niikyangw pay yaw pam paasat qa
pas hin hönginiiqey qa pas pan'i. Pay yaw pam aqw kwangwawari-
kiwta. Pay yaw pam oovi qa hikwismokiwkyangw yaw aqw
warikiwta. Yaw oovi pam aqw warikiwta haqami puma mootininiqw
pumuy amumi tutaptaqw pangsoq yaw pami'. Pam yaw oovi paasat
pay pan heenakhooya'yma.

Naat yam pam oovi pam panmaqw piw yaw himu atsva, niikyangw a'ni yaw himu hoyta. Noq yaw pam angk taymaqw yaw kur
yoyviikwa. Yaw yoyviikwaniqw pay yaw pam put qa pas aw hin
wuuwanta. Pay pi yaw puma piw pangqe yesqw oovi pay yaw pam
put qa pas aw hin wuuwankyangw pay yaw aqw warikiwta. Pu' yaw
oovi pam panmakyangw hisatniqw pu' yaw puma haqami mootini-
qat pangsoq yaw kur pam pitu. Pu' yaw pam aqw pitutoqe pu' yaw
piw ahoy as yorikqw pay yaw pas mi'wa qa haqaqw mamatsila. Pu'
yaw pay oovi pam put qa nuutaytat pay yuumosa pangso haqaminiqey. Pu' yaw puma haqam put naatoylay peenaniqw pu' yaw pam
pangsoniqw yaw oovi aw pituqw pay yaw kur pam se'elhaq pep'e.
Niiqe oovi yaw put naatoyla'at pay yaw ep pe'yta. Yaw pam ep
pituuqe yaw aw taynumqe yaw naami pangqawu, "Is uti, ya pay i'
kur hisatniqw peqw pitu? Pas as qa suusa haqam inuupewtay," yaw
yan pan wuuwa. Nit pu' yaw pay pan paasat suuwuwa kur pay kya
pi antsa qa naapniqe oovi'o. "Pay suyan powaqay akwa'. Pay pi antsa

Meanwhile, the two boys were running along. True enough, it was not long before the Coyote Boy went into the lead. No wonder, for he was strong and in excellent shape. Soon the two disappeared from the view of the spectators. But even though they were gone from view, the spectators felt no urge to go home. Everybody was curious about the outcome of the race, so they remained at the starting line.

Coyote Boy kept running straight along without stopping anywhere. Already the two were quite far away. At one point when Coyote Boy glanced over his shoulder, the other was nowhere in sight. He scanned the area looking back, but to no avail. Halting his run for a while, he looked about, but nobody came into view. So he decided not to wait any longer and continued on. However, he did not run as fast as he could. Instead, he ran at a relaxing pace, heading toward the first destination they had been instructed to aim for. He was now trotting along slowly.

Coyote Boy was still moving along in this manner when something rushed past him overhead with great velocity. Looking after it, he saw that it was a nighthawk. Since it was a bird, he did not give the matter much thought. After all, nighthawks were living in that area. Without considering the matter further, he ran on. In due time, he reached the first destination of the race. Upon nearing it, he again looked over his shoulder, but the witch boy was nowhere to be seen. So without any further delay he headed straight to his goal. Upon reaching the place where they had been instructed to put their clan symbols, he noticed that the other one had already been there. His clan mark was already incised on the rock. Inspecting it, Coyote Boy muttered to himself, "Gee, when did he get here? No one ever passed me," he thought. Then it hit him. His opponent could not have been on foot. He must have used his witchcraft. That was the explanation. "I remember now," he said. "My uncle warned me that he would do this by means other than on foot."

ura pi itaataha inumi pan tutapta pay i' son naapniqat," yan yaw pam
wuuwa.

Pu' yaw pam oovi pep put himuyat atpip pu' tuwat naatoylay
peenat qa sööwunit pu' yaw pay piw aapiyta. Paasat pu' yaw pam
hoopoqwat. Yaw pam hoopoqwatniiqe pu' yaw pam paasat oovi pas
hin hönginiiqey pas yaw paasat pan wari. Noq pu' mi'wa tiyo kya pi
pay paasat naapniqe pu' yaw pay ahoy napwataqe pu' piw ahoy
hopiniwti. Noq pay yaw antsa kur pam qa naap. Pay yaw kur pam
put atsva puuyawma. Niiqe pay yaw pam oovi put ep haqtiqey
wuuwaqe pu' pay yaw antsa pan napwatat pu' yaw pay paapiy oovi
naap. Niikyangw pay yaw qa mitwat an hongviniiqe pay yaw oovi qa
pas a'ni warikiwma. Pay pi yaw suyan mitwat ep haqtiqe pay yaw
oovi pam qa pas hin wuuwankyangw yaw aqw warikiwta.

Pu' yaw mi'wa iswungwtiyo suyan angkniiqe yaw oovi pam
pangqw a'ni wari. A'ni yaw pam warikiwta. Pas pi yaw hin hönginiiqey pani'. Pu' kya pi haqami maangu'yqe pu' pay yaw pep pay
hiisavo naasungwnat pu' piw aapiytangwu. Panmakyangw pu' yaw
pam haqami pituqw paapiy pu' yaw mi'wa piw kuuku'yta. Yaw pam
put tuwaaqe pu' pan wuuwa, "Pay kya naat qa pas yaapti. Pay pi son
pam qa piw naat pantini," yan yaw pam wuuwaqe paasat pu' yaw
pam piw put ngöytaqe pu' yaw piw hin hongviniiqey pas pan piw
wari. Yaw oovi pam panmakyangw yaw aqw hoopoq tunatyawkyangw warikiwta haqaqw sen yaw maatsiltiniqat oovi. Niikyangw
pay hapi pam mooti'ymaqa pan suhopiniikyangw paasat aqwniqw
oovi pam yaw paasat pas qa naatusita. Pu' yaw pam oovi pangqw
angk warikqe pay yaw antsa naat qa wuuyavotiqw pay yaw kur pam
put angk pitu. Angk pituuqe pu' yaw eepeqta. Eepeqtaqe pay yaw qa
aw hingqawt pu' pay aapiy aqle' piw a'ni wari. A'ni yaw pam pangsoq hoopoqhaqami wari.

Pu' yaw pam powaqtiyo pangqw yaw put as ngöyva. Ngöytakyangw pay yaw pam kur put son wiikini. Pay yaw oovi pam pas
suyan yaaptiqw pu' yaw pam piw yoyviikwaniwtit pu' yaw aapiy
pam pangqw put akwniikyangw pu' piw put ngöyva. Noq pay
mi'wa kya pi pas a'ni hönginiiqe pay yaw oovi pas kur yaapti. Pay
yaw pas yaaptiqw pu' pam hisatniqw tuwat eepeqtaqe pu' yaw piw
atsva puuyawma. Noq pu' mi'wa pay yaw paasat ahoywat taatatay-
tima. Noq pay yaw oovi pam angkniiqa pay yaw as qa haqaqwnii-
kyangw yaw pam haqe'niqw pay yaw piw atsva pam yoyviikwa
puuyawma. A'ni pi yaw pam himu kur puuyaltingwuniiqe pas pi
yaw oovi haqami suutuwayama. "Kur pay i' piw qa naap'a," yan

Without delay he pecked his clan symbol underneath the one left by the witch boy. Then he continued on again. He now headed northeast, running as fast as his feet would carry him. Apparently, the other boy had now used his legs again after changing back into his human form. Before he had not run on foot, but had flown over Coyote Boy. When he believed that he was far ahead of him, he had transformed himself back and continued on foot. But he was not as strong as the Coyote Boy and could not run very fast. That did not concern him, however, since he was far in the lead.

Coyote Boy sped along in pursuit of the witch boy. He ran as fast as he was able to. At one point, when he grew tired, he rested for a while. Then he resumed the race. Eventually, he reached the place where the other had again left his human footprints. When Coyote Boy spotted them, he thought, "He's not too far yet, but I bet he's going to use that trick again." Thinking like this, he dashed along in pursuit of the witch boy, his eyes focused in a northeasterly direction. Maybe his opponent would become visible somewhere. The boy in the lead, who was now running in his human shape, did not over-exert himself. Finally, Coyote Boy came in sight of him, and before long was right behind him. The moment he reached the witch boy, he overtook him. Having passed him without saying a word, he ran on at top speed in a northeasterly direction.

The witch boy tried to keep up with Coyote Boy, but he soon realized that he would not catch up with him. So, when the Coyote Boy was far ahead, the witch boy changed into the nighthawk again and resumed his pursuit. Coyote Boy, who was exceedingly fast, was already far gone. But even though, at some point, witch boy passed him flying over his head. Coyote Boy kept looking over his shoulders. At first, his pursuer was nowhere to be seen, but then somewhere the hawk flew past him. Being a creature with wings, he soon disappeared from view. "There he goes again, not using his legs," he thought, speeding along in pursuit.

yaw pam wuuwaqe pu' yaw pam piw pangqw paasat oovi pay pas a'ni wari. A'ni yaw pam put oovi ngöyva.

Noq pu' yaw puma kur ayoq hopoqkimiq yawni. Pangqe pi paayuniqw pangso yaw puma haqamiwatni. Pay yaw Katistsay akwniwihaqami yaw puma. Pangso yaw puma hoytaqe yaw oovi puma pep piw naatolay hapi peenat pu' paasat kwiniwiqwatni. Pu' yaw oovi puma pangsoq naangöyva. Naangöyta yaw puma pangsoqniqw pay yaw kur pam piw yoyviikwat akwniiqe pay yaw kur piw aqw mooti pituuqe pay epeq put naatolay peena.

Pu' yaw pam angk aw pituuqe pay yaw as hihin itsivuti. Niikyangw pay yaw kur pam hintiniqe pu' yaw pay oovi pam pep tuwat naatoylay peenat pu' paasat piw pangqw kwiniwiqwat wari. Noq yaw oovi pam naat haqe'niqw pu' yaw hak aw pitu. Niikyangw pay yaw kur pam hak pumuy kiiyamuy angqw. Niiqe pu' yaw pam put aw pangqawu, "Pay um sonqa navotay," yaw aw kita, "pay hapi pam qa naap'o. Noq pay antsa haq'iwtay," yaw aw kita. "Niikyangw pay pam haqte' son naat hiisavo qa piw naapni. Pay pam piw putwat akwnen sonqa maangu'yniy," yaw aw kita. "Niikyangw ason hapi um piw aapeqtaqw pu' paasat kur piw pantikyangw pu' paasat uupeqtaniqw um hapi paasat pay put mu'ani," yaw aw kita. "Pay um paasat put qa naapniqw um mu'ani. Oovi um hapi aapeqte' ahoy tunatyawmani. Ahoy taatataytime' ason hapi ung hisatniqw wiikikyangw utsvaniqw paasat pay um itakw mu'aniy."

Yan yaw aw tutaptat pu' paasat put hoomatsvongtoynat pu' yaw piw awtat aw tavi. "Noq naato hapi i'wa piiwuy," yaw aw kitat pu' yaw aw hiita tavi. Noq yaw kur pam i' tawiyaniikyangw sunasavaqe yaw pam kwanakpu. Pu' yaw piw it tahut enang maqana. "Ta'ay, pay hapi ason pas pamwa qa naapniqey qa tuuqayqw paasat pu' hapi um tuwat itakwniy. Noq pay um sonqa tuwi'ytani hin um it hintsanniqeyuy. Pu' pay um sonqa navoti'ytani hisatniqw it aw taqa'nangwtiniqeyuy," yaw aw kita. "Pay um itakwnen son put tuwat qa wiikiniy," yaw aw kita. Yan yaw aw tutaptat pu' aw pangqawu, "Ta'ay, pay um warikniy," yaw aw kita. "Niikyangw pay itam son ung tatamtotani. Noq pay ima uutaham pepeq kivaapeq tsovawtay," yaw kita. "Noq pay ason um itamumi taqa'nangwtinik ason um pan naawaknaqw pay itam sonqa nanaptaniy," yaw aw kita.

Pangqw pu' yaw pam oovi put hoohutnit put awtat matsvongkyangw wari. Antsa yaw pam piw an a'ni wari. Naat yaw oovi pay kur qa pas angk pitut pay yaw pam hihin maangu'i. Maangu'yqe pu' yaw pam pep pay oovi huruutiqe pu' kya pi antsa son pi hiita aw qa

The two were supposed to aim for the Eastern pueblos. There was a river there, and their destination was somewhere nearby, northwest of Katistsa. Toward this goal the two runners were now advancing. Here they had been told to incise their clan symbols again, and then continue in a northeasterly direction. So they were headed toward this place in pursuit of each other. But since the witch boy had again resorted to the guise of the hawk, he reached the place first and drew his clan mark.

When Coyote Boy arrived after him, he became slightly angry. However, there was nothing he could do. So he too pecked his clan symbol on the rock, and then ran on in a northwesterly direction. He had not gotten very far when he encountered a man. The man was from his home village and said, "I'm sure you've noticed that the witch boy is not using his legs. He's far ahead already. But he's bound to use his legs again for a while. When he does that, he'll get tired. You'll be able to pass him again, but when he uses his old trick and overtakes you in the form of a hawk, I want you to shoot him. You can shoot him because he's not on foot. Therefore, watch out for him after passing him. Keep looking back. As soon as he catches up with you and flies overhead, shoot him with this."

This is how the man instructed the Coyote Boy, whereupon he thrust a bundle of arrows in his hand and gave him a bow. "This too is yours," the man added, and handed him something else. It turned out to be a gourd which was split in two halves. Along with it came a piece of sinew. "Well now, if the other does not quit using means other than his legs, you can make use of this device. You'll know what to do and when to use it," he said. "With the help of this gourd you're bound to catch up with him." With these words of advice he said, "Now, run. We won't forsake you. All your uncles are assembled in the kiva. Whenever you need our assistance, speak a prayer, and we'll surely hear you."

With that, Coyote Boy ran off, clasping the arrows and the bow in his hands. He really tore along. However, before he came in view of the other he felt exhausted. He stopped and uttered a prayer to some spirit. True enough, his uncles in their kiva at Sikyatki heard him.

naawaknaqw pay yaw antsa pepeq Sikyatkiveq kivaapeq puma taahamat nanapta. Yaw puma nanaptaqe paasat pu' yaw puma pepeq
tsootsonglalwa. Soosoyam kya pi puma taahamat pepeq tsootsong-
lalwaqw yaw antsa ima put kwiitsingwuy hooyintotaqw yaw pam
pangqw kivangaqw yaymakkyangw pu' yaw pangsoq hoopoqwatsa
hoyta. Aqw yaw pitutokyangw pay yaw pam oomawniwtingwuniiqe
yaw oovi pangsoq hopoqkimiq oo'omawt huru'oopokya. Pantotit pu'
yaw puma a'ni yoknaya. A'ni yaw puma yoknaya. Pu' pam hapi naat
yoyviikwat akwniiqe yaw paas mowati. Paas yaw pam tseekwekqw
pay yaw put homasa'at, pöhö'at soosoy himu ang mowatiqe pay yaw
paapu a'ni pituuti.

Pu' yaw pam putakw ani putuutiqe pay yaw maangu'yqe pu'
yaw pay nawus oovi qatuptu. Qatuptuqe pu' yaw pay ahoy hopiniwti. Pay yaw kur pam himu pan tseekwekye' pay paapu qa a'nini-
ngwu. Pay yaw paasat pam ööwiti. Pay yaw kur pam son paapu
putakwni. Pangqw pu' yaw pam yoksonaq tuwat as naap wari. Noq
pan hapi kya pi a'ni yokvaqe pas pi yaw oovi itsehe'tutskwati. Pu'
yaw pam pangqw tsötsqasat ang okiw waqtima. Pay yaw oovi pam
pas qa hoyta.

Noq pu' mi'wa angkniiqa yaw pu' paasat haqami piw kukyat
tuwaaqe paasat pu' yaw pam piw ahoy qa naatusita. Pangqw pu'
yaw pam oovi piw pas hin hönginiiqey pan warikqe antsa pay yaw
hiisavoniqw pay yaw piw aapeqta. Pay yaw oovi pam piw qa aw
hingqawt pay yaw piw aqle' a'ni wari. Pu' yaw pam oovi paapiy pay
ahoy taatataytimakyangw pay yaw pas suhaq'iwma pami'. Pangqw
pu' yaw pam oovi paasat pangsoq kwiniwiqhaqamiwat yaw pam
piw oovi wari. Niiqe pay yaw oovi pam pas suyan haqti. Nawis'ewtiqw pu' yaw oovi mi'wa kur pang yoksonaq yamakqe paasat pu'
yaw pam haqam piw naasungwna tuwat. Pam pi pay qa pas put an
hongviniiqe pay yaw oovi sumangu'yngwuniiqe pay oovi nawus
pephaqam mooti naasungwni'yta. Naasungwnat pu' paasat piw yaw
pam himuniwti, yoyviikwaniwti.

Noq paasat pay yaw kur put masa'at, pöhö'at soosoy himu ang
lakyaqe pay yaw oovi pam paasat qa putuwya'iwkyangw pangqw
piw put akwa'. Pam hapi yaw suyan navoti'yta son paapu put sung-
kiniqey. Pay hapi suyan pam haq'iwta.

Noq pu' mi'wa mooti'ymaqa antsa pay yaw pas yaapti. Pay yaw
pas yaaptiqe pu' yaw pam oovi piw haqam pay hihin huruusalte' pu'
piw aqw ahoy taynumngwu, aqw tunatyawtangwu. Tunatyawtangwu sen pi naat qa angqaqwniqw. Pantit pu' yaw piw aapiytangwu.

They were all gathered there, smoking their pipes. The puffs of smoke they kept exhaling were leaving the kiva and drifting in one direction only, northeast. Upon reaching this direction, they were transformed into clouds. As a result, the sky over the Eastern pueblos became thick with thunderheads. Then they began to release their rain. It really poured. The witch boy, who was still using the guise of the hawk, became drenched. So thoroughly drenched did he become, that all his wing and breast feathers were soaked with moisture.

As a result, his feathers became so heavy that he grew exhausted and had to stop. In doing so, he changed back into his human form. When a bird gets dripping wet, it is not strong any more. The hawk had gotten weak due to the rain, and now the witch boy could not use its disguise any more. Instead, he had to rely on his own legs. Because of the heavy downpour, however, the ground had turned soft, so that the poor wretch was now sloshing through nothing but mud. As a result, he did not make much headway.

By now Coyote Boy, his pursuer, had come across his tracks again. Exerting himself, he ran as fast as he was able. Sure enough, it paid off. Before long, he overtook his rival the witch boy. Again, Coyote Boy said nothing to him as he dashed past. Looking back every so often, he saw that he was drawing way ahead. He now turned in a northwesterly direction. No doubt, he had gained a lot of ground and was far in the lead. Eventually, however, the witch boy managed to escape the rain. He took a break to catch his breath. Because he was not as strong as Coyote Boy, he quickly tired and had to pause there. After resting, he changed back into the nighthawk again.

By now, all his wing and breast feathers were dry, so being light-weighted, he could use the hawk guise again. He knew that he would catch up with Coyote Boy, who was far away.

Coyote Boy, who was in the lead, truly was way ahead. For this reason, he would halt in his tracks once in a while and scan the area behind him. He wanted to see whether his rival was approaching. Then he continued on again. He pressed on as fast as he was able to run, always in the same direction.

Niikyangw paasat pay yaw pam pas hin hönginiiqey pay paapu pas pani'. Pu' yaw pam pantsakma aqw'a.

Noq pu' yaw hisatniqw kur powaqtiyo angk haykyalaqe yaw antsa aqw pay warikiwtaqw tuwa. Tuwaaqe pu' yaw pay pan wuuwa, "Pay hapi sonqa pu' navota nu' qa naapniqw'öy. Pay nu' oovi nawus pas haq atsvaniqw pay kya as nuy qa tuwaniy," yan yaw pam wuuwaqe pu' yaw pam oovi pavan pas ooveti. Oovetit paasat pi yaw pam pas oovi oovahaqe' puuyawma.

Noq pay yaw mi'wa mooti'ymaqa kur navotqe pu' yaw put hoy kya pi as tumostsokya. Niiqe pu' put nuutayta. Niiqe yaw pam oovi pep haqam huruutuqe pu' yaw as put nuutaytiqe yaw aqw oomiq taytaqw antsa yaw angqaqö. Pu' yaw pam as aqw pookyaqw pay yaw ho'at qa aqw pitu. Yaw qa hin aqw pitut pay yaw ahoy posma. Pu' yaw piw sukwat. Piw yaw as aqw pookyakyangw pay yaw piw qa aqw pitsina. Pu' yaw pay pam nawusta. "Pay pi nu' son kur itakw put hintsanni. Pay pi pas oovahaqe'niqw i' qa aqw pituy," yan yaw pam wuuwaqe pu' pay yaw pam nawus put tunipiy pephaqam maspa.

Pangqw pu' yaw pam put oovi piw ngöyva. Pu' yaw pay pamwa aqwhaqami. Pu' yaw pam angk tayma. Nuwu yaw pay haq'iwma. Pay yaw oovi pas haqtiqe yaw aqwhaqami tuuwaqalngwamiq kya pi tuuwayama. Pam yaw pangsoq tuuwayamaqw paasat pu' yaw pam piw huruuti. Pep pu' yaw pam put tawiyat makiwqey horokna. Put yaw horoknaqe pu' yaw pam put pep tutskwave tavi. Noq pay pi yaw as pam tawiya piw qa wuuyaqa. Pu' hin pi yaw pam put aasonmiq pakikyangw pu' yaw pam oovi pep put aqw papkikyangw piw yaw aqw nanaptu. Pu' yaw pam mitwat akw naamiq uuta. Naamiq uutat pu' yaw pam pep tawiya sipna'ytangwuniqw put aasonngaqw pu' yaw pam put tahut naahoy laanata, atkyamiqnit pu' sipnayat aqw enang. Pantit pu' yaw pam mapqölöy akw yaw put tahut pu' murukna. Muruknaqw pay yaw kur pam paasat puuyalti. Pu' yaw pam put aasonaq pakiwkyangw pu' yaw aqwhaqami put murukinma. Pas pi yaw kur pam himu a'ni puuyaltingwu. Pas pi yaw oovi pam suyaapti. Paysoq yaw pam himu aqwhaqami a'ni puuyawmakyangw a'ni toovovotima.

Niiqe pay yaw oovi qa wuuyavotiqw pay yaw pam put mooti'ymaqat aapeqtakyangw pas pi yaw paysoq aqle' toovomti. Pantikyangw pu' yaw pay oovi qa wuuyavotiqw pay yaw pam aqw haqaminiqey kwiniwiq yaw suptu. Pangsoq yaw pam pituuqe pepeq pu' yaw pam put angqw hawt pu' paasat pepeqwat pu' naatoylay yaw

In due time, the witch boy was closing in on Coyote Boy. He could see where he was running. Seeing him he thought, "He must be aware by now that I'm not using my legs. This time I'll fly high over him so that he can't spot me." With that, he rose way up in the sky and that's where he flew along.

The boy in the lead was aware of this and placed an arrow on his bow, waiting for his opponent. Waiting where he had stopped, he was looking up when he saw the bird approaching. He fired his arrow, but it failed to reach the bird. Way short of its aim, it fell back to the ground. Coyote Boy shot a second arrow, but it too failed to reach its target. Coyote Boy gave up. "I can't harm him with an arrow. He's flying too high. He's way out of reach." This is what he thought, whereupon he discarded his weapon.

Once again Coyote Boy resumed his pursuit. The witch boy was way out of range as he looked after him. The distance between the two was growing even larger. Farther and farther he flew until he finally disappeared over the horizon. The minute he was out of sight, Coyote Boy halted his run and took out the gourd he had received. He placed one half on the ground. It was not very large, and he did not really know how to get inside. After several attempts he finally managed to fit himself into it. Then he closed the other half over himself. Having done that, he noticed the spot where the gourd has its stem button. From the gourd's center he now stretched sinew in both directions, so that it formed a line from a point at the bottom to the stem of the gourd. Next, he began twisting the sinew between the palms of his hands. Miraculously, the gourd began to lift off. Inside, Coyote Boy kept up the twisting of the sinew cord. The magic gourd was flying quite fast by now. Before long, it had covered a great distance. As the flying contraption zoomed along, it emitted a humming noise.

It did not take long before Coyote Boy passed his rival in the lead. He just whirred past him. Soon he reached the destination in the northwest. There he climbed out of the gourd and incised his clan symbol on a rock. This time he was the first to do so. Thereupon he

tuwat mooti owat ep tapamvena. Tapamvenat paapiy pu' yaw pam piw aapiyta. Nit pay yaw pam oovi qa pas putakw wuuyavonit pay yaw put angqw haawi. Put angqw hawqe pu' yaw pay pas naap höngiy paasat pu' piw akwa'.

Noq pu' yaw mi'wa angkniiqa yaw tuwat pepeq haqam pam mooti peenaqw pangso yaw pituuqe pu' yaw pay oovi panis pam pepeq naatoylay peenat pay piw aapiy. Pay yaw pam pas qa ahoy napwatat pay pankyangw pu' piw tuwat pangsoq kiimiqwat Sikyat-kimiq. Pangqw pu' yaw pam put piw tuwat ngöyva.

Noq pay yaw mi'wa kur pas haqti. Pay yaw oovi pam kya pi Kawestimay aakwiningye'haqe'niqw paasat pu' yaw pam yoyviikwat akwniiqa pu' piw put tuwat wiiki. Wiikikyangw pay yaw paasat put pas aw qa tunatyaltit pu' yuumosa kiimiqhaqam puuyawma. Pay yaw oovi pam naat qa pas tuuwayamaqw pu' yaw pam tiyo naap-niiqa paasat pu' yaw piw tawiyay horokna. Paasat pu' yaw pam put aqw pakiiqe pu' pangqw piw tuwat put akwa'. Pay oovi naat qa wuuyavotiqw pay yaw pam put piw tuwat wiikiqe pay yaw oovi aapeqta pay yaw naat qa angqw haawi.

Pu' yaw pay pam pas Sikyatkimi haykyala. Pep pu' haqam put qa tutwaniqat pangso pu' yaw pam qatuptuqe pu' yaw paasat pay put tawiyat angqw haawi. Pam angqw hawt pu' yaw pam pu' tawiyat pay haqe' qa hak tuwaniqat pangqe tupkya. Pu' yaw pam put pep tupkyat pu' pay paasat pangqw naap piw wari. A'ni yaw pam pangqw wari.

Paasat pu' yaw i' tuwat yoyviikwat akwniiqa pu' yaw paasat tuwat haqami pituuqe pu' yaw pay paasat nawus napwata. Son pi yaw pam pankyangw pangso pakitoniqe oovi. Pu' yaw oovi pam ahoy napwatat pu' yaw pam pangqw put ngöyva. Paasat pu' yaw pam as pas hin hönginiiqey okiw pani'. Nit pay yaw pam pas mitwat qa wiiki'yma. Pay yaw pam suyan se'elhaq aqwhaqaminiqw pay yaw pam oovi put kukyat ang hinma. Panmakyangw pu' yaw kur i' iswungwtiyo kiimi haykyalaqe yaw tsuyakiwma. Pangqw pu' yaw pam oovi pas piw qa naatusita. Pangqw pu' yaw pam piw kiimi a'ni wari. Pu' yaw puma haqaqw warikqw pangso yaw pami'. Niiqe pay yaw oovi qa pas wuuyavotiqw pay yaw pam aw pitu. Noq pay yaw ep naat sinom pan wukotsovawtaqe yaw angqaqwniqw kur tutwaqe yaw pangqaqwa, "Angqw pay'uy. Angqw pay haqawa maatsiltiy," yaw kitota.

Pu' yaw puma pangsoq oovi taayungwa haqawa hapi yawniqw. Pu' yaw pam amumiq haykyala. Pu' yaw himuwa pangqawu, "Pi

continued on again. He only flew a short distance before he dismounted. Then he ran on his own strength.

By now his rival had reached the place where Coyote Boy had arrived first to draw his mark. No sooner had he added his own than he continued in his flight. This time, he did not change himself back into his human shape; instead, he flew on in the guise of the hawk. Heading for his home village of Sikyatki, the witch boy was the pursuer now.

Coyote Boy was far away, but as he was coming through the area northwest of Kawestima, the witch boy, who was using the nighthawk, caught up with him. Without paying attention to him, he flew right on in the direction of Sikyatki. He had not vanished out of sight when Coyote Boy, who was running on foot, extracted his gourd a second time. Once more he got inside and resumed the race with his flying machine. It only took a short while before he was abreast of his rival. He passed him, but this time he did not dismount.

Coyote Boy soon neared Sikyatki. He landed at a place where he could not be seen and climbed out of the gourd. After hiding it where it could not be found, he once more started running on foot. He ran off at full speed.

His rival, who was using the hawk, now too had reached a point where he was forced to change himself back. After all, he could not afford being seen arriving in the disguise of the bird. So having completed the transformation, he resumed his pursuit of Coyote Boy. The poor thing ran as fast as his feet would carry him. But he did not gain on the other. It was quite obvious that Coyote Boy had come through here already. So the witch boy just followed his footprints. Meanwhile, Coyote Boy was nearing the village, rejoicing in his heart. One last time he summoned up all his strength, hurtling towards the finish line where the two had started. Before long, he came into view of it. The crowd was still gathered there. Now the spectators had spotted him and exclaimed, "There he comes. One of them can clearly be seen."

pay i'wa kur'ay! I' sumataq iswungwtiyoy," yaw peetu kitota. Pu'
yaw himuwa piw pangqawu, "Qa'ey, pay qa pamway, pay mi'way,"
pepeq yaw puma kitota.

Pu' yaw amumiq haykyala. Pu' yaw kur haqawa pas suyan maamatsqe pu' pangqawu, "Qa'ey, pi pay kur pamway, pam kwusi'y-
taqay. Pay pam mootitay. Pay pi kur sonqa pam put maanatniy," yaw
kitota. "Noq pay mi'wa pas haqaqw naat qa mamatsilay," yaw kitota.

Yanhaqam yaw puma hintiqw pay yaw pam oovi mooti aw pitu.
Pam yaw mooti aw pituuqe pu' pep haqam pam poyot tsööqökiwtaqw pangso pu' yaw pamniiqe pu' yaw put poyot kwusuuqe paasat
pu' yaw pam pep mitwat nuutayta. Pay yaw oovi pas hihin nawutstiqw pu' yaw pam angqaqw tuwat kuyva. Angqw kuyvakyangw pay
yaw nawus pam pas yuumosa pangso. Niiqe pay yaw paapu okiw
pas hihin heenakhooya'yma. Pay yaw pamwa pas kur pas maangu'i.

Panmakyangw hisatniqw pu' yaw pam tuwat amumi pitu. Yaw
amumi pitutoqe pay yaw okiw pas wiwtima. Pu' yaw oovi paasat
pam amumi pituqw pu' yaw pam iswungwtiyo put aw warikqe pu'
paasat put angayat aakwayngavoq tsöqö. Put tsöqöt pu' yaw poyoy
akw put tiyot hiikwamiq söökwikna. Pantit pu' yaw pam pep put
kwaptuku. Pay yaw oovi pam pas sumoki. Yan yaw pam pep put
powaqtiyot yukuna. Yan yaw pay pam mootita.

Niiqe yaw pu'sa mitwat powaqtiyot sinomat yaw qa haalaytoti.
Pu'sa yaw puma pep tsaykita. Pu' yaw oovi kwusi'ytaqa powaqtiyot
niinat pu' yaw pam paasat put taahayat aw nakwsu. Pam haqawa
kya pi pep pumuy kiiyamuy ep pan tuu'awvaqw put yaw aw
nakwsu. Niiqe pu' yaw aw pangqawu, "Ta'ay, pay nawus yantani.
Pay uma naap it yan naanawaknakyangw uma put kwayya. Pay pi
uma kya pi put pas qa kyaakyawnayaqe oovi aw unangwtatvey,"
yaw pam amumi kita. "Pu' pay kya as uma qa pas umuutuwiy
akwyaqw pay kya nu' as son pas niinani," yaw pam aw kita. "Uma
naap qa naahaalaytapnaya. Pay kur uma pas qa nun'okwatuy. Uma
a'ni hiituniiqe oovi qa nun'okwatu. Pay uma oovi qa yep itamum
yesni. Pay oovi uma hiita umuuhimuy ömaatotat pay uma yangqw
nöngakniy," kita yaw pam pumuy amumi.

Noq pay yaw puma popwaqt qa naanakwha. Pu' yaw pam
powaqtaha'at ahoy aw pangqawu, "Qa'ey. Pay itam son pantotiniy,"
yaw aw kita. Pu' yaw pay put tiw'ayay awniiqe pu' yaw pep put
aama. Pantit pay yaw pam sinomuy tsamkyangw ahoy nima. Pay
yaw puma pumuy isngyamuy qa tunatyayamuyyani. Puma yaw pay
qa naakiqötotani. Puma yaw a'ni ö'qaltniiqe pay yaw qa naanakwha

Everybody was staring into the direction from which either of the two runners was expected. The boy was getting closer and closer. Suddenly a voice shouted, "It's him!" Others joined in, "Yes, it seems to be Coyote Boy!" Someone else was of a different opinion. "No, it's not him, it's the other boy!"

Ever closer Coyote Boy was approaching. One of the spectators who was sure by now that he had recognized the runner exclaimed, "No way, it's not him. It's the boy who has the girl. He's the winner. He's bound to get the girl. The other is not even visible yet."

This is how the two runners fared. The Coyote Boy had arrived first. Since he was first, he ran over to where the knife was stuck in the ground and grabbed it. Then he waited for the witch to come in. After a good length of time had passed, the witch boy appeared on the horizon. He had no choice but to head straight towards the finish line. The poor thing was trotting slower and slower. Apparently, he was completely worn out.

Eventually, he was in everyone's sight. As he drew nearer, he could be seen stumbling along. The moment he arrived, Coyote Boy ran up to him and grabbed his long hair from behind. Then he thrust the knife into the boy's throat, and cut off his head. The witch boy died instantly. This is how Coyote Boy dispatched his rival. In this way Coyote Boy won.

The relatives of the dead witch boy became unhappy. Regretting what they had done, they were crying. Coyote Boy, who had won the bride and killed the witch boy, now stepped up to the uncle who had delivered the news about the race at his house. "All right," he said to him, "it had to be this way. It was your own wish, and now you have lost your nephew. In helping him, you showed that you did not care for him at all. If it hadn't been for your special powers, there would have been no need for me to kill him," he said. "You caused your own misery, because you are people without compassion. You are so mighty that you could not show any pity. Therefore, for you to live here with us is out of the question. Pack your belongings and leave this village."

But the witches refused, and the witch boy's uncle retorted, "Never. We won't do that." That's all he said. Then he went to his dead nephew and buried him there. Thereupon, he took his relatives and went home with them. Under no circumstances were the witches going to submit to the wish of the Coyote clan people. They had no

haqamiyaniqey.

Yaniwtiqw pu' yaw paasat pam maana oovi pep piw aapiy mö'öngqatqw pay yaw paasat qa hak paapu amumi hin hepta. Pam yaw oovi pan aapiytaqw pu' yaw put engem ova yukuyaqw paasat pu' yaw puma kya pi naama aasi.

Pay yaniwtiqw aapiy pay yaw puma pep as ahoy yeskvakyangw pay yaw qa kwangwayese. Puma popwaqt, kwitavit, pö'yyaqe qa naaniyaqe pay yaw puma pas nuutungem qa ankiwakwsa tunatyaw-yungwa. Pay yaw pas son himuwa qa hintingwu. Pay yaw qa iswu-ngwasa hintingwu. Pay yaw naap hak himu hintingwu.

Noq yaw oovi pep Sikyatkive kikmongwi pay timuy soosokmuy kyaakyawnaqe oovi pam yaw as haqami hakiy aw taqa'nangwtiniqey wuuwanta. Pay yaw son puma panhaqam nukusyesniqat pam naawakna. Niiqe oovi yaw powaqa as sulawtiniqat yaw pam pan naawakna. Noq pay yaw oovi pam Sikyatkive mongwi pas put kitsokit kiiqötiniqat yaw pam naawakna. Pu' yaw pam yanhaqam tunatyawkyangw aapiy yaw qatu. Pu' yaw pay hisat pu' yaw pam hakiy haqami tuwa, hakiy aw taqa'nangwtiniqey. Niiqe pu' yaw paasat pam yaw Qöötsaptuvelay ep kikmongwit awi'. Niiqe pu' pam hin pep Sikyatkivituy amungem tunatyawtaqey put aw put lalvaya. Pay yaw pam pas pep kiiqötiniqat yaw kita.

"Haw'owi?" yaw Qöötsaptuvelngaqw mongwi aw kita. "Noq hintotini itamu?" yaw aw kita. "Hin nu' ung pa'angwaniy?" yaw aw kita.

"Owiy," yaw kita, "pay nu' ason it sopkyawuy tunatuytaqw pu' ep pu' uma kiipokni. Ason imuy hohongvituy, taataqtuy pasmi hanqw paasat pu' uma pangso kiimi ökye' pu' uma pep pi pay kitsokit uwiknayani. Pu' pumuy taataqtuy pasngaqw umumiyaqw pay uma pumuy qöqyani."

"Kur antsa'ay," yaw kita. "Pay nu' ason yep itimuy aa'awnani. Pu' ason um hisat pangso uutimuy hanqw pu' piw itamuy aa'aw-naqw pu' itam awyani." Yanhaqam yaw puma pumuy engem pasiw-na.

Pu' yaw pam ahoy Qöötsaptuvelngaqw pitu. Pu' qavongvaqw pu' pam yaw tsa'akmonwit aa'awna pam tsa'lawniqat puma naalös taalat epeq sopkyawmaniqat, yan yaw pam put aa'awna. "Kur an-tsa'ay," yaw pam kita, tsa'akmongwi. "Pay nu' ason qaavo tsa'lawqw pay navoti'yyungwe' aqwhaqami pan wuuwankyaakyangw itam nenngem hiita hintsatskyaniy," yaw aw kita.

Noq yaw ep tsa'lawqat ep mihikqw pu' Sikyatkingaqw mongwi

intention of causing their own ruin by leaving. They were extremely powerful and declined to leave.

After these events the bride was able to continue her stay at the groom's house, and no one challenged the two any more. As soon as her wedding dress was finished, she had her hair washed and tied with Coyote Boy's, which symbolized their marriage.

Following these events, the people at Sikyatki settled down to their daily routine again, but life was not very peaceful. The sorcerers, or Turds, resented the fact that they had been beaten and were causing every possible trouble for the rest of the villagers. Things kept happening to people, especially those of the Coyote clan, but also to others.

The chief of Sikyatki, therefore, who held all of his children dear, was thinking of seeking someone's help. It was his desire to terminate this corrupted way of life. He wanted the witches wiped out and the village destroyed. With these intentions on his mind he lived there. One day it occurred to him whose help he might seek. He went to the village leader of Qöötsaptuvela. With him he shared his plans and explained that he wanted Sikyatki destroyed.

"Is that so?" the Qöötsaptuvela chief replied. "How are we going to accomplish this? How can I help you in this matter?"

"Yes," the Sikyatki headman said, "I plan to hold a communal harvesting party. On that occasion you can attack the village. As soon as all my capable men have gone down to the field, you can come over and set the houses on fire. And when the men come running from the field, you can kill them."

"Very well, I'll tell my people about it. As soon as you let us know that your people have left for the field, we'll come." This is how the two forged their plans.

The day after the chief returned home from Qöötsaptuvela, he informed his crier chief. He was to announce publicly that there would be a communal harvesting party four days hence. "All right," the crier chief agreed. "I'll make the announcement tomorrow. Once people know, they can think about the coming event and make their preparations."

piw ahoy Qöötsaptuvelay ep mongwit aw tuu'awva. "Ta'ay, yaapiy um uuqaqleetaqtuy aa'awnaqw yaapiy naalös taalat epeq pu' uma aw kiipokni. Oovi uma yaapiy haqaapiy umuutunipiy aw tumala'y-vayaniy," yaw aw kita.

"Kur antsa'ay," yaw kita. "Pay itam sonqa pantotini."

Pu' yaw ep sopkyawmaniqat aw talöngwiwtaqat ep talavay iits pay puma Qöötsaptuvelngaqw qaqleetaqt nankwusa. Pu' yaw puma pay Sikyatkimi haykyalayat pu' pay puma pangqw amumi maqap-tsi'yyungwa. Pu' yaw soosoyam sopkyawwisniqam hangqw paasat pu' yaw puma pangqw yuutu. Pu' yaw puma kiimi suuyayva. Pu' kiinawit momoymuy, tsaatsakwmuy ang yesqamuy yaw saqhönya. Pantotit pu' yaw puma put uwiknaya. Pu' yaw peetu santsami'y-vayaqe put yaw tuupelpa palqeqnayat pu' yaw aw uwiknayangwu. Noq pu' yaw pam su'wikngwu.

Paasat pu' yaw taataqt pasve höhöqyaqam kwiitsingwuy tutwa. Pangqw kiingaqw yaw a'ni kwiikwitsi. Pu' yaw pay puma pan wuuwaya, pay hapi yaw himu hinti. Pu' yaw puma pay pangqw ahoy aqw naanangk yuyutya. Pu' yaw puma pep qaqleetaqt put uwiknayaqam pay kur piw pumuy tutwaqe pu' yaw pay amumiq yuutukqe pu' pay himuwa amumiq pituqw pay suuninayangwu. Pay pu' puma qa hiita tunipiy akw rohomtotiniqey himu'yyungqe pay okiw himuwa qa pas rohomtit pay mokngwu. Pay yaw puma okiw pumuy soosokmuy qöqya.

Pu' yaw ima peetusa isngyam yaw ayo' nönga watqaqe. Pu' yaw pay puma son kur pepeq yesniqe pu' yaw pangqw puma pay Oraymi nönga. Niiqe oovi puma yaw isngyam pay pas nuutungk Oraymi sinoti.

Yanhaqam yaw Sikyatki kiiqöti. Pay yaw pas ima popwaqt, kwi-tavit, soosoyam so'a. Pu' i' kikmongwi amungem pan tunatuytaqe pay yaw piw amumum mooki. Pay yuk pölö.

The night of the announcement, the Sikyatki chief returned to the leader of Qöötsaptuvela to bring him the news. "You can now tell your warriors that they are to make their attack in four days. They can start working on their weapons," he said.

"Very well, we'll surely do that," the other promised.

Early in the morning, on the day of the communal harvest party, the warriors from Qöötsaptuvela set out. Upon reaching the vicinity of Sikyatki, they waited. When everybody who was going to participate in the harvest party had descended to the field, they rushed the village. In no time they were inside. Quickly they pulled the ladders out from the houses where the women and children were. Having accomplished that, they set everything on fire. Some of the warriors had come with pitch they had gathered. This they smeared on the walls of the houses; as a result they quickly caught fire.

The men who were harvesting at the field spotted smoke. They saw that it was coming from the village. Thinking that something had happened, they ran back, one after the other. When the warriors who had set the fire saw them, they fell upon them. As soon as a man reached them, he was dispatched. Since the Sikyatki men had no weapons with which to resist, they died without being able to fight back. They were all killed, poor things.

Only a few Coyote clan members managed to survive by running away. As they were no longer able to live at Sikyatki, they fled to Oraibi. The Coyote clan, therefore, became the last group to be absorbed into the community of Oraibi.

This is how Sikyatki was destroyed. And all the witches, those excrement people, perished. The village chief, who had hatched out the scheme, lost his life with them. And here the story ends.

5

The Abandonment of Huk'ovi

The ruin of Huk'ovi, which translates approximately as "Windy Place-on-High," lies about three miles northwest of Old Oraibi. The site, never excavated or seriously investigated archaeologically, was "occupied in the twelve hundreds," according to Colton and Nequatewa (1932: 8). This assumption is based on the occurrence of a number of characteristic ceramic remains, among them Jeddito Black-on-orange and Jeddito Black-on-white, types that do not seem to have been in use after 1300 A.D. He concludes that the pueblo was "abandoned, like so many others in northern Arizona, because of the great drought of 1291-1299."[1]

The mytho-historical events leading up to the ruin of Huk'ovi have been published twice before. Courlander's version, "The Flight from Huckovi," closely resembles the narrative presented here (1971: 151-56). On the other hand, Nequatewa's tale significantly differs from Courlander's and mine in a number of key elements (Colton and Nequatewa 1932: 2-12).

Thus two girls, rather than just one, are interested in the boy protagonist. His overall role in the ritual of the Ladder Dance is more prominent. Two Spider Women are featured, one with her grand-children Pöqangwhoya and Palöngawhoya. The trees employed for the dance grow in height through the magic of the chanting kachina gods. There's a rather unmotivated episode featuring an old man who has survived the kiva debacle. Finally, the avenging woman ghost who expels the Huk'ovi residents drives them westward, rather than eastward or over the cliff, at the request of the protagonist.

Most significantly, however, Nequatewa's story incorporates several more elements of witchcraft. Not only are the two girls vying for the boy witches, the kachina in charge of the ladder ritual is also a wizard who succumbs to a bribe by the girls "to do crooked work." An additional sorcerer is hired by them to cause the catastrophic collapse of the kiva roof.

As the Hopis of today forego their native language for English, as the old-time Hopi *homo religiosus* abandons traditional beliefs, the phenomenon of black magic, once a powerful controlling agent in Hopi society, is rapidly losing its grip. Simmons's view "that the Pueblos are obsessively preoccupied with the threat posed by adher-ents to the black craft and that this fear is endemic" no longer holds for the present (1974: 76). Modern Hopis no longer suffer from witch phobia and are not averse to sharing their knowledge of the subject with cultural outsiders. Yet, if the frequency with which the destruc-tive motif of witchcraft is encountered in Hopi oral traditions is any indicator, it must have been extremely pervasive and deeply in-grained in Hopi culture at one time. Of the hundreds of narratives I have recorded in the field, dozens feature the sinister machinations and misdeeds of witches. Of the seven villages presented here, the destruction or ruination of four—Awat'ovi, Qa'ötaqtipu, Sikyatki, and Huk'ovi—is directly or indirectly attributable to the evil uses of sorcery.

As not much ethnographic information is available on Hopi sorcery, outside of what can be gleaned from the published body of Hopi oral literature, I would like to present an overview sketched through a series of folk statements volunteered to me by Hopi consultants. Only some of the major aspects of Hopi witchcraft can be highlighted here. A more thorough treatment of this topic would easily fill a book of its own.

The general Hopi term for a sorcerer or witch, male or female, is *powaqa*. While this animate noun pluralizes as *popwaqt*, the same word, when used as an inanimate noun, conceptualizes the abstract notion of "witchcraft" or "sorcery." In this meaning the word occurs in singular form only. Morphologically, the word *powaqa* is composed of the root *powa-* and the element *qa*, "one who/that which." Although this analysis ultimately may not be verifiable, the core semantics of *powa-* imply something like "change." Elsewhere I have, therefore, suggested the gloss "transform" for this morpheme (Malotki 1983: 461). This can be deduced from such words as *powata*, "to make right/cure/exorcise," *powalti*, "become purified/healed (as from insanity)," *powa'iwta*, "be purified/be back to normal," and others. The element is likewise manifested in the lunar appellation *Powamuya*, literally "transform-moon/month" (approximately February), during which the great "purification ceremony," popularly known as the "Bean Dance," takes place. While the stem *powa-*, which is not attested by itself, embraces positive denotations in these words, predominantly negative ones adhere to it in *powaqa*, "1. sorcerer 2. witchcraft," *powaqqatsi*,[2] "way of life based on sorcery," and the affiliated verb *povowaqa*, "to practice witchcraft/exercise black magic." In the light of its etymology, the term *powaqa*, "witch," can thus be understood as "negative transformer," and *powaqa*, "witchcraft," as "practice of negative transformation." As will become evident below, the sorcerer attempts to "transform" the world around him for his own personal gain and advantage, usually with "negative" consequences, including death, for his fellow humans.

Hopi definitions of the *powaqa*, or "sorcerer," typically employ the label *nukpana* which denotes "bad, wicked, evil person/evildoer/villain." The special knowledge of black magic which he commands is characterized as *tuhisa*. It is exploited for totally selfish purposes only.

Text 34

Pay antsa it powaqat pangqaqwangwu, pam nukpana. Pam naap hiita himuniwtingwu, pu' piw napwatangwu. Pu' piw a'ni

They say the sorcerer is really an evil person. He can transform himself into just about anything and then change back again. In

hiita tuwi'yta. Pu' powaqaniiqe
oovi nukpana a'ni hiita tuwi'y-
taqe putakw hakiy hintsanngwu.
Pam pi pay tuhisa himu powa-
qatsa tuwi'atniiqat it kitotangwu.

addition, he's endowed with a
great deal of special know-how
which he uses to harm people.
This know-how of the sorcerer is
referred to as *tuhisa*, "magic
power."

Text 35

Noq pu' i' powaqa pay tuwat
neengemsa hiita nukngwat
hintiniqeysa wuuwantangwuniiqe pam oovi it tuhisay akw
tuwat a'ni naamongvasnangwu.
Noq pu' i' nukpana, powaqa pay
pam piw qa taaqasaningwu. Pay
puma soosoyam hiitu pumaya,
mamant, tootim, momoyam.

A sorcerer only thinks of doing
something nice for himself.
Therefore, he uses his magic
powers to benefit himself. It's
not only a man who can be that
evil person or sorcerer but also
girls, boys, and women.

In the context of a narrative, sorcerers, when operating individ-
ually, are often specified according to gender and age. Thus, one
encounters *powaqtiyo*, "witch boy," *powaqmana*, "witch girl," *powaq-
wuuti*, "witch woman," and *powaqtaqa*, "witch man," as well as their
respective plural forms. When acting as a whole conclave, however,
Hopi oral literature frequently refers to them under the derogatory
term of *kwitavit*,[3] "excrement/feces people/turds." The following text
constitutes a Hopi rationalization for the motivation of this supposedly self-imposed cover term on the part of the sorcerers.

Text 36

Popwaqt antsa hisat pi puma
hiitu pay naap kiva'yyungngwu.
Pay pumuy qa pas powaqkiva
kitotaniniqw oovi puma pay
naatupki'yyungqe oovi panwat
pangqaqwa, "Itam pi pay kwitavit. Itam pay qa hiitu." Yan
puma naalavayta. Puma a'ni
hiituniikyangw yan yaw naatupki'yyungqe oovi pangqaqwa,
"Itam pi pay kwitavit. Kwitat

The witches of long ago had
their own kiva. But as they did
not want to refer to it openly as
witch kiva, they covered their
ways up by saying, "We're feces.
We're nothings." This is how
they talked about themselves.
They were powerful beings, but
to camouflage their activities
they said, "We're turds. No one
likes excrement. And since peo-

hak qa himuningwuniqw itamuy
qa himuyaqw oovi itam pay yep
okiw naap kiva'yyungwa."
Puma okiwaysa yu'a'atikyaa-
kyangw hintsatskya. Oovi
kitotangwu, "Pay okiw itam yep
kiva'yyungwa qalavehaqam. I'
yep itaakiva, i' kwitakiva." Puma
pay putakw qa pas pas suyan
powaqnatngwaniwta. Qa pumuy
powaqlalwaniqw oovi puma
paniqw pan naatuwi'yyungwa,
kwitavit.

ple don't like us, we wretched lot
have our own kiva here." Feign-
ing humility, they practiced their
evil craft. "We poor things have
our kiva here at the edge [of the
village]. This is our kiva, the excrement kiva," they kept saying,
hoping that through this ruse
they would not be called out-
right sorcerers. They did not
want people to refer to them as
witches. That is why they used
the term "turds" for themselves.

According to Hopi mythology, witchcraft previously reigned in
the underworld. It and the general chaos of koyaanisqatsi were the
primary motivation for all remaining good Hopi to seek a new beginning in the upper surface world. However, evil succeeded in emerg-
ing with them from their ancestral home. Interestingly enough, First
Witch is a female.[4] She justifies her showing at the emergence place
of Sipaapuni with the excuse that she felt obliged to introduce the
Hopis to the idea of life after death. Indirectly, she also hints at her
responsibility of maintaining the institution of death in the new
world.

Text 37

Noq pu' yaw i' Hopi as hapi put
nukpanat atkyangaqw apyeve
waayaniqe pu' yaw pam oovi as
pay nana'uyvewat angqw pew
yukwat it tutskwat aw yamakkyangw pu' yaw pay pam kur
powaqat enang pew horoknakyangw pay pam yaw put qa
navota. Noq pu' yaw puma
Hopiit pep haqam naat pu'
yesva, haqam puma nöngakqey-
niqw pep pu' yaw i' hak suukya
manawya tuutuytikyangw pu'
pay yaw mooki.

The Hopi tried to escape the evil
in the underworld by running
away from it. Secretly, he
emerged into this world, but
evidently without noticing, he
brought the sorcerer with him.
The Hopi had just settled down
at the place where they had
emerged, when a little girl fell ill
and died.

Pu' yaw paasat puma pepeq wukw'aymat pangqaqwa, "Is ohiy," yaw kitota. "Ya sen pam okiw hinti? Pay hapi itam suma-taq piw powaqat enang pew ho-roknaya. Noq i' hapi as qa yanta-niqw oovi itam pewya. Itam hapi as paapu qa it mokiwuy enang aw ökimantaniqe oovi pewya. Itam hapi as sutsep qatsit yep himu'yvayaniy," yaw kitota. "Noq pay hapi nukpana itamuy yantiqw oovi i' sulawtiy," yaw kitota. "Pam pay putakw son pi qa yaaptiniqe pu' oovi put pan-tsana. Noq oovi itam put hakiy ang hepyani. Pay pi son hak qa piw a'ni himuniiqe oovi itamuy hin hepta," yaw kitota.

Noq pu' yaw pam pantiqw pu' yaw pay puma put ep qa haalaytotiqe pay puma piw put aw pavan wuuvaya. Pu' yaw pam hak pumuy mongwi'am yaw it hoomat ömaatat pu' yaw pam put huur pölöla. Pantit pu' yaw pam imuy sinmuy pepeq-yaqamuy soosokmuy sumitsova-la. Niikyangw pay puma oovi pep tsovaltiqw pu' yaw pam amumi pangqawu, "Nu' hapi it oomiq tuuvani," yaw kita. "Nu' hapi it oomiq tuuvaqw i' hakiy aw posqw pam hapi powaqani. Pu' itam pay put ahoy taviyani sen pay itam pas niinayani. Pay hinwat hapiniy," yaw kita.

Paasat pu' yaw pam put hoomavölölnit oomiq tuuva. Pu' yaw antsa poskyangw yaw antsa

The elders cried out, "Oh my, why on earth did this hap-pen to that poor thing? We prob-ably brought a sorcerer out with us into this world. This was not to be. That's why we came here. We were not supposed to en-counter death anymore; instead, we were to come to have eternal life. An evil person must have caused the girl's death. He prob-ably wanted to prolong his life with her death. So let's search for this person. Whoever he is, he must be extremely powerful. That's why he is testing us."

The people were unhappy about this event and seriously reflected on the matter. Their leader now took some cornmeal and shaped it into a ball. Having done so he asked all the people to gather in one place. When everybody was assembled there, he said to them, "I'll throw this ball up into the air. The one it falls on will be the sorcerer. We'll put him back down into the underworld or kill him. I don't know yet what it will be."

With that, he hurled the cornmeal ball up in the air. Sure enough, as it came falling down, it landed directly on a beautiful girl. Immediately, they grabbed

hakiy lomamanat su'awi. Paasat
pu' yaw puma put hakiy maanat
ngu'aya. Ngu'ayaqe pu' yaw aw
pangqaqwa, "Um kur'a. Um kur
pay piw itamum yama. Um kur
powaqa. Ura uma pay qe'yani,"
yaw aw kitota. "Noq oovi pay
itam nawus ung ahoy atkyamiq
tuuvayaniy," puma yaw put aw
kitotaqw pu' yaw pam paklawu.
"Qa'e, pay uma qa pas nuy pantsatsnani. Pay nu' as antsa pi
nukpananiikyangw nu' yep hapi
pay umumi hiita maataknaniqe
oovi paniqw pew umumum
yamay," yaw pam pumuy
amumi kita. "Pay atkya piw naat
yeesiwa. Meh, uma pewyani,"
yaw pam amumi kita.

Paasat pu' yaw pam pumuy
ahoy pangso haqaqw puma nöngakqw pangso pumuy tsaama.
Naat pi yaw pam pangsoq qa
uutsiwta. Pu' yaw amumi pangqawu, "Ta'ay, kur uma peqw
yoyrikyani. Pay hapi pam tsayhoya piw ahoy taatayi. Pay pam
hapi oovi naat hintangwuqey
pay naat piw ahoy panti. Niikyangw pay pam hapi naat
yepeq atkyaveq nuutum qatu,"
yaw pam pumuy amumi kita.

Paasat pu' yaw puma oovi
awyaqw pu' himuwa yaw aqw
yan yorikqw piw yaw epeq
sinom yakta. Noq pam yaw ura
hak tsayhoya mokqa antsa piw
ahoy qa hinkyangw pay piw
pepehaq nuutum angqe' wawar-
tinuma, hohonaqtinuma. Nuu-

the girl and said to her, "It's you
then. You must have come out
with us. You're the witch. Remember, your lot was not supposed to go. Now we'll have to
throw you back down again."
The girl started crying. "No,
don't do that to me. Yes, it's true,
I'm a witch, but I came out in
order to show you something
here. There's life down below.
Look, come here," she said to
them.

Whereupon she led them
back to the location of their
emergence. The hole there was
still not sealed. "All right," she
said, "look down here. That little
girl is alive again. She's as
healthy as before and is living
with all the other people down
in the underworld," she explained.

The people went to the hole
and as they looked down, they
could see the people walking
about. The little girl who had just
passed away was in good health
and running around playing
with the others. She was happy
with them. "This is how someone will fare for all the future,"
the witch explained. "So don't

tum yaw pam pepehaq haalayi.
"Yantimantani hak'i," kita yaw
amumi pam powaqa. "Pay oovi
uma nuy qa pas niinayani. Pay
uma nuy qa ahoy aqw taviyani.
Pay naat piw qatsimantani. It
hapi nu' aw tunatyawmani. Oovi
pay himuwa mookye' pam pay
naat atkyaminen pep pay nuutum haalaymantani. Yaniqw
oovi nu' umumum pew yamay,"
yaw kita.

Yuk pay yaw pam pumuy
pan tuptsiwnaqw pu' pay yaw
puma oovi put qa ahoy pangsoq
tuuvaya. Noq pay yaw hak pas
antsa oovi mookye' pay yaw hak
pas antsa pangsoq haqami
ahoyningwu, pangsoq haqami
haqaqw ima Hopiit pew nö-
ngakqw pangsoqa'. Noq pay
itam pi pu' put pangsoq "Maski"
yan tuwi'yyungwa. Noq pay hak
oovi yaw piw pangsoq ahoynen
pu' pay piw pepeq nuutum
qatungwu.

Noq pay yaw pam powaqa
pan piw kur nuutum pew
yamakkyangw pu' pay yaw pam
haqaapiy piw peetuy sinmuy
naami tuuwikta. Pay pi pam son
pi hiita qa pas öqalay akw
pumuy uunatoynat pu' pumuy
naami sinota. Noq pu' pay yaw
puma oovi qa pas pepehaq suus
yesvaniqe pu' pay yaw puma
pangqw nankwusakyangw pay
yaw puma paasat qa suupwat
toonavit pangqw angqe' aatsavala. Pu' yaw pay puma piw qa

kill me, don't put me back down.
There will be life after death. I
will see to that. Therefore, when
a person dies, he will enter the
underworld and be happy there.
For this reason I came out with
you."

This was enough to convince
the people. They did not cast the
witch back down. Thus, it's
really true that a Hopi who dies
returns to the netherworld from
which he emerged. We call this
place Maski, "Home of the
Dead." Once a person returns
there, he lives on there with the
others.

So now that witchcraft had
made its entrance into this world
it was not long before the witch
began to recruit people for herself. She must have persuaded
them with her evil powers and
thus brought them on her side.
The people, meanwhile, had no
desire to stay there [by the Sipaa-
puni] forever. They started out in
many groups and scattered over

hopiitsaniikyangw pangqw aapiyya. Pay yaw puma oovi piw hintaqat akw qa sun sinomniikyangw pangqaqw nankwusa. Niiqe paniqw yaw oovi i' nukpana pay qa Hopiituysa amumum peqwhaqami pitu. Pu' yaw pay paniqw oovi ima soosoyam himusinom piw put hiita enang tuwi'yyungwa, it hiita powaqat.

the land. Not only Hopi departed from there, but others also. Somehow they were not one and the same people when they left. For this reason, evil did not come here only with the Hopi. All the people in the world, therefore, are familiar with witchcraft.

According to Hopi belief, Palangwu is the universal headquarters of all practitioners of black magic. It is located somewhere northeast of Hopi territory. Occasionally, a Hopi will identify it geographically with Canyon de Chelly. The *powaqki*, "Home of the Sorcerers," at Palangwu, is modeled exactly after the Hopi subterranean kiva. As may be gathered from the text below, its division into an upper and lower floor has hierarchical implications for the double caste system of witches.

Text 38

Palangwuy pi pay nu' qa tuwi'yta pam haqamniqw pay sutsep pi pay pangqaqwangwu, pam hopqöyvehaq'a, kitotangwu. Antsa yaw pepehaq pam pas wukoki himu, wukopowaqkiniqw kitotangwu. Noq oovi yaw puma pangsoq kya pi naangemnaye' pu' pangsoqhaqamiyangwu.

Himuwa na'uynömay pu' na'uykongyay amum naami tokilte' pu' pangsoq puma naamaniqey oovi pangsoqningwu. Himuwa wuuti koongya'yte' put hurupuwvitsnat pu' aqle' qatuptungwu. Pu' taaqa piw pantingwu. Nöömay

I don't know where Palangwu is, but everybody always says it's far in the northeast somewhere. A huge house is supposed to be there, the Powaqki or "Home of the Sorcerers." The sorcerers usually invite each other to go there.

For example, if someone has a date with a secret woman or man, they go there in order to be together. If a woman already has a husband, she puts him into a deep sleep and then she gets up. The man does likewise. After putting his wife to sleep, he visits his secret lover at the Powaqki. After meeting there,

puwvitsnat pu' pangsoq na'uynömay aqwningwu. Pu' pepeq
kya pi antsa naanami ökye' pu'
pepeq antsa kya pi naanama
panyungwa, kwangwa'ewlal-
wangwu. Pay it yanhaqam piw
nu' navota. It yanhaqam hintsakwisa. Puma popwaqt qa yep sus-
talpuva naanami nuvö'iwyungw-
niqe paniqw oovi pangsoq yaw
puma piw tsotsvalwisngwu.

the couples have a good time
together. This is what I heard.
That's how they do it. Sorcerers
never want to demonstrate their
sexual desire for one another in
the open. That is why they go to
Palangwu.

Text 39

Palangwuy epeq yaw puma
suvotsotsvala. Noq pepeq yaw
pay kivat su'anta. Noq puma
yaw qa suup tsovawtangwu
pepeq. Peetu yaw atkyamiqwat
tsotsvalqam pas qa nun'okwat.
Noq puma oovi pan natngwani'yyungwa, atkyapopwaqt. Pu'
yaw tuuwingaqwyaqam puma
yaw pay hihin nun'okwat. Pumawat oovi tuuwingaqwpop-
waqt.

All sorcerers gather there, at
Palangwu, in one place. This
place is just like a kiva. Actually,
they are not all assembled in the
same area. Those who meet on
the lower floor of the kiva are the
really cruel and merciless ones.
For this reason, they are referred
to as *atkyapopwaqt* or "lower-
floor sorcerers." Those who
assemble on the upper platform
of the kiva are less cruel and can
be somewhat merciful. These are
the *tuuwingaqwpopwaqt* or
"upper-floor sorcerers."

Travel to Palangwu is effected by the witches in many different
disguises. According to Hopi belief, one frequent mode of flying is as
a crow.

Text 40

Hopiit pi pangqawangwu it
angwusit powaqaningwuqat.
Ima antsa popwaqt mihikqw
Palangwuy aqwyangwu, haqami
hopqöymiq powaqkimiq. Pepehaq kay pi haqam hopqöyvehaq

The Hopis claim that the crow is
a sorcerer. As is well known,
sorcerers travel at night to Palangwu, their witch home, somewhere in the northeast. There,
somewhere on the northeast

haqam wukopowaqkiniqw ima
peetu popwaqt a'angwustuy aw-
niwtotingwu. Pumuy akw aqwyangwu. Pu' pay piw ahoy
pumuy akw angqw ninmangwu.
Nen pu' talavay iits pay pangqaqw puma a'angwust puuyaw-
wisngwuniqw pu' oovi pumuy
pangqaqwangwu, "Pu' hapi
popwaqt ökiwisa. Oovi pi pisoq'iwwisa." Ephaqam himuwa
nuutungkniqw pu' pangqaqwangwu, "Is okiw, i' powaqa kur
qa tawasangwna. Kya pi qa taatayqe oovi nuutungk yangqaqw
puu'u," kitotangwu. Noq paniqw oovi pumuy piw pangqaq-
wangwqu, "Puma powaq'a'a-
ngwust," kitotangwu.

side, are the headquarters of all
sorcerers. Some of them transform themselves into crows and
travel in this guise to their destination. In this guise they also
return home. Early in the morning, when the crows are flying in
from their meeting place, people
say, "Now the sorcerers are
arriving. That's why they're in
such a hurry." Occasionally,
when one crow is late behind the
others, they say, "Oh my, this
sorcerer did not make it home
before sunrise. He probably
didn't wake up in time." That's
why people refer to these crows
as witch crows.

One important reason for sorcerers to congregate at Palangwu is
to induct *powaqwiwimkyam*, or "witch neophytes," into the *powaqwimi*,
their own demoniacal order.

Text 41

Noq pu' pay hak hiita pi hintsakye' pay hak piw sonqa sinohaq-
tangwu, pu' tis it hiita wiimit
epe'. Pay hakim hiita ep wuu-
haqniiqamye' hakim sun
loma'unangwa'ykyaakyangw
hiita hintsatskyaqw himu aw
aniwtingwu, hakim hiita
tuunawakniy aw yoyrikyangwu.
   Noq pu' pay i' powaqa piw
oovi panta. Pam pi put powaqat
songyawnen wiimi'yta. Niiqe
pay pam piw oovi pan sinohaq-
ni'ytangwuniiqe oovi pam hakiy
naami sinotaniqey itsa pam piw

Whenever someone undertakes
something special, he needs a lot
of people, especially if it is a ceremony. With many participants
during such a ceremonial event,
who all focus on doing something with good thoughts in
their hearts, things turn out successfully and everyone's most
heartfelt longings are realized.
   The sorcerer is not different
in this respect. Witchcraft is his
ritual, so to speak. Since he also
needs a lot of participants, he is
out to recruit people. He engages

tuwat wuuwankyangw put hiita
pay qa antaqat hintsakma. Pay
pam hiitakw hakiy put aw
kwangwa'ynangwu, hiita akw
hakiy huwngwu.

in evil activities with which he
makes witchcraft attractive to
people or with which he traps
them.

As Text 42 explains, a person can become a sorcerer of his own
free will. Or, a practitioner of witchcraft may attempt to persuade a
child to join the ranks of evildoers. To protect their children from this
danger, parents discourage them from sleeping over at other people's
homes.

Text 42

Noq pu' ima peetu pay piw
powaqat pas antsa naap naanawakna. Pay puma put akw
hiita nukngwat aw ökiniqey
oovi. Noq pu' put tuwi'yvaniqa
paasat oovi son pi hakiy qa
hepngwu.

    Pu' ephaqam hakimuy tsaa-
tsakwmuyniqw powaqa haki-
muy amumi pu' pangqawngwu,
"Um qa powaqvakni? Um put
qa tuwitani? Hak put tuwi'yte'
hak akw a'ni mongvasningwu."
Hakiy aw yanhaqam hing-
qawqw yaw hak qa uunatingwu.
Taq hak yaw wuuyoqniiikyangw
wuwni'ysaynen pay a'ni
hopiituqaykyangwnen yaw hak
powaqvakye' pay yaw hak put
qa mongvastingwu. Pu' hak yaw
mokngwu. Hakiy aw kitota-
ngwu.

    Ephaqam hiitawat hak
kwaatsi'ytangwu sen maanat
sungwa'ytangwu. Pu' pumuy
yumuyatuy pangqaqwangwu
puma powaqatniiiqat. Pu' hakiy

Some people are interested in
witchcraft on their own in order
to acquire precious things. The
one who wants to learn this business surely looks around for a
sorcerer.

    Once in a while, a sorcerer
will say to young children,
"Don't you want to get initiated
into witchcraft? Don't you want
to learn about it? Whoever
knows witchcraft benefits a great
deal from it." One is not to be
swayed by this kind of talk. For
when the child is old enough to
reason and speaks Hopi well,
and it has been initiated into
witchcraft, it does not profit from
it at all. Instead, it dies because
of it.

    Whenever a boy or girl has a
friend whose parents are said to
be witches, children are warned
not to go there. Especially, they
are told, "Don't you ever sleep at
their house. When they invite
you to spend the night, always

oovi pangso meewantotangwu,
"Um qa hisat pep kiiyamuy ep
puwni. Ung puwngemintaqw qa
nakwhamantani, taq ung powaq-
vanyani," hakiy aw kitotangwu.

say no. Otherwise, they are
going to initiate you into witchcraft."

Another method of recruiting novices is by kidnapping infants.
To enter the parents's home, the sorcerer is often disguised as a fly.

Text 43

Noq pu' pay piw pangqaq-
wangwuniqw pay pam himu
nukpana piw a'ni tuhisa-
ningwuniiqe oovi pam kur
hakimuy amungaqw hiitawat
neengem sinotaninik pam pay
piw pas mihikqwsa, hakimuy
hurutokvaqw, pu' hakimuy
amumi hin pakiqw pay hakim qa
nanaptangwu. Pay ephaqam
himuwa oovi mooti
tootovi'ewayniwtit pu' yaw
hakimuy amumi pakingwu. Pay
pi hak oovi piw naamahin qa
puwkyangw pay hak paasat-
niqwhaqam son pas piw put
tootovit aw pas hin wuuwantangwu. Pay pi pam naap hisatniqw angqe' waynumngwuniqw
oovi. Paasat put naat pas tiposit
yaw hepngwu. Nen pu' pam put
tuwe' paasat pu' pam put it yuy
aqle' wa'ökiwtaqat pang kwusu-
kyangw pu' pam put pangso
haqami pumuy tsotsvalkiyamuy
aqw, Palangwuy aqw, wikngwu.
Yan pay puma imuy pas naat
tsaatsakwmuy naami sinolalwa.
Noq pay puma pep ki'yyungqam oovi put pakiqw son nanap-

People say that a sorcerer is an
evil person with great magical
skills. Thus, when he wants to
get someone to become his fol-
lower, he enters a house at night
when its residents are asleep and
can't hear him. Once in a while,
he changes into something like a
fly first before entering. For even
if someone is not asleep yet, he
usually won't be concerned
about a fly at that time. After all,
flies are around at any time of
the day. The sorcerer then looks
around for a baby. Upon finding
one lying next to its mother, he
picks it up and takes it to the
witches' meeting place at Palangwu. In this manner, sorcerers
add little children to their ranks.
As the household members normally are not aware of a sorcerer
making his entrance, they have
no way of knowing who among
their relatives the evildoer is.

tangwuniiqe pay puma son oovi piw put navoti'yyungngwu pam hakimuy amungaqw pam himuniqw.

Noq yaw tiposit naat muupiwtaqat powaqvanyaqw pam yaw pay qa hintingwu, pam yaw pay qa mokngwu.

They say that when a baby that is still on its cradleboard is initiated into witchcraft, nothing will happen to it. It will not die.

As Titiev has pointed out, the initiatory proceedings of sorcerers "are modeled on those of the highly regarded secret societies which conduct Hopi ceremonies. Thus, the novice must be introduced by a ceremonial father chosen from the ranks of the sorcerers, his head is washed in yucca suds, and he is given a new name" (1942:550). Most importantly, through this initiation, the candidate acquires the faculty of transforming himself into the animal familiar of his godfather. By drawing on the supernatural powers inherent or attributed to it, he can now exercise his evil craft.

Text 44

Pay pi lavaytangwuniqw yaw antsa hak hakiy na'ykyangw sonqa powaqvakngwuniqw oovi kya pi puma namaqyangwu antsa pepeq piw sonqa. Antsa kya pi piw hak hiita na'yvaqw pu' pam hakiy sonqa tungwangwu, hakiy powaqtungwangwu.

They say that it's probably true that someone has a godfather as he is initiated into the business of witchcraft. Therefore, sorcerers probably select a godfather there [at Palangwu]. Also, when one acquires a godfather, the latter names the new initiate. He gives him a witch name.

Text 45

Pu' yaw puma piw pepehaq tsotsvalye' pu' yaw puma piw imuy hiituy popkotuy akw enang tumala'yyungngwu, pumuy akw enang mongvasya yaw puma. Noq pu' it powaqat ep pay pam piw hiita na'yve' pay pam oovi piw as antsa put angqw hiitaningwu. Niikyangw

Whenever sorcerers gather at Palangwu, they work there through their animal familiars. It is from their powers that they derive benefits. Of course these animal godfathers are acquired in an evil way. They are not selected by the candidate's parents. Rather, he does it himself without

pam pay tuwat nukpanvewat put oovi namaqangwu. Pay qa hisat hakiy yumat put hakiy engem namortota. Put pay pam naap pantikyangw pu' pay piw qa awinit akwa. Niiqe puma popwaqt oovi imuy hiituy pas qa atsa ii'istuy, momngwutuy, a'angwustuy pay puuvumuy hiituy pan mihikqwsa pas yaktaqamuy pumuy puma tuwat nalalwa.

telling anybody. Therefore, no one knows who the godfather of a sorcerer is. The animals they choose are particularly those that roam at night, such as coyotes, owls and crows.

By assuming the shape of his godfather beast, a sorcerer is believed to acquire a second heart in addition to his human one. For this reason, the locution *lööq unangwa'ytaqa*, "two-hearted one," is commonly applied to him.

Text 46

Ima popwaqt, put hakiy pan tuskyaptaniqey tuwi'yyungqam, löölöqmuy unangwa'yyungqat lavaytangwu. Noq puma hapi ima popwaqt namu'yyungwa, ii'istuy, momngwutuy, kwaatuy. Ura himu piw tatamotshoyaningwu. Puuvumuy tsöötsöptuy, tohootuy, hoohontuy, tsayrisamuy, puuvumuy soosokmuy hiituy puma namu'yyungwa. Noq puma piw nanap unangwa'yyungqw oovi paniqw pangqaqwangwu, powaqa lööq unangwa'yta, lööq tuwit akw hinma.

Those sorcerers who know how to make a person go mad are said to possess two hearts. They have coyotes, owls, and eagles for godfathers. Even a little mouse may qualify for this role. In addition, antelope and mountain lions, bears, elk, and other animals can be godfathers. All of these animals have their own hearts. That is why they say that a sorcerer has two hearts and two sets of practical know-how that he can draw on as he lives.

Nagualism, a phenomenon which involves animal metamorphosis paired with the faculty of deriving powers from it, is not the privilege only of the *powaqa* in Hopi society (Parsons 1939: 63). It equally applies to the *tuuhikya*, "medicine man," and the *povosqa* or *poosi'ytaqa*,[5] which may be rendered as "seer" or "shaman." Etymologically, the two words incorporate the word *poosi*, "eye," which alludes to the fact that these practitioners diagnose a disease by examining the patient through a *ruupi*, or "quartz crystal."

Obviously, sorcerer, medicine man, and shaman have much in common. All three undergo some sort of initiation. They all seek out tutelary assistants from whom they hope to obtain certain magico-religious powers for their own personal advantage (Eliade 1964: 297). But while the medicine man and shaman are essentially curers through the practice of "white magic," the black magic of the *powaqa* achieves the very opposite, sickness and death.

Unfortunately, nearly all knowledge of the ancient Hopi shamanic tradition is lost. One of my consultants, however, had a vague recollection that the Hopi shaman also went into some sort of a trance or ecstasy before he undertook his healing.[6] An additional clue may have been preserved in the word *tuskyavu*. This word, which is frequently applied to the *powaqa*, designates "the crazy, mad person," and may at one time have been associated with the ecstatic experience of the shaman. The fact that it is now used in reference to the sorcerer may, therefore, be an indication that Hopi sorcery is a version of an ancient shamanic complex.[7] A good portion of this ancient shamanic ensemble could perhaps be reconstructed by integrating all the customary practices of the *tuuhikya*, "medicine man," the *povosqa*, "shaman," the *yaya*[8] "magician" and the *powaqa*, "sorcerer," now scattered and only found in isolation, into one ideological schema.

Text 47

Pay ima tuutuhikt hiituy imuy tuutuvosiptuy hiituy yang yaktaqamuy popkotuy hiitawat na'muyyungwa. Pam it hiitawat an a'ni hongvininik put namaqngwu. Nen pu' put na'ykyangw pu' yep tuuhikyat hintsakngwu.

Pu' i' povosqa ephaqam himuwa it kwewuy namaqe pu' put an yuwsit pu' povoslawngwu. Pu' himuwa hoonawuy, pu' himuwa kwaahut, pu' piw hikis pi it pösawyat, homitshoyat put pi himuwa na'yvangwu. Pi

Medicine men can also have animal familiars. They receive the aid of game animals or other creatures that roam the land. As a rule, the animal called upon as a godfather is that which one desires to equal in power. With the help of this animal the medicine man then practices healing.

The seer or shaman will sometimes call on a wolf as a godfather and even dress like one when he shamanizes. Others come to have the bear or eagle as

yaw pam tuhisaniqw oovi'o. Pay oovi yan ima imuy namaqye' pu' qa pas ephaqam pas pumaniwtotingwu. Pay puma pumuy unangwyamuy unangwa'ykyaakyangw amun yuwsi'ykyaakyangw pep hakiy aw hintsatskyangwu. Pay pumuy tuhisayamuy naami pani'ykyaakyangwyangwuniiqe oovi.

Noq ima popwaqt hiituy namaqye' pas pumuy amuntote' pumuy akw yaktangwu. Iisawuy namaqe' iisawniwtingwu. Niikyangw qa hisat himuwa tuuhikya iisawuy na'yva. Hintiqw pi oovi. Pay pi pangqaqwangwu, iisaw nu'an uuna. Pam hiita suutuptsiwngwuniqw qa put hapi anyungwniqe oovi it iisawuy piw qa katsintota.

a helping spirit. Even the little mouse will qualify, for it is very skillful. However, while medicine men will call on the powers of these animals, they never change into them. Still, they possess their hearts and may dress like them as they treat a patient. They have incorporated the magic skill of these animals.

On the other hand, when sorcerers select animals as their godfathers, they really change into them and go about in their guise. For example, if a sorcerer has a coyote as an animal benefactor, he becomes transformed into a real coyote. No medicine man has ever acquired a coyote as a godfather. I don't really know why, but people say that the coyote is gullible. He believes things right away and they don't want to be like him. This is also the reason that the coyote was not made into a kachina.

Metamorphosis into the animal familiar by the sorcerer is accomplished by somersaulting over a rolling hoop. It is not clear whether each sorcerer owns his own hoop or whether it only exists at Palangwu. Text 48 seems to indicate the former, since the hoop act is carried out in order to reach the Home of the Sorcerers. Text 49, on the other hand, presents the act as being performed at Palangwu only. Text 50 adds a cannibalistic component to the hoop rite, in that the sorcerer is said to consume part of his familiar's heart. I suggest the term "cardiophagy" for this custom.

Text 48

Antsa kya pi powaqa haqamininik pu' ngölat atsvaqe kopang-

Whenever a sorcerer wishes to travel somewhere, he somer-

tsööqökye' pu' hak hiita antsa
namaki'yte' pamniwtingwu. Pu'
putakw powaqkiminen pu' ahoy
kya pi talhayingwtiqw pite' pu'
piw himuwa ahoy atsvaqe
kopangtsööqökye' pu' pay ayaq
piw hopiniw'iwkyangw yee-
vangwu.

saults over a hoop and then
changes into the animal that he
has called upon as his godfather.
In its form, he journeys to
Powaqki, the "Home of the
Sorcerers," and returns when the
time is close to daybreak. Once
more he somersaults over the
hoop, this time to land on its
other side in human shape again.

Text 49

Noq pu' puma yaw pepeq tso-
valte' paasat pu' puma yaw piw
it hiita ngölat atsvaqe kopang-
tsötsöqyangwu. Pu' yaw puma
pantsatskye' puma yaw piw
yangqw it saaqat ahopqöyva
naanangk maqaptsi'yyungngwu.
Noq pu' paasat yaw himuwa
papte' paasat pu' yaw pam it
hiita ngölat aqw ayoq kwiniwiqwat muumat paasat pu' yaw
pam put angk warikye' paasat
pu' pam yaw put atsvaqe ko-
pangtsööqökngwu. Pantikyangw
paasat pu' yaw pam ayoqwat
yeevakyangw pay yaw pam
himuniikyangw pepeqwat
yeevangwu, pami' himu, hiita
pam akw mongvasniiqey. Pay
pam paasat oovi qa hopinii-
kyangw pang ahoy qatuptu-
ngwu. Noq pay yaw puma oovi
pepeq naanangk pantsatskyaqw
pas pi oovi hiisavoniqw son
pepeq qa hin töötöqngwu, tis
puma hiihiitu pepeq naap töötökiy töötöqyaqw. Meh, puma pi
soosoy hiituyangwu, ima

When the sorcerers are assembled at Palangwu, they somer-
sault over a hoop. To do that,
they all wait in line on the northeast side of the kiva ladder. As
soon as it is someone's turn, he
rolls the hoop over towards the
northwest, then dashes after it
and flings himself over it. As he
lands on the other side, he
becomes transformed into the
animal from whose powers he
benefits. Now he is no longer in
his human form. One after the
other the sorcerers go through
this procedure. Before long, there
is a pandemonium of sounds, for
all sorts of creatures can be heard
uttering their peculiar cries.
There are crows, bears, and
cougars. Shouting all at the same
time, they pay no heed to each
other.

a'angwust, hoohont, totokotst.
Suusaq puma sa'akye' qa nami-
tuqayvayaqw pavan pep hin
töötöqngwu.

Text 50

Pay pi popwaqt powaqkimiqye'
pepeq ökye' pu' kya pi antsa
haqamiyanik pu' hintsatskya-
niqw pu' himuwa hiita na'yte'
pu' put kya pi lavaytiqw yaw
put antsa engem unangwayat
tuupeyaqw pu' pam put sowangwu hiita na'ytaniqey. Put kya
pi pay oovi hingsakw angqw
sowantangwu. Pay panhaqam
tsotsvalyaniqw put awniwtinik
put kya pi pay oovi pam yaw-
numngwu. Niiqe oovi haqam
tsotsvalyaqw pu' himuwa
haqami yaavoq ayatiwe' put kya
pi unangwtuupey angqw sowangwu. Put kya pi angqw sowat
pu' put ngölat atsvaqe kopangtsööqökye' pu' ayaq pay himu-
niw'iwkyangw kya pi qatuptungwu. Puma pi pay pumuy
hiituy öqalayamuy akwye'
haqami suptuniqey oovi. Pu' piw
qa suhopiniikyangw haqam
kiimi pituniqey ooviyo.

Whenever sorcerers come to the
Powaqki and intend to go out
and do something, they announce what animal they have
for a benefactor. After its heart
has been roasted, the witch eats
some of it. He keeps eating only
little bits from it. Later, when the
sorcerers have the meeting in
which they transform themselves
into their godfather, they always
take that roasted heart around
with them. As they finally assemble then, and one of them is
ordered to go on an errand far
away, he takes a bite out of the
roasted heart. Having done so,
he somersaults over a hoop to
land on the other side, transformed into his particular animal. Sorcerers draw on the
powers of that animal in order to
quickly reach their destination.
Also, they do this to avoid
getting to the village as humans.

Sorcerers, in addition to the animal benefactors mentioned above,
are believed to operate in the guise of bats and shiny big flies, also
known as skeleton flies. Of the domestic animals, cats and dogs qualify, but only if they are black. The appropriate Hopi terms for the latter are tu'alangwmosa, "witching cat" and tu'alangwvooko, "witching
dog." Witch dogs are said to attract attention through their odd behavior. Either they bark and whine for no apparent reason, or they
dig up the ground around the house, which is usually interpreted as a

bad omen. Hopis are very suspicious of all of these creatures and either avoid them or destroy them.

Text 51

Pam mastotovi kya pi antsa popwaqtuy pok'am. Sen pi pam tuutu'amit angqwniqw oovi. Pu' piw as pam mihikqwsa puuyaw-numngwu. Oovi paniqw piw pangqaqwangwu, mastotovi as mihikqw qa puwngwuniqw ooviyo. Noq oovi hak mihikqw haqam tootovit tuwe' hak antsa pangqawngwu, mastotovi.

I guess the skeleton fly is truly the pet of the sorcerer. Perhaps because it comes from the grave-yard, or perhaps because it only flies around at night. People say that the skeleton fly does not sleep at night. When someone spots a fly at night, one calls it a skeleton fly.

Text 52

Ephaqam i' powaqa sawyani-ngwu. Noq oovi sawya ephaqam hakimuy aw pakiqw pu' hakim uutaye' pay hakim put pas suuninayangwu. Pu' hakim put tuupeye' kwasinayaqw kur pam Hopi sawyanen pam pay pas qa haqami pitungwu.

Once in a while, a sorcerer comes in the form of a bat. When a bat flies into a house, people close it up and quickly kill it. They roast it until it is done, for if the bat was a Hopi, he no longer has a way of getting about.

Text 53

Pay antsa pangqaqwangwu, pay hak powaqanen moosaniwti-ngwu. Suqömmosaniwte' pan-kyangw waynumngwu, mi-hikqw yawi', tutu'alangwtinum-ngwu. Oovi hakimuy amumi pangqaqwangwu, "Uma pay qa moomostuy pokmu'yyungwni. Uma qa qömvit moosat pooko'y-yungwmantani. Pam hapi pas tu'alangwmosa. Put hapi akw hakimuy tutu'alangwyaqw hakim qa nanaptangwu." Pam pi pay hakimuy moosa'amningwu-

People claim a sorcerer can change into a cat. As a rule, he changes into a black cat and then roams about at night, practicing witchcraft. That is why they tell us, "Don't have cats as pets, es-pecially not a black one. A black cat is a witch. When sorcerers go witching in its guise, people are generally not aware of it." A cat usually belongs to someone and is together with people in the house. That is why people are unaware that it is a witch.

niiqe hakimuy ep amumum
pakiwtangwuniqw oovi hakim
qa nanaptangwu pam tu'alangw-
niqw.
    Pay ephaqam suqömvookot
piw tuwa'ynumyangwu mi-
hikqw. Pam yaw pay piw pas
tu'alangwvooko.

Then, once in a while, people
see a black dog at night. That,
they say, is really a witch dog.

One of the prime objectives of the Hopi *powaqa* is to lengthen his
own existence on this earth. This he achieves by causing the death of
one of his relatives.

Text 54

Pay pi imuy popwaqtuy pangqaqwangwu, puma himuwa
powaqa pas wuuyavo qatunik
pu' imuy sinomuy pay naap
hiitawat kya pi tavingwu. Pu'
naami pangqawngwu kya pi,
"Pay um inungem mokqw pu'
nu' piw yaapiy hiisavo qatuni."
Yante' pu' hiitawat tiw'ayay
taviqw pu' antsa pam aapiy
tuutuylawngwu. Pu' pam put
taviiqa navote' pu' awnen pu'
aw pakmumuylawngwu, "Okiw
um himu itiw'aya. Okiw um
himu itupko," kitikyangw put
aw pakmumuylawngwu. Pam pi
pay qa neengem pakmumuy-
lawngwu. Pam put tavi'ytaqa
put yaw engem pakmumuy-
lawngwu iits mokniqö. Yan it
piw popwaqtuy yu'a'atotaqw
itakw puma it qatsiy wuupa-
lalwaqw oovi himuwa powaqa
naat wuutaqaniikyangw
qatungwu.

They say that if a sorcerer wishes
to live a long life, he will sacrifice
the life of any one of his relatives. I guess he argues like this,
"If you die for me, I'll live for a
while longer." With that, he
chooses one of his nephews, and
the latter promptly falls ill.
When the witch responsible for
this learns of the illness, he goes
to his relative and with tears ex-
presses his sympathy. "My poor
nephew. You, my younger brother, poor thing," he says, lament-
ing his illness. But it is only a
charade. After all, he caused his
illness and only sheds tears
hoping that he will soon die.
This is what people say about
sorcerers. They are believed to
prolong their lives through the
deaths of their relatives. It is for
this reason that some sorcerers
live to be old men.

To kill his relative, the sorcerer must extract his heart. This is accomplished, symbolically, with an instrument described as a spindle (Text 55). After the heart has been extracted, it is taken to Palangwu and deposited in a special receptacle. Sorcerers who are reluctant to bring a relative's heart and try to cheat by substituting the heart of a domestic animal are found out and fail to extend their lives (Text 56).

Text 55

Ima pi popwaqt yaw himuwa kya pi hakiy tavingwu. Hak hakiy akw qatsiy wuptanik pu' kya put antsa unangwhoroknangwu. Nen pu' put powaqkimiqhaqami yawmaqw pepeq pay engem put hin yukuyangwuniqw pay pi pangqaqwangwuniqw puma yaw antsa it hiita patukyat akw hakiy unangwayat horoknayangwu. Noq hin pi pam hinta himu patukya. Put nu' qa hisat hiita aw yori. Pu' qa hak hisat piw inumi pangqawu hin pam soniwqö. Hin put hak hinte' hak hakiy unangwhoroknangwuniqw pay popwaqt hapi songqe it kyaakyawnayaqe oovi put qa yu'a'atinumya. Pam hapi kya pi hakiy tuwitoyne' pu' put songqe hakiy aa'awnangwu hak hin put akw hakiy unangwhorokknangwu. Hin pi oovi pas hinma, pam himu unangwhorokinpi himu.

They say that if a sorcerer wants to lengthen his life by sacrificing one of his relatives, he will usually extract his victim's heart. This he takes to the Home of the Sorcerers, where something is done to it. People claim that a spindle is employed to extract a person's heart. I have no idea what that spindle looks like. I've never seen one. No one ever told me what it looks like. Who knows what someone has to do to take out the heart. Sorcerers guard this kind of knowledge and, therefore, don't go around talking about it. At the time someone is initiated into witchcraft, he is informed how to go about this task. I, therefore, have no clue how this heart extraction is carried out.

Text 56

I' powaqa yaw hakiy oovi piw unangwhoroknangwu. Pas qa atsat hakiy pam yaw unangwayat nana'uyvewat horoknangwu. Niikyangw puma yaw

It is said that a sorcerer will extract a person's heart. This is really true. He does it in a secret way. He has a special tool to accomplish this feat, a spindle.

piw oovi put hiita pas awiwa'y-
yungwa. Puma yaw it hiita
patukyat akw tuuvantsatskya.
Niiqe pay yaw pam piw oovi
pan hakimuy tokvaqw pu' pam
put hiitawat tiw'ayay namorte'
pu' pam put awnen paasat pu'
pam yaw put patukyat unangwmi tavit pu' yaw pam put putakw unangwhoroknangwu.
Nen pu' pam paasat put yawkyangw pu' nuutum pangsoq
haqami Palangwuy aqwningwu.
Noq pu' yaw pam pepeq pite'
pu' pam yaw put haqami siivut
aqw panangwu. Pam yaw siivu
pay piw pas paniqw pepeq
pumuy amungem maskya'iw-
tangwu. Pu' yaw pam put
pangsoq panaqw pu' yaw pam
kur pas antsa it hopit unangwa'atnen pu' yaw pam pas
susmataq pan pangqw paklaw-
ngwu.

Noq pu' pay yaw himuwa as
naamahin put naawaknakyangw
pay yaw pam piw ephaqam qa
suutaq'ewningwu pas pan naap
tiw'ayay unangwhoroknaninik,
put pan tavininik. Tis put aw pas
unangwa'yte'. Noq pam pi put
tungla'ytangwu. Put tuwi'ytaniqw pam put pi hiikya'yta. Hiitawat pam pas aw unangwa'yte'
pu' yaw pam nawus put tavingwu. It yaw pam piw hiikya'-
yta. Niikyangw pay himuwa
yaw piw oovi pan qa suutaq'ew-
nen paasat pu' pam pay oovi
hiita unangwayat haqamnen pu'

As soon as people are asleep, he
selects a nephew or niece and
visits them. Then he places the
spindle on their chest and takes
out the heart. With this heart he
then travels to Palangwu. Upon
his arrival, he places it into a
vessel which is kept ready there
for this purpose. In this vessel,
the human heart can clearly be
heard crying.

Even though a person wants
to be a witch, he is sometimes
not willing to extract the heart of
his own nephew or niece to sacrifice them. Especially when he's
fond of them. Yet, he desires to
learn witchcraft; learning that
demands a price. He must sacrifice the relative he loves. That is
the price he has to pay. Still, if
someone is not willing to go
through with it, he will get the
heart of an animal and then go to
the meeting at Palangwu. Instead of with a human heart, he
arrives with the heart of a pig, a
sheep or a chicken.

put pangsoq yawkyangw pu'
nuutum tsotsvaltongwu.
Niikyangw pay qa it hopit piw
oovi unangwayat, pay it hiita
pitsootit, kaneelot, kowaakot,
put hiita unangwayat pam
pangso yawkyangwningwu.

Paasat pu' pam piw epeq
pite' pu' pan put pay naap hiita
unangwayat kwusivaqw pay
yaw puma piw pepeq nanap-
tangwu. Pam pepeq siivu hapi
yaw kur pay piw qa paysoq
pepeq pantangwu, puma pumuy
hakimuy unangwayamuy
pangsoq pan tangalalwaniqat
oovi. Pay yaw pam piw pumuy
pepeqyaqamuy aa'awnangwu
hiita unangwayat himuwa pangsoq panaqw put yaw pam piw
tuu'a'awnangwu. Niiqe pu' yaw
pam oovi pangsoq put panaqw
pu' pay yaw pam put hiita
unangwa'atniqa pay yaw piw
put an pangqw töqtingwu. Kur
pam it kowaakot unangwa'atnen
pam yaw piw pay pan paklaw-
ngwu.

The minute he enters with an
animal heart, the other sorcerers
notice it. For the vessel into
which the hearts are placed is
not just an ordinary pot. It
announces to all those present
what kind of a heart is in it. The
moment the heart is inside, it
produces the characteristic
sounds of the being it belongs to.
In the case of a chicken, for example, the heart clucks like a
chicken.

By killing a relative, the sorcerer adds four years to his life expec-
tancy. Titiev's claim that heart extraction must be performed annually
was not confirmed by my informants (1942: 550). Since many things
in Hopi culture occur or exist in sets of four, I would give their statements more credence.

Text 57

Noq pu' pam oovi hiitawat pan
unangwhorokne' paasat pu' pam
yaw oovi piw putakw naalöq
yaasangwuy akw qatsiy piw aw

When a person's heart has been
extracted by a sorcerer, he can
prolong his life by four years.
When those four years are gone,

hoyoknangwu. Pu' paasat put
naalöq yaasangwuy aqw pituqw
paasat pu' pam piw nawus
sukwatningwu. Pay pas piw
hiisavo qatuniqey oovi. Noq
puma popwaqt yaw pumuy
pantsatskyaniqat yan kya pi piw
pumuy amumi tutavo. Ispi pam
hopit unangwa'at yaw hiikya'y-
tangwu, tis oovi hakiy pan pas
naat tsaakwhoyat, naat qa hiita
wuwni'ytaqat. Noq pu' it hiita
pitsootit, kaneelot'ewakw unangwa'at pay yaw qa hiikya'y-
tangwu. Niiqe pay pam oovi
yaayanhaqam hintsakmakyangw
aqwhaqami qatungwu, kur naat
qa hak put aw maamatsqw, kur
qa hak put nu'ansanqw.

he must sacrifice another life in
order to continue living. Sorcerers have been instructed to kill.
A human heart is worth a great
deal, especially if it belongs to a
child, one who is still innocent. A
pig's heart or sheep's heart, on
the other hand, is not worth anything. In this manner, sorcerers
live long lives; that is, as long as
they're not recognized and
caught in the act.

While death-dealing witchcraft is restricted to the sorcerer's own
relatives, disease-causing black magic is not. One method employed
involves lodging a pathogenic object in the body of the human target.
The Hopi term for this "foreign object charged with malignant
power" is *tuukyayni*. According to Titiev, "stiff deerhairs, red or black
ants, centipedes, bits of bone or glass, and shreds of graveyard clothes
are favorites" (1942: 551). Beaglehole and Beaglehole add porcupine
quills, bones of a dead person, and excrement to this list of injurious
objects (1935: 6). As Eliade has pointed out, these injurious objects are
not introduced *in concreto*, but are created by the mental power of the
sorcerer (1964: 301). According to Beaglehole and Beaglehole the
Hopi *tuukyayni* bullets are symbolically projected from the sorcerer's
"left hand by flicking the fingers at the intended victim" (1935: 6).
Stephen reports that the missile, which was also referred to as *powaqat
ho'at* "sorcerer's arrow," was launched by a "magic bow" (1894:212).
It was usually sucked out by the shaman, who thereby becomes "the
antidemonic champion" (Eliade 1964: 508). My text below additionally mentions cowry shells and teeth of the dead as potential disease
inflictors.

Text 58

Pay pi piw pangqaqwangwu pam hak himu powaqa hakiy hiita akw so'on unangwa'yte' sen hiita akw hakiy aw qa kwangwatayte' pu' pam hakiy hiita akw tuukyayangwu. Noq pu' pam kur su'an yukuqw pay hak putakw tuutuytingwu. Noq ima popwaqt a'niyaqe antsa hakiy hin hintsatsnanik pu' hakiy antsa sotsapmu'ayangwu, pay naap hiitawat hak tuutuy- tiniqw oovi. Piw pay mastamat akw yaw e'nang hintsatskya. Pu' pay hiihiituy ööqayamuy akw kya pi piiwu. Putakw yaw pam hakiy hintsanqw paasat pu' hak pan hiita na'palngwu, sen sulawtingwu. Ii'it puma hiihiita popwaqt kya pi akw tuumumu'- tiwiskyaakyangw hin pi puma put hakiy aw panayangwu.

Noq oovi hak tuuhikyat awniqw pu' pam hiisa'haqam hakiy ang hiita ipwangwu. Haqam tuutuyqw pep hakiy sokotkye' hakiy ep hiita horok- nangwu.

It is said that if a sorcerer does not like a particular individual or looks unfavorably upon some- one, he will magically insert a foreign object into him. If he does it successfully, this person then falls ill. Because sorcerers are very powerful and intend to harm a person, they shoot cowry shells into the body, causing the person to become ill with a disease. In addition, they use the teeth of dead humans as well as all sorts of animal bones. As a result, the person then contracts a disease and even dies. How sorcerers manage to shoot these missiles into people, I have no idea.

When the [ailing] person consults a medicine man, the medicine man always extracts a few items from the person's body. He usually pinches the patient where it hurts and removes something.

A second technique of inflicting misfortune or disease on a victim makes use of a bait object. Generally, it is a person's hair that the sor- cerer will try to acquire as the bait.

Text 59

Powaqa pu' pay naap hiita hakiy angqw sokopte' pu' put hin- tsankqw pu' hak hintingwu. Ephaqam meh hakiy höömiyat angqw sookyaknangwu. Pu' put

A sorcerer will steal anything from a person to do something to it. As a result, harm is done to that person. For example, the sorcerer will pluck a hair from a

hintsangwu sonpiqee. Pu' hak
paasat hintingwu, tuutuytingwu.

person and then treat it in such a
way that this person meets with
bad fortune or falls ill.

One favorite pastime of sorcerers is the pursuit of illicit sex. Both
male and female converts to witchcraft are believed to enter clandes-
tinely the homes of people they are lusting after in order to satisfy
their sexual desires.

Text 60

Pantotit paasat pu' yaw puma
piw pas soosovik it natkot oovi
angqe' nankwusangwuniiqat
piw peetu yan it navoti'yyungwa. Pay yaw himuwa piw kya
pi hisat haqe' waynumkyangw
pu' haqam hakiy aw yorikye'
pay pam put aw tungla'ytingwu.
Aw kwangwa'ytuswe' paasat
pu' yaw pam hak haqam ki'y-
taqw pangso yaw pam put ooviningwu, naamahin pi yaw pam
hak haqam pas yaaphaqam ki'y-
tani, sen Si'ookive, sen Hopaq-
kivehaq. Pay pi pam paasat qa
naap waynumngwuniiqe pay
yaw pam oovi piw paasat
pangsoq suptungwu. Nen pu'
pam haqami hakiy awniiqey pay
piw naat it tuhisay akw pangso
put qa navotnakyangw pu'
pangso put aw pakingwu. Paasat
pu' pay pam piw put qa nanvot-
qat aw hintsangwu, tsopngwu.
Pu' i' wuuti, maana pay piw put
antingwu. Pay pam piw haqami
hakiy tiyot sen taaqat kiiyat awnen pu' piw paasat pep putwat
tsopt pu' paasat piw hisatniqw
ahoy pangso Palangwuy

After changing into their animal
forms, sorcerers are believed to
roam about in search of a sexual
partner. Whenever a sorcerer
spots a female he takes a fancy
to, he goes after her wherever
she may live, even if her home
should be far away, such as at
Zuni or a Rio Grande village. Of
course, he does not travel on foot
in order to quickly reach his
destination. Then he enters the
home of the desired female by
means of his magical powers. As
a result, the victim is unaware of
his coming. Thereupon, he has
intercourse with her without her
being aware of it. A woman or
girl does the same thing. They
too enter a boy's or man's home,
have intercourse with them and
then return to Palangwu again.

awningwu.

Niiqe paniqw piw oovi peetu pangqaqwangwuniqw antsa
yaw hak haqe' waynume' pay
yaw hak hakiy pas naap kiy
angqwniiqat pas su'an soniwqat
son haqam piw aw qa yorik-
ngwu. Naamahin pi yaw hak
haqe' pas yaakye' waynumni.
Pu' piw naamahin piw yaw pam
naap himusinoni, sen Kastiila,
sen Pahaana. Pu' pay peetu hikis
pas it paatuwaqatsit yupqöymi
sasqayaqam pay yaw piw imuy
tuwimuy su'amun sosniwqamuy
amumi yortota. Ispi pam hakimuy yaw kitsokiyamuy angqwniiqa put hakiy pepehaq panhaqam tsopqw pu' pam paasat put
engem tiitangwu. Noq pay yan it
piw peetu navoti'yyungwa.

This is the reason that some
say they encounter on their
travels people who look just like
someone from their home village. This is true even when
journeying in distant places. The
familiar-looking face can also be
from another tribe, a Spaniard,
or an Anglo. Some people even
travel to lands across the ocean
and see others who resemble
their friends. Which is of course
due to the fact that a sorcerer
from their own village had intercourse there with a woman who
then gave birth to a child.

Within the complex of sexual witchcraft one special form produces what is generally referred to as *tuskyavu*, "love craziness," in its
victim. To bring about this state of love madness, the love magician
renders an individual helpless against his sexual desires by means of
a *tuskyaptawi* or "charming song."[9]

Text 61

Pay antsa ima popwaqt kya pi it
hiita tuskyaptawit taawi'yyungqe oovi putakw hakiy tuskyapto-
tangwu, it maanat, wuutit. Pam
pi antsa powaqa it maanat hiita
tuskyapte' taawiy akw put naami pitsinangwu. Pay popwaqt
kya pi hakiy pantsatsnangwu-
niqw pam himu tuuya antsa i'
tuskyavu. Pan pam maatsiwa.

It's a fact that [male] sorcerers
possess charming songs which
they use to bewitch a girl or
woman. Once a sorcerer has
charmed the female, he gets her
to come to him by singing that
song. In doing this, witches
actually cause a disease in their
victim known as love madness.
They brainwash the female and

Hakiy pan naanaphin wuwnito-
toynayangwu. Hakiy naanaphin
unangwayat hintsatsnaqw pu'
hak antsa pantingwu, hoonaq-
tingwu.

mess up her heart. She then goes
mad.

Text 62

Pu' ima popwaqt haqawat tuskyaptawi'yyungqam pu' piw put
haqam taalawlalwangwu, qa
maataqpuve. Pu' hak powaqa
hakiy aw tunglaytaqey taawit
akw angwutaqw pu' antsa pam
qa navoti'ykyangw hakiy awningwu, haqaqw, sen kiy angqw
sen haqam hiita nuutum hintsakkyangw angwutiwe' pangqw pu'
pam nakwsungwu. Pu' haqaqw
put himuwa pan taawit akw
wangwaylawqw pu' pam put aw
pitungwu, qa navoti'ykyangw.
Ispi okiw tuskyaptingwuniiqe'e.

Some sorcerers who know
charming songs sing them where
they cannot be overheard. With
the help of such a song, the
sorcerer can gain the affection of
the female he desires. She then
comes to him without being
aware of why. Wherever she
happens to be, at home or some
place else where she is doing
something with other people,
once she has been overpowered
by the charm, she starts out. Not
knowing what is going on, she
arrives at the place of the person
who has summoned her with the
help of the song. No wonder.
The poor thing has become love
mad.

Charming songs of a different nature also serve to assure the sorcerer's hunting success. Casting a spell on the game animals, with the
song, the animals offer themselves freely as prey.

Text 63

Pu' piw tuskyaptawit akw imuy
tuutuvosiptuy maqwisngwu,
popwaqt. Maqtoqa haqam sun
qatuwkyangw put taatawlawqw
pu' pam tsööviw, sowi'yngwa
warikngwu. Pu' yaw susmataqningwu. Taawit akw wariknaqw
qötmok'iwta mo'angaqw. Pay-

Sorcerers also go hunting for big
game animals with a charming
song. The hunter simply sits still
somewhere, chanting the song.
As a result, an antelope or deer
will come running. It's quite obvious that witchcraft is involved
because, having been compelled

soq mo'angaqw wisaavi mun-
ngwu. Put taawit akw yuutuk-
nayat, qöqyat panyungqamuy
hapi kiimiq oo'oyaya. Qa
powatotat panyungqamuy
kiimiq kivantaqw pu' pumuy
kwipyangwu. Pu' angqw sinom
noonovangwu.

by the song, the animal is
foaming at the mouth. Saliva is
dripping from it. After flushing
out a number of animals like this
and killing them all, the sorcerers
lug them home. Without bothering to purify them, they bring
them in and cook them. Then
people eat the meat.

Of course, the antisocial practices a sorcerer engages in are not
limited to individuals only. Epidemics and famines are typically
blamed on witches. Thus, cloud control, which within the realm of
agriculturists and horticulturists ultimately implies life-sustaining
moisture control, is frequently attempted by the sorcerer, because it
will impact a large group of people. To this extent, witches either
channel clouds exclusively to their own fields and garden plots, or
they cause rain-laden clouds to withdraw. In the text samples below,
offensive odor is used to make the clouds recede.[10]

Text 64

Pu' yaw pangqw hoopaqw,
Kiisiwuy angqw, yooyangw qa
taala. Puma oo'omawt kya pi
pay pas nun'okwatniiqe pay hiitawat aw suu'unangwtatve-
ngwu. Noq kya pi hin'ur yokvani'ewakw soniwa. Noq pu' ima
popwaqt kwayngyaq pay hakiy
pi engem hiita nukushintsatsna-
ngwuniiqe pu' pan yokvaniqw
pu' yaw pooyantotangwu,
mas'öqat ang pooyantotangwu.
Pam yaw hin'ur hovaqtingwu-
niqw oovi put ang pantsatskyaqw pu' pay yooyoyangwt qa
kiimi ökingwu.

Rain that comes from Kiisiwu in
the northeast is usually so thick
that it obscures the light. I guess
the clouds there are very compassionate, because they come to
the aid of a person [who needs
rain on his fields] without delay.
Soon, it looks as if it's really going to pour. But the sorcerers at
the refuse and toilet area always
interfere in an evil way. Thus,
when it is about to rain, they
blow through a bone, preferably
the bone of a diseased human.
This produces a terrible odor. As
a result, the rains do not approach the village.

Text 65

Pay pi ima popwaqt pi' a'ni hiita
tuwi'yyungngwuniiqe it tuwiy
akw pumuy oo'omawtuy piw
hin uutayangwu. Sen pay haqamiwat laalayyangwu. Paasat pay
puma oo'omawt hakimuy
amumi qa ökingwu. Paasat pay
qa yokvangwu.

Noq pu' pay ura hisat
haqawa pangqawqw pam yaw
piw pas hakiy aw taytaqw yaw
pam hak pepehaq tumpaqniqw
pu' yaw pam i' pas qöötsa
oomawniikyangw pu' piw pas
pavan tuukwiwta. Naanatsve
yaw kwap'iwtaqa yaw haqaqwwat yaw pangsoqwat kiimiq as
hoytaqw pu' pam hak wunuuqa
yaw it hovinapnay sirokna.
Siroknat pu' yaw pam po'olti.
Pantit paasat pu' yaw pam put
oomawuy pas su'aqwwat kuriy
iitat kwanaltit pu' yaw pang
qas'aatsava put oomawuy
aqwwat pooyanta. Noq pay pi
hakiy pi kuringaqw a'ni hovaqtungwuniqw pay pi pam oomaw
son pi qa putakw hovalangwu-
yat akw pay piw oovi qa pangso
pitu. Pay pi pam as son pi qa
yoknaniqe oovi pangso tuwat
pan hoytaqw pu' pay pam hak
panhaqam hintiqw pay pam
paasat kur haqami.

Sorcerers have extraordinary
powers. They can use them, for
example, to close in the clouds.
Then the clouds cannot reach
people, and the rain won't fall.

Once someone related that
he observed a man at the mesa
edge while there was a really
white cumulus cloud up in the
sky. It was stacked several layers
high and kept moving in the
direction of the village. Suddenly, the man who was standing
there slid down his pants. Next
he bent over, and sticking his
buttocks directly towards the
cloud, blew at it through his
spread legs. As a person's
behind stinks a great deal, the
cloud did not come nearer
because of the odor. It definitely
had intended to shed its moisture, that's why it was approaching. However, due to the action
of that man, it went somewhere
else.

In addition, practitioners of witchcraft are believed to unleash a
host of crop-destroying pests. These agents of destruction, combined
with the sorcerers's own powers of averting imminent rain, constitute
the classic formula for bringing about an ever-dreaded famine.

Text 66

Pay pi pangqaqwangwu yaw antsa ima popwaqt hiihiituy poktotangwu, it hiita natwanit sakwitotaniqö. Antsa imuy töötöltuy pu' imuy piw hiituy peetuy, tukyaatuy, pu' imuy antsa pöövöstuy, aatuy.

People say it's true that sorcerers recruit all sorts of creatures to ruin crops. Certainly, they employ grasshoppers, kangaroo rats, prairie dogs, mice, and cutworms.

Realizing the ever-present danger of witchcraft, Hopi society prescribes a whole array of safeguards and taboos to separate a person from its malevolent influence. These prophylactic measures pertain both to the ceremonial and the secular context of Hopi life. Since the scope of this book does not permit a listing of these, suffice it to say that sorcerers are not immune to discovery. As a rule, when found out they will do their utmost to bribe their way out of what is a potentially fatal predicament. Note that the correct Hopi term for a witch that is seen or heard is *tu'alangw*,[11] not *powaqa*.

Text 67

Hak tu'alangwuy ngu'aqw wuutinen yaw sutsep hakiy aw naakuwaatingwu. "Um qa pangqawe' inuupe haalaytini." Pu' hak yaw uunate' paasat put tutu'alangwqat qatsiyat ayo' tavingwu. Paasat pu' hak qatsiy kwayngwu.

Pu' yaw taaqa tutu'alangqw pu' hak put ngu'aqw pamwa yaw hakiy aw sutsep tuukwavit tuwat kuwaatingwu. Pu' hak tuukwaviyat nakwhe' paasat pu' hak piw putwat qatsiyat ayo' tavingwu. Oovi yaw hak tu'alangwuy ngu'e' hiita hakiy aawintaqw hak yaw qa nakwhangwu. Hak yaw qa nakwhaqw paasat pu' pam pay naapningwu.

When someone discovers a witch, and it is a woman, she will always offer herself sexually to that person. "If you don't say anything, you may enjoy my body." They say that if one then gives in to her, one spares the witch's life but forfeits one's own.

If the recognized witch is a man, he always offers that person a necklace. If the necklace is accepted, once again the witch's life is spared [and that of the other is forfeited]. Therefore, if one catches a sorcerer, one must say no to whatever he or she has to offer. Then the sorcerer is bound to die.

Text 68

Pay pi pangqaqwangwu piw
sinom, yaw hak antsa it powaqat
haqam nu'ansane' pay hopiniqw
awnen pay yaw ngu'angwu.
Hak yaw ngu'aqw pu' hakiy pay
son pi qa aw hepngwuqat kitotangwu. Pu' ephaqam wuutinen
pu' hakiy aw pangqawngwu,
"Ta'a, pay antsa um nuy maamatsi. Noq pay um qa it lalvayni.
Oovi um inuupe haalaytini. Um
inumi hintsanniqey naawakne'
pantini. Nit pu' um pantit pu'
um it hapi qa lalvayni. Taq um
pante' pay um naap songqe
hintiniy," yaw itakw hakiy aw
wuutiningwu.

   Pu' taaqa himuwa pante' pu'
yaw antsa lomasivakwewta-
ngwu, lomatukwapngöntangwu.
Pu' himuwa a'ni kanelvokmu'y-
te' pu' yaw hakiy aw pangqawngwu, "Ta'a, antsa um nuy
maamatsi. Um it qa lalvayni. Um
it qa lalvaye' ivokmuy ikanel-
vokmuy, ivakasvokmuyni. Pu'
yep piw sipkwewa. Pu' um put
piwni, pu' itukwaviy." Yan yaw
hakiy aw hingqawngwu.

   Pu' hak antsa ngasta put
hiitanen pu' put hak nakwhe'
pu' hak pay yaw put engem
mokngwuniqw oovi yan itamumi tutavoniqw oovi hak hakiy
haqam yaw pan powaqngu'e'
hakiy aw kuwaatiqw yaw hak qa
nakwhangwu. Yaw hak put

People say that if a person actually catches a sorcerer practicing
and he is in his human form, that
one should walk up to him and
seize him. They say any witch
caught like this will definitely try
to tempt this captor. In the case
of a women she will say, "All
right, you've truly recognized
me [for what I am]. Don't tell on
me. In return, you can enjoy
yourself with me. If you want to
have sex with me, that's fine. But
when you're done, you must not
tell anyone. If you do, something
bad will happen to you."

   If it is a man, he will probably be wearing a beautiful concho belt or a necklace. If he owns
lots of sheep or cows, he will say,
"All right, you truly found me
out. Don't tell on me. If you
don't, you can have my sheep or
cows. Also, here's a concho belt.
And my necklace you can have
too."

   In case a person has none of
the things offered to him and
agrees to accept them, he dies for
the sorcerer. For this reason,
there's an instruction that says to
refuse everything a sorcerer
offers when caught red-handed.
For he who accepts the offer will
definitely regret it.

pante' pay sunengemningwu-
niqw yan i' piw itamumi tutavo.

As soon as the recognized sorcerer realizes that his discoverer
cannot be bribed, he resorts to pleading for his life. As one might
expect, however, this plea is loaded with trickery.

Text 69

Noq pu' yaw oovi himuwa pan
nu'ansaniwqa paasat pu' yaw
hakiy pan aw as hiita kuwaatiqw
pu' pay yaw hak put pas qa
nakwhaqw paasat pu' yaw pam
piw hakiy pas sonqa aw na'o-
kiwa'ytangwunen pu' yaw pam
hakiy aw pangqawngwu, "Pay
as nu' ngas'ew naalös it taawat
aw yorikt pu' paasat pi pay ason
haqamini," yaw pam hakiy aw
kitangwu. Noq pu' pay wuwni'ytaqa pay yaw paasat piw qa
nakwhangwunen pu' put aw
piw tuwat pangqawngwu, "Pay
so'oni. Pay um naap nukpananiiqe um oovi naap it aqw
naavitsina. Pay pi um oovi tatam
haqamini," yan hak yaw as put
aw lavaytingwu.

Paasat pu' pam pas qa
okiwte' pu' paasat pam yaw naat
piw hiisavo qatuniqey hakiy aw
tuuvingtangwu, sen paayis taalat
anga, löös, suus piw taawat aw
yorikniqey piw hakiy aw yaw
pam naawaknangwu. Noq pay
yaw hak pas qa nakwhe' pay
yaw hak paasat put pö'angwu.

Noq pay yaw pam piw kur
qa paysoq naalöq taalat pangqawngwu. Pam yaw naalöq

When a sorcerer gets caught red-
handed, and his discoverer
rejects what is offered to him [for
not revealing his identity], he
begs for sympathy and says, "If
only I could see the sun four
more times and then die." A
person with brains will reject this
plea also and reply, "No. You are
completely evil and brought this
upon yourself. You must die."

The sorcerer, however, will
not give up and will plead to live
a little longer, maybe two or
three days. He will even ask to
see the sun just one more time.
When the person stands fast, he
beats the sorcerer at his game.

Of course, the sorcerer was
not just asking for four days.
When he said four days, he was
actually asking for four years.
Were someone to grant his
request for four days, he would
actually live another four years.

taalat pangqawe' pam yaw hakiy
aw naalöq yaasangwuy tuuving-
lawngwu. Pu' kur hak pay
paasat put nakwhanaqw pam pi
pay paasat oovi piw paasavo
naalöq yaasangwuy ang
qatukyangw pu' pay piw aqw
pituqw pay pam paasat son piw
hakiywat akw qa yaaptiniqe oovi
hakiy aw pangqawngwu. Pu'
hak oovi pay pas qa nakwhaqw
paasat pu' pay yaw pam aapiy
pay panis nalöstalqw pu' pay
yaw pam mokngwu.

Upon reaching the end of that
time, he would have to lengthen
his life again with another
person's death. Thus, when the
offer of a witch is declined, the
sorcerer has four more days to
live and then he dies.

As Titiev rightly points out, "one of the most telling features of
the Hopi attitude toward sorcerers is found in their religious notions.
On the whole, Hopi religion is decidedly nonethical, but *poakam* [cor-
rectly *popwaqt*] are severely punished in the other world" (1942: 556).
Once again, lack of space prohibits any enumeration of the manifold
ordeals[12] the sorcerer is subjected to along his journey in the underworld. The example cited below focuses on the last leg of this journey, when he reaches the flaming fire pit, his final destination. Here
Kwaani'ytaqa, in his role as psychopomp, makes sure that evildoers
receive their deserved punishment, while the souls of the pure are
permitted to proceed to paradise.

Text 70

Noq pu' pam oovi pan mookye'
pam as pay piw paasat pangsoqhaqami itam sulaw'iwmakyangw sasqayaqw pay yaw
pam as piw pangsoq nakwsu-
ngwuniikyangw pay yaw pam
qa pas aqw haqami pitungwu,
pepeq ima qa hinyungqam
yesqw pangsoqa. Pepehaq
haqam yaw i' Kwaani'ytaqa yaw
piw it koysöt aw tunatyawkyangw pu' pam yaw piw

When a sorcerer is dead, he
heads for the place where we go
when we die. But he never
reaches the location where the
pure ones live. Rather, he comes
to the fire pit that the Kwaani'y-
taqa is tending. He has a huge
fire going in the pit. As the
sorcerers line up at this pit, they
are cast into the fire. They line
up on all four sides of the hole:

pangsoq a'ni qööhi'ytangwuniqw pam yaw pay pangso
paasavoningwu. Pangso yaw
puma popwaqt yaw tuwat
tsotsvalqw pep pu' yaw ima
hakim piw tuwat pumuy pangso
put qööhit aqw maspitota. Noq
pep pu' yaw puma piw naana-
n'i'vaqw aqw leetsiwtangwu.
Yangqw kwiningyaqw, taa-
vangqw, tatkyaqw, hoopaqw
yaw puma aqw panyungngwu.
Noq pu' paasat yaw pam pep
put qööhit aw tunatyawtaqa yaw
pangqawngwu, "Taa', huvam
pumuy pangsoq maspaya'a!"
yaw pam kitaqw paasat pu' yaw
ima hakim piw tuwat pumuy
pangso oovi pan naanangk
maspitotangwu. Puma yaw ima
hakim pumuy amutsviy haqa-
miyaqam puma yaw pepeq
tuwat pumuy pantsatskya. Niiqe
puma hapi oovi paasat pumuy
amumi ahoy nana'o'ya. Meh,
himuwa naat qatukyangw pu'
hakiywat taviqw pam pu' yaw
pepeq put pangsoq na'atsqök-
nangwu.

Noq pu' piw yaw himuwa
powaqa hintaqat akw piw pay
a'ni mokhurunen pay pam piw
hintaqat akw qa uwikngwu, qa
mokngwu. Paasat pu' pay yaw
pam i' hohoyawniikyangw piw
pangqw ahoy yamakngwu. Pay
yan it piw lavaytangwu.

the northwest, southwest, southeast, and northeast. As they
stand there, the Kwaani'ytaqa
who is looking after the fire commands, "All right, throw them
in!" Whereupon, all those who
died because of these sorcerers,
cast them in, one after the other.
The victimized now exact their
revenge. Everyone who murders,
once he dies, is pushed into this
fire pit.

Once in a while, for some
peculiar reason, a sorcerer is not
easily killed. He simply does not
burst into flames and die. Such a
sorcerer will return in the shape
of a stinkbug. That's what people
say.

Endnotes

1. Today, due to better palaeoclimatological information, based on more accurate dendrochronological data, the "Great Drought" is assigned a much longer period. As a rule, it is said to have lasted from 1276-1299 A.D. (Haury 1986: 70).

2. *Powaqqatsi* is the movie title adopted by Godfrey Reggio for his sequel to *Koyaanisqatsi*, which has become an international cult movie. Both movie titles, which were suggested by me, name ancient Hopi concepts. However, while *koyaanisqatsi*, "corrupted life," is a static idea that describes social disorder and chaos, *powaqqatsi* is more dynamic, in that it portrays an active pursuit of willful, malicious change.

3. The term *kwitavit*, or "turds," is limited in its linguistic usage to the dialect of the Third Mesa villages. Second Mesa speakers prefer the form *kwitam* for the same meaning.

4. According to Titiev, "the Hopi believe that all witches are the descendants of a mythological character known as Spider Woman, who plays a prominent part in their stories of the beginning of human life on earth" (1942: 549). All of my informants unanimously disagreed with this statement. Spider Woman is considered a powerful, yet benevolent earth goddess who, like a *dea ex machina*, always appears to help those in distress. To quote the rebuttal of one of my consultants: Kookyangwso'wuuti qa powaqa. Pam pay hiita lolmatsa tuwat wuuwanta, hakimuy sinmuy pa'angwantaniqey. "Old Spider Woman is no sorceress. On the contrary, she constantly thinks of helping people."

5. *Poosi'ytaqa*, the Third Mesa term, literally means "one who has an eye." Among Second Mesa speakers, the expression *povosqa*, "one who [does] seeing/a seer," is more prevalent. *Poovost* and *povosyaqam* are the respective plural forms. In addition to the rendition as "shaman," one also encounters "crystal gazer," "crystal diagnostician," and "eye-seeker" (Stephen 1894). *Poovost* were once organized in *poswimi*, secret societies of their own. An individual initiate into such a *poswimi* was consequently known as a *poswimkya*.

Whether the *yaya'*, or "magician," who practiced white magic, also employed helping spirits in performing his feats of illusion, I have not been able to determine to date. Regardless of this, Eliade's observations that the terms "shaman," "medicine man," "sorcerer," and "magician" designate certain individuals endowed with magical

and religious powers, and that they are found in all "primitive" societies, are certainly true regarding the Hopi (1964: 3).

6. Interestingly enough, the ancient Hopi shaman used to employ
a special medicine to induce ecstatic behavior reminiscent of his
nagual, or "animal familiar," whose form and power he magically
assumed. This may be gathered from the following statement: Poosi'ytaqa aw pitsinanik hiita ngahuy angqw sowangwu. Pu' paasat
pam ang pakiqw pu' paasat pam hintsakngwu. Pu' hiita na'ykyangw
nuutuupa ma'ynume' pan pam nay an hintsakngwu. Pu' piw pan
töqnumngwu. "Whenever a shaman is about to practice, he eats from
his medicine. As soon as it has been digested, he acts strangely. As he
uses his hands on his patients, he behaves just like his alter animal.
He will even utter similar sounds."

7. That the borderline between shamanism and witchcraft is a
narrow one which is easily transgressed is underlined by Hodge's
remarks: "Witchcraft may be defined as the art of controlling the will
and well-being of another person by supernatural or occult means,
usually to his detriment. If shamans possessed supernatural powers
that could be exerted beneficially, it was naturally supposed that they
might also be exerted with injurious results, and therefore, where
shamanism was most highly developed, the majority of supposed
witches, or rather wizards, were shamans" (1910: 965).

That a close connection between witchcraft and curing was once
also observable at Hopi, can be gathered from the following statement by Titiev: "On the basis of a widespread belief that the same
kind of power which causes an ailment can also cure it, the Hopi tend
to equate their shamans with witches" (1956: 54). For this reason, "all
medicine men are regarded with a mixture of respect and fear."

8. While in Hopi oral literature initiation into the business of curing almost regularly involves death, dismemberment, and resurrection for the *tuuhikya*, "medicine man," this seems also to have been
the case for the *yaya'*, "magician." This is evident from a legend of the
origin of the *yaya't*, or "members of the Yaya' society," recorded by
Voth (1905: 41-47). Here, the candidates are put to death in fiery pits
and then miraculously brought back to life. This ritual death and
resurrection scenario, according to Eliade, is typical of a shaman's
initiation (1964: 38).

9. Beaglehole and Beaglehole also report that a *tuskyaptiiponi*,
"love sorcerer's medicine bundle," was used in conjunction with the
practice of love magic (1935: 8).

10. Titiev cites what he calls "a standard technique" for driving off rainstorms. "The two-hearted one takes four reeds, about half an inch in diameter and four inches long and fills them lightly with a mixture of ashes (*qötsvu*) and a vaginal discharge (*hovalangwu*). The ashes represent dust. The other substance is thought to be highly displeasing to the sky gods. When rain appears imminent, the male-factor blows the contents of one of the reeds upward, whereupon the clouds promptly recede. This is done four times, after which, the deities give up and take their rain elsewhere" (1942: 551).

11. The following is a Hopi folk-definition of *tu'alangw*: Tu'ala-ngwuy hak tuwangwu hakiy aw hintsanqw sen hinwat hakiy tsa-tsawinaqw. Pu' powaqat pay hak qa tuwangwu hakiy aw tutu'a-langqw. Pam pay qa susmataq tu'alangwningwu. "A *tu'alangw* is visible when practicing. For example, when he is scaring someone. The *powaqa*, however, one cannot see when he is practicing his witch-craft against a person. He is clearly not a *tu'alangw*."

12. Hopi oral literature contains several Orpheus myths, in conjunction with which, details of the sorcerer's fate in the underworld are presented. In addition to the ones published by Voth (1905: 114-119), Courlander (1971: 121-131) and Yava (1978: 100-104), I have recorded four such myths, one of which features Coyote on a visit to the afterworld.

Hin Huk'ovi Kiiqöti

Aliksa'i. Yaw Pivanhonkyape yeesiwa. Pu' yaw pay put atpip
Huk'ove piw yeesiwa. Pay yaw pep nan'ip sinom pay wukoyese.
Noq yep Pivanhonkyape yaw hak tiyo ki'yta, suhimutiyo yaw haki'.
Pu' Huk'ove piw yaw hak maana ki'yta. Noq i' Huk'ove maana yaw
Pivanhonkyape tiyot aw tungla'yta. Noq pay yaw i' tiyo pas piw put
maanat qa naawakna. Pay yaw as i' maana pi'ep aw hinwat tuwanta-
ngwuniqw pay yaw pas qa aw uunati.

Pay yaw as pam maana qa suus haqam put tiyot aw pituuqe yaw
oovi as aw naap yu'a'aykungwuniqw pay yaw pam tiyo pas qa hisat
aw hingqawu. Pu' yaw mihikqw pu' yaw pam maana ephaqam
hakiywat tiyot ayatangwu yaw as pam put tiyot kiiyat aqw engem

The Abandonment of Huk'ovi

Aliksa'i. They say people were living at Pivanhonkyapi. Below this place, at Huk'ovi, was another settlement. Both villages had a lot of people. At Pivanhonkyapi lived a young man who was very handsome. And at Huk'ovi lived a girl who wanted the boy from Pivanhonkyapi. But he did not care for her at all. The girl had tried repeatedly to get him, but he never gave in to her.

More than once, the girl had encountered the boy and spoken to him without being prompted, but he had never answered her. Occasionally, at night she would tell another youth to bring that boy over to her house. When informed of his mission, the Pivanhonkyapi boy refused to go and at times actually became angry. "No way will I go

wiktoniqat. Noq pu' yaw pam hak oovi pangsoq put wiktoqat yaw as aw pangqawqw pay yaw pam pas qa nakwhangwuniiqe ephaqam pay yaw itsivutingwu. "Son pi nu' pangsoqhaqaminiqw piw uumi pan naawakna. Oovi um aw pangqawqw pay paapu qa hakiy angqw ayalawmantani," yan yaw pam haqawat aw lavaytingwu.

Noq yep Pivanhonkyape kya pi puma saqtivangwu. Noq put yaw aqw haykyawta piiwu. Pephaqam tump puma yaw saqtiva-ngwuniqw pang yaw pas tumpoq owat ang naalöp qölöwyungwa. Pang puma it löqöt yaw hongnatotangwu saqtivaninik. Noq pep yaw puma put angk haykyalaya, saqtivaniqat. Niiqe yaw oovi puma kya pi yungya. Niiqe pu' yaw puma kivaapeq tsootsongyangwu, naa-nawaknangwu.

Qavongvaqw pu' yaw i' tiyo yumuy amungem komokto. Noq pu' yaw yangqw Huk'ongaqw i' maana piw yaw su'ep kur komokto. Sunaasaq yaw puma oovi komokto. Noq yaw i' tiyo haqami komok-toqey yaw pep kootinuma. Noq naat yaw pam oovi pep kootinumqw yaw hak haqaqw aw hingwawu, "Taaqay," yaw kita.

Pu' yaw pam aw yorikqw yaw kur hak maana. Noq yaw pam put hakiy maanat pay qa tuwi'yta. Noq pam yaw kur Huk'ongaqw. Pay yaw pam qa aw hingqawniqe pu' yaw pay pam aapiy. Pu' yaw piw angqw hingqawu, "Ya nu' pas nuutsel'ewayniqw oovi um inungaqw waayay?" yaw aw kita. Piw yaw pam qa aw hingqawu. Pu' yaw piw, "Ya nu' pas so'wuutit an soniwqw oovi um inungaqw waytiwnu-may?" pu' yaw yanwat piw.

Pas paasat pu' yaw i' tiyo aw pangqawu, "Qa'ey," yaw aw kita, "pay um as lomamanay," yaw aw kita.

"Noq um hintiqw pas inungaqw sonqa waayangwu?" yaw aw kita. "Pay nu' navoti'yta um pu' komoktoniqw oovi nu' ung yep nuutaytay," yaw pam maana aw kita. "Noq oovi itam pay haak qa kolawqw um pewniy," yaw pam maana put aw kita. "Um pewnen inuupe haalaytiniy," yaw aw kita.

"So'on piniy," pu' yaw i' tiyo kitaaqe pay yaw qa nakwha. "Son pi nu' panhaqam hintsakni. Itam pep itaakiy ep hiita angk hoyoyota. Noq son nu' oovi panhaqam hintsakniy," yaw aw kitaaqe pas yaw qa hin nakwha. I' tiyo pi yaw kiy ep nuutum put wunimangwu, saqti-vaqö'. Pam yaw suukyawa. It yaw pam lavaytiqe yaw oovi qa nakw-ha.

"Pay pi son hintiniy," pu' yaw pam maana as piw aw kita. "Pay pi itam qa hakiy aa'awnaqw son pi hak navotniy," pu' yaw as piw aw yanwat.

to her place, and yet she has the nerve to ask you to get me there. So tell her not to have anyone else come after me any more." This is how he used to react to the girl's invitation.

Pivanhonkyapi was a village that frequently staged the Ladder Dance. Once again, this event was close at hand. Right at the rim of the mesa where the dance was usually performed were four holes in the bedrock. Into these holes, trunks of pine trees were inserted whenever the ceremony was to be held. As the day for the Ladder Dance was drawing near, the participants retreated into their kiva to go through their more esoteric rites. There they would smoke ritually and chant prayers.

The morning after the ceremony got under way, the youth set out to fetch firewood for his parents. By chance that very day the girl from Huk'ovi, too, was going out for wood. The two went at the same time. The boy was already gathering fuel in the area where he intended to prepare his load. He was just going about his business when, all of a sudden, someone spoke to him. "Man," a voice said.

When he looked up to see who it was, he noticed that it was a young woman he did not know. Evidently she was from Huk'ovi. As he had no intention of speaking to her, he wandered off. Again she spoke. "Am I so ugly that you must run away from me?" she inquired. "Do I look so much like an old woman that you're avoiding me?"

At long last the boy replied. "No," he said, "you're a pretty girl."

"Then why do you move away from me? I knew that you were coming here to fetch firewood. That's why I came to wait for your arrival," the girl explained. "Stop gathering wood for a while, and come here to me," the girl invited the youth. "Come over here and enjoy yourself on me. You can have my body."

"Oh no," the boy exclaimed, refusing. "I can't do such a thing. At our village we are nearing an important event. For that reason I can't be doing that," he said, vehemently rejecting the girl's offer. After all, he was going to participate in the Ladder dance. He was one of the men selected to climb on the pole. This he pointed out to the girl as he turned down her offer.

"Don't worry, it'll be all right," the girl assured him. "If we don't tell anyone, no one will know."

"Pay kya nu' son nakwhaniy," yaw aw kita. "Taq tooki pay puma tsovaltiqe pay pi inungem enang sonqa hin pasiwnayaqw oovi pay nu' son pantiniy," yaw aw kita.

Pu' yaw pay pam maana as pi'ep hinwat piwningwu. Pan yaw as aw natsop'ö'qala. Pay yaw pam tiyo pas qa uunati. Yaw qa uunatit pu' yaw pay pam komokiy iikwiltat pu' yaw pam pangqw nima.

Pangqaqw pu' yaw maana itsivu'iwkyangw nima. Qa aw tiyo unangwtapqw pavan yaw pam itsivu'iwkyangw pangqaqw kiy tuwat awi'. Naat yaw pas oovi pam itsivu'iwkyangw pituuqe yaw pangqawu, "Pay nu' pas kur hin qa hinwat yukunani. Pas nu' yan itsivu'iwkyangw pitu," yaw pam naami kita.

Pu' yaw pam tiyo pituqw paasat pay yaw kur puma put ang hongnatota, uuyiyamuy. Put ang puma yayvat pu' tiivangwu. Noq pam hapi pay oovi ang hoongi. Paasat pu' ep mihikqw i' maana tuwat pi naat itsivu'iwtaqe pay yaw pas kur hin put tiyot qa hinwat yukunani. Noq pam pi yaw powaqmana kur piw, a'ni yaw pam hak tuhisa. Paasat pu' yaw pam tuwat ep mihikqw hiita pi sonqa tumala'yta. Niiqe pu' yaw pam pep Pivanhonkyapiy ep sukw qölöt aqw uuyit pakiwtaqat yaw pam yooha, pay pi a'ni himuniiqe'. Pay hin pi yaw pam put piw yooha. Pantiqw pu' hapi yaw i' tiyo pay sonqa posni. Noq pam qölö hapi yaw kwanakye' pu' yaw paasat pam lestavi put ang pam tiyo wuviwtaqw put yaw pam enang pangsoq tumpoq posni. Yan yaw pam put aw naa'oyniqe oovi put yooha.

Qavongvaqw pu' yaw ep pay suus qa himu. Ep yaw oovi piw taataqt kivaapeq tsovawtaqw yaw Kookyangwso'wuuti ep pitu. Pituuqe pu' kivayamuy paki. Pu' yaw amumi pangqawu, "Yangqw Huk'ongaqw maana sukw umuuqölöy aqw umuu'uyiy pakiwtaqat yoohay," yaw amumi kita. "Noq uma oovi awye' uma ahoy aw yukuyani; son hapi pam pantaniy," yaw amumi kita. "It uma akw aw yukuyaniy," yaw kitat pu' yaw pam amumi pay hiita wutaq'iwtaqat tavi. "Pay uma umuu'uyiy angqw tsoopayat pu' it uma ang lelwiyaqw pay sonqa huurtini," yaw kita amumi'.

"Antsa kya'iy," pu' yaw kitota pepeq taataqtniiqe pu' yaw puma hiisa'niiqam angqw awya. Pu' yaw antsa puma put pas sustumpoqniiqat tsoopaya. Pu' yaw puma ang hepyaqw pay yaw kur pas antsa yoohiwta. Paasat pu' yaw puma put so'wuutit ngahuyat ang lelwiya. Pantotit pu' yaw ahoy piw uuyiy aqw panayat pu' aqw huurtota. Yantoti yaw pumanit pu' ahoy piw kivay awya. Pu' puma ep mihikqw piw naat hintsatskyat pu' piw tookya.

Qavongvaqw pu' piktotokpe piw yaw ep Kookyangwso'wuuti

"I don't think I'll go along with you," the boy insisted. "Last night the men already had their first assembly. They most certainly included me in their ceremonial plans. Therefore I cannot do what you ask."

Again and again the girl pressed the boy, each time in a different manner. Over and over she urged him to have intercourse with her. But he would not be swayed. Without giving in to her temptations, he picked up his bundle of firewood and departed for home.

The girl also headed home. She was furious that she had been rejected. She was still in this frame of mind when she arrived home. "One way or another I'm going to fix him," she said to herself. "I've come back seething with anger, so I'll do something about it," she vowed.

When the boy returned to Pivanhonkyapi, the pine trees had already been erected. These the kachinas would climb to dance on, so they were all set up. That evening the girl was still fuming. She was determined to do something to that boy. And she would find a way, for she was a witch and a master at her craft. So that night she worked on her plan. By using her magic powers she caused a crack in one of the holes into which the pine poles had been inserted. Yes, she was skilled at her sorcery. Who knows how she accomplished this, but now she was certain the boy would fall. With a crack running though the hole, the pole would give way and crash down over the rim with the boy still on it. This was how she would get her revenge.

The following day was called Suus Qa Himu, as nothing special happens on this day, three days prior to the ceremonial climax. The men were gathered within their kiva when quite unexpectedly, Old Spider Woman called on them. She entered their kiva and said, "A girl from Huk'ovi has caused a crack alongside the hole in which your tree is planted. I urge you to go over and fix it. It can't stay the way it is," she warned them. "Here, take this to mend the crack." With that, she handed the men a mushy paste, and instructed them, "Pull out the pole and repair the damage."

"Perhaps this is true," some of the men said as they proceeded to the dance site. They removed the pole closest to the mesa rim. Sure enough, they discovered that the hole was cracked. They took the magic medicine Old Spider Woman had given them and plastered it over the crack. They then replaced the tree and made sure that it held fast. That done, they returned to their kiva. Once more that night they carried out their ritual, and then they slept.

pitu. "Pay piw sukwata," yaw amumi kita. "Uma oovi piw awye' piw
aw yukuyani." Pu' pay yaw piw put hiita amumi tavi.

Pu' puma oovi piw awyaqe pu' piw aw yukuya. Pay yaw antsa
kur piw yoypu. Pu' yaw puma put aw piw yukuyat pu' aqw ahoy
paas uuyiy panayat pu' aqw huurtota. Pu' yaw pay aapiy piw löös
puma mimuywatuy aw yukuya. Pam yaw kur soosok put yongoyta.

Pantoti yawniqw pu' yaw aw talöngvay, tiikimii'. Pu' yaw Pivanhonkyape sinom pu' Huk'ongaqw piw peetu tiimaywisa. Kyaasta
yaw sinom. Pu' yaw antsa talavay katsinam nönga. Pu' yaw puma
kiisonmiyaqe pu' yaw aw pitsinaya, tiiva. Kwangwativa yaw,
kwangwatötöqa. Paasat pu' lööyöm kya pi put pep ang mooti wuuvi.
Lööyöm yaw put ang pantingwu. Ang wuuve' pu' pepeq ooveq
taawit an pu' puma hiihin wunimangwu, pangqe oovaqe put löqöt
ooveq. Pas pi yaw himuwa ooveq ngu'ykyangw pu' angqw haayiwtangwu, tumpoqwat. Pu' piw yaw angqe kwangwariyayatangwu. Pu'
pay ang naahoy wungwupkyangw haahawngwu. Pay yaw hiihin
puma put ang wunimangwu. Uru, yaw tatkyaqöymiqhaqami', qa
ngas'ew yaw puma hin suusuykyangw put ang pantsakngwu.

Pu' yaw himuwa sukw uuyit angqw piw ayo'wat aw tso'omtingwu, pay yaw piw kwangwangu'angwu. Pu' yaw pepwat put piw
epningwu, kwangwariyayatangwu angqe. Pu' ephaqam yaw pas
sunaasaq naahoy tso'omte' pas oova puuyawmakyangw naasaw-
vangwu. Pu' yaw puma pante' suupan yaw puma naamiq ongok-
niqat antingwu. Pu' yaw sinom tiitimayyaqam yaw sa'akmangwu.
Yaw a'ni töqtotingwu. Pantsatskya yaw puma pephaqamo.
Kwangwavususuta yawi', kwangwarukukuta. Pu' yaw ayayatoy-
nayaqw putakw yaw piw enang pay pavan hin töötöqa.

Pan yaw pumawat mootiwatniiqam yukuqw paasat pu' yaw i'
tiyo piw sukwwat amum tuwat ang wuuvi. Pu' yaw piw amun puma
put ang pantsaki. Pay yaw qa himu hinwat hintiqw yaw taawanasapti. Taawanasaptiw pu' yaw puma nöswisa. Pay yaw oovi kivay
ahoy awya. Pangsoq yaw puma oovi yungya. Pu' yaw puma nöönösaqe pu' pay nasungwni'yyungwa. Noq pangqw yaw kivangaqw pu'
i' mongwi hom'oytoqe yama. Yamakqe pu' yaw haqam pi son pam
qa hom'oyto. Pam pangsoniqw pu' yaw i' powaqmana yaw kur
navota, pay yaw kur hak ahoy qölöyamuy aw yukuuta. Pay pi son
hin piw aw qa pootaqe pay yaw kur navota. Niiqe yaw pam itsivutiqe yaw pangqawu, "Pay kur piw hak aw yukuy", yaw kita. "Noq
pay nu' son naat qa piw hinwatniy," yaw kitaaqe pu' yaw naat
katsinam kivaapeyaqw pu' yaw pam pepeq kivaapeq piw tuhisay

The next day, on Piktotokya, Old Spider Woman showed up again. "The witch has done it again," she informed the men. "Therefore, go over and mend the crack." And as before she handed them something.

The men did as bidden. They went to the ladder hole. Sure enough, there was a new fissure in the rock. After repairing the damage as they had done the previous time, they fastened the pole. Twice more the men had to repeat this routine as they fixed the remaining holes. Apparently, the girl had caused cracks in all of them.

By now the day of the dance was at hand. The people of Pivanhonkyapi and some from Huk'ovi went to see the event. There was a crowd of spectators gathered. And, indeed, the kachinas came out in the morning. They headed to the plaza and began their performance. They danced beautifully and uttered cries which were pleasing to the onlookers. Presently, two of the kachinas proceeded to climb the poles. It was customary for two to do so at the same time, and dance on the top of the poles. Next, one would hold on to something at the top and, hanging downward, swing out to the mesa edge to the beat of the chanting. And then he would spin nicely round and round the pole. Up and down the dancers climbed. They performed all sorts of acrobatic acts up there. And in spite of the steep drop-off on the south side, not one of them ever got dizzy.

Now one dancer would jump from one post to another, skillfully grabbing it. There he would repeat this performance, spinning nicely around the pole. At times the kachinas exchanged poles by jumping simultaneously from one to the next, crossing each other in mid-air. When they jumped, it appeared as if they were going to collide. Whenever this happened, the spectators below roared. The screaming from the crowd was deafening. This is what happened there during the Ladder Dance. In addition, there were the pleasant sound of the drum and the grating noise of the bone scapulae as they were scraped across the notched sticks. The kachinas shaking their rattles added to this symphony of sounds.

When the first kachina pair had finished, it was the boy's turn. He, too, climbed the pole with a companion. They performed just as the first two did. None of the dancers were hurt, and the dancing continued until noon, when the men took a break to eat. They returned to their kiva and descended into this underground chamber. Having eaten lunch, they sat around resting. Meanwhile, the leader of the ceremony left for a shrine to deposit prayer feathers and sacred

akw lestavit qöhikna. Epeq yaw taataqt tangawkyaakyangw yaw qa
nanapta lestavi qöhikqw. Naat yaw oovi puma panyungqw pay yaw
pam pumuy aw saapu. Lestavi yaw qöhikkyangw soosokmuy
kivaapeq tangawtaqamuy amumi saapu.

Pu' yaw as puma pangqw okiw nöngakniniqw pay hak pi hiisavo hintsakt pay hikwismokngwu. Pu' yaw oove sinom nanaptaqe
pu' as angqw ayo' hiita maspitotakyangw pay yaw puma put qa
angqw ayo' soosok maspayaqw pay yaw soosoyam puma pangsoq
so'a. Pu' yaw pep sinom tsaykita. Pas pi yaw hin unangwa, pavan
yaw puma qatsitota. Pas yaw pep ki'yyungqam soosoyam haqawatuy
kwayya pangsoq kivamiq.

Yanhaqam yaw puma pep qa kwangwa'ewtota. Niiqe pay yaw
oovi pangso tiitso'a. Paasat pu' yaw ima Huk'ovit pay pangqw ninma, puma pep tiimaymayaqam. Pu' yaw okiw ima Pivanhonkyapit
qa haalayya. Noq Huk'ovewat sinom pay yaw qa hin unangwa'y-
yungwa, pumuy pi pay amungaqw qa hak hintiqw.

Yantoti yaw puma pep'e. Pu' yaw yan mihi. Mihikqw pu' yaw
pay qa hak yaw haqe' waynuma, naat pi yaw son haalayya sinomuy
kwa'yyaqe oovi. Noq i' yaw hak suukya taaqa qa kiy ep pakiwtaqe
yaw kiy ooveq qatu. Noq angqw atkyaqw yaw qööhi maatsilti. Niikyangw yaw Pivanhonkyapiy su'aqw yaw hoyoyota. Pay yaw pas
suupangsoq hoyoyotat pu' pay yaw hintiqe pu' yaw pay piw suuta-
töqwat ahoy. Pangqw pu' yaw piw ahoy su'aqw. Pay yaw pantsakma
pam pangqw qööhi. Noq pam yaw aqw tayta. Pay yaw hiihintsak-
tima. Naanahoy yaw leeletstima. Panmakyangw yaw aw tupohaqami'i. Naat yaw pam oovi pepeq yantaqw pay yaw angqaqw wuuvi.
Pay yaw kur pas qööhi. Pu' yaw pang Pivanhonkyapiy qaqlava yaw
hintsakma. Niiqe pas yaw pam put oovi qönilti. Pu' yaw pas ang
kiinawit kuyva. Pantit pu' yaw angqw kiisonmi'. Kiisonve pu' yaw
pahokit yaw ep huruuti. Niikyangw piw yaw kur wuuti. Pep yaw
pam qatuwkyangw yaw hingqawlawu. Noq yaw pam aw taytaqw
pas yaw pam a'ni hin soniwa, nuutsel'eway yawi'. Noq pam yaw kur
Tiikuywuuti.

Pu' yaw kur pam pep qatuwkyangw yaw put taaqat tuwa. Pu'
yaw pam put aw pangqawu, "Um pewniy," yaw aw kita. Noq pi yaw
nuutsel'eway. Pay yaw pam oovi qa suutaq'ewa awniqe. "Pay um
nuy qa mamqast pewniy. Pay nu' son ung hintsanniy," yaw aw kita.

Pu' yaw pam oovi put aw haawi. Pam yaw aw pituqw pu' yaw
pam put aw pangqawu, "Pay nu' navotqe oovi angqö," yaw aw kita.
"Uma hapi yep hiniwtapnayaqw nu' put navotqe nu' umuy ookwa-

cornmeal. As he went on this mission, the witch girl overheard that the damaged holes had been mended. To find out for sure, she went to see for herself. When she noticed that they had indeed been repaired, she grew angry. "Oh no! Darn it. Someone fixed the cracks. There's got to be another way," she swore. So, by means of her witchcraft, she broke one of the roof beams in the kiva where the kachinas were. They had no inkling that the beam had been broken. Thus, they were still resting there when the roof suddenly caved in. As it broke it crashed down on all those inside.

Everyone tried to get out, but soon died of suffocation. The people on top, aware of the disaster, came scrambling and cleared away the debris. But it was to no avail. All the men had already perished. How the people lamented! They were in hysterics about the terrible event. What a day of horror it was! Each of the villagers lost at least one relative or acquaintance in this tragedy.

Now the fun was gone. The dance performance was terminated and the spectators from Huk'ovi returned home. The people of Pivanhonkyapi were all saddened and grieving. This was not so with the Huk'ovis, for they had not lost anyone to this calamity.

This is what took place at Pivanhonkyapi. As night fell no one could be found wandering about, for most of the people had lost a loved one and were sad. It so happened, however, that one man was not in his house, but was sitting outside on top of the roof. All of a sudden, from down in the plain a light became visible. It was coming straight toward Pivanhonkyapi. At some point, however, it went back toward the south, then again reversed its course and headed for the village. This is what the flame was doing. The man kept watching. It was really strange to him that it was going back and forth. Finally, it disappeared below the mesa edge. The man was still sitting there when it came up the mesa. It really was a fire. It continued along the outskirts of Pivanhonkyapi and made a complete circuit around it. Then it appeared in the village and entered the plaza. Then it stopped at the shrine. To his amazement, the man now discovered that it was a woman. As she rested there, she muttered something. She was terrifying to look upon. Apparently, she was Tiikuywuuti.

As she sat at the shrine she spotted him. Beckoning to him she said, "Come here to me." She was so ugly, however, that he hesitated to approach her. "Don't be afraid of me. I won't harm you," she assured him.

The man came down from the housetop. When he reached the

tuwqe oovi angqö. Noq pay nu' navoti'yta hak put pantiqw'öy," yaw aw kita. "Yep i' Huk'ove powaqmana yep tiyot aw tungla'ytaqw pam put qa aw unangwtapqw pam put ep itsivutiqe oovi pam pas paasa'niiqamuy qöyay," yaw kita. "Noq pay pi uma naanawaknaqw nu' umungem aw naa'oyniy," yaw aw kita. "Kur uma naanawakne' qaavo uma inungem hiisa'niiqam paahototat pay uma yep o'yaqw pay nu' paasat aw pitsinaniy," yaw pam put aw kita. Pay yaw panis aw kitat pu' pay yaw piw qööhit akw ahoy aqwhaqami'. Pu' yaw aqwhaqami hawmat pu' yaw ang pay piw an aqwhaqami hiihintsakma. Hisatniqw pu' yaw teevengehaqami'.

Yan yaw pam hak pep taaqa yori pam himu put aw pituqw. Qavongvaqw pu' yaw pam kiinawit hiisa' ep akwsingqamuy amuupa nakwsuqe pu' yaw pumuy yan aa'awna. Pu' yaw pam pep kiinawit put tuu'awnuma pan himu put aw pangqawqat. Pu' yaw pay kur naanakwhaqe pu' yaw oovi puma hiisa'niiqam son pi qa paahototaqw pu' yaw pam put kiisonmi kima. Pep pu' yaw pam put pahokit aqw oya. Yan yaw pam pep hinti. Taalö' yaw pam pep put hom'oya. Pantiqw pu' yaw piw tapkikyangw pu' mihi. Pu' yaw qa hak paasat puuwi. Sinom yaw kits'ova tsokiwyungwa, hiita nuutayyungwa hapi.

Pay yaw oovi pas lomamihikqw pu' yaw angqaqw atkyangahaqaqw piw maatsilti. Pang pu' yaw piw hiihintsakma pam qööhi. Pay as hinte' pas Pivanhonkyapiy su'aqwnit pu' pay piw poniltingwu. Pantsakma yaw pam pangqwniikyangw pu' yaw pay ayo' huk'omiwatniiqe pu' pep piw put angqe pas qöniwma. Pep put kitsokit angqe pas qöniltit pu' yaw kiisonmi paki. Pu' yaw pam pep ngumanta. Hiita yaw tawkyangw pam pep yaw kiisonve ngumanta. Niiqe yanhaqam yaw pam tawma:

Tutaahe, tutaahe.
Tutavunaahe, tutavunaahe.
Heh, heh, heh, heh.

Kitangwu yaw. Pay yaw panis kitat pu' yaw pay piw angqw kiisongaqw teevengehaqami ahoy.

Noq pay yaw kur peetu sinom nanapta pep himu hingqawlawqw. Pu' yaw as peetu angqw aqw suukukuyvaqw pay yaw paasat pam teevenge piw pan qööhisa hoyoyota. Paasat pu' yaw puma pangqaqwa, pep sinom nanaptaqam, "Ya himu yep pitu? Noq naap hisat kya qaavo piwniniqw paapu itam moqmani'yyungwni. Itam qaavo paapu moqmani'yyungwe' itam hiita ngu'ayaniy," yaw kitota.

monstrous woman she said to him, "I've heard what happened here. That's why I've come. I took pity on you. I know the person who is responsible for the tragedy that took place here. She is a witch girl from Huk'ovi who is full of desire for a young man here. When he remained steadfast and refused to submit to her, she grew so angry that she killed all those men. But if you so wish, I will take revenge for you. If that is your desire, I want some of you to make prayer sticks for me and deposit them here at this shrine. I will then take on this task." This was all the woman said, whereupon she departed, using the fire as a cover. She descended over the mesa rim and, following the same zigzag course, disappeared in a southwesterly direction.

This was what the man experienced in his encounter with the ghastly being. The next morning he went about the village among the survivors, telling them what he had learned, and conveying to the others the instructions Tiikuywuuti had left with him. The men agreed with her proposal, and some of them set to making prayer feathers. It was still daylight when the man who had first seen her took them to the shrine on the plaza. But gradually day turned to late evening and then darkness fell. No one was asleep. The people were crowded on the rooftops, waiting for the things to come.

It was late at night when, once again, the flame made its appearance down below. Once more it approached in a zigzag line. Every so often it seemed to head straight for Pivanhonkyapi, but then it turned in the opposite direction again. Finally, it approached Huk'ovi. The fire circled the village and then entered the plaza. There the monster woman went through the motions of grinding corn and singing:

Tutaahe, tutaahe.
Tutaavunaahe, tutaavunaahe.
Heh, heh, heh, heh.

These were the only sounds she uttered. Thereupon she made her way out of the plaza and headed west.

Some of the Huk'ovi people apparently had heard the chanting of the creature, because they came out of their houses to see what all the commotion was about. Some ran to the same direction the creature had taken, but by now she was already moving southwest in the guise of a flame. Those who heard the strange song asked each other, "Who on earth was that creature? It might return, so let's plan an ambush. We can lie in wait tomorrow and then grab it."

Pu' yaw oovi puma hiisa'niiqam naanakwhaqe pu' qavongvaqw mihikmi pu' yaw natsvalaya. Pu' yaw antsa pay piw aasathaqamti. Pay lomamihikqw pu' yaw pay angqw piw hoyta. Pu' pay piw antsakmakyangw pu' piw kiisonmi paki. Pu' yaw pay piw anti. Pay put yaw piw tawkyangw pep ngumantat pu' yaw oovi ahoyniqw pu' yaw puma pang na'uyi'yyungqam pu' aw yuutu. Pu' yaw as himuwa aw warikye' pay yaw tsawne' pay paasat ahoy waayangwu. Pi a'ni yaw himu soniwqw oovi; nuutsel'eway yawi'. Pas pi yaw kori'vo'yta. Pu' yaw sutsiirumta.

Pay yaw kur son puma put aw ökini. Pay yaw himuwa panis tuwat pu' pay piw ahoy waayangwu. Yan pay yaw puma put piw qa ngu'aya. Pu' yaw pay pam piw aqwhaqami ahoy. Noq ima tuwat Pivanhonkyapewat sinom pangqw aw taayungwa. Susmataq puma put qööhit tuwa'yyungwa. Noq pay yaw ima Huk'ove sinom pay as mootiniqw qa pas aw hin wuuwayaqw pu' pay pan löösta. Pu' yaw aapiy pam pangso pantsaki. Aasakis yaw mihikqw pay yaw piw ep pitungwu. Pu' piw pep kiisonve pan ngumantat pu' pay piw ahoyningwu. Pu' pay yaw puma put aw hin wuuwaya. "Pay pi son i' qa hintiqw pew sasqay," yaw kitota pep sinom. "Noq pay pi itam kur hin ngu'ayani. Pas himu nuutsel'eway'oy." Pay yaayan kya pi naapa hingqawnumya puma pep sinom.

Nuwu pay hapi yaw naalösta, nungwu tsivotsikista. Yaw qa hin pam himu pumuy maatapniqey unangwa'yta. Paasat pu' yaw nawus pep Huk'ove momngwit tsovaltiqe yaw pangqaqwa, "Pay i' himu pew sasqaqa pas sumataq itamuy qa maatapniy," yaw kitota. "Noq pay pi son pam qa hintiqw oovi pew sasqaqw pay tsangaw naat itamuy qa hintsana. Noq pay itam oovi yangqw aapiyyaniy," yaw kitota. "Pay itam yangqw aapiyye' pay pi itam nawus haqam piw kya as qatsitutwaniy," yaw puma momngwit kitota.

Pu' yaw puma pay sun unangwtoti. "Ta'ay," yaw kitota, "pay itam pas qaavo payyani." Pay puma pas oovi aw suptsinaya. Pu' kya pi oovi pay puma qavongvaqw taalawvaqw pu' pay pangqw tee- vengewat nankwusa. Haqami pu' mihiknayaqe pu' yaw pep yesva.

Pu' yaw ep mihikqw pay yaw piw qööhi angqw atkyangaqw amumiq hoyta. Pu' yaw puma haqam tsovawtaqw pay yaw as pumuy tuwakyangw pay yaw pumuy amuqle'niikyangw pay yaw naat piw kiimi'i. Ep pituuqe pu' pep soosovik poota. Hakiy pi songqe heeva naap hisat pi yaw hak ep akwsingqw put yaw hapi pam amungk laalayniqe oovi. Noq pay yaw qa hak haqam. Pay yaw kur soosoyam watqa. Pangqw pu' yaw pam ahoy amumiq.

The following evening those who had agreed to this plan assembled. Finally, the right time came. It was well into the night when the creature approached. It behaved as on the previous occasion, and then entered the plaza. As before, the Tiikuywuuti went through the grinding motions, and once again, she accompanied her grinding with the same eerie song. When she finished and was about to depart, those who lay in hiding rushed upon her. But as the men converged on her, they became terrified and fled in fright, understandably so, for she was a horrifying creature and exceedingly hideous. Her eyes were two hollow pits and her teeth were bared.

The men simply could not get near her. As soon as a person's eyes fell on her, he became frightened and ran. And so she escaped again, taking the same route as before. The people of Pivanhonkyapi watched her from afar. They could easily discern the flame. The Huk'ovi men, at first, did not pay heed to the fire; but then it happened a second time. This occurrence now repeated itself on a regular basis. Each night the creature made its nocturnal visit. It would grind in the plaza, and then return where it came from. The people wondered why all this was going on. "She's coming here for a reason," they kept saying. "We must catch her by any means, this ugly demon."

Meanwhile, four days went by, then five days. Still, the creature did not let them be. Seeing this, the leaders of Huk'ovi gathered and said, "This thing which keeps coming here will not leave us alone. Perhaps it has a purpose for doing this. We must be thankful that it hasn't harmed anyone yet. So let's move away from here," they decided. "We're bound to find a place to live somewhere else." And, therefore the leaders agreed to abandon the village.

Everyone agreed with the decision. "All right," they said, "we'll go tomorrow." Immediately they began to prepare for the exodus. The next morning, at the crack of dawn, the people started out in a southwesterly direction. When darkness fell, they made camp.

Once more the flame came from the plain. It seemed to be coming straight for them. When it spotted them where they were gathered, it moved past them and on toward their village. There the creature inspected everything. It was looking to see if, perchance, someone had remained behind who needed to be driven out. But not a soul was left, and the fire headed back toward the Huk'ovis.

Pu' yaw puma put qööhit tutwaqe pay yaw paasat piw nankwusa, naamahin pi yaw mihikiwta. Pangqaqw yaw pam pumuy layma,
qööhi. Haqami pu' yaw puma taalawnaya. Paasat pay yaw pam qööhi kur piw haqami. Qavongvaqw mihikqw pu' pay yaw piw amungk
nakwsu. Pay yaw pam sutsep oovi pangqe' pumuy laynuma. Pay
yaw pas mihikqw pu' yaw amungkningwu.
     Pu' yaw puma nawus hoyoyotangwu. Panmakyangw pu' yaw
pam pumuy maatavi. Pepeq kya pi pam himu ki'yta. Pangso yaw
pam pumuy Huk'ovituy ökinat pu' maatavi. Noq pay yaw puma
Huk'ovit pas qa huruutotiqe pay yaw puma pas oovi sutsepnankwu-
sa. Niiqe puma yaw haqami ökiiqe pepehaq pu' pas piw kitsoktota.
Pepehaq pu' yaw oovi Huk'opsinom yeese. Put hapi yaw puma hakiy
powaqmanat atsviy pangqw aapiyyaqw oovi pu' Huk'ove kiiqö. Pay
yuk pölö.

When the people of Huk'ovi spotted the fire, they got up and trekked on again, even though it was night. By the time the morning came, the creature disappeared. However, the next evening it was back and followed them anew. Wherever the people turned, it prodded them on, usually at night.

So the people had no choice but to move on. Finally, at a certain place the Tiikuywuuti let go of them. Apparently she had her abode there. The Huk'ovis, however, did not settle there but continued on. Eventually, they reached a site where they established a settlement. There, far away from their previous homes, the people of Huk'ovi were living now. Thus, it was because of a witch girl that the village of Huk'ovi was abandoned and fell into ruin. And here the story ends.

6

The End of Hovi'itstuyqa

Hovi'itstuyqa is the Hopi place name for Mount Elden, a ridge-shaped volcanic dome along the southern flank of the San Francisco Mountains near Flagstaff, Arizona. Distinguished by thick, pasty extrusions of hardened magma, its promontory features a little point that juts skyward. This topographical configuration, which is clearly discernible against the horizon as one approaches the mountain from the northeast, apparently reminded the Hopi of "buttocks" (*hoovi*) "sticking out" (*itsta*), for this is what Hovi'itstuyqa implies: "Buttock sticking out point."

To date, it has been impossible to positively locate the ruin site associated with the place name. Nequatewa, who published the only other version on the demise of Hovi'itstuyqa (1938: 37), believed that it was identical with Elden Pueblo at the foot of Mount Elden in Flagstaff. However, Eldén Pueblo after which the archaeological period between A.D. 1130 and 1200 has been named Elden Phase, is generally known as Pasiwvi to the Hopi (Pilles in Malotki and Lomatuway'-ma 1987: 115). During the Elden Phase, termed the "Golden Age of the Sinagua" culture by Pilles, the Sinagua populated the entire region from Wupatki to the north, Anderson Mesa to the east, and the Verde Valley to the south of the San Francisco Mountains. Farmer has consequently suggested (1955: 44) that Hovi'itstuyqa could have been one of many sites known to have been occupied in late prehistoric times in the Flagstaff area (Turkey Hill Pueblo 1150 to 1200 A.D. and Old Caves Pueblo 1250 to 1300 A.D.), along Anderson Mesa (Kinnikinick Pueblo 1200 to 1325 A.D., Grape Vine Pueblo 1300 to 1400 A.D., and the Pollock Site 1250 to 1325 A.D.), and in the Verde Valley (Montezuma Castle, which was occupied as late as 1425 A.D.).

According to the present legend, Tupats'ovi, the home village of the protagonist, was situated on Nuvakwewtaqa, the Hopi name for the Chavez Pass area approximately one hundred miles south of the Hopi mesas. On the basis of archaeological evidence indicating that Chavez Pass and Anderson Mesa were inhabited at the same time, Farmer decided on Grape Vine Pueblo as a possible candidate for Hovi'itstuyqa. However, since Grape Vine Pueblo has not been excavated to date, its identification with Hovi'itstuyqa must remain unsubstantiated. As Farmer himself submits, "it will be of some interest some day when this site is excavated to see if there is any evidence of such a destruction" (1955: 45).

Nor has Elden Pueblo, initially explored by Fewkes in 1926 and currently being reexcavated by Pilles, yielded any archaeological clues that it was destroyed by enemies from the south, as revealed in the story. Two Hopi sherds of Jeddito Black-on-yellow with the rather late date of 1300 to 1400 A.D., recently discovered by Pilles, in his opinion, point to the possible conclusion that Elden Pueblo, first dated to about 1150 to 1200 A.D. on the basis of ceramic finds, was occupied later than originally presumed or underwent "periodic visitation by later inhabitants of the region" (Pilles 1991).

While the likelihood is rather high that the present legend garnishes a true historic event, the exact location of Hovi'itstuyqa may never be resolved satisfactorily. As to how the Hopi came to learn of the destruction of the village, one can only speculate. Sinagua people emigrating to Hopi country after the final eruption of Sunset Crater in 1250 A.D. may have transmitted word of the extinction of one of their settlements. As I have shown elsewhere (Malotki and Lomatuway'ma 1987: 9), Ka'nas, which identifies a Hopi kachina associated with Sunset Crater about ten miles north of Elden Pueblo, may be linguistic proof that some of the Sinaguas were absorbed by the Hopi. Since it is an axiom of Hopi phonological structure that native words only occur with the syllable initial sound sequence *qa, ka* in a word invariably betrays its foreign origin. Thus, nonnative Ka'nas might actually represent the ancient tribal name of the Sinagua immigrants.

Another possible scenario could be, of course, that the destruction of Hovi'itstuyqa has no historic foundation whatsoever. The Hopi's familiarity with the ruin could simply stem from the fact that they discovered it while on pilgrimage to one of the shrines located at Nuvatukya'ovi, the home of their kachina gods. The Hopi must have come across many ruin sites in this way, any one of which could have served as the inspirational departure point for the present legendary account. To satisfy their curiosity as to the possible fate of the ruin's former residents, an "explanation" came about in the form of the present mytho-historical account.

The story itself contains many of the stock ingredients distinguishing Hopi storytelling and constitutes oral entertainment at its best. Pitsinsivostiyo, or "Cotton Seed Boy," against the incredible odds of near-outcast social ranking and unattractive physiognomy, wins the girl of his dreams. He does so by meeting the condition the girl has set for accepting one of her suitors as a future mate: he must bring her a live yellow fox. Pitsinsivostiyo accomplishes this challenge with the aid of his grandmother, whose true identity is revealed as Old Spider Woman in the course of the story. When Pitsinsivostiyo's wife, who all along had really been interested in a handsome young man from Hovi'itstuyqa by the name of Sikyaatayo, "Yellow Fox," gives in to the adulterous advances of the man and follows him to his home at Hovi'itstuyqa, Pitsinsivostiyo, heartbroken over the loss of his wife, ponders revenge. He realizes his revenge when, at the suggestion of his grandmother, he manages to entice a band of mercenaries living far to the southwest of Tupats'ovi, to raid Hovi'itstuyqa and destroy its population. Pitsinsivostiyo personally kills his rival Sikyaatayo and allows his former wife to be carried off by the chief of the enemy party as one of the rewards for the insidious attack.

Although the present tale, in its main points, closely resembles the story told by Nequatewa in 1938, it is nearly four times as long. As is also the case with the other legends of this collection, when compared to previously published accounts, I attribute this difference in length to my method of tape-recording the story in the original Hopi vernacular.

Both stories agree on the proper names of the protagonist and antagonist and their respective home villages. They also concur in the appellation of the *Kisispayam*, the raider group to the southwest of Chavez Pass. The name, which is etymologically obscure, is assigned by Nequatewa to the Yavapai from the Verde Valley. None of the Hopis I consulted as to the ethnic origin or tribal affiliation of the Kisispayas was able to shed any light on this question. Farmer believes (1938: 45) that to identify them with the Yavapai "is of interest and does fit with the present trend of thinking that these groups to the west and southwest of Flagstaff may be the descendants of the people of prehistoric times, in the area, or at least that some element of the past groups is represented in the historic tribes found in the Verde Valley by the first Spanish explorers."

Unlike Nequatewa, who gives the name of the girl as Nagai-si, the girl remains unnamed in the version recorded by me.

In addition to the obvious difference in narrative length, the percentage of dialogue is larger in this version. The story is also richer in detail. Thus, the socially inferior standing of Pitsinsivostiyo, as compared to the girl he woos, receives greater emphasis. The episodes in which his grandmother explains to him how to fashion bow and arrows contain lengthy didactic passages. The actual ruse applied in trapping the fox is played out in more elaborate fashion. The scene depicting a woman anxious to satisfy her curiosity as to who might be grinding corn in the old woman's house is psychologically much more convincing than the summary statement in Nequatewa which, incidentally, shows a man in this role. A higher degree of specification also holds for the planning and execution of Pitsinsivostiyo's revenge. In one major deviation from Nequatewa's story line, the fox that is endowed with the faculty of speech and human emotions is not returned to the animal world of his peers after the discovery of the woman's adultery, but only at the very end of the tale. The entire episode, missing in Nequatewa, is highlighted by an explanation why henceforth the fox pelt will be part of the kachina costume.

Curiously enough, both stories concur in identifying Pitsinsivostiyo's grandmother as Old Spider Woman, although this narrative element is not in conformity with traditional Hopi mythology. As a rule, Old Spider Woman is portrayed as living with her grandsons Pöqangwhoya and Palöngawhoya. Nor is her abode normally confined to the toilet and refuse area of the village, as in the story here. This location may, however, be connected to the standard mode in which the earth goddess contacts a person in need of help. The initial encounter generally takes place at the time when the person is about to relieve himself inadvertently in the spot where she has her subterranean house.

Hin Hovi'itstuyqa Kiiqöti

Aliksa'i. Yaw yep Homol'oviy tatkyahaq Nuvakwewtaqay ang
yeesiwqw pep yaw pam kitsoki Tupats'ovi yan maatsiwa. Pu' yaw
ayam Nuvatukya'oviy hopqöyngaqw pep piw yaw yeesiwa; niikyangw pam pi pep Hovi'itstuyqa. Pay yaw yangqe Hopiikivaqe qa
suup piw kitsokiniqw yaw oovi yepeq suskwiningyaq pay naahayp
ima lööyöm kitsoki Orayviniqw pu' suukyawa Pivanhonkyapi yan
maatsiwa. Pu' yaw Tupats'oviy pay pas hihin hoopaqw yaw piw
suukyawa kitsokiniikyangw pamwa yaw Awat'ovi yan maatsiwa.
Noq pay yaw ima yang kitsokinawit yesqam pay yaw sun hopiitniiqe
pay yaw puma oovi naanan'i'vo hiita oovi sasqalalwangwu. Ephaqam pay yaw himuwa hiita tutkya'yte' pu' yaw pam put kima-

The End of Hovi'itstuyqa

Aliksa'i. People were living southeast of Homol'ovi. There on the ridge of Nuvakwewtaqa was a village by the name of Tupats'ovi. Way over on the northeast side of Nuvatukya'ovi, the San Francisco Mountains, there was also a settlement. It was known by the name Hovi'itstuyqa. Here in Hopi land there were villages in several locations. Far in the northwest were the two communities of Oraibi and Pivanhonkyapi situated close together. And somewhat northeast of Tupats'ovi was the village of Awat'ovi. The people at home in these villages were all Hopis. Therefore, they were wont to travel into all directions for something or other. Once in a while when a man had a particular trade item, he would come with it and barter for it in the

kyangw ang kitsokinawit huuyannakwsungwu. Pu' pay yaw ephaqam haqamwat tiikiveniqw pay yaw himuwa qa ööne' yaw aw
tiimaytongwu. Noq yan pay yaw puma peetuy tuwimu'yyungwa.

Noq pu' yaw pay piw it tuuwaqatsit aasupoq ima soosoyam
himusinom pay tuwat naap yeese. Niiqe pay yaw puma peetu piw
tuwat yukiq Hopiikimiq pan hiita himuy nahoyngwanhuuyawis-
ngwu. Niikyangw peetu yaw pay soq tuwqamniiqe pay yaw oovi
kiipokwise'sa pu' ökingwu. Noq pay yaw ima Hopiit pumuy kiiyamuy qa pas aqw sasqaya. Pay pi yaw pangqe' naala waynumqw
qatuvosniqw oovi yaw himuwa hiita oovi haqamininik pay yaw pam
qa suukw sungwa'ykyangwniqw pu' yaw puma pay pas son it tunipiy qa enang yanwisngwu. Yanhaqam yaw puma pay tuwat angqe'
qatsi'yyungwa.

Noq pu' yaw yep Tupats'ove yaw i' hak tiyo Pitsinsivostiyo yan
maatsiwqa ki'yta. Niikyangw pam yaw okiw pay panis so'ytaqe pam
yaw oovi pay put amum ki'yta. Pu' yaw puma pay piw söqavungsi-
notniiqe pay yaw puma kiitavanghaqam pay qalavehaq ki'yta. Niiqe
pay yaw oovi pu' pumuy kiiyamuy pay ahayp puma Tupats'ovit
kwayngyavi'yyungwa. Pu' yaw puma naamöm pay piw qa pas hiita
tuwa'ynumqe pay yaw ngas'ew qatuuqe pay qatu. Pay niikyangw
yaw ephaqam himuwa pay hiita himu'yte' pay yaw pumuy ookwatuwe' pu' pumuy angqw hiita himuy maqangwu. Pu' yaw pam
Pitsinsivostiyo pay okiw piw tuwat hin'ewayhoyaniqw oovi pay yaw
qa haqawa pep put aasayniqa put sungwalawu. Pay yaw pam oovi
pas sutsep nalahinnuma. Noq pay yaw piw qa hak pas pumuy
amumi suutaq'ewniiqe pay yaw oovi qa hak hisat pumuy amumiq
kiikinumto.

Noq pu' yaw pay piw pep kitsokive yaw i' hak maana pay kong-
tanisay piw tuwat qatukyangw pas yaw pam piw lomamana. Noq
pam yaw pay hakimuy pay pavansinmuy amungaqwniqw puma
yaw oovi pep kiisonviy kwiningyaqw aw ki'yyungwa. Pu' yaw pam
piw tuwat qa na'önaniiqe pam yaw oovi sutsep yuy pay engem hiita
hintsakngwu. Pu' yaw pam piw a'ni novahaskyeniiqe pay yaw pam
oovi pas sutsep noovalawqw pay yaw put yu'at qa hisat pas noovalawu. Pu' yaw pam ngumantive' pas pi yaw pam mihiknat pu' puwtongwu. Pam hapi yaw naat pay pu' puhumantikyangw pay panwat-
niiqe pay yaw oovi nanap'unangway hiita ep pisoq'iwtangwu. Pu'
hin hak yaw kiy qeni'ytangwuniqw puuvut yaw pam paas tutwi'y-
taqw oovi yaw mimawat momoyam put aw kwangwa'ytutuswa.
Panyungwni as yaw pumuy timat.

various villages. Then again, if there was a dance somewhere, and a person was not lazy, he would go see the dance. This is how people all had some acquaintances somewhere.

In turn, there were all the other Indian groups living all across the land. Some of them ventured far into Hopi territory to trade their belongings. Some were enemies and therefore only came to raid. The Hopi, as a rule, did not visit their settlements. Since it was difficult to travel in those areas on one's own, someone would go with several companions if he wanted to go somewhere for a specific purpose. Travelers then usually took some weapon along. This is about the way life was in those days.

At Tupats'ovi lived a boy by the name of Pitsinsivostiyo. The poor lad had only a grandmother, so he lived with her. The two were lower-class people and had their abode somewhere at the southwestern edge of the village, in an area used by the villagers as a dump and to relieve themselves. The grandmother and her grandchild were destitute and had hardly any food. They eked out a bare living. Once in a great while, when a villager had something to eat and felt sorry for them, he would share a portion of his food with them. In addition to being poor, Pitsinsivostiyo was quite homely. For this reason, no one of his age group befriended him. He always puttered around alone. Nobody really wanted to get acquainted with the two, which meant that they never had any visitors.

It so happened that a girl was living in the village of Tupats'ovi who was of marriageable age and exceedingly beautiful. She was a member of the influential upper class people who had their homes on the northwest side of the plaza. She was quite industrious and always did chores for her mother. Also, she was most willing to cook. Therefore she was always busy preparing a meal and her mother never had to cook. Whenever she started grinding corn, she ground long into the night before going to bed. She had just reached young womanhood, which explained why she constantly did the work of her own free will. She was so well versed in all aspects of housekeeping that all the other women were envious of her and wished they had daughters like that.

Pankyangw pu' yaw pam piw pas lomavitsangwa'ykyangw pu' piw yaw kwangw'ewakw toko'yta. Niiqe pas yaw pam oovi qa hakiy anta. Son yaw hak haqamwat kitsokive panta. Noq yantaqat akw yaw pam tuwat naatuwiwtaqw pay yaw kur angqe' ima tootim, sinom it nanapta. Pay yaw qa pepsa puma tootim it navoti'yyungwa.

Niiqe mootiniqw pay yaw as pumasa pep tootim put aw tutu-maywisngwuniqw pu' pay haqaapiy yaw ima kiyavaqtotim kur nanaptaqe pu' yaw puma pas naap pangso hin navotwisniqe pu' yaw oovi himuwa awnen pu' yaw antsa pas naap yorikqw pay yaw pas kur qa atsa. Pu' hapi yaw puma put aw sasqalalwa. Pas hapi yaw qa haqaqw kitsokingaqw yaw qa aw tootim tutumaywisngwu.

Noq pay yaw pam maana naat put manqatsiy kwangwa'iwtaqe pay yaw qa hin naat kongtaniqey unangwa'yta. Noq yaw ima tootim yaw as okiw pisoq'iwyungwa put mantuwtote' pu' nöömatotaniqey. Son pi yaw puma haqam hakiy pantaqat nukngwat maanat tutwa-niqe oovi. Pi yaw hak put amumte' sakinani.

Noq pay yaw oovi puma tootim as soosokivaqw put aw tutumay-wisngwuniiqe yaw oovi put kiiyat aqw homta. Noq pay yaw pam pas qa hakiy naawaknaqe pay yaw pam oovi as pay hiitawat aw yu'a'ay-kungwuniikyangw yaw himuwa amumtiniqey aw pangqawqw pay yaw pam paasat qa nakwhangwu. Noq haqaapiy pu' yaw pam maana pay pumuy tutumaytuy iingyalti. Pay pi yaw pam as pumuy amumi su'angqawngwuniqw naat yaw puma put aqw sasqaya. Pu' yaw pam oovi put ang wuuwantangwu, hin as yaw pam pumuy amumi lavaytiqw pay puma paapu pangsoq tuutuqayyani. Niiqe pam yaw oovi ephaqam hiita hintsakye' pay put ang wuuwan-kyangwningwu, ngumante', noovalawe'. Pu' yaw piw puwninik pay yaw pam ephaqam put aw wuuwante' qa iits puwvangwu. Panma-kyangw nawis'ewtiqw pu' yaw pam hisat neengem yewatuwa.

Noq pu' yaw oovi himuwa aw pan amumtiniqey ö'qalqw pu' yaw pam oovi hiitawat aw pangqawngwu, "Pay pi um pas qa atsat inumumtiniqey naawakne' um tur angqw inungem it sikyaatayot wikqw pu' nu' put pooko'ytani. Ason haqawa inungem put wikvaqw paasat pu' pam hapi pay nuy pö'aqw pay nu' paasat son put qa amumtini," yan yaw pam hiitawat paapiy aw lavaytingwu.

Noq pu' yaw ima tootim pay pas put maanatyaniqe pu' yaw puma oovi qa naatusi'yyungwa haqawa hapi mooti put engem wik-ve' putniqat oovi. Niiqe pu' yaw puma tootim as okiw sutsep put sikyaatayot oovi angqe' yakta. Ephaqam yaw himuwa pay sen ko-mokte' pay yaw put enang tunatyawkyangw oovi pantsantongwu.

The girl's facial features were beautiful and the skin of her body light-complected. She was different from anyone else. No one in the entire village was like her. She was known for these qualities, and all the boys and other people had heard of her.

At first it was merely the boys of her home village who came to court her at night. But before long those from the other villages, too, had gotten word of her. They were curious to find out for themselves, so they would go to see her with their own eyes. And it was true. Now they kept flocking to her. There was not one village from which the suitors were not coming.

The girl, however, was still enjoying her girlhood and had no desire yet to take a husband. Each one of the boys, on the other hand, was anxious to make her his girlfriend and wife. They knew they couldn't find anyone else so attractive. The one who married her would be a lucky man.

From all corners of the land the boys kept arriving to woo her. They swarmed to her house. But she did not love any one of them. She would talk to a boy, but when he expressed an interest in marrying her, she simply refused. Eventually, she became tired of all the suitors. Even though she was frank with them and told them how she felt about them they kept coming. She was racking her brain for what she could possibly say to stop them from coming. Whenever she was doing something such as grinding corn or cooking, this was on her mind. Sometimes she was thinking about it when she went to bed so that she could not fall asleep right away. Finally she hit upon an idea.

If any man should ask her to marry him, she would answer him like this, "If you're really serious about living with me, I'd like you to catch me a yellow fox. It's my wish to own one as a pet. Whoever can fulfill my wish, will have won me, and I promise to marry him." This was her reply from then on.

The boys were really anxious to win the girl, so they made every effort to be the first to procure the animal for her. The poor things were constantly roaming about in search of a yellow fox. Once in a while one would go after wood, but the fox too was on his mind.

Pas pi yaw puma hiihin tutuvotya put sukw ngu'ayaniqey oovi. Noq pay pi yaw pam himu a'ni tumqaningwuniqw pay yaw oovi qa hak sukw haqam sakinaqw nuwu pay yaw hisatti. Noq yan pay yaw pam maana naat qa kongta. Hikis pi yaw pam imuy pay pavansinmuy amungaqwyaqamuy tootimuy qa naawakna. Put maanatniqw pi yaw i' himu himu'ytiwqa pay qa himu. Okiw yaw as himuwa aw pang- qawlawngwu kur yaw pam put amumtiqw pam yaw son put engem qa hiihiita nunukngwat tsovalani. Noq pay yaw pam pas qa hiitawat aw uunati. Qa hakiy yaw pam aw unangwtavi. Yantaqat akw pay yaw peetu tootim okiwtotiqe pay yaw oovi paapu qa aw sasqaya- ngwu.

Noq pu' yaw yangqw Hovi'itstuyqangaqw piw i' hak tiyo nuu- tum put aw tuwanlawu. Noq pam hak tiyo piw yaw as suhimutiyo- niqw pay yaw pam maana tis imuy kiyavaqtotimuy qa amumi pas suyan su'paningwu. Noq piw yaw pam tiyo kur Sikyaatayo yan maa- tsiwa. Noq pay yaw as pam maana put Sikyaatayot aw qa su'pataqw pam yaw kur tuwat pas hak wuko'nangwaniiqe yaw oovi pi'ep put awningwu. Noq pay yaw pam maana piw putwat aw mimuywatuy su'an lavaytingwu.

Noq pay yaw pas qa haqawa hisat haqam put hiita sikyaatayot ngu'aqw nuwu pay yaw aapiy navayhaqam yaasangwva. Noq pay yaw paasat ima tootim put qa haqamyaqe pu' yaw puma oovi pay paapu qa put maanat aqw sasqayangwu. Pay kya pi yaw pas qa haqawa put amumtiniqw oovi yaw pas qa haqawa hisat sakina. Hikis pi yaw as ima peetu nasungwtotaqe pu' yaw as oovi put sikyaatayot oovi haqamiye' pu' yaw haqam put tutwe' pu' yaw put ngöyakngwu. Pu' yaw puma put pan ngöyakye' pu' yaw put aw nana'uyve hoyto- taqw pay yaw kur pam piw navote' pay yaw paasat haqawatuy amuutsava haqamiwat suymaktongwu. Noq pay yaw puma qa hin put wungvayaniqey wuuwayangwu. Tis pi yaw puma put pantotiqw son pi yaw pam qa putuniniqw oovi. Pu' yaw puma qa pantaqat yaw as put aw wikvayani. Pay yaw as puma hiihin put ngu'ayaniqey tuwanlalwa. Ephaqam yaw himuwa pas naat kiy angqw pakiwtaqat as horokintaqw pay yaw pam sikyaatayo hin hintsakkyangw put aqle' yamakngwu. Pu' ephaqam yaw himuwa naat kiiyat aqw yaahantaqw pay yaw pam put kuukiqw paasat pay yaw pam nawus put maatapngwu. Pu' haqawa yaw as tis naat sukw pu' tiitiwput yuyat aangaqw uu'uyqe pu' yaw pay ason pas kiy ep wungwnaniqey wuuwankyangw kiy aw wiiki. Noq pay yaw pam naat qa wuuyavo- tat pay yaw okiw pas qa atsat piitsöngmoki. Pam hapi yaw naat put

They tried all sorts of tricks to capture one. But since a yellow fox is quite skittish, no one ever managed to catch one. Meanwhile, a great deal of time had passed, and still the girl had not taken a husband. The eligible sons of upper class villagers, too, did not interest her. Material possessions meant nothing to her. These upper class suitors kept saying they would spoil her with all kinds of valuables if she consented to marry one of them. But the girl remained steadfast. She was not persuaded by any one of them. So, quite a few of the boys lost heart and stopped frequenting her place.

Among those trying their luck was a boy from Hovi'itstuyqa. He was very handsome, but to suitors from villages outside her own the girl showed even less kindness. It so happened that this boy's name was Sikyaatayo, "Yellow Fox." The girl did not treat him very kindly, but because he was stubborn, he repeatedly called on her. Still, the girl's reply to him was the same as to the others.

Some six years passed, but still no one had succeeded in catching a yellow fox. The boys, who so far had failed to get the animal, discontinued visiting the girl. They thought she might never get married, because none of them had lucked out with the fox. As it was, some of the boys had even banded together. They had thought that if they went in search of the fox and found one, they could surround him. But each time they did so and sneaked up to him, he somehow became aware of them and managed to escape. They did not consider throwing their hunting sticks at him, for this would probably have injured him, and the girl would not want an injured animal. So they attempted all sorts of approaches in capturing one. Once in a while a boy tried to extract the fox while he was still in his den, but somehow the animal managed to slip by him. At other times, a hunter dug into the burrow, but the fox bit him, and he had to let go of the animal. On one occasion a boy actually succeeded in stealing a new-born pup from his mother, thinking he could raise the little thing at home. But it did not take long before the poor creature got hungry for milk. He had taken a pup that was still suckling. He knew this when he kidnapped the pup, so when he arrived home, he tried to have him drink

yooyongqat wiiki. Pu' yaw pam as pay put navoti'ytaqe yaw as oovi wikkyangw pituuqe pu' yaw as put pookoy naat pu' piw tiitaqat piihuyat yooyongnaqw pay yaw pam as put angqw yooyongniqey nakwhaqw pam yaw pokwuuti put yooyongnaniqe qa nakwha. Niiqe yaw pam tiyo put wikvaqa yaw as put pookoy piihuyat moytoynaqw pay yaw pam pokwuuti ahoy yorikye' yaw a'ni höykitangwu. Pu' yaw pam tiyo pas qa ayo' taviqw paasat pu' yaw pam pokwuuti pay put pas aw yootokngwuniiqe pay yaw oovi pam put lööshaqam kuu-kiqw pu' yaw pam pay nawus qa piw tuwanta. Niiqe aapiy pay yaw qa pas wuuyavotiqw pay yaw pam sikyaatayhoya mooki. Yan pay yaw pam tiyo oovi put qa nöömata.

Noq pay yaw as puma totim hiihin okiw tuwanlalwaqw, pay yaw pas qa himuwa put engem put sikyaatayot wikva. Paapiy pay yaw puma oovi paapu put maanat qa aqw poptaya. Pay yaw pas i'sa Hovi'itstuyqangaqw tiyo, Sikyaatayo yan maatsiwqa, pas mimuy amun aw pas tungla'ytaqe yaw naat as aw sasqangwuniqw pay yaw pam put piw as qa naawaknaqw pay yaw pam naap put aw qa tuuqayqe oovi naat aasakis mihikqw pangso put aw tutumaytongwu.

Noq pu' yaw i' Pitsinsivostiyo pay yaw tuwat wuuyoqtiqe pay yaw oovi tuwat nuvösayti. Niiqe pu' yaw pam oovi pep Tupats'ove kiy ep pay mihikqw pay soy qa aa'awnat pu' yaw pay angqe' kii-nawit nakwsungwu, pay yaw pam as okiw hakiy mantuwtaniqey yan wuuwankyangw. Noq pu' yaw oovi pam ang waynumqw pu' yaw haqam maana ngumantaqw pu' yaw pam put awningwu. Pu' yaw ephaqam haqawa pay put ngumantaqat aw yu'a'ataqw pay yaw pam paasat qa awningwu. Pu' yaw pam piw aapiytangwu. Noq pu' yaw qa hak haqam hiitawat maanat aw yu'a'ataqw pu' yaw pam awnen pu' aw yu'a'aykungwu. Noq pu' yaw pam maana pay pisoq ngu-mante' pay yaw qa aw hingqawqw pay yaw pam paasat okiwte' pu' yaw pay aapiynen pu' piw haqamiwatningwu. Pu' yaw ephaqam himuwa pay naamahin pisoq ngumamate' pay yaw qa aw kwuupukt pu' yaw pay aw yu'a'atikyangw ngumantangwu. Pas yaw pam ason maangu'e' pu' naasungwnanik pu' qe'te' pu' yaw aw yorikye' paasat pu' yaw navotngwu pay yaw kur hak okiw hin'eway qa suhimu tiyoniqw pay yaw pam paasat put aw qa su'pangwu. Pay yaw pam yanhaqam angqe' okiw nanvota.

Panmakyangw pu' yaw pam kur hisat it pas lomamanat kiiyat aqw pituqw pay yaw paasat piw i' Hovi'itstuyqangaqw tiyo piw aqw yantaqw pu' yaw pam pay qa awnit pu' yaw pay puwto. Pay yaw aapiy piw pas hiisakishaqam taalaniqw pu' yaw pam piw ahoy aqw-

the milk of his dog that had just given birth to a litter. But the bitch refused to let the little fox suckle. The boy put her tit into the baby fox's mouth, but each time the dog turned her head and growled fiercely. When the boy did not remove the fox, the bitch snapped at him, and after she had bitten him twice, he stopped trying. Soon thereafter the little fox pup died. So this boy too failed to win the girl as a wife.

Try as they might, not one of the boys, poor things, had ever managed to catch a yellow fox. They now completely stopped calling on the girl. Only the boy from Hovi'itstuyqa, whose name was Sikyaatayo, and who like the others desired the girl, was still calling on her. And even though the girl felt no love for him, he did not give up. Every night he went for a rendezvous with her.

Pitsinsivostiyo, meanwhile, had grown up and reached an age where he became interested in the other sex. Without telling his grandmother at home in Tupats'ovi, he would roam the village, thinking he might make friends with a girl. Wherever he came across a girl on his nightly excursions, he would go up to her. When he saw someone else talking to that girl, however, he did not approach her. Only when he found a girl alone did he venture up and address her. When the girl was busy grinding and did not respond, he lost heart and left, going somewhere else. On a rare occasion a girl, even though busy grinding corn, actually talked to him without looking up. When she grew tired and stopped to rest, and looked up at him, she would realize that he was homely and totally unattractive. She was then no longer nice to him. This is how the poor lad fared.

One day when Pitsinsivostiyo strayed over to the house of the beautiful girl, the boy from Hovi'itstuyqa was at her vent hole, so instead of going up to her he went home to bed. A few days later he returned and, much to his surprise, did not see the boy from Hovi'itstuyqa. He stepped up to the vent, regardless of the consequences.

niqw piw yaw pam Hovi'itstuyqangaqw tiyo ep qa awi. Noq pu' yaw pam pay oovi naap hiniwqat awi. Niiqe pu' yaw pam aw pituqw pay yaw pam maana piw naat antsa pisoq ngumanta. Noq pam pi yaw qa hisat put aw yorikqe pas pi yaw qa yan unangwti pam panhaqam lomamananiqw. Pas pi yaw pam qa hin tuptsiwni'ewakw lomavitsangwa'yta. Pu' yaw pam pay put qa hingqawt pay yaw pam pas pangqw iipaqw put aqw qatukyangw put paysoq tiimayi. Yan pay yaw pam put qa aw yu'a'aykut pay yaw pam pangqw puwto paasat pay pas mihikqw.

Niiqe aapiy yaw pantaqw pay yaw pam naat qa piw awi. Niikyangw pas pi yaw pam putsa piptsantangwuniiqe yaw qa nanvoti'ynuma. Niiqe oovi yaw so'at as aw hingqawqw pay yaw pam pas put qa hu'wanangwu. Pay yaw pam maana okiw put pas kur hintsana. Paapiy pay yaw pam okiw hiisavo pas qa nanvoti'ynuma. Pu' yaw pam pay piw putakw qa nöösa'ytangwu. Pu' yaw pam piw puwninik pu' wa'ökye' pay yaw pam paasat piw put maanat piptsantangwu.

Panmakyangw pu' pay yaw pam put akw pas suupan pay hintini. Pas pi yaw pam okiw putsaniiqe hakiy as yaw pam put aa'awnani. Niikyangw pay pi yaw pam qa hakiy sungwa'ytaqe pu' yaw pam oovi pay put qa hakiy aawintaqe pas yaw pam putakw maqsoni'yta. Yanti yaw pam putakwniiqe pu' yaw pam pay nawus naap hiniwqat akw it soy aa'awnani. Noq pay yaw pam Pitsinsivostiyo piw mimuywatuy amumum navoti'yta pam maana pas piw put sikyaatayot oovi hakiy amumtiniqey, yan hakiy aw lavaytingwuniqw. Niiqe pay yaw pam oovi piw put as ang paas wuuwa hin pam su'annen pay kya as haqam put ngu'aniqey. Nit pay yaw kur pam son put haqamni. Pay yaw pam as piw nuutum tuwantat pay yaw pam tis naalaningwuniiqe pay yaw pam oovi put pas qa hisat sakina. Pay itakw piw yaw pam oovi pas son nawus qa soy aa'awnani. Pay yaw pam kur hakiy aw qa tuwiheve' kur yaw son nawus qa soy awni.

Noq pu' yaw suus puma naama talavay tuumoytaqw pu' yaw pam ep pu' soy aw pangqawu, "Itaasoy, nu' as ung hiita tuuvingtaniy. Niikyangw nu' ung piw mooti hiita aa'awnaniy," yaw pam put aw kita.

"Ta'a, ya himu'u?" yaw pam kitaaqe pu' yaw pam pay paasat oovi tunösqe'tiqe pu' yaw pay pas putsa aw yuki'ytaqw pu' yaw pam put hiita aa'awnaniqey put yayna. "Owiy," yaw pam put aw kita, "pay um sonqa navoti'yta antsa yep itaakitsokiy ep yangqw kiisonviy

When he got there, he found the girl grinding corn. He had never seen her before, so he almost swooned when he saw how beautiful she was. Her facial features were unbelievably beautiful. Not daring to speak a word, he sat outside the vent hole watching her inside the grinding chamber. Finally, without saying a word, he left to go to bed. It was already dark night.

For the time being, Pitsinsivostiyo did not return to the girl's house. In his mind, however, he kept picturing only her, so much so that he was almost in a daze. His grandmother had told him to forget her, but as usual he paid no attention to her. The girl had touched Pitsinsivostiyo to the quick. He became absent-minded, and finally was so affected by the experience that he did not eat any more. Whenever he went to bed, he just lay there, picturing the girl.

At last it seemed that even Pitsinsivostiyo's health was being affected by his encounter with the girl. She was constantly on his mind, so he had the desire to talk to someone about her. But since he had no friend, he could not do so, and was really suffering. He became so desperate that he decided to say something to his grandmother, regardless of the consequences. Pitsinsivostiyo was of course fully aware, just like all the others, of the girl's requirement for marriage. He knew that she would only marry in return for a yellow fox. Consequently, he too pondered how best to capture the animal. He tried like all the rest, but since he was all by himself, he had no luck. This was another reason to talk to his grandmother. Since he had no one else to teach him how to hunt this animal, he had no choice but to consult his grandmother.

One morning when the two were having breakfast together, he said to her, "Grandmother, I'd like to ask you something. But first I must tell you something."

"Very well, what is it?" she replied and stopped eating. She was all ears when her grandson began. "Yes," he said, "you've probably heard of this girl who lives in our village on the northwest side of the plaza. She's a ravishing beauty, but shows no love for anyone. Boys flock to her from all over. She chats with them briefly, but keeps telling everyone that she's not interested in a husband."

akwningyaqw i' maana ki'yta. Niikyangw pas pam piw lomamana-niikyangw pas hapi pam qa hakiy naawaknay. Pay as pas soosoki-vaqw ima tootim aw tutumaywisngwuniqw pay pi as amumi yu'a-'aykungwuniikyangw pay yaw pam pas qa puwsungwnawaknaqey pay pas yansaningwuy," yaw pam put soy aw yan lalvaya.

"Hep owi, pi pay nu' antsa navotqw yaw antsa put hakiy maanat aw puma tootim homtaqw pay yaw antsa pam pas qa hakiy aw unangwtavi," yaw pam kita.

"Owiy, pay um suuput yu'a'ata. Niikyangw pay pi as soosokmuy amumi yu'a'aykungwu, niikyangw pay pas qa inumi yu'a'ayku. Pay pi pam as oovi piw it hiita himu'ytiwqat qa pas naawakna. Pay as oovi imuy tootimuy pay hiita namat tuwa'ynumyaqamuy piw put aw sasqayaqw pay yaw pam qa put hiita oovi hakiywat amum qatuptuniqey pay yan pumuy navotnay. Pu' piw pam hapi pas qa na'öna, pas na'alasvu. Niiqe pam yaw oovi sutsep yuy engem noovalawqw oovi pam pay yaw qa hisat pas novawuwanta. Niiqe nu' aw wuuwaqw pay kya as itam naamaniikyangw hin aw wuu-waqw pay kya as hin inungem pasiwtani. Noq pu' nu' put amum-tiqw pay um paapu qa maqsonlawt paysoq kwangwaqtuqw pay ason pam itamungem noovalawmantani. Pu' nu' piw okiw pas as aw tungla'ytay." Yan yaw pam put soy aw tu'awi'ykyangw pay yaw pam naat put sikyaatayot qa pangqawu.

Noq pu' yaw pam so'wuuti put mööyiy aw pangqawu, "Is uti okiw himu imöyhoya. Ya um as okiw panhaqam tuwat wuuwanta? Pay pi antsa um pu' nuvösaytiqe oovi'o. Is uti, noq antsa hin sen pasiwtani? Pi um okiw pay yan'ewayhoya. Pu' ima sinom piw pay itamumi qa pas suutaq'ewyaqw oovi itam yepehaq qalaveq yan okiwqatu. Noq itam pi pay tis söösöqamniqw son piw himu itamumi suutaq'ewni itamumiq lööqökninik'i. Pu' itam yan naalaniiqe son itam naalaniikyangw hakiy yuwsinani. Noq oovi pay um nawus qa panhaqam wuuwantat pay um ngas'ew qate' pay qatuni," yaw pam put aw kitaaqe pay yaw oovi put qa aw okiw unangwtavi. Niiqe yan yaw pay pam okiw put unangwmoknaqw pay yaw pam Pitsinsivos-tiyo qa piw aapiyta.

Noq pu' yaw aapiy pantaqw pay yaw kur pam son put maanat suutoknikyangw pay yaw pam naat qa piw soy aw hingqawu. Pay yaw aapiy pas piw hiisakishaqam talqw pu' piw yaw puma ep tapkiwtaqw pu' yaw puma piw tuumoytaqw pu' yaw pam piw put aw pangqawu, "Itaasoy," yaw pam put aw kita.

"Ya himu'u?" yaw pam put aw kita.

"Sure, I've heard of a girl who's being courted by droves of boys, but has succumbed to none of them."

"Yes, that's the one. She briefly chats with everybody, but she never talked to me. She's not after any material possessions. She's told all those boys whose fathers are rich, that she wouldn't marry any one of them for this reason. She's hardworking and self-motivated. She's constantly cooking for her mother, so the latter never needs to worry about fixing meals. It occurred to me that if we put our minds together, we might convince her to marry me. If I could marry her and she would cook for us, you would not need to toil anymore. You could live a pleasant life. I desire her with all my heart." This is what Pitsinsivostiyo told his grandmother. He did not mention the yellow fox yet.

The old woman replied, "My poor grandchild. Is that what has been going through your head? I see, you've gotten old enough to be interested in sex. Dear me, how do you figure we might succeed? Look how homely you are. The people show no concern for us. That's why we live poor and destitute at the edge of the village. We're nothing but dregs, so no one will be willing to become related to us through marriage. Being completely alone, we can't prepare the wedding outfit for a bride. Just forget the whole thing and live your life as you always have." This is what she said to Pitsinsivostiyo. She had no sympathy for him. Her reply made the boy so sad that he could not go on with the conversation.

Thus the matter remained, but Pitsinsivostiyo could not forget the girl. A few days later, when the two were having supper, he spoke to her once more, "Grandmother," he said.

"What is it?" she replied.

"Owiy, pay antsa ura nu' puunathaqam uumi it maanat yu'a'a-
taqw pay um ura as nuy meewaqw pas hapi nu' pay putsa wuuwantangwuniiqe nu' oovi piw uumi as tuuvingtani. Niikyangw nu' pu'
nuutungk ung qa soosok hiita aa'awna. Noq it nu' ung qa aa'awna.
Yaw haqawa it sikyaatayot put maanat engem wikvaqw pay yaw
pam paasat son put hakiy qa amumtini. Pay yaw haqawa put engem
wikvaqa pay yaw put paasat sonqa pö'ani. Pay yaw naamahin naap
hak engem wikvani. Pay yaw pam son paasat put nawus qa amumtini. Noq pay pi nu' pas antsa put as amumtiniqe qa naatusi'ytaqe
pay nu' as oovi qa suus naalaniikyangw put ngu'aniqey tuwantaqw
pas piw kur pam himu a'ni tumqaningwuniiqe hak naat qa hin aw
haykyalaqw pay pam waayangwuy," yan yaw pam soy aw lalvayqw
pay yaw pam naat panis put hu'wantoyna, "Noq pay pi as um
naamahin wuyniikyangw pay um naat a'ni wuwni'ytaqw oovi nu'
ngas'ew piw uumi tuwihevay," yaw pam put aw kita.

"Is uti, ya pam piw panhaqam hiitawat aw lavaytingwu? Pay pi
pam son piw paysoq pan hiitawat aw lavaytingwu. Pay antsa pam
himu sikyaatayo hin'ur tumqaningwu. Son pay naap hak nu'anhimu
put naap paysoq ngu'a. Pam hapi pay piw tuwat hin'ur wuwni'y-
tangwu. Pam qa it iisawuy an uuna. Pam it huuwit piw paas tuwi'y-
tangwuniiqe oovi pam son hisat haqam kwisni. Niikyangw pas as
su'annen pay as son put qa ngu'a. Noq pay pi kur pam maana pas qa
atsalawqw pay pi itam kur ungem tuwantani. Pay pi itam kur
atsangwkini. Pay pi naap unangwayniqw kur atsalawe' pay pi naap
hintaqat aqw naavitsinani," yaw pam kitaaqe pay yaw oovi aw hin
tutaptaniqey yaw aw pangqawu.

Niiqe pam yaw oovi paas put soy aw tuuqaytaqw pu' yaw pam
oovi put aw tutaplawu, "Ta'a, imöyhoya, qaavo hapi um su'its tayte'
um hapi yuk teevenge it Löhavutsotsmot ahopqöyminen pang um it
mongpuwvit hepnumni. Pay pam pan hin'ur kuytaqw pay um oovi
put tuwe' pay um son as qa niitini. Niikyangw pay um qa tsaa' put
angqw kimani. Pay pi um naat puvu'niiqe son pas hin itunawakniy
kivaniniqw paniqw oovi pay um tatam pas niitit pu' um angqw ahoyni. Pay um sonqa su'aw yaasathaqam ahoy pituni. Pi pay yangqw
pangso hihin yaavo'o. Pay um oovi pay ang aapate' pay um pay
puwni," yan yaw pam put aw paas tutaptat pu' yaw piw put paas
aa'awna hin pam mongpuwvi soniwngwuniqw.

Paasat pu' yaw pam oovi pay paas ang aapatat pu' yaw as ang
wa'ökt pay yaw pam qa iits puwvaqe paysoq yaw pam aapay ang
namtötölawu. Pas pi yaw pam kwangwtoya put sikyaatayot haqam-

"Yes, I'm sure you remember that I talked to you about that girl recently. You told me to stay away from her, but she's always on my mind, so I'd like to ask you a question. I did not tell you everything the last time. I did not mention that she will marry whoever can bring her a yellow fox. The one who accomplishes that will win her hand. It does not matter who he is, she will have to marry him. And because I've made every effort to get her, I tried on several occasions to catch this animal all by myself. This fox, however, is so skittish that it ran away long before I got close to him." His grandmother merely listened and acknowledged what he was saying. Pitsinsivostiyo continued, "You're old, I know, but you've still got a lot of brains. That's why I'm seeking your advice."

"Dear me, is that what she's been saying to her suitors? Maybe she has a special reason. For surely that yellow fox is very shy. He won't be captured by just anyone who's doing this on his own. A fox is much too smart for that, and not gullible like a coyote. He's quite familiar with traps, so he won't allow himself to get caught. But if one goes about it in the proper way, this feat can be achieved. If the girl really speaks the truth, we can give it a try for you. We'll see if she means what she says. If she lied, it'll be her own fault and she'll have to bear the consequences." This is what his grandmother said, whereupon she gave him some instructions.

Pitsinsivostiyo listened carefully to every word. "Well then, my grandson," she started, "tomorrow you get up first thing in the morning and head out to a place northeast of Löhavutsotsmo. There I want you to look for some Apache-plume. When you find a nice good stand, gather a good amount. Be sure not to bring too few. You're new to this and might not pick the sort I want. So cut as much Apache-plume as you can. You should be back home around this time of day. Mind you, it's quite far to that place. You better make your bed now and go to sleep." These were his grandmother's instructions. She also explained to him in great detail what Apache-plume looks like.

Pitsinsivostiyo did as told. He spread out his bedding and lay down. He could not fall asleep right away, and kept tossing and turning on his sheepskin. He was looking forward to getting a yellow fox.

niqe. Niikyangw pu' yaw pam pas ang wuuwaqe pas yaw kur hin wuuwa. Pay pi yaw pam paas navoti'yta hak it mongpuwvit ang hootangwuniqw. Niiqe pam hapi yaw oovi suyan hoongapto. Noq pam maana pi yaw qa pan hakiy aw tutaptangwu. Noq son pi yaw pam oovi put mokput put aw wikvani. Nit pay yaw pam qa pas soy tuuvinglawu hintiqw pam put pangsohaqami ooviniqey. Hisatniqw pi yaw pam oovi puwva.

Niiqe qavongvaqw pu' yaw pam oovi pay pas su'its tayta. Pay yaw naat oovi qa hin qöyangwnuptuniqw pay yaw pam qatuptuqe pu' yaw naat aapay tsovalantaqw pay yaw put so'at kur navotqe pu' yaw pam pay paasat taatayi. Niiqe pu' yaw iits taatayt pu' yaw puma sunösa. Sunöst pu' yaw tiyot so'at aw put pikya'yngwhoyat tavi. "Itakw hapi um put tutkitaniy," yaw aw kita. "Niikyangw um wuu-haq tutkitani. Ephaqam himuwa qa lomahintaqw pay hak put tuuvat pu' piw sukwatningwuniqw oovi um it wuuhaq tutkitaniy," yaw kitaaqe pu' put mit ngat'at yaw aw tavi, putakw iikwiwtaniqw.

Pangqw pu' yaw pam nakwsuqe pay yaw oovi pas Wupatkiy aatatkye'niqw paasat pu' yaw pam taawa yama. Pay yaw pam kur a'ni hönginiikyangw pu' piw a'ni hikwis'öqalaniiqe pay yaw pam pas as yuumosa henanatimakyangw pay yaw naat qa pas maangu'yt pay yaw pangso pitu. Nit pay yaw pam qa hiita nitkyaynit pu' kuuyiy angqw hintit pay yaw pam aapiyta. Pay yaw pam pas panis pep hiisavo huruusaltit pu' yaw piw nakwsu.

Noq antsa pay yaw naat pu' töngvakyangw pay aapiy hiisavo-tiqw pay yaw pam pangqw Löhavutsotsmoy ahopqöyngaqw pangso wupto. Pu' yaw pam pangso pas soosok wupqe paasat pu' yaw pam pangqe' put hiita mongpuwvit hepnuma. Noq pay yaw pam pang niitiwtaqa pay yaw pam oovi suuputniiqey wuuwankyangw pay yaw pam oovi pas wuuhaqlawu. Hisatniqw pu' yaw taawanasaptiqw paasat pu' yaw pam nitkyakweway taviiqe paasat pu' yaw pam pep haqam it löqötskit atpip qatuwkyangw yaw kwangwatumoyta. Pu' yaw pam nöst pu' yaw pam pay mooti hiisavo pep qatuwkyangw pu' yaw pam pay angqe' taynuma. Niiqe pam yaw pang kyaataynuma. Qa hisat pi yaw pam pangqe' waynumqw putniqw pi yaw oovi pang a'ni soniwa. Hiihiitu yaw angqe' töötökiy qa pevewwisa, tis pi yaw kwangqatniqw oovi. Niiqe pay yaw pam oovi pay hihin nawutsnat pu' yaw pan wuuwa, "Han nam qa sööwu yep yantat piw ang put oovinen pay iits ahoy pitu." Yan yaw pam wuuwaqe pu' yaw pam oovi piw aapiytaqe pay yaw antsa su'aw taawa pay hihin atkyatiqw pay yaw pam qe'ti. "Pay kya i' niitiwta," yaw pam yan wuuwaqe pu'

But as he thought about the matter, he did not know what to think. He was familiar, of course, with the fact that arrows are fashioned from the Apache-plume. He was clearly going to go after arrow-making material. However, how did that relate to the girl? He could not bring her a dead fox. He refrained from further probing why his grandmother wanted him to do this, and eventually dozed off.

The following morning Pitsinsivostiyo awoke early. It was not yet even gray dawn when he rose to gather his bedding. His grandmother, who heard him, also woke up now. They quickly had breakfast, whereupon the old woman handed Pitsinsivostiyo an axe. "This you can use to cut the Apache-plume. Be sure to cut a lot. Once in a while a branch is not good and one has to throw it away and take another, so bring a large amount." With that, she also gave him a tumpline to carry the load on his back.

Now Pitsinsivostiyo started out. By the time he passed the area southeast of Wupatki, the sun was up. The boy was an extraordinary runner. His strong lungs allowed him to breathe longer. He had been trotting in a straight line and reached Wupatki without being the least bit tired. He paused for a brief time before he set forth anew, without touching his journey food or taking a drink from his water.

Sure enough, the sun was just a little past its mid-morning point when he ascended the northeast side of Löhavutsotsmo. Upon climbing all the way up, he went in search of the Apache-plume. He found a lot growing there; so convinced that this was the right kind, he chopped off many branches. By the time it was noon, he set down his food belt and, relaxing under a pine tree, ate with great relish. Having stilled his hunger, he lingered a while, taking in the view. He had never been in this area before, so he was very impressed with what he saw. He could hear the constant sounds of all sorts of creatures, for the weather was nice and warm. After Pitsinsivostiyo had stayed for a good length of time, he thought, "I must not waste my time here. If I cut some more, I'll be home soon." So he continued chopping off more Apache-plume. Just as the sun got a little low on the horizon, he stopped. "I guess this is plenty," he thought. With that, he carefully tied the sticks, loaded the bundle on his back, and set out for home.

Eventually, he noticed that he was getting closer to home. He was quite familiar with the area now. He had not been moving very rapidly and so was glad when he realized how quickly he had arrived. The sun had not completely set yet when he arrived from southwest of his house. Upon reaching his house, he deposited his bundle behind the

yaw pam oovi paasat put paas somt pu' yaw pam put iikwiltat paasat
pu' yaw pam pangqw ahoy nimanhoyta.
Panmakyangw pu' yaw pam pay kiy aw hayingwnaqey pay yaw
navota. Pay yaw pam pang haqe'niiqey pay yaw pang paas tuwi'yta.
Noq pay yaw pam as pangqw qa pas ahoy a'ni hoytakyangw pay
yaw kur pam pangso suptuqe yaw tsuya. Pay yaw oovi naat pam
taawa qa pas pakiqw pay yaw pam pangqw kiy taavangqw angqw
aw pituto. Pu' yaw pam pas kiy aw pituuqe pu' yaw pam pay pep
saaqat aakwayngyap put somiy tavit pu' yaw kiy aqw paki.
Noq pu' yaw pam kiy aqw pakiqw pay yaw pam so'at kur put
tuwaaqe yaw put aw haalayti. "Askwali pay um pitu. Pay um
puye'em yaasatniqwhaqam pituniqw oovi pay nu' angwu pay aw
noovalawu. Noq oovi ason nuy novayukuqw pu' itam ason paasat
pay tuumoytani," yaw pam kitaaqe pu' yaw pay oovi hihin pisoqti.
Nit pay yaw pam put qa tuuvinglawu sen pi pam put tuunawakniyat
tuwaaqat.
Pu' yaw pam so'wuuti yukuuqe pu' yaw pam aw tunösvongyaa-
tat pu' yaw pam put aw pangqawu, "Ta'a, pewii'. Itam tuumoytani,
taq pi um sonqa tsöngmokiwkyangw pitu," yaw pam put aw kitaqw
pu' yaw pam oovi aw hoyokqw paasat pu' yaw puma tuumoyvaqw
pu' yaw pam Pitsinsivostiyo put soy aawinta haqe' pam hinnumqey.
Noq pay yaw pam put piw qa hiita tuuvinglawt pay yaw pam panis
put aw tuuqaykyanqw pu' hu'wantoyna. Pu' yaw puma oovi tuumoykyangw pu' yaw puma hisatniqw öyqw paasat pu' yaw pam
so'wuuti ang ayo' qenilawqw pu' yaw pam Pitsinsivostiyo yamakma.
Niiqe yaw su'aw put so'at pumuy tunösvongyayamuy ayo'
oyaqw pu' yaw pam angqaqw ahoy pakikyangw paasat yaw pam put
hiita yukumaqey put yaw pam iikwiwkyangw ahoy paki. Noq pu'
yaw put so'at put tuwaaqe pu' yaw pam put aw pangqawu, "Is askwali, pi pay kur um suuput kiva. Askwali, pay kur itam kya son hin
ungem qa yukuni. Niikyangw pay naat son i'sani. Noq pay ason
itamuy it pas mooti yukuqw pu' nu' ung piw hiitawat ayatani," yaw
pam put aw kita. "Pay um tsangaw piw kur wuuhaqtay," yaw kita.
"Qaavo talavay pu' it itam aw tumala'yvaniy," yaw kita.
Pu' yaw oovi puma piw puuwi. Nit qavongvaqw kay pi iits taatayi, pay tiyo piw kya pi iits aw tumala'ytaniqey oovi. Pay yaw puma
kya pi oovi sunöst pu' put aw tumala'yta. Pu' yaw puma put siipan-
lawu. Pu' yaw so'at pay pi as so'wuutiniikyangw pay kya pi put hisat
sonqa nuutumi taytangwu put hin yuykuyangwuy hoohutniqw. Kur
yaw pam hoongapma, pam tiyo. Pam so'at yaw put ayata, hoohut.

ladder and entered.

As soon as he was inside, his grandmother saw him. Overjoyed, she welcomed him. "Thanks, you have returned. I knew you would be back about this time, so I started making supper ahead of time. The minute I'm done cooking, we can eat." This is what she said, hurrying a little more. She still did not inquire of him whether he had found what she was interested in.

When the old woman was done, she set out the food and said, "All right, come here. Let's eat. You must be starving." Pitsinsivostiyo moved up to the food and as they ate he told his grandmother how he had fared. Again she asked no questions of him, but merely listened and nodded to what he had to say. When the two were finally satiated, the old woman cleared the area where they had eaten and Pitsinsivostiyo went outside.

Just when his grandmother had removed everything, he came back in, toting on his back the Apache-plume sticks he had been sent to fetch. No sooner did his grandmother see them than she exclaimed, "Thanks a lot, you brought the right thing. Thank you. Now we can make this for you. We'll need some other things, though. But let's finish this task first before I tell you what to do next," she said. "I'm so glad you brought so much of the arrow-making material. Tomorrow morning we'll start working on it."

The two now went to bed. The next morning they were up early because the boy was anxious to get going. They quickly ate breakfast and then they began. Their first job was to peel the branches. Since Pitsinsivostiyo's grandmother was an old woman, she must have observed at some time in her life how arrows are made. After all, the boy had brought arrow-making material. That's what she had told him to get. Eventually, when all the branches were pared down, she straightened them. Wherever a stick was bent slightly, that part was pulled through the perforated horn of a mountain sheep, a device she

Pu' yaw oovi puma pep pantsaklawkyangw pu' yaw pay put paas papsit pu' yaw so'at put antsa sutskwuplawu. Yaw haqam hihin himuwa ngölöwtaqw pu' pam put pangw'alat ang popromvut ang panat pu' ang yaw langaknangwu. Put yaw pantsakkyangw pan pam put sutskwuplawu. Pu' yaw put tiyot aw tavingwu. Pu' yaw pam tuwat owat ang put ruukwanlawu suphingpulawqe. Pantsakkyangw pu' yaw pay so'at piw hiihiita oyi'ytaqe pu' yuumoqhaqami pakiiqe pangqaqw yaw hiita pöhömokiy ipwaqe pu' ang peehut homasat ayo' oyaaqe pu' put yaw pam hoohut aw homastotoyna. Pantsakkyangw pu' yaw puma pas put wuuhaq yukuuta.

Pu' yaw so'at pangqawu, "Askwali, yantani," yaw pam so'at kita. "Noq ura nu' uumi pangqawqw pay naat son yantani. Noq nu' it itaamötsikvuy ang ayo' tsovalat pu' qöönani. Noq um pay inuusavo ang aapate' pay um ang haak wa'ökiwtani. Pay pi um wuuyavo nakwsuqe sonqa mangu'iwta. Pay ason nu' it yukye' pu' ang neengem tuwat aapataqw paasat pu' nu' ason uumi piw hinwat tutaptani itamuy pay wa'ökiwtaqw'ö," yaw pam put aw kita.

Paasat pu' yaw pam oovi ang qenilawqw pu' yaw pam tiyo ang neengem aapataqe pu' pay pang wa'ökiwkyangw pu' soy aw maqaptsi'yta. Noq pu' yaw pam hisatniqw tuwat yukuuqe pu' yaw pam ang neengem aapatat pu' yaw pay pep qatuptu. Pantit pu' yaw pam pangqawu, "Ta'a, imöyi. Qaavo hapi pu' um pay piw teevengewat awtangaptokyangw pay um pu' qa pas aasavoni. Niikyangw um hapi it kwingvit ooviniikyangw um hapi put pay piw qa suukw susutskwivut ang tsaaqakyangw pu' um uumay pölölaqw pam hiisayhaqamniqw pay um pangsakw oovi mamavisni. Um ang hepni yangsakwniikyangw um tsiipuyat ep qaapuknaqw kur pam aasonva taskyap'iwtaqw put hapi umniy," yaw aw kita. "Pantaqat hapi um kivani. Mit um qa pantaqatniqw pam qa hongvi. Pam sonqa qöhikni. It hapi um pangsoq hawt heptoni, it awtangavitay," yaw aw kita. "Put hapi itam ungem awtatani. I' hoohu yankyangw i' pay qa hiita aw apitingwu i'sanene'. Pam hoohu mit awtat enangningwu. Noq pay um yang aqw sikyanawitniikyangw haqami pituqw pay pam kwingvi son pang qa susmataqni." Yan yaw pam put aw tutaptaqw pu' yaw puma oovi pay paasat puuwi.

Qavongvaqw pu' yaw puma pay iits piw taytaqw pu' yaw pam tiyo pay piw aapiy tuumoytaqw pu' yaw put so'at put engem nitkyalawqe yaw su'aw yukuqw yaw pam tiyo öyqe pu' yaw pam oovi put kwewtat paasat pu' yaw pam pangqw piw nakwsuqe pay yaw oovi antsa naat qa taawanasaptiqw pay yaw pam pangso haqami

used as a shaft-straightener. Next, she handed the shaft to the boy who rubbed it with a stone to make it nice and smooth. The old granny now trudged to the back room, where she stored all sorts of things, and came back with her feather bundle. Putting a few wing feathers aside, she fletched the arrows. In this manner the two manufactured a great quantity.

"Thanks, this will do," his grandmother finally said. "Remember, I said this would not be all. Well, let me gather our trash and burn it. You go ahead and spread out your bedding and lie down for the time being. You travelled far yesterday and must be tired. When I'm done with this, I'll make my bed too. Then I'll give you some further instructions."

Thereupon the old woman cleaned up the mess on the floor. The boy put out his bedroll and lay there waiting for his grandmother. Soon she was done and made her bed too. After settling down on it she said, "Now, my grandson, tomorrow you must go southwest once more, this time to get bow-making material. But you won't need to go far and stay away so long. What we need is oak. Again you must hack off a good many straight branches. Select the ones about the size of your fist in diameter. When you find any this size, peel off the bark. If the inside is a brown color, then that's the kind you want to get. Anything else does not have the proper strength and is bound to break. So this is what I want you to search for, this bow-making material. We'll make that into a bow for you. An arrow by itself is no use whatsoever. An arrow needs a bow. Just go along the valley here until you come to an oak grove." After giving him these new instructions the two slept.

The following morning the two were up early again. While the boy breakfasted, his grandmother fixed a journey lunch for him. Just when she was done, the boy was satiated. He tied the food to his belt and departed. True enough, it was not yet noontime when he reached an area where young oaks were growing. These were the ones his grandmother had told him to look for. Even if they are small in size,

pituqw pay yaw pam kwingvi pay naat tsaatsay pang susmataq. Noq pu' yaw put aw hin so'at tutaptaqw pam yaw oovi panyungqat ang hepnuma. Noq pam pi yaw naat pan naamahin as hingsayhooyaniikyangw naat tayte' yaw kur a'ni huruningwuniqw pam yaw naat oovi qa pas wuuhaq awtangapqw pay yaw piw taawanasaptiqw pu' yaw pam oovi nitkyamokiy taviiqe pu' yaw haqam kiisi'ytaqat atpip nöösa. Nöst pu' yaw pam piw tapkimi ang peehut ooviniiqe yaw pay su'aw tawimoksa'tat pu' yaw pay ahoy nima.

Niiqe pay yaw pam ep ahoy pituuqe pay yaw piw pep kits'ove put oyat pu' yaw piw kiy aqw pakiqw yaw so'at navotqe yaw haalaytiqe yaw aw askwallawu. Noq pay pi yaw pam pu' tavoknenniiqat aape pay iits pituqw pay yaw pam so'wuuti pay paasat aw noovativaqe pu' yaw yukuqw pu' yaw puma piw nöösa.

Pu' yaw pumuy pas öyqw pu' yaw pam so'wuuti ang ayo' qenitaqe pu' yaw pam put mööyiy aw pangqawu, "Ta'a, kur aw uu'awtangaviy yukutoo'. Pay sen pi um suuput kivaqw itam pay putwat piw aw hintsaktivani," yaw pam put aw kitaqw paasat pu' yaw pam oovi iipohaqami yamakmaqe pu' yaw put iikwiwkyangw ahoy pakiiqe pu' yaw pay put qöpqöt akwningye' oya. Noq pu' yaw put so'at awniiqe pu' yaw put ang pootaqw pay yaw kur pam suuput kivaqw pas yaw pam haalaytiqe yaw mööyiy aw pangqawu, "Askwali, pay um suuput kiva. Pay nu' it tutaplawu."

Niiqe pu' yaw pam aapamiqhaqami pakimaqe pu' yaw pam pangqw lööq wukovoyot yawkyangw yama. Paasat pu' yaw pam put mööyiy aw sukw tavit pu' yaw aw piw pangqawu yaw pay pam haak put aw taytaqw pu' yaw pam ason put hin hintaniqat paas yukuqw pu' yaw pam ason tuwatni. Niiqe pu' yaw pam oovi put sukw ang kwusut pu' yaw pam haqam ngungu'ypi'ytaniqat pangsoq nan'ivoq put ang paas lomatsatsvi. "Yantangwu hapi i'i," yaw pam put aw kitat pu' yaw pam put pay paasat saaqat ang hootakna. Pu' yaw pam paasat put awtatniqat ngungu'ypiyat nan'ip sööngöt enang saaqat aw soma. Paasat pu' yaw pam mööyiy aw pangqawqw pu' yaw pam tuwat put sukw aw hintsaktivakyangw pay yaw kur pas qa atsat a'ni ang tsatsviqw pay yaw pam put hootaknaniqe yaw ngölölaqw pay yaw pam okiw suqwhi.

Noq pay yaw put so'at aw pangqawu, "Pay um qa pas aw hin wuuwantani. Pay nu' paniqw oovi ung qa sukw angqw kimaniqat uumi tutapta. Pay um oovi piw sukw ang kwuse' um piw kur putwat aw tuwantani," yaw pam put aw kitaqw pu' yaw pam oovi piiw. Pantsaklawkyangw hisatniqw pu' yaw pam su'an yukuuqe pas hapi

as long as they are alive, they are extremely tough. He had not chopped many branches before it was noon. So he took his lunch and ate in a place that provided some shade. Having satisfied his hunger, he went in search of more oak. By early evening he had a good arm load together, so he left for home.

Upon his return, Pitsinsivostiyo placed the oak on the rooftop and entered. His grandmother happily greeted him and thanked him. This time he was back earlier than the day before, so the old woman started cooking and when she was done, they ate.

When the two were full, the old granny cleared the table and said to her grandson, "All right, go get your bow material. If you brought the right kind, we can get underway." Pitsinsivostiyo went outside as bidden and lugged the oak in on his back. He placed the bundle down northwest of the fireplace. Inspecting it closely, his grandmother found the oak branches just right. Glad about this, she said to her grandchild, "Thank you, you brought the right sort. This is what I told you to get."

With that, she disappeared into the room next door, and returned with two big knives. One she handed the boy, telling him to watch her for a while and not try himself before she had finished one properly. With that, she picked up an oak branch and trimmed it nicely on both sides where the grip of the bow was going to be. "That's the way its supposed to be," she said, whereupon she stretched the oak stem across the ladder. She did this by tying the bow down with grass which held the bow in place to the left and right of the bow grip. Then she encouraged her grandson to start working on one himself. Sure enough, he hacked off all the little twigs, but when he was about to stretch it on the ladder, he bent it too much. As a result, the bow broke.

"Don't worry about it," his grandmother said. "That's why I had you bring more than one piece of oak. Just pick another and try again." So Pitsinsivostiyo tried once more. Finally he got it right. He really finished it nicely. Thereupon, he tied it to the ladder to stretch it.

yaw pam piw lomayuku. Paasat pu' yaw pam tuwat put hootakna.
Noq pu' yaw aapiy pantaqw paasat pu' yaw pam pan hootakiw-
kyangw pu' yaw pam paas lakqw pu' yaw put so'at piw peehut tahut
haqamniiqe pu' yaw pam put lööqmuy awtat aw aptsiwtaqat murukna. Pam hapi yaw put awatvostoynaniqe pu' yaw pam oovi pumuy
pantsana. Noq pas hapi yaw puma put kur lomayukuqw pas yaw as
pam awta qa pas a'ni hongviniikyangw yaw pam put aw tuwantaqw
pay yaw put ho'at ang a'ni öqalat yamakngwuniikyangw piw yaw
yaavoningwu. Yanhaqam yaw pam lööq pas loma'awta'yva.
Paasat pu' yaw put so'at piw aw tutapta, "Ta'a, pu' hapi um put
sikyaatayot oovi yuk teevenge owatsmomini. Niikyangw um hapi
pay paasat it uutunipiy kimakyangw pangsoni. Pu' um awniikyangw
pu' um haqam huruute' pep pu' um it kwaakwit pay tatam wuuhaq
mokyaatat pu' piw aapiytani. Nen pu' ason um pangso owatsmomi
pite' pang pu' um haqam wuuyaq qeni'ytaqat heeve' pu' um pang
pay naanahoy waynumlawkyangw um pep put tutskwat pay tatam
paas pöhingputani. Pu' um piw ang kuklaqvutani. Ason um pantit
paasat pu' um it uuhoy pangso qeni'ytaqat aw naanan'i'vaqw pok-
lawni. Pu' um pantaqat ang wa'ökqw pay himu uumi pite' pay sonqa
pan wuuwani, 'Kur it yephaqam hiitu aw kiipokqe oovi it yep niinaya,' yan sonqa wuuwamantani. Pu' um piw uukutsipsömiq sukw
piw tsuruknat pu' um sukwat pay sunasavahaqe' qöhiknat pu' um
put qalaveq it saanat aw piitaknat pu' um put uu'unangwmi pii-
taknani. Niikyangw um ason pay pas taawa pakiqw pu' um pang
wa'ökni. Ason um pang wa'ökye' paasat pu' um it kwaakwit naapa
siwuwuykinani. Pu' uumo'ay aqw um pay piw hiisa' oyani. Pam
hapi imuy aatuy su'amun soniwngwuniqw put pay akw sonqa
tuptsiwni'ewaytini um pay wuuyavo pang mokqatniqw oovi ima
tootopt pay uumi tiitota. Noq yep nu' imuy pöövöstuy huwqw
pumuy um piw enang kimani. Puma hapi pay paas peekyewyungqe
hin'ur hovaqtuyaqw pumuy um pay sikwiyamuy hingsakw tutkitat
pu' naapa tsurumnaqw pay um peekyewtaqat sonqa pan hovakuy-
tini. Noq paasat tapkiwtaqw hapi ima hiihiitu ii'ist sisikyaatayt,
kweekwewt angqe' hiita nöönösaniqey oovi tunöshepnumyangwu.
Noq himuwa ung hova'ikwqa ung mooti tuwaaqa pay hapi naat
sonqa pas yaayavaqwni. Pas pam ason pu' uumi nakwse' paasat pu'
pam uupa sominumni. Pu' pam put kwaakwit tuwakyangw pu' ung
pekyehovaqtuqat navote' paasat pu' pay pam sonqa tuptsiwni um
pang mokpu wa'ökiwtaqata. Niikyangw son um pas paasavo haqam
qa hiikwistaniqe oovi ason um hikwismangu'e' um pay hiisavawyat

In this position the wood dried. Next, the boy's grandmother procured some sinew which she twisted into a cord long enough for the two bows. This bow string she attached to the bows. They really did a good job. The bow was not very strong, but when the old lady tested it, the arrow zoomed off with great force and flew quite far. Now Pitsinsivostiyo had two nice bows.

Once more the grandmother had instructions for Pitsinsivostiyo. "Well," she said, "now it's time to go after the yellow fox by the rocky hill southwest of here. Be sure to take your weapons along. Once you get there, stop somewhere and collect a large amount of the giant drop seed grass. Then continue until you reach the rock mound. Look for a large, empty place there. When you find one, walk back and forth across it until the earth is really messed up. Be sure to leave many tracks behind. Having done that, shoot your arrows into the ground over all the empty space. Then lie down on the ground so that when someone comes up to you, he will think that you were attacked by enemies and killed. Stick one arrow into your armpit. Break another in half, smear it with pitch at one end, and then glue it to your heart. You must be lying there ready when the sun goes down. Then sprinkle the giant drop seed all over yourself. Be sure to put some also into your mouth. These seeds look just like maggots. With that it will be quite believable that you've been dead for quite some time, and the flies have laid their eggs. Now here are some mice which I trapped for you. Take those with you too. They are pretty much decayed already and stink terribly. Cut their meat into little pieces and stick them on your body. Then you're bound to give off the odor of a rotten corpse. In the early evening creatures such as coyotes, yellow foxes and wolves roam in search of something to eat. An animal that smells you and finds you will first keep its distance. Then it will come up close and sniff you all over. When it sees the drop seeds and notices your decaying odor, it will be convinced that you are dead. Of course, you can't afford not to breathe for that long. If you get out of breath, just inhale a little bit of air at a time. When the drop seeds start moving then, the animal will think they are live maggots. With a happy heart it will then announce to the other creatures that it has come across some food. Once they hear the call, they will all assemble there." This is how his grandmother laid out her instructions for him.

hikwsut pu' piwmantani. Pan pay piw pam kwaaki poniniykye' pay puma taayungqam aatu pangyaqat pam sonqa yan wuuwani. Paasat pu' pam hapi haalay'unangway mimuywatuy aa'awnani pam tunöstuwqeyu. Noq pu' pumawat nanapte' paasat pu' puma sonqa pangso tsovaltini," yan yaw pam put aw tutapta.

Noq pu' yaw pam oovi ep qavongvaqw pay yaw pangso owatsmominiiqe yaw put soy tutavoyat aa'antsakmakyangw pu' pephaqam tapkinaqe pu' yaw pam oovi pangqe' wa'ö. Is, pavan yaw ep a'ni soniwa. Pas pi yaw put aw tuwqam wukokiipo'eway.

Hiisavoniqw pay yaw taawa pakiqw pay yaw hiita navota. Niiqe yaw poosiy puruknaqw yaw pam pep suukya iisaw ep antsa aw yanta. Yanta yaw aw taynumkyangw put qöqönlawu. Pu' yaw iisaw aw wuuwa, pas yaw kur a'ni hiniwtapna. Yaw tuwqamuy kur aw a'ni naayawva. Ang hoohu yanyungwa. Pu' yaw suukya hoohu tiyot aqw tsööqökiwta. "Is uti, pas kya hak a'ni taaqay," yaw kita. "Meh, hiisa'haqam hoohuy akw aw pookyayat qa mu'aya. Son kya haqawa qa pas mavastat aw pookya. Oovi yangqe' yanta," yaw yan aw wuuwantaqe put ep aw moto'ta pami'. "Sen pay pas mokpu," yaw yan wuuwaqw pu' piw ang qöniltingwu. Pu' yaw suutsepngwat aw hoyta. Noq pu' yaw pam awniiqe aw yanta. Yaw pas pas mokpu. Pay yaw pas qa poniniyku. Pu' yaw aw yorikqw pay kur i' pay wuuyavo mokpu. "Oovi pu' pay ang tootopt kur aw tiitotay," yaw yan wuuwa. Yaw ang totopnöhu yanyungwa. Pu', "Is, nangpi haqami hakiy wangwayi. Son pi nu' it naalaniikyangw soosok sowaniy," yaw kitaaqe pu' yaw oovi angqw hiisavo kwiniwinit pep pu' yaw a'ni wahahalawu.

Wahahalawqe pu' yaw qe'tit pu' yaw teevengeniiqe pu' pangsoq piw yaw wahahalawu. Qe'tit pu' piw yaw hoopoq. Pas oovi pam naanan'i'ivoq pantit pangqw awniiqe pep yaw yantaqw pu' yaw hiisavoniqw pay kwiningyahaqaqw yaw hak warikiwta. Pu' yaw sungnuptu put aw, "Ta'ay," yaw kiita, "ya hak yepehaq itamuy wangwaylawuy?" yaw kita.

"Pay nuu'uy," yaw kita. "Pay nu' it yep tuwa yep mokpuniqw pas kya hak a'ni taaqaniiqe oovi a'ni hiniwtapna. Pay pi itam it soswaniqw oovi nu' paniqw umuy wangwaylawuy," yaw kita.

Hiisavoniqw pay yaw puma hiihinyungqam popkot pep put aw tsovalti. Noq paasat pay yaw naat hihin taalaniqw puma yaw pep put aw ökiiqe pu' yaw puma tuwat put aapa sominumya. Noq naat yaw puma put qöqönyaqw pu' yaw pam pay suuvaqw poosiy puruknaqe pu' yaw pam pumuy amumi as taynumt pay yaw pam pumuy qa pas

The next morning Pitsinsivostiyo headed out to the rocky hill. He did exactly as his grandmother had told him. His preparations took until early evening, and then he lay down. What a terrible sight he presented! The whole scene gave the impression that he had been attacked by a large number of enemies.

Not long before the sun went down Pitsinsivostiyo heard something. Opening his eyes, he saw a coyote. The animal kept circling him, inspecting him from all sides. It concluded that the victim evidently had been in a tremendous fight. He must have been attacked by enemies, for there were arrows all over, with one actually sticking in the boy. "What a brave man," the coyote said. "Look at all the arrows that were shot at him and missed. But one of the attackers' shots was well aimed. That's why he is lying there now." This is what went through the animal's mind as it craned its neck toward the boy. "I wonder if he's really dead," it thought as it circled his prostrate body. The coyote came closer and closer until it stood right by Pitsinsivostiyo. No doubt, the victim was dead. He no longer stirred. From the looks of him he had been dead for a long time, because the flies had already laid their eggs. There were fly eggs all over him. "Why don't I call someone," the coyote thought. "I can't devour all of him by myself." So he trotted a little ways northwest and then emitted a series of barking howls.

Stopping its howling, the animal ran southwest and howled once more. After that it went to the northeast. When it had howled into every direction, it returned to the boy and stood by him. It was not long before someone came running from the northwest. The animal stopped and asked, "Well, who's calling here?"

"It's me," the coyote replied. "I found this dead boy here. He must have been brave and fought hard. I called all of you so that we can feed on him."

Before long, all sorts of creatures had gathered. There was still a little bit of daylight, so they came up to the boy and sniffed around him. They were still circling Pitsinsivostiyo when he opened one eye.

pas suyan tuwa'ynuma. Niiqe pu' yaw pam pay oovi ahoy uviiti-
kyangw son yaw kur pam pante' pumuy tuwa'ytani. Niiqe pay yaw
pam oovi as tuutuskyangw pay yaw pam nawus putsi'uvita. Pantaqe
pu' yaw pam pay pumuy hihin pavan tuwa'ytaqw pay yaw puma
popkot qa nanapta.

Naat yaw pam oovi pumuy amumi tunatyawtaqw pay yaw
puma sumataq put soswaniqe pay yaw paasat qe'toti put qöqönyaqe
pu' yaw pay put pas aw hoytota. Niiqe pu' yaw puma put aw ökiqw
pay yaw himuwa put naat pay qa pas angqw kyatkut pay yaw put
mooti ang lengitsmingwu.

Noq pu' yaw puma soosoyam put aw ökiqw piw yaw put putngaqwwat maayat su'aqlap i' pas suslomasikyaatayo nuutum put aw
wunuwta. Niiqe putwat yaw pamniqey yan yaw pam wuuwankyangw yaw pam putwatsa aw tunatyawta. Noq pu' yaw puma popkot naat pu' yaw put soswaniqw pu' yaw pamwa pas suslomasikyaatayo put maayat atsva kwilaktoq pu' yaw pam tiyo put aw yootok-
kyangw piw yaw pam put suhokyavaqe ngu'at pu' yaw pam pang
ahoy suqtuptuqe pu' yaw pam ayangqwwat put hokyayat ngu'aaqe
pu' yaw pam pep a'ni töötöqlawu, "Yap pahaha, yap pahaha," yaw
pam kitalawqw pu' yaw pay mimawat soosoyam naanahoy kwee-
tsikma. Pu' yaw pam sikyaatayo as a'ni rohomnumqw pay yaw pam
tiyo put pas qa maatavi. Pu' yaw pam sikyaatayo pay piw tsawnaqe
pay yaw pam qa hin put kuukiniqey unangwa'yta.

Noq pu' yaw mimawat soosoyam haqami tuutuwayamaqw pu'
yaw pam Pitsinsivostiyo put sikyaatayot aw pangqawu, "Haakiy, pay
um qa pas hintsakniy. Pay nu' son ung hintsanniy. Pay nu' son ung
niinaniqw oovi pay um nuy qa mamqasniy," yaw pam put aw kitaqw
paasat pu' yaw pam sikyaatayo sun yukuqw pu' yaw pam put maanat aw tu'awi'yta. Pu' pam put sikyaatayot pas naawaknakyangw
pu' yaw ason hak put engem wikvaqw paasat pu' yaw hak put pö'e'
pu' yaw put amumtiniqat. "Noq nu' oovi okiw wuuyavohaqam it aw
yan hintsaklawkyangw pu' itam isoy amum aw yan wuuwaqw pu'
nu' oovi angqw umumi piw taqa'nangwti. Noq kur antsa um kya pi
pay nakwhaqw oovi inumi nakwsuqw oovi nu' ung ngu'ay," yaw
kita. "Oovi um qa hin naawaknat inumumni. Pam pay maana sonqa
ung paasniy," yaw kita. "Ason pi pay hisat sonqa um ep wuuyavo
amum qatuqw pay sonqa ung ahoy piw yuk uusinmuy aw laalay-
niy," yaw pam aw kita.

Noq oovi yaw, "Kur antsa'ay," yaw kita, "pay nu' umumniy,"
yaw kita.

With this one eye, he had a hard time seeing them properly. With his eyes closed, however, he could not have seen them at all. So he carefully observed them through his eyelashes. Now he could make them out a little bit better. They in turn were not aware of this.

Paying close attention to the animals, Pitsinsivostiyo realized that they clearly intended to eat him. They had quit circling by now and were creeping up closer. Upon reaching his body, one of them licked him with its tongue, but did not bite a chunk out of him yet.

When all the creatures were by his side, Pitsinsivostiyo noticed that next to his right hand stood the most beautiful yellow fox. He knew this was the one to get, so he focused his attention on it. The animals were about ready to sink their fangs into him, when the handsome fox stepped over the boy's hand. At this moment Pitsinsivostiyo grabbed for the fox and got hold of its leg. He quickly jumped up, and getting hold of its other leg, let out a series of screams. "Yap pahaha, yap pahaha," he yelled, and the other animals scurried in all directions. The yellow fox fought back as hard as he could, but the boy would not let go of him. The animal became frightened now, but showed no intention of biting his captor.

When all the other creatures had disappeared, Pitsinsivostiyo spoke to the fox. "Wait before you do anything. I'm not going to harm you. I don't want to kill you, so you need not be afraid of me," he said. The fox calmed down, whereupon Pitsinsivostiyo told him all about the girl. He explained to him that her heart was set on a yellow fox and that the one who brought her one would win her hand in marriage. "I tried to accomplish this for a long, long time until both my grandmother and I came up with the idea of seeking help from all of you. You consented and came to me, and that's how I managed to catch you," he said. "So don't fuss now. I'm sure that girl will be gentle with you."

The fox replied, "Very well, I'll go with you."

Paasat pu' yaw pam oovi pangqw put wikkyangw nima. Noq pu'
yaw pam kiy ep ahoy pitukyangw put wikvaqw pas pi yaw put so'at
engem haalaytiqe yaw pangqawlawu, "Askwali, is askwali! Pay kur
um su'an yukuuqe oovi pay um put wikva. Askwali. Pay pi um pu'
put maanat aw wikve' pay um son put qa pö'ani. Pu' pi pay pam son
nawus qa umumtini. Is uni, paypa um pu' naa'aptsina," yaw pam
kitaaqe yaw haalaylawt pu' yaw pam aapamiqhaqaminiiqe pu' yaw
pam pangqaqw tsaqaptatnit pu' hiita mookiwtaqat pangqaqw yawma. Niiqe pu' yaw pam put tsaqaptat aqw kuyt pu' yaw pam put
pantaqat aqw put hiita momrit pu' paasat put neyngala. Pantit paasat
pu' yaw pam put mööyiy aw pangqawu, "Ta'a, kur pangqw pew put
uuvokoy wiikii'!"

Pu' yaw pam oovi pangqw put soy aw wikqw pay yaw pam naat
rohomtit pu' piwningwu. Niikyangw pay yaw pam put soy aw pitsi-
naqw pu' yaw put so'at may akw put tsaqaptat aqw moroknat paasat
pu' yaw pam put sikyaatayot may akw soosovik ang maamapri. Noq
pay yaw pam panis put pantsanqw pay yaw pam kur kwakwhatiqe
pay yaw pam pep pumuy naamömuy amuqlap qatuptuqe qa hin yaw
waayaniqey unangwa'yta. Noq pam so'wuuti hapi yaw kur put
kuuyit aqw hiita ngahut oyaqw pu' pam put aw la'yvaqw paniqw
yaw pam oovi kwakwhati. Noq pu' yaw put mawpilawu. Pas yaw
suphingpu, lomahinta. "Is askwaliy," yaw kita, put sikyaatayot awi.
"Pay itam yuk it tuwat maanat aw pootaniqe itam oovi ung poktay,"
yaw pam aw kita, sowuuti.

"Owiy," yaw kita. "Pay itam nanapta. Nanaptaqe oovi awyaqw
kur antsa i' nuy qa peevewnaqe nuy namortaqe oovi nuy ngu'ay,"
yaw kita.

"Owiy," yaw kita, "askwal pi um naataviy," yaw aw kita.

Yan yaw puma put engem put pas hiita tumqat tuyqawva. Niiqe
yaw pam Pitsinsivostiyo qavomi mihikmi kwangwtoya. Noq pay
yaw pam sikyaatayo paasat paas kwakwha'iwtaqe qa hin yaw
yamakniqey unangwa'ytaqw pu' yaw puma oovi ang neengem
aapataqe pu' yaw puma oovi puwvaniqw pu' yaw pam sikyaatayo
pay put tiyot aqle' tuwat wa'ö.

Qavongvaqw tapkiqw pu' yaw puma piw nösqw pu' yaw pay
pam tiyo put maanat kiiyat awniqey yaw put soy aw pangqawu. Noq
pay yaw pam so'wuuti naat put meewa. Ason yaw pay hihin too-
kiwqw pu' yaw pam put wikkyangw pu' yaw ason aw pootatoni.
Noq yaw pam Pitsinsivostiyo okiw as qa nakwhani'yta. Niiqe pay
yaw suupan putniqw pay yaw as se'elhaqtiqw pas piw yaw pam put

Thereupon Pitsinsivostiyo went home with the fox. When he arrived with the animal, his grandmother was overjoyed. "Thank you, thank you," she kept saying. "You did what I told you perfectly. That's why you caught the fox. Thanks. With this animal you're bound to win the girl. She will have to marry you now. How nice, now I guess you have yourself a wife," the old woman said gratefully. She then disappeared into the back room and came back with a bowl and something in a bundle. Pouring water into the bowl, she crushed something into it and mixed it with the liquid. Then she said to her grandchild, "Now, bring me your animal."

Pitsinsivostiyo obeyed and brought her the fox. He was still resisting his captor. The old granny now dipped her hand into the bowl and rubbed the liquid all over the fox's body. No sooner had she done this than the fox became completely tame. He sat down next to the two and showed no more impulse to flee. The old woman had put some medicine into the water, which produced its magic effect on the fox. For this reason, he became tame. She kept stroking his fur. How soft and beautiful it was! "Thank you," the old woman said to the animal. "We also want to give it a try with this girl. That's why we made you into a pet," she explained.

"Yes," the fox replied, "we were aware of that. That's why we came. And sure enough, this boy had confidence in me and selected me and caught me."

"Of course," Pitsinsivostiyo replied. "Thanks for giving yourself to me."

In this manner the two came into possession of that extremely skittish animal. Pitsinsivostiyo was already looking forward to the following night. And since the yellow fox was tame and showed no sign of trying to escape, the two spread out their bedding in order to sleep. The yellow fox, in turn lay down next to the boy.

Early in the evening the following day, right after supper, Pitsinsivostiyo told his grandmother that he was ready to go to the girl's house. But his grandmother suggested he wait a little longer. Later, when some of the people were in bed, it would be better to visit the

qa nakwhana. Noq pay yaw naat as qa wuuyavoti.

Nawis'ewtiqw pu' yaw put so'at put aw pangqawu, "Ta'a, kur aw hin navottoo'. Pay sen pi pas qa atsalawe' pay pam sonqa naap pangqawni pay um pö'aaqata. Noq pay pi um hin'ewayhoyaniqw pay sen put ung akw qa himunen pay uumi qa unangwtapni. Naamahin pi um as it aw engem wikniniqw pay kya uumi yorikye' pay paasat qe'watani," yaw pam put aw kita.

Paasat pu' yaw oovi pangqw kiy angqw put sikyaatayot tsöpkyangw put maanat kiiyat aqwa. Niiqe pay yaw pam naat qa pas aqw pitut pay yaw pam put taviqw piw yaw pay pam put angk wawartima. Pas pi pay yaw pam put pokooya'atniiqey pan angk hinma.

Noq pu' yaw puma put maanat kiiyat aqw pituqw pu' yaw pam tiyo pay paasat piw put ahoy tsöpaatat pu' yaw put kiiyat tupatsmiq wuuvi. Niiqe yaw pam aqw wupqw pay yaw pam maana naat piw ngumantaqw pu' yaw pam tiyo pangqw haqaqw aqw poksö'ytaqw pangqw pu' yaw pam put sikyaatayot mavoko'ykyangw pangsoq qatuptu. Pu' yaw pam aqw qatuptuqw pu' yaw pam pay qa paasat aw hingqawu. Pay yaw pam put mooti tiimayt paasat pu' yaw pam put aw pangqawu, "Soh, meh, yep nu' ungem it wikvay," yaw pam put aw kita.

Noq pay yaw kur pam maana sunvotqe pu' yaw pam oovi pay suungumanqe'tit pu' yaw pam put aqw yorikqw piw yaw pangqw pam tiyo put sikyaatayot mavoko'ykyangw qatuqw pas pi yaw pam hin unangwtiqe pu' yaw pam pay pangqw matangaqw suyma. Niiqe pu' yaw pam put aqw warikt pu' yaw put aw pangqawu, "Is uni, ya um piw put pooko'yta? Um qa sööwu pangqw pantat um pew pakye' um yep inumi yu'a'atani," yaw pam put aw kitaqw pu' yaw pam oovi pangsoniiqe pu' yaw pep put haqami qatu'a'awnaqw pep pu' yaw pam qatuptukyangw pay yaw pam naat put sikyaatayot pep mavoko'yta.

Noq pu' yaw pam pep qatuptuqw pu' yaw pam maana pay qa sööwu put tuuvinglawu sen pi pam tsöngmokiwtaniqw pay yaw pam paasat aapaminiiqe pu' yaw pam pangqaqw it piikit hiisa' tawimokkyangw yamakqe pu' yaw pam put atpipo oya. Pantit pu' yaw pam put piw engem hiita aqw kuyt pu' yaw piw hiisa' kwiptosit enang aqw oyat pu' piw putwat atpipo tavit pu' yaw aw pangqawu, "Ta'a, um yep tuumoykyangw inumi yu'a'atani. Noq nu' son haak as uuvokoy ungem tsöptani?" yaw pam put aw kita.

Paasat pu' yaw pam put maanat aw pangqawu, "Pi pay nu' ungem put wikvay. Pi yaw um put pas naawaknaqw oovi nu' antsa

girl with the animal. Poor Pitsinsivostiyo was restless. According to him it was already quite late, but his grandmother did not see it that way. Not much time had passed yet.

Finally, his grandmother said, "All right, this is the moment to go and find out. If the girl did not lie, she will tell you herself that you have won her. However, you're quite homely. She may dislike you for that and not accept you. Even though you bring her the animal she wants, she may but cast a glance at you and change her mind," she said to him.

Pitsinsivostiyo left the house with the fox in his arms and headed over to the girl's place. On the way he set the animal on the ground and let it run after him. The fox trotted after him just like a dog.

Upon reaching the girl's house, the boy picked up the fox and ascended to the upper story. Sure enough, the girl was grinding corn, so he sat down at the vent to her grinding chamber with the fox in his arms. He still did not say anything to her. He watched her first, then he said, "Hey, listen, I brought this for you."

The girl heard him at once and immediately stopped grinding. She looked up at the vent hole. When she spotted the boy squatting there clutching a yellow fox, she got very excited. Quickly she arose from the grinding bin, ran up to the vent and exclaimed, "How nice, is that your pet? Don't waste your time out there. Step inside. Then you can talk to me." The boy complied and sat down where she had offered him a seat, still embracing the fox.

No sooner had he taken his seat than the girl, not wasting any time, asked him if perhaps he was hungry. Quickly she disappeared into the room next door and returned with a few rolls of piki. These she placed next to Pitsinsivostiyo. "Here, you can eat this while you talk to me. May I hold your pet for you for the time being?"

Pitsinsivostiyo said, "Sure, I brought this fox for you. From what I heard, this is the animal you wanted. I caught it especially for you. The yellow fox is yours."

put ngu'aqw pay pi um oovi pu' putniy," yaw pam put aw kita.

"Is uni, ya um inungem it wikva? Pi antsa nu' hiitawat aw pan lavaytingwuniqw pay qa hak hisat yangqaqw inungem it wiiki. Pay pi nu' as pas qa hakiy amumtiniqe oovi antsa hakiy pan lavaytingwu," yaw pam put aw kita. "Noq pay pi um it angqw kur inungem wikvaqe pay um nuy pö'a. Noq pay pi nu' oovi sonqa umumtiniy," yaw pam put aw kita. Pas pi yaw pam put sikyaatayot tsuya. Pu' piw yaw pam maana qa hin put Pitsinsivostiyot hin'ewakoyat tuwa'ykyangw yaw put amumtiniqey put aw pangqawu. "Is askwaliy," yaw kita, "pay nu' sonqa umumniy," yaw kita. "Niikyangw yaapiy hapi naalötok ep pay hapi nu' uumi lööqöktoniy," yaw aw kita. "Oovi um haqaqwniiqey uusinmuy aw tuu'awvaniy," yaw kita. "Niikyangw nu' pi pay it sonqa yep tavi'ytaniy," yaw kita. "Ispi nu' it oovi yep tootimuy amumi pangqawlawu. Tsangaw kur um hak hin'urniiqe it inungem wikvay," yaw kitaaqe put sikyaatayot ang mawpitikyangw uninita. "Niiqe it oovi um kimaniy," yaw kitaaqe pu' yaw oovi engem hiita mokyaata, put tiyot engem.

Pangqw pu' yaw pam haalaykyangw wari. Warikqe yaw ahoy kiy ep pituqw yaw naat so'at kur qa puuwi. "Iso'oy," yaw kita.

"Ya himu'u, imöyhoyay?" yaw kita.

"Pay maana nakwhay," yaw kita.

"Is askwaliy," yaw kita, "is askwali."

"Niikyangw it nuy mokyaatoynay," yaw kitaaqe pu' soy aw purukna. Yaw kur pam muupi. Pu' yaw piw somiviki. Pu' yaw pam kuyapkuyqe aw taviqw pu' pep puma put tuumoyta. Yaw qa hisat puma put hiita nöösa. Noq pas yaw kwangwa himuniqw puma yaw kwangwanösa puta. "Niikyangw pam maana inumi tutapta, 'Yaapiy naalötok ep pay nu' angqw wikniy,' yaw kita. Yanhaqam inumi lavayti."

"Tih, pay pas aw suptsinay," yaw kita.

"Owiy," yaw kita.

"Kur antsa'ay," yaw kita, "yaapiy pu' nu' ikiy qenilawni, itam okiw nukuski'ytaqw. Noq pay pi nu' hihin qö'awpani. Nen paavalwikqw hihin kwangw'ewakw aw pituniy," yaw kita. "Niikyangw pam hapi sonqa lööqökniqw oovi pangqawu. Niikyangw itam hapi kur hin hiita engem yukuni. Itam naala'ay," yaw kita. "Pay pi itam ngas'ew hiita hiisakwhoyat sen hiita engem yukuqw pankyangw pu' itam ahoy piw kiiyat aw wikyaniy," yaw pam put aw kita, tiyot awi'.

Noq aapiy pu' pay yaw pam Pitsinsivostiyo put maanat aqw sasqalawu. Niikyangw ep nalöstalqat ep pu' yaw pam pay hihin qa

"How nice, you really brought it for me? Yes, it's true, that's what I used to tell my suitors, but no one ever brought me one. I said that to them because I had no desire to get married," she continued. "But since you came with the animal, you beat me at my game. I will therefore become your wife." She was very pleased with the fox. Without noticing Pitsinsivostiyo's homeliness, the girl had promised to marry him. "Thank you so much," the girl said again. "I will surely live with you. Four days from now I'll come to your house to grind corn as your bride. So tell your relatives to attend the wedding ceremony. The fox, however, I will keep here. For he is what I kept talking about to the boys. I'm glad you were powerful enough to fulfill my wish," she said, stroking the yellow fox and uttering words of delight at the same time. "So take this home with you," she said and wrapped something up for the boy.

Pitsinsivostiyo ran home in happy spirits. When he arrived, his grandmother was still up. "Grandmother," he cried.

"What is it, my grandson?"

"The girl said yes."

"Oh thank you, thanks," the old woman replied.

"Look, this is what she wrapped up for me." He opened the bundle in the presence of his grandmother. There was rolled piki and also *somiviki*. The old woman ladled some water into a bowl for him and then the two ate. They had never tasted anything like this. The food was delicious and they ate with great gusto. "The girl also gave me some instructions. 'Four days from now I will come and get you.' Those were her words."

"Gee, she's really in a rush."

"Yes," said Pitsinsivostiyo.

"Very well. I'll start cleaning up the house," his grandmother said. "We really live very poorly here. I'll dust a bit and whitewash the walls. Then it will look a little more pleasant. By the way, I'm sure she said she will come here to grind as a bride. What on earth are we going to do? We're all alone. Maybe we can get at least some of the things that are part of her wedding outfit before we take her back to her home," she said.

Pitsinsivostiyo now visited the girl on a regular basis. On the fourth day he was a little late, but when he finally arrived, she was all

iits aqwniiqe pu' yaw pay pas hisatniqw pu' epeq pituqw pay yaw pam maana paas kur pay na'sastaqe pu' yaw pay oovi put nuutayta. Niiqe pay yaw pam antsa oovi paas yumuy put awini'ykyangw pangsoq hisat lööqökniqey aqw hoytaqw pay yaw puma oovi paas piw navoti'yta. Noq pay yaw puma put engem pay hihin tusitsuya. Pay pi yaw puma suyan navoti'yta pam Pitsinsivostiyo pay okiw söqavungsinoniiqe pay kya yaw son pas pumuy maanayamuy engem pas hiita hin yukuni. Niikyangw pay yaw as puma tsuya pam maana nawis'ew kongtaniqw. Pay pi yaw pam as pu' wuuyoqtikyangw naat qa koongya'ytaqw suupan yaw as pam pay okiw siwahovaniikyangw wuyootiniqat puma wuuwanta. Pu' pay pi yaw pam put pö'aqw pay yaw puma oovi nawusta.

Noq pu' yaw pam antsa put epeq wiktoqe pu' yaw epeq pituqw pu' yaw puma put oovi pay nawus aw no'a. Noq pu' yaw pam oovi put nguman'iniyat iikwiwkyangw pu' yaw pam put kiy aqw wiiki. Niiqe pu' yaw pumuy pangsoq pituqw pu' yaw pam aqwhaqami pangqawu, "Haw, kuwawatotangwuy! Nu' qa naala waynumay," yaw pam aqwhaqami kitaqw pu' yaw pam so'wuuti antsa angqaqw kuwasveveta.

"Peqw huvam yungya'aa. Antsa kya hak waynuma," yaw pam angqaqw kitaqw pu' yaw pam tiyo oovi put maanat wikkyangw aqw paki.

Noq pu' yaw pumuy epeq pakiqw pu' yaw pam so'wuuti put maanat aw haalaytiqe pu' yaw put engem haqami atsvewtoynaqw pu' yaw pam maana pep qatuptu. Nit pu' yaw pam put mööyiy paas aw tutapta haqami pam put nguman'iniyat taviniqat. Pantit pu' yaw pam piw paas put maanat nopna. Pu' yaw pam put aw pangqawu, "Is uni, pi kur antsa itam nawinmö'wi'yvayani. Pi antsa kur um hak sonewmana. Noq askwal pay itam as yan'ewayomniikyangw piw ung tuyqawva. Pay pi um as antsa itamuy pevewin'ewakwmuy amumi lööqökqw pay itam son hin ungem hiita qa yukuyani," yaw pam put aw kita.

Noq pu' yaw pay paasat hisatniqw pam tuumoytaqe qe'tiqw pu' yaw pay puma tokniqat yaw pam pumuy amumi pangqawu. Paasat pu' pep hötsiwmiq yaw tiyot engem aapata. "Yang um puwniy," yaw kita. "Noq itam pay yepeq puwniy," yaw kitaaqe haqami pösömiq yaw pam put maanat engem aapata.

Noq yaw pam tiyo tuwat itsivuti. Pi yaw as nööma'yvaqe yaw put amum as puwniqw pay yaw piw so'at naat put amum puwni. Pay aw yaw so'at pangqawu, "Yantay," yaw kita, "pay itam Hopiit

prepared and was waiting for him. In the meantime she had also informed her parents when she was going to the boy's house to grind corn as a bride, so they knew about it. Their joy, however, was tempered by the fact that Pitsinsivostiyo was a low-class person and that he and his grandmother would not be able to provide much for their daughter. Still, they were glad that she had finally found a husband. After all, she was quite old already and still not married. They were concerned she might become a spinster. But now that Pitsinsivostiyo had beaten her at her game, her parents too had to resign themselves to the situation.

So Pitsinsivostiyo came to pick her up and when he arrived, they gave their daughter to him. The girl gave him a tray filled with corn flour which he loaded on his back. The two proceeded to his house. Upon arriving he called inside, "Hey! How about some words of welcome. I'm not alone." At once one could hear the old woman's inviting chatter. "Please, come in, whoever is about." Thereupon Pitsinsivostiyo entered with the girl.

The old woman thanked the girl for coming and offered her a seat. The girl sat down. Then the grandmother told her grandson where to place the tray with the flour. After that she fed the girl. "How nice," she cried, "we truly have gotten a beautiful in-law. You are really a gorgeous girl. We must be grateful to have won you, being as destitute as we are. And because you came to grind for us, who are so despised, we'll surely manage somehow to make something for you."

When the girl was finished eating, the old granny announced that it was time for them to go to bed. For Pitsinsivostiyo she made the bed by the door. "You sleep here," she pointed out to him. "We'll sleep over here," and went into a corner to roll out the bedding for the girl.

Pitsinsivostiyo got quite upset. He thought he had gotten a wife and could sleep with her. Instead, his grandmother was going to sleep with her. The old woman said, "This is how we customarily do this. When a bride comes to grind, one cannot sleep with her during the first four days. Once your hair has been washed and tied together with hers, you can sleep with her," she explained. The boy could not change that, so he slept alone.

The next morning the girl was up early, gathering her bedding. When the old woman heard that, she also got up. Then she asked the girl to accompany her outside to speak the morning prayer. Both of

yan tuwi'yyungwa. Hak naat pu' lööqökne' paasat naalös hak qa amum puuvuwngwu. Ason hakim naama asqw paasat pu' pay pi sonqa um amum puwvaniy," yaw aw kita. Yaw nawus tiyo qa hingqawu. Niiqe pay sunala yaw puuwi.

Qavongvaqw pu' yaw pam maana pay as su'its taytakyangw pay yaw pam oovi paasat aapay tsovalantaqw kur yaw pam so'wuuti navotqe pu' yaw pam oovi pay paasat tuwat qatuptuqe pu' yaw pam oovi aapay ang tsovalat pu' yaw put maanat aw pangqawu puma yaw naama kuyvatoniqat. Niiqe pu' yaw puma oovi naama pepeq hiisa' hommatsvongtat pu' yaw aw iipo yamakqe pu' yaw puma talpewi naawakna. Noq pam maana yaw as okiw qa pas hiita akw kyaanavot yukuni. Pu' pam piw hiita noovataqw pam yaw okiw naakya'ytaniqat yan yaw pam tuwat naawakna. Noq pu' yaw pam so'wuuti pumuy tuwat hin put mö'wiy yuwsinayaniqat put tuwat tuuvinglawu.

Yanti yaw pumaniqw paasat pu' yaw puma ahoy pakiqw pu' yaw puma paasat noonova. Noq pam maana yaw pay paasat pas hihin nösqe pu' yaw pam oovi pay put so'wuutit aw maqaptsi'ytaqw pu' yaw pam oovi hisatniqw öyqe pu' yaw pam put matamiq panat paasat pu' yaw pam put piw pay paas kur engem huumiqe pu' yaw pam oovi put matamiq engem tangata. Paasat pu' yaw pam oovi pep ngumanta pay paasat su'its talavay.

Noq naat yaw pam oovi pep pan ngumantaqw piw yaw hak suupaasat pang pumuy naamömuy kiiyamuy aqle' kwayngyavoq mötsikvuy maspatokyangw piw yaw navota hak pep ngumantaqw. Niiqe pay yaw pam put qa pas pas aw hin wuuwankyangw panga. Pas yaw pam angqw ahoyniikyangw pu' yaw piw pan navotqe pu' yaw pam pan wuuwa, "Maataqpa hak pep ngumanta. Son pi suupan pep so'wuuti ki'ytaqani. Pi pam pay paapu wuyo'iwtaqe pay as qa hisat suupan pu' ngumanta," yan yaw pam wuuwaqe yaw pam oovi kur hin put aw wuuwani. Niiqe pu' yaw pam hak kiy ep ahoy pakiiqe pu' yaw pam pep mimuywatuy pep ki'yyungqamuy amumi yan lalvayqw pu' yaw pumawat tuwat put aw wuuwanlalwaqw pay yaw pas qa haqawa navoti'yta hak sen pephaqam ngumantaniqat.

Noq pu' yaw puma pas hin nanaptaniqe pu' yaw puma oovi put hakiy pumuy amungaqwniiqat pangso hoonaya. Niiqe pam yaw oovi pangso kookostoqey pan atsa'ykyangwniiqe pu' yaw pam ep pakiiqe pu' yaw put so'wuutit aw pangqawu, "Nu' as se'elhaq aw noovataniqw piw kur itaaqöhi pay tsootso'a. Noq nu' piw se'elhaq yang umuukiy iikye' imötsikvuy maspatoq piw paasat yangqwsa naat

them helped themselves to some cornmeal, then they went out and prayed in the direction of the rising sun. The girl prayed that she would complete her four-day stay without any hardships. Also she hoped that if she cooked some food there would be plenty for everyone. The old woman, on the other hand, was asking how she could provide the wedding outfit for her daughter-in-law.

This is how the two prayed. Then they went back in and ate breakfast. The girl only ate a tiny portion. She was waiting for the old woman, and when the latter was satisfied, she led the girl to the grinding stone. She had already shelled the corn and placed it on the stone for her. Now the bride was grinding there early in the morning.

It so happened that just at that hour a woman passed by the house, on the way to the dump to throw out her trash. She clearly heard the grinding sounds. She went by without giving it much thought. On the way back she heard the noise again. This time she thought, "I wonder who is grinding corn there. That can't be the old woman who lives here. She's far too old for that chore and never seems to be grinding." The woman was at a loss. Back in the village, she told the others about this. They were all racking their brains, but nobody knew who could possibly be grinding corn there.

The women were all dying from curiosity, so they sent one from their group over. She pretended to be coming for some live embers, and when she entered, she said to the old woman, "I wanted to do some cooking a while back when I realized that our fire was out. And when I came by your house earlier this morning to throw out my trash, I saw smoke coming out of your chimney. That's why I came here," she said.

"Sure. Here, I just added wood to the fire, so there's bound to be some good hot coals. Just put your torch in and light it," she encouraged the visitor. While the visitor had her torch in the fireplace, she was biding her time. Standing around, she carefully inspected the house and once more heard grinding noises in the back room. Since the old woman who lived there was still with her, it could not be her.

kwiikwitsqw oovi nu' angqw pew'i," yaw pam put aw kita.

"Pi kur antsa'a. Ta'a, pay naat nu' pu' piw aqw qöönaqw pay son oovi naat angqw qa hin'ur töövu'iwtani. Pay um antsa oovi uukopitsokiy aqw pane' angqw paalatani," yaw pam put aw kitaqw pu' yaw pam oovi put kopitsokiy pangsoq pumuy qöpqöyamuy aqw pani'ykyangw yaw pay pep wununumlawu. Niikyangw pam yaw pumuy kiiyamuy paas ep yorikkyangw pu' piw yaw tuqayvaasi'ytaqw pay yaw pas hak antsa pepehaq pumuy aapaviyamuy epeq ngumanta. Noq paasat pi yaw pam so'wuuti pep ki'ytaqa naat pepwat put amum pakiwtaqw pay yaw oovi qa pam kur ngumanta.

Noq pu' yaw pam pas qa nang'eknaqe pu' yaw pam oovi put tuuvingta, "Is uni, ya um piw hakiy nguman'aya'ytaqw oovi piw hak ungem ngumanta? Sen pi um piw hakiy maanat pu' tavi'yta," yaw pam put aw kita.

Pay yaw pam mooti tayatit pu' yaw pam put aw pangqawu, "Pi pay as uma puye'em son tuutuptsiwniniqw pay pi nu' ung aa'awnani. Pi tooki i' imöyi yep maanat wikvaqw pam oovi yep lööqökiwtaqe pam oovi yep ngumanta," yaw pam put aw kita.

"Is uni, ya pam piw hakiy naa'aptsina?" yaw pam put aw kita.

Noq pu' yaw pam put aa'awna pam tiyo pep ki'ytaqa kwusi'yta. Noq pu' yaw pam yan put aa'awnaqw pas pi yaw pam as qa tuptsiwkyangw pay qa hingqawu.

Noq paasat pay yaw put kopitsoki'at nuwu pas uwikqw pu' yaw pam oovi put angqw suuhoroknat pu' yaw payniqey yaw put aw pangqawu. Pas pi yaw pam pisoq'iwta mimuywatuy put aa'awnaniqey. Pas pi yaw antsa qa hin tuptsiwni'ewayniqw pam yaw oovi put kiy aw tuu'awmaniqe kwangwtoya. Noq pu' yaw pam oovi pep pituuqe pu' yaw pam pumuy put aa'awnaqw antsa yaw puma qa hin tuutuptsiwa. Pu' yaw pam pumuy put aa'awnat paasat pu' yaw pam piw sutsvowat hakimuy kiiyamuy awniiqe pu' yaw piw pumuywatuy aa'awnaqw pay yaw pumawat piw qa tuutuptsiwa. Paapiy pu' yaw puma pep kitsokive put naa'awintota. Noq pu' yaw ima pas qa tuutuptsiwyaqam puma pu' yaw paasat pangsoqwat put maanat kiiyat aqw put yumuyatuy tuuvingtawisngwu. Noq pay yaw pas antsaniiqat yaw puma hiitawat aw kitaqw pu' yaw pam pay paasat piw panwat haqami tuu'awmangwu. Naat yaw pay oovi qa taawanasaptiqw pay yaw puma sinom pep soosoyam it navoti'yyungwa.

Paapiy pu' yaw pam maana oovi pep mö'öngqatkyangw pu' yaw payistalnaqw pu' yaw pam put tiyot amum ep qavongvaqw asni. Noq ep mihikqw pu' yaw put Pitsinsivostiyot so'at iipohaqami

The visitor could no longer refrain herself and asked, "How nice. Did you ask someone to grind corn for you? Maybe you have a girl back there."

The old woman laughed and replied, "I know you won't believe this, so let me tell you. My grandson came home with a girl last night, who's grinding here as a bride."

"Isn't that nice. So he got himself a wife?"

The old woman replied in the affirmative. The other woman was so surprised that she could not utter a word.

Meanwhile the torch had flamed up. The woman quickly extracted it and excused herself. She was in a great hurry to relate this news to the others. It was an unbelievable story, so she was looking forward to bringing the surprising news. Sure enough, when she told the others, they refused to believe it. She hurried from house to house, telling her story everywhere. The people could not believe what they heard. And thus the news spread throughout the village. But no one took it seriously, so they all went to the girl's house and asked her parents who confirmed that it was true. It was not even midday yet when all the villagers were informed.

Meanwhile, the girl who was staying at the groom's house had completed her third day grinding corn. The next day was going to be the hair washing ceremony. That night Pitsinsivostiyo's grandmother went outside and made an announcement. "All of my off-spring that live out there, come and gather at this house. Tomorrow we want to wash the hair of my daughter-in-law. We'll be eating her food from this day on." After the announcement she went back in and they slept.

Early the next day the girl's mother arrived with a few of her relatives for the hair washing ritual. Much to their surprise, upon their arrival, they found a large crowd of people gathered inside. They were all related to Pitsinsivostiyo's grandmother. It was incredible how many relatives she had! They were sitting there in great numbers. They all washed the couple's hair. Ahead of time, Pitsinsivostiyo's uncles also had fashioned all of the wedding garments, which

yamakmaqe pu' yaw pam pep tsa'lawu, "Pangqe' kya uma inatkom yeese. Uma pew itaakiy aw tsovawmani. Itam qaavo mö'wit put it imöyiy Pitsinsivostiyot enang asnaye' pu' itam put itaamö'wiy engem hiita yukuye' itam put noovayat yaapiy noonovaniy," yan yaw pam tsa'lawt pu' ahoy pakiqw pu' yaw puma tookya.

Qavongvaqw pay yaw su'its yaw put maanat yu'at pumuy pee-tuy sinomuy tsamkyangw yaw epeq pituqw pu' yaw puma pumuy asnayani. Noq piw yaw pumuy epeq ökiqw pas hapi yaw pepeq ha-kim sinom wukotangawta. Noq puma yaw kur it Pitsinsivostiyotnit pu' put soyat sinomat. Pas pi yaw puma kur a'ni hakimuy sino-mu'yta. Pas pi yaw puma haqe' kur wukoyese. Niiqe puma yaw oovi soosoyam pumuy asnaya. Pu' yaw put Pitsinsivostiyot taahamat pay aapiy angqe' ii'it hiita mö'öngyuwsit yukuutotaqe pu' yaw puma put pep naanangk kivanta. Niiqe pay yaw puma oovi pas soosok hiita aptsiwtaqat yukuya. Pu' yaw pam maana oovi tuwat novavisoq'iwta. Noq pay pi yaw puma as piw kyaysiwqw pay yaw pam piw pumuy hin nopni'yta. Noq yan pay yaw puma put mö'öngna'yat suyukuya.

Noq pu' yaw pam maana pay qa pas naat wuuyavo pep mö'öng-qat pu' yaw pam pay ahoy nimani. Niiqe pu' yaw pam tiyo oovi pay piw naap put nöömay kiiyat aqw wikqe pas pi yaw pam wukosikwi-mokta. Pas yaw pam navayhaqamuy imuy pas wukososowi'yngwa-muy pangsoq mö'önangwsikwimokta. Noq pu' yaw put maanat yumat it yan yorikqe pas pi yaw puma haalayti.

Noq yan yaw puma naamöm pumuy sinomuy tsovalaqw pu' yaw puma pumuy amumi unangwtatveqw pu' yaw puma oovi put mö'wiy pay naat qa pas wuuyavotiqw pay yaw puma put engem soosok hiita mö'öngyuwsiyat yukuya. Pu' yaw puma as piw naa-mahin pan put suyukuyakyangw pas pi yaw puma soosok hiita lomayukuya. Qa hisat pi yaw hakim haqam pan mö'öngna'yat suyukuya.

Noq yan yaw mimawat sinom piw ep nanapta yaw kur puma naamöm qa paysoq hiitu. Puma hapi yaw as kur pas hiituniqw yaw puma pep sinom pumuy okiw as pay tuuvi'yyungwa. Qa hak yaw as okiw pumuy amumi suutaq'ewa. Noq yaw pam so'wuuti yaw kur i' Kookyangwso'wuuti. Noq pu' yaw pam Pitsinsivostiyo yaw kur it pösövit himu'ytaqw put hapi yaw angqw ima soosoyam Hopiit it hiihiita hiihinyungqat yuwsiy yuykuya, katsinyuyuwsitniikyangw pu' pay pöpsaalatniikyangw pu' pay puuvut hiihiita puma naaqavo yuuyahiwtaqw puta. Noq oovi yaw pam maana pas hakimuy amumi mö'witiqw paapiy pu' yaw puma oovi naama qatu.

they were now bringing in one after the other. The girl in turn was busy preparing the food. There were many guests, but somehow she managed to feed them all. This is how the wedding party came to a close.

The bride's stay really had not been very long. She was now ready to return home. Pitsinsivostiyo took his wife home in person. He had bagged a large amount of venison, six big deer in all. When the girl's parents saw all the meat the bridegroom brought, they were happy.

This is how the old woman and her grandchild assembled their relatives, who helped with the wedding. In no time they finished the wedding outfit, but even though they worked fast, everything was finished beautifully. Never had preparations for a wedding party been completed so soon.

By now the other people had realized that the old woman and her grandson were not just ordinary people, but were endowed with greater than human powers. No one had been willing to accept them, and they were cast out by the villagers. As it turned out now, Pitsinsivostiyo's grandmother was actually Old Spider Woman. And Pitsinsivostiyo, or "Cotton Seed Boy," owned all the cotton from which the Hopis fashioned all kinds of clothes, kachina costumes, blankets and everyday garments. To these people the girl had now become an in-law, and she and Pitsinsivostiyo lived together.

The girl, of course, also had the yellow fox as a pet. He had really gotten attached to Pitsinsivostiyo's wife and always stayed on her heels. The girl loved him dearly.

Noq pu' yaw pam maana paapiy piw put sikyaatayot pooko'y-
kyangw pu' yaw aapiy qatuqw pas yaw pam sikyaatayo put Pitsinsivostiyot nöömayat paas natuwi'ytaqe pam yaw oovi sutsep put
angk yannuma. Pas pi yaw pam sikyaatayo put qa tukingwu. Pu'
yaw pam maana piw put aw unangwa'yta.

Noq yep hapi yaw Hovi'itstuyqave i' hak tiyo piw pan Sikyaatayo maatsiwqa ki'ykyangw pam yaw piw hak pas suhimutiyo. Noq
pam yaw suus hisat pep tupats'oveniiqe pam yaw ep suus mihikqw
put yaw maanat aqw tuwat tutumayto. Noq ep yaw pam maana pay
as put aw yorikkyangw pay yaw pam naat put qa aw ya'a'ayku. Pam
hapi yaw wuuwantaqw pay yaw pam son naat qa piw put aqw poo-
taniniqw oovi. Noq pay yaw pam maana as kur put naayongqe yaw
oovi pangqawngwu pam sikyaatayot naawaknaqey. Noq pay yaw
pam naat qa piw aw pootaqw pay yaw pam Pitsinsivostiyo pas qa
atsat put sikyaatayot ngu'aaqe pu' put aw wikvaqe put pö'aqw pay
yaw pam kur paasat nawus hinte' qa put amumtiniqe pu' yaw pay
oovi put aw lööqö.

Noq pu' yaw pam Sikyaatayo pep Hovi'itstuyqave ki'ytaqa yaw
kur navota pam maana pay kongtaqw. Noq pay yaw pam tuwat pay
a'ni himuniiqe pay yaw piw a'ni unangwa'yta. Niiqe pay yaw pam
oovi pas son put Pitsinsivostiyot qa nömanawkiniqey yan yaw pam
neengem yuku. Pan yaw pam su'qawta.

Niiqe pu' yaw pam oovi pangqw kiy angqw pangso Nuvakwewtaqay awi'. Niiqe pu' yaw pam pep pituuqe pu' yaw pam it hakiy
tuwiy kiiyat awniiqe pay yaw pam pep qatukyangw pam yaw
naaqavo Pitsinsivostiyot nöömayat aw tunatyawtangwu hiita pam
hintsakqw. Niiqe pam yaw oovi put aw navota pam yaw aasakis
talavay put pookoy sikyaatayot wikkyangw kuyvatongwuniqw.

Pu' yaw pam oovi yan it navoti'ykyangw pu' yaw pam haqam
put hisat ngu'aniqey yaw naawini. Niiqe pu' yaw pam oovi suus piw
hisat pay naat aapiy qa wuuyavotiqw pu' yaw pam piw put pookoy
wikkyangw kuyvatoq pu' yaw pam put pay nana'uyve angkniikyangw pu' yaw pam haqam pay hihin na'uypikya'ytaqat ep huruutiqe pu' yaw pam put pep moqmani'yta.

Niiqe pay yaw pam oovi pay naat qa wuuyavo pep pantaqw pay
yaw Pitsinsivostiyot nööma'at angqaqw ahoy. Niiqe pu' yaw pam
oovi put Hovi'itstuyqangaqwniiqat tiyot naat pu' aasawvaqe pu' yaw
naat pu' lööshaqam piw aapiy kwilakit nakwsuqw paasat pu' yaw
pam put aw warikqe pu' yaw pam put aw pitut pu' yaw pam put
aakwayngyangaqw sumavokta. Noq pu' yaw pam as rohomnum-

Now this boy from Hovi'itstuyqa, whose name also happened to be Sikyaatayo or "Yellow Fox," was very handsome. Long ago he had also been at Tupats'ovi and one night had gone to court the girl. But when the girl saw him that night, she had not yet spoken to him. She thought he would surely visit her again. She had taken a liking to him and that is why she kept saying she wanted a yellow fox. But when he failed to return, Pitsinsivostiyo had captured the animal and gained the girl's hand by bringing the fox. There had been no way out but to become his wife, and that's why she went as a bride to grind at his house.

Evidently, Sikyaatayo, who lived in Hovi'itstuyqa, had heard that the girl had taken a husband. He was a powerful lad and also quite aggressive. He therefore decided to take Pitsinsivostiyo's wife away. He was fully determined to do this.

So he went over to Nuvakwewtaqa, where the village of Tupats-'ovi was located. Upon arriving there, he looked up an acquaintance, and while living there, spied on Pitsinsivostiyo's wife to see what she was doing on a daily basis. He soon learned that every morning she went to pray to the sun, accompanied by the yellow fox.

Once Sikyaatayo had found this out, he started scheming where and when to grab her. One day soon thereafter, when Pitsinsivostiyo's wife was going out with her pet to speak the morning prayer, he followed her secretly. He stopped at a hiding place and lay in wait for her there.

Soon Pitsinsivostiyo's wife was on her way back to the house. She had just reached the hiding place of the boy from Hovi'itstuyqa, and had taken a couple of more steps, when he ran up to her and embraced her from behind. The woman struggled but he easily overpowered her and forced her to the ground. Revealing himself to her by name he said to her, "Don't resist. It's me." Evidently she recognized the boy, for she held still. The boy now had intercourse with her right there on the ground, and she let it happen without resistance.

As it was, the little fox pet witnessed the scene. He was barking furiously, but apparently no one heard him, because no one came to them. Pitsinsivostiyo had actually heard the barking, but did not go see what it was all about. Instead, he waited for his wife to return.

kyangw pay yaw pam put qa angwutaqw pu' yaw pam pay put wa'öknaqe pu' yaw put aw naatungwakyangw pu' yaw aw pang- qawu, "Pay um qa pas rohomnumniy. Pi pay nuu'uy," yaw pam put aw kitaqw pu' pay yaw pam put kur maamatsqe pay yaw paasat sun yuku. Paasat pu' yaw pam put pay pep suututskwavehaqam tsopqw pay yaw Pitsinsivostiyot nööma'at pas qa rohomtit pay yaw put nakwhana.

Noq pu' yaw pam pok'at yan yorikqe pu' yaw as okiw pep wahahalawqw pay yaw pas qa hak kya pi navotqe yaw oovi qa hak pumuy amumiqa'. Noq pay yaw as i' Pitsinsivostiyo kur navot- kyangw pay yaw pam qa aqwnit pay yaw pam panis put nöömay ahoy pituniqat maqaptsi'yta.

Pu' yaw Pitsinsivostiyot nööma'at ahoy kiy ep pituuqe pay yaw pam kur hin pas hintani. Pay yaw pam oovi qa pas pas put koongyay aw suyan hu'wantoyna pam aw yu'a'ataqw.

Noq pu' yaw pam Pitsinsivostiyo pay put nöömay aw kur hin wuuwanta, hintiqw pam qa suyan unangwa'ytaqw. Niiqe pu' yaw pam oovi pay pangqw yamakqe yaw oovi ahoy soy kiiyat aqwniqw pay yaw piw pumuy pok'am pam sikyaatayo pangqw put angk yamakt pu' yaw pam pay put pangqw ngöyva.

Niiqe pu' yaw pam Pitsinsivostiyo pepeq kiy epeq ahoy pituuqe pu' yaw pam pay pephaqam qatuptuqw pu' yaw pam sikyaatayo put aqlavoniiqe pu' yaw put aqlap qatuptu. Pantit pu' yaw pam pep put aqlap ponikiwkyangw pay yaw naat qa wuuyavotiqw piw yaw pam suposvalmunkyangw pu' yaw somisvevetaqw pu' yaw pam Pitsin- sivostiyo paasat navotqe pu' yaw pam put aw yorikqw piw yaw pam okiw pakmumuya. Niiqe pu' yaw pam put qötöyat mapritikyangw pu' yaw pam put as paysoq aw pangqawu, "Ya um hintiqw okiw panhaqam hingqawlawuy?" yaw pam put aw kita.

Noq pu' yaw pam put aw pangqawqw piw yaw pam put aw kwuupukt pu' yaw pam put aw pangqawu, "Owiy, pay nu' ung ookwatuwqe'ey. Pas nu' se'el uunömay amum kuyvatokyangw piw nu' hiita qa nukwangwyoriy," yaw pam put aw pangqawkyangw pu' yaw pam paasat aapiytaqe paasat pu' yaw pam hin yorikqey put yaw soosok lalvaya.

Noq pu' yaw pam tiyo yan it pas put naap yorikqat angqw navot- qe pu' yaw pam tuwat qa haalayti. Niiqe pu' yaw pam it yantaqatsoy aw lalvayqw pu' yaw pam pay tuwat qa haalayti.

Noq pu' yaw pam tiyo pangqw Hovi'itstuyqat angqwniiqa pas yaw kur a'ni haskyeniiqe pay yaw pam paapiy pangso Tupats'omi

When his wife arrived, she did not feel the same about her husband any more. She did not respond to him as clearly as before, when he talked to her.

Pitsinsivostiyo was at a loss. Thinking about his wife, he felt that she was not her normal self. So he decided to go over to his grandmother's house. The yellow fox jumped up and ran after him.

Back at his grandmother's he sat down. The fox came up and settled down next to him. Lying there with his legs tucked under, it was not long before tears were rolling down his face and he was sniffing. When Pitsinsivostiyo heard that, he looked at him and noticed that he was crying. Stroking his head he said, "Why on earth are you making these noises?"

The fox lifted his head and replied, "Because I feel sorry for you. This morning when I ran along with your wife for the prayer to the sun, I saw something unpleasant." Whereupon he related everything he had witnessed.

When Pitsinsivostiyo heard what the fox had witnessed with his own eyes, he became unhappy.

So now the boy from Hovi'itstuyqa, who was very aggressive and had come all the way to Tupats'ovi because of Pitsinsivostiyo's wife, had gained the upper hand over the woman. He was extremely handsome, and since the girl was not really in love when she married Pitsinsivostiyo, she readily succumbed to him. Pitsinsivostiyo was still with his wife, but no longer slept with her.

It was not long thereafter that Sikyaatayo returned home to Hovi'itstuyqa with Pitsinsivostiyo's wife. Pitsinsivostiyo was most disconsolate about this turn of events and told his grandmother about it. He was bent on revenge.

put Pitsinsivostiyot nöömayat oovi sasqakyangw pay yaw pam kur put angwuta. Pay pi yaw pam piw pas suhimuniiqe oovi. Pu' pay yaw pam maana as kur qa pas put Pitsinsivostiyot naakwaknakyangw put amumtiqe pay yaw oovi naap piw mitwat aw nakwha. Noq pay yaw pam Pitsinsivostiyo as naat pay put nöömay amum piw aapiy qatukyangw pay yaw pam put qa aw hintsakma.

Niiqe pay yaw oovi aapiy naat qa pas wuuyavotiqw pay yaw pam Sikyaatayo put Pitsinsivostiyot nöömayat kiy awhaqami wikkyangw nimaqw pu' yaw pam it ep qa haalaytiqe pu' yaw pay oovi paasat put aw hin as naa'oyniqey yaw yan soy aa'awna.

Noq pu' yaw pam oovi put aw paasat hintiniqat put tutapta. Pay pi yaw pam son put aw qa ahoy naa'oyniqat pam yan wuuwa. Niiqe pu' yaw pam oovi put yukiq pas taavangqöymiq imuy hiituy Kisispayamuy pangsoq heptoni. Puma yaw himusinom pay tuwat pas sutsep kiikiipoktinumyaqe pay yaw oovi son put aw qa unangwtatveni pam pumuy amumi pan ö'qalqw. Pay yaw pam panis yan put aw tutaptaqw pu' yaw pam oovi pay ep qavongvaqw pay pangsoqhaqami.

Niiqe pay yaw pam oovi naat pay qa pas mihikqw pay yaw pangsoq haqami pitukyangw pu' yaw aqw haawi. Nit pay yaw pam aqw hawqe pay yaw pam qa piw aapiyta. Pay yaw pam pep haqam qatuptuqe pu' yaw angqe' as pumuy hiituy kiiyamuy as hepnumkyangw pay yaw put qa tuwa. Pas yaw masiphikiwmaqw pu' yaw paasat haqaqw yaw i' kwiitsingw wunuptukyangw pu' pay yaw aapiy hiisavoniqw pay yaw piw pangqaqw kootalawvakyangw pay yaw sumataq qa suup qööhiwta. Noq pu' yaw pam pay naat qa paasat pay pangso nakwsu. Pay yaw pam pangqw pas wuuyavo qatuwkyangw pay yaw maqaptsi'yta.

Pay yaw pas oovi mihikqw pu' yaw piw pang pam qööqöhiwyungqa peep soosoy tsootso'qw paasat pu' yaw pam pangso nakwsuqe pu' yaw aw pituuqe pay yaw pam pep haqam qalave huruutit pu' yaw angqe' paas taatayi. Noq pay yaw paasat puma soosoyam tookya'eway. Noq pu' yaw pep suusunasavehaqam yaw i' suukya pay mimuywatuy amuupeniiqe pay pavan pas hihin wuuyoqa homoki. Noq pay yaw pam suupan wuuwa pay yaw pep son pam hak pumuy mongwi'am qa ki'ytaqat. Niiqe pu' yaw pam oovi piw paas ang yorikqw pay yaw paasat qa hak ang waynumqw paasat pu' yaw pam oovi pangso nakwsu. Niiqe pu' yaw pam aw pituqw pay yaw pangqw naat kootalqw pu' yaw pam oovi aw paki.

Pu' yaw pam aw pakiqw pay yaw antsa hak ep qatukyangw pay

The old woman advised him how to go about this. She fully concurred that he would need to avenge himself. She told him to seek the assistance of the Kisispaya people far in the southwest. This Indian tribe was always about raiding. She was convinced that they would help him if he asked. The next day Pitsinsivostiyo was already on his way.

It was not yet completely dark when he came to a place where he had to descend. Having made the descent, he did not continue on, but sat down scanning the area for the dwellings of this tribe. But he could not see anything. Meanwhile it was getting dusk, and the light of fires became visible in the locations where smoke was rising in the air. There were clearly several fires. But Pitsinsivostiyo did not go up to them yet. He just sat there waiting.

Finally, when the night was totally dark and all of the fires had burned down, he left his place and crawled up to the campsite. He halted at the edge and carefully scrutinized the area. Everybody seemed to be asleep. Right in the center of the camp he saw a roundish hut which was much larger than the rest. Pitsinsivostiyo reasoned that this had to be the living quarters of the chief. Inspecting everything carefully one more time, and seeing that no one was about, he went over to the hut. Seeing the light from a fire, he entered.

Sure enough, there was a man inside. He noticed Pitsinsivostiyo, but did not say anything. After a while he merely got up, went to the door, and disappeared. No sooner was he gone through the door than he yelled out a loud war whoop. While he was yelling, he kept slapping his mouth. Following this signal he remained outside.

yaw pam aw pakiqw pay yaw pam as navotkyangw pay yaw put qa
aw hingqawu. Pay yaw pam panis aw pakiqw pu' yaw pam hak as
wunuptukyangw pay yaw pam qa pas sungwnuptu. Niiqe pu' yaw
pam wunuptut pu' yaw pay hötsiwmiqwat nakwsuqe pu' yaw pay
yamakma. Pu' yaw pam pay panis yamakt pu' pay yaw pam a'ni
kipoktöqti. Niiqe pam yaw oovi a'ni töötöqkyangw yaw mo'ay pala-
latoyna. Pu' yaw pam pantit pu' yaw pam pay qa ahoy pakit pu' yaw
pam pay pepeq iipaq wunuwta.

Hiisavoniqw pay yaw hakim pas sumataq kyaysiwqam iipaq
mowawataqw yaw pam navota. Niiqe pay yaw oovi naat qa wuuyavotiqw pu' yaw pam pumuy mongwi'am pumuy amumi pangqawu,
"Ya pay uma soosoyam taataqt, tootim tsovalti?" yaw pam pumuy
tuuvingtaqw pay yaw puma soosoyam pepyaqey yaw aw pangqaqwaqw pu' yaw pam paasat aapiyta, "Pi hak piw yep pituqw oovi
nu' paniqw umuy navotnay. Noq hiita pi ooviniqw pay nu' naat put
qa tuuvingtakyangw pay ason pas nuy aa'awnaqw paasat pu' nu'
pay sonqa umuy piw navotnaniy," yaw pam pumuy amumi kitat pu'
yaw pay ahoy homokiy aw paki.

Noq yaw pam Pitsinsivostiyo as mootiniqw pay tsawnat pay yaw
puma iipaqyaqam sun yukuyaqw paasat pu' yaw pam pay ahoy yan
unangwti. Noq pay yaw pam piw kur pumuy lavayiyamuy tuuqayta.
Pay pi yaw puma hisatsinom angqe' haahaqe' yaktangwuniiqe pay
yaw soosokmuy hiituy sinmuy amumi ökiqw pu' pay yaw piw i'
naap himuwa naamahin tuwqa pay ephaqam pep kiive huuyanvi-
tungwuniqw pay yaw puma pan peetuy lavayiyamuy tuuqayvaya.

Noq oovi pay yaw pam pepeq pumuy mongwi'am put aw ahoy
pakiiqe aw hingqawqw pay yaw pam navota. Niiqe pam yaw oovi
put aw pangqawu, "Ta'ay, qatuu'. Um pas hak yangqaqw itaakiy
papkiqe um son hapi pay paysoq hiita oovi'oy," yaw pam put aw
kita.

"Owi hapiy," yaw pam put aw kitat paasat pu' yaw pam put aw
put Hovi'itstuyqangaqw tiyot put aw lalvaya hin pam hintikyangw
pu' put nömanawkiqe pu' put nöömayat pas wikqat. Niiqe pay pam
pas son put aw qa ahoy naa'oyniqey yan yaw pam put aw tu'awi'yta.
"Noq i' itaaso nuy angqw peqw hoonaqw oovi nu' antsa umuy
angqaqw peqw heptokyangw umuy angqaqw peqw ayatato uma as
inumi unangwtatveniqat oovi'oy. Niiqe oovi uma as su'patote' uma
as inungem pangso put kiiyat aw kiipokye' pay uma tatam pas
pumuy pep kiiqötotaniy. Pu' pay uma hin naanawakne' pay uma piw
pantotiniy. Sen uma imuy momoymuy mamantuyyanik pay pi uma

In a little while Pitsinsivostiyo could hear the noise of many voices outside. Before long the chief spoke. "Are all the men and boys assembled?" he asked, whereupon they all said yes. "A stranger just arrived. That's why I alerted you. I've not yet inquired of him the reason for his coming, but as soon as he tells me, I'll let you know." With that, he reentered the roundish hut.

At first Pitsinsivostiyo had been scared, but when the people outside quieted down, he felt relieved. Surprisingly enough, he understood the language of this group. This was nothing unusual, because the ancient ones used to roam far and wide, encountering all kinds of other people. Enemies would even come to trade at the village once in awhile. In this way they learned the languages of other tribes.

For this reason, Pitsinsivostiyo understood when the chief came back in and said, "All right stranger, have a seat. Having entered my house so purposefully, you must be about for something important."

"Yes, that's true," answered Pitsinsivostiyo, whereupon he narrated how the boy from Hovi'itstuyqa had managed to steal his wife and take her with him. He now wanted to avenge himself on this boy. "It was my grandmother who sent me here. So I came in search of you and to request that you help me in my endeavor. If you're kind enough to comply, I would like you to raid the village of Hovi'itstuyqa in my behalf and destroy it. You can do whatever you want. If you're interested in the women and girls, you can round them up. If you want to kill them along with the rest, that's all right too. The loot such as food and other items of value that you find, you can distribute however you see fit. My only wish is to see that place destroyed." This is what Pitsinsivostiyo said to the chief.

The man did not waste much time and quickly agreed. "Very well. That boy truly committed a wrong. He got himself into this mess through his own doing. By the same token he got all of his people into trouble. It's hard for someone to cope with adultery. We have the same customs. When two people get married, they have to live together. You can rely on us. We'll help you." The chief's reply pleased Pitsinsivostiyo greatly.

ason pumuy tsamyani. Pu' pay uma piw pumuy enang qöqyaninik pay uma piw pantotini. Pu' it hiihiita nöösiwqayamuy it himu'ytiwniqat pu' pay ason uma piw enang angqw ahoy kiwise' pu' put uma aw naap hin wuuwaye' put pay uma pan naahuyvani. Niikyangw pay pam pep pas kiiqötiniqat nu' yan naawaknay," yaw pam pumuy mongwiyamuy aw kita.

Noq pay yaw pam taaqa qa sööwunit pay yaw put suhu'wana. "Kur antsa'ay. Pay antsa pam kur pas qa antiqe pay pam oovi naap it yantaqat aqw naavitsinakyangw pu' pay pam piw soosokmuy sinomuy amungem qa antiy. Noq pay son hak antsa put tsönawuy ang kuytaniy. Pay itam piw pan put tuwi'yyungway. Pay hak as hakiy amumte' pay hak as sonqa putsa amum qatungwuy. Noq pay itam antsa son oovi uumi qa unangwtatveniy," yaw pam put aw kitaaqe yaw pam put pi'oysana.

Noq pu' yaw pam Pitsinsivostiyo yaw paas put aw tokiltaqe yaw oovi naalötokmiq yaw put tavi. Pu' yaw pam ason haqam pumuy nuutaytaniqey paas yaw put aw yan yukut paasat pu' yaw pam pangqw pay ahoy nima.

Noq pay yaw naat as put tokilayat qa aqw pituqw pay yaw pam pas qa nakwhani'ytaqe pu' yaw pam pay oovi naat payistalqat ep tapkiqw pay pangso Hovi'itstuyqami nakwsu. Niiqe pu' yaw pam pay qa pas aw kiimi pitut pu' pay yaw pam pephaqam naat pay huru'iwta. Pas yaw hisatniqw qa taalawvaqw paasat pu' yaw pam pas aw kiiminiiqe pu' yaw pam pang kiinawit kukuytinuma. Pam hapi yaw kur put Sikyaataytiyot kiiyat hepnuma. Niiqe pay yaw oovi naat qa wuuyavotiqw pay yaw pam put kiiyat tuwaaqe pu' yaw pam angqw oongaqw kivaytsiwat angqw aqw kuyva. Noq antsa yaw puma naama pepeqniikyangw pay yaw puma paasat kur wa'ökqe pay yaw piw paasat naatsopta. Noq pu' yaw pam yan pas naap yorikqe paasat pu' yaw pam pas itsivuti. Pas pi yaw pam naatuhota. Niiqe pay yaw pam paasat oovi pangqw ayo'nit pu' yaw pam pay pangqw pangso haqami pam pumuy tuwqamuy aa'awnaqey. Noq pu' yaw pam ep pituqw pay yaw puma paasat pay pep yeese. Puma hapi yaw pas kur qa atsat kwangwtapnayaqe pay yaw oovi iits tuwat pep ökiiqe yaw oovi naanaqle' qööqöhi'yyungwa. Niikyangw pay yaw puma piw qa susmataqpuveyaqw pay yaw oovi ima Hovi'itstuyqaveyaqam qa nanvotya puma pephaqam yesqw.

Pu' yaw pay pam tsuya. Pay puma pas kur qa atsatotaqe oovi pay aapiy ep ökiqw. Niiqe pu' yaw pam hin pumuy mongwiyamuy amumi lavaytiqey pay yaw piw put ang ahoy. Niikyangw paasat pu'

Pitsinsivostiyo now set the date for the attack. It was to take place in four days. After arranging where he would wait for them, he departed from the Kisispayas.

Waiting for the appointed date Pitsinsivostiyo became increasingly restless, so on the evening of the third day he left for Hovi'itstuyqa. He stopped before coming in sight of the village. When darkness fell, he ventured inside. He peeked into every house, searching for the one where Sikyaatayo lived. Before long he succeeded, and looked in through the opening in the roof. Sure enough, the couple was down there. Sikyaatayo and Pitsinsivostiyo's wife had evidently just laid down and were making love. When he saw the two with his own eyes, he grew furious. The sight really pained him, so he left again and headed to the meeting place arranged with the enemies. Upon his arrival, he found the Kisispayas already encamped there. Full of anticipation, they had come early. There were many fires burning next to each other. But they were camped in a spot out of sight of Hovi'itstuyqa so that they would not be discovered.

Pitsinsivostiyo rejoiced in his heart. They had truly kept their word and were even there ahead of time. Once more he went over everything he had discussed with the chief. Then he added, "I want to kill that boy myself. No one else is to harm him." Thereupon he described where the boy lived. "As soon as I have dealt with him and emitted the war whoop, you can rush the village and fall upon its people. Deal severely with them. I don't want you to spare any man or boy. But that will be tomorrow. So let's catch some sleep this night. Tomorrow we'll attack." These were Pitsinsivostiyo's instructions. The Kisispayas agreed with everything. And since a villager might by chance be about, they slept without any fires that night.

The following morning they built a fire in one spot and then, one after the other, cooked something for themselves. When everybody was satisfied, they began working on their weapons. They did not extinguish the fire, but warmed up their arrows over it to straighten them. They also refurbished their bows. By noontime they were finished, and then they waited for the evening. Pitsinsivostiyo was going to issue some final instructions at that time.

yaw pam pumuy pan aa'awna, "Nu' hapi put tiyot pay pas naap ason niinaniqw oovi pay qa hak hapi haak aw hintsakniy," yaw pam pumuy yan aa'awnakyangw pu' piw haqam pam ki'ytaqw. "Noq pay ason nu' oovi put niinakyangw pu' paasat tuwat kipoktöqtiqw paasat pu' uma ason tuwat pep kiive pumuy amuupa nankwuse' pu' pay uma pumuy hintsatsnaniqey pay uma tatam pumuy pantsatsnani. Niikyangw pay imuy taataqtuy tootimuy amungaqw pas qa haqawa akwsingwniqat nu' naawakna. Noq pay pi itam naat pas qaavoya- niqw pay oovi itam haak yep pu' mihikqw tookye' pu' ason itam qaavo pu' aw kiipokwisniy," yaw pam pumuy amumi yan tutaptaqw pay yaw puma oovi suunanakwha. Noq pay pi yaw naap hisatniqw haqawa waynumniniqw pay yaw puma oovi ep mihikqw qa qööhi'y- kyaakyangw tookya.

Qavongvaqw pu' yaw puma pay suup haqam qööyaqe pu' yaw puma pang pangso oovi nenngem hiita naanangk noovalalwakyangw pu' hisatniqw pu' puma öö'öyayaqe pu' yaw puma paapiy pu' it tunipiy aw tumala'yvayaqe puma yaw oovi pay put qööhiy qa too- kyayaqe puma yaw oovi put aw it hoy mukintotaqe pu' yaw puma put tsiikwantota. Pu' yaw it awatvosiy pu' yaw puma piw aw puu- hulalwa. Niiqe pu' yaw puma pay taawanasami put yukuyaqe pu' yaw puma oovi pay paasat tapkimi maqaptsi'yyungqw pu' yaw pam Pitsinsivostiyo piw naat pumuy amumi hintotiniqat tutapta.

Hisatniqw pu' yaw pay pas mihikqw pu' yaw pam Pitsinsivos- tiyo pumuy tuwqamuy amumi pangqawu, "Ta'ay, pay hapi aw pituniy. Noq oovi itam pay angwu aw hoytotani. Ason itamuy ep ökiqw paasat pu' nu' hapi haak pay naala awnen pu' umuy hinwat navotnaniy. Niikyangw uma hapi pay ason inuusavo put kitsokit ngöyakni," yan yaw pam pumuy amumi lavaytiqw paasat pu' yaw puma oovi soosoyam pangso Hovi'itstuyqami nankwusa.

Niiqe pu' yaw puma ep ökiqw pu' yaw puma tuwqam ayatiw- qam pay yaw ang put kitsokit qaqlava na'uyi'ykyaakyangw put Hovi'itstuyqat ngöyakiwkyaakyangw maqaptsi'yyungwa.

Noq pu' yaw pam Pitsinsivostiyo pay pumuy amuusavo awniiqe pu' yaw pam pay haqami kiihut tupatsa'ytaqa kits'oviyat aqw wupqe pu' yaw pam pay pangqe tsoorawkyangw pep pumuy sinmuy amu- mi tunatyawta. Noq pangqe' taala' pi pay i' tookila qa pas wuupani- ngwuniqw pay yaw pam oovi naat qa pas wuuyavo pangqe pantaqw pay yaw kur tookilnasaptu. Noq pu' yaw pay oovi paasat angqe' too- kiwqw pu' yaw pam pangqw hawt paasat pu' yaw pam pumuy ayamuy amuminiiqe pu' yaw pam pumuy mongwiyamuy aw pang-

Finally, it was dark and Pitsinsivostiyo said to the enemies, "Well, the moment has come. Let's start moving. As soon as we reach the village, I'll enter all by myself and then I'll give you the signal. Some of you can go ahead already and surround the village." With these words, they all set forth toward Hovi'itstuyqa.

Upon getting to the village, those of the enemies who had been ordered were in their hiding places along the village edge. They had Hovi'itstuyqa encircled and were waiting.

Pitsinsivostiyo now ventured forth alone. He ascended the roof of a two-story house and from up there observed the villagers. This was summertime, so the nights were not long. Soon it was midnight. By now the people of Hovi'itstuyqa were in bed and all the lights were out. So Pitsinsivostiyo climbed down from his lookout post and went to his helpers. He reported to their chief, "All right, all the people are asleep. You can enter the village now and wait somewhere in the dark. After I've dispatched that Sikyaatayo, I'll yell a war whoop at the top of my voice. Then pounce on the people and start killing the men and boys. When I'm done, I'll go back to where we spent the night and wait for you." With these words Pitsinsivostiyo reentered the village. This time he did not bother to hide and without any concern for his safety made straight for the house of Sikyaatayo.

When he arrived there, he looked in through the hatch in the roof. The two were not asleep yet. They had unfolded their bedding and were sitting on it clinging to each other.

qawu, "Ta'ay, pay pu' puma pep sinom soosoyam tokvay. Noq oovi uma pay pu' pas aw yungye' pu' pay uma haqe' qa susmataqpuva na'uytotaniy. Noq ason nu' pangso put Sikyaataytiyot kiiyat awnen pu' nu' ason put niine' paasat pu' nu' hapi sonqa a'ni kipoktöqtiqw paasat pu' uma pumuy ki'yyungqamuy amuupa nankwuse' pu' pay pumuy taataqtuy, tootimuy qöyantivayaniy. Noq nu' hapi pay put niine' nu' pay paasat hapi yuk ep itam tokqw pangsonen pu' pay pep umuy haak nuutaytaniy," yaw pam put aw kitat pu' yaw pam pay paasat piw ahoy kiiminiiqe paasat pay yaw pam qa pas nana'uytikyangw pay qa hiita tuutuskyangw pay yaw yuumosa put Sikyaataytiyot kiiyat awi'.

Niiqe pu' yaw pam oovi pangso pituuqe pu' yaw pam pangqw kivats'ongaqw kivaytsiwat ang aqw kuyvaqw piw yaw puma kur naat qa puwkyangw pay yaw puma kur paas pay ang aapataqe puma yaw oovi pay pep put atsve qatuwkyangw pas pi yaw huur naamiq pilniwta.

Yan yaw pam yorikqe pas yaw pam itsivutiqe pu' yaw pam oovi pay qa sööwunit pu' yaw pam sukw hoy hotngay angqw horoknaqe pu' yaw pam put awtay aw tsokya. Noq puma pi yaw pay naat qa puwqe pay yaw naat oovi qööhi'ytaqw oovi pay yaw naat pepeq taala. Noq pu' yaw pam oovi put tumostaqe pu' yaw pam put Sikyaataytiyot suu'unangwmi mavastat pu' yaw pas hin hongviniiqey pan yaw pam put langaknat pu' yaw pam put maatavi. Noq pu' yaw pam pantiqw pas pi yaw put hoo'at ang suymakkyangw piw yaw a'ni öqalat yama. Panti yaw pamniqw piw yaw pam put naat pas pep kwangwaqtuqat yaw suu'unangwpa mu'aqw pay yaw pam paasat sumokqe yaw oovi angqe' mootokma. Pu' yaw pam hoohu piw a'ni öqalat aqw pituuqe pas pi put peep hotmiqwat yama. Pas yaw pam mongaqwwat soosoy tuuwayama. Pay yaw pam panis pantit pu' yaw pam antsa a'ni kipoktöqtiqe yaw mo'ay palalaykina. Pantit pu' yaw pam pay waaya.

Noq pu' yaw mima tuwqam yaw put töqtiqw nanaptaqe pu' yaw puma tuwat pep kiinawit aatsavalqe pu' yaw puma tuwat pang imuy taataqtuy tootimuy qöyantiwiskyangw pu' imuy momoymuy mamantuy suuvo haqami laayintota. Noq puma Hovi'itstuyqave sinom yaw qa hin yan wuuwantotaqe naat yaw puma pu' tunipiy ömaativayaqw pay yaw puma Kisispayam pumuy qöyantivayqe pay yaw qa hin kyaananaptat pay pumuy soosokmuy qöqya. Pantotit pu' yaw puma pang kiinawit piw yungqe pu' yaw piw pang hiihiita nunukngwayamuy ipwantivaya. Tuutukwavit, tu'oynaaqat, nöösiwqaya-

When Pitsinsivostiyo saw this, his anger flared up again. Without wasting any time, he extracted an arrow from his quiver and placed it on the bow. Since the couple was still up, the fire was still going and it was light inside. Pitsinsivostiyo got ready to shoot and aimed right at the heart of Sikyaatayo. He pulled the bowstring back as hard as he could and let go. With great force the arrow rushed across the bow. It hit Sikyaatayo, who was still sitting there enjoying the girl, right through the heart. He was killed instantly, and his head fell forward. So powerfully had the arrow struck him that it went clear through his back. In the front one could not even see it anymore. Immediately Pitsinsivostiyo let out a war whoop, slapping repeatedly on his mouth. Then he fled the scene of his revenge.

When the enemies heard Pitsinsivostiyo's war whoop, they scattered throughout the village. Rushing from house to house they killed the men and boys. The woman and girls were all herded together. The people of Hovi'itstuyqa had of course not suspected anything. They had barely reached for their weapons when the Kisispayas had already cut many of them down. The Kisispayas had an easy time murdering them all. After the slaughter they entered the houses and started plundering the people's valuables. Necklaces, earrings, provisions, and everything of value were plundered.

In the end they took the married and unmarried women, as well as the little girls they had rounded up, to the place where Pitsinsivostiyo had promised to be. When they arrived, Pitsinsivostiyo already had a fire going and was waiting for them. He greeted the arriving Kisispayas, "Sit down a while. Thanks for coming. Did you do as requested?" he asked.

muy, puuvut yaw puma kiwisniqe yaw put oovi pang kiinawit nankwusa.

Pantotit paasat pu' yaw puma imuy momoymuy, mamantuy, mamanhoymuy tsamkyaakyangw pu' pangso haqam pam Pitsinsivostiyo pumuy nuutaytaniqey pangqawqw pangso yaw pumaya. Pu' yaw puma pangso ökiqw pay yaw pam antsa pep pumuy amuusavo qööhi'ykyangw yaw pumuy nuutayta. Noq pu' yaw puma pep ökiqw pu' yaw pam pumuy amumi pangqawu, "Ta'ay, haak huvam yeese'ey. Kwakwhay uma ökiy. Pay uma su'an yukuya?" yaw pam pumuy amumi kita.

"Owiy, pay itam uututavoyyaqe pay itam qa hiitawat taaqat, tiyot ayo' yamaknayay. Nit pu' itam hiitayaniqey pay put mokyaatotaqe pay put oovi enang kivayay. Pu' imuy momoymuy, mamantuy, mamanhoymuy itam pay qa amumi ma'yyungwt pay itam pumuy angqw tsamyay," kita yaw pam pumuy mongwi'amnit pu' yaw piw pangqawu, "Niikyangw nu' hapi pay itwat pas sunengem wikniy," yaw pam put aw kitat pu' yaw pam put sukw wuutit pangso qööhit aqlavo langaknaqw piw yaw kur pam put nöömayat neengem namorta.

Noq pu' yaw pam Pitsinsivostiyo put aw pangqawu, "Kur antsa'ay. Ta'ay, pay pi nu' nuwu umuy imuy momoymuy aa'awna. Noq pay pi pam qa nuyniqe oovi angqaqw pewhaqami put amumniqw pay nu' son oovi pas pu' put kyawnaniy. Noq pay pi nu' yan naawaknaqe oovi antsa pi umuy pangsoqhaqami wayaknaqw oovi kwakwhat pi uma su'patotaqe oovi inungem itunatyay aw antsatsnay," yaw pam put aw kita. "Noq pay uma oovi aqwhaqamiye' pay uma epehaq tuwat umuuqatsiy ö'qalyaniy," yan yaw pam pumuy amumi lavaytiqw pu' pam pumuy yaw pöötapna ahoy kiiyamuy aqwniqw paasat pu' yaw puma naanahoyya.

Paasat pu' yaw pam Pitsinsivostiyo kiy ep ahoy pituuqe pu' yaw pam it soosok soy aw lalvaya. Noq pay yaw put so'at pumuy sinmuy ookwatuwkyangw pay yaw pam qa hingqawu. Nit pu' yaw hötsiwmiq yorikqw yaw angqw himu piw pooko hötsiwngaqwniqw yaw kur Pitsinsivostiyo put ura engem wikva. Noq yaw pam put yaw kur piw qa niinaya. Noq pam yaw kur pep pi pay mooti pituma. Yaw aqw pakiqw pu' yaw pam put wangwayi awi. "Ta'a, yep'ey," yaw kita. Noq pu' yaw pam so'at paas yaw hiita kur piw yuku, nakwakwusit engem. Noq pu' yaw pam put tiyot aw pangqawu, "Ta'ay," yaw kita, "um it ahoy wikni haqam it ngu'aaqe. Um pepeq it paas tavini. Um ahoy sinomuyatuy aw hoonaniy," yaw kita. "Pay tsangaw

"Yes," replied their chief, "we went by your orders and did not spare any man or boy. All the things we wanted, we bundled up and brought along. We did not lay our hands on the womenfolk, though, and drove them here. This one here I'll take for myself," he said, whereupon he dragged one woman next to the fire. He had chosen Pitsinsivostiyo's wife.

Pitsinsivostiyo replied, "Very well, I promised the women to you. This one here did not want me and followed that boy here. I can't treasure her any more. It was my desire to have this done, that's why I hired you. So thanks for fulfilling my wish. When you get back home, I hope you will live a long life." After these words of farewell he laid out a road marker in the direction of their homes and they parted.

When Pitsinsivostiyo arrived back at his house, he told his grandmother everything that had happened. The old woman felt sorry for the people of Hovi'itstuyqa, but did not say anything. Then she looked to the door and saw the fox pet sitting there. Evidently, Pitsinsivostiyo had brought him along. He had not been killed in the raid. He ran into the house, whereupon the old woman called him over. "Here," she said. She had made a prayer feather for the fox. Next, she turned to her grandson and said, "All right, I want you to take him back where you caught him. Put him down there and send him off to his people. I'm glad that because of him we at least briefly met our in-law. So go and happily join your people again." With this, the old woman handed Pitsinsivostiyo the prayer feather.

Pitsinsivostiyo took the yellow fox and carried him back to the place where he had captured him. There he gave him the prayer feather and said to him, "Take this to your relatives. We made it for them."

atsviy itam mö'wit pay pi panis aw yoriy," yaw kita. "Pay pi oovi
antsa um haalaykyangw ahoy uusinmuy awniy," yaw pam so'wuuti
aw kitaaqe pu' put nakwakwusit Pitsinsivostiyot aw oya.
Pangqw yaw pam put wiiki. Pu' haqam put ngu'aaqe pangso aw
wikqe pepeq pu' yaw put nakwakwusit pay maqa. Pu' yaw aw pan
tutapta, "Ta'ay," yaw kita, "um it uusinmuy aw kimani. It itam
amungem yukuuta."

"Is kwakwhay," yaw kita. "It hapi itam as sutsep tungla'y-
yungqw qa hak hisat it itamuy hiita nakwakwusit maqanaqw kur um
itamuy maqaniy," yaw kita. "Niikyangw antsa yaapiy uma it hiihiituy kakatsinye' uma put yuwsi'yyungwni. Pay uma qa nanahinki-
nayakyaakyangw yaapiy itaapukyay yuuyahiwtani," yaw pam sikyaatayo Pitsinsivostiyot aw kita.

"Kur antsa'ay," yaw kita. Pam haalaytiqe pangqw yaw pam ahoy
piw nima.

Paapiy pu' yaw puma oovi piw yeese. Noq pu' yaw i' Pitsinsivostiyo pay aapiy put wuuwanlawngwu hin pam pep Hovi'itstuyqave
pumuy sinmuy hintsanqey. Pam yaw pi'ep pi put ang ahoy wuuwa-
ngwuniiqe pay yaw pam put naasos'onti. Pay yaw as kur pam qa pas
soosokmuy pep sinmuy qöyanikyangw pas piw yaw pam panti. Pay
pi yaw as puma qa pas soosoyam put hintsatsna. Pay pi yaw as pam
Sikyaataytiyo naalaniikyangw put tsöntaqw pas piw yaw puma
soosoyam put qa'antipuyat ep okiw so'a. Noq ii'it yaw pam ang
wuuwantangwuniiqe pay yaw pam pas qa kwangwahintangwuniiqe
pu' yaw pam oovi it yantaqat soy aw soosok nöngakna.

Noq pu' yaw put so'at aw pangqawu, "Is uti okiw imöyhoya. Pay
antsa um hiita akw suyan qa kwangwahintaqw pay nu' uumi maamatsi. Noq pay puye'em sonqa pam ung wuwnitotoyna. Noq pay as
antsa um qa su'antaqat pumuy amungem ankiwakwlawqw pay nu'
qa uumi pi hingqawt pay nu' ung nakwhana. Noq pay nu' oovi piw
tuukopana qa uumi hingqawqe'e," yaw pam put aw kita. "Noq pay
kya antsa itam yep yante' pay kya itam son put suutokni. Noq oovi
itam pay pas qa hakiy awini'ykyangw pay itam yangqw yukiq taa-
töqni. Pay pi itam pangqw pew pitu. Noq pay pi son pas himu itamuy kyawnani. Pay pi itam yep qa hakiy aw yankyangw peqwhaqami pitu. Pu' pay pi piw ima yepwat ki'yyungqam itamumi qa
suutaq'ewya. Noq pay oovi itam pangsonen pay itam pepeqwat son
hin qa qatuni," yan yaw pam put mööyiy aw lavayti.

Paapiy pay yaw oovi naat qa pas wuuyavotiqw pu' yaw puma
oovi hisat mihikpuva pangsoq haqami pas ahoy kiy aqw nakwsu.

"Thanks," the yellow fox replied. "We always desired to have a prayer feather, but no one ever gave us one, until you came along. From this day, whenever you stage a kachina dance, you are to dress with it. And without hesitation you are to wear our pelt as part of the kachina costume." This is what the yellow fox said to Pitsinsivostiyo.

"Very well, we'll do that," Pitsinsivostiyo promised. Happy about this, he returned home.

From that day on life resumed its usual course again, but Pitsinsivostiyo was troubled by what he had done to the people of Hovi'itstuyqa. He repeatedly thought about the events until he became completely preoccupied. He should not have murdered all the people there. After all, not all of them had wronged him. Sikyaatayo alone had hurt him by stealing the love of his wife, yet all of the villagers had perished. Such thoughts kept going through Pitsinsivostiyo's mind. As a result, he was not feeling well. Finally, he blurted it all out to his grandmother.

"My dear grandson," she exclaimed, "I've indeed been aware of your discomfort. I knew when you plotted this wicked scheme that it would be troubling you one day. I did not want to say anything, but sided with you. By failing to talk to you, I am myself at fault too," she said. "I guess if we stay here, we'll never be able to forget. I think we should just get up and go southeast without telling anyone about it. After all, that's were we came from in the first place. Nobody will miss us. We came here not depending on anyone. If we go back to our original place, we'll be able to live there."

Soon thereafter the two started out in the dark of the night. The few belongings they had they did not bother to take along. And since all sorts of edibles were growing along their way, they also went without journey food.

Sure enough, the people along Nuvakwewtaqa soon realized that the old woman and her grandson were gone. Nobody had seen them leave, and now that the two were gone, their cotton was beginning to give out. Since they had neglected to keep some seeds, they were not able to grow it any more.

Niiqe pay yaw puma hiisa' hiita himu'ytaqe pay yaw put qa enang kima. Pu' pay pi yaw ang aqwhaqami hiihiimu nöösiwqa kuuyungqw pay yaw puma oovi piw qa hiita nitkya'yma.

Noq antsa pay yaw pas wuuyavotiqw pu' yaw puma sinom pep Nuvakwewtaqay ep nanapta yaw kur puma hisat haqaminiqw. Noq pay yaw oovi qa hisat hak haqam pumuy amumi yori. Pi yaw pumuy aapiyniqw paapiy pay yaw pumuy pösövi'am sulaw'iwma. Pu' yaw pam pay paasat piw qa poosi'yvangwuniqw pay yaw pam kur paapu hiita angqw aniwtimantani.

Noq pas yaw ep pu' ima sinom nanapta pam Pitsinsivostiyo hapi yaw kur put himu'ytaqe pu' pam aapiyniiqe pam yaw kur pay put enang kima. Ep pu' yaw puma sinom nanapta pam hapi yaw kur qa paysoq pan maatsiwa. Pumuy hapi wuuwantotaqw pam pay put aw maatsiwa. Paasat pu' yaw puma put kyaakyawna pam aapiyniqw. Yan pay yaw puma paapu aapiy qa hiita pösövit a'aniwnaya.

Noq yanhaqam yaw oovi Hovi'itstuyqa kiiqöti. Put puma pep tiyot nöömayat nawkiyaqw pam itsivutiqe pu' pangsoq pumuy tuwqamuy yaw antsa pan ayataqe pu' pumuy angqw tsamvaqw puma yaw oovi pumuy pep pan kiiqötota. Yanhaqam yaw oovi pep kiiqöti. Pay yuk pölö.

It was at this point that the people fully realized that Pitsinsivos-tiyo, or "Cotton Seed Boy," had actually owned the cotton. When he left, he took it with him. The people now also understood that his name was not just a coincidence. He was named after this plant. Now, too late, they treasured what they had had in him. But now he had left. From that day on they could no longer grow any cotton.

In this way Hovi'itstuyqa was destroyed. Enraged that his wife was taken from him, Pitsinsivostiyo ordered destruction of the village by enemies he took there himself. They did his bidding, and now the village lies in ruin. And here the story ends.

7

The Destruction of Awat'ovi

Of the seven pueblos portrayed in the legendary accounts of this collection, Awat'ovi[1] stands apart, in that its destruction occurred in historic times and is datable with a high degree of accuracy. Located some nine miles southwest of Keams Canyon, Arizona, along the eastern edge of Antelope Mesa not far from its southernmost point, Awat'ovi was probably the largest and most populous of all the Jeddito villages[2] that once flourished in this part of Hopiland.

The town's name, which literally means "Bow-High-Place," apparently owed its origin to the *aawatngyam*, or "Bow clan people" who, according to Fewkes, were the most prominent and influential of its founding clans (1893: 363).

Perhaps no other ancient Hopi village now in ruins is mentioned with greater frequency in historic documents and in the published literature. For the Spanish *conquistadores* arriving from Mexico, Awat-'ovi constituted the gateway to the province of Tusayan, their appellation for the Hopi country. No wonder then that the town became intimately linked with many of the major events precipitated by the Spanish presence in the Southwest. The following synopsis of some of these events, as they were of particular concern to Awat'ovi, is based on information compiled in the writings of Hargrave (1935: 17-18), Montgomery et al. (1949: 1-43), and James (1974: 33-64).

Awat'ovi was initially discovered in 1540 by a contingent of the Coronado Expedition under Pedro de Tovar. This first encounter with the white-faced strangers[3] from Spain and their accompanying "man-beasts" (men on horseback) must have been traumatic for the residents of Awat'ovi. That same year the pueblo experienced a second visit by the *Kastiilam*, "Castilians," as the Spaniards came to be referred to by the Hopi. This time, the caller was García López de Cárdenas on his way to the "great river," the Grand Canyon. His assignment was to find the best route from New Mexico to the "South Sea." Disenchanted that none of the rumors about a new El Dorado north of the fabled "Seven Cities of Cibola"—the latter had turned out to be the mud-and-stone villages of the Zuni—had proven true, the Spaniards did not return to Tusayan until forty-three years later. In 1583 "*Aguato*," as the pueblo is referred to in the annals of the expedition, played host to Antonio de Espejo, followed by Juan de Oñate in 1598 and 1604.

Contact between Awat'ovi and the Spaniards, who were busy consolidating their power in the Rio Grande region of New Mexico, remained sparse until August 20, 1629 when three Franciscan missionaries—Francisco Porras, Andrés Gutiérrez, and the lay brother Cristóbal de la Concepción, all known for their zeal to convert the Indians—dedicated the mission of San Bernardo de Aguatubi. An architecturally impressive mission complex was erected over the site of a kiva in order to demonstrate the "superiority" of Christianity over the "pagan religion" of the natives. While few details are known about the Mission Period, there are indications that San Bernardo may have served as headquarters for all missionary endeavors by the Franciscans in Hopiland. While a good number of the people of Awat'ovi adopted the Catholic faith, many others remained unconverted, deeply resenting the ideological subversion of their native beliefs and the forceful abandoning of their religious ceremonies.

This resentment against the proselytizing missionaries,[4] and general hatred of everything Spanish, was not limited to the Hopi. The cruel inhumanity of the Spaniards toward the Indians of the Southwest, which included their conscription for the performance of slave labor, the abuse of women, and the suppression of "idolatrous" practices was prevalent throughout the Southwest and finally exploded in the great Pueblo Rebellion of 1680. This well-organized revolt was spearheaded by Popé, a religious leader from San Juan Pueblo. Those in Awat'ovi who joined the concerted uprising against the Spanish yoke stoned Father José de Figueroa to death and destroyed the mission church. The resulting period of independence from Spanish domination was soon terminated however, when Diego de Vargas resubjugated rebellious New Mexico and, in 1692, marched into Tusayan territory. After the resubmission of Awat'ovi was secured for the Spanish Crown, the church was rebuilt and reconsecrated. Apparently, the residents of Awat'ovi were more willing to accept Spanish sovereignty and Catholic Christianity than the other Hopi villages, for in 1700, they welcomed Father Juan Garaycoechea. He was permitted to visit the town and resumed baptizing the natives. Brew feels "there must have been strong motivation for their choice to face death and destruction, on the side of the Christian God and the Spaniards, and against their native kachinas and fellow Hopi" (1979: 520). According to Bandelier, Awat'ovi "had virtually become again a Christianized pueblo" (1892: 372).[5] The overall Hispanophile attitude and pro-Catholic gestures and overtures so outraged some of the Hopi communities to the west that they conspired to jointly attack the apostate village and burn it to the ground. Awat'ovi, which may have had some eight hundred inhabitants at the time, was successfully sacked late in the fall of 1700. While most of its population was killed, some of the surviving women and children were distributed among the villages of the avengers. Following the massacre, no attempt was ever made to resettle Awat'ovi. The uninhabited site has since lain in ruin.

James has called the destruction of Awat'ovi "one of the most significant events in Hopi history" (1974: 62). It certainly proved a turning point in Hopi relations with the Spanish. With their relatively strong ally of Awat'ovi gone, the Spaniards were never again able to reestablish the stronghold they had enjoyed in Tusayan.

The earliest contemporary testament to the destruction of Awat-

'ovi is found in a Spanish document dated 1701. Written by Pedro Rodríguez Cubero, who had replaced Vargas as governor of New Mexico in 1697, it refers to the campaign he waged in the summer of 1701 "in the province of Moqui [i.e., Hopi] against apostate Indians there, following the annihilation which they committed upon the converted Indians of the pueblo of *Aguatubi*" (Wilson 1972: 129). However, Cubero's expedition proved a failure. The Hopi, prepared for reprisals by the Spanish, were not intimidated, and their punitive action resulted only in intensifying Hopi "determination to remain free of any Spanish influence, secular or religious" (James 1974: 64).

Of the many references to Awat'ovi in the published literature the first one belongs to Bourke who paid a visit to the ruin in 1881. Interestingly enough, he refers to the site by its Navajo designation of "Tolli-Hogandi"[6] (1884: 109). This term, which translates "Singing House," rather than its proper Hopi name, was apparently used also by the First Mesa village chief of Walpi when he remarked on the site to Bourke (Fewkes 1893: 363). Bourke himself concludes that Tolli-Hogandi must be identical with the "*Aguato*" of Spanish records and that "the singing men" whom the Hopis did not like had been the "missionaries who, at Tolli-Hogandi, had gathered about them a colony of neophytes, whose rapid increase gave alarm and disquietude to the old heathen element, and that the latter, upon the first favorable pretext and opportunity, rallied to wipe out at one fell stroke the hated innovation and its adherents" (1884: 91).

The first scientific work at the ruin was carried out by Mindeleff who was involved in a study of Pueblo architecture at the time. He published a brief assessment of the ruin (1891: 49-50) and charted the ground-plan of its eastern section which, almost in its entirety, takes up the ancient Mission complex (1891: Plate IV).

Fewkes was the first to actually undertake its partial excavation. While he drew up a complete ground plan of the pueblo, which also includes the older, western section omitted by Mindeleff, his cursory investigation, which lasted a mere ten days, was primarily designed to verify some of the oral traditions of Awat'ovi's downfall (1893: Plate II). The fact that in nearly every excavated chamber remnants of charred wood, ashes, and other evidence of fire were unearthed, was ample proof to him that the village had perished in a great conflagration. However, since the number of human bones retrieved was judged too small by him "to answer the requirements of the legend," Fewkes renewed his investigative efforts during a second dig in 1895

(1893: 373). This time, many skeletons were found, "evidently thrown promiscuously in a heap, without pious regard or the sympathetic offering of food in mortuary vessels." In his view, this discovery attested to the wholesale slaughter that had taken place and to "one of the most brutal tragedies of the times" (1895: 572).

The most extensive archaeological exploration of the ruin to date was that by the Peabody Museum Awatovi Expedition under the direction of J.O. Brew. During its five seasons of field research in the Jeddito Valley and on Antelope Mesa, a total of twenty-one sites was excavated, chronologically ranging from approximately 500 A.D. to 1700 A.D. (1935-1939). At Awat'ovi alone, thirteen hundred rooms were unearthed, twenty-five of them kivas (Brew 1941: 40). The Franciscan missionary establishment that came to light in the course of the excavation comprised "two churches and foundations for a third; a friary; a suite of offices and schoolrooms; a row of workshops, storerooms, etc.; and the foundations for a barrack-stable" (Montgomery et al. 1949: 47).[7] Among the most sensational discoveries by the Awatovi Expedition were the exquisite mural frescoes that adorned many of the kiva walls. Awat'ovi's mural art, which has been presented in an exhaustive monograph by Watson Smith, allows a wealth of ethnographic insights not only into the ritualistic aspects of Hopi culture but the complete ramifications of the Hopi cultural complex at the time (1952).

Excepting the Hopi emergence myth from the underworld, probably no other tale is attested to more often in the published body of Hopi oral literature than the one relating to the tragic end of Awat'ovi. While Bourke had been the first to briefly comment on the ruin, a slightly more informative account of Awat'ovi's violent demise is found in Bandelier (1892: 371-372). The extended version published by Fewkes was actually obtained for him by Alexander Stephen (1893: 364-366). Containing a much greater number of details than the succinct references by Bourke and Bandelier, its summary presentation is not marked, however, by the style which distinguishes traditional Hopi narratives. James, who published his account under the title "The Storming of Awatobi," admits that Fewkes was his source (1901: 497-500). Retold in romantic kitsch fashion, so typical of the popular literature of the times, it constitutes but an exercise in fictional prose. His claim that he heard the story, much as he told it, "from Hopi lips," has nothing in common with Hopi narrative tradition.

Voth recorded two versions of the end of Awat'ovi. The first, told by a Second Mesa man from Shipaulovi, is an abortive sketch of the actual events at Awat'ovi (1905: 254-255). The motive given for the destruction—unhappiness on the part of the village chief's son because the marriageable women of the village gave him the cold shoulder—is utterly ludicrous and completely incongruent in the light of the bloody consequences that it entailed for the community. His second account was related by an Oraibi man (1905: 246-253). That it genuinely reflects the spirit of Hopi story-telling, can, among other things, be deduced from the many dialogue passages it contains. It too, however, is relatively weak in its motivation for the wholesale slaughter of an entire village. This version relates that, during a rabbit hunt, in which both sexes participate, one of the mounted hunters accidentally rides down the chief's daughter and kills her. This incident so infuriates the chief that he devises a plan that ultimately leads to the eradication of Awat'ovi.

Unlike Voth's second account which, in great detail, unfolds the Awat'ovi chief's scheme to gain the support of the Oraibis, Walpis, and Mishongnovis for his planned revenge and devotes a good portion of the narration to the actual attack and ensuing massacre, Curtis's account focuses almost exclusively on a string of mythological events prior to the town's fall (1922: 184-188). Nearly all of these events center around the deity of Aaloosaka and his six sons. The town's actual destruction is mentioned in only one sentence, almost like an afterthought: "In the fifth year, they [i.e., the inhabitants of Awat'ovi] became so bad that Tapólo, chief of the Tobacco clan, secured the aid of the Horn clan at Walpi in destroying most of the people of Awatobi" (1922: 188). However, when the legend is read in conjunction with Curtis's ethnographic section "Migrations of the Tobacco Clan," a more rounded picture emerges regarding Awat'ovi's end (1922: 83-89).

Waters's chapter "The Destruction of Awatovi" contains no narrative passages (1963: 258-266). Rather, it is a mixture of historic facts and legends, interspersed with reflective and philosophical observations by its author.

Courlander's first published version of the demise of Awat'ovi also does not reflect the true flavor of Hopi story-telling (1971: 209-220). It constitutes, in fact, a composite based on input from six different informants, as is admitted by the author himself (1971: 268). Several of its passages read like summary statements from sources in the literature. Often, they are analytical and quite specific, which runs completely counter to the style of Hopi narrative tradition.

These observations do not hold, however, for Courlander's second version (1982: 55-60). Its authenticity is easily recognized. It features one detailed episode of wife-stealing as an example of the life style bordering on *koyaanisqatsi* brought on by the Awat'ovi *kwitavit*, or "Turds." The immoral behavior displayed between men and women in the kivas moves the *tsa'akmongwi*, or "crier chief," rather than the *kikmongwi*, or "village chief," to initiate the doom of the village.

Finally, Yava's remarks, edited by Courlander, once more constitute a mixture of analytic comments and narrative sections (1978: 88-97). Among other things, he suggests that the sacking of Awat'ovi had a great impact on how the Hopi came to regard themselves. "They had always been the Peaceful People, but, after the destruction, they had to live with guilt feelings for violating their principles" (1978: 88). He claims that the Hopi are ashamed of what happened and that nowadays they "want to forget the whole Awatovi affair" (1978: 95).

The present Third Mesa version is the most comprehensive narrative available on Awat'ovi's destruction to date. Obviously, it mirrors or is reminiscent of a good number of plot elements in the other accounts. On the other hand, it introduces a host of details missing in the previous versions. Of course, this is not surprising in a situation where traditions are passed on orally. Good storytellers are frequently familiar with more than one variant of the same tale. In addition, they may inadvertently drift into the context of another story. They will even freely borrow anecdotal events from another tale to enhance the impact of their narrative. Occasionally, a certain subplot may be fleshed out to such an extent, by a skilled narrator, that it will turn into an independent tale. Due to the fallibility of human memory, as Fewkes reminds us, "errors too must be expected, and the personal equation should always be considered. These folk-tales are not mathematically exact, although capable of scientific treatment, and versions vary" (1893: 366). My narrator's version reflects all of the above techniques, whether intentional or unintentional, and, therefore, constitutes a typical product of the Hopi narrative tradition.

Thematically, the legend, as presented in this book, is divided into two major parts. The first part, rich in mythological content, is, foremost, the story of Pavayoykyasi,[8] a moisture deity who is said to command the rainbow. The second part, which exudes a much stronger historical flavor, relates to Ta'palo,[9] the Awat'ovi village chief, and his involvement in the fate of the pueblo. Pavayoykyasi, the protagonist of the first part, is said to reside at Tuutuwki, the "(Hopi) Buttes" south of First and Second Mesa. When the girl he falls in love with is abducted by the evil Lepenangwtiyo, "Icicle Boy," who lives in an ice cave at Nuvatukya'ovi, the "San Francisco Mountains," Pavayoykyasi sets out to rescue her. In the process, he defeats the abductor, who embodies polar weather, and banishes him, in culture-heroic fashion, to a region in the north, where snow and ice are naturally at home.

While in many ways reminiscent of Curtis's version,[10] the plot in the first half nevertheless shows more differences than similarities (1922: 184-188). The protagonist, in the account Curtis has preserved, is Aaloosaka, a two-horned germinator god. He resides at Alosak-tûqi [Aaloosaktukwi], which is also located in the "San Francisco Mountains."[11] After Aaloosaka ferries the girl, who accompanies him of her own free will, from Awat'ovi to his home aboard a flying shield, Hahay'iwuuti, the mother of all the kachinas, imposes a number of grinding ordeals upon her. Successfully passing these tests with the assistance of Spider Woman, the girl is found worthy of an alliance with the god.

Owing to their supernatural powers, both Pavayoykyasi and Aaloosaka prove immensely beneficial to Awat'ovi where, in accordance with Hopi matrilocal marriage customs, they take up their residence. Aaloosaka, in addition to providing bountiful harvests and plentiful rains, is portrayed as the heroic savior of Awat'ovi in an episode related by Curtis outside the legendary account (1922: 84). When the village was threatened by a firestorm burning across the plain, he "ran forth from the village and met the wall of fire. He ran his horn into the ground in the path of the flames and tore up the earth in a narrow furrow. There the fire stopped: it could not cross the furrow."[12]

Both my version and Curtis's share the fact that six sons are born to their protagonists Pavayoykyasi and Aaloosaka.[13] The children's names, Sakwyeva, Moomo'a, Hoyniwa, Siisivu, Wuktima and Patösqasa, which are also the same in the two accounts, may symbolically emphasize the good life which reigned under their fathers' tutelary influence at Awat'ovi. Thus, according to Curtis, Sakwyeva, the name bestowed on the first-born, denotes "the greenness of the fields covered with flourishing crops" (1922: 186). The Hopi will generally concur with this interpretation. *Sakw-*, the combining form of *sakwa*, "blue/green," is the color typically used to describe plants. Moomo'a, "mouths," according to Curtis, is supposed to signify "that the mouths of the people would be full." My informants were not able to confirm this interpretation, because the regular plural form of *mo'a*, "mouth," is *mom'a*, not *moomo'a*, in the Third Mesa dialect. Hoyniwa, the name of the third child, which is glossed as "winnowing" by Curtis, is, instead, associated with ritual smoking by a consultant of mine. Although the simplex *hoyna* may indeed mean "winnow," an unrelated, homophonous form refers to the "releasing of smoke out of one's mouth, after retaining it momentarily, while in prayerful thought." This would make the name symbolic, in a religious sense. Siisivu, explained as the plural of *siivu*, "pottery vessel," according to the view of Curtis, implies "the desire that everybody have full cooking-pots." My informants rejected this interpretation, suggesting, instead, that it referred to *siivu*, the "black soot" left on the pot from the burning wood. Wuktima, defined simply as "stepping" by Curtis, is explained as a description of the gait of a bear, by one of my informants. Since the bear is one of the animal familiars customarily selected by medicine men, the name may have magico-religious implications regarding healing. Finally, Patösqasa, the name of the youngest son, cannot be satisfactorily unlocked as to its etymological meaning. Curtis's suggestion that it refers to "the sound made by thumping a watermelon to determine if it is ripe" is rejected by the people I consulted. While there exists a verb *patöqsamti*, "to pop," which comes close to the name, this term cannot be used with regard to a watermelon. The noun *patöqsasa*, defined as a legume of the *Astragalus* genus with inflated pods which children pop, may be a more likely source for the name, although its phonetic shape too does not accurately match that of the name (Whiting 1939: 79-80).

A story song, which enumerates the children's names in the version presented here, is still familiar to many elderly Hopi and is held to be an ancient Wuwtsim song. Linguistically no longer transparent in every aspect—several words are already obsolete—it poetically condenses the bad life at Awat'ovi, precipitated by the Catholic Church and its Hopi converts.

While the presence of a moisture and fertility deity in Awat'ovi turns out to be a tremendous boon to its residents, it eventually also becomes the catalyst for disaster. Extraordinary powers and greater-than-average achievements are generally perceived with great suspi-

cion by Hopis and arouse their jealousy and envy. People who excel
in certain ways or distinguish themselves from their fellow humans
by their unconventional attitudes and nonconformist ways are typically vulnerable to a charge of witchcraft. The act of accusing someone
in this way has been conceptualized in the Hopi language by the verb
powaqsasvi, literally, "strike someone as witch." This way of mind and
action control, which is easily achieved in a small society, has left a
long-lasting impact on the Hopi psyche, and the dread of being
accused of sorcery explains many behavioral traits of the Hopi. As
Parsons points out, "in such a social code or theory of conduct innovation is discouraged, and any show of individualism is condemned"
(1939: 107). Titiev confirms this observation (1942: 556). "The constant
terror of witchcraft under which the Hopi labor has had a marked
effect on their characters. Brought up in an atmosphere of dread and
helplessness in the face of evil attacks, they quickly learn to avoid all
appearance of having exceptional ability, and to emphasize modera-
tion in all things. They constantly decry their powers, make frequent
professions of humility, and, through fear of arousing the envy or
jealousy of the two-hearted, prefer not to seek great honors or to hold
high offices."

That jealousy is indeed responsible for a great deal of factional-
ism, dissension, and overall social disruption in Hopi society, is easily
observed in the body of Hopi oral literature, where this detrimental
sentiment occurs as a motif that wreaks havoc time and time again.
Jealousy also pollutes the dealings of the inhabitants of Awat'ovi with
their benefactors Pavayoykyasi and Aaloosaka. According to Curtis, a
faction of sorcerers and witches "believed that the children of Alosaka
had had nothing to do with the prosperity the people had been
enjoying. They were jealous, and desired to kill the Crier Chief, his
wife, his daughter, his grandchildren, and Alosaka" (1922: 187). The
Hopi term for the emotion of jealousy or strong resentment toward
others is *qa naani*, literally "not laugh/not be amused," for the one-
time manifestation, and *qa nanani* for an ongoing or repeated experience of this feeling. This latter term, though in pluralized form, is also
the expression used by the narrator in the Hopi original, here, to
characterize the sorcerer faction of Awat'ovi.

Although modern Hopi are no longer as vulnerable to an accusa-
tion of witchcraft as in former times, they are nonetheless painfully
aware that actions and decisions in their daily lives are still governed
occasionally by this deep-seated fear. Since it is central to under-

standing the Hopi character, the following three testimonials, which
analyze this phenomenon from a Hopi point of view, are cited in full.

Text 71

Pay Hopi pas nukpananiiqat
pangqaqwangwu. Itam sutsep
naayuyuynaya. Itam qa
nami'nangwa'yyungwa. Itam
hiihiita ang naanami qa kwa-
ngwataayungwa. Pas hak hihin
haqam hiita nukngwat hintiqw
pay piw paasat peetu sinom
hakiy piisalayangwu. "Pam
powaqa," pay ephaqam kitotangwu. Pu' qa pangqaqwaninik
pu' piw ayanwatyangwu, "Pam
mashuyi'ytaqe oovi put nukngwat haqam," pay kitotangwu
piiw.

Noq pay i' Hopi as hiita
nukngwat haqamnen pam pay
put as piw oovi qa kwivilal vay-
ngwu. Pu' piw hiita pay kyaa-
hinte' put pay pam piw oovi as
qa pan kwivilalvayngwu. Pay pi
itam lavayit mamqasyaqe oovi
pay qa panhaqam as neengem
yu'a'atota. Pu' it hiita himu'y-
tiwqat itam soosoyam put aw
kwangwa'ytutuswaqw hak oovi
piw put hiita lomahintaqat
himu'yte'ningwu. Noq pay hak
oovi as piw qa öönakyangw put
hiita haqamniqw pay piw himuwa qa naane' pu' pay hakiy
aqw panhaqam hingqawe' pu'
pay hakiy piw unangwmokna-
ngwu.

Noq pu' ima hisatsinom piw
angqe' yan utuhu'puva kotskiw-

They say that the Hopi are evil.
We're always bothering one
another and have no love for
each other. There are all sorts of
things which arouse our envy in
our fellow man. When someone
achieves something good, people
criticize him. "That guy is a sorcerer," they say. Or if they don't
want to say that, they say, "He
must have sold a corpse in order
to get that precious thing."

Therefore, when a Hopi
acquires something nice, he's not
supposed to boast about it. Or if
he does something outstanding,
he must not brag. We are afraid
of talk; therefore we do not
speak about our accomplish-
ments. Since we all long for
material possessions, everybody
wants to have beautiful things.
But no sooner does one get
something by working hard than
there's a person who is jealous
and calls him a sorcerer. As a
result, one loses heart.

The old people used to labor
during hot weather and on burn-

qat ang maqsonlalwakyangw pu'
piw hiita a'aniwnaya. Noq pu'
pay himuwa su'annen pay pam
piw hiita aniwnaqw pay paasat
piw himuwa qa naane' pay piw
put powaqsasvingwu. Hak
haqam loma'uyi'taqw pu' pay
himuwa qa naaningwu. Put aw
qa kwangwatayte' pay piw
hintsanngwu, aw soyaknangwu.
Noq pu' pay pam piw qa pas
lomawungwiwmangwu.

ing sand in order to grow their
crops. But if one of them succeeded, someone else was envious and branded him a sorcerer.
Or, when a man has some nice
plants, someone else will get
jealous. Looking unfavorably
upon that, he will do something
to them to bewitch them. Then
they won't grow well any more.

Text 72

Pay himuwa haqam pas qa atsat
naap maqsoniy akw a'ni hiita
naami sen timuy amungem
tsovalantaqw pay himuwa piw
put powaqsasvingwu. I' put aw
qa kwangwataytaqa pay piw put
aqw pas sonqa yan hingqawngwu. Noq pay it ima hisatsinom, ima wuuwuyoqam piw
pangqaqwangwuniiqe oovi piw
pangqaqwangwu yaw Hopi
nukpananiiqat. Pam yaw pay
put natngwaniy Hopit akw
naatupki'yta. Pay yaw qa hak
haqam hopi. Pay yaw itam soosoyam panyungwa, nukpanat
himu'yyungwa. Qa hak yaw qa
haqam qa hovariwta. Paniqw
yaw itam sutsep naanamiq hingqaqwa. Pay yaw hak naamahin
piw qa pas hakiy aw ma'ytangwu. Pay yaw hak it lavayit
akw hakiy tuuhotangwu, tis oovi
it hiita atsat akwa'.

Noq pay yaw pam son naat
itamuupa sulawtini. Pas ason

Whenever a person, by his own
hard work, assembles a few
things for himself or his children,
he will be called a sorcerer by
someone. One who is envious of
him is bound to speak against
him. The old people and the
elders also used to say that the
Hopis are evil. They say the
Hopis simply use their name
[which means "civilized"] to
hide behind, in order to cover
their evil ways. There is no good
person. We're all like that. We all
have evil in us. Nobody is innocent. For this reason, we constantly talk against each other.
Even though no one actually lays
hands on another person, he will
hurt him with his words, especially with lies.

This problem will not go
away. Not until we come to the
judgment day, when our creator
will purify us. Therefore, our
elders used to say long ago,

yaw itam it nuutungk
talöngvaqat aqw ökiqw pepeq
pu' yaw i' hak itamuy yukuuqa
pam pu' yaw itamuy powatani.
Ep pu' yaw pam piw imuy pas
nuunukpantuy pay haqami
hintsanni. Noq oovi hisat ima
wuuwuyom hakimuy amumi
pangqaqwangwu, "Hak pay qa
pas a'ni unangway qatungwu.
Hak hakiy waynumqat paas tavingwu. Hakiy kiiyat pakiiqat hak
ngas'ew hiisakw nopnangwu."
Ii'it puma hiita naavaasqatsit-
niqat hakimuy amumi as yu'a-
'atotangwuniqw pu' pay qa hak
haqam put enang qatu.

"One must not live with a mean
heart. A traveller is always to be
welcomed. The person who
enters someone's house must be
fed some food." They were talking about a life of mutual respect
and caring, but no one lives like
that.

Text 73

Pay pi hak hin'ur himunen pu'
hiita tuwi'yte' hak hakiy ayo'wat
pan yuuyuynangwu. Noq pay i'
himu powaqa pantangwu.
Himuwa hihin pavan hiita ep
nukwangwhintiqw pu' pay pam
paasat qa naane' pay pam paasat
put hinwat hintsanngwu. Pay
sen pam put engem hinwat hiita
eepewi tunatuytangwu.
Ephaqam pam put engem qa
hiita nukwangwlavay'oye' pu'
put hin yu'a'ataqw pu' pay
aye'wat mima sinom tuutup-
tsiwe' pu' pay put hin yu'a'atotangwu. Noq pu' pay pam
unangwmokye' pay pam okiw
hiita aw qa antingwu.

If someone has extraordinary
powers and has special
knowledge in things, he usually
causes trouble for other people.
A sorcerer is just like that. For
example, if a person is successful, the sorcerer becomes jealous
and then does some harm to
him. Maybe he plans something
against him. Or he spreads a
rumor about him. The other people then believe the bad things
he said about him and talk about
him in the same manner. As a
result, the person gets so dis-
heartened that he no longer
succeeds in his affairs.

While the version recorded by Curtis lists jealousy as the single
factor which prompts the murdering of five of Aaloosaka's children—

he himself, with his youngest son, escapes to his home at the San Francisco Mountains—additional reasons are introduced to motivate the massacre in the account recorded here. As a consequence of the crime, drought and famine befall the inhabitants of Awat'ovi. When Pavayoykyasi eventually returns and miraculously saves the remaining survivors from starvation, they elect his son Patösqasa as their new leader. Thereafter the people's lives return to normal. Before long, however, this state of happiness and harmony is shattered by a new inroad of evil. By now, Ta'palo is the village head of Awat'ovi, who, according to Curtis, invites the neighboring inhabitants of Walpi to destroy the town.

The whole scenario of the violent end of Awat'ovi, which Curtis sums up in a couple of lines, takes almost the entire second part of this version (1922: 188). While in many instances it confirms the general unfolding of happenings depicted in the recorded materials by Fewkes, Voth, and Courlander, it builds a much more dramatic case for the state of *koyaanisqatsi*, the social disease of turmoil and corruption which affects the community. Ultimately, three major events induce Chief Ta'palo to seek the annihilation of the pueblo. First, his daughter is killed during a communal rabbit hunt, as a result of reckless riding by one of the hunters. Next, the pueblo succumbs to a gambling craze. This craze reaches its culmination when the crier chief, one of the most respected officials in a Hopi community, is publicly compromised by the participation of his wife. Finally, the residents of Awat'ovi engage in social dancing. After the people's decision to stage a Butterfly dance, the nightly practice sessions soon degenerate to a level of unabashed sexual promiscuity. The general atmosphere of *koyaanisqatsi* comes to a climactic crisis for Ta'palo when he witnesses an act of adultery between his wife and her dance partner.

The subsequent events leading to the conflagration of the town and the fratricidal butchery of its population, more or less parallel those in the versions recorded by Fewkes, Voth, and Courlander. Overall, however, the present version is more graphic in detail, which is probably due to the fact that it was recorded in the Hopi vernacular.

To be sure, there are a number of differences between the various versions, some of which may be worth pointing out. Thus, the murderous scheme with the *wawarkatsinam*, or "Runner kachinas," in which Ta'palo attempts to entrap the village leader of Shungopavi into sacking Awat'ovi, also occurs in Voth (1905: 247-250).[14] While his four Runner kachinas are identified as Hömsona, Angwusngöntaqa, Tsilitosmoktaqa, and Sikyapku, the latter two are replaced in this account by Leetotovi and Sikyaatayo. Voth's version has the Awat'ovi chief, whose name we never learn, offer two small clay figures to the village head of Oraibi: one symbolizing "the males, the other the females of his village." The Oraibi chief is, thereby, given the option to select whatever group he fancies as a reward for this assistance in the mission of revenge. The same anecdote is alluded to in Curtis (1922: 86). In this version, Ta'palo, the night before the raid, hands over his *tiiponi*, or "chief's medicine bundle and status emblem," to the joint war chiefs of the enemy forces as a gesture of forfeiting his "children."

In Mindeleff, the signal for the attack is given when the Walpi war chief utters his war cry (1891: 34). In Voth, it is conveyed by the chief's son, who is supposed to leave the roof on which he is sitting when the right moment for the attack has arrived (1905: 252). According to Voth's narrator, the son had been bewitched by his father, who is characterized as a *powaqa*, or "sorcerer." In Courlander (1971: 217), the Awat'ovi chief waves a firebrand as a signal. In Courlander (1982: 59), it is the crier chief who uses a blanket for this purpose. In this version, Ta'palo himself gives the signal with the blanket.

In the aftermath of the storming of the town, many of the villagers are tortured and slaughtered at various locations. Fewkes identifies one place by the name of Maski, "Home of the Dead," another as Mastsomo, "Death Mound" (1893: 366). Voth only refers to Mastsomo (1905: 253). Curtis also gives Mastsomo (1922: 88), as does Waters (1963: 264). Courlander mentions three places: Masqötö, "Skull," Mastukwi, "Death Butte," and Mastsomo (1971: 218). The same is true for his 1982 version. Yava speaks of "Skull Ridge" or "Skull Mound," which I assume to be translations of Masqötö (1978: 93). The account given here mentions Masqötö and Mastsomo.

Of course, information on the geographic location of these torture and execution sites varies from version to version. Fewkes claims that Mastsomo was pointed out to him by the Hopi, but that he did not excavate it "to try and find the bones of the unfortunates" (1893: 369). Voth puts Mastsomo "at a place between Walpi and Mishongnovi" (1905: 253). Masqötö, "Skull," where a number of female prisoners were decapitated, according to Courlander, lies not far from a site called "Five Houses" (1971: 218). Mastukwi is placed at "the wash just a little to the east of where the village of Polacca now stands," and Mastsomo "near Wepo Wash, on the west side of Walpi" by his narrator. In my account, Masqötö remains unspecified as to its location, and Mastsomo is rather vaguely placed somewhere "on the west side of Walpi."

Turner and Morris, after analyzing the fragmented human bones excavated at a multiple burial site "on the left bank of Polacca Wash ten miles south of the Hopi villages," found that "thirty Hopi Indians of both sexes and all ages were killed, crudely dismembered, violently mutilated, and probably cannibalized some 370 years ago" (1970: 320). According to the two researchers, "the location of, dismemberment of bodies in, and radiocarbon age of this mass burial" indicate the bodies were indeed those of the captive Awat'ovis slain following their departure from the razed village. Both agree that "southwestern archaeological evidence fitting legendary events has seldom been better" (1970: 330).

There are various explanations as to what happened to Ta'palo, the Awat'ovi village leader. Whereas Fewkes makes no mention of his fate, Voth indicates that both he and his son were destroyed in the kivas with the others (1905: 258). According to Curtis, he went into hiding before the raid, only to return after the event and single-handedly contribute to the general slaughter by suffocating a survivor he finds in one of the kivas (1922: 87-88). Waters claims that, according to Oraibi tradition, Ta'palo went to live in a Rio Grande pueblo (1963: 265). In Courlander, he chooses to die with the rest of his people (1971: 219). Yava reports that he, together with several clan relatives, is supposed to have escaped from the village before the raid (1978: 94). The legend here simply states that Ta'palo perished in the inferno.

Survivors of the massacre, who were transplanted to Oraibi, Mishongnovi, and Walpi contributed a number of significant new cults to the ceremonialism of these villages. There is consensus in the narratives that among the Awat'ovi rituals perpetuated in this fashion were two women's ceremonies: the Maraw (Fewkes 1893: 366; Curtis 1922: 89; my account) and the Owaqöl (Voth 1905: 253; Curtis 1922: 89; Courlander 1982: 60). Agreement furthermore exists that the Wuwtsim, Al, "Horn," and Taw, "Singer," societies continued in the Hopi villages to the west (Curtis 1922: 89; Courlander 1971: 219; Yava 1978: 95). The version presented here is the only one that also includes the Lakon, the third of the three women's ceremonies that are part of the Hopi ceremonial year. Since none of the other accounts corroborates this fact, my narrator may have been in error.[15]

Generally, 1700 is the year accepted now as the one which marked the end of Awat'ovi. Both the ample evidence from Spanish chronicles and other sources gathered by Brew (Montgomery et al. 1949: 20-24), as well as the Spanish document from 1701, recovered by Wilson (1972: 125-130), strongly suggest this date. As to when in 1700 the actual attack took place, several of the legendary references point to the month of November. Mindeleff mentions the annual "feast of the Kwakwanti [Kwaakwant]," always held in November (1891: 34). Fewkes confirms this (1893: 369). He gives the "Na-ac'-nai-ya [naa'as-naya]" or "New Fire" ceremony, regularly celebrated in November, as the time of the tragic event. Curtis simply says that it was the "season of the New Fire ceremony" (1922: 87). Waters specifies that the attack was planned for "the first night of Wuwuchim [Wuwtsim], when all the men would be meeting in the kiva" (1963: 264). My narrator gives *suuwuwtsimtotokpe*, which translates "exactly on Wuwtsim eve."

Wuwtsim was once one of the most important ceremonials in the course of the Hopi ceremonial year. Now extinct save in the Second Mesa village of Shungopavi, it is generally characterized as a "manhood initiation rite." Jointly performed by the Wuwtsimt, Taatawkyam, Kwaakwant, and Aa'alt, initiates into the "Wuwtsim," "Singer," "Agave," and "Horn" societies, it usually lasted eight days. When staged in the form of a *wuwtsimnatnga*, or "Wuwtsim initiation," it was announced sixteen days in advance. This is the form to which Fewkes's locution refers. *Naa'asnaya* simply describes the initiatory act during the sacred night of Astotokya. However, it is not the idiomatically established term for this ritual. Its culturally appropriate name is Wuwtsim. Since *totokya*, "eve," always refers to the day prior to the ceremonial climax, *wuwtsimtotokya*, "Wuwtsim eve," in my account, designates the seventh day within the eight-day ceremonial span. Assuming that the ideal period for the Wuwtsim ceremony is November 20-28 and that the narrator did not err—in the course of nearly three centuries that the legend has been handed down orally, mistakes must naturally be expected—Awat'ovi would have been destroyed sometime during the last week of November, 1700 (Malotki 1983: 372).

Overall, the account of the destruction of Awat'ovi follows the rules governing Hopi storytelling tradition. This is particularly evident in the first half, the story of Pavayoykyasi. If any historical events underlie this part, they are camouflaged beyond recognition. Many of its episodes are the stock material of a good storyteller and could easily be exchanged for anecdotes from other tales. The second half, on the other hand, which presents the story of Ta'palo, violates several of the established narrative rules. What was clearly mytho-historical in the first part, in the second part assumes much more the flavor of an historical account. To be sure, the general camouflage of factual information continues. However, it is pierced by historical fact in several instances. Thus, we not only learn the name of the village chief, but it is also revealed that the *popwaqt*, or "sorcerers," respon-sible for much of the social turmoil in the town, are identical to the Spaniards. The term *popwaqt* here is not used in its narrow definition of "witchcraft practitioners," but in the broader sense of ideological trouble makers. Characterized as an evil, uncivilized lot, they are reported to be baptizing the residents of Awat'ovi, thereby confusing minds and dividing the population into two factions.

By adding this explanatory note to the tale, the narrator indirectly also exposes the function of the same cover term of *popwaqt*, "sorcer-ers," in the first part. I believe that it there, too, denotes the Spaniards and the missionized Hopi of Awat'ovi. Based on this interpretation, which must remain speculative of course, the narrative segment featuring Pavayoykyasi would represent the historic events leading up to the Pueblo Revolt of 1680. The killing of five of Pavayoykyasi's six sons could then symbolize the deadly blow Hopi religion at Awat-'ovi suffered under the missionary onslaught of Catholicism. The return of Pavayoykyasi and his remaining son Patösqasa, on the other hand, would signify the recovery of the ancient religion during post-Rebellion times. Free of the Spanish priests and their proselytes, indi-cated by the perishing of the sorcerers during the famine, the town can once again enjoy harmony and peace. However, as soon as Awat-'ovi submits to Vargas and welcomes the padres anew, the Hopi devotees of the Christian faith, previously branded as evil sorcerers, once more make life untenable for the traditionalists. *Koyaanisqatsi*, with all its social aberrations, having reigned prior to the Pueblo Rebellion, reasserts itself. This reassertion of *koyaanisqatsi*, read Catholicism, prompts Ta'palo into action.

Whether the attack on Awat'ovi was indeed masterminded by its leader or the other Hopi villages simply took matters into their own hands, we will never know. Ta'palo's initiative certainly runs to type with Hopi narrative traditions.[16] Parsons has advanced the hypothesis that Awat'ovi was not destroyed by the Hopi at all (1939: 12). She believes that the motivation for Awat'ovi's destruction "is given in such fictitious terms of personal revenge or outrage or of desire to capture young women and children" that it seems more probable that the town was destroyed by nomadic tribesmen, such as the Utes. One of the arguments she proposes in support of her theory is the fact that Walpi, fearing it might be next on the hit list of the nomadic raiders, invited the Tewas from the Rio Grande area to establish a colony on First Mesa. While Parson's point has some merit, it seems to me, on the basis of both the documentary and legendary evidence, that Awat'ovi was destroyed by Hopi from other Mesas.

Waters thinks that the tragedy that took place at Awat'ovi forever dealt a devastating blow to the Hopi intrinsic commitment to peace, a notion supposedly anchored in their very tribal name. "Their complete destruction of one of their own villages, and their ruthless massacre of their own people for betraying a human tolerance toward a new faith, was an act of religious bigotry that equaled if it did not surpass the cruelty of the hated 'slave church' itself. For the Hopis were a People of Peace, dedicated since their Emergence to a universal plan of Creation which ever sought to maintain in unbroken harmony the lives of every entity—mineral, plant, animal, and man. Now, in the one act of unrestrained hate and violence, they had committed a fratricidal crime of mass murder that nullified their own faith and stamped forever an ineradicable guilt upon the heart of every Hopi" (1963: 266).

I believe that Waters greatly exaggerates his case when he states that the Hopi have been guilt-ridden ever since the atrocities of Awat'ovi. At least, none of the Hopi I consulted in matters of Awat'ovi showed signs of guilt. Nor were they in any way reluctant to discuss the events surrounding the downfall of the village. The argument Waters submits, critically hinges, of course, on the meaning he assigns to the word *hopi*. In interpreting the tribal name as "People of Peace," he unjustifiably characterizes the Hopis as elitist pacifists. Such pacifists the Hopis have never been.

As I have shown elsewhere *hopi* does not signify "peaceful" (Malotki 1991: 45). Rather, it denotes "good" in the sense of "well-behaved." Considering that the sedentary Hopi compared themselves favorably with their predominantly nomadic neighbors, the term is perhaps best rendered as "civilized." The Hopi achievements in agriculture, architecture, and ceremonialism must have induced a feeling of ethnic superiority in them, which is reflected in the onomastic label they gave themselves.

The fantasy that *hopi* means "peaceful" is both erroneous and misleading. Not only has it created "the unreal Hopi," it has also contributed to the widely held view that the Hopi constitute an edenic society living in tranquility and harmony on the high plateau (Shorris 1971: 148). This falsehood about them has led people from around the world to expect something of them that is impossible.

As it turns out, there is not a single word in the entire Hopi lexicon which captures our idea of "peace." On the other hand, the Hopi language contains an extensive vocabulary that relates to the business of "war." Thus, in addition to the term *naaqöyiw*, "the killing of one another," which approximates our concept of "war," the language provides two verbs for the notion "to kill." While *niina* refers to the killing of one or two persons (or animals), *qöya* implies the killing of three and more. Based on this observation, one could easily turn the tables on the mistaken peace-exegetes and claim that Hopi are obsessed with killing. After all, their language operates with terms for single as well as mass murder.

Obviously, nothing could be further from the truth. Conclusions of this sort are fallacious, if not ludicrous, because the lexical differentiation into *niina* and *qöya* is entirely a grammatical one. Hopi has a number of verbs that behave this way, that is, lexicalize differently according to whether the object or target they act upon is singular/dual or plural. Thus, *tavi* means "to place one thing or two things," *oya*, "to place many things." Normally, native speakers are not even aware of such suppletive stem packages in their respective languages. How many speakers of English pay attention to the fact that the present tense form of "go" changes to "went" when it is used in a past time context? Grammatical irregularities of this kind do not affect the mind. Nor do they sum up the psychological makeup of a people or determine the world view of their speakers.

Hence, one noun for "war" and two verbs for "killing" do not make the Hopi a warlike people. Neither does the fact that the domain of warlore was quite extensive in Hopi culture (Malotki 1991: 47). Also the fact that Hopi oral history is brimming with violence, feuding, and death, on an individual as well as a communal scale, as is evident from the stories in this book, must not be taken too literally. After all, even the Hopi kachina gods, whom one would expect to be spiritual role models, are portrayed as death-dealing avengers when they are wronged in Hopi mythology.

None of these observations preclude the Hopi from striving for peace and harmony within religious or philosophical parameters. They only make the Hopi appear more like the rest of humankind. Both Hopi and Christian theology aim high at such ideals as brotherly love and peace, being fully aware that the most hideous crimes have been perpetrated in the name of their respective gods.

Endnotes

1. A total of twenty-seven spellings of Spanish and Anglo provenience has been compiled for the village name in Montgomery et al. (1949: XXII). They range from such renditions as Abattobi and Ahwat-tenna to Waterby and Zuguato. In accordance with the principles of Hopi standardized orthography, the correct transcription of the town's name is Awat'ovi.

2. Other well-known villages on Antelope Mesa, which lie in ruin today, were Mösiptanga, "wild gourd," Kookopngyam, "Kookop clan members," Tsaaqpahu, "small spring," Lölöqangwtukwi, "bull snake butte," and Kawayka'a. The latter place name is of non-Hopi origin.

3. The Hopi belief in the return of a white elder brother—he is commonly referred to as *itaapava*, "our elder brother" or *itaaqötsapava*, "our white elder brother"—who would establish peace and justice throughout the land, may have helped the Spaniards in their initial confrontation with the Hopi. The belief, which is probably traceable to the widespread Pre-Columbian myth of the return of Quetzalcoatl or Kukulcan, the Toltecs' and Mayas' bearded white god in the form of a plumed snake, was quickly shattered, however, when this white brother, in the person of Pedro de Tovar, demonstrated aggression and brutality against the Indians.

4. The Hopi term for the Catholic priests during the time of the Spanish occupation was *tota'tsi*, "dictator, demanding person." Still applied today to a particularly "bossy person," the word turns out to be a Nahuatl loan (Kenneth Hill, personal communication 1991). Pronounced *totahtzin* in the Valley of Mexico accent, it originally meant "our honored father." The fact that this word found its way into the Hopi vocabulary, though with a radically different denotation, indicates that Nahuatl speakers not only accompanied the Spanish missionaries to the Hopi but also resided among them.

5. Yava reports that the Spanish padres were so successful at converting the people of Awat'ovi that "eventually more than half the population allowed itself to be baptized, and the ones that resisted were a minority" (1978: 89). Waters claims that, early in the spring of 1700, Garaycoechea "persuaded seventy-three Hopi to be baptized" (1963: 259).

6. The Navajo name is additionally encountered in such spellings as Tolla-Hogan, Talla-Hogandi, Tally-Hogan, and the Navajo-Hopi hybrid Atabi-hogandi.

7. For a conjectural restoration of the Mission San Bernardo de Aguatubi see Montgomery et al. (1949: Figs. 35 and 36).

8. As the god of the rainbow, Pavayoykyasi is linked with moisture and fertility. He is occasionally impersonated as a kachina. When several of them dance, they are referred to as *Pavayoykyasim*. Etymologically, the initial segment of the god's name seems to relate *pava-* to *paavahu*, the plural form of *paahu*, "water/spring." The element *yoy-* is the combining form for *yooyangw*, "rain."

Pavayoykyasi also designates the rectangularly shaped frame carried on the back of the *Kwaakatsina*, "Eagle kachina," and *Leenangwkatsina*, "Flute kachina." As a rule, this board is called a "moisture tablet" or "rain water shield" in the Hopi ethnographic literature. Hartmann, in an extensive comparison between the two germinator gods Muy'ingwa and Aaloosaka, shows that Aaloosaka was closely linked with the *Alwimi*, or "[Two] Horn society," at Walpi (1975: 293-346). Fewkes's collection of Hopi kachina renditions depicts Aaloosaka with a *pavayoykyasi* on his back and a rainbow forming over his head and shoulders (1903: 180). This shared attribute of the "moisture tablet" seems to explain the substitution of Aaloosaka in Curtis's First Mesa legend for Pavayoykyasi in our Third Mesa version.

9. The name of the Awat'ovi village chief, which has a foreign ring to it, occurs in a variety of different spellings, for example as Ta-po'-lo in Fewkes (1893: 364), Tapólo in Curtis (1922: 84), and Tapolou in Waters (1963: 263). Two of my informants, who were familiar with the name, pronounced it Ta'palo.

10. For a considerable length of the narrative, Curtis's account relating to "The Origin of the Awatobi Fraternities and the Alosaka Cult," runs closely parallel to the Hopi legend of the eruption of Sunset Crater recorded in *Earth Fire* (Malotki and Lomatuway'ma 1987). The same is true for "The Hisanavaiya Myth" collected by

Titiev (1948: 32-37).

11. The place name commonly heard for the home of Aaloosaka at Third Mesa is Aaloosakvi. It is either identified with one of the peaks of the San Francisco Mountains or located to a point west of the mountain range.

12. Without mentioning the heroics of Aaloosaka, Stephen also reports the occurrence of a great fire during the Spanish period. "The valleys around all the mesas were burned up, excepting the valley around Awat'tobi" (1936: 388).

13. In his version, Courlander speaks of "a priest of the One Horn Society who had three sons—Sakieva [Sakwyeva], the eldest, Momo'a [Moomo'a], the second, and Pakushkasha [Patösqasa], the youngest" (1971: 209). Since the two-horned Aaloosaka is considered the patron deity of the Al or "[Two] Horn society," the statement that the priest is associated with the "One Horn society" is obviously in error. The proper Hopi term for what is often referred to as the "One Horn society" is *Kwanwimi*, which translates "Agave society."

Yava also mentions only three sons (1978: 94). His reference to "a Two Horn priest dressed up in an Alosaka costume," correctly reflects the cultural reality. Curtis introduces Sákuyeva [Sakwyeva] as "chief of the Al-wimi fraternity," and Sísivu [Siisivu] as the "Kachina chief" (1922: 84).

14. My corpus of hitherto unpublished Hopi stories contains one which elaborates this incident into a fully fledged, independent tale. It was entitled "Awat'ove Neyangmakiwta," or "Mixed Hunt at Awat'ovi," by its Second Mesa narrator.

15. Parsons, who refers to Awat'ovi as a "treasure town of ceremonies" due to all the rituals reputed to be derived from it, assigns the Lakon to Walpi (1939: 869).

16. Communities embroiled in *koyaanisqatsi*, a life marked by social chaos of irredeemable proportions, are typically "cleansed" through some scheme of catastrophic punishment devised and orchestrated by their own chiefs. As a rule, the chief perishes in the course of the disaster. The pattern encountered in the present legend also applies to the ones relating the destruction of Sikyatki and Pivanhonkyapi in this book.

Hin Awat'ovi Kiiqöti

Aliksa'i. Yaw Awat'oveq yeesiwa. Pas pi yaw pepeq qa an'ewakw yeesiwa. Sinom yaw peetu qa naatuwi'yyungwa. Noq pu' aapiy pay aqwhaqami kitsokinawit piw sinom yeese. Noq puma Awat'opsinom pay yaw hiihintsatskyangwu. Pu' pay yaw hiihiituy tiilalwangwu.

Noq pepeq yaw hakim pay wuuyoqam naawuutim piw nuutum qatu. Noq yaw pam taaqa pepeq tuwat tsa'akmongwiniqw yaw puma pay suukw hakiy manti'yta. Noq pam maana pas yaw loma-mananiqw yaw aw tootim tungla'yyungwa. Yaw as aw tutumaywis-ngwuniqw pay yaw pas qa hakiywat aw unangwtapngwu. Pay pas qa hakiywat naawakna. Pay yaw oovi qa hin kongtaniqey una-ngwa'yta.

The Destruction of Awat'ovi

Aliksa'i. They say they were living at Awat'ovi. Great numbers of people were at home there, so many in fact, that some people did not know each other. In addition, there were settlements all across the land. The residents of Awat'ovi were wont to do all sorts of things. In particular they would perform various kachina and social dances.

Among the residents of the village was an elderly couple. The man held the rank of crier chief. The couple had a beautiful daughter who was desired by all the unmarried men. They courted her, but in vain, for she gave in to no one. She felt no love for any of her wooers, nor was her heart set on finding a husband.

This is how things were when it turned early summer and people

Pu' yaw oovi panmakyangw pu' yaw tal'angwmiq pituqw pu'
yaw oovi soosovik sinom pasvaya, pu' hiihiita uylalwa. Uu'uyaqe pu'
yaw oovi puma paapiy uuyiy aw naaqavo sasqaya. Pu' yaw pam
tsa'akmongwi piw uuyi'ytaqe nuutum pangso sasqangwuniikyangw
pay yaw pas kur wuuyoqtiqe pay paapu qa an hongviniiqe pay yaw
ephaqam pas hihin ahoy pitungwu. Pay yaw paapu okiw pas mangu'iwkyangw ahoy wupngwu. Noq yaw pam pantsakqw yaw put
manti'at ookwatuwngwu. Noq yaw pumuy na'am suus piw pan
mangu'iwkyangw ahoy pituqw yaw pumuy tapkiqw noonovaqw
yaw pam maana put nay aw pangqawu, "Himu as nu' suus tuwat
qaavo uu'uyiy awniqw um suus qaavo haak yep pay qa put
wuuwankyangw nasungwni'ytani," yaw aw kita.

Noq yaw pam aw yan lavaytiqw pas pi yaw put na'at haalayti.
"Is kwakwhay. Ta'ay, tsangaw pi kur um pan wuuwanta. Pay nu'
ason qaavo ung su'its taataynaqw pu' um tuwat awniy," yaw aw
kita. "Noq um ason ep pite' um ep neengem qööniy. Pay nu' ep ta-
qatskive paas kohot maskya'ytay. Ason um mooti put aw namkinat
pu' paasat pi pay um ang uuyit ang hintsaknumniy." Yan yaw pam
put tiy aw tutapta.

Noq pu' yaw puma pay hiisavo yeskyaakyangw yu'a'totat pu'
tokva. Qavongvaqw pu' yaw pam taaqa tiy su'its qatuptsinaqw pu'
pam neengem nitkyamokyaatat pu' pangqw nakwsu. Pu' yaw pam
aqw kiitavangqöymiq hawtaptimakyangw pu' aw tutskwami hawqe
pu' pay yuumosa nay paasayat awi'. Noq pay yaw naat qa qöyangwnuptuqw pay yaw pam ep pituuqe pu' yaw pay oovi yuumosa ta-
qatskimi. Yaw pam ep pituqw antsa yaw ep koho pangawtaqw pu'
yaw pam put hikikw ep ömaataqe pu' neengem aw qööha. Pu' yaw
hihin pavan uwikqw pu' pam yaw aw qatuptu, naamukinaniqe.

Noq naat yaw pam pu' aw hiisavo qatuptuqe pay angqe' taynumqw piw yaw himu tatkyahaqaqw mamatsiltima. Noq paasat pi
yaw naat pay qa pas suyan taalaniqw oovi himuniqw pay yaw pam
maana qa pas suyan maatsi'ytaqe pay yaw paysoq angksa tayma ang
hoytimaqw. Pam yaw lööq nakwakwusit matsvongkyangw pam
uysonaq waymakyangw naahoy maasanmakyangw hiita maspima-
'ewakw hintsakma. Angqw tatkyaqw yaw hoytimakyangw pu' yaw
ang hintsakmakyangw pu' yaw angqw maanat aqwwat yamaktokyangw pu' put su'aqwwat nakwsu. Pu' yaw put aw haykyalaqw kur
yaw hak tiyo. Pas yaw hak suhimutiyoniqw piw yaw hak lomayuwsi'ynuma. Hak yaw pitkunkyangw pu' mötsapngönkwewkyangw
pu' yaw hiita iikwiwta. Niikyangw pu' yaw tsaqaptat piw oovi

everywhere were in their fields planting crops. Day in and day out, they trekked to their plants. The crier chief, too, had sown and, like the others, constantly went to and from his field. But since he was already quite old, he was no longer as strong as he used to be, and once in a while barely managed to return home. Each time he grew more exhausted as he returned to the mesa top. Whenever this happened his daughter felt sorry for him. One day as her father had returned tired again, they were eating their supper when suddenly the girl said to him, "Why don't I go check on your plants tomorrow, and for once, you can stay here and rest without worrying about them."

When her father heard her say this, he became happy in his heart. "Thank you so much, I'm glad you're suggesting this. I'll wake you up early in the morning and you can go in my place," he said. "As soon as you get there, build a fire for yourself. I have wood by the field hut set aside for this purpose. Warm yourself first by the fire before you take care of the plants." This is how the crier chief instructed his daughter.

After sitting there for a while talking, the family finally went to bed. At daybreak the following morning the man woke up his daughter. She fixed a lunch for herself, descended the northwest side of the village and, upon reaching the plain below, headed straight to her father's field. It was not yet the time of yellow dawn when she reached her destination. She went directly to the field hut where she found the pile of wood, selected a few pieces, and built a fire for herself. As it flamed up a little stronger, she settled down by it to warm herself.

The girl had only been sitting there a short while when she spotted a person coming from the southeast. Since it was not yet full daylight, she was not quite able to determine who it was. She simply followed the person with her eyes. As he moved along, he traversed the field, heading straight toward the girl. He held two prayer feathers in his hand and, as he strode through the planted field, kept motioning to and fro, seemingly throwing something. As the stranger got closer, she saw that he was a very handsome young man wearing beautiful clothes. He wore an embroidered kilt with a colorful kachina sash, and carried something on his back. He had eagle down in his hair and in his hand he held a sort of wand.

yawkyangw piw kwavöönakwa'yta.

Noq piw yaw pam maana qa hin mamqast pay yaw aw suuyu'a-
'ayku. "Yeese'e, um hak piw waynuma," yaw aw kitaqw pu' yaw
oovi pam tiyo ayangqw kwiningyaqwwat qööhit aw qatuptu. Pu'
yaw pam maana qa sööwunit yaw nitkyamokiy tsawiknaqe pu' yaw
put tunös'a'awna. "Yep it um nösni. Um kya tsöngmokiwta," yaw aw
kitat pu' yaw put engem aw piikit oyat pu' yaw hiita piw aqw kuyqe
pu' yaw put aqw kwiptosit hiisa' oya.

Paasat pu' yaw pam tiyo tuumoyva. Noq yaw pam maana put aw
wuuwanta hak pamniqw. Pay pi yaw pam kiy ep peep soosokmuy
tootimuy tuwimu'ytaqw pay yaw suyan i' hak qa pangqw. Noq pu'
yaw pam tiyo kya pi öyqe pu' qe'ti. "Ya pay um ööyi?" yaw pam
maana aw kita.

"Owiy. Kwakwhay, nu' nöösay," yaw aw kita. "Noq nu' pay hihin kyaktayqe oovi songqe pay hoytani. Niikyangw nu' mooti uumi
hin tutaptaniy. Um hapi tapkiqw yangqw pite' umuy noonovaqw pu'
um unguy unay aw maqaptsitani, itam hapi as naamatiniy. Kur puma
nakwhe' yaapiy naalötok hapi ung una angqw pew ahoy wikqw pu'
nu'wa ason paasat ung yangqw tuwat ikiy aw wikkyangwniy," yaw
pam tiyo put aw kita.

Yaw aw kitakyangw pu' yaw pam tiyo nakwsuniniqw pu' yaw
pam maana pay put nitkyamokiy pay aw tavi. Pu' yaw pam put yawkyangw aqw taatöqhaqami ahoy. Pu' yaw pam maana pay hiisavo
angk taytaqw pu' yaw aqwhaqami tuuwayama. Pu' yaw pam piw
hiisavo qööhiy aw naamukini'ytaqw paasat pay yaw sikyangwnuptu.
Pu' yaw pam oovi pumuy paasayamuy awniiqe pu' angqe' hintsak-
numa, pastinuma, uuyit tsaatsa'tinuma, pu' yaw piw aamaqnuma.
Pantsaknumkyangw pu' yaw pam tapkinaqe pu' ahoy niman'öqalti.
Pu' yaw pam oovi pangqaqw nimakyangw put tiyotsa wuuwanma.
Pay yaw kwangwtoya amumtiniqe.

Noq pu' yaw pam kiy ep ahoy pituqw yaw yumat haalayti. Pu'
yaw na'at aw pangqawu, "Is kwakwhay, um pituy. Pas um antsawat
nuy tsuyaknay. Pas nu' tuwat antsa kwangwanasungwni'ytaqw um
i'uyiy tumaltay," yaw aw kitaaqe haalaylawu.

"Pay um haak tuwat nasungwni'ytaniy. Pay itam sonqa pay hisatniqw noonovaniy," yaw aw yu'at kita.

Pu' yaw oovi pam antsa pay naat hiisavo qatuqw pu' yaw yu'at
aw tunösvongyaataqw pu' puma aw yesva. Pu' yaw puma noonovaqw pu' yaw pam pumuy amumi tu'awi'yta hin pam pep hintiqey,
pu' piw hak aw pitukyangw pu' piw hin aw tutaptaqw. "Pay nu' yep

Without the slightest trace of fear the girl addressed the stranger. "Have a seat, whoever you are," she said, whereupon the boy sat down northwest of the fire. Without delay the girl opened her lunch and bade him eat. "Here, eat this. You must be hungry," she said, offering him her piki. Then, she poured some water into a bowl and put some *kwiptosi* in it.

The boy began to eat, while the girl wondered who he might be. At the village she knew nearly all the young men, and this one was definitely not from there. After a while he stopped eating. "Are you full?" inquired the girl.

"Yes, thank you for the food," the young man replied. "I'm somewhat in a hurry, so I have to move on," he said. "But there's something I'd like you to do. When you get home tonight and you and your parents eat supper, ask them if they'd permit us to get married. If they will, have your father bring you back to this place four days from now. I will then take you home from here."

Having proposed to the girl like this the boy got ready to leave. Before he set out, however, the girl handed him the rest of her lunch. With that he started out in a southeasterly direction. The girl looked after him until he disappeared from sight. After warming herself for a while by the fire it finally became yellow dawn. Now it was time for her to go and work in her father's field. All day she hoed weeds, thinned out the plants and hunted for worms, and when early evening came she headed for home. On the way back all her thoughts were of the boy and getting married to him.

When she arrived back at her house her parents were happy to see her. Her father exclaimed, "I'm glad you're back. Thank you, you really caused me a lot of joy. I rested nicely while you worked on my plants." He was full of gratitude.

"You too rest a little now," the girl's mother added. "We'll eat shortly."

Soon her mother set out the food on the floor and the family sat down to eat. During the meal the girl told her parents how she had fared at the field. She also mentioned the visitor and his marriage proposal. "I know everybody here, so he must be from another village. He was dressed in beautiful clothes. He wore an embroidered

pas qa hakiy qa tuwi'ytaqw pay pi son hak haqaqw qa kitsokit angqwniqw oovi hakiy qa tuwi'yta," yaw amumi kita. "Pas hak nawinyuwsi'yta. Pitkunkyangw mötsapngönkwewkyangw pu' hiita iikiwta. Kwavöönakwa'ykyangw pu' hiita piw yawta," yaw amumi kita.

Paasat pu' yaw na'at pay kur maamatsi. Kur yaw pam sonqa Pavayoykyasi. Pam hapi paasathaqam soosokmuy uuyiyamuy ang maakwannumngwuniiqe put hapi oovi sonqa makwanpiy yawta. Pay kur sonqa pam'i," yan yaw aw lavayti. Noq pay yaw puma sunakwha. Pay yaw as puma engem kongwuwantaqey aw pangqawu. Pay yaw na'at nuwu paasaytiqe paapu mangu'iwkyangw pasngaqw pitungwu. Noq pay yaw antsa pam put amumtiqw pay yaw pam put aw enang tatqa'nangwtimantani. Yan yaw na'at lavayti, pay yaw yu'at piw su'an lavayti.

Yantiqw pu' yaw puma hiisavo pay yest pu' wa'ömti. Qavongvaqw pu' yaw pam maana yuy amum tumtsokqe pu' noovat pu' pay hiihiita na'saslawu. Pu' pay nalöstalmiq piklawu, pu' piw ngumanta. Pay pi son puma qa nana'waklawu. Pu' yaw oovi ep aw talöngvaqw pu' pam maana hiita hinmaniqey su'its na'sastaqw pu' yaw put na'at put tiyot tutavotyatniiqe pu' yaw oovi put mantiy wikkyangw pangso paasay awi'. Noq pay pi yaw naat su'itsniqw puma pasmi pituuqe pu' oovi pam taaqa pep taqatskiy atpip hiisa' piw kohot pay panhaqam maskya'ytangwuniiqe oovi pay yaw hiisakw piw qööha. Pu' yaw puma pep put aw naamukini'ykyangw pu' put hakiy nuutayta.

Pay yaw naat oovi qa wuuyavotiqw pay yaw piw tatkyahaqaqw mamatsiltimakyangw pu' piw yaw uuyiyamuy aasonmihaqami paki. Pu' yaw puma aw tunatyawtaqw pay yaw pam piw an uysonaq hintsakmakyangw pu' pangqw yamaktokyangw pu' amumi nakwsu. Pu' yaw amumi pitukyangw pay yaw kur piw pami, pam hak put maanat aw pituuqa. Pu' pay yaw pam oovi put suumamatsqe pu' qatu'a'awnaqe pu' piw peehut piikiy engem ipwa. Pu' piw engem kuyqe pu' aqw kwiptsosit oyat pu' tunös'a'awna. Pu' pam maana yaw put nay aw pangqawu pay pam puunat pep aw pituqw. Noq pay yaw na'at haalayti. Pu' yaw pam tiyo oovi paasat tuumoyvakyangw pay yaw pas pisoqtumoyta. Pu' yaw pay oovi hikis angqw yukut pu' amumi pangqawu, "Ta'ay, pay itam sonqa payni. Pay nu' hihin kyaktayi," yaw kita.

"Kur antsa'ay, pay pi tur uma antsa pay hoytaniy," yaw put maanat na'at amumi kita. Pangqawt pu' yaw put tiyot put tiy nguman-

kilt, had a kachina sash around his waist and carried something on his back. In his hair was tied eagle down and he held some kind of wand in his hand," she explained to her parents.

Right away the girl's father recognized who the stranger had been. It must have been Pavayoykyasi. It is he who at that time in the morning asperses all the plants. For that reason he probably carried the aspergill in his hand. "It could not have been anybody else," he said. No question, the parents approved of the match. They told their daughter that they had already been thinking of getting her a husband. Her father had grown quite old and was always exhausted when he returned from the field. If Pavayoykyasi should marry her, he would have a helper for his farming chores. This is what the girl's father had to say, and her mother concurred.

The three of them sat together for a little while, then lay down for the night. The next day the girl built a fire under the piki griddle to make piki with her mother. The two wanted to prepare all kinds of things for the set date in four days. They were baking piki and grinding corn and to better cope with these chores they both took turns. When the agreed day arrived, the girl got everything ready that she planned to take with her. The father, doing the young man's bidding, took his daughter out to the field. It was still early when the two arrived there. The girl's father built a little fire with the wood he kept stored below the field hut and he and his daughter warmed themselves waiting for the stranger.

Before long a man came into sight from the southeast. Just as the first time, he strode toward the middle of the plants, doing something amidst them as he came, and then headed straight toward them. She recognized him at once as the boy who had come before and, after bidding him sit down, took some piki out of her bundle. Once more she poured water into a vessel, added the *kwiptosi* and invited him to eat. Then she told her father that he was the boy who had recently approached her. Her father was elated. The boy began to eat, but he seemed to be pressed for time. He only tasted the food a few times, and then said, "All right, we'll have to go now. I'm somewhat in a hurry."

"Very well, you two be on your way then," replied the girl's father. With that he loaded his daughter's corn bag on the boy's shoulders and as he looked after them, they set out in a southeasterly direction. Before long, the two had disappeared behind a ridge.

mokiyat iikwiltoynat pu' amungk pay taytaqw puma aqw taatöqhaqami nakwsu. Pangqw pu' yaw pam tiyo put maanat wikkyangw
yaw aqw taatöq namurmiq tuuwayama.

Pu' yaw pam maanat na'at pay paasat uuyiy ang hintsaktiva.
Noq puma pi pay yaw naat pas su'its pangsoniqw yaw oovi naat pu'
qöyangwnuptu. Naat yaw oovi pam pang uuyiy ang hintsaknumqw
piw yaw hak aw pitu. Noq yaw pam put qa tuwa aw pituqw pas yaw
aw hingqawqw pu' yaw pam aw yan kwuupu. Noq yaw pam hak aw
pangqawu, "Ya pay um uutiy qa wikvaqe oovi naala yepey?" yaw aw
kita.

"As'ay, pi pay itam se'el yep as naama pituqw pi pay hak naat
pu' se'elhaq wikkyangw taatöqhaqamiy," yaw aw kita.

"Haw'owi? Is ohi antsa'ay. Ya um hintiqw piw put aw no'ay?
Pam hapi pay nukpanay. Pam Nuvatukya'ove ki'ykyangw pangso
mamantuy oo'oykyangw pep pumuy tusungwqöyantay. Pam hapi
Lepenangwtiyo. Noq kur um piw kyan'ew put aw no'ay," yaw aw
kita.

Paasat pu' yaw puma pep qa haalaykyangw naama pep qa hingqawlawu. Pas yaw hisatniqw pu' pam tiyo yaw put maanat nayat
aa'awna yaw pam Pavayoykyasiniiqey. "Pay pi nu' nawus payni. Pay
pi nu' pi as mooti aw yu'a'aykuqe nu' himu'yvaqw kur pay pamwa
wiikiy. Noq pay nu' son paysoq nakwhaniy. Pay nu' sonqa amung-
kniy," yaw kitat pu' pam pangqw tuwat ahoy taatöqhaqami.

Paasat pu' yaw put maanat na'at okiw qa haalaykyangw pangqw
pay nima, pay qa piw uuyiy aw hintsant. Pu' yaw pam Pavayoykyasi
pangso taatöhaqami hiisavonit pu' yaw pam pephaqam pookoy, it
hiita paatuwvotat, himu'yta. Noq pam yaw lööp natsve yukiwta. Noq
yaw pam atkyaqeniiqa riyakngwu, pu' oovaqeniiqa pay qa riyakngwu. Pu' yaw pam oovi aw wupqw pu' yaw pam paasat oomi hölöltikyangw pu' pay puuyalti. Noq paasat pu' yaw pangqw kiy awi'.
Noq yaw pam kur Tuutukwive haqam ki'yta. Niiqe pep hapi yaw
Tuutukwive pep yaw Siipa yan maatsiwqat ep yaw pam ki'ykyangw
pay yaw tuwat panis so'yta. Pu' yaw pam kiy ep pituuqe pu' yaw soy
aw yan tu'awi'yta. Hintiqw put qa wikvaqey yaw aw lalvaya. "Pay
nuy ep pituqw pay na'atsa ep naala paasay ang hintsaknumqe pas
nuy aw hingqawqw pu' navotqe pu' inumi yan lalvaya, pay yaw hak
se'elhaq put kur wikqat. Noq kur i' yangqw Nuvatukya'ongaqw
nukpana pay mooti ep pituuqe put nuy nawki," yaw aw kita. "Noq
pay nu' sonqa oovi amungkni. Pay pi pas nu' mooti aw yu'a'aykuqe
pay as sonqa nu' putniy," yaw kitaaqe pay yaw pas amungk su'qaw-

Now the girl's father began to tend his plants. They had gotten there so early, that only now was it turning gray dawn. A short time later, the crier chief was hoeing weeds among his plants when a second stranger arrived. The chief had not noticed his arrival and it was only after the stranger addressed him that he looked up. "You're all alone. Didn't you bring your daughter with you?" said the stranger.

"Sure I did. We were both here quite early. A young man just took off with her in a southeasterly direction."

"Is that so? Oh my, why did you give her to that man? He's evil. He lives at Nuvatukya'ovi, the San Francisco Mountains, where he abducts these girls and freezes them to death. He's called Icicle Boy. It's too bad that you handed your child over to him."

The crier chief and the stranger talked there for a while, feeling quite depressed. At one point the newcomer confessed that he was Pavayoykyasi. "Well, I must go. It was I who first talked to the girl. I therefore gained her, but Icicle Boy has made off with her, and I can't tolerate that. I must follow them," said Pavayoykyasi, heading off in a southeasterly direction.

The girl's father no longer felt like caring for his plants and decided to go home. Pavayoykyasi, meanwhile, had walked a little ways southeast where he had left his pet, a magic flying shield. The shield had two parts, with the lower one spinning and the upper one remaining still. Climbing aboard, Pavayoykyasi rose up into the air and flew off. He was traveling to his home, in the Buttes Area, where he lived with his grandmother at a place called Siipa. Upon his arrival he told his grandmother how he had fared and why he had come without the girl. "When I got there, only her father was working in his field. He did not notice me until I spoke to him. Then he explained to me that someone had already led away the girl. Evidently it was that evil boy from Nuvatukya'ovi who got there first and took her away from me. I'll have to go after the two. After all, it was me who spoke first to the girl and therefore I should be entitled to her." This is what Pavayoykyasi said, all bent on following the evil one and his victim.

ta.

Pu' pay yaw as so'at meewa, "Pam son uumi put no'ani. Pi pam hin'ur himu'u," yaw so'at aw kita. Noq pay pi yaw pam naatatamtani. Pay pi yaw put hinwat hintsanniqat yan wuuwankyangw yaw pam kiy angqw yama. Pu' yaw pam pookoy awniiqe pu' put aqw wuuvi.

Noq pu' paasat yaw i' nukpana put maanat pookoy paatuwvotat aqw tsokyaqw pu' puma pangso Nuvatukya'omi hoytaqw yaw puma aw tupo pitutoq yaw pam maana put aw pangqawu yaw kwayngyavomokqey. "Um as haak uuvokoy qatuptsinaqw nu' hiisavo haawe' nuy ason kwayngyaptaqw pu' itam piw aapiytani," yaw aw kita.

Noq pu' yaw pam oovi put pookoy qatuptsinaqw pu' yaw pam maana angqw hawqe pu' haqami hiisavo nakwsut pu' pephaqam na'uytat pu' pep tsukunilti. Naat yaw oovi pu' siisiniqe tu'qaltiqw piw yaw hak haqaqw aw hingqawu, "Itse, yaavonitningwu. Um ayo' hihinnit pep siisit pu' ason angqwnen peqw pakini," yaw himu aw kita. Pu' yaw pam oovi hakiy tutavoyatniiqe pu' ayo' hihin yaavonit pu' pephaqam siisi. Siisit pu' yaw pam pangqw ahoy awi'. Pu' yaw pam haqam mootiniiqey aw pituqw pep yaw aqw tutskwamiq hiisayhoya hötsiniqw pu' yaw pam aqw pangqawu, "Ya nu' haqe' uumiq pakini? Pi uumiq hiisaqhoya hötsi."

"Pay um uukuktönsiy peqw rooyoye' pay um sonqa hin peqw pakini," yaw hak angqw aw kita.

Pu' yaw pam oovi awniiqe pu' kuktönsiy aqw rooroyaqw pay yaw antsa aqw pavan wuuyaq hötsiltikyangw piw yaw angqw saaqa wunuptu. Pu' yaw pam put saaqat ang aqw kivaytsiwat aqw paki. Pam yaw epeq pakiqw yaw hak so'wuuti epeq naala qatu. Pu' yaw pam put qatu'a'awnaqw pu' pam yaw oovi pangqw qöpqöt kwiningyaqw aw qatuptu. Pu' yaw pam so'wuuti put aw pangqawu, "Is okiwa, imöyhoya, um hapi pay suus yanma. Pam ung wikqa hapi pay nukpananiqw piw um put aw uunati. Pam hapi Lepenangwtiyo. Pam yep kiy ep imuy mamantuy tusungwqöyanta," yaw aw kita. "Noq uma hapi ep pituqw put kiiyat aw saaqa wunuqw put saqleeta'at hapi hin'ur qala'yyungwa. Noq oovi nu' ung it ngahut maqaqw umuy panis haqam qatuptuqw pay um aapiy it mömtse' umuy put saaqat ang wupniniqw pu' um it aw pavoyaqw pay sonqa ahoy saqleetaniwtini." Yan yaw pam put aw tutaptat pu' put hiita ngamaqa. Pu' yaw piw aw pangqawu, "Ta'a, pay um nawus amum awhaqamini. Niikyangw pay nu' haak umumni. Nu' hapi Kookyangwso'wuuti. Noq nu' hapi uunaqvuy aakwayngyangaqw tsokiwmani.

In vain his grandmother tried to talk him out of this intention. "That Icicle Boy won't give her up. He's full of extraordinary powers." But Pavayoykyasi did not worry what might happen to him. Fully aware that the other might destroy him, he left his house, went to his magic vehicle, and climbed aboard.

Meanwhile, his evil rival also had put the girl aboard a flying shield and was on his way to Nuvatukya'ovi. The two of them were nearing the base of the mountain range when the girl told him that she needed to relieve herself. "Why don't you land your pet for a while? I have to go the bathroom. Then we can continue."

Icicle Boy complied and landed his flying shield. The girl climbed out and walked away for a short distance, where she squatted down. She was straining to defecate when suddenly she heard a voice. "Phew! Go further away. Move a little further over there to do your business. When you're done, I want you to enter my abode here." The girl obeyed the instructions of the voice and stepped aside to relieve herself. When she was finished, she came back. At the spot where she had stood before there was a tiny hole in the ground. Into this she spoke, saying, "How on earth can I get in there? The entrance is much too small."

"All you need to do is rotate your heel into the hole and you'll be able to enter," the voice replied.

The girl did as she was told and rotated her heel into the little opening in the ground. Sure enough, the circumference of the hole widened, and a ladder protruded from it. By means of this ladder the girl climbed down the kiva opening. Inside she found an old woman sitting all by herself, who bade her take a seat. The girl obeyed and sat down to the northwest of the fireplace. Thereupon the old woman said, "Dear me, my grandchild, you will never return from where you are going. The man taking you with him is evil, yet you fell for him. He's the Icicle Boy, and he freezes young maidens to death at his house. When you get there, you'll see that the rungs of his entrance ladder are extremely sharp. For this reason I'll give you this medicine. When you land, chew it, and as socn as you step on the ladder, spray the medicine on it. The rungs will change back into the ordinary kind." This is how the old woman instructed the girl. Handing her the medicine, she added, "Well, you'll have to go on and accompany this boy to his home. But I'll come with you for the time being. I'm Old Spider Woman and I'll ride along behind your ear. Be sure, therefore, that you don't scratch there when you itch. I'll watch over you at

Um hapi oovi kuktsukvaqw qa naaritani. Pay ason nu' ung ep tumaltat pu' piw ahoy angqwni. Pay nu' son ung tatamtani," yaw pam put maanat aw kita.

Put' yaw pam maana okiw qa haalaykyangw pay nawus put nukpanat amum kiiyat awi'. Pu' yaw pam maana put pokyat aqw piw wupqw pu' pam piw hölöltikyangw pu' pangso Nuvatukya'omi yuumosa pumuy wiiki. Noq yaw puma haqami pas oomi wupqw yaw antsa piw pephaqam kitsoki. Pu' yaw puma pay pephaqam put kitsokit qalavehaqam qatuptu. Pu' puma pep hawqe pu' pay pangqw naap kiimi nakwsu. Pu' yaw puma pangqw pangso haqami kiimi nakwsukqw pu' yaw pam maana pay aapiy put ngahuy moytaqe pu' pangqw put mötskyangw put tiyot angk. Pu' yaw puma kiimi pakikyangw pu' kiisonmi pakikyangw pu' aw kwiniwiwat nakwsu. Noq pangqw kiisonviy kwiningyaqw yaw kur pam ki'ytaqw yaw antsa aw wupasaqa wunu. Noq yaw puma put saaqat aw pituqw yaw antsa put saqleeta'at susmataq a'ni qala'yyungwa. Pu' yaw pam tiyo pay mooti ang aqw wuptoq pu' pam angknikyangw pu' mooti put ngahuy saqmi pavoyat pu' angk aqw wupto. Pay yaw pam put aw pavoyaqw pay yaw antsa pam pas saqleetaniwtiqe pay put qa hintsana. Pu' yaw puma oomiq wupqw pepeq yaw put kiiyat aqw kivat su'an hötsiniqw pangsoq pu' yaw pam put wikkyangw paki.

Noq pam nukpana yaw kur lööqmuy siwamu'ytaqw puma yaw kur pepeq qatuuqe yaw pumuy pakiqw amumi kuwawata. "Is askwali, uma pitu," yaw amumi kita. Noq yaw puma kur naat as ngumantaqw pu' yaw pam wuuyoqwa maana pangqw matangaqw suymakqe pu' put ngumanmokiyat tsöpaatoynat pu' haqami paas tavi. Pantit pu' yaw pam put maanat saaqat ahoop qatuptsina. Pu' yaw pam tiyo put wikvaqa yaw aapamihaqami pakiiqe pu' pep yuwsiy oyat pu' angqw yamakkyangw pu' yaw kivaminiiqey amumi pangqawu. Pu' yaw pay puma hiisavo pep yesqw pay yaw tapki. Tapkiqw pu' yaw pam tiyo ahoy pituqw pu' puma noonova.

Pu' yaw pam Kookyangwso'wuuti put maanat aw pangqawu, "Um hapi pavan nösni, taq taltimiq haqtini," yaw aw kitaqw pu' yaw oovi pam pas pavan öyt pu' tunösvongyat angqw ayo' waaya. Pu' yaw puma nöönösaqe pay yaw pep hiisavo yesqw pu' yaw pay puma tokni. Pu' yaw paasat pam suukya maana put naat pu' pituuqat pangso kwiniwi wangwayi. "Um pewwatnen yepeq aapaveq puwni," yaw aw kitaaqe pu' engem yaw pangso kwiniwiwat höta. Pay yaw pam panis put pangso panat pay qa hiita ang puwniqat maskyatoynat pay yamakma.

Icicle Boy's place and then I'll come back again. Don't worry, I won't abandon you," she assured the girl.

The girl was most unhappy about these revelations, but she had no choice. She would have to go to the evil boy's house. Once again she climbed aboard his flying pet, and it rose into the air and transported them both directly to Nuvatukya'ovi. There they flew to a village located high up in the mountain range. At the edge of that village the magic shield landed, and after disembarking, the two walked toward the boy's house. Immediately, the girl put the medicine in her mouth, and chewing it, followed the boy. Soon after entering the village they reached the plaza, from where they continued in a northwesterly direction. Icicle Boy had his home at a point northwest of the plaza, where a gigantic ladder stood. True enough, when they reached the ladder, the girl could see quite clearly that its rungs were as sharp as knife blades. The boy climbed up first with the girl right behind. But first she sprayed her medicine on the ladder. As a result, the rungs became quite normal, and did not cause her any harm as she stepped on them. At the top was an entrance similar to the one a kiva has. Through this entrance Icicle Boy led the girl inside.

Apparently, the evil boy had two younger sisters who were living there. They welcomed the pair, "Thanks for coming," they exclaimed. They had evidently been grinding corn, for the older of the two came out of her grinding bin to receive the bag of ground corn from her brother. After storing it away somewhere, she had the girl sit down northeast of the ladder. The boy, in turn, disappeared into the inner room. There he took off his clothes and after he came back out, announced that he was going to the kiva. Before long it was late afternoon and upon Icicle Boy's return they all ate supper.

Now Old Spider Woman said to the girl, "Eat your fill. It's still a long time till daybreak." The girl obeyed and only after she had really satiated her hunger, did she leave the area where the food was set out. After supper all of them sat around for a while until they were ready to go to bed, at which time one of the evil boy's sisters asked the girl to move to the northwest side. "Come here. You can sleep in the inner room," she said as she opened the northwest door. She urged the girl to go in, and without leaving any bedding for her, was gone again.

Noq pep yaw kur patusungwtanganiqw pas pi yaw ep iyoho'o.
"Pay puye'em ima sonqa ung yanhaqam hintsatsnaniqe oovi ung
angqw pew wikkya. Noq pay um qa hin wuuwantani. Pay nu'
ungem it yep paas maskya'yva," yaw aw kitat pam put engem ang
lööq pas sussuphingput koyongpöhöt aapataqw pu' pam put atsva
wa'ö. Pu' yaw piw lööq put usiitoyna. Noq pay yaw antsa hiisavoniqw pay yaw pam mukiiti. Pu' pay yaw oovi pam kur hisatniqw
puwvaqe pay qa suusa tuusungwtiqw pay taalawva.

Qavongvaqw yaw pam tuqayvastaqw yaw aapavehaqam mimawat susmataq noonova. Noq pay yaw pas qa hak okiw put tuutsa-
ma. Pas yaw hisatniqw kya pi puma öö'öyaqw pu' haqawa angqw
wiktoqe pu' pay okiw akwsingputsa aw tunösvongyaata. Pu' yaw
oovi pam pep tuwat tuumoyta. Pu' paasat yaw pam maanat naat pu'
öyqw pay yaw puma nukpanat siwamat put matamiq panaaqe pu'
yaw aapangahaqaqw hiita inkyangw awi'. Noq kur yaw puma
patusngwat pangqaqw kima. Put yaw pam ngumantaniqat puma
yaw pangqawu.

Yaw pam okiw as qa haalayti. Noq pay yaw Kookyangwso'wuuti
naat kur put amumniiqe yaw aw pangqawu, "Pay it nu' uumi taviqw
pay um piw put mömtsat pu' ngumankyangw aw pavoyamantani.
Pay pam paasat sonqa paatimantani." Pu' piw yaw aw pangqawu,
"Pay um uumapqölmiq töhahaykye' akw piw naamamapre' pay son
tuusungwtini." Yaw aw kitat pu' yaw piw hiita put maqat pu' yaw
pam pay aapiy. Pu' yaw pam put mötskyangw pu' matamiq pavoya-
kyangw ngumantaqw pay yaw antsa pam patusngwa paa'iwma. Pu'
yaw piw antsa pay qa tuusungwti.

Pu' yaw puma nukpanat siwamat as qa tuptsiwa pam maana qa
hintiqw. Pu' yaw puma put paa'iwmaqat kuysivut ang kuukuy-
kyangw pu' haqe' koltsivaqe put kwaplawu. Pu' yaw tapkimi pay
pam put soosok piingya. Pas yaw puma qa yan unangwtoti.

Pu' paasat ep mihikqw puma nöönösaqw pu' yaw paasat put teevengewat pu' panayaqw pay yaw piw pep kwiniwiqwat an patusu-
ngwtanga. Pu' yaw pam oovi piw pep nawus puwniqe pu' pam
pangso put panaaqa angqw yamakqw pu' pam pay paasat naap put
koyongvöhöt aapatat pu' ang wa'ö. Pu' pay yaw piw put uskyangw
puwvaqe pay yaw qa suusa piw tuusungwtiqw taalawva.

Ep qavongvaqw pu' yaw pay put pas qa nopnayat pay panis
horoknayat pay matamiq panaya. Pu' yaw piw pam haqawa angqw
aw hiita inkyangw nakwsu. Noq yaw kur pu' lepenatwat aw ini'yma.
Pu' yaw paasat pam nawus piw ngumanta. Pu' yaw pam pay naat

The chamber was a veritable ice cave. It was extremely cold. "I anticipated this," said Old Spider Woman. "I knew they would do this to you when they brought you here. But don't worry, I came prepared for this." With that she made a bed for the girl out of two down feathers. They were the softest turkey down. The girl lay down on them, and the old woman covered her up with two more feathers. It was not long before she was nice and warm. Soon the girl fell asleep and she made it to the following day without freezing to death.

In the morning she could clearly hear the others eating in the front room, yet no one bothered to invite her to breakfast. After a while, when they were full, one of the sisters came in and served her the leftovers. Now she ate too, and as soon as she was full, the two sisters took her to the grinding bin. Next they hauled something in from the inner room. It was ice, which the girl was told to grind on the metate.

The poor girl's heart sank. But Old Spider Woman was still with her and said, "Chew what I give you and spray your saliva on the ice while you grind. I assure you, the ice will melt quickly. Also, spit into the palms of your hands and rub your body with the saliva. You'll see, you won't get cold." With that she handed her some medicine, and departed again. The girl chewed it as told and kept spurting it onto the grinding stone. Lo and behold, the ice was thawing. Also, when she rubbed herself, she did not suffer from the cold any more.

The two sisters of the evil boy could hardly believe their eyes when they saw that the girl was unharmed. Pouring the melted ice water into pottery vessels, they kept storing them on top of a wooden shelf. By late afternoon the girl had crushed all the ice. Both Icicle Boy and his sisters were at a loss to comprehend this.

That night after supper they placed the girl into a chamber in the southwest. This, like the one to the northwest, was also an ice cave. Again she was compelled to sleep there. As soon as the one who had put her in there had left, she made her own bed with the turkey plumes and lay down. After covering herself in the same fashion, she fell asleep and slept through the night without suffering from the cold.

This time the girl received no breakfast whatsoever. Instead, they simply dragged her out of her chamber and put her to work at the grinding bin. Again, one of the boy's sisters brought something in. This time it was icicles on a flat tray. Once more the girl was forced to grind. However, she still had some of the medicine which, mixed

ngahu'ytaqe put aqw pavoyankyangwniqw pay yaw piw pamwa suupa'iwma. Pu' yaw nukpanat siwamat piw put angqw kuukuy-kyangw put koltsiva kwaplawu.

Ep mihikqw pu' yaw taatöwat paasat put panayaqw pay yaw pam paapu paas hintiniqey navoti'ytaqe pay yaw qa hin wuuwan-kyangw pepeq puwqe pay yaw antsa piw qa hintit talöngva.

Noq pu' yaw i' Pavayoykyasi amungkniiqe pu' pep haqam pam mantuwa'at kwayngyaptaqw pay yaw pam piw suupangso pitu-kyangw piw yaw tuwat siisimokqe pu' tuwat pephaqam pookoy qatuptsinat pu' angqw haawi. Angqw hawqe pu' yaw pam angqw ayo' hiisavo nakwsut pu' pephaqam naat pu' kwangwatsukuniltiqw yaw haqaqw aw himu hingqawu, "Is itse, yaavonitningwu," yaw aw himu kita. "Ason um kwayngyaptat pu' pew ahoynen pu' um peqw pakini."

Yaw aw hak kitaqw pu' oovi pam haqami sutsvowat naalakqe pu' pepwat siisi. Yukut pu' yaw pam pangqw ahoy pangso haqami pep hak aw hingqawqw. Pu' yaw ep pituuqe yaw ep taynuma. Pay pi yaw pas hiisaqhoya aqw hötsiniqw yaw pam aqw pangqawu, "Pi nu' kur kya pi hin uumiq pakini. Pi aqw hiisayhoya hötsi," yaw aqw kita.

Pu' yaw hak angqw aw pangqawu, "Pay um uukuktönsiy peqw rooroyaqw pay sonqa wuuyoqtini," yaw hak kita.

Pu' yaw pam paasat kuktönsiy aqw rooroyaqw piw yaw antsa aqw wuuyaqtikyangw angqw yaw saaqa wunuptu. Pu' yaw pam put ang aqw pakiqw yaw hak so'wuuti epeq pakiwtakyangw pay yaw piw naala. Pu' yaw put paas taviiqe yaw put pangso qöpqöt akwniwi tavi. Pu' yaw pam tiyo put Kookyangwso'wuutit aw lalvaya hintiqw pam pangqe' waynumqey. Pam nukpana yaw put mantuwayat pang-sohaqami wikqw pam yaw put as hin naaptiniqe pas pan tunatyaw-kyangw pumuy pangso amungk.

"Is uti antsa'a, pay antsa pam pangso pumuy mamantuy oo'oy-kyangw pumuy pep tusungwqöyanta. Noq pay antsa pi yep huruu-tiqw pay nu' aw piw hin tutaptaqey pay nu' uumi pan piw tutaptani. Pay um ason ep haqam kiqlave huruute' it ngahut pay aapiiy möm-tsani. Pu' um pangqw kiisonmi pakiqw pay angqw kwiningyaqw puma ki'yyungwa. Pu' aw hapi wupasaqa wunuqw put hapi saq-leeta'at hin'ur qala'yyungwa. Noq put hapi um ason uungahuy aw pavoyaqw pay pam powalte' son ung hintsanni. Noq pay nu' naat sonqa ung piw tuwat aw pootani." Yan yaw pam so'wuuti aw lavay-tiqw pu' pam pangqw yamakqe pu' piw pookoy aqw wupt pu' piw aapiyta.

with her saliva, she kept spurting on the icicles, causing them to melt right away. As before, the two sisters poured the water into pots which they stored on a shelf.

That night the girl was closed into another chamber facing southeast. Knowing full well that nothing would harm her, she fell asleep without worry and, indeed, woke up in the morning safe and sound.

Meanwhile, Pavayoykyasi, who had been following the two, arrived at exactly the same spot where his girlfriend had felt the urge to relieve herself. He, too, felt the need to defecate, so he landed his flying pet and climbed out. Having walked a little ways off he had just squatted down when a voice cried, "Phew! Go further away. And when you're done with your business, come back and enter my abode."

Pavayoykyasi did as bidden and moved aside, where he relieved himself. When he was finished, he returned to where the voice had spoken to him. Scanning the area, he discovered a tiny hole in the ground. "There's no way I can enter this hole here," he protested. "The opening is much too small."

The voice replied "Just rotate your heel in the hole. That will make it larger."

Pavayoykyasi obeyed and rotated his heel. Lo and behold, the hole widened into a big opening with a ladder standing there. On climbing down it, he found an old woman sitting there all alone. She welcomed him, bidding him sit northwest of the fireplace. Of course, she was Old Spider Woman. Thereupon Pavayoykyasi told her why he was about. He explained that the evil Icicle Boy had abducted his girlfriend and that he was following him with the intention of getting the girl back somehow.

"Oh dear," said Old Spider Woman, "I know he keeps taking girls there to freeze them to death. Your sweetheart actually stopped here, so let me give you the same advice that I gave her. When you land at the edge of the village where Icicle Boy lives, chew this medicine. Only then go to the northwest side of the place where he and his two sisters live. His big entrance ladder, as you will see, has rungs which are as sharp as knives. Onto those you must spray your medicine, whereupon they will be transformed and be unable to harm you any longer. Also, I will personally check on you to see how you're faring on your venture." This is how the old woman spoke. With that Pavayoykyasi left, once more climbed aboard his magic pet, and continued his journey.

Noq pu' yaw pam tiyo yamakqw pu' yaw pam Kookyangw-so'wuuti tuwat yamakqe pu' yaw haqam muumuyt ki'yyungqw pam yaw pangso'. Pu' yaw pam pep pituuqe pu' yaw pumuy amumi put tiyotnit maanat tu'awi'yta, pam yaw pumuy pa'angwaqw yaw qa nukpana put maanat tuyqawvaniqat oovi. "Noq nu' as umuy tuwaa-qe oovi angqw umumi tuwat taqa'nangwti," yaw amumi kita.

"Ta'ay, pay pi itam sonqa umumyani. Noq pay pi um hin itamu-mi tutaptaqw pay itam sonqa pantotini."

Yan yaw puma aw lomalavaytotiqw pu' yaw oovi pam amumi tutapta, "Askwali, yan hapi uma nuy nukwangwhu'wanayaqw nu' qa nanahinkinakyangw umuy ayalawni," yaw amumi kita. "Pay uma Nuvatukya'oviy tupoye' pep uma aqw oomiq kiitiwiskyangw hoyto-tani. Pay uma haqamwat oomi poroknayat pu' piw aapiytotamantani. Ason uma pangso it nukpanat kivayat su'atpipo ökye' pu' paasa-voyani." Yan yaw pam pumuy amumi tutapta.

"Kur antsa'ay, pay itam sonqa pantotiniy," yaw kitotaqe pay yaw sunanakwha. Yan yaw pam Kookyangwso'wuuti nukwangwnavot pu' pangso Nuvatukya'omi put Pavayoykyasit angk.

Noq pu' yaw pam Pavayoykyasi pangso oomi wupqe pu' yaw put kitsokit tuwaaqe pu' pay haqam qalavehaqam pookoy qatuptsi-naqe pu' angqw hawt pu' ngahuy mömtsat pu' angqw kiimi nakwsu. Pu' yaw pam aw pakiiqe pu' kiisonvit heptimakyangw pu' tuwaaqe pu' ang taynumqw yaw antsa aw kiihut aw wupasaqa wunuqw yaw susmataq saqleeta'at a'ni qala'yyungwa. Pu' yaw oovi pam aw nakw-suqe pu' aw wunuptut pu' yaw put ngamakiy aw pavoya. Pantit pu' yaw pam put ang wupqw pay yaw antsa powaltiqe pay yaw put piw qa hintsanqw pam yaw aqw oomiq wuuvi. Pu' yaw pam pep kivaytsiwat aw pituuqe pay qa sööwunit pay aqw supkito. Pam yaw epeq pakiqw naat yaw puma mamant pisoq ngumantotaqe yaw pakiqw tutwaqe yaw suuqe'toti. Pu' yaw pam mantuway pay suumamatsi. Noq pay mimawat hakimniqw pam yaw pumuy qa tuwi'ytaqe yaw amumi pangqawu, "Ya ki'ytaqa haqami'iy?" yaw kitaqw qa himuwa yaw aw hingqawu. Pu' yaw piwniikyangw paasat yaw hihin pavan öqalatniqw pu' yaw suukya nukpanat siwa'at aa'awna pam kivamihaqaminiiqat. "Nu' yep put aw pituqw oovi um aw pay wiktoniy," yaw kitaqw pu' yaw pam suukya maana pangqw suymakt pu' iipohaqami suymakma paavay wiktoqe.

Pu' yaw pam paavay kivayat ep pituuqe pu' put pangqw horok-na. "Um sonqe nawus itamumini," yaw aw kita. "Pi hak piw ep pa-kiiqe pas ung kyeteynawakna. Hak sumataq qa paysoq waynumqe

No sooner had he departed than the Old Spider Woman also left. She went to the place where the gophers were living. Upon her arrival she told them all about Pavayoykyasi and the girl. She said she was helping them both so that the evil Icicle Boy would not win the girl. "It occurred to me that you could be of some assistance. That's why I came."

"Very well, we'll certainly go with you. Let us know what you expect of us, and we will do it."

Old Spider Woman was pleased with the gophers' reply, so she instructed them, "Thank you for agreeing so kindly to my request. Now I can ask you without hesitation what I want you to do. Go to the base of the mountain range of Nuvatukya'ovi. There I want you to tunnel your way to the top. If you surface, just continue until you arrive directly below the house of the evil boy. That's as far as I want you to burrow."

"Agreed, we will do that. You can rely on us," the gophers replied. Old Spider Woman was elated with this response. She now started out after Pavayoykyasi who was already bound for Nuvatukya'ovi.

Pavayoykyasi, meanwhile, had advanced to the top of the mountain, where he found the village he was looking for. He sat down his flying shield right by its edge, climbed out, and after chewing his medicine headed for the village. Entering its confines, he searched for the plaza. When he found it, he looked around. Sure enough, there was the house with the gigantic ladder and, no doubt, its rungs were sharp as knives. He stepped up to them and spurted on them the medicine he had been given. Then he climbed up, and since the sharp edges of the rungs had been dulled, he reached the top unharmed. He entered the kiva opening and without delay stepped inside. The three girls were still busy grinding, but when they spotted the newcomer they abruptly halted. Pavayoykyasi recognized his girlfriend right away. Of course he did not know the two other females, so he asked them, "Where is the owner of this house?" There was no reply. Once more he asked but more forcefully. This time one of Icicle Boy's younger sisters answered. She said that her brother had gone to the kiva. "I've come to see him. Go get him," Pavayoykyasi commanded. Quickly one of the girls ran out to fetch her older brother.

As soon as she arrived in her brother's kiva, she begged him, "You must come over to our place. There's a stranger there who wants you right away. It seems he's not around without a purpose.

pay pas itamumi hihin kyee'ew yu'a'ata," yaw aw kita.
"Ya hakniiqe pas piw panhaqam hintsakiy?" yaw pam nukpana
kitaaqe yaw itsivuti. "Pay nu' ungk awniy," yaw pam siway aw kita.
Noq pu' yaw oovi put siwa'at ep pakiqw pay yaw naat qa
wuuyavotiqw pay yaw Lepenangwtiyo ep angk paki. "Ya um hintiqw piw yangqaqw pew papkiy? Son hak pay yan'eway ikiy pap-
kingwuy," yaw put aw kita.
"Owiy, pay um kur it maanat inupyeve pewhaqami wiikiy. Pay
pi nu' nuwu pi as mooti aw yu'a'aykuqe pay son as qa nu' amumtiniqe oovi nu' umuy angqw pew ngöyvay," pam yaw aw kita. "Noq
pay nu' son oovi qa wikkyangw nimaniy," yaw Pavayoykyasi kita.
"Pay kya nu' so'on uumi no'aniy," yaw nukpana kita. "Pay pi nu'
pew it panaaqe pay nu' oovi put himu'yva," yaw as mooti kitat pu'
pay yaw piw hinwatti. "Pay naato hintaniy. Pay itam mooti naami
hin hepniy. Itam naami nanavö'niy. Kur ason um nuy pö'e' paasat
pu' pay nu' sen uumi no'aniy. Noq oovi itam ikivay awniy," yaw aw
kita.
Paasat pu' yaw puma naama yamakmaqe pu' put kivayat awhaqami'. Noq yaw su'aw puma nukpanat kivayat aw pakiqw yaw kur
ima muumuyt put kivayat su'atpipo hangwaya. Pu' yaw puma pep
kivaape pakiiqe pu' qöpqöt kwiningyaqw aw naama qatuptuqw pu'
yaw pam nukpana pangqawu, "Ta'ay, nu' ungem it yep ang tanga-
taqw um hapi it tsootsongniy. Niikyangw um hapi put kwiitsingwu-
yat qa nööngantoynani. Um hapi put kwiitsingwuy pas qa suusa
nöngaknakyangw pas put soosok sowe' pu' um hapi nuy pö'aniy,"
yaw aw kita.
Noq suupaasat yaw piw Kookyangwso'wuuti put Pavayoykyasit
angk pituuqe pu' yaw put naqvuyat aakwayngyaveq tsokiltiqe pu'
aw pangqawu, "Pay um qa hin wuuwantani. Pay son um qa hin ang
ayo' yamakni," yaw pam aw kita. "Niikyangw uukuringaqw kuktsukvaqw um hapi pay sun yantani. Pay puma ung pa'angwawisqam
ung pantsatsnani. Pay um put kwiitsingwuy kwukwu'ni." Yan yaw
pam so'wuuti aw tutapta.
Noq pu' yaw pam nukpana kivay teevengeniiqe pu' pangqw
poksöt angqw pipmokiynit pu' tsoongot horoknaqe pu' put aw yawma. Noq pas pi yaw pam piw hiita wukotsongo'yta. Pu' yaw pam
piw aqlap qatuptuqe pu' yaw put tsoongot ang tangativa. Pas pi yaw
oovi wuuhaq aqw tangatat pu' put aw iitat pu' aw piw pangqawu,
"Ta'ay, yepee', pay pi um hin pi naami navotniy. Pay pi nu' uumi
tutaptaqw pay pi um oovi pu' pas naapeniy," yaw aw kitat pu' yaw

He talked to us in a somewhat agitated voice."

"Who on earth would be doing a thing like that?" the evil boy exclaimed, quite angry. "Well, I'll follow you," he said to his younger sister.

It was not long after her return that Icicle Boy came in. "Why are you entering our home like this?" he asked reproachfully. "No one dares do that here."

"Yes, but you took off with my girl. I was the one who first talked to her, and I was going to marry her. That's why I came after you," Pavayoykyasi retorted. "And I won't go home without her."

"I won't give her up under any circumstances," the evil boy shot back. "I'm the one who brought her here, so she's mine." But then he changed his tune somewhat. "At least for the time being. Let's first test each other's power. We'll compete for her. If you beat me in this contest, I may give her back to you. So let's go to my kiva."

Both men left the house and headed over to the kiva. The very moment they entered the subterranean abode, the gophers arrived, digging directly underneath. The two sat down on the northwest side of the fire pit, and the evil boy announced, "Well, I'll fill a pipe for you which I want you to smoke. However, no smoke must escape from it. If you smoke up all the tobacco without exhaling any smoke, you'll be the winner."

Just then Old Spider Woman caught up with Pavayoykyasi. Perching behind his ear she whispered, "Don't you worry. You'll survive this test. Just make sure you sit still when something tickles your behind. That will be the ones who came to help you. You simply keep swallowing the smoke." These were the old lady's instructions.

Icicle Boy now went to the southwest area of the kiva. From a niche there he removed his tobacco bag and his pipe and brought them over. The pipe was enormous. Icicle Boy sat down next to Pavayoykyasi and started filling it. When it was filled to the brim, he held it out to Pavayoykyasi and said, "Well, now you can find out how good you are. I told you what to do, so you'll be on your own." With that he lit the pipe.

put tsoongot taqtsokt pu' put aw iita.

Pu' yaw pam naat pu' put kwusunaniqw yaw antsa kurivehaq kuktsukya. Pu' yaw pam put so'wuutit tutavoyatniiqe pay yaw nawus sun yankyangw put tsoongot kwusuna. Noq kur yaw paasat puma muumuyt piw put Pavayoykyasit kuriyat su'atpip oomi poroknaya. Kur yaw puma paasat pangso porokinkyaakyangw put kuriyat tongtoynayaqw pam kuktsukva. Pu' yaw pam oovi put kwusunaqe pu' pep tsootsongo. Pu' yaw pam aasakis angqw tsootsone' pu' pay put kwiitsingwuy kwu'ukngwu. Pu' yaw pam put kwiitsingwuy kwu'takyangw yaw pam put enang siikingwu. Pu' yaw pam siikiqw pay yaw pam kwiitsingw aasonaq yamaktokyangw pu' pay kuringaqwwat yamakngwu. Pu' pam pangqw yamakkyangw pu' yaw haqe' ima muumuyt hötayaqw pay yaw pangsoqwat yungtakyangw pu' pay aapiy haqamwat hihin yaaphaqam piw oomi yamakngwu. Kur yaw panniqw pam so'wuuti pumuy muumuytuy pan kii'ayata. Yan pay yaw pam qa hin pas kyaanavota. Pu' yaw pam hisatniqw put piivat pas soosok sowaaqe pu' paasat put tsoongot ahoy nukpanat aw taviy.

Aw yaw taviqw pam put tsoongot aw yorikqe pas yaw qa yan unangwti. "Is uti, pay kur um qa pay himu'uy," yaw pam Lepenangwtiyo aw kita. "Niikyangw pay naato piw hintani. Itam pu' it natwanit akwni," yaw aw kita. "Itam pu' soosok it poshumit uyni. Pu' haqawa mooti put aniwnaqa paasat put maanatni," yaw aw kita.

Kitat pu' yaw pam yamakmaqe pu' hiisavoniqw pay yaw hiita iikwiwkyangw ahoy paki. Noq yaw pam kur tuuwat haqam moktamaqe put yaw qöpqöt kwiningya pangalat pu' yaw piw yamakmaqe pay yaw naat qa wuuyavotiqw pay yaw piw ahoy pitukyangw piw yaw an hiita mokkyangw paki. Pay yaw kur piw tuuwat pam ahoy mokkyangw paki. Pay yaw pam qa suus panti. Pu' kya pi hiisaq naawaknaqe pu' yaw paasaq qöpqöt kwiningye' möyiknaqe pu' angqw kwiningyaqw qöpqömiq hoomat akw sunasava pu' tuuwuha. Yaw pumuy nan'ik put tsiikyana. Pantit pu' yaw put Pavayoykyasit aw pangqawu, "Um hapi yukwat hoopoqwat ang uyniy. Noq pu' nu' yukwat teevenge tuwatniy." Noq yaw i' Kookyangwso'wuuti kur it tawaktsit poshumtaqe put yaw enang kivaaqe pu' put Pavayoykyasit aw oya. "It um enang uyni. I' hapi pay pas a'ni halayviniiqe supsiwtangwu," yaw aw kitat pu' put aw oya.

Noq pu' yaw puma naama nan'ik uytiva. Pu' yaw puma pay pas soosok hiita natwanit nan'ikye' uuya. Pu' pam Pavayoykyasi put tawaktsit enang. Pu' yaw puma soosok uyyukuqw pu' yaw pam

Pavayoykyasi was about to grab it when he felt an itching at this behind. Heeding the old woman's advice he sat still and did not move when he accepted the pipe. It was, of course, the gophers that had pierced the ground right under his behind. As they were coming through now, they kept touching his buttocks, which tickled him. Pavayoykyasi started smoking. Each time he drew on the pipe, he swallowed the smoke. Each time he swallowed the smoke he would fart. Each time he farted, the smoke inside of him escaped and came out from his behind. As it did it entered the tunnel the gophers had dug and eventually exited above ground quite a distance away. For this reason the old woman had asked the gophers to burrow the tunnel. In this fashion Pavayoykyasi did not have to suffer. Soon he had finished all of the tobacco and handed the pipe back to the evil one.

Icicle Boy was surprised when he inspected the pipe. "Gee, you are no ordinary man," he had to admit. "But this won't be all. Now we'll compete with crops. We'll plant all our seeds, and whoever gets them to mature first will win the girl."

With that Icicle Boy left, only to return a short while later with a load on his back. Evidently he had bagged some sand which he piled up northwest of the fireplace. He disappeared again, but before long reentered with another bundle, also containing sand. This he repeated several times. When he had spread out as much sand as he wanted, he drew a line with cornmeal across its middle, from a point in the northwest to the fireplace, dividing the area into two sections. That done he said to Pavayoykyasi, "You can plant on this portion here which extends to the northeast. I, in turn will sow on the part that extends to the southwest." Fortunately, Old Spider Woman had gathered up some sweet corn seeds which she had brought along. These she now gave to Pavayoykyasi. "You use these when you plant. These are very fast and grow without complication."

Thereupon both contestants began sowing on their sandy lots. On both sides they planted all the crops they had. Pavayoykyasi, of course, also included sweet corn. As soon as the owner of the kiva was finished, he opened a chamber to the northwest. All of a sudden clouds emerged from this chamber in large quantities. They shed their moisture on the two men's fields. After soaking them thoroughly they retreated again. No sooner had they disappeared than fog followed them out of the chamber. It kept billowing out until the entire kiva was filled. So thick was it that it became dark inside. Old

kiva'ytaqa pu' kwiniwihaqami hötat pu' angqw ahoy yama. Pu' yaw pangqw kwiningyaqw angk oo'omawt wukonöngakkyangw pu' yaw pumuy paasayamuy ang a'ni yokyanakyangw pu' piw yaw paas mowanayat pu' piw pay ahoy aqwhaqami yungiwma. Yaw puma aqwhaqami yungiwmaqw pu' yaw amungk paasat i' pamösi angqaqw tuwat wukoyamakqe pas piw yaw epeq oopo. Pas pi yaw epeq qa taalawva. Noq yaw i' Kookyangwso'wuuti piw kur maahut enang wikvaqe yaw pam put haqam pay naat na'uytoyna. Pu' yaw pan epeq qa taalawvaqw pu' yaw pam put maahut qa talpuva pu' pana. Pam yaw put panaqw pu' yaw pam tutskwave pu' kwangwaqtuwkyangw leelena. Taatawlawqe pas pi yaw sosonkiwa.

Noq pu' yaw pam nukpana pi'ep yamakye' pu' pakye' pu' yaw ep hiita hintsaklawngwu. Teevep yaw pam yaymaklawu. Noq pay pi yaw qa taalaniqw oovi yaw kur pam hintsaki. Pay yaw mimawat put qa suyan tuwa'yyungwa. Noq pam hapi yaw kur it lepenat tuwat pep yuyku. Put yaw kur pam pep koplawu. Pu' yaw pam put koptaqe pu' kyeevelngaqw put haytaqw yaw epeq iyoho'iwma. Pu' pay yaw i' maahu tuusungwtiqe pay okiw paapu hihin leelena.

Pu' yaw i' so'wuuti paasat piw hiita u'naqe pu' yaw put tiyot aw pangqawu, "Is uti, taq pi nu' kur supwat hiita qa u'naqw oovi pay itaavoko sumataq mangu'iwma. Um oovi iipo yamakye' ep haqam it suwaptsokit tuwe' pay um pas pantaqat ep horoknat pu' um angqw ahoy yawmani," yaw pam aw kita.

Pu' yaw pam oovi awhaqami yamakmaqe pu' angqe' put suwaptsokit hepqe pu' haqam tuwaaqe pu' put pep horoknat pu' put yawkyangw pangso kivami ahoy. Pu' yaw ep put yawkyangw pakiqw yaw so'wuuti haalayti, "Askwali, pantani," yaw kitat pu' yaw put aw pangqawu yaw put pep qöpqöt aqw tsööqöknani. Pu' yaw pam oovi pantiqw pu' yaw pam so'wuuti put pookoy put suwaptsokit atsmiq tsokya. Pay yaw panis pantiqw pay yaw pam maahu kur ahoy öqawtaqe pu' yaw pay piw ahoy a'ni leelentiva. Noq paasat pam yaw pantiqw pay yaw suukwangqat'iwmaqe pay hiisavoniqw pay yaw pas taala'niiqat an utuhu'ti. Pu' yaw pay paasat pay soosoy himu ang kuyva, patnga, kawayvatnga, melooni, uuyi. A'ni yaw himu ang wungwiwma. A'ni yaw himu aniwti. Pas pi yaw Pavayoykyasit himu'at hiihiimu a'ni aniwtiqw pay yaw puma nukpanat pö'i'yma. Pu' yaw i' sami'uyi'at pay suyan tayvayaqw pu' i' so'wuuti put Pavayoykyasit aw pangqawu, "Ta'ay, pay uu'uyi sonqe tayva. Oovi um awnen sukw angqw aakiknat siingye' pu' yukiq qöpqömiq tu'tsani. Ason kwasiqw pu' um suushaqam angqw yukut pu' um put nukpanat aw

Spider Woman also had brought a cicada along that she had kept hidden. But now that the light was gone, she sat the insect down in the dark. No sooner had she done so than the cicada started singing, squatting comfortably on the ground. As it sang, the air was filled with nice sounds.

The evil boy, meanwhile, kept leaving and reentering the kiva, all the while engaged in some mysterious activity. Again and again he would go out. Since it was dark, there was no telling what he was up to. It was impossible for the others to see. As it turned out, he was making icicles which he tied into bundles. Then he hung them from the ceiling with the result that the air was turning colder. Now the cicada began to freeze. As it shivered from the cold, its singing grew fainter and fainter.

At this point Old Spider Woman recalled something, for she turned to Pavayoykyasi and cried, "Darn it, why didn't I think of this? Now our pet is growing weaker. Go outside quickly and bring back a whole saltbush."

Pavayoykyasi did as bidden and ran outside. There he searched for a saltbush until he found one. Having uprooted it he came back inside the kiva with it. The old woman was overjoyed. "Thanks, that will do it," she exclaimed, whereupon she ordered him to insert the bush in the pit of the fireplace. That accomplished, she placed the cicada on top of the saltbush twigs. Immediately, the cicada gained its strength back and started singing quite loud again. As a result, the air was rapidly warming up, and before long it was like summer. Now everything began to grow—squash, watermelon, muskmelon and corn. Things were really growing. It was incredible how fast the crops came along. Maturing as quickly as they did, Pavayoykyasi's crops were winning the upper hand over those of the evil boy. When it was evident that his sweet corn was ready for harvesting, Old Spider Woman said to Pavayoykyasi, "Well now, your corn is mature. Go over and pick an ear. Then husk it and roast it in this fireplace. When its done, taste it once or twice and then throw it over to the evil one." Pavayoykyasi obeyed her instructions. He stepped up to the plants and broke off an ear of fresh corn. Then he husked it and roasted it. When the corn was done, he took two bites out of it and threw the rest at the feet of Icicle Boy. Pavayoykyasi had beaten his opponent in the contest.

tuuvani." Yan yaw pam aw tutaptaqw pu' yaw pam oovi uuyiy awniiqe put suukw angqw samiitaqe pu' siingyat pu' paasat aw tu'tsa. Pu' yaw kwasiqw pu' yaw pam angqw löös kyatkut pu' pay put tuuvetiy nukpanat aw tuuva. Pay yaw pam paasat put pö'ay. "Pay kur um qa pay hak'iy," yaw Lepenangwtiyo aw kita. "Niiqe oovi um pay mooti hiihiita aniwnay. Pay oovi um nuy pö'ay," yaw nukpana kita.

Noq pay yaw paasat ahoy suyan taalawva. Pay yaw paasat pamösi haqaqw yamakqey aqwhaqami pakimaqw pay yaw piw paasat ahoy taalawva. Noq pam yaw kur söhöt tangalawkyangw put koplawqw pam yaw pangqw kyeevelngaqw haayiwyungwa. Noq pam yaw kur pangqw lepen'iwwisa. Niiqe pu' puma put pö'i'ymaqw pay yaw pam ahoy paa'iwmaqw pay yaw söhösa kop'iwtaqa pangqw haayiwyungwa. Noq put yaw pam so'wuuti put Pavayoykyasit aw pangqawu, "Um awnen aw pangqawqw iipo yamakye' tsa'lawqw put sinomat angqwye' pay it yep uu'aniwniy ang höqye' pay put naap hinwat hintsatsnaniqat amumi pangqawni," yaw pam aw kita.

Pu' yaw pam oovi put nukpanat awniiqe pu' put so'wuutit lavayiyat aw tuwat tutapta. Pu' yaw pam oovi iipohaqami yamakqe pu' pan ephaqam tsa'lawt pu' piw ahoy pakiiqe pu' put pö'aaqat aw pangqawu, "Ta'ay, pay pi um nuwu pi nuy pö'ay. Pay pi nu' yan lavayti, pay ura haqawa moopeqtiqa put maanatniy. Noq pay pi um nuy suyan pö'aaqw pay son pi qa um putni. Pay oovi itam ikiy awniqw pay pi um wikniy," yaw aw kitat pu' pam put pangqw wikkyangw ahoy kiy awi'.

Pu' yaw puma ep pakiqw pu' yaw pam Lepenangwtiyo put maanatwat aw pangqawu, "Ta'ay, pay pi ura nu' it aw yan yukuy. Noq pay pi nuwu pi nuy pö'ay. Noq pay oovi son nawus i' ung qa wikkyangwniy," yaw aw kita. Paasat pu' yaw pam matapkingaqw yamakqe pu' angqw put Pavayoykyasit awi'.

Noq pu' yaw pam nukpana amumi piw pangqawu, "Pay haakiy, pay haak uma qe'niy. Ason uma yukiq kuyvat pu' paasatniy," yaw amumi kitat pu' kiy kwiniwiqhaqami höta. Paasat pu' yaw puma angk awniiqe pu' naama aqw kuyva. Noq yaw pangsoq kur wupa'atvela'ytaqw yaw aqwhaqami mamant naanangk tatsimiwta. Pam hapi yaw kur pumuy pephaqam tusungwqöyankyangw pumuy so'pumuy pangsoq paysoq wahitaqw puma yaw pangsoq naanangk tatsimiwta. Naato yaw peetu pas kur pu' so'qam naat qa pas hinyungwa. Qa pas paas patusungw'iwyungwa. Pu' yaw pam amumi pangqawu, "Yantsanni hapi nu' as it'ay. Naato nu' hapi as it tusungwninat pu' imuy

"You're a formidable man," the evil boy conceded. "You were the first to grow all sorts of things. I admit, you've won."

Now it became light again in the kiva. The fog disappeared into the chamber from which it had first emerged. Once more one could see clearly. From the ceiling bundles of wild grass, which had been icicles before, could be seen hanging. When the evil boy began to lose, they had started melting so that once again only bundled grass was dangling here. At this moment the old woman said to Pavayoykyasi, "Go to him and command him to go outside and make an announcement from the roof top. Tell him to have his relatives come and harvest these crops and do with them whatever they please."

Pavayoykyasi approached Icicle Boy and explained to him what the old lady wanted him to do. Obediently he went outside and cried out the public announcement. Then he came in again and said to the winner, "Well, there's nothing I can do. You beat me. Remember I said that the better one should have the girl. Since you defeated me, she is yours. So let's go to my house. There you can take her with you." With that he led Pavayoykyasi to his house.

Upon arriving there Icicle Boy said to the girl, "Well, this was my decision. He beat me in the contest, so he can take you with him now." The girl got up from the grinding bin and went to Pavayoykyasi.

However the evil boy spoke once more, "Wait a minute! Don't go just yet. Look in here first and then you can be on your way." With that he opened a door leading into a room on the northwest side. Pavayoykyasi and the girl followed him inside. There was a big slope there and all the way down girls were stacked against each other. Some of them had died only recently. They were still in good shape and had not completely turned into ice yet. Icicle Boy said, "This is what I intended to do with her. After freezing her to death, I would have thrown her down here with the others, but you came after me.

amungk yukiq it tuuvaniniqw pay um inungk pituy. Noq pay pi nu' antsa yan uumi yuku. Itam naami nanavö'niqat nu' pangqawu. Pu' haqawa pas pavanniiqa pu' ason itniqat antsa pi nu' pangqawqw pay pi um nuwu pi nuy pö'aaqe pay pi oovi um pu' wikniy," yaw aw kitaaqe pu' yaw nawus pay put maanat put aw no'a.

"Owiy, kur uma hakim nuunukpant yep yeesey. Noq pay uma yaasavo yep yest pay uma ayoq pas kwiniwiqhaqamiyaniy. Pay uma pas haqami nuutuukwangyavoqye' pepehaq pi pay uma yesvaniy. Niikyangw ason pas ima yang sinom hiita natwaniy aniwnaye' pu' put soosok kiikiy ang o'yaqw paasat pu' pay uma pephaqam tuwat qeni'yyungwmantani." Yan yaw pam Pavayoykyasi put nukpanat aw lavayti.

Paasat pu' yaw pam mantuway ngumanmokiyat iikwiltat pu' put wikkyangw pangqw yama. Pangqw pu' yaw puma put tiyot pokyat awniiqe pu' pep puma naama put aqw wupqw pu' yaw pam piw hölöltikyangw pu' pumuy pangqaqw tsoki'ykyangw pu' puuyawma. Pu' yaw put tiyot pok'at kya pi pay piw put kiiyat tuwi'ytaqe pay yaw oovi yuumosa pumuy pangso Tuutukwimi wiiki. Noq pu' yaw pam antsa pephaqam put maanat wikva. Noq yaw put tiyot pok'at pep kiiyat oove qatuptuqw pu' yaw puma angqw hawqw pu' yaw pam tiyo kivats'ove aqwhaqami pangqawu, "Haw, kuwawatotangwuy! Nu' qa naala waynumay," yaw aqwhaqami kita.

Pu' yaw put so'at pumuy paki'a'awnaqw pu' puma naama aqw paki. Pas pi yaw so'at supakhaalaytiqe yaw amumi haalaylawu. "Is askwali, um wikva. Pas nu' umuy awhaqami wuuwantaqe hiisavo akw qa haalayi. Noq pay kur tsangaw uma su'an yukuqw oovi itam mö'wi'yvayani," yaw kitaaqe pas pi yaw pumuy amumi haalaylawu.

"Owiy, pay niikyangw nu' qa naalaniikyangw put nukpanat pö'ay. Piw nuy pam hak so'wuuti hakimuy amumum pa'angwaqw oovi nu' it ahoy naapti. Pas nu' oovi pumuy hakimuy tsuya," yaw pam soy aw kitaaqe pu' yaw puma hin pep hintotiqw put yaw pam soosok soy aw lalvaya.

Noq pu' yaw pam so'tapnaqw put so'at aw pangqawu, "Hep owi, pi pay antsa pam so'wuuti pep ki'ytaqa pay pam piw soosokmuy so'amu. Pay himuwa hiita ep öwihiniwtiqw pay pam hakiy ookwatuwe' pay pam hakiy pa'angwangwu. Noq pay kur tsangaw pam uumi unangwtapqw oovi pay kur um ang ayo' yama," yaw pam kitaaqe put Kookyangwso'wuutit haalayti. Pu' yaw oovi pam so'wuuti tuwat put puhumö'wiy engem qaa'öt ipwaqe pu' engem huumi. Pu' pam put mataptsömiq panaqw pu' yaw pam pepwat pas

At that point I decided that we would measure our powers. I said the stronger one would get the girl. As it turned out, you won. So you have her now." With that he gave Pavayoykyasi the girl.

"Yes," Pavayoykyasi replied, "all of you who live here are evil, but you can no longer remain here. Instead, you will go as far northwest as you can. There you will live as remote from people as possible. And this is how it will be from this day on: People will first harvest their crops and gather them into their houses before you can have your turn with the cold weather." This is what Pavayoykyasi said to the evil boy.

Thereupon he loaded the girl's corn bag on his shoulders and went out to the girl. They headed to their flying shield and stepped aboard. Soon it rose up into the air and with both of them riding in it, it flew along. Evidently the flying shield was familiar with the boy's home, for it took them straight to the Buttes Area. Pavayoykyasi had finally brought his bride home. The craft landed right atop the boy's house. After climbing out, the boy shouted inside from the roof, "Haw! Say some words of welcome. I'm not alone."

Pavayoykyasi's grandmother asked them to enter, and the two went in. The old woman cried from joy. She was really glad. "Thank you, you've brought her! I was worried about you being that far away and quite unhappy for a while. I'm glad you succeeded, for now we have a bride," she exclaimed, airing her joy again and again.

"Yes, but I did not conquer that evil one by myself. It was an old woman and other beings who helped me to get her back. I'm most grateful to them," Pavayoykyasi explained. With that he told his grandmother in detail how they both had fared.

When Pavayoykyasi ended his account, his grandmother said, "Yes, indeed. The old woman who lives there is the grandmother of all people. Whenever someone is in need, she takes pity on him and helps him. I'm so glad she came to your rescue, for this is how you survived," she said, expressing her gratitude to Old Spider Woman. She then took out some corn for the new in-law, shelled it for her, and had her kneel by the grinding bin, this time grinding real corn. Finally, she got some cotton, twisted it into a string, and tied it into the ear lobe of the bride.

humitat ngumanta. Pu' yaw pam piw haqaqw pösövit horoknaqe pu' put muruknaqe pu' yaw put mö'wiy naqvuvawtoyna. Pu' yaw pam oovi pep paayis teevep ngumanta. Pu' yaw nalöstalqat ep su'its talavay i' so'wuuti put mö'wiy wikkyangw iipo yamakqe pu' pep tsa'lawu. "Pangqe' kya uma inatkom yeese. Uma angqw pewye' yep inumum it itaamö'wiy asnayani," yan yaw tsa'-lawu.

Noq pay yaw naat qa wuuyavotiqw pay yaw naanan'i'vaqw oo'omawt kuukuyvakyangw pay yaw pumuy amumiq naakwusta. Pu' yaw puma pumuy su'amutsve naanami ökiiqe pu' yaw pumuy amumi yoknaya. Kur yaw puma put asnawisqam pep öki. Yanhaqam yaw puma put mö'wiy asnayat pu' piw haqaqw ökiiqey aqwhaqami ahoyya.

Qavongvaqw pu' yaw pam so'wuuti piw pay pan su'its qatuptuqe pu' piw iipohaqami yamakmaqe pu' piw ep tsa'lawu. "Pangqe' kya uma inatkom yeese. Uma angqw pew tsovawmani. Itam yep pu' puhumö'wi'yvaya," yanhaqam yaw pam pep tsa'lawt pu' piw ahoy paki.

Noq pay yaw naat oovi qa nawutstiqw pay yaw hakim yungtivaya. Noq yaw kur puma kookookyangwt pep paasat ökiwta. Pas pi yaw kur puma pephaqam kyaastaqe pas pi yaw pangso naspawmaqe yaw hiisavoniqw pay puma pepeq opopota. Noq pay yaw sumataq puma soosoyam ökiqw pu' it Pavayoykyasit so'at aapamiqhaqaminiiqe pu' pangqaqw it pösövit ipwantiva. Pay yaw pas wuuhaq pam pangqaqw tsaama. Pu' yaw pay ima kookookyangwt peetu tusqentivaya. Yaw puma pepeq pantsakkyaakyangw pu' haqami sutsvowat put oo'oyaya. Pu' yaw peetuwat put awyaqe pu' put pösövit pep tuwat noonova. Pu' yaw himuwa hiisa'haqam sowat pu' kyeevelmoq wupngwu. Aqw wupt pu' yaw aqw oomiq kuriy iitat pu' siisingwu. Yaw pan oomiq siisiqw pu' yaw kuringaqw hiisay pösövi yamakkyangw yaw pangsoq kyeevelmoq kwangwaviitakngwu. Pantit pu' yaw pam pangqw muruwsusuwtikyangw ahoy hawtongwu. Puma hapi yaw kur pan put pösövit murikintotakyangw pu' piw tonlalwa. Pu' yaw himuwa oovi atkyamiq hawqw yaw oongaqw wupavösöptoni hayiyitangwu. Pu' yaw piw peetu put pangqw hannayaqe pu' put namikwaplalwakyangw pu' pölölantota. Pu' yaw oovi puma qa suup pölöt yukuyaqe pu' paasat piw yawi'o'oytivaya. Pu' yaw paasat pas ima wukokookookyangwt tuwatya. Yaw himuwa pas pantaqat tonvölöt kwu'ukt pu' put siisitimakyangw ayoqwat warikngwu. Pu' yaw puma pep naahoy yuyutyaqe pay yaw pan piw pep suuyawi'o'-

For three whole days the girl ground corn. Early in the morning of the fourth day, the old woman took her by the hand and led her outside. There she cried out, "You, my offspring, who live out there! Come here and wash our bride's hair with me!"

Before long clouds began to gather from all directions, moving toward the two. Right above them they merged and then released their rain. They had come to wash the bride's hair. Having accomplished this they disappeared again to where they had come from.

The following morning the old woman rose early. Once again she went outside and made an announcement. "You, my offspring, who live out there! Come and gather here! We have a new bride here!" Then she went back in again.

It did not take long, and some beings began to enter. This time it was the spiders that kept arriving. There were lots of them. They came in droves and soon filled the entire house. When it appeared that all had arrived, Pavayoykyasi's grandmother vanished into the back room and started bringing out cotton. She brought out large quantities of it. Immediately, some of the spiders set to carding the cotton. This they kept doing, always putting the clean cotton to one side. Other spiders now fell upon the cotton and began to devour it. Whenever one of them had gobbled up a good portion, it crawled up to the ceiling. There it would stick its rear end up in the air and extrude from its behind a little cotton which became attached to the ceiling. Then the spider would lower itself back down, spinning around and around as it descended. In this fashion they twisted the cotton and made it into thread. By the time they were all down, long cotton strings were dangling from the ceiling. Next, a few of the spiders ran the threads back up rolling them up into balls. When they had made several balls, they began to set up the loom. Now the big spiders got their turn. Each of them swallowed an entire ball of yarn and defecated it as it ran over to the other side of the loom. Back and forth they ran, and in this way completed the warp. Then they set the loom upright and, scuttling to and fro between the warp threads, began the actual weaving. Since there were multitudes of spiders the work was finished in no time.

ya. Pu' yaw puma put yawi'oyiy hongvanayaqe pu' piw put amuu-
tsatsava yuyutyaqe pay yaw piw put aw suupööqantivaya. Niiqe pay
pi yaw puma kyaysiwqe yaw oovi hiihiita soosok suyuki'ywisa.
Noq pu' yaw i' hak suukyawa piw hakiy iikwiwkyangw paki.
Noq yaw put hakiy iikwiwtaqw pamwa yaw piw hiita wukotori-
kiwkyangw amum paki. Noq pu' yaw pam put panat pu' pay qöpqöt
akwningya tavi. Noq yaw pam kur tuhavit iikwiwkyangw pakiqw
pam tuhavi yaw kur it wukosowi'yngwat torikiwkyangw pitu.
Pamwa yaw kur put sowi'yngwat ep mö'wit engem totstaniqe pu'
yaw oovi put ep taviqw pay yaw pam paasat aw pitsinaqe pas pi yaw
piw a'ni halayviniiqe yaw putwat piw suyuki'yma.
    Pay yaw oovi naat qa taawanasaptiqw pay yaw pam yukuuqe
pu' put mö'wiy aw taviqw pu' yaw pam put ang tuwanta. Noq pay
yaw piw pam pas kur put su'aapeniiqat yuku. Pay yaw oovi pam
mö'wi ang kwangwasupki. Pu' pay yaw piw pas qa haqaqwat put
tuuholawu. Yanhaqam yaw puma pep mö'wiy engem yewasvi-
soq'iwyungqe pay yaw piw suyuki'ywisa.
    Noq pu' yaw puma pep pantsatskyaqw pu' yaw i' Pavayoykyasi
tuwat maqto. Pu' pay yaw pam tuwat maakyaniiqe pay yaw oovi qa
pas wuukonakwsut pay yaw lööqmuy pas wukotsayrisatuy niina.
Pay yaw oovi naat ima pööqantotaqam qa yukuyaqw pay yaw pam
ahoy pumuy iikwiwkyangw pitu. Pay yaw pam kur paas pumuy
siskwaqe pay yaw oovi put paas sikwi'iwtaqat iikwiwva. Pu' yaw put
pituqw yaw so'at haalaylawu. Pu' yaw pam pay paasat sukwat aw
nöqkwiva.
    Noq pu' yaw pay naat qa pas taawansaptiqw pay yaw puma pep
soosok hiita yuki'ywisa. Pu' yaw oovi pam mö'wi'am yaw kur pik-
taqe yukuuqe pu' yaw piw novangumanta. Yukuuqe pu' yaw pumuy
amungem aw noovalawu. Su'aw yaw pam oovi novayukuqw yaw
mimawat piw tuwat yukuya. Pu' yaw puma pep oovi put noovayat
aw yesvaqe pu' noonova. Pas pi yaw puma pep put noovayat naanasna. Pas pi yaw pam kur wukonovataqw puma qa hin soosok
soswa. Pu' yaw himuwa kya pi a'ni ööye' pay paysoq tunösvongyat
angqw ayo' hihin qalavonit pay pangqe' wa'ökmangwu. Yaw puma
pephaqam naanaqle' öyvuusukiwyungwa. Pu' pay kya pi himuwa
hisatniqw pas sööpukye' pu' qatuptut pu' pangqw yamaktongwu.
    Noq pu' yaw pumuy nööngantaqamuy amumi ima ki'yyungqam
haalaylalwa. Pu' yaw so'wuuti piw amumi pangqawngwu, "Uma
angqw mö'wit noovayat paatsonlalwani. Pam qa hin sulaw'iwma."
    Pu' yaw oovi puma put angqw paatsontikyaakyangw pu' nöö-

Now a man entered carrying someone on his back—a lame man who himself carried a big buckskin on his shoulders. The man put the lame one down on the floor northwest of the fireplace. No sooner had the lame man been put down on the floor than he began to fashion wedding boots for the bride from the buckskin he carried. He was extremely quick and soon finished the footwear.

It was not yet noontime and he was already done. He handed the boots to the bride, who tried them on. They were exactly her size. She had no problem putting them on, and they did not hurt her anywhere. In this way they were all busy making the wedding garments for the bride. Everything was finished in no time.

Meanwhile, Pavayoykyasi went hunting. He was an expert hunter, and had not advanced very far when he killed two big elks. The weavers were not even finished when he returned with his prey on his back. He had already taken out the innards and only brought back the meat. His grandmother thanked him profusely and immediately set to making stew from one of the animals.

It was still not yet the noon hour when everything was ready. The bride had finished baking piki and was grinding corn for the somiviki. When that chore was done, she prepared lunch. By the time she was ready, the others also had finished their work. Everybody settled down to her food and ate, gorging themselves. There was so much, however, that they could not eat it all. Whenever someone felt satiated, he moved away from the place where the food was set out and lay down by the edge. The guests were lying all over, relaxed, with full stomachs. Later, as their fullness passed, one after the other got up and went outside.

Pavayoykyasi and his family thanked those who were leaving. The old woman kept saying, "Help yourselves to the bride's food and save some for later. It's not getting less."

nganta. Pu' yaw piw amumi pangqawngwu, "Uma hapi ason tapkimi angqw ahoyye' pu' pas nöqkwivityani. Tsangaw i' imöyi sakina," yaw amumi kitangwu.

Noq pas pi yaw puma pangqaqw a'ni noova'ywisa, wukovatsona'ywisa. Noq pu' yaw pantaqw yaw antsa tapkiwmaqw yaw puma kwangwtotoykyangw ep ahoy ökiwta. Pu' yaw pay soosoyam ep öki'ewakwniqw pu' yaw pam so'wuuti put mö'wiy amum aw tunösvongyalawu. Pu' yaw puma yukuuqe pu' pumuy pep sinmuy tunös'a'awnaqw pu' puma yaw piw aw yesvaqe pu' piw noonova. Pay yaw puma piw an naanasna. Pas pi yaw kur pam wukotaqat niinaqw pas pi yaw nöqkwiviyamuy angqw sikwisa wukotangawta. Pu' yaw himuwa kya pi ööye' pu' piw pay an hihin qalavonit pu' pay pangqe' wa'ökmangwu. Pay yaw puma piw taawanasaveniiqat su'an hintoti. Niikyangw pay yaw puma paasat naat qa nöönganta. Pu' yaw puma soosoyam öö'öyaqw pu' yaw puma ang ayo' paas qenita. Pu' yaw puma ang qenitaqe pay yaw nuutum pepeq qatu.

Noq paasat pay yaw kur mihi. Noq pay yaw naat puma qa wuuyavo yesqw yaw oovehaqam sumataq hiitu piw öki. Noq pay yaw qa nawutstiqw yaw angqaqw ayayayku. Pu' yaw paasat i' so'wuuti aqwhaqami kuwawata. "Yungya'a, pay itam umuy nuutayyungwa," yaw aqwhaqami kitaqw pu' yaw paasat angqaqw hiitu yungtiva.

Noq yaw kur puma katsinam paasat öki. Yaw kur puma tuwat put mö'wiy tayawnawisqe öki. Pas pi yaw piw a'ni na'mangwu'yvaya. A'ni yaw kur kya pi puma haqam uuyi'yyungqe put kivaya. Tuupevu pas yaw wukotuupevuniikyangw wuuwupa. Pu' yaw piw meloonitnit pu' kawayvatngat soosok hiita natwanit yaw puma wukokivaya. Noq yaw oovi qa suukya Hehey'a amumum pituuqe yaw put iikwiwkyangw pakit pu' piw ahoy yamakye' pu' piw peehut iikwiwkyangw ahoy pakingwu. Pay yaw puma Hehey'am panis pantotit pu' yaw pay kur haqamiya. Pu' mimawat katsinam pay yaw epeq huruutotiqe pu' yaw puma pepeq pumuy amumi tiikive'yyungwa. Pas pi yaw puma kwangwa'ewyaqw puma yaw qa hingqawkyaakyangw kwangwatitimayya. Pu' yaw puma tiitso'qe pu' ang pepeq tangawtaqamuy put na'mangwuy huylalwa. Pu' yaw put mö'wit pas soosoyam qa suukw hiita maqayaqw pas pi yaw pam hiita niiti.

Pu' yaw puma pantotit pu' nöngakma. Naat yaw oovi pu' pumuy nöngakmaqw pay yaw piw peetu ökikyangw pay yaw piw pumuy su'amun yukuya. Pu' yaw puma katsinam naanangk pep ökiwta. Pay

So, as the guests filed out, they put some food aside for later. As they did, the old woman urged them, "Toward early evening I want you to come back and have some stew. I'm so glad my nephew was lucky enough to bag some meat."

People were leaving with large quantities of food. As it turned evening, they returned, looking forward to the feast with great anticipation. When everybody appeared to have arrived, the old woman and the bride set out the supper. That done, they once more invited everyone to eat. All the guests sat down and ate to their hearts' content. Pavayoykyasi had killed a large buck, so the stew was mostly meat. As soon as a guest was full, he moved to the edge and lay down. People did just as they did during the midday meal. When all were satiated, the old woman and her in-law cleared the table and joined the others.

By now it had turned black night. The whole group had not been sitting there long when some newcomers could be heard on the rooftop. Soon a rattle sounded from above, and the old woman welcomed them in. "Come on down, we're waiting for you!" she shouted, whereupon they entered.

The new arrivals were kachinas who had come to entertain the bride. With them they had brought loads of gifts, especially crops. The ears of baked sweet corn were big and long in size. In addition, they had muskmelon, squash, and all the other field fruits in great quantities. There were several Hehey'a kachinas who kept coming and going, hauling these things on their backs. As soon as they had brought everything in, they departed. The other kachinas, however, remained and staged a dance for the bride and her guests. The kachinas were very good and the spectators all watched in silence. After ending their dance they distributed their presents to the people inside. And since the bride received more than one gift from each of them, she accumulated a large pile.

Thereafter the kachinas filed out. No sooner had they left, than a new group arrived that did exactly what the first had done. In this manner the kachina groups kept coming, one after another. Each group only danced once. To the departing kachinas the bride handed somiviki, which they were to take along on their journey home.

yaw puma pas yuki'ywisa. Pu' yaw katsinmuy nööngantaqamuy pu' yaw pam mö'wi pumuy noovay nitkyatotoyna. Piw yaw kur pam wuwni'yhintiqe yaw kur aw wukonovataqe pumuy yaw pam soosokmuy naanan'ik novahuyta. Pu' yaw Hehey'amuy amungem piw supwat mokyaataqe pu' sukwat aw tavi pumuy amungem moktaniniqw. Son pi qa puma pi hiihiita aniwnaya. Puma pi yaw a'ni pasvaya.

Hisatniqw pu' yaw sutmakma. Paasat pu' yaw pam so'wuuti pangqawu, "Ta'aa, pay sumataq yantani. Pay askwal puma piw itamuy angqw pootayaqe oovi itamuy hin'ur tayawnaya. Pu' uma askwal itamumi unagwtatveqw oovi itam it mö'wit yuwsinaya. Pay uma oovi haalaykyaakyangw angqe' umuukiy ang nankwusani," yaw kitaaqe yaw pumuy amumi haalaylawu.

Pu' yaw puma oovi paasat tuwat ninma. Pas pi yaw puma pangqw naanan'ik hiihiita mokyungwa, tsaatsakwmuy aqwhaqami. Yanhaqam yaw puma pep put mö'wiy tayawnaya. Pu' yaw pam so'wuuti put mööyiy aw pangqawu, "Ta'aa, pay uma qaavo son nawus qa it mö'wit kiiyat awni. Pay son it ephaqam qa nuutayyungwa. Pay hapi wuuyavoti i' pangqw aapiyniqw'ö. Pay son it yumat qa ephaqam sölmokiwta. Noq pay oovi itam tokvani. Ason qaavo pu' nu' piw uumi hinwat tutaptani," yaw pam mööyiy aw kitaqw pu' yaw puma oovi tokva.

Qavongvaqw pu' yaw pam so'wuuti pumuy iits pay taataynaqe pu' yaw pu' mö'wiy aw torikuyna. Pantit pu' paasat mö'wi yuwsi'ykyangw nimangwuniqw pan yaw pam put yuwsina. Put yaw pan paas yuwsinaqw pu' yaw puma pangqw antsa nöngay. Nöngakqw pu' yaw pam so'wuuti amungem pöötavi. Pangqw pu' yaw puma put ang nakwsu. Pu' yaw pam tiyo oovi put sukw sikwimokiy put puma qa nöqkwipyaqw put yaw pam mö'önangwkiy aw iikwiwma, put nöömay tavitokyangw. Niiqe pu' yaw puma pokyat piw aqw wupqw paasat pu' yaw pam hölöltikyangw pu' yaw antsa pay piw puuyaltikyangw pay yaw puma kur pangso pumuy paasayamuy aw kur paasavo put akwni. Noq pay yaw oovi pok'am pep kisve qatuptu. Paasat pu' puma angqw hawt pangqw pu' yaw pay puma naap aqw kiimiq, Awat'omiq. Pam maana hapi oovi koongyay wikkyangw.

Noq angqe' pi yaw tootim iits pay kits'ovaqe yesngwuniiqe yaw put hiita tutwaqw yaw pangqaqw himu qötsmamatsila. Noq yaw aw tupohaqami. Pu' yaw angqaqw wupqw yaw kur hak mö'wi. Niikyangw yaw hakiy tiyot wiiki. Noq yaw so'at aw pan tutapta, "Um

Fortunately she had had the foresight to prepare a lot of it. She now distributed all of it to the succeeding dance groups. For the Hehey'as she also bundled up some somiviki, which she gave to one of the kachinas to take along for the group. No doubt the Hehey'as had raised all sorts of crops, for they were really good farmers.

Eventually the night became still. Now the old woman said, "Well, I suppose that's that. I'm grateful the kachinas came to visit us and provided us with a good time. And I'd like to thank you for helping us make the wedding outfit for the bride. Now go back to your homes with happy hearts." This is how she kept expressing her thankfulness to everyone.

Thereupon the guests started leaving for home. Everybody had some food wrapped in a bag, even the children. This is how the bride was entertained at the wedding. Now the old woman said to her grandson, "All right, tomorrow you must return to your wife's home. I'm sure her relatives are already waiting. It's been quite some time since your bride left. Her parents must be missing her. So let's go to bed now. In the morning I'll have some more to say to you." With that they all went to bed.

The next day the old woman woke up the couple early. First she wove the bride's hair into a braid, then she dressed her the way a bride is supposed to be dressed when she returns home after the wedding. That accomplished, all three of them went outside, where the old woman laid down a road marker for the couple. Along that Pavayoykyasi and his wife started out. On his back he carried a bag full of meat which had not been used for the stew. Along with his wife, he was taking this meat to the home of his in-laws. Once again the two boarded the flying shield, which soon rose up in the air. They were going to fly with it all the way to their fields at Awat'ovi. After landing at a field hut there, they climbed out of their pet and walked the remainder of the way to the village. The girl was finally bringing home her husband.

In those days young boys used to be up on the roofs early. No wonder they noticed a whitish speck in the distance. As the speck approached the base of the mesa, they realized that it was a woman in her bridal outfit, and that she was bringing a young man with her. Now prior to the couple's departure, the old woman had instructed her grandson as follows, "When you arrive at your bride's home, say this to her father, 'I want you to cut up all this meat and cook it. In the evening then you can invite all the villagers to come and feast.'"

hapi ep it kiiyat ep pite' it nayat um aw pangqawni, 'Pay it soosok um sikwit tutkitaqw aw hapi kwipye' pu' tapkiqw uma soosokmuy sinmuy tuutsamtotaqw soosoyam aw nöswisni.'" Yan yaw so'at aw tutaptaqw pu' yaw puma oovi maanat kiiyat ep pituqw pu' antsa yaw yu'at puma haalayti. Paasat pu' yaw pam Pavayoykyasi put maanat nayat aw pangqawu, "Itam it pay soosok pu' aw kwipyani. Kwipyat pu' ason tapkiqw uma angqe' soosokmuy sinmuy tuutsamtotaqw soosoyam angqw hapi nöswisniy," yaw pam mö'önangw'at aw kita.

Paasat pu' yaw puma soosok put sikwit aw kwipyay. Kwipyaqe pu' paasat yaw antsa tapkiqw pu' yaw puma naatim tunösvongyaata. Paasat pu' yaw put yu'at yamakmaqe pu' yaw soosovik pan kiinawit pam tuutsamtinuma. Tuutsamtinumqe yaw pangqawnuma, soosoyam yaw aqw nöswisniqat. Paasat pu' yaw antsa aqw sinom sasqativaya, nöswisqam. Pu' yaw antsa himuwa nööse' yaw haalaytingwu. Pantsatskyaakyangw pu' yaw soosoyam öö'öyayaqe nöngakqw paasat pu' yaw pam maana ang ayo' qenita.

Noq paapiy hapi pay oovi pam mö'önangw'am iits talavay qatupte' pu' yaw pay pangso uuyiyamuy awnen pang pu' yaw pam maakwannumngwu, soosokmuy uuyiyamuy anga'. Pam yaw aasakis talavay pantingwu. Pas yaw pam qa na'öna. Niiqe pu' yaw tal'angvaqw yaw put maanat na'at uyqw yaw pam Pavayoykyasi put uuyiyat ang pastinume' pu' yaw pay suyukuye' pu' yaw pay naap hakiy haqam qa yuki'ymaqat pa'angwangwu. Pu' pay yaw piw putwat engem piw suupastiyukungwu. Paavantsaklawu yaw pami'. Panwiskyaakyangw pu' yaw puma paapiy a'ni yaw yooyoknayangwuniiqe pas pi yaw a'ni hiita aniwnayangwu.

Noq pu' oovi yaw pam pepehaq yan mö'önangw qatuqw pu' pay yaw put nööma'at nö'yilti. Nö'yiltikyangw yaw tiyooyat tiita. Niiqe paasat pu' yaw it Pavayoykyasit so'at put tiposhoyat asnaqe pu' yaw put Sakwyeva yan tungwa. Pu' yaw pam wuuyoq'iwma. Naat pu' yaw yaasangwvaqw pay yaw piw nööma'at nö'yilti. Pu' yaw pay piw tiita, pay yaw piw tiyooyat. Pamwa pu' yaw Moomo'a. Pi yaw pay piw nö'yiltikyangw pu' piw tiita. Pamwa pu' yaw Hoyniwa. Pu' pay yaw pam aasakis yaasangwvaqw pay yaw piw tiitangwu. Aapiy yaw piw paykomuy tiita. Noq i' yaw naalöq epniiqe yaw Siisivu, pu' angkniiqa Wuktima. Pu' yaw nuutungkniiqa Patösqasa. Yan yaw puma maamatsiwya. Navayniiqamuy yaw pam put engem ti'oya. Noq pay yaw puma piw pas a'ni hiituhooyamu, puma naanatupkom. Pay yaw pas a'ni wuwni'yyungwa. Noq oovi pam suswuyoqa, Sakwyeva,

When the couple arrived at the girl's house, her parents were elated. And Pavayoykyasi said to his wife's father, "Let's boil all of this meat. Then, in the evening you can invite all the people to join us and eat with us." This is what his son-in-law said.

When all the meat was cooked, the new husband and wife set out the food for the feast. The girl's mother left and went from house to house inviting everybody to come and eat with them. Soon those people who cared to eat started arriving. Whenever one had eaten, he was happy. This went on until everybody was satiated. Soon they had all departed again and the girl cleared everything away.

From that day on Pavayoykyasi, the new son-in-law, would rise early at dawn to head out to the village crier's fields and sprinkle the plants with dew. Every morning he would do this to all the plants. He was a most industrious man. And when summer came and the girl's father had sown, Pavayoykyasi hoed weeds and cared for the plants. As soon as he was done with this, he would assist whoever was not finished. As a rule, it did not take him long to complete the work. In this manner Pavayoykyasi spent his days. From that time on it always rained a lot and the Awat'ovis harvested a great abundance of crops.

As the days went by with Pavayoykyasi living there, his wife became pregnant and gave birth to a boy. His grandmother washed his hair and named him Sakwyeva. He quickly grew bigger, a year passed, and the woman was again with child. Once more she gave birth to a boy. His name was Moomo'a. A third time she became pregnant. This child too was born a boy, and was called Hoyniwa. Each year Pavayoykyasi's wife bore another boy. The fourth one was named Siisivu, the one after him Wuktima, and the last Patösqasa. Six sons in all she bore for Pavayoykyasi, and all of them were endowed with greater than human powers. All were extremely intelligent. Sakwyeva, the oldest, was barely six years old when he was made village leader of Awat'ovi in charge of all the villagers. This happened because he did so much for the welfare of the people. Each

yaw naat panis tiyosaytiqw pay yaw put kikmongtatve. Niiqe yaw put kikmongtatveqw yaw oovi pepehaq tiyoniikyangw yaw pumuy amumi kikmong'iwta, Awat'opsinmuy amumi'. Yaw pam kikmongwi piw pumuy a'ni hiitakw pa'angwantaqw oovi a'ni yaw puma hiita aniwnayangwu uu'uye'. Pu' yaw sutsep yooyoki, pu' tömö' a'ni nuvatingwu. Pas hapi yaw puma Awat'opsinom pepehaq kwangwayese. Pay yaw puma sutsep haalayya. Naavaasya yaw puma'. Pay yaw Pavayoykyasit atsviy puma pan yeese. Pu' pay yaw put timat piw pas qa nana'önt a'ni hiituniqw oovi yaw puma pumuy amutsviy piw a'ni mongvasya. Pu' yaw puma oovi pay pephaqam lomayese.

Noq puma pep Awat'ove suupwat toonavit pay yaw pas qa nananyaqe it Pavayoykyasitnit pu' i' Sakwyeva kikmongwtiqw pumuy pas qa no'a. Niique puma yaw pay pas kur popwaqtsa. Haqam yaw pep kwitave kiva'yyungwa. Noq yaw oovi pumuy kwitavit yan tuwi'yyungwa. Niiqe puma yaw pumuy aw sutsep wuuwantota, hin as yaw puma hiita aw alöngtotaniqey pu' sen yaw pumuy angqw haqawa kikmongwtini. Noq pay yaw kur puma hin it Pavayoykyasit atpik hiita hintotini.

Noq paasat pay yaw Sakwyevat ima tupkomat wuuwuyoqamtoti. Wuuwuyoqamtotiqw pu' yaw tsaatsayom poktinumyangwuniqw puma yaw put kwangwa'ytutuswa pumuy amumi. Kwangwa'ytutuswaqe pu' put nay aw pangqaqwa, "Um as itamumgem hootani. Itam put tsaatsakwmuy amumi kwangwa'ytutuswa. Itam nuutum poktinumyani," yaw puma nay aw kitotaqw paasat pu' yaw oovi pam amungem hootay.

Hootat pu' awtataqw paasat pu' antsa puma nuutum tsaatsakwmuy amumum poktinumyangwu. Noq pam yaw pi i' Pavayoykyasiniiqe pu' pam hapi yaw kur it talwiipikit amungem hoolawu. Hootaqw pu' yaw oovi aapiy puma pumuy tsaatsakwmuy amumum poktinumyakyangw pu' hiitawat hoy akw panis aw tongokyaqw pay yaw paasat pam himuwa mokngwu. Pantsakkyaakyangw pay yaw wuuhaqniiqam puma tsaatsayom pantaqat akw puma pay so'a.

Noq pay yaw wuuhaqniiqam pan so'a hooyamuy akw tongokyaqe. Noq yaw kwitavit tsutsyakya. Pay yaw pu' kur hin qa hiita akw amuupewiyaniqey oovi puma yaw tsutsyakya. Niiqe pu' puma yaw oovi sinmuy amungem hiita nukushiita tunatyaltoti. Niiqe pu' yaw pay puma oovi sinmuy tuskyaptotaniqey yan yukuyaqe oovi pumuy amumi soyaknayani. Niiqe pu' yaw puma oovi pumuy sinmuy tuskyaptote' pu' yaw puma pumuy Pavayoykyasit timuyatuy

year they planted, they had big harvests. It always rained, and in winter there was plenty of snow. Life in Awat'ovi was pleasant. The people were always happy and kind to each other. All of this was due to Pavayoykyasi. His sons, too, were endowed with special powers. Since they were never lazy, the villagers profited from them in many ways. Because of them they lived a most agreeable life.

However, there was one group of people in Awat'ovi that could not stand Pavayoykyasi. Also, the fact that Sakwyeva had become the village leader did not please them at all. This group consisted of sorcerers and witches. They had their kiva at Kwitavi, the "Excrement Place," and for this reason they were known as the Turds. They were constantly racking their minds, thinking how they could change things for the worse, and how one of them might succeed in becoming village chief. However, they were not able to do much because of Pavayoykyasi's powers.

Meanwhile, Sakwyeva's brothers were getting older. They reached an age where they wanted to go around shooting with bow and arrows like the other boys, so they spoke to their father about it. "Please," they asked, "make us some arrows. We're envious of the other kids who have them. We would like to shoot around with arrows too." So their father fashioned bows and arrows for them.

Now Pavayoykyasi's sons were able to play bow and arrows with the village children. But since their father was Pavayoykyasi, the arrows he had made for them were actually lightning bolts. As his sons were now shooting around with the other kids, they only needed so much as touch one of them and as a result the child would die. As time went by, a great number of children perished for this reason.

When so many children died because they came in contact with the boys' arrows, the sorcerers and witches were filled with joy. After all, they now had some reason to confront Pavayoykyasi. Now they would be able to plan some detrimental things for the people. They therefore decided to make the villagers crazy. This they would accomplish by bewitching them. If, indeed, they should succeed in driving the people mad, they could blame this on Pavayoykyasi's sons. This is what the sorcerers thought.

tukopnayani. Yan yaw puma wuuwaya.

Noq pu' pay yaw sinom hintoti. Pay yaw puma hintotiqe yaw qa naakyaptsi'yyungwa. Panis yaw naangwu'yyungngwu, naanaywangwu. Pu' yaw hiita nöösiwqat tuunawkilalwangwu. Pu' yaw wuutit haqe' piikit intaqw pay yaw piw nawkiyangwu. Pas yaw qa hak hakiy kyaptsi'yta. Soosok hiita akw yaw naa'itsivulalwa. Haqam yaw himuwa taaqa, tiyo wuutit, maanat aw pite' pu' yaw pay piw aqw maakwutsngwu, pu' yaw paasat tsopngwu. Pas pi yaw puma pepehaq qa unangwtalya. Pantsatskya yaw puma. Pu' yaw haqam wuy siisisiqw pu' tsaatsayom aw ökye' pu' yaw puma put wuukw kwitayat akw put okiw soosok lelwiyangwu. Pas yaw qa hakiy o'okwatuwi'yyungwa. Pu' yaw ima wimmomngwit paapu hiita himuy qa antsakwisa. Pas yaw soosoy paas tuskyap'iwyungwa. Noq yaw puma Awat'ove sinom koyaanisqatsi'yyungwa. Pu' soosoyam naanami itsivu'iwyungwa. Pas yaw qa hak hakiy haalayi.

Noq pu' yaw ima kwitavit yaw pangqaqwaqw pay yaw sonqe i' Pavayoykyasit ti'at kikmongwiniqw oovi yaw puma put atsviy pan koyaanisqatsi'yyungwa. Niiqe pu' yaw oovi puma kivay ep nanawinya yaw pumuy naanatimuy qöqyaniqey. Noq pumuy kwitavituy amungaqw yaw i' Pavayoykyasi piw hakiy sungwa'yta. Pu' yaw oovi puma mihikqw pep kivay yaw ep tsovaltiniqat yaw kwitavituy mongwi'am pangqawu, "Uma mihikqw nöönösat angqw pew tsovaltiniy. Itam yep pumuy amungem hin pavasiwnayaniy," yaw kita mongwi'amniqw pu' yaw oovi tapkiqw pu' puma kiy ang nöönösat pu' yaw puma angqw aw tsovawma. Soosoyam tsovaltiqw paasat pu' yaw pam mongwi'am amumi pangqawu, "Pas hapi itam yepeq qa lomaqatsi'yyungway. Noq pay pi son pi qa it itaamongwiy atsviy itam yantoti. Oovi itam as pumuy pay qöqyani. Itam pumuy qöqyaniqat nu' naawaknay," yaw kita. Pu' pay yaw puma kivapt pas sunya. "Noq oovi yaapiy pay naalötok hapi itam pumuy qöqyani," yaw kita amumi mongwi'amniqw paapiy pu' yaw oovi puma put ngöytotay.

Pu' yaw it Pavayoykyasit sungwa'at pangqw yamakt pu' pam yaw pangso kwaatsiy aw pasiwniyamuy tuu'awma. Pu' yaw kiiyat ep pakiiqe yaw aw pangqawu, "Pas hapi umungem qa hin lomavasiwnaya. Yaapiy yaw naalötok puma umuy qöqyaniqat pep pasiwnaya. Pay hapi itam pu' qa lomaqatsi'yyungqw paysoq i' uuti pu' mongwiniqw oovi put qa lomahintaqat mamqaya."

"Haw'owi?" yaw pam aw kita.

"Pay nu' it oovi ung angqw aa'awnatoqe oovi angqöy," yaw aw

And this is exactly what happened. People began to change in their ways. There was no mutual respect any more. They were constantly arguing and fighting with one another. People were robbed of their food. A woman would be taking piki somewhere, only to have others snatch it away from her. No one had any concern for his fellow man. For all kinds of reasons people would get angry at each other. Men and boys would reach under the dresses of women and girls and rape them. People seemed to be blind to what they were doing. They got worse and worse. For example, if children encountered an old person relieving himself, they would smear excrement all over him. They showed no compassion for anyone. The leaders of the religious societies, too, grew increasingly negligent in their ceremonial duties. Everything was completely insane. The life the inhabitants of Awat'ovi were living was one of utter chaos. They were all pitted against each other. No one displayed any fondness for his fellow man.

The Turds insisted that this life of turmoil and corruption was all the fault of Pavayoykyasi's son, who was the village leader. As a result, they planned in their kiva how to kill the entire family. It so happened that one of the Turds was a friend of Pavayoykyasi's. That night they decided to assemble in their kiva, so their headman said, "When you've eaten supper, come back. We need to decide what to do with Pavayoykyasi and his lot." The sorcerers did as told, and after they had finished eating in their houses, they met in their kiva again. When everyone had gathered, their chief declared, "Life here in Awat'ovi is not good any more. Obviously, this is the fault of our leader. We must therefore kill him. It is my wish that we do away with the entire family." The kiva members consented. "Well, in that case let us kill them four days from now," their leader declared. This was the goal they were pursuing now.

Pavayoykyasi's friend left the kiva and went over to his friend's house to reveal the intentions of the sorcerers. Upon entering Pavayoykyasi's house he said, "They've hatched out some evil plans against you. They've decided to kill you four days from now. They claim life in the village is so bad because your son is in charge. They put all the blame on him."

"Is that so?" exclaimed Pavayoykyasi.

"Yes, that's why I came to let you know." With that his friend departed again.

pam kwaatsi'at aw kitat pu' yaw pam angqw yama.

Pu' yaw it Pavayoykyasit kwaatsi'at yamakmaqw pay naat qa nawutstiqw piw yaw hak ep paki. Noq yaw pam kur imuy kwitavituy mongwi'am. Noq pu' yaw i' Pavayoykyasi pay naat qa tuuvingta hintiqw pam waynumqw. Pay yaw put paas mooti tavit pu' yaw puma piw pas paas naatsotsongnaqw paasat pu' yaw pam put tuuvingta, "Ta'ay, son pi um qa hiita oovi waynumay," yaw aw kita.

"Hep owiy," yaw aw kita. "Pay i' uuti mongtiqw naat panis naalöq yaasangwuy ang pam mongwiniqw pay pas itam nukushintotiy," yaw kita. "Pay kur itam qa umutsviy a'ni yooyoknaya, qa umutsviy kur itam hiita a'ni a'aniwnayangwuy. Umutsviy itam pas qa unangwtalyay," yaw aw kita. "Pay itam oovi son umuy nawus qa qöqyaniy," yaw kita awi'.

"Pay pi kur antsa'ay," yaw aw kitaaqe pay yaw piw qa aw pas hingqawu, i' Pavayoykyasi. "Pay pi antsa uma pantotinik pantotiniy," yaw aw kita.

Pu' oovi yaw naalös taalat ep yaw pumuy qöqyani. Paasat pu' yaw pam yan it nöömay aa'awna, "Itamuy naanatimuy yaw qöqyaniy," yaw aw kita. "Noq pay nu' nakwhay. Pay pi itamuy pantsatsnaniy," yaw kita. "Pay pi tuwat pan kya pi wuuwantotay," yaw kita put awi'.

Pu' yaw paasat pam oovi panhaqam qa lomanavoti'ykyangw paasat pu' soy kiiyat awi'. Pu' yaw pam ep pituuqe yan yaw soy aw lavaya, "Pas itamungem qa hin lomavasiwnaya. Yaw yaapiy naalötok itamuy qöqyaniqat yan yaw kwitavit itamungem pasiwnaya. Yan nuy ikwatsi it aa'awnaqw oovi um aw itamungem hin wuuwani. Yaniqw nu' oovi angqöy," yaw aw kita.

Pu' yaw so'at aw pangqawu, "Is uti, hintiqw piw umungem panhaqam naanawakna? Pas pi as umutsviy ephaqam hin'ur pu' qatsi'ykyaakyangw piw umuy kur pantsatsnani," yaw aw so'at kita. Pu' yaw aw pangqawu, "Pay ason qaavo um piw angqwni," yaw kita. "Ason um ep piw angqwniqw pu' nu' paasat uumi hinwat piw tutaptani," yaw aw kita.

Kitaqw paasat pu' yaw pam pangqw ahoy piw kiy awi', timuy awniiqe pu' pep piw pumuy amumum talöngna. Noq oovi qavongvaqw pu' i' Pavayoykyasi soy piw yaw ahoy awi'. Pu' ep pituqw pu' yaw paasat pam so'at aw piw tutapta, "Um hapi pay it sustsaakw uutiy Patösqasatsa yuk Nuvatukya'omi waatavitoni. Niikyangw um Awat'ove ahoy pite' um it tuu'oyit angqw it nana'löngöt qaa'öt tsotspitaqw pu' uma put huumiyani. Pu' uma put hiita aw intotani.

Not long after, someone else arrived at Pavayoykyasi's house. It was the chief of the sorcerers in person. Pavayoykyasi said nothing. He did not inquire why he was about. He simply welcomed him in, whereupon they smoked, exchanging the pipe between them. Only then did he speak. "Well, you must have come for a specific reason."

"Yes, indeed," the head sorcerer replied. "Ever since your son became village leader four years ago, we've been thrown into turmoil. Because of you and your family, the rains have ceased, and our crops have failed. It's because of you that we've not come to our senses," he accused him. "We must therefore kill you."

"Well, I suppose so," answered Pavayoykyasi, who did not try to contradict him. "If that's your intention, go ahead and do it."

In four days the sorcerers planned to perpetrate the deed. Pavayoykyasi conveyed this news to his wife. "They want to kill our family," he said. "I did not object. 'Do to us what you want,'" I said. "Anyway, that's what they've been thinking about."

With this terrible news Pavayoykyasi went to his grandmother. He related to her what had happened. "The sorcerers have instigated an evil scheme against us. Four days hence they want to kill us. My friend confirmed this. Maybe you can come up with a plan for us. That's the purpose of my visit."

Pavayoykyasi's grandmother exclaimed, "Dear me, why on earth do they want to do that? It used to be because of you and your family that life was flourishing at Awat'ovi. So why would they wish to do this to you? Come back tomorrow. At that time I should be able to advise you," she said.

With that Pavayoykyasi returned home again to his children. He spent the night there and in the morning once more visited his grandmother. Upon his arrival she instructed him as follows, "First I want you to take your youngest son Patösqasa to a shelter at Nuvatukya'ovi. Next, after your return to Awat'ovi, have your family remove ears representing all the different kinds of corn from your corn stock. Have them shell the ears and place the kernels into a shallow receptacle. Also add seeds from all the other crops. Then you must dig a hole

Pu' soosok hiita poshumiyat piw enang intotani. Pu' ason uma put soosok hiita poshumtotat pu' uma pep umuukiy ep tutskwamiq hangwaye' pu' uma put poshumit pangsoq wukotangatotani. Pantotit pu' uma qötsvit enang pangsoq tangatotani. Pam hapi putakw qa mowatiniqw oovi. Pu' piw qa kwaayatini."

Yan yaw pam put mööyiy aw tutaptaqw pu' pam pangqw nima. Pu' yaw puma oovi put soyat tutavoyatyaqe pu' hin aw tutaptaqw yaw puma pantoti. Puma yaw put poshumit pangsoq wukotangatotat pu' yaw piw ahoy aqw ootsoknayat pu' atsva piw ahoy paavalwiya. "Yantaniy," yaw Pavayoykyasi kita.

Paasat pu' yaw oovi payistalqat ep pu' yaw i' Pavayoykyasi sustsaakw tiy, Patösqasat, yaw wikkyangw pu' yaw nuvatukya'omihaqamini. "Pay nu' itwatsa wikniy," yaw kita. "Noq ason pi pay umuywatuy hin pi yukunayaniy," yaw amumi kita. "Oovi itam payniy." Kitat pu' yaw pam paasat qöpqömiq pas a'ni qööna. Pu' yaw oovi paasat angqw pavan uwikqw pu' yaw pam ngaakuyiy aqw wuuta. Wuutaqw paasat yaw angqw söviwtikyangw pu' yaw aqw poksömiqhaqami yamakma. Noq pam söviwangw yaw kur pamösiniwtiqe pu' yaw pep Awat'ove oopo. Pam yaw pep oopokqw pu' yaw pumuy kiiyamuy angqw tangaqwunu laholtikyangw pu' yaw Nuvatukya'omiwat. "Ta'ay, itamniy," yaw kita. Pu' yaw puma naatim put tangaqwunut atsmiq wuuvi. Pu' yaw puma aqw wupqw pu' yaw pam tangaqwunu piw laholtikyangw pay yaw pumuy tsoki'ykyangw Nuvatukya'omi pumuy pitsina.

Paasat pu' yaw oovi puma naatim nakwsuqw pu' ima ep akwsingqam aa'aslalwa, naavahomlalwa. Pu' yaw paas puma yuuyaha, lomavitkuntota, kwewtota. Lomatsöqa'asya pu' kwavöönakwatota. Pankyaakyangw pu' yaw puma talöngni'ywisa. Pu' paasat yaw tuwat kwitavit tunipit yuykuyaqe yaw pisoqya, haalaytsutsuytikyaakyangwya. "Itakw hapi nu' Sakwyevat niinaniy," yaw himuwa kitangwu. Pay yaw himuwa naap hiitawat tungwangwu. "It hapi nu' akw Siisivut niinani," pay yaw yan hingqawkyaakyangwya, tututsiwtikyaakyangwya yaw puma'.

Pu' yaw oovi aw talöngvaqw pu' pay su'aw töngvaniwtaqw pu' yaw puma pangqw kiisonmiya. Sakwyeva yaw mooti'ymaqw pu' angk mimawat tupkomat. Puma yaw oovi pumuy kiisonmi yungqw pu' yaw ima kwitavit amumi yuutu. Pumuy amumi yuutukqe pu' pephaqam pumuy wuvinumya. Pay yaw puma qa amumi rohomtoti. Yaw puma pumuy oovi soosokmuy qöqya. Pantsatsna yaw puma pumuynit pu' yaw puma pumuy naanatupkomuy tatkyaqöymiq-

in the floor of your house and store everything there. Mix ashes in with the seeds so they don't get wet. They will not spoil that way."

With these instructions Pavayoykyasi returned home again. He and his family did exactly as he had been told. They buried large amounts of seeds, and after the hole had been covered with dirt, they sealed it with plaster. "This should do it," Pavayoykyasi remarked.

On the third day Pavayoykyasi decided to take Patösqasa, his youngest child, to Nuvatukya'ovi. "He's the only one I'm taking to safety," he said. "The rest of you will have to suffer what they're going to do with you. I'll be on my way now." With that he vigorously stoked the fire. When it really flamed up, he poured a liquid medicine on it. As a result, clouds of mist billowed up which drifted out through the vent hole. Outside the mist changed into fog. It enshrouded the entire village of Awat'ovi. Now a rainbow began to arch from Pavayoykyasi's house all the way to Nuvatukya'ovi. "Let's go!" he shouted, whereupon he and his son climbed atop the rainbow. Once more the rainbow arched up, and carrying the two on its back, delivered them at the foot of the mountain range.

After the departure of Pavayoykyasi and his youngest son, the rest of the family bathed and washed their hair. Then they dressed, putting on their beautifully embroidered kilts and belts. Finally, they decorated their bodies with paint and tied eagle plumes in their hair. Prepared like this they awaited the morning. The Turds, in turn, were busy readying their weapons, gloating with anticipation. "With this I'll kill Sakwyeva," one of them would declare. Another would say, "With this I'll kill Siisivu." This is how they were boasting and laughing with malicious glee.

Then the new day arrived. The moment the sun was in its midmorning position, Pavayoykyasi's family filed out to the village plaza. Sakwyeva led the group with his younger brothers following. No sooner had they entered the plaza than the Turds pounced on them. The brothers, who offered no resistance, were clubbed down, and every one of them was killed. After this deed the Turds hauled their victims, one after the other, to the southeast side of the mesa.

haqami naanangk tsötsöptiwisa. Noq yaw kur pepehaq haqam yaw Pavayoykyasiniqw pu' timat koysö'yyungwa. Noq pangsoq yaw puma pumuy naanatupkomuy maspayat pu' amungk aqw ootsoknaya. Maspayaqe pu' yaw puma piw aapiy pepeq haalayya, tiitikive'yyungngwu.

Noq ep puma pumuy qöqyaqat aw tal'angwmi pay yaw qa yokva, pu' tömö' qa nuvati. Pas yaw qa hin an hiita aniwnaya. A'ni yaw hukve' yaw uuyiyamuy yaahangwu. Pu' yaw puma nawus piw ang ahoy uu'uyangwu. Pu' yaw piwningwu. Naat yaw puma ang uylalwaqw pay yaw tal'angwnasapti. Pu' pay yaw paasat tis qa hiita aniwnaya. Lööq yaasangwuy ang yaw pay qa yokva, nuwu pay paayis yaasangwuy anga'. Naalöq yaasangwuy aqw pu' pay yaw pumuy himu tunösmaskya'am pay yaw pas hingsa' pee'iwta. Pu' peetu pay yaw tis pas soosokya. Tsivot yaasangwuy aqw pu' pay yaw pas qa hak hiita haqam himu'yta. Pu' yaw paasat pay himuwa ngas'ew haqami yöngöt'ewakw oovi nakwsungwu. Yaw put kivaqw yaw puma yöngötsa nöönösangwu. Pu' yaw pam puma sinom pepeq tsöngso'iwma pu' yaw pangqaqwa, "Kur pay itam as pumuy amutsviy yooyoknayakyangw pas itam suhintsatskyay," yaw kitota. "Pas kur itam qa antoti," pu'sa yaw yaayan hingqaqwa.

Oovi yaw navay yaasangwvaqw pay yaw pas hikiyom peeti. Paas yaw okiw laakiwyungwa, pas yaw okiw öö'öqamsa. Yaw hiitu wukotamö'yyungwa, kori'vo'yyungwa. Noq puma yaw pep kivapt naanatupkomuy amumi kiipokyaqam pay yaw oovi pas wuukoso'a. So'qw pu' yaw paasat talavay hapi yaw himuwa taaqa kivami tontsokiy yankyangwniqw pu' yaw pay put nawkiyangwu. "Um hintiqw put piw pantsaki? Taq itamuy yokvaniqatsa naanawaknaqw um put piw pannuma." Kitote' pay yaw put nawkiyangwu. Pu' yaw aapiy pay naap haqam pösöve piw paaholalwangwu asniqw yaw kur okiw son yokvani. Pu' yaw pay piw naap haqam saqtsave pu' yaw piw paaholalwa. Pay yaw kur son yokvaniqw yantsatskyangwuniikyangw pu' yaw paasat antsa pay wuukoso'a.

Pas yantiqw pu' yaw i' Pavayoykyasi put sustsaakw tiy amum ahoy Awat'omi'. Yaw puma ep pituqw qa hak yaw haqam waynuma. Pu' yaw puma angqw haqam hisat ki'ytangwuniiqey pangso yaw puma paki. Ep pakiiqe pu' yaw puma tutskwamiq yaahaqw naat yaw angqw poshumi'am wukotangawta. Noq yaw ima naatim tömöngvaqw pep ahoy pitu. Noq yaw puma pep ki'yyungqam soyalyungiwta. Pu' yaw i' Pavayoykyasi nuutum pakiniqey wuuwanta piktotokpe mihikqw. Pu' yaw pam pan wuuwantaqw pu' yaw puma naatim put

Pavayoykyasi and his sons had a ground oven there to roast corn. Into this ground oven the sorcerers hurled the dead bodies and closed it up with dirt. Having disposed of the brothers, they displayed their joy by staging dances.

The summer following this atrocity it did not rain. The winter passed without snow. As a consequence, people's crops were smaller than usual. In addition, the wind blew fiercely and unearthed their plants. When they planted anew the subsequent year, the same thing happened. People were still planting, and already it was the middle of summer. This time they harvested even less. By now, two years had passed without rain. It was the same during the third year, and by the end of the fourth year, nearly all of the food reserves were depleted. Some people had used up everything. By the fifth year no one had anything left. People would go out in search of cactus and plants of that sort. That's all they were eating. At this point when people were dying from starvation, they would say, "We used to get plenty of rain because of Pavayoykyasi and his sons. But we had nothing better to do than to destroy them. We committed a great crime," they kept saying with deep regret.

By the beginning of the sixth year only a few villagers were left. The poor wretches were all dried up and nothing but skin and bones. Their knees were swollen and their eyes were like empty sockets. The members of the sorcerer kiva who had attacked the brothers perished in great numbers. The sorcerers were dying, but in the mornings when they came across a man who was taking his spun yarn to the kiva to make prayer feathers, they snatched it away from him. "Why are you doing that? We are the ones who are praying for rain, not you. It's none of your business to carry this yarn around." And they would rip the ball of yarn away from him. Just about anywhere, in a corner or behind the ladder, people were trying to make prayer sticks, but it was not going to rain. As a result, many of the Awat'ovi residents lost their lives.

At this point Pavayoykyasi returned to Awat'ovi with his son. When the two arrived, they found no one walking about. Upon entering the house where they once had lived, they dug up the floor where their big seed cache was. Father and son had arrived on the morning of the day when the members of the Soyal society were in ceremonial session. Pavayoykyasi therefore decided to enter the kiva with the initiates on the night of the second day of their ritual gathering. He made this decision while he was uncovering the seeds with

poshumiy ahoy yaahat pu' mokyaata.

Noq pu' yaw it Pavayoykyasit kwaatsi'at naat yaw pay kur qatuuqe yaw navotqw yaw i' Pavayoykyasi kur ahoy pitu. Noq pam yaw panis yan navot pu' yaw pam aqw suukuyvato. Noq paasat pu' yaw i' Pavayoykyasi put kwaatsiy pitsinaqe yaw haalayti. Pu' yaw pay puma pepeq hiihiita naami yu'a'ata. Yaw Pavayoykyasit kwaatsi'at put aw tu'awi'yta hin puma pepeq hiniwtotiqw. Noq pay yaw puma oovi nawutsna. Pu' yaw pay pam ahoy kivaminiqey pangqawqe pu' as yamaktoq pu' pay pamwa put ahoy wangwayi. "Haaki, pay haak um qe'ni. Pay naat nu' uumi hingqawni," yaw Pavayoykyasi kwaatsiy aw kita. "Um hapi pu' mihikqw suutokihaq angqw ahoyniqw pu' nu' paasat piw uumi hinwat tutaptaniy," yaw aw kita. Yan yaw pam oovi navoti'ykyangw pu' pangqw yama.

Pu' yaw ep mihikqw pay qa taalawvaqw aapiy hiisavoniqw yaw pam Pavayoykyasi tsöqa'asi. Pu' yaw pam imuy Aa'altuy amun tsöqa'asi. Maynit pu' hokyava tuumat tsokokoykina. Pu' yaw löövaqw yöngösonat hokyaasomta. Pu' yaw pam piw tiy pay piw pan yuwsina. Nit pu' yaw pam kur piw nan'ik pumuy amungem hiita aqw naatöngtaniqey put paas yuku. Ooveq yaw pam natöngpi'am ngölökiwta. Pu' yaw natöngpiyat ep ngölöwtaqat pay atpiphaqam yaw nana'löngö qaa'ö aw somiwta. Pankyangw pu' yaw puma pep put kwaatsiy nuutayta.

Pantaqw pu' yaw antsa kwaatsi'at ep pitu. Pu' yaw ep pakiqw pu' yaw pam put kwaatsiy paas tavi. Pu' yaw pam aw pangqawu, "Kwakwhay, um pituy. Pay antsa pi nu' uumi yan naawaknaqw kwakwhat um nakwhaqe oovi angqöy," yaw aw kita. "Noq antsa pi nu' ura naat piw hinwat uumi lavaytiniqey pangqawu. Noq itam hapi yangqw nöngakye' yuk kwitavituy kivayamuy aw mootiyakyangw pu' aapiy pay itam soosovik kivanawit hapi nankwusani. Noq itamuy hapi haqamwat kivamiq pakiqw um hapi pay oongaqw itamumiq tuuqaytamantani. Noq pu' hapi itam haqamwat yukye' angqw yamakqw pu' hapi son pepeq qa hinwat lavaytotimantani. Pu' um put aw paas tunatyaltini. Pu' itamuy soosokiva nakwsukyangw pu' yukuqw paasat pu' um angqw itamungk ahoy pewni. Nen paasat pu' um nuy aa'awnani hinwat haqamwat kivapt lavaytotiqw put um nuy paasat aa'awnani." Yan yaw pam kwaatsiy aw tutapta.

Noq pu' yaw puma oovi nöngakwisniniqw pu' yaw puma naatim nan'ik poshummokit tori. Paasat pu' yaw puma pangqw nöngakqe pangso kwitamiya. Puma hapi yaw pumuy naanatimuy amungem qa lomavasiwnayaqw oovi puma pangso hapi yaw mootini. Paasat pu'

the help of his son. When this task was finished, they filled bags with the seeds.

It so happened that Pavayoykyasi's friend from the sorcerers' kiva was still alive. After hearing the news that Pavayoykyasi was back, he hastened to call on him. Pavayoykyasi was filled with joy to see him, and the two began to talk about all sorts of things. Pavayoy-kyasi learned from his friend how people had fared at the village. They talked for a long time. Finally, his friend said that he had to return to his kiva. He was already on his way out when Pavayoykyasi called him back, "Wait a minute, don't leave just yet. There's something I need to tell you. I want you to come back again at midnight. I'll have some instructions for you then." With this information his friend left.

That evening, shortly after darkness had fallen, Pavayoykyasi painted his body in the fashion of the Al society initiates. He dotted his arms and legs with white clay, and tied a tortoise shell rattle to both of his legs. He dressed his son in the same way. For both of them he also made something to lean on, sticks which were curved at the upper end. Below the curved handle all kinds of corn were tied to the shaft. In this guise father and son were waiting for their friend.

Before long Pavayoykyasi's friend arrived, and Pavayoykyasi welcomed him politely, saying, "Thanks for coming. This is what I had hoped you would do. I'm grateful you consented. You remember, I told you I'd have something to say to you. I'd like us to leave now and go from kiva to kiva, first the Excrement kiva and then the rest. While I and my son enter, I want you to listen from the roof top. When we're done inside and have come out, the people down below will surely comment on us. Pay careful attention to what they have to say. After we've visited every kiva, follow us back here again. You can then reveal to me what you heard." This is how he instructed his friend.

As the three of them were leaving now, both father and son slung a bag full of seeds over his shoulder. Then they headed to the Excre-ment Place, the kiva of the sorcerers. Since it had been them who had instigated all the evil plans for Pavayoykyasi's family, they went to

yaw puma kivats'omi ökiqw pu' yaw pam Pavayoykyasi poshumiy
angw wukomatsvongtat pu' kivamiqhaqami put tsalakna. Tsalaknaqw yaw epeq tangawtaqam yaw pösaalay akw huur naamoki'y-
kyaakyangw yaw qa hingqaqwa. Noq pu' yaw puma pepeq tangawtaqam yaw kur nanapta himu pang aasaqaltiqw. Pu' yaw puma pang
put naanaqastivaya. Paas yaw peetu mangu'iwkyaakyangw yungiwta. Noq yaw peetu angqe' put pongikyaakyangw pay yaw paasat put
ngarorotota. Pu' yaw peetu pay naat qa pas mangu'iwyungqam pu'
yaw pay put paas oo'oyaya ang pongikyaakyangw. Pu' yaw pam
naalös put pangsoq tsalaknaqw paasat pu' yaw puma aqw pakini.
Kivamiq yaw puma pakiiqe yaw puma amuupa yorikqw yaw epepq
hiitu a'ni sosniwqam yeese. Yaw pumuy amumi taayungwa, hiitu
pata'inyungwa. Paas yaw laakiwyungwa, sutsi'rumyungwa, kori'-
vo'yyungwa. Pu' yaw puma aqw pakiiqe pu' yaw qöpqöt kwiningyaqw wunuptu. Pangqw pu' yaw puma wunimantiva. Niikyangw
yanhaqam yaw puma taawi'yta:

> Meeheheyeye heyewloohoo'o'o
> Meeheheyeye heyewloohoo'o'o
> Haa'o'o haa'o haa'a'a'oo'oha'a'o'o'o'o
> Haa'o'o haa'o ohaa'o'ohaa'a oo Sakwyeva, Moomo'a
> Haa'o'o haa'o ohaa'o'ohaa'a oo Hoyniwa, Siisivu
> Uulavayi aniwti'i.
> Uutingavi aniwtiqö'ö
> Awat'ove kyaysiwa'a.
> Meeheheyeye heyewloohoo'o'o
> Meeheheyeye heyewloohoo'o'o
> Haa'o'o haa'o ohaa'o'ohaa'a oo Sakwyeva, Moomo'a
> Haa'o'o haa'o ohaa'o'ohaa'a oo Wuktima, Patösqasa.
> Uulavayi aniwti'i.
> Uutingavi aniwtiqö'ö
> Awat'ove kyaysiwa'a.
> Naap uma'a hiita'a oovi'o tuutalahoyintangwu'u.
> Qa soq vinur piikit tuunawkilalwangwu.
> Qa soq vinur tonit tuunawkilalwangwu.
> Qa soq vinur saqpe paaholalwangwu.
> Qa soq vinur pösömi paaholalwangwu.
> I' yantaqa umu'nangwa tunway'o
> Naatutukopanmuyiwa.
> Hya'aw, hya'aw a'a'a'aw

this location first. As they arrived on top of the subterranean chamber, Pavayoykyasi took a large handful of seeds and threw them inside. The men down below were squatting there in deep silence, tightly wrapped in their blankets. When they noticed the seeds scattered across the floor, they vied for them. Some of them were too weak to do so. They were at the end of their strength. A few managed to pick up a seed here and there and began to chew them. Others who still had some stamina left carefully tucked the seeds away as they picked them up. Four times Pavayoykyasi dispersed the seeds, then he and his son made their entry. When the two reached the floor below, they glanced around among the men. They looked terrible. The men, in turn, with their hair all messed up, were staring at Pavayoykyasi. They were mere skeletons, with their teeth bared and eyes hollowed. Pavayoykyasi and his son positioned themselves at the northwest end of the fireplace and started dancing. The song that accompanied their steps went as follows:

Meeheheyeye heyewloohoo'o'o
Meeheheyeye heyewloohoo'o'o
Haa'o'o haa'o haa'a'a'oo'oha'a'o'o'o'o
Haa'o'o haa'o ohaa'o'ohaa'a oo Sakwyeva, Moomo'a
Haa'o'o haa'o ohaa'o'ohaa'a oo Hoyniwa, Siisivu
Your words came true.
Your plans for the killing came true.
Many people came to be in Awat'ovi.
Meeheheyeye heyewloohoo'o'o
Meeheheyeye heyewloohoo'o'o
Haa'o'o haa'o ohaa'o'ohaa'a oo Sakwyeva, Moomo'a
Haa'o'o haa'o ohaa'o'ohaa'a oo Wuktima, Patösqasa.
Your words came true.
Your plans for the killing came true.
Many people came to be in Awat'ovi.
For no good reason at all you are waking people.
Wrongfully you are taking the piki away from people.
Wrongfully you are taking the yarn away from people.
Wrongfully you are making prayer sticks by the ladder.
Wrongfully you are making prayer sticks in the corner.
Your hearts being this way are painful.
Blaming one another.

Hya'aw, hya'aw yepehaq
Yepehaq yaw unangwa taalawva,
Lavayi taalawvaqö'ö
Nu'an yeesiwa kiinawita'a.
Yan'i, yan ura i' lalvaya
Sakwyeva, koysöy angqö'ö
Yoytukyayniyu tövutsitsingyat'a
Takurit qaa'öta, sakwaput qaa'öt
Inguyu sona'ipwat'a
Akw'a nalwi'ykyango'o.
Tuma'i, soosoyamu'u, tupqölmiya.
Qa hak nam yep qatu'u.
Yan ura i' lalvaya, Sakwyeva.
Mee'ee'yeeye aa'a'ahayaw
Ayayaw yeehay
Uu'i, uu'i, uu'u'u'u'iy.
Hapi meh,
Haa'o'o haa'o haa'o'o'oo'oha'a'o'o'o'o
Haa'o'o haa'o ohaa'o'ohaa'a oo Sakwyeva, Moomo'a
Haa'o'o haa'o ohaa'o'ohaa'a oo Hoyniwa, Siisivu.
Umuukwayngyap itamu tuutuptala.
Umuukwayngyap itamu unangwa tsaamiwa'a.
Hapi meh,
Yo'o'hoy uu'u'u'u'iy
Okiw iti'i tsöngpaklawu,
Wupölangvikita tsokinvikit tuuvinglawu.
Qa soq vinur tiy saanay nopna.
Qa soq vinur tiy pösöhikwna.
It kinvi kur
Yankiwako oovi.
Pövöngmi natsvalantangwu.

Yanhaqam yaw puma taawi'yta. Wunimat pu' yaw puma piw amumi hiisa' humitat tsalaknat pu' pangqw yama. Yan yaw puma pepeq yukuqw pu' yaw puma paayomniiqam piw sutsvowat kivamiya. Pu' yaw puma pay piw an pepwat yukuya. Pu' yaw puma soosokiva kivanawit yukuuqe pu' yaw oovi puma pay paasat ahoy nima. Noq pu' yaw i' kwaatsi'at pumuy amungk yannumqe pu' yaw haqamwat hin lavaytotiqw put yaw pam aw paas tunatyawma.

Noq yaw pep Kwitave puma yukuqw yaw antsa pam kwaatsi'at

Hya'aw, hya'aw a'a'a'aw
Hya'aw, hya'aw here somewhere.
Even if the heart gets pure,
Even if the words get clear,
People just live in their houses without caring.
This way, this way, remember,
Spoke Sakwyeva from the earth oven.
His rain power he let steam up in the fire.
From yellow corn, from blue corn,
Our mother, he took the embryos out,
Smearing his body with them.[1]
Let us go, all of us, to the spirit world.
No one shall remain here.
Remember, this is how Sakwyeva spoke.
Mee'ee'yeeye aa'a'ahayaw
Ayayaw yeehay
Uu'i, uu'i, uu'u'u'iy.
For sure,
Haa'o' haa'o haa'o'o'oo'oha'a'o'o'o'o
Haa'o'o haa'o ohaa'o'ohaa'a oo Sakwyeva, Moomo'a
Haa'o'o haa'o ohaa'o'ohaa'a oo Hoyniwa, Siisivu.
Because of you we have been hidden,
Because of you our hearts have been destroyed.
For sure,
Yo'o'hoy uu'u'u'u'iy
Oh my poor child crying from hunger
Thick piki, white and blue piki you are asking for.
Wrongfully she does not feed her child chewed food.
Wrongfully she lets her child drink in the corner.
For this evidently,
For this kind of thing,
They have been gathering at Pövöngvi,[2] the sorcerers' kiva.

This was the song Pavayoykyasi and his son sang. Finishing their dance performance, they once more scattered some corn in front of the men and exited from the kiva. Together with their friend they moved on to the next kiva. There they staged the same dance and sang the same song. This performance they repeated in every single kiva. Only then did they return home. Their friend followed them listening carefully to what the men had to say.

aqw tuuqaytaqw yaw pepehaq haqawa pangqawu, "Pas kur pay kya
as itam antsa pumuy amutsviy yephaqam hisat a'ni qatsi'yyungngwu. Niikyangw itam pumuy amungem panhaqam qa antaqat
pasiwnaya. Niiqe oovi itam yanhaqam qa lolmat aqw naa'ökinaya.
Sinom hapi wuukosulawti," pepehaq yaw suukya kita.

Yan yaw pam pep navot pu' yaw pam pangqw oovi pumuy
amungk pantsakmakyangw pu' puma soosokiva kivanawit yukuqw
pu' yaw pam Pavayoykyasit kiiyamuy amungk awi'. Noq pay yaw
puma naatim antsa ep pakiwtaqw yaw pam piw aw paki. "Ta'ay,
qatu'uy," yaw pam Pavayoykyasi put kwaatsiy aw kita. Aw kitat pu'
yaw put tuuvingta, "Ta'ay, ya hin um navotay?" yaw aw kita. Noq
pu' yaw pamwa put aw lalvaya hin pam pang kivanawit navotqey.
"Noq pay pas yansa ang aqwhaqami lavayta," yaw kita.

Noq talavay yaw mooti puma yanti. Nit pu' taawanasave piw.
Pu' yaw puma oovi su'aw tapkimi naalösta. Aasakis yaw puma an
wunimat pu' paasat aasakis amumi piw hihin hoyokput humitat
maspangwu. Pu' yaw puma pepeq okiw put ang naanaqasyangwu.
Panis yaw himuwa ang poopongt pay yaw mo'amiqhaqami tsalakna-
ngwu. Tsöngmokiwyungwa yaw puma. Putakw pu' yaw pay peetu
hihin angqwtoti. Pay yaw hihin öqawtota. Pay pi pam humita piw
a'ni himu. Yantoti puma yawniiqe pay paasat yaw puma hihin
ööyiwyungwa.

Pu' yaw puma naatim oovi paas yukuuqe pu' yaw kiy ahoy awi'.
Pu' yaw puma pep pituuqe pu' yuwsiy paas soosok oyaqw pu' yaw
pam put tiy aw pangqawu, "Pay um hapi pu' yep qatuniy," yaw aw
kita. "Nu' hapi pu' pay naala ahoyni." Kita yaw awniiqe pu' yaw
pam pay pep Awat'ove oovi tiy tavi. Yan yaw pam put tiy aw lavaytit
pu' pangqaqw ahoy haqami pas kiy aw ahoy nima.

Noq pu' yaw oovi pam Pavayoykyasi nimaqw pu' yaw i' tiyo
kiinawit nakwsuqe pu' yaw humitat oo'oytinuma. Pu' yaw hiitawat
aw pangqawu, "Haak uma it qa soswat uma umuutu'oyqeniy aqw it
o'yani. Pu' ason pas qavongvaqw pu' uma aqw pootayani."

Pay yaw okiw peetu qa mangu'iwyungqe pay yaw hiisa' angqw
soswangwu. Pu' peetu yaw pay tis pas soosok soswa. Pu' mimawat
qa soswaqam pu' yaw tu'oyqeniy aqw put o'ya. Qavongvaqw pu'
yaw puma ang yoyrikya. Noq yaw pay piw qaa'ö ang ahoy opom'iwyungwa. Yan yaw puma oovi qa soosoyam so'a, qa pas sulawti. Yanhaqam yaw pam pumuy pephaqam ahoy öqawtoyna.

Noq paasat pu' yaw puma pepehaq put kikmongtatve, it Patösqasat. Pam hapi yaw sustsay ura pumuy Pavayoykyasit angqw pam

And indeed, after they finished at the Excrement Place, the friend listened while someone remarked, "I guess it was really because of Pavayoykyasi and his sons that once we enjoyed a great life here. But we committed a heinous crime against them. For this reason we brought this awful situation upon ourselves, and people here have died by the hundreds."

This is what he overheard. Then he followed the two to their next destination and finally to Pavayoykyasi's house. Father and son entered, so he went in after them. "Sit down," Pavayoykyasi greeted his friend, and then he inquired, "Well, what did you hear?" His friend repeated the various comments he had listened to. "In all the kivas they were saying the same," he explained.

The first time Pavayoykyasi and his son toured the kivas was in the early morning hours. They did the same thing at noon. By early evening they had repeated their rounds for the fourth time. Each time they danced, they threw away a larger amount of corn kernels. The men inside, poor wretches, were scrambling for the food. No sooner had a man picked up a seed than he stuffed it in his mouth, for every one of them was famished. The corn kernels handed out by Pavayoykyasi were magical in their effect. The corn revived them and their strength grew a little. This is what happened to the men. They stilled their hunger a little.

When father and son were through, they returned to their house. Arriving there, they took off their costumes, and Pavayoykyasi said to his son, "I want you to remain here. I'll go back alone." And so he left his son in Awat'ovi while he returned to the Butte Area.

After Pavayoykyasi had departed, the boy went from house to house distributing corn kernels. As he did so, he would say, "I don't want you to eat these for the time being. Instead, put them where you usually keep your corn stacks. But you must not look at them before the next morning."

Some of the people, however, were so weakened from starvation that they could not refrain from eating a few of the seeds. Others devoured them all. But those who did not eat them placed them in the empty spaces of their corn stacks. The following day when they checked on them they found, to their great amazement, that the formerly depleted spaces were bursting with corn. Due to this miracle, not all of the villagers perished. They were not all wiped out. Pavayoykyasi's youngest child gave them their strength back.

ti'at, pam hapi oovi kikmongwi. Paapiy pu' yaw pam pepehaq tuwat oovi mong'iwta. Pu' yaw pam mongtiqat aapiy panis tömöngvaqw pay yaw piw a'ni nuvati. Panmakyangw pu' yaw piw ahoy yooyok-tiva. Pu' yaw puma tal'angwnayaqe piw uu'uyaqw yaw piw hisat-niiqat an a'ni natwaniy aniwti.

Yantiqw pu' yaw puma pepehaq ahoy angqwtoti. Pankyaa-kyangw pu' yaw puma pepeq ahoy qale'yki. Pu' pay yaw puma kwangwayese aapiy. Yaw qa tsöngmokiwyungwa, a'ni hiita a'aniw-naya. Pu' yaw sinom wuuhaq'iwma ahoy, qa okiwhinyungwa. Pu' peetu pas yaw tis lomavasa'yyungqam a'ni pasvayaqam a'ni hiita a'aniwnaya, kyahaksinom. Niikyangw pu' paasat paapiy haqaapiy pu' yaw peetu kawaymuy poktota piw. Kawayvoktotaqe pu' yaw pumuy akw enang, pu' puma pasva tumala'yyungwa. Pu' yaw akw piw maqnumya. Yan yaw puma pepehaq yeskyaakyangw pu' pay nuwu hiisa' yaasangwnaya.

Noq pu' yaw pay panmakyangw pu' pay puma ahoy piw hisat hin qatsitotaqey pay put yaw aqw piw puma naa'ökini'ywisa, pepeq sinom. Noq pu' yaw paasat pepeq Awat'oveq pu' ima hiitu popwaqt pas yaw qa hakiy puma kyaptsi'yyungwa, qa hakiy puma hiita'yyu-ngwa, qa hakiy aw kyaataayungwa. Nukushiitasa puma yaw wuuwantota. Pay yaw hiita haqam hovalayaniqeysa puma tunatyaw-yungwa ima hiitu popwaqt. Yaw himuwa oovi haqam taaqa paasay ephaqam tumala'ytaqw ima yaw aw ökye' hiita himuyat nawkiya-ngwu, a'ni hintsatsnangwu. Naap yaw hinwat qa lomahintsatsnat maatatvet pu' piw aapiyyangwu. Ephaqam yaw niinayangwu. Pu' imuy momoymuy piiw. Yaw haqam piw wuutit aw ökye' naanangk-totangwu. Pu' yaw piw yuwsiyat oyanayangwu. Yaw pumuy pi lo-mamamantuy ngöynumyangwu. Pas yaw qa hakiy puma hiita'y-yungwa. Yantaqat akw pu' yaw son wuuti, maana naala kiy angqw haqaminingwu, kuytongwu. Pas yaw kur hin qa hakiy amumnen pu' naami taqa'nangwtingwu. Pas yaw puma hiitu a'ni unangwa'yyu-ngwa. Puma pas yaw hiitu qahopiit. Pu' yaw imuy maamaakyamuy piw pay pan tumala'yyungwa. Yaw hiitawat haqam aw ökye' tuu-niyamuy nawkiyat hiita yaw himuyat ang poswayat a'ni hintsatsnat pu' piw maatatvengwu. Yan yaw puma qatsi'yyungwa.

Pu' yaw nuwu yan qatsiniqw pu' yaw pay qa an yooyoki. Pay pi as yaw naat himu a'aniwkyangw suutsepngwat yaw qa ani'. Qa an yaw aniwtingwu. Paasat pu' yaw ima put tumala'yyungqam, pop-waqt, qa hakiy puma aw tuuqayyungwa. Namuy amumi qa tuuqay-yungwa piw taahamuy. Pu' it hiita tuptsiwniy yaw piw qa aw tunat-

As a result, the Awat'ovis made Patösqasa their new village leader, and from that day on he was the chief there. The first winter after this event it snowed a great deal. Also, it began to rain again. By the time the people reached summer, they resumed their planting activities and, just as in the olden days, harvested great amounts of crops.

In this fashion the Awat'ovis recovered and everything came back to life again. Living was pleasant once more. No one was starving, for the crops were bountiful. The suffering was over and the population of Awat'ovi was increasing again. Those who had nice fields worked hard in them and reaped large harvests. They were rich. As time passed, some of the villagers even acquired horses. By raising horses they were able to use them for their farming chores. They also went hunting with them. This is how the inhabitants of Awat'ovi were living.

A number of years went by. Then, ever so slowly, people began to drift into the same corrupt life style they had experienced before. Once again it was the sorcerers and witches that neither showed respect for their fellow villagers nor thought them worthy of anything. Their minds were focused on bad things only. Wasting and undoing things was what they paid attention to. If a man was working on his field somewhere, they would go up to him, take his tools away and rough him up. All kinds of nasty things they did to people and then left them in their misery, only to continue somewhere else. Once in a while they actually committed murder. Prime targets were women, of course. Wherever they encountered a single woman, they ripped off her clothes and raped her one after the other. They also pursued the girls, for they had no respect for anyone. For this reason a girl or woman dared not go after water or leave her house unattended. They accompanied each other and helped each other in this way. The behavior of the sorcerers was disgusting. The hunters, too, they molested. They would take from them the game they had stalked. They stripped them of their other belongings, too, beat them up and then abandoned them. This is the kind of life that was going on.

Before long the rainfall became sparser and sparser. Although crops were still growing, they did not grow as lushly any more. The harvests, too, were not as large as in prior years. The sorcerers who were responsible for these changes did not listen to anyone, neither to their fathers nor their uncles. They also paid no attention to their religious beliefs. The words of their kachina godfathers and Powamuy

yawyungwa. Pu' piw katsinnamuy, Powamuynamuy lavayi'am pay yaw pumuy aw qa himu. Paasat pu' imuy mongwimuy pay yaw pas qa hiita'yyungwa, pas naap mongwimuy, kikmongwiy, qaleetaqmomngwituy, wimmomngwituy, pumuy yaw qa hiitatota. Pu' yaw it tuptsiwniy, wiimiy qa aw tunatyaltoti. Pu' yaw put hiihin oovelantota, pu' pay aqw naayuyuynaya. Pu' pay yaw pep kitsokive hiihiimu nukurhintoti. Naanami yaw soyakintota. Pay yaw hisat atkya pan qatsi'yyungngwuniqw pay yaw piw ahoy soosoy himu panwisa. Yanwat puma yaw tuwat hintsatskya. Pas yaw naapeya. Yanyungwa yaw pumaniqw paapu yaw sinom pumuy maqastotiqe pay kiikiy ang yan tangawtangwu, sun yanyungngwu.

Noq pu' yaw pay pi hiisakishaqam pi pas yaasangwvaqw pay pi Patösqasa sonqa wuyooti. Noq pu' pay kikmomngwit pu' piw naanangk oo'oytiwngwuniqw i' yaw hak Ta'palo kikmongwi. Pam yaw put aw hin wuuwanta. Qa hin yaw lomahinta. Qa hak yaw hakiy haalayi pas suyan. Yan yaw pam pepeq kitsokiy pay piw ahoy aqw pituto, nangwu'yqatsi.

Yankyangw pu' yaw hisat neyangmakiwni. Noq yaw ep pi mamant nuutumyangwu. Niiqe oovi yaw puma nuutumya, mamant. Niikyangw puma pi pay naapyangwu. Pu' yaw tootim peetu kawaymuy akwyangwu, pokmu'yyungqam. Noq yaw oovi puma ep aw talöngvaqat ep maknöngakiwma. Pu' yaw oovi puma haqamiyaniqey pangsoq ökit pangqw pu' ahoy poniltoti. Paasat pu' pantoti yaw puma'a. Noq yaw hisat haqam neyangmakiwqw pay yaw himuwa tiyo, taaqa sowit, taavot niine' pu' put tutskwava tavingwuniqw paasat pu' ima mamant put aw naanaqasye' aw yuutukngwu. Pu' hak mooti aw pite' pam put tuyqawvangwu, tuunit, sowit, taavot, hiitawat. Pantikyangw pu' paasat pam put paavay, nay, taahay himuwa epniiqat put aw pam put taviqw pam paasat pu' put engem iikwiwtangwu, tumsiy engem. Yan yaw puma hintotingwu neyangmakiwqw.

Noq yaw puma ep pan maqwisqw it kikmongwit ti'at, maana, lomamana yaw, nuutuma. Noq yaw oovi puma angqw ahoy nimiwwisqw pephaqam yaw hak tiyo piw sukw warikna. Sowit warikna qe pu' kawayvookoy akw pu' yaw pam put ngöyva. Pam yaw put oovi ngöytakyangw pam it kikmongwit tiyat, maanat, yaw pam enang wari, kawayvookoy akwa'. Warikqe pay yaw pam okiw sunina. Pam yaw put sunina. Noq pu' na'at nuutumniiqe pu' yaw pangqawu, "Is ohi, um hintiqw piw okiw pantsana? Pay pi kya pi um qa tuwaaqe oovi'o. Pay pi nuwupi. Pay itam qa naanami it ep hinyungwni," yaw

godfathers meant nothing to them. They only had contempt for people in leadership positions, no matter what their rank—village leader, warrior chiefs or those in charge of religious societies. They neglected their old beliefs and kept criticizing and ridiculing their religion. For this reason all kinds of evil things took place in the village. People were even bewitching each other. The situation was as grave as it had been long ago in the underworld. People were on their own. They became more and more scared of the sorcerers and preferred to stay inside their homes.

Meanwhile years had passed and Patösqasa had gotten old. And since village chiefs are successively put into their position, a certain Ta'palo was now in charge. He was worried about the situation, for it was not good. There was no happiness among people. Strife and turmoil were returning to the village.

One day there was going to be a mixed hunt. On such an occasion girls participate in the hunt. And this is exactly what happened. The girls were going to join the men. They would go on foot, of course. A few of the boys, however, those who owned horses, would ride them. On the morning of the event people were leaving for the hunt. Upon reaching their destination they turned around to head back. Long ago it was customary during such a mixed hunt that if a boy or man killed a jackrabbit or cottontail, it was placed on the ground somewhere and the girls competed for it by running. The one who reached the prey first was entitled to keep it. She then handed her prize to a brother, father or uncle of hers, who carried it for his clan woman. This is what typically took place during such a mixed hunt.

At the occasion of this hunt, the daughter of the village chief, a beautiful girl, decided to go along as well. The group was already homeward bound, when one of the young men flushed out a jackrabbit. Immediately, he set to pursuing it on his horse. But alas, during his pursuit he rode over the daughter of the village chief, and the poor girl was killed on the spot. Ta'palo, her father, who was also a member of the hunting party, cried out, "My, why did you do that to her? Perhaps you did not see her. Well, it can't be helped now. Let's not be angry with each other about this." In his heart, however, Ta'palo was furious. "I'm sure that was no accident. He did that intentionally. That was all planned." This is what he said in his heart even though he had assured the boy that he was not upset. But he had only said that with his mouth. To himself, he swore that somehow he would avenge his daughter's death.

aw kita. Niikyangw unangwngaqw yaw pam itsivuti. "Pay son pam paysoq put enang panti. Pay son piw pam qa pas pasiwni, yukiwta," kita yaw pam unangwngaqwniikyangw pam qa itsvutiqey pang-qawu. Pam pay yaw mo'avesa pangqawu. Niiqe yaw oovi kur hin tuwat qa naa'oyniqey kita pam naami pepe'.

Paasat pu' yaw oovi pay yukhaqam pay yaw qa kwangwa'ewti. Pay yaw maakiw yukilti pam yaw put enang warikqö. Pay yaw puma qa kwangwa'ewtota. Qa haalaykyaakyangw yaw puma pangqaqw ninma. Pankyaakyangw yaw öki. Yantiqw paasat pu' yaw Ta'palo pangqawu, "Pay itim pas qahoptoti. Pas qa hakiy qatsiyat yeese, qa hakiy aw tuuqayyungwa," kita yaw pami'. Itsivuti yaw pami'. Pam pas yaw itsivutiqe pay yaw pas kur hin qa naa'oyni, tiy hapi engem.

Pantsakkyaakyangw pu' yaw pay kya pi himuwa pangqawu, "Ya itam hintiqw qa sosotukwye' putakw nanavö'yamante' piw pavan naatayawni'yyungwniy?" yaw hak kita. Noq pu' yaw antsa pay ima tootim, taataqt amumyaqam aw su'patota. "Pas hapi antsa pantaniy," yaw kitota. "Pay pi itam tuwat haalayyaniqe oovi yepeq yanyungwa. Pay pi kiinawit kur pi itam hintsatskyani. Pay pi yepeqsa itam tuwat haalayyangwu," yaw kita hak antsaniqw pu' pay sa'akmaqe, "Ta'ay, pay itam antsa put piw aw pootayani," yaw hak kitaaqe pu' oovi puma tootim taataqt pay naat nanalt sosotukwyangwu.

Pantotit pu' puma ninme' pu' yaw put yu'a'atotangwu, kiy anga'. Pas hapi pam sosotukwpi kwangwa'ewa. "Noq pay pi sen itam kwangwa'ewyangwuniqw pay sen ima mamant haqawat kwangwtotoye' itamumyamantaniy," yaw yanhaqam lavaytoti pumaniqw pu' yaw oovi puma haqawat siwamu'yyungqam, qööqamu'yungqam yaw amumi pangqaqwa, "Uma awyani. Pas kwangwa'ewa."

Noq pu' yaw pay peetu pangqaqwa, "Itam umuy pay aw tsam-yaqw pay uma oongaqw haak aqw taayungwni. Nen uma hin aw wuuwaye' kur antsa kwangwa'ewakwniqw pu' pay pi ason uma itamumtotiniy," yaw yanhaqam puma siwamuy, qööqamuy amumi lavaytotiqe pu' yaw oovi pumuy aw tsamya. Yaw aw tsamyaqw pu' pay yaw oovi kivats'ongaqw puma aqw taayungwa, ep puma tootim, taataqt sosotukwyaqw. Pu' yaw kwanonota. Yaw haalaykyaakyangw a'ni taatawlalwakyangw antsa put hiita nanavö'ya, sosotukwpit. Pu' yaw puma ahoy ökiiqe pu' pay pangqaqwa, "Pas antsa himu kwa-ngwa'ewa. Pas as itam umumumyani," yaw yanhaqam lavaytoti puma mamant. Pu' put aw yorikyaqam pu' yaw pay peetuy maman-tuy aawintota, "Pay itam amumumyani, taq pas sumataq himu kwa-ngwa'ewa," yaw kitotaqe pu' oovi puma yumuy namuy amumi

This tragedy, of course, took the enjoyment out of the event, and the hunt was terminated. It was no longer fun, and with subdued spirits the group headed back. In this frame of mind the hunters and girls arrived at home. Ta'palo, however, said, "My children have turned bad. Things are out of hand. They're not listening to anyone any more." He was full of rage and he knew he would have to seek revenge for his daughter's death.

While all this was going on someone suggested, "Why don't we play Sosotukwpi? With this gambling game we can cheer each other up again." Sure enough, all of the boys and men in his company agreed with him. "Yes, that's a great idea," one of them replied. "We're here in the kiva to be happy. We don't know what to do in our homes. Only here do we truly have a good time." The others shouted their consent. "All right, let's indeed try this game." So all the menfolk, young and old, began playing Sosotukwpi.

Each time the players returned home after the game, they were raving about it. After all, Sosotukwpi is great entertainment. "Maybe some of the girls would enjoy joining us when we're having so much fun." This is how the players kept talking, so those who had younger or older sisters said to them, "Why don't you come over? Sosotukwpi is great fun."

Others, in turn, suggested, "We'll take you over to the kiva and you can watch from the roof top. You can then make up your minds. If it really is fun, you can join us later." Soon they were taking their younger and older sisters to the kivas where they gambled. Then they observed the players from the rooftop. There was laughing and shouting. The boys and men were merrily singing along as they competed with one another. Returning from the kivas the girls agreed, "Yes, that game is fun. Why don't we participate." The girls who had witnessed the game told friends about it. "We're going to play with the boys because that game is a great deal of fun." First they asked their parents for permission. "Can we go with them if we don't go inside the kiva? The boys and men shouldn't be the only ones having fun. Just watching them would be really enjoyable." It was the month of Paamuya, the time of year when Sosotukwpi was normally played.

maqaptsitota, "Ya sen itam qa awye' amumumyani? Pas puma nanalt pepeq haalayya, ima tootimniqw pu' taataqtu. Noq pas itam amumi taayungqw pas himu sumataq kwangwa'ewa", yaw puma kitota mamantniiqe yumuynit namuy maqaptsitota. Noq pay yaw sonqa paamuyve. Paamuynawit pi put hiita hintsatskyangwuniqw oovi pay paamuyve puma sosotukwya. Noq pu' pay ima yumat, namat yaw amumi pangqaqwa, "Pay pi uma awyaniy," yaw kitota. "Tsangaw pi put hiita hintsatskyaqe haalayya. Yangqe' hapi tamö'vamuyva hapi Hopi haalayngwuniqw oovi pay pi uma awyani. Pay pi uma awye' ephaqam nuutum haalayyaniy," yaw yanhaqam yumat, namat amumi lavaytotiqw pu' puma mamant yaw kwangwtapnaya.

Niiqe qavongvaqw pu' yaw oovi puma siwamuy, qööqamuy yaw aw tsamkyaakyangwya. Himuwa put siway, qööqay aw wiikye' kivats'ongaqw aqw pakinikyangw pu' aqw pangqawu, "Haw! Uma kuwawatotani. Nu' qa naala waynumay," yaw aqw kitangwu.

Pu' yaw angqaqw sa'akma. "Yungya'ay," yaw kitota.

Pu' yaw himuwa tiyo aqw pakkye' yaw qööqay, siway wik-kyangwningwuniqw pu' yaw amumi kuwawatota. "Ta'ay, huvam yungya'ay. Uma paas yungtani. Yangqe pay haak uma yesniy," yaw amumi yanhaqam kuwawatota. Pu' yaw ima mamant amumumto-tiqw amumi yaw haalaytoti. "Pay kur antsa kya qa hintani itam umumumyaqw'ö." Yaw yanhaqam puma pumuy amumi lavaytoti mamant.

Noq pu' yaw puma tootim, taataqt pumuy mamantuy aw pang-qaqwa, "Uma paas itamumi taayungwni, hin itam itakw nanavö'ya-ngwuniqw'ö. Nen uma tuwi'yvaye' pu' uma itamumyaniy," yaw yanhaqam pumuy mamantuy aw lavaytoti pepeq kivaapeq.

Paasat pu' yaw oovi aw pitsinaya. Pu' haqam pakwsivu oyiqw pu' yaw pangqw put puma o'yaqe paasat pu' yaw sosotukwya. Pantsatskya yawniiqe antsa yaw ang kwangwa'ewlalwa. Pas yaw a'ni kwanonota. Mamant yaw amumi taayungqw yaw antsa pas kwa-ngwa'ewlalwa. Pu' yaw puma angqw ninma. Pu' qavongvaqw mihikqw piw awyaqe pu' piw pay sosotukwyakyaakyangw pu' yaw mamantuy amumi öqaltoti, "Ta'ay, uma tuwat tuwantotani. Nii-kyangw itam umuy nan'ivo o'yani. Noq uma nan'ivaq mamant too-timuy amumum naanami nanavö'yaniy," yaw pam mongwi'am kita.

Noq pu' yaw oovi kya pi puma pumuy pantoti. Nan'ivo mamantuy o'ya. Paasat pu' aw yaw pitsinaya. Pitsinayaqe pu' yaw nanavö'ya. Naaqavo yaw puma pantsatskya. Pantsatskyakyaakyangw yaw nuwu puma hiita himu'ytiwqat aqw oo'oyayat pu' put oovi puma

So the parents replied, "Sure, you may even go inside. We're glad they are playing there and are having a good time. During the winter month of Paamuya a Hopi is supposed to be happy, so there's nothing wrong with you going there. Enjoy yourselves with the boys." The girls were elated about this reply.

The next day the players all brought their younger and older sisters along to the kiva. Whenever one of them arrived accompanied by a younger or older sister, he shouted down from the roof just before entering, "Haw! How about some words of welcome. I'm not coming alone."

Right away one could hear boisterous shouting from below. "Come on in!" they yelled.

Every boy arriving with a sister received a great welcome upon entering. "All right, do come in! Be careful as you climb down the ladder! Have a seat here!" The girls who accompanied their brothers replied merrily, "There can't be any harm in participating."

The boys and men explained to the girls, "Watch carefully how we play. Once you learn the rules, you can join us." That's what they said to them down in the kiva there.

Before long the game got underway. They took out the cottonwood cups from where they usually kept them and began to play. Everybody was enjoying it. There was a great deal of laughter and boisterous shouting. The girls who were only watching also had a good time. Then they went home. The following night they returned, and when the game resumed, the men urged the girls, "All right, now you can try. But first we'll divide you into two groups. Then you can play mixed in with the boys against each other."

And this is what they did. They divided the girls into two groups. Then the game got underway. Both sides were competing with each other. This went on day after day. Meanwhile, the players began to bring some of their possessions to the kiva. These were the stakes they gambled for.

nanavö'yangwu.

Pantsatskyakyaakyangw pu' yaw pay taavangwatyaqamuy amungaqw pay pumuy pas pö'i'ywisa. Pu' hoopaqwwat maana, lomamana, yaw nanavö'qamuy amumi qatuptu. Qatuptuqw pu' yaw nanavö'niqa tiyo aw hoyokqe pu' put pakwsivut ang ma'ynumkyangw yaw yorikqw angqw maana aw qatuuqa yaw it kwasay oomi hölökni'ytaqe yaw tamöy maatakni'yta. Noq is yaw pas lomamana hakniqw pas yaw qötsatatmö'yta. Pu' yaw pam put maanat tamöyatsa aw taykyangw ang ma'ynuma. Niikyangw pay yaw kur put soomokit hepnumqe pay naat qa tuwat pay yaw kur soosok wa'ömnaqw pay yaw ayangqwwat pö'aya puma'a. Yanhaqam yaw hiniwtiqw pu' pam maana pan put aw naamaataknaqw pu' yaw pantsaktivayaqw pu' pay ayangqwwat hiituwat pö'i'ywisqw pu' yaw pay mimuywatuy angqw maana piw tuwat pantingwu.

Pay as yaw oovi pantsatskyangwuniikyangw pu' yaw paapu nuwu haqaapiy puma pas qa unangwtalawvayaqe yaw qa ökingwu. Pu' yaw paapu himuwa maana put kwasay oomiqhaqami tsovale' yaw wukoqaasi'ytangwu. Qötsaqaasi'ytangwuniqw pay pi tiyo pi taaqa nuvöningwuniiqe yaw pas pantaqw tsangaw pi yaw aw naahölökni'ytangwuniqw oovi pay himuwa sonqa hiitawat qaasiyat aw tongokqw pu' ayangqwwat pay puma pö'yyangwu. Paniwma yawniikyangw pu' haqaapiy pu' pay ima tootim yaw qööqamuy, siwamuy kuwaatoti. Pu' yaw ayangqwwat haqawa pangqawu, "Ta'ay, itam naami nanavö'ni. Kur nu' ung pö'e' pu' nu' uusiway aw hintsanni. Pu' kur um nuy pö'e' pu' um iqöqay, isiway aw hintsanni." Yan yaw puma naanami yukuyaqe pu' yaw aapiy pantsatskyangwu.

Pantsatskyakyangw pu' yaw nuwu pay pas qa unangwtalawvaya. Yaw taltimiqhaqami pantsatskyangwu. Pantsatskyangwuniikyangw pu' ima mamant ahoy ökiiqe pu' yumuy amumi yan lavayta, pas yaw kwangwa'ewniqw. Kwangwa'ewniqw pu' pay yaw ima haqawat momoyam pay naanami pangqaqwa, "Pas hapi yaw kwangwa'ewniiqat itaamana pituuqe yan kwangwalalvaya. Noq sen pi yaw itam qa amumumyaniqat pangqawu. Yanhaqam inumi pam imana lalvaya," yaw naanami kitota.

Pu' yaw piw suukyawa pangqawu, "Hep owi, pay piw imana pan tuu'awvaqe pay oovi inumi piw panhaqam lavayti sen pi itam qa aqwyaniqw. Pas yaw himu kwangwa'ewa. Yanhaqam lavayti inuminiqw pay pi oovi itam itaakongmuy tuuvingtotani pay pi puma naanakwhaqw pay pi itam songqa amumumyani."

Yaw yan puma momoyam naanami yukuyaqe pu' antsa kong-

On one occasion the group on the southwest side was about to win, when all of a sudden a beautiful girl sat down close by the players. The boy who was supposed to guess moved up to the game. As he held his hand over the gaming cups, he looked at the girl who had squatted down beside him. That instant the girl pulled up her dress and revealed her knee. The girl was exceedingly beautiful and had light-complected knees. The boy's eyes were riveted on the girl's knee as his hand moved along the gaming cups. He was searching for the hidden object under one of the cups. He knocked all of them over and still did not find it, so the other side won. This happened, of course, because the girl had teased him with her exposed knee. Now all of them started using this trick, and when one group came close to winning, a girl from the opposing group would bare her knee.

This went on and on until they became so wrapped up in the game that they would not hear of going home on time. As a next step, a girl would now pull her dress all the way up so that her big thighs became bared. With the view of an exposed white thigh the boys or men could not help but get all aroused. Excited that a girl had revealed herself, they would feel compelled to touch the girl's thigh, and their side would lose. Finally, the boys made it a practice to offer their older or younger sisters as prizes. One player would challenge another and say, "All right, let's play each other. If I beat you, I can sleep with your sister. If you beat me, you can have mine." This is what they agreed to; so that's what they did from then on.

Things started getting more and more out of hand. Without letting up, the gambling continued until the early morning hours. Upon coming home all the girls told their parents how much fun the game had been. Some of the married women shared this news with each other. "Upon coming home our daughter was raving how much she enjoyed herself. She thought that maybe we should also give it a try. Anyway, that's what she said."

Thereupon another woman replied, "Sure enough, my daughter came home with the same news and also suggested that we go there. It's supposed to be a lot of fun. I think we should therefore ask our husbands if they will allow us to participate."

This is what the women decided to do. Indeed, they asked their husbands for permission. The latter were anxious to please their wives and answered, "Sure, why don't you go there. That game must really make everybody happy, for that is what our daughters are reporting. Go there and enjoy yourselves with the rest."

muy amumi maqaptsitotaqw pay yaw kongmat su'patotaqe pay pangqaqwa, "Ta'ay, pay pi uma awyani. Pay pi antsa kya pi pam haalaypi himuniqw oovi ima itaatim, mamant, pangqaqwa. Pay uma awye' nuutum haalayyani," yaw yanhaqam puma kongmat pay amumi hingqaqwa.

Noq pu' yaw imuy peetuy momoymuy kongmat epeqyangwuniiqe pu' yaw pay pangqaqwa amumi, "Owi, pas kwangwa'ewa. Pay uma itamumtotiniy," yaw pay himuwa kitangwu.

Noq pu' yaw oovi pay momoymuy enang tangatotakyangw pu' pay pas qa unangwtalawvayaqe pu' qa tootokya. Qa tootokqe pu' haqaapiy pu' pay it sosotukwpit öönatote' pu' tiivanlalwangwu. Yaw tiivanlalwangwu taltimiqhaqami. Pantsakwiskyangw pu' pay yaw antsa nuwu imuy peetuy ang momngwituy nöömamuyatuy enang tangatota. Pu' yaw pay as puma antsa ökingwu. Nuwu paapu yaw pas nu'an hintotiqe pu' ima momoyam paapu yaw aw nitkya'ywisngwu. Pu' yaw pay hiita noovatote' put aw kiwisqw pu' yaw pay ima momngwit taataqt qa nuutumyaqam okiw tsöngmokiwyungngwu. Yaw qa amungem noovatotat pangsosa pas pisoq'iwyungngwuniiqe kongmuy qa nopnayangwu. Pay yaw puma pay naap noovalalwa hiita, niikyangw pay pi taaqa qa novatwi'ytangwuniqw. Noq pay yaw puma hin noonova angqe'. Pu' yaw peetu ima momoyhooyam timu'yyungqam pu' pumuy qa aw tunatyawyungqe puma okiw yaw tsöngmokiwyungqw pu' yaw himuwa taaqa tiy kwusut pu' kivaminingwu. Aqw taytaqe epeq yaw tsaakwhoyat yu'at nuutum qa unangwtalngwu. Pu' yaw haktonsa as oongaqw tungwantangwu. Pu' yaw epeq a'ni kwanonotangwuniiqe yaw qa nanvotyangwu. Yaw himuwa oongaqw tiy tsöpkyangw put yuyat tungwantaqw yaw qa navotngwu. Haqaapiy pas nu'an qa unangwtalawvayakyangw pu' yaw pay antsa it tsa'akmongwit pu' nöömayat enangtota. Pas yaw taalawvaqw qa qe'totingwu. Naat yaw töngvamiqhaqami tiivanlalwangwu.

Noq yaw it tsa'akmongwit nöömayat enang panayaqw pas yaw pam qa haalayti tsa'akmongwiniiqe pu' antsa put kikmongwit awniiqe pu' pangqawu, "Ta'ay," yaw kita, "pay pi antsa it piw inömay pu' songyawnen nuy nawkiyaqe nuy tuuhotota. Pay antsa pay nu' tuwat itsivutiqw pay pi itam yep tur soosoyam sulawtini. Yan hapi nu' tunatyawtaqe oovi pay ungsa it hapi aa'awna. Oovi um it qa hakiy aw lalvayni," yaw yanhaqam aw lavayti.

Noq yaw antsa aapiy pantaqw pu' ima hakim tiyot haqamwat kivaape yaw hiita naawini. Yaw hiituy wunimaniqe yan naawinqe pu'

Some of these women's husbands had already been at the kiva, so they were able to confirm this. "Yes, it's true. It's great fun. Come on over and join us."

Now the women also came to the kiva. So engrossed did everybody become in the game that no one considered going to bed. When the players finally tired of Sosotukwpi, they began dancing. They danced and danced until daylight came. Meanwhile, the wives of some of the priests also became involved in this gambling craze. They, too, would not return home on time. It got so bad that the women even took their food to the kiva. They would cook something and take it along, with the result that the priests and the other men who did not participate would go hungry. So busy were the women getting to the kiva that they did not feed their husbands. The men tried fixing various things, but alas, a man does not know how to cook, so they did not eat properly any more. Some of the women also had little children, whom they began to neglect. Thus, the poor wretches were starving. The men finally had to pick up the children and take them to the kiva. Looking inside, they could see the mothers of the children all engrossed in the game. They called their wives by name, but to no avail. The noise of the players was so deafening that they did not hear. The men just stood there with children in their arms calling down, but there was no response. The gambling craze finally reached a climax when the wife of the crier chief became involved. The gambling did not stop at daybreak any more and the dancing continued until the sun was up in the sky.

The crier chief was very upset when they got his wife to join. Because of this he sought out the village leader. He said to him, "You know, I feel as if my wife has been taken from me. They have caused me great pain. I'm so angry, I wish we could all die. At least, this is how I feel, so I came to let you know about it. But don't tell anybody else."

In this manner things continued at Awat'ovi. One day, a couple of young men were making plans in their kiva to stage a social dance. They told their kiva partners about it and asked if there were any objections. The kiva mates were delighted about their plan. "Sure, that's

yaw puma oovi pep kivasngwamuy aa'awna. Yaw tuuvingta sen pay qa hintani put hiita wunimaniniqw. Noq pu' pay yaw kwangwtapnaya, "Qa'ey, pay pi son hintani," yaw kitota. "Pay pi antsa uma tuwat yephaqam put tunatyawtaqw pay pi itam umungem put ang kuukuyvaniy," yaw kitotaqe pu' oovi pumuy lööqmuy manmongtapya. Pu' yaw sukw it hakiy wuukoq pas mongtapya, pam amungem tsootsongniqö.

Noq pu' yaw oovi pay yan naanakwhaqw pu' yaw puma oovi ep qavongvaqw mihikqw ang piw tsa'lawu, kiinawit. Ang yaw tsa'lawkyangw yukut pu' nöst pu' piw ang tsa'lawu. Pantsakkyangw pu' yaw antsa epeq taataqtuy tsovala mooti. Noq pu' yaw puma oovi mooti tatawkosya epe, mihikqw, ep suus tsovaltiqat epe'. Pantikyangw qavongvaqw pu' yaw pay pam mongwi pumuy ayata, "Ta'ay, uma pu' hapi mihikqw mamantuy tsovalaniy," yaw amumi kitaqw pu' yaw oovi puma ep mihikqw pu' ang piw tsa'lawu. "Ta'ay, uma kivamiqyani. Uma iits aqwyaniy," yan yaw ang tsa'lawu.

Pantikyangw pu' yaw piw lööstakyangw pay piw an ang tsa'lawkyangw pu' yaw mongwi'am amumi pangqawu, "Ta'ay, pu' uma mamantuy tsovalaniy," yaw amumi kitaqw pu' yaw oovi puma antsa angqw yamakqe pu' piw ang tsa'timakyangw pu' antsa pumuy oovi mamantuyniiqe, "Ta'ay, uma kivamiqyani, mamantuy," puma yaw yan ang tsa'tima.

Niikyangw pu' yaw mamantuy tsovalanmakyangw tsovalaqe pu' angqw kivami pumuy tsaama. Pu' yaw kivats'omi pituuqe pu' aqw tsa'lawu, "Haw, kuwawatotangwuy!"

Pu' yaw antsa tootim kur taataqt tsutsyakyaqe angqaqw sa'akmaqe, "Ta'ay, yungya'ay. Hakim paas yungtangwuy. Uma yangqe yesniy," amumi yanhaqam lavaytoti. Antsa angqe mamant yesvaqw pu' mongwi'am pangqawu amumi, "Ta'ay, uma tootim, taataqt uma tawlalwani. Son pi ima mamant taawit qa aw tuuqayye' hin maasantotaniqey tuwi'yvayani." Amumi haqami yaw yan lavaytiqw pu' oovi hak pusukin'aya'am pusukinpit kwusuuqe pu' pam oovi mooti tawkuynaqw pu' paasat ima tawlalwa. Noq pu' pay ima manmongwit mamantuy aw pangqawu, "Hakim paas tuuqayyungngwu taawit awi. Nit pu' pay hakim angwu masasatotangwu." Amumi yaw yanhaqam lavaytiqw pu' oovi mamant put aw tuuqaykyaakyangw yaw angwu pay antsa masasatota.

Pay antsa put taawit aw tuuqayyaqw paasat pu' mongwi'am piw amumi pangqawu, "Ta'ay, uma tuwantotani. Itam tuwanlalwe' itaatotokyay aqw pituqw itam sonqe taawi'ykyaakyangw tiivani," yaw

fine with us," they replied. "If that's your intention, we'll see to it that you complete it successfully." Immediately they selected two men to be in charge of the female dancers. Then they chose an elderly man who would do the ritual smoking for them.

Now that permission for the dance had been obtained, the organizers broadcast it publicly from the rooftop the following night. After the announcement they had supper, whereupon they repeated the announcement. Next they recruited the menfolk into the kiva. During their first nightly gathering they memorized their songs. The next morning the leader said to them, "All right, I want you to bring in the girls tonight." Once more an announcement to this effect was made in the evening: "All right, come to the kiva. Come early!"

The announcement was repeated twice, whereupon the man in charge said, "Well, it's time to assemble the girls." They left the kiva and went from house to house, inviting the girls as follows: "All right, you girls, go to the kiva!"

Slowly but surely they picked up the girls and took them to the kiva. As they arrived on top of the roof, they hollered in, "Haw! How about some words of welcome!"

The boys and men down below were delighted to comply and many voices could be heard shouting, "Well, come on in. Be careful as you enter. Sit down here on the benches." When all the girls were seated, the leader commanded, "All right, I want you boys and men to sing. The girls must hear the songs so they can learn how to make their dance gestures." No sooner had he spoken than the drummer picked up the drum. He started the song, and they began to sing. The two men in charge of the girls now said to them, "Listen carefully to the song and make your dance gestures." The girls complied and started moving their arms.

They were still listening to the song when the leader said, "All right, now you practice this. If we keep practicing, we're bound to be able to dance to the song by the time we reach the eve of our event."

amumi kita.

Paasat pu' puma oovi hongvaqe pu' puma mamant namortota hakimuy tootimuy. Noq pu' oovi aw pitsinayaqw paasat pu' puma tiiva. Niikyangw yaw imuy hiituy Wukoqalvoliituy hongva. Pumuy yaw tootim naanawakna. Pu' yaw antsa puma tuwanlalwa. Noq pas yaw hiitu kwangwa'ewya antsa. Pu' puma tuwanyukuyaqe angqw ninma. Ninmaqw pu' yaw qavongvaqw taalawvaqw yaw pumuysa yu'a'atota, pumuy hiituy Wukoqalvoliituy. Pas yaw hiitu kwangwa'ewya. Pas yaw soosovik kitsokiva pamsa lavayi. Pu' yaw piw oovi aqwya. Ep qavongvaqw mihikqw pu' pay piw anhaqam hiniwtapnayaqw pu' pay angsakis mimhikqat ang puma tuwanlalwangwu. Niikyangw pay kur puma pas qa hisat taalö tiivani. Paysoq yaw puma kwangwa'ewlalwaniqey oovi pantsatskyangwu.

Tiivanlalwaqw pu' i' kikmongwit nööma'at kya pi navota. Noq pu' aapiy puma pantsatskyangwuniiqe pas yaw qa tokngwu ephaqam. Puma qa tokngwu, qa iits tokwisngwu. Pantsakkyaakyangw pu' yaw nuwu paapu pas nu'an hintotiqe pu' yaw pay pas talhahayingqw pu' piw ökingwu. Yanhaqam kya hiniwma epniqw pu' pay put kikmongwit nööma'at kya pi navotqe pu' pay put koongyay aw put maatsikinta. Pas yaw tuwanlalwaqam kivaapeq pas hiitu kwangwa'ewya.

"Pay nu' ang wuuwanta," yaw pam kita koongyay awniqw pu' koongya'at aw pangqawu, "Hin um put aw wuuwantay?" yaw kita.

"Owiy," yaw aw kita, "pay hapi sen nu' nuutumniqey oovi pu' pi pas yaw kwangwa'ewya. Hikis pay yaw peetu momoyam nuutumya. Qa pas mamantuysa yaw naanawakna. Oovi pu' piw peetu momoyam nuutumyaqw inumi pangqaqwa pas pam himu kur kwangwa'ewa. 'Um itamumnikyangw', yanhaqam puma inumi yu'a'atota, ima momoyam nuutumyaqamniqw pu' nu' oovi pay hapi as nuutumniqe oovi ung tuuvingta. Sen antsa nu' nuutumniniqw sen um put ang hin wuuwani," yaw put koongyay aw kita, kikmongwit.

Noq pu' kikmongwi aw pangqawu, "Pay pi um nuutumninik nuutumni. Pam pi pay uupe'e. Pay pu' uma tuwat haalayya. Pay itim soosoyam haalayyaniqw oovi nu' yephaqam umuy timu'ytaniqw kur antsa puma pepeq put hiita tuwanlalwaqw pay pi kwangwa'ewniqw pay pi uma haalayyani. Noq pay pi um nuutumninik nuutumni," yaw yanhaqam pam kikmongwi put nöömay aw lavayti.

Pu' paapiy oovi nööma'at nuutumningwu. Pay as iits pitungwu. Nit pu' haqaapiy pay pas yaw qa pitungwu. Qa pitungwuniqw pu' nuwu yaw pas talhahayingqw pitungwu. Noq pu' yaw pay puma

The girls rose from their seats and each picked a boy. Soon the dancing got under way. They had decided to do the Butterfly dance in which the female dancers wore no bangs but had their foreheads exposed. This had been the boys' request. And so they kept practicing. The dancers were really good. When the practice session was over, everybody went home. Early in the morning of the next day, people were talking about nothing else but the Butterfly dancers and how good they had been. That was the talk in every house. That night the procedure of the night before was repeated. Thereafter they practiced every night. Evidently, there were no plans to stage a dance during daytime. They continued doing this because they greatly enjoyed themselves.

Eventually, word of the nightly dancing also reached the wife of Ta'palo, the village leader. By now it already occurred once in a while that the dancers failed to go to bed, or if they went to bed, it was very late. Soon this habit got so bad that nobody returned home before daybreak. Just when this started happening, the wife of the village chief heard of it. On several occasions she mentioned to her husband that the dancers practicing in the kiva were really good. "I've been thinking," she said to her husband.

"What have you been thinking about?" he replied.

"Well, I might participate. I hear they are really enjoyable. Quite a few women are already there. They don't just need girls. Those women who went told me that it was a great deal of fun. 'You should come with us,' they've been urging me. That's what I wanted to ask you about. Maybe I should go too. What do you think?" she asked her husband.

The village leader replied, "If you want to be with the others, go ahead and join them. It's up to you. You all can be happy. I have you as my children so that all of you can be happy. Since they are having a good time practicing for a dance, you should be happy. By all means, join the dancers if that's what you want."

From that time on Ta'palo's wife never missed a dance practice. As a rule, she returned late. Eventually, she did not come home at all, or rather not before it became daylight. And always there was laughing and shouting in the kiva where they were practicing. Her husband, on the other hand, stayed at home smoking and pondering the ways of the villagers, his children. Meanwhile, the boisterous noise at

epeq tuwanlalwaqam pas a'ni kwanonotangwu. Kwanonotangwuniqw pam kya ep kiy ep yankyangw pay tuwat tsootsonglawngwu,
hiita tuwat timuy engem wuuwantaqe. Nit pu' pay yaw pas epeq a'ni
kwanonotangwuniqw pu' it nööma'at pay yaw pas aapiy pankyangw
nuwu pay pas yaw taalawvaqw pitu, suus. Noq pu' pay yaw i'
kikmongwi pay hin wuuwaqe pay sen pi haqam himu qa lomahinta.
"Sen hintiqw oovi iwuuti pas taalawnat pitu?" yaw yan pam wuuwaqe pu', "Pay pi as pu' mihikqw piw tuwanlalwaqw pu' nu' hapi piw
aqw kuyvani. Hin pi hintaqw oovi pas a'ni kwanonotangwu epehaq
tootim, taataqtu," yaw pam yan wuuwa.

Noq pu' oovi ep piw suus nööma'atniqa pas kwangwtoynaqe pas
yaw pavan yuuyuwsilawu. Naawuslawqe pavan yaw ngumnit wu-
koqömata. Pantit pu' yaw höömiy aw lomayuku. Pantit pu' kwasay
yaw ang tsiwta. Paas yaw naanaapa hiita lomahintsanqw pu' antsa
yaw manmongwit wiktoq pay antsa yaw suyma. Pu' yaw koongyay
aw pangqawu, "Ta'ay, nu' hapi piw aqw'a."

"Ta'ay, pay pi uma haalayya. Pay pi um aqw piw nuutumni,"
yaw pam yanhaqam lavayti put nöömay awniqw pu' oovi pam aqwniqw pu' pay epehaq hongva. Pu' yaw tiivantivaqe tawkuynayaqw
pam navotqe pu' pay tuqayvaasi'ytaqw pu' antsa yaw a'ni epehaq
pay kwanonoyku piw. Pu' yaw töötöqya. Pas sumataq yaw pavan
haalayya. Pas yaw qa unangwtalya'ewakwniqw pu' yaw pam oovi
aqw kuyvaniqe pu' yaw oovi wunuptu. Wunuptuqe pu' patsvuy
haqe' kwimikni'ytaqe pu' yaw put pam usiitat pangqw pu' yaw
kivami nakwsu, pangso kivami haqam puma tuwanlalwaqw.

Noq pu' yaw oovi pam pangso pituuqe yaw kivats'omi pitutoq
pay yaw epehaq kwanonota. Pavan yaw hak hin töna'yte' pan ang
a'ni töötöqngwu. Antsa yaw angqw kivats'omi pituuqe pu' yaw aqw
kuyva. Noq antsa yaw epeq tiiva. Noq antsa yaw pam nööma'at
nuutum. Is pavan yaw tsoni'ytaqe pavan yaw suusaykyangw pavan
yaw masasata. Pas yaw qa unangwtala. Pu' hapi yaw tawvongya'y-
yungqamuy aqw pam nööma'at pituqw pu' yaw pavan a'ni kwanonoykungwu. Noq pu' yaw pay kikmongwi aqw taytat pu' yaw
pangqawu, "Kur yanhaqam ima yepeq hintsatskyangwuniiqe oovi
kwanonotangwu." Noq pam yaw naatuhota. Pam nööma'at tawvongya'yyungqamuy aqw pituqw a'ni yaw kwanonoykungwuniqw pay
yaw pam naatuhotaqe pay yaw pam hihin qa naani. Qa naaniqe pu'
oovi paasat pu' pay pan wuuwa, "Pay tur han pas paas hin yori.
Hintotingwu pi pas ima'a," kitaaqe pu' yaw pangqw oovi kivaytsiwat angqw aqw qatuptuqe pu' pas aqw tayta.

the kiva went on and on. Once again Ta'palo's wife did not come home before daybreak. The village leader grew concerned. Maybe something was not right. "Why on earth would my wife remain so long? I have to go over there and see for myself when they practice tonight. Who knows why those boys and men are making so much noise." This is what he thought.

Once more Ta'palo's wife was looking forward to the evening. She spent a lot of time putting on some fine clothes. Next she combed her hair and powdered her face with a lot of cornmeal. That done, she nicely fixed her hair and brushed off her dress. By the time the ones in charge of the female dancers came around to pick her up, she had meticulously prepared herself. She left right away, saying to her husband, "I'm going to the kiva again."

"All right, enjoy yourselves. Go on, take part," he replied. And so his wife went to the kiva and the dancers lined up. Ta'palo could hear how they started dancing and singing. He kept listening. Sure enough, there it was again, the roaring laughter and the shouts of merriment. The dancers were clearly having a great time. When it seemed that things would not calm down, he rose from his seat. He was curious about what was going on in the kiva. Picking up a tanned hide he usually kept draped over a beam, he slung it across his shoulders and headed over to the kiva where the practicing was taking place.

Upon arriving there Ta'palo climbed up to the roof, with the laughing and shouting as loud as ever. People were yelling at the top of their voices. Now he had reached the edge of the hatch in the roof and looked in. Sure enough, there they were dancing, and his wife very much part of it. Dancing with great enthusiasm, she was smiling broadly as she motioned with her hands. No doubt, she was really enjoying herself. As she neared the men in the chorus, the shouting increased markedly. The village leader who noticed all of this said to himself, "So this is the reason for this merriment." It really hurt him. Each time his wife was approaching the chorus, the shouting and laughing increased. That caused the village leader a great deal of anguish. It was no laughing matter for him. Still, he thought, "Why don't I watch a little more. I'd like to see what really goes on." With that he squatted by the kiva opening and looked down.

Pay yaw as mima peetu momoyam tawvongya'yyungqamuy
aqw ökiqw pumuy yaw pay qa pas aw pas hin a'ni kwanonoykungwu. Pay yaw put nööma'at aqw pituqwsa pu' yaw pas a'ni
kwanonoykungwu. Pantote' put pas yaw tuuhototangwu. Noq pu'
yaw pam amumi hin wuuwaqe pu' pay pepeq nakwhani'yta. Noq
pu' yaw antsa tiitso'naya. Pu' yaw tiitso'nayaqe kohalmokiwyungqe
pu' angqw naahukyanawisniqe pu' yaw angqw nöönganta. Nööngantaqw pu' yaw pam ang nööma'at yamakto it hakiy amawtaqey
amum. Noq pu' yaw pay pi qa taala angqeniqw pay yaw oovi puma
put kikmongwit qa maamatsi. Nit panis yamakt pu' pay pam yaw
kikmongwit nööma'at put amaway aw pangqawu, "Itam inungem
kwayngyavoni," yaw pam kita put awi'.

"Kur antsa'ay," yaw kitaaqe pu', "Tume'iy," yaw kitaqw pangqw
pu' puma kivangaqw yaw nakwsu, taatö. Taatönit pu' pangqw hop-
qöymiqhaqami.

Noq pu' yaw pam kikmongwi amungk tayta. Noq pay yaw pas
nuwu hisatniqwti. Pay yaw pas wuuyavotiqw pay yaw qa angqaqw
ahoy puma. Pu' pam pay hin wuuwaqe pangqw yaw oovi amungk.
Amungkniiqe haqami pumaniqw yaw angqw amungk kuyva. Yaw
panis angqw aw kuyvaqw yaw ep kiihut pösömiq pam amawa'at put
nöömayat yaw tsopta. Yan yaw pam yorikqe pas yaw unangwmoki.
Pas yaw pam itsivuti. Nu'an itsivutiqe pu' yaw pay antsa pumuy qa
aw ma'ytat pangqw pu' yaw pay pam nima, kiy awi'. Niiqe pu' yaw
oovi ep pakiiqe pu' pay aapiy tsongomokiy kwusuuqe pu' yaw put
tangata. Nit pu' tsootsongi. Pas yaw itsivutiqe kur hin wuuwankyangw tsootsongi. Pas yaw qa suyan unangwa'ykyangw tsootsonglawu. Pu' yaw tsootsonglawkyangw pu' itsivu'iwtaqe pu' yaw naanap hin tuwat hin wuuwanta. Qa hin hiita lolmat yaw timuy engem
wuuwanta. It hiita lomahiita wuuwantaniqw pam yaw qa haqaqw
aw pitu. Noq yaw pam pas naatuhota nöömay nu'ansanqe. Pas yaw
kur puma koyaanisqatsi'yyungwa. Yanhaqam yaw pam wuuwanta.

Niikyangw ura hayphaqam it antsa neyangmakiwqat ep ura i'
kawayo put tiyat enang warikqe ura put niina. Pay yaw as ep pas
naatuhota put tiy haqami hintsanqe. Niikyangw pu' yaw it piw nöö-
mayatyaqw paasat pu' yaw pam pas itsivutiqe pas yaw kur hintiniqe
pu' yaw oovi naanap hin wuuwantaqe pu' yaw pangqawu, "Ta'ay,"
yaw kita, "pay pi nuwupi. Pay pi nawus tur yep itam sulawtiniy,"
yaw yanhaqam pam tuwat wuuwankyangw tsootsonglawu.

Niiqe pu' yaw paasat pu' oovi pam kikmongwi put aw tumala-
la'yva. Pay yaw pas kur hin qa naa'oyni, timuy hapi amumi'. Pay

It was obvious to him that the noise level was not as high when some of the other women neared the chorus. The shouting occurred when his wife came closer. Each time they did that, Ta'palo's heart ached. All kinds of thoughts crossed his mind, but outwardly he remained calm. Now the dancing stopped. Since the dancers were hot, they were filing out of the kiva to cool themselves off. His wife, too, emerged accompanied with her dance partner. It was so dark, however, that the two did not recognize the village leader. No sooner had his wife exited than she said to her partner, "Why don't you come with me to the bathroom?"

"Sure, why not," replied the man. "Let's go." With that they headed away from the kiva in a southeasterly direction. Then they continued on down the northeast side.

The village leader looked after them. When quite a bit of time had passed, and still the two were not back, he decided to go after them. Following the path they had taken, he finally caught sight of them. The instant he did, he saw that the man was having intercourse with his wife in the corner of a house. This sight broke his heart. He became furious. He was outraged, yet he did not lay hands on the lovers. Instead, he went home. Upon entering his house he grabbed his tobacco pouch, filled his pipe, and smoked. He was beside himself and was hardly able to think straight while he smoked. He felt terrible, but he smoked on and on. All sorts of thoughts kept crossing his mind. The thoughts he had for his children, however, were not good. He should have been thinking of good things, but none came to mind. The fact that he had caught his wife in the act of adultery caused him great pain. Life was out of joint. Awat'ovi was living *koyaanisqatsi*. This is what Ta'palo thought.

Only recently, at the occasion of the mixed hunt, a horse had run over his daughter and killed her. The loss of his child had grieved him a lot. But now they had gotten to his wife, and he was full of rage. Not knowing what to do, he considered all kinds of options. Finally, he said, "Well, what's done is done. We'll all have to be wiped out here." This is the conclusion the village leader reached as he was smoking there.

So Ta'palo set to work. There was no other way: he would seek revenge on his children. The village of Awat'ovi was not to exist there any longer. Nothing good was going to be forthcoming from it.

yaw pas pam pepeq kitsoki, pas qa pepeqni. Pay yaw paapu qa himu nukngwa pepeq a'aniwni. Haqam yaw kitsokiniqw pay yaw tuusaqasa pang kuyvamantani. It yantaqat pam yaw a'ni aw wuuwanta. Pay pi yaw naap puma songyawnen it yan yukuya, pepeq sinom, timat, qahoptotiqe, powaqtotiqe.

Pu' yaw oovi puma pankyaakyangw yeese. Noq i' mongwi pi put an tumala'ytakyangw pu' paasat pay aapiy piw hiisavohaqamtiqw pu' yaw pam hisat nöömay aw pangqawu, "Pas hapi itam pay wuuyavotiy," yaw kita. "Pas itam pay wuuyavo pu' piw nukusyese, qa lomayese. Noq nu' wuuwaqw pay kur paapu himuni. Pay qa himu haqam itamungem nukngwa ayo' taviwniqa pu' peeti. Noq nu' oovi walminiy," yaw aw kita, nöömay awi'.

Pu' yaw nööma'at nakwhana. "Ta'ay, pay pi um awniy," yaw aw kita.

Pangqw pu' yaw oovi pam Walmi'i. Pu' pam Walpe pituuqe pu' pep pu' mongwit kiiyat aw'i, pu' paki. Paasat pu' put paas taviqw pu' paasat pay son puma qa maamatsi. Son pi hak paysoq pi mongwinen piw mongwit aw paysoq kokoliyawtongwu. Niiqe pu' yaw paasat puma oovi kivamiqhaqami paki, son pi qa pep mongwit kivayat aqw. Pangsoq yaw puma pakiiqe pep pu' puma naatsotsongna. Pay yaw oovi puma pas su'awwuyavo naatsotsongnaqw paasat pu' yaw Walpe mongwi pu' Awat'ongaqw mongwit aw pangqawu, "Ta'ay," yaw aw kita, "son pi um qa hiita oovi waynuma. Son um paysoq yangqaqö. Ya himu'uy?" yaw kita awi'.

Paasat pu' yaw i' Awat'ongaqw mongwi pu' aw pangqawu, "Owiy," yaw aw kita, "pay antsa nu' kur haqami hakiy awniqe pewhaqami nu' ung tuwaaqe oovi angqöy," yaw aw kita. "Pas nu' a'ni hiita wuuwantay," yaw aw kita. "Pas nu' qa haalayi piiwu. Pep itaakitsokiy ep ima popwaqt, nuunukpant, pas puma qa hakiy ayo' yamakni'ywisay," yaw kita. "Pas puma pay paapu pas tuqyanta. Pu' piw imuy mamantuy a'ni pumuy sokoplalwa. Hiitawat haqam tsopyangwu. Pay pas hisatniiqat put aape pu' pas nu'an hintay," yaw kita. "Noq hintani sene'? Hintini sen nuu'u? It oovi nu' angqöy," yaw Walpe mongwit aw kita.

"Owiy," yaw aw kita, "owiy. Hiita hin um wuuwantaqey, pangqawni um'iy," yaw aw kita.

"Owiy," yaw kita, "pay yanhaqam hapi itam piw atkya qatsinaya. Yantaqat hapi akw itam pewya as'a. Noq pay kur piw itamum yama Kastiila, nukpana, qahopi. Pam yep tuu'a'asnaqe, itaasinmuy aa'asnaqe, pay pam pumuy put öqalanta. Qa hakiy kyaptsi'yyungw-

Where the village site was now, only weeds would be sprouting in the future. Things of this nature Ta'palo was pondering. It was as if the people there, his children, had actually decided upon this fate when they had turned bad and become sorcerers and witches.

The people of Awat'ovi continued living in this corrupt fashion. Ta'palo, however, kept nursing his plan. Quite a bit of time had gone by, when one day he said to his wife, "Things really have come to a head here. We've been living immorally for too long. I can't think of anything else. There's nothing good left that could save us. I will therefore go to Walpi," he told his wife.

His wife did not object. "All right, you do that," she replied.

So Ta'palo headed over to Walpi. Upon his arrival he sought out the house of the village leader and entered. The latter welcomed him in, realizing at once that the headman of a village does not call on a peer merely to gossip. The two of them repaired to a kiva, probably the one the Walpi leader was associated with. Upon entering, the first order of business was a ritual smoke. The two passed the pipe back and forth between them. After a while the Walpi leader said to the headman of Awat'ovi, "Well then, you must be about for a purpose. You can't just have dropped in for nothing. What is it?" he asked.

Thereupon the Awat'ovi leader said, "Yes, I did not know whom to turn to. Then I thought of you and came," he replied. "I've been mulling over a terrible plan in my mind, for I've been unhappy for quite some time. In our village the sorcerers, those creatures of evil, do not let anyone go free any more. Their influence is devastating. They are destroying people whenever they can. They are seducing the unmarried girls and have intercourse with them wherever they can. It's a lot worse than it was ever before. I'm at my wits' end. I don't know what to do any more. That's why I came."

"Yes, I see," replied the Walpi leader. "So what do you intend to do? Tell me."

"Well, you can see that once again we're leading a life of corruption, just as we did in the underworld. That's why we emerged to this upper world. But the Spaniard, this evil, uncivilized person, also came up with us. He's baptizing people here. In doing so he's encouraging them not to respect anyone or anything, neither the elders nor

niqat, wuuwuyoqamuy qa kyaptsi'yyungwniqat, tiitikivet qa kyaptsi'yyungwniqat, it hapi pam pumuy songyawnen ayalawu. Pay itam
pep atkya yantoti. Pas qa hakiy antsa pi qatsi'ata. Naanaphin itam
yeese," yaw kita awi.

Paasat pu' yaw Walpe mongwi aw pangqawu, "Noq hiita um
inungaqw naawaknay?" yaw aw kita.

Paasat pu' yaw Awat'ongaqwwat mongwi aw pangqawu, "Owi,
hiita hapi nu' pas wuukoq uumi tungwla'yta ung ayataniqey," kita
yaw awi. "Um as yangqw Walngaqw Awat'omi um itamumi kiipokni. Pangso um kiipokni. Uuhongvi'aymuy um pangso hoonani.
Soosok hiita oovi um tunipit na'sastani, awtat, hoohut, pikya'yngwat.
Himu tunipiniqw put um na'sastani. Pantit pu' um yangqw pumuy
aw laalayni. Pumuy laalaykyangw pu' amumi um pangqawni, 'Pay
uma Awat'opsinmuy pas höönayani, pas yukuyani. Soosokmuy qöqyani. Pay qa hak pep qatuni.' It nu' uumi tuuvinglawu. Um pantiqw
pu' paasat Awat'oviy aqle' tutskwava himu a'aniwqat put nu' uumi
sisviniy," kita. "Put um oovini. Inungem um yante' put um aasataniy," yaw aw kita.

Paasat pu' yaw pep Walpe mongwi ephaqam yaw yooko'ta,
wuuwanlawu, qa hingqawkyangw. Pas yaw oovi nawutstiqw pu'
yaw lavayti, "It um oovi waynumay?" yaw aw kita.

Pu' yaw Awat'ongaqw mongwi aw pangqawu, "Owi, it nu'
oovi'o. Noq hin um hingqawni um'iy?" yaw aw kita. "Hin um aw
wuuwa?"

"Owiy," yaw kita, Walpe mongwi, "pay pep uukitsokiy pi ep
kyaastay," yaw kita. "Itamuupeniiqe wuuhaqya. Puma itamumi ahoy
rohomtote', itamumi ahoy naanaywe', pas kya puma son itamuy qa
angwutotaniy," yaw aw kita. "Pay antsa pi as itam a'ni taataqt piw
yep'e. Pay itam a'ni taataqt, nayawtuwi'yyungwa. Payotsim itamumi
kiipokqw itam amumi naanaywangwu. Pu' Yotsi'em piw itamumi
naanaywaqw piw itam amumi ahoy naanaywangwu. Pay puma
itamumi kikiipokyaqw itam amumi naanaywangwu, nenngem. Ispi
qa itam so'niqey put oovi itam naanaywangwuniqw pu' um yep
inumi pangqawu, pangso nu' uusinmuy ungem soosokmuy haqami
hintsanniqat it um inumi naawakna. Pam pi pep Hopikitsoki, pu' i'
piw Hopikitsoki. Noq itam yangqw pangso Hopit aw naanaywaniqw
pam qa lomahintay," yaw aw kita. "Pas pam qa lomahinta. Pam qa
haqam pantay," yaw aw kita. Kitaaqe pay pi songyawnen qa nakwha.

"Pay kur antsa'ay," yaw Awat'ongaqw mongwi kita. "Pay kur
nu' piw tur haqamiwat hakiy aw piw hepniy," yaw kitat pu' yaw

our ceremonial dancers. The same thing we once experienced in the underworld. It was total chaos, and we lived any old way."

The Walpi headman asked, "So what is it you want from me?"

Thereupon the leader from Awat'ovi replied, "I'm requesting you to do something big. I want you to come from Walpi to raid our village at Awat'ovi. That's the place I want you to attack. Send over your strong fighters. Have them prepare weapons such as bows, arrows, and stone axes. Whatever the weapon, get it ready for the raid. Then lead your men over, instructing them to this end, 'Wipe out the Awat'ovi people, finish them off. Kill each and every one of them. No one is to live there any more.' This is what I'm asking of you. If you do this, I'll pay you with all the crops that grow near Awat'ovi. If you fulfill my wish, that shall be your reward."

The Walpi leader just sat there in silence, bent forward, thinking and thinking. After a lengthy pause he said, "So this is the reason for your coming?"

"Yes," answered Ta'palo, "that's why I came. What do you have to say to that? What's your opinion?"

"Well, the population of your village is large. Your people outnumber us by far. If they offer resistance and fight back, they're bound to overpower us," he said. "To be sure, we are brave men here. We are courageous and know how to fight. When the Paiutes attack us, we fight them. The same is true for the Apaches. When they raid us, we fight them. But when they attack us, we fight back in our own interest. We fight because we don't want to die. But you just told me that you want me to destroy all of your people. Awat'ovi is a Hopi village, and so is Walpi. We would be fighting against Hopis there, and that is not right," he said. "That would be bad. That's impossible." Arguing like this the village leader of Walpi refused Ta'palo's request.

"Very well," the Awat'ovi leader replied. "I guess I'll have to look for somebody else, some other place."

wunuptu.

Wunuptit pu' yaw pam pangqw yama. Yaw qa nukwangwnavota hapi. Pangqw pu' yaw pam teevenge nakwsu. Teevenge pam nakwsukyangw yaw pam Songoopami pitu. Yaw Songoopami pam wuuvi. Pangso wupqe pu' yaw pam paasat yuumosa Songoopapmongwit kiiyat awi. Aw pituuqe pu' yaw pam aqw paki. Noq yaw mongwi pay as puuwi. Pu' yaw pam put qötöyat wayayaykina. Qalpeq yaw palalaykinaqw pu' yaw taatayi. Taatayqe pu' yaw qatuptu. Pu' yaw oovi qöpqömiq tsoyla. Paasat pu' yaw puma put qöpqöt nan'ivaqw qatuptu. Paasat pu' yaw Awat'ongaqw mongwi pu' pipmokiy horokna. Tsoongoy pu' yaw tangata, taqtsokya. Taqtsokqw yaw angqw hikis tsootsonat pu' yaw mitwat aw tavi, Songoopave mongwit awi'. Pamwa pu' yaw put pas soosok tsootsongqw sulawtiqw pu' yaw ahoy aw tavi. Paasat pu' yaw Owat'ongaqw mongwi paas put angqw haarit pu' taviqw pu' yaw Songoopapmongwi tuuvingta, "Ta'ay, hiita oovi um waynumay?" yaw aw kita.

"Owiy," yaw aw kita, "pas nu' qa haalayi. Antsa yep Awat'ove ima itim pas puma a'ni unangwa'yyungwa. Pas puma qa hakiy aw kyaptsi'yyungwa. Pas puma ilavayiy qa aw tuuqayyungwa. Noq hayphaqam itam pep maakiwa. Noq ep imanay enang yuutukqe put niinaya. Noq pay pi nu' as naamahin oovi paas put tumaltakyangw nu' itsivu'iwtay," yaw kita. "Piw nu' qa haalayi. Noq oovi pay as pas pam pep kitsoki pas as tuuvoyniqat nu' naawaknay," yaw kita. "Pay as pas pam pep tuuvoyni. Pisatsmoniwtiqw pay pas tuusaqasa ang kuyvamantani. It nu' yantaqat oovi waynumay," yaw aw kita.

"Haw'owi?" yaw aw kita.

"Owiy. Oovi um yep uutotimuy, hohongvituy, um aa'awnaqw yuyutyani, naahongvilalwani, kitani um amumi'i. Noq yaapiy naalös taalat ep nu' piw ahoy pituniy," yaw aw kitat pu' yaw pay wunuptu.

Pu' yaw pam pangqaqw ahoy nima. Noq pam ahoy pituuqe pumuy sinomuy, tootimuy yuyut'ayata. Pu' yaw oovi puma paapiy haqaapiy pantsatskya, yuyutya, naahongvilalwa. Noq pay yaw sinom nan'ip kitsokive qa aw hin wuuwantota. Awat'ove qa hin sinom navoti'yyungqw pu' Songoopave piw qa hak hapi navoti'yta, puma hiita ngöytaqw. Qa hak put aw hin wuuwanta. Noq oovi naalös taalat ep mihikqw pu' yaw Awat'ongaqw mongwi pu' piw Songoopami. Pu' Songoopapmongwi pay yaw as wa'ö. Niikyangw suyan pam Owat'ongaqw kwaatsiy nuutaytaqe pay yaw pam qa puuwi naato. Niiqe yaw oovi pituqw pam navotqe pu' qatuptu. Pu' yaw qööha

With that Ta'palo rose and departed. He had not received a favorable response. Heading southwest he came to Shungopavi. After climbing up to the village he made straight for the house of its leader. Arriving there, he entered. He found the village leader asleep, so he shook his head and he tapped on his forehead until he awoke. Right away he got up and threw some wood on the fire. Then the two men sat down by the fireplace, facing each other. Ta'palo took out his tobacco pouch, filled his pipe, and lit it. He puffed a few times, then passed the pipe to the headman of Shungopavi. When the headman had smoked it empty, he handed it back to the Awat'ovi leader. The latter carefully cleaned the bowl and put the pipe away. Now the Shungopavi leader asked, "All right, tell me why you are about at this time of night."

"Well yes," he replied, "I'm not a happy man. These children of mine at Awat'ovi are out of control. They have no respect for anyone, nor do they listen to my words. Recently we had a mixed hunt. They rode over my daughter and killed her. Of course, I took care of her in the proper way, but I'm still furious inside. I'm very depressed. I want the village erased from the earth. Awat'ovi is to disappear completely. Let it turn into a mound of dirt with nothing but grass growing over it. This is the reason I came," he explained.

"Is that so?"

"Yes. That's why I want you to tell your young men, your best runners, to practice running and get in shape. Four days from now I'll come back again." With that he got up.

Thereupon the Awat'ovi leader returned home. Upon arrival he ordered his own young men, relatives of his, to practice running too. They did as bidden and from that day on ran to make themselves strong. The people in both villages did not give it any thought. Neither in Awat'ovi nor in Shungopavi did anyone know what the two headmen were after. No one paid any attention to the runners. On the fourth day, at night, Ta'palo once again went to Shungopavi. The leader there had already gone to bed, but since he was expecting his friend from Awat'ovi, he was not asleep yet. When he heard that his visitor had arrived, he got up and stoked the fire. "You've come," he said as Ta'palo entered.

piw. "Um pituy?" yaw aw kita, pam aqw pakiqw.

"Owi. Ura pi nu' uumi tutapta. Ura um uuhongvi'aymuy nana-munwa'ayalawni. Ya um panti? Ya pay suutaq'ewya?" kita yaw awi'.

"Owiy," yaw kita, "pay nanamunwa; pay suutaq'ewya.

"Antsa'ay," yaw kita. "It hapi nu' yantaqat yan wuuwankyangw nu' ung pu' ayatay," yaw kita aw pam Awat'ongaqw mongwi. "Um hapi yangqw uuhongvi'aymuy ikitsokiy aqw hoonani. Wawarkatsin-muy uma akw hapi aqwyaniy," yaw aw kita. "Naalöyömniiqam uuhohongvit katsinmuy yuyaani. Nen pu' puma pumuy akwyani. Pankyaakyangw uma ikitsokiy aqwye' itam nanamunwaniy," yaw kita awi'.

"It um yantaqat wuuwantay?" yaw pam Songoopapmongwi aw kita.

"Owi, it nu' naawakna. Paayis taalat hapi ep uma yuuyaat pu' ason naalös taalat ep hapi uma aqw ikitsokiy aqwyani," kita yaw kur piw awnit pu' yaw aapiy'o.

Meh, yaw naalös hapi taalat aqw tavi. Noq pu' yaw oovi pep Songoopave puma hongvi'a'yat paayis piw natwantota, nanamunwa. Ep pu' paayis taalat ep pu' yaw puma hakim naalöyömniiqam yaw yuuyahiwta. Pu' yumat yaw amungem hoy'ankwivi'yyungwa, pu' piw tuupevut. Put yaw amungem paas ep tumaltota. Noq suukya yaw tiyo Hömsonat yuwsi, pu' suukya yaw Angwusngöntaqat, pu' suukya Leetotovit pu' i' nuutungkniiqa Sikyaatayot yawi'. Paasa'-niiqamuy yaw puma yuuyaha. Pu' yaw oovi nalöstalqat ep pu' puma awat'omiqya, put na'mangwuy yankyaakyangwya. Pu' yaw puma epeq ökiiqe pu' kiisonmi yungya. Pay yaw pepeq kiisonvi Songoo-pavit ep kiisonvit amum namihayawta. Pep pu' yaw puma pahokive pu' yaw puma put na'mangwuy o'ya. Paasat pu' yaw pepeq Awat'o-veq pu' tsa'akmongwi pu' yaw tsa'lawu, tootimuy yaw wangway-lawu: "Tootimuy, pangqe' uma sonqa yeesey," yaw kita. "Uma pew kiisonmi tsovawmaniy. Yep ima katsinam ökiiqe umumi nanamun-wan'ökiqw oovi uma qa sööwuyat pan tsovawmaniy," yanhaqam yaw tsa'lawu.

Pu' son pi tootim, taataqt, hohongvit qa nanaptaqe pu' yaw aw wukotsovalti, kiisonmi. Paasat pu' yaw aw pituni. Paasat pu' yaw puma pephaqam oovi pan nanavö'ya, yuyutya yaw puma. Pay yaw ephaqam katsinam mootitotangwu, pu' pay mimawatyangwu, Awat'ongaqw tootim. Pantsatskya yaw puma pepniqw pay yaw nuwu na'mangwu'am tsaa' pee'iwma. Tsaa' pee'iwmakyangw nuwu yaw suukw wikit aqw pitu. Suukya yaw tuupepwiki peeti. Paasat pu'

"Yes. Remember I instructed you to ask your strongmen to practice running. Did you do that? Were they willing to do so?" he asked.

"Sure," he replied. "They are racing and they are doing it willingly."

"Very good. Now this is what I had in mind when I told you to do this," said the Awat'ovi leader. "Send your best runners over to my village. Have them come in the guise of Runner kachinas, just four of them. Upon their arrival at my village, we'll race each other."

"So this is what you were thinking?" the Shungopavi leader exclaimed.

"Yes, that's what I want. Three days hence have your men put on their costumes and on the fourth I want you to come to my village." With that Ta'palo departed again.

So the date had been set four days hence. For the next three days the Shungopavi runners practiced again and raced each other. At the end of the third day, four of the men were getting ready. Their mothers had prepared the customary gifts of boiled corn and roasted sweet corn for them. One of the young men dressed as Hömsona, another as Angwusngöntaqa. The third costumed himself as Leetotovi and the last one as Sikyaatayo. On the fourth day the four kachinas went to Awat'ovi with their presents. As soon as they arrived, they headed to the plaza. The Awat'ovi plaza is similar to the one in Shungopavi. They laid down their gifts at the shrine located in the plaza. Right away the crier chief of Awat'ovi made an announcement from the rooftop. He was calling all the boys: "You boys out there, gather at the plaza. These Runner kachinas have arrived to compete with you. Don't tarry, but come at once." This is what he announced publicly.

Obviously, boys and young men who were able runners had heard the announcement, for they assembled in large numbers at the plaza. Soon the races got under way. And so they competed there, running against each other. Once in a while the kachinas were first, then the other side, the boys from Awat'ovi. As this continued the kachinas' presents, which were bestowed on the winners, were getting fewer and fewer. Finally, only one bunch of baked sweet corn remained. A boy from Awat'ovi picked it up and put it aside. "I'm going to win this," he proclaimed. "I'll race anyone for it. But I know it will be mine," he boasted.

yaw Awat'oveq hak tiyo put ep kwusut pu' ayo' tavi. "Nu' hapi it
pö'aniy," yaw kitat ayo' tavi. "Nu' oovi hiitawat amum warikni. Pay
sonqa nu' itniy," yaw kita. Paasat pu' yaw oovi pantiqw pu' yaw Hömsona yaw amumni.
Pam yaw naatavi. Paasat pu' yaw oovi puma wari. A'ni yaw hak
wari, Awat'oveq tiyo. Pas pi yaw Hömsona qa hin wiiki'yma. Pay
yaw put qa nawip qa wiiki'yma kura'. Pam yaw pay put angk. Noq
pu' yaw i' Hömsona pay haq oovi angkniikyangw haqam pu' pam
put nuutayta. Pu' tiyo pi naala pas aqw pitut pu' angqw pay ahoyniikyangw it Hömsonat aw pituqw paasat pu' yaw pam kur put ngu'a.
Ngu'at pu' yaw put tuuva, tiyot. Tuuvat pu' yaw atsmi wuuvi. Atsmi
wupt paasat pu' yaw poyoy horokna. Hömsona pi poyo'ytangwu.
Putakw pam hakiy höömiyat tukungwu, hömsomayat. Pu' yaw oovi
pam put atsve pas tsokiwkyangw paasat pu' pam poyoy akw pu' put
hiikwamiq yaw söökwikna. Paysoq yaw ungway pavoya. Yantsana
yaw pam putniqw pay yaw hapi kur puma nuutungk. Noq oovi i'
na'am'iwtaqa, katsinna'am'iwtaqa, pep Awat'oveq paas yaw amungem nakwakwusit kur tumalta. Pu' put paas pam yaw ep inkyangw
nuutayta. Yaw hapi yukiltiqw pu' yaw pam pumuy put huytaqw pu'
ahoyyani. Pay yaw panis oovi Hömsona put tiyot pantsant, wunuptut, pu' angqw mimuy sungwamuy amumi pitutokyangw pu' yaw
amumi maasakna. "Tume'ey!" Son pi qa yan maasakna. Pay yaw
paasat puma yuutu. Qa sööwu yaw puma nakwakwusiy, paahoy
tungwla'yyungwt pay yaw puma paasat pangqw yuutu, watqa.

Noq yaw oovi paasat pay puma aapiy yuutukqe pay haq'iwyungqw pu' tiyo yaw qa ahoy pitu. Pu' yaw sinom pay hin wuuwaya, "Kya pam hinti haqamo. Pas kya pam put hintsana." Pay pi
yan sino wuwni'ytangwuniqw yan yaw suuwuwaya.

Pu' yaw peetu aqwya. Aqw yuutu haqe' pi pan yuyutyaqw pangsoq yaw hakim suupootayaqe pay yaw tutwa. Pepehaq yaw mokpu
wa'ökiwta. Paasat pu' yaw pangqaqwa, "Pay kur pam it niinay," yaw
kitota. Paasat pu' yaw sinmuy aa'awnaya. "Pay kur pam it niinay,"
yaw kitota. Pavan yaw hin unangwa. "Itam amungkyani. Itam qöqyani," yan hingqawkyaakyangw pu' yaw totim, taataqt kiikiy ang
yuutu, tunipiy oovi. Pay yaw hak naap hiita tunipiy kwuse' put
yawkyangw pangqaqw pu' yaw puma pumuy amungkningwu. Pu'
yaw peeti kawayvokmu'yyungqam pumuy ang yayvaqe pu' pumuy
akw pu' puma pangqaqw pumuy ngööngöyay, katsinmuy.

Pu' yaw puma pumuy amungkya. Antsa yaw paasat ima katsinam pay Awat'ongaqw haani tutskwami. Tutskwami awyaniiqe

The Hömsona kachina stepped forward, ready to meet the challenge. The race was on. The boy from Awat'ovi ran extremely fast, and the Hömsona was not about to catch up with him. Or rather, he pretended not being able to catch up. He just ran after him. When the kachina had fallen way behind, he simply waited somewhere for the boy to return. By now the latter had reached the turning point all alone and was dashing back. The instant he came upon the Hömsona, the latter grabbed him and threw him on the ground. Having the boy down, he jumped on top of him and drew his knife. A Hömsona always carries a knife, which he uses to cut off a loser's hair, usually the knot that is tied behind the head. But instead of cutting off the boy's hair, he thrust his knife into his throat. The blood just spurted out. This is what Hömsona did, and for this reason he had raced this boy last. Meanwhile, the kachina father who was taking care of the Runner kachinas at Awat'ovi had fashioned all the necessary prayer feathers for them and was waiting with the feathers in a tray. At the close of the race he was going to distribute these prayer offerings to the kachinas, whereupon they were supposed to return home. The Hömsona who had murdered the boy now got up. Approaching his partners, he motioned to them, "Come on, let's go!" With that all four Runner kachinas dashed off. They did not waste any time accepting the prayer feathers and prayer sticks, but sped off as fast as their feet could carry them.

The kachinas were already far away, yet the boy who had challenged the Hömsona still was not back. The spectators began to worry. "Something must have happened to him. Maybe the Hömsona did something to him." These were some of the thoughts that crossed the people's minds.

A few of the spectators decided to go and check. They went along the same course where the runners had raced, and found what they were looking for. The boy was lying in his blood, dead. They exclaimed, "The Hömsona must have killed him." They informed the other spectators. "He was killed!" they shouted. The ensuing commotion was tremendous. "Let's go after them. Let's kill them," the voices of the boys and men could be heard as they ran to their houses for weapons. Grabbing any weapon they could find, they rushed after the fleeing kachinas. Some of those who owned horses mounted them and galloped off in pursuit of the fugitives.

pangqw pu' yaw puma naanangk yuutukiwta, pönawit. Oovi yaw puma Walpiy tatkye'haqe' Huktuwivahaqe' pangqe' yaw pumayaqw pangso yaw Hömsona maangu'iwma. Pay yaw puma suntoti, pay yaw maamangu'a puma, katsinam. Pay yaw oovi aapiy qa wuuyavotiqw pangsohaqam pu' yaw Hömsona pay tis pas qa wiiki'yma pumuy. Noq oovi yaw pangqe' kya pi pumayaqw pu' yaw ima Awat'ongaqw kawaymuy akwyaqam pu' yaw Hömsonat wiikiya. Pu' yaw puma put pongo. Pongokqe pu' yaw puma put niinaya. Mumuutota yaw hoohuy akw. Puma yaw put niinayat paapiy pu' puma mimuywatuy piw amungkya. Su'aw yaw oovi pephaqam puma tsomooya'ytaqat aw ökiiqe put aw tupo ökiwisqw pangso pu' yaw it Angwusngöntaqat pu' yaw wiikiya. Pu' yaw piw put an yukunaya. Yaw pongokqe piw niinaya. Paapiy pu' yaw puma lööqmuy paasat ngöytota. Yaw aw taavangqöymihaqami, Musangnuviy yuk hopqöymihaqami, pangqe ura wukovöva, put pangso puma yaw haykyalni'ywisqw pangso pu' Leetotovit pu' yaw piw wiikiya. Pu' yaw put piw an yukunaya. Paapiy pu' yaw Sikyaatayo peeti. Pam pu' yaw aw pövami pitut pu' ahoy yorikqw pay yaw naat qa pas angk haykyalaya. Pep pu' yaw paasat pu' pam kwaatsiy tsoopa. Kwaatsiy tsoopat yaw akw naavootsiwa. Naalös yaw oovi pam put akw naavootsiwt pu' himutskit atsmiq put tsokya. Pantit pu' yaw pam aqw pövamiq hawt pu' ayo'wat wuuvi.

Noq ima pi Songoopapmongwi pu' Awat'opmongwi pan yaw kur puma put pasiwni'yta. Kur yaw hiituywatuy naat pangso pövami qa ökiqw wiikiye' pay pi yaw qöqyani. Pu' yaw kur himuwa pay pöövat yamakqw pu' sen pay piw soosoyam nöngakqw yaw aw ökye' pay qa hiitawat niinayani. Yan yaw kur puma put yuki'yta, mongwit. Noq yaw oovi Awat'ongaqw puma tootim, taataqt pumuy katsinmuy amungkyaniqw yan hapi yaw kur mongwi amumi tutapta. "Kur hapi pay pöövat nöngakqw uma amungk ökye' pay uma qa amumi hintsatskyat angqw ahoyyani. Pu' kur naat himuwa pöövat qa yamakqw sen piw soosoyam qa nöngakqw pay uma soosokmuy qöqyani. Pu' piw kur himuwa ayo' yamakqw pay uma qa aqwhaqami angkyani." It yaw kur paas pam amumi tutaptaqw puma pangqw pumuy amungkya.

Yantiqw pu' yaw oovi puma pangso pövami ökiiqe pu' put kwaatsiyat tutwa. Himutskit yaw atsveq tsoki. Pep pu' yaw puma pangqaqwa, "Pay kur pam yamay," yaw kitota. "Pay ura yamakqw pay itam qa awhaqami angkyani." Kitotaqe pu' yaw pay pangso puma paasavo put oovi angkyat pu' ahoy pangqaqw ninma. Noq

The chase was on. Sure enough, the kachinas could be seen hurrying down to the plain below Awat'ovi. Upon reaching level ground they sped on, one behind the other, following the contours of a wash. They were moving along the southeast side of Walpi, past Huktuwi, when the Hömsona began to tire. Soon it happened to all of them. The kachinas were getting tired. A little while later they came to a place where the Hömsona who killed the boy could not keep up with the others any longer. It was at this place where the riders from Awat'ovi caught up with the kachina. They quickly surrounded him and killed him by shooting their arrows into him. No sooner had they cut him down than they resumed their pursuit of the others. They had just reached a little hillock and were nearing its base when the Angwusngöntaqa was caught. He was dispatched in the same manner. The men surrounded him and shot him to death. Then they went after the remaining two. At a place in the southwest, northeast of Mishongnovi, there is a large wash. The pursuers were approaching this wash when they caught up with the Leetotovi. Again they dealt with him in the same way. Now only the Sikyaatayo was left. He had reached the wash by now and when he looked back, he saw that his pursuers were not too close yet. He took off his mask and discharmed himself by swinging it repeatedly over his head. Four times he did the discharming act, then placed the mask on a bush, jumped down into the wash, and climbed out again on the other side.

This happened exactly according to the plan the leaders from Shungopavi and Awat'ovi had hatched out. Should any of the kachinas be caught before reaching the wash, they were to be killed. In case one managed to cross the wash, however, or even if all of them should do so before the pursuers' arrival, they were to be spared. This is what the two headmen had agreed upon. Apparently, the leader from Awat'ovi had instructed the boys and men to this extent before they took up their pursuit. "If the kachinas cross the wash before you, you are not to harm them. They can return home. But if you catch up with them before one or all of them escape across the wash, you may kill them all. The one who crosses the wash, however, you are not to chase after any longer." This is what Ta'palo had impressed on the men prior to their departure.

The Sikyaatayo had just crossed the wash when his pursuers reached the place where he had left his mask. They found it perched on a bush. They said, "It looks like he got across. As you recall, we are not supposed to follow him any longer." With that they stopped their

Sikyaatayot hapi yaw oovi qa wiikiya. Put yaw suukw qa niinaya.
Paasat pu' yaw antsa pam oovi suukya ahoy pitu, Songoopave.
Pu' yaw mongwi aw pangqawu, "Kwakwhay, um pituy," yaw aw
kita. "Kwakwhay, kur ung qa enang niinaya. Yantaniy," yaw kita.
"Pay oovi um yep qatuniy," yaw kita, put hakiy awi, put Sikyaatayot
akwniiqat.

Paasat pu' yaw ep mihikqw pu' pay pam pi suyan hakiy nuutayta piiw, Songoopapmongwi. Niiqe pay yaw as oovi pam piw wa'ökt
pay yaw pam qa puuwi. Noq pu' yaw antsa Awat'ongaqw mongwi
piw hisatniqw ep pitu. Pu' piw yaw an pam Songoopapmongwi qööt
pu' tuuvingta, "Ta'ay, um son pi qa hintiqw waynumay," yaw aw
kita.

"Owiy," yaw aw kita, "pay antsa pi it nu' ura uumi naawaknaqw
itam hapi aw antiy," yaw aw kita. "Itam paykomuy uukitsokiy
angqw katsinmuy qöqya. Pu' inuupeq uma suukw. Noq itam hapi aw
antiy," yaw kita Awat'ongaqw mongwi. "Noq nu' oovi haalaytiy,"
yaw kita. "Noq oovi qaavo um aqw pumuy itimuy tsamtoniy," kita
yaw put Songoopapmongwit awi. "Momoymuy, mamantuy angqw
um tsamni. Taataqtuy, tootimuy, wuuwukwmuy pay um qöyani. Pay
pi tsangaw um nuy nakwhanaqe aw inungem antiqw. Nu' haalay-
tiqw oovi yantaniy," yaw kita awi'.

Paasat pu' yaw Songoopapmongwi ephaqam yanta, wuuwanlawu. Pas yaw wuuyavotiqw pu' yaw aw pangqawu, "Qa'ey," yaw
aw kita, "pay itam sukw uusinoy niinaya. Suhimutiyot itam niinaya.
Pu' uma paykomuy isinmuy piw qöqya. Pay itam naami antsanay.
Pay itam sunantiy," yaw kita. "Pay itam qa piw peetuy qöqyani. Pu'
pay nu' uusinmuy piw qe'ni. Pay nu' son pumuy pangqaqw pew
tsamni. Pay nu' put qa naawakna. Pay nu' son pantiniy," yaw aw
kita, Awat'ongaqw mongwit awi'.

Pu' yaw tuwat ephaqam yanta. Nit pu' yaw pangqawu, "Is ohi,
antsa'ay," yaw kita. "Suupan pay as itam nan'ivaq sunan qa antiqw
um pay sonqa nakwhaniy," yaw kita. "Pay nu' as pas pepeq put
ikitsokiy tuuvoyniqat naawaknaqe oovi yan it naawaknaqw pay pi
um qa nakwhay," yaw aw kita. "Noq pay pi oovi yantani. Pay pi
yantani," kitat pu' yaw wunuptut pu' yaw nima.

Yanhaqam yaw pam pep navota Songoopavenit pu' pangqaqw
nima, qa haalaykyangw. Pituuqe pu' yaw pam put aw wuuwanta.
A'ni yaw pam put aw wuuwankyangw pu' yaw paasat Orayvit pam
piw tuwa. Kur yaw pam pangso. Pay oovi ep mihikqw pu' yaw pam
pangqw Oraymiqa. Orayve yaw pituuqe pu' mongwit kiiyat aw'i. Pu'

pursuit and headed for home. Thus the Sikyaatayo was the only one they failed to catch. He alone was not killed.

Meanwhile, the boy who had impersonated the Sikyaatayo kachina had returned to Shungopavi. The village leader said to him, "Thank you for coming. I'm grateful they did not kill you. This is how it will be now. You can live here now."

That same night the village leader from Shungopavi was clearly expecting a visitor again. Once again he had bedded down, but he was not asleep. Sure enough, it was not long before the headman from Awat'ovi arrived. As on the previous occasions the Shungopavi leader stoked the fire, then he asked, "Well, you must be around for a reason."

"Yes," Ta'palo replied, "you did indeed do what I asked you to do. We killed three kachinas from your village, you killed one of our boys. We did just as agreed." The Awat'ovi leader continued, "I'm happy the way things worked out. So tomorrow I want you to come to the village and round up my children. You can gather the women and girls. The men, young and old, however, you must kill. I'm glad you consented to my plan and did exactly what I asked you to do. I'm happy that it shall be this way now."

When the leader from Shungopavi heard this, he just sat there, speechless, mulling things over in his mind. Finally, after a long pause, he spoke. "No," he said, "we killed one of your people, a handsome boy. You, on the other hand, killed three of my relatives. So we are even. We did the same thing to one another. No more killing. I refuse to do that to your people. I can't bring your womenfolk over here. That's not what I wanted. I simply can't do that."

Now the Awat'ovi leader sat there, all surprised. "Too bad, indeed," he replied. "It seems we committed the same crime, so I thought you would agree to my scheme. It's my desire that my village get erased from the earth. For this reason I came up with this plan. I was under the impression that you were for it. But now, I think, this was all in vain." With that, Ta'palo got up and left for home.

This is the reply the Awat'ovi leader received in Shungopavi. Understandably, he was unhappy. Upon arriving home, he mulled over the situation. As he was wondering what to do, it occurred to him to try the Oraibis. That same night he headed over to this village. Upon reaching his destination he went straight to the village leader's house. The two headmen exchanged the customary smoke. When

yaw pan puma piw naatsotsongna. Paas yaw puma puuvut oovi mongvastiqw paasat pu' yaw Orayve mongwi put Awat'ongaqw mongwit pu' yaw aw pangqawu, "Ta'ay," yaw aw kita, "um yaavahaqaqw hak waynuma," yaw aw kita. "Son pi um qa hiita oovi'o. Son pi um paysoq waynuma. Hiita oovi um waynumay?" yaw aw kita.

"Hep owiy," yaw aw kita. Pu' yaw pam put pep aw lalvaya hintiqey. "Nu' Walmi as mooti taqa'nangwtit pu' Songoopami piw. Noq puma nuy qa nakwhanaya. Noq um ikwatsiy," yaw aw kita. "Um isungwa. Kur nu' hakiy piw aw taqa'nangwtiniqe oovi nu' angqaqw peqw ung tuway," yaw aw kita. "Pas pepeq Awat'oveq itim pas qa unangwtalyay," yaw kita. "Pas qa hakiy puma kyaptsi'yyungwa, qa hakiy aw tuuqayyungwa. Wuuwuyom qa hiitu'u. Momoymuy, mamantuy kwangwa'ewlalwa. Pu' yang it tuutuskyat pu' tiitikivet sakwini'ywisa, qa hiita'yyungwa. Pay ima Kastiilam, popwaqt, pay puma pas yep pas yesniqey pu' it puma tunatyawkyaakyangw ahoy öki. Pay yaniwti ura atkya naat itam yesngwuniqw'ö. Noq pay as pam pas ikitsokiy pas tuuvoyniqat nu' naawakna. Pay pam pas qa haqamni. Pu' um oovi inumi unangwtave' soosok hiita umni. Momoymuy, mamantuy um angqw tsamni. Puma yep umuy pa'angwayani uma wuuhaqtiniqat. Itaavavasay uma uylalwe' ang hiita a'aniwnayani. Soosok it nu' hiita uumi no'ani um nuy pa'angwaqöy," yaw aw kita. "Um ipava," kita yaw awi. "Pay pas pam qa haqamni, Awat'ovi," kita yaw pam Orayve mongwit awniqw pu' yaw pam piw tuwat aw pas wuuwa.

Pas aw wuuwat pu' yaw aw tuwat lavayti. "Ta'ay," yaw aw kita, "pay pi put um naawakna. Niikyangw put um inumi pangqawqw puma hapi uutimuy," yaw aw kita. "Ya pay hak naap timuy qöyangwuy?" yaw aw kita.

"Nuu'uy," yaw kita. "Nu' pan naawakna. Owi, pante' i' hapi pay ihimuni, qa hakiy piiwu. Pay nu' ason ep hin naami navotni. Pay son yantani, son pam qatsini. Qa lomaqatsi."

Yaw kitaaqe pay pi pam pas suutaq'ewa. Yaw suutaq'ewa Awat'ovit pas kiiqötiniqat, naawakna pay pas qa haqamniqat. Paasat pu' pay oovi Orayvi yaw nakwha. "Niikyangw nu' pay tutskwat qe'ni. Pas haq'urniqw oovi'o. Pay nu' imuy mamantuy, momoymuysani. Niikyangw pay nu' son naalaniy," yaw kita. "I' hoskaya. Pay nu' son naalani. Pay son nu' hakiy piw qa sungwa'ykyangwniy," yaw kita put mongwit awi, Awat'ongaqw. "Pay son aye'wat kitsokivit qa inumumyani," kita yaw kur pam Owat'opmongwit awi'.

Noq paasat pu' yaw Owat'opmongwi pu' Orayepmongwit aw

they were done, the leader from Oraibi said to the headman of Awat-
'ovi, "Well now, you've come a long distance. This must be for a
reason. You can't just be walking around. What's on your mind?" he
asked.

"I certainly have a reason," the Awat'ovi leader replied. He then
gave an account of what he had done so far. "The first place I went to
ask for help was Walpi, then Shungopavi. But they both declined.
You're my friend and partner. I need someone's help, so I selected
you. That's why I came here." Ta'palo went on, "My children over in
Awat'ovi are out of control. They have no respect for people nor do
they listen to anyone. The elders are nothing to them. They are ravishing the women and girls. Our shrines and ceremonies are in
shambles. They don't mean anything. These Spaniards, nothing but
sorcerers and witches, are hoping to settle here for good. That's why
they came. The same thing took place when we still lived in the
underworld. Now I want my village erased from the surface of the
earth. It is to disappear completely. If you assist me, therefore, you
can have everything. You can bring women and girls here. They can
help you to increase in number. If you plant our fields, they will yield
large crops for you. I'll let you have all these things if you help me.
After all, you're my older brother. Awat'ovi is to be no more." This is
what Ta'palo said to the Oraibi leader. The latter, in turn, reflected
about the proposal.

When he was done thinking he said, "All right, so this is what
you want. What you said refers to your children. Does one kill one's
own children?" he asked.

"Yes, I do," Ta'palo replied. "That's the way I want it. It will be
my responsibility, no one else's. I'll find out what will happen to me.
But life in my village cannot go on the way it is. Life there is bad."

By responding in this manner Ta'palo showed his determination
to follow through with the deed. He was willing to have Awat'ovi
totally destroyed. It was his desire for the village to disappear. Now
the Oraibi leader accepted. "But I don't want your land. It's too far
away. I'll take the girls and women. Also, I can't do this alone. This is
an enormous task. I can't be the only one. I must have partners in
this," he said to the Awat'ovi leader. "The other villages will probably support me."

Ta'palo replied, "The Walpi headman refused, explaining that
this was not their custom. I think the two of us should go there. We'll

pangqawu, "Walpeq mongwi pay qa nakwhay. Qa pan yaw pam
pumuy tuwi'amniiqat kitaaqe qa nakwhay. Itam naama aqwniy,"
yaw kita. "Itam naama aqwniqw hingqawni pi," kitaaqe pu' yaw
puma oovi naama pangsoqa, Walmiqa. Niikyangw pu' yaw pay
puma qa kikmongwit awnit yaw puma qaleetaqat hakiy awi, qalee-
taqmongwit awi'. Pep pu' yaw puma pituqw pu' yaw piw puma
tsootsongi. Paas yaw put mongvastotiqw yaw pumuy tuuvingta
hintiqw waynumqat. Paasat pu' yaw Owat'opmongwi put aw hin
iqwniiqey put yu'a'ata. Soosok yaw pam put aw yu'a'ata hiita
Orayvit aa'awnaqey, momoymuy, mamantuy, paavasat aa'awna. Pu'
yaw Orayvi tutskwat pay qe'ni. Yaw yaavaq pami', Orayngaqw. Noq
yaw kur pantaniqw. Noq yaw oovi Orayvi hapi mamantuy, momoy-
muyni. Pu' yaw Walpi pa'angwanik pu' pam tutskwat, Awat'oveq
tutskwayat.

Yuk pu' yaw paasat pay qaleetaqmongwi nakwha. "Ta'ay," yaw
kita, "kur antsa pantani. Pay nu' sonqa umumi unangwtapniy," yaw
kita. "Itam kur oovi mongwit awyaniy," kitaaqe paasat pu' puma
pangqw kikmongwit awya. Pep pu' paasat piw puma pan hintoti-
kyaakyangw put mongvastotikyaakyangw paasat pu' i' qaleetaqa pu'
put mongwit aw pangqawu hin puma naawinyaqat. "Orayvit pay
naanakwha kiipokyaniqey. Noq oovi itam hapi Orayvituy pa'a-
ngwayani Awat'opsinmuy qöqyaniqey."

Paasat pu' yaw mongwi pangqawu, Walpeq mongwi, "Pay i' pi
as qa itaatuwiy," yaw aw kita. "Itam yangqw pangso naat piw Hopi-
sinmuy aw itaasinmuy aw itam songyawnen pi kiipokye' qöqyani,
itaasinmuy, naap itaasinmuy. Qa itaatuwiy. Noq um pi put aw
mongwi, um pi qaleetaqa. Noq um nakwhaqw pay kur nu' put hin
angqw ayo' yamakniy," kitaaqe pay yaw paasat pi pay kur hin nawus
qe'ni. Yantiqe pu' pay yaw songyawnen hapi oovi qaleetaqat pam qa
anguukye' ö'qalniqe pu' pay yaw oovi nakwha. Pay yaw aw
unangwtapna. Niikyangw pam hapi Walpi pay Awat'ovit tutskwayat
oovi, paavasayat.

Pu' yaw puma it yu'a'aykuyaqe pay aw pi sunti. Pay qaleetaqa
nakwhaqw pay mongwi pi kur hintiniqe pu' pay oovi qaleetaqay aw
tuqayvastaqe pu' pay oovi nakwha. Yanhaqam yaw puma pepehaq it
yu'a'aykuyat pu' pay pangqw naanahoy ninma.

Niikyangw naalös taalat ep hapi yaw masiphikqwhaqam ima
yaw pangqw awyani Awat'omi, Walngaqwniqw pu' Orayngaqw pu'
haqam owatpelpahaqe' pay haak yaw na'uyi'yyungwni. Ason yaw
sinom tokvaqw paasat pu' Awat'opmongwi yaw pumuy pay pangqw

go together and see what he has to say." With that the two headed over to Walpi. But instead of going to the village leader, they sought out the warrior chief. Once again they first smoked. Upon completion of the smoking ritual the warrior chief inquired about the reason for their coming, and Ta'palo explained. He repeated what he had told the Oraibi leader, that he had offered him the Awat'ovi womenfolk and fields. That the Oraibis were not interested in the fields because they were too far away. That it was going to be that way. He could have the girls and women. If the Walpis were to help, they could have the Awat'ovi land.

At this point the Warrior chief agreed. "All right," he said, "let it be this way. You can count on me. I'll help you. So let's go to my leader." Thereupon they went to the village chief. After completion of the customary smoking ritual, the warrior explained to the leader what they had planned, that the Oraibis had agreed to the attack and that they would assist Ta'palo in wiping out the people of Awat'ovi.

Once more the Walpi leader asserted his position. "This is not our custom. We would be raiding Hopis. This would mean killing our people, our very own people. That's not our tradition. But you are in charge, you are the warrior chief. If you have no objections, there's no way out for me." The Walpi leader was forced to go along now. He did not want to interfere with his warrior chief, which meant that he had agreed to the undertaking. He too threw in his support. In return, the Walpis were to be awarded the Awat'ovi land, its fields.

All three of them had discussed the matter now and they were of one mind. Because the warrior chief consented, the village leader had no other choice but obey him and go along with his decision. This is how they talked there, and then the three men parted, each going home in his own direction.

What had been agreed upon was that four days hence, at dusk, they would come over to Awat'ovi, both from Walpi and Oraibi, and would hide along the boulder-strewn slopes there. Once the people of Awat'ovi were asleep, Ta'palo would let them know about it or give them a signal. Therefore, with four days at their disposal, the three departed for home. They would need to work on their weapons, such as bows and arrows, and ready what it takes to hide out. Everything that relates to killing and war had to be prepared.

Awat'ongaqw son pi hin pumuy qa aa'awnani, maasaknani amumi. Oovi yaw puma paasa' hapi taalat makiwa'ykyaakyangw, naalös taalat makiwa'ykyaakyangw, pangqaqw naanahoyya. Pay hapi puma tunipit tumala'yyungwni, awtat, hoohut, pu' hiita hak akw naatupkyangwuniqw puta. Pay puuvut hiihiita naqöyhiita, naqöy'a'wiwat.

Paasat pu' yaw pam oovi Orayngaqw mongwi kiy ep ahoy pituuqe pu' yaw pam qaleetaqmomngwituy tsovala. Tsovalaqe pu' pumuy aa'awna, yan Awat'oveq mongwi itamumi naawaknay. It yaw pam soosok amumi lalvaya. "Noq oovi yaapiy uma put tunipit tumala'yyungwni. Naalös taalat ep hapi itam yaw aqwyani. Uma oovi put tumala'yvayaniy," kita pam pep pumuy momngwituy, qaleetaqmomngwituy.

Nit pu' paasat Orayve mongwi pu' yaw pam lööq tiw'aymuy yuk Musangnuminit Songoopami piw hoona. Amumi yaw pangqawu, "Uma pangsoni. Uma aw tuu'awmani, uma itamumyani. Uma itamum Awat'opmongwit pa'angwani. Yan pam itamumi naawakna. Noq oovi uma pangso nan'ivo tuu'awmaqw itamumi unangwtatveqw itam soosoyamyaniy." Yan yaw pumuy ayataqe pangso pumuy hoona. Ephaqam naat Supawlavi pay qa haqam.

Pu' yaw oovi pam suukya Musangnumi, pu' suukya Songoopami. Musangnuvi pay yaw nakwha amumumniqey. Pay yaw sunakwha. "Antsa'ay, pay nu' sonqa amumumniy," kitaaqe pam pay yaw qa hin naawaknat sunakwha. Pu' Songoopave hapi pay mooti ura Awat'opmongwi piw putumaqw pep pu' paasat mongwi put tuwa'ykyangw pu' pangqawu, "Pay itam pi ura it hiniwtapnaya. Noq oovi pay pi aw aniwti. Noq pay naat nu' piw oovi son nakwhaniy," yaw kita. "Nu pay qe'ni. Nu' pay son pangqaqw pumuy mamantuy, momoymuy pew tsamni. Nu' son yep ikitsokiy ep pumuy oyi'ytani. Noq pay pi oovi pam hakiy epmantani. Hak nukpananen, qahopinen, pay pi amumumninik amumumni. Hak amumi unangwtapninik amumumni. Nu' pay qe'niy," kitaaqe pay yaw pam qa nakwha. Pam pay yaw sinmuy amumi no'a, pam pay hakiy epmantani. Yanti yaw pami', Songoopavi. Yaw qa nakwha.

Paapiy pu' yaw oovi puma put tumala'yvaya, tunipit, naalös taalat aqw hapi puma tokila'ykyaakyangw. Pu' yaw oovi puma put pan tumaltota. Noq pu' yaw naalös taalat aqw pitu. Ep pu' yaw puma yuuyahiwta. Yuuyahiwtaqe pu' yaw tapkiwmaqw pu' yaw paasat puma nankwusani tuwvöötayaniqey oovi. Pu' yaw oovi haqami pi songqa tsovaltiqw pep pu' yaw Orayve mongwi pu' amumi nakwsuqe pu' pumuy amumi haalayti. "Kwakwhay," yaw amumi kita,

As soon as the Oraibi leader arrived back home, he gathered his warrior chiefs. Having done so, he told them that the Awat'ovi leader had requested their assistance. He shared every detail with them. "Start at once to get your weapons ready. We'll march in four days. So go to work," he bade his warrior chiefs.

Next, the Oraibi leader decided to send two of his nephews to Mishongnovi and Shungopavi. He told them, "I want you to go to these villages and ask them to join our forces. Tell them to come with us to help the Awat'ovi leader. He needs us. If you inform them at both places and they agree to help us, we can all fight together." This is what he ordered his nephews to do, and then sent them on their way. The village of Shipaulovi did not exist yet at that time.

One of them headed to Mishongnovi, the other to Shungopavi. The Mishongnovis were all for joining them. They agreed right away. "Sure, you can count on me," said their leader. He consented without hesitation. The Awat'ovi leader had, of course, already been to Shungopavi in the very beginning. Upon receiving the messenger from Oraibi the Shungopavi chief said to him, "As you recall, the race we staged with its tragic ending was a terrible thing. Beyond that I can't agree to anything. I won't go. I don't want to bring the Awat'ovi girls and women here. I will not allow them into this village. Let every man here decide for himself. If someone is so evil and bad that he wants to join in with you and the others, let him do so. I, for one, will not go." He absolutely refused to be part of the attack. With that he gave his people permission to decide for themselves. This is what the Shungopavi leader did. He remained steadfast.

From that day on the men concentrated on their weapons, knowing full well that they only had four days. Soon the fourth day, their deadline, arrived. Now they were getting ready. It was toward late afternoon when they were about to set out on the warpath. The Oraibi leader made it a point to meet with the warriors where they had assembled. He was grateful to them. "Thank you all," he said. "With happy hearts go forward to your destination. Go in strength," he encouraged them. "I'll be waiting here for you. Don't worry about anything as you go along. It was the Awat'ovi leader who wanted it this way." After these words the Oraibis started out. There was a huge number of them, boys and men.

"pay uma haalaykyaakyangw aqwhaqamiyani. Hakim öqawwis-
ngwuy," yaw kita. "Pay nu' yepeq naat umuy nuutaytani. Pay uma
qa hin wuuwanwisni. Pay pi yan naawakway." Yanhaqam yaw
amumi lavaytiqw paapiy pu' yaw puma. Tathihi yaw kyaysiwa,
tootim, taataqt.
    Pu' yaw Musangnuve piw pumawat oovi pantoti. Piw yaw puma
pep yuuyaaqe pu' pangqw piw hisatniqw piw yaw oovi tuwat nankwusa. Pi yaw son pi amumi mongwi'am qa lavaytiqw, pu' Walpeq
piiw. Pay yaw oovi taawa su'aw pakiqw puma haqami Awat'oviy ep
haqami amumi mongwi pangqawqat pangso yaw puma su'aw pay
masiphikiwtaqw pu' tsovalti. Is tathihi yawi, kyaasta, Orayvit, Musangnuvit, Walpit. Qa an'ewakw yaw hinta. Pephaqam pu' yaw puma
oovi yesva, masiphikpuva. Pephaqam haqam paahuuniqw pay pep
put aqlaphaqam, Awat'oviy kwiningqöyve. Paasat pu' yaw Awat'o-
veq pu' mongwi pam pi it tunatya'ytaqe pu' pam yaw tiiponiy
horokna. Put yaw horoknakyangw pu' paasat pipmokiy, tsoongoy.
Paasat pu' yaw pam hisat paasatniqwhaqam pangqw pu' tuwat
nöömay amum pu' puma Awat'oviy kwiningqöymi haawi. Nööma'at
yaw piikit wukomokta son pi qee'. Yaw puma amumi pituqw yaw
mongwi haalayti. Awat'opmongwi amuupa yorikqe yaw kyaastaqw.
"Kwakwhay," yaw kita, "kwakwhay uma naanakwha. Yan hapi nu'
naawaknay," yaw amumi kita. "Noq oovi uma mooti nöönösaniy,"
kitaqw paasat pu' yaw nööma'at pumuy son pi qa piikit huytima
anga'. Paas yaw oovi puma soosoyam nöönösat pu' yaw tsoongoy
horokna, Awat'opmongwi. Pu' puma piw hiisa'niiqam hapi songqa
tsootsongya mongmatsiwtaqam. Yanti yawi'. Haalayti yawi'.
"Kwakwwhay," yaw kita, "kwakwhay, uma kur nuy nakwhanayaqe
oovi yaasa'haqam tsovalti. Isinmuy uma hapi ayo' tuuvoynayaniqey
put hapi nu' naawaknaqw kur uma yaasa'haqam nuy nakwhanayaqe
oovi yep tsovawtay," yaw kita amumi. "Nu' haalaytiy," yaw kita.
    Noq yaw oovi pan puma tsotsongyukuyaqw pu' yaw amumi
paasat pu' pangqawu, "Noq oovi pay uma haak pi yepyani. Pay uma
haak yepyakyangw ason hihin pas mihikqw, talhahayingqw, pu' uma
oomi tuuwimo qöötsaptsomomi yayvaniy," yaw kita. Paas yaw
aa'awna haqaminiqat. "Pu' paasat taawa yamakqw nu' hapi ikivay
ooveq qatuniy," kita yaw amumi. "Pepeq pu' qatuqw inumi uma
tunatyawyungwni. Pu' nu' hisatniqw wunuptit ipösaalay wiiwilaqw
paasat pu' uma yuutukniy," yaw kita. "Pu' uma inumiq yuutukye'
nuy ngu'aye' pu' nuy kivamiq tuuvayani. Pay nu' qa paapu qatuni.
Pay nu' pi yan naawakna yepeq i' kiiqötiniqw. Niikyangw ima pop-

The same happened at Mishongnovi. The men there, too, dressed and then, in turn, marched off. Most likely, their headman had addressed them prior to their departure, and the same was probably true for the leader of the Walpis. By sundown the warriors reached the hiding place below Awat'ovi that Ta'palo had pointed out to them. It was about dusk by the time all of the contingents had assembled. What a huge throng they made up, the Oraibis, Mishongnovis, and Walpis. Their number was incredibly large. It was nightfall now and the men were encamped at the northwest side of Awat'ovi, next to a spring. Ta'palo, who was ultimately responsible for all this, now got his chief emblem out. In addition, he picked up his pipe bag and pipe. Then he descended the northwest side of the mesa accompanied by his wife, who carried a large bundle of piki. When the two arrived at the enemy camp, the Awat'ovi leader was elated. Looking about among the warriors, he saw that there were many of them. "Thanks," he exclaimed, "thanks for consenting to my wish. This is how I wanted it. But first you must eat," he said, whereupon his wife distributed the piki among the men. When they were satiated, he took out his pipe, and then they smoked, he and several of those with the rank of war chief. Ta'palo was overjoyed. "Thanks again," he said. "Thank you for agreeing to my plan and for gathering in such large numbers. I want my people wiped off from the surface of this earth, and I see that all of you assembled here share my desire. I'm most happy," he explained.

When the smoking ritual was over, Ta'palo said to the warrior chiefs, "I'd like you to remain here for the time being. Later, while it's still dark but getting closer to daylight, climb up to the trash piles on the ledge." With that he pointed out to them precisely where that location was. "After the sun rises, I'll be sitting on top of my kiva. Watch me carefully. The minute I get up and wave my blanket, I want you to launch the attack," he said. "Run up to me first, grab me and throw me inside the kiva. I don't care to live any longer. For it is my wish that this village here become a ruin. These sorcerers must all die. As soon as you have thrown me in, take the ladder. Then run from kiva to kiva and at each one, pull out the ladder. We're just celebrating the eve of the Wuwtsim ceremony, so the men and boys are bound to be sleeping in their kivas. And then when you are up there, divide the village among yourselves and spread out. Pick up chili bundles, set fire to the wood stacks on top of the roofs and, after lighting the chili, cast it into the kivas. Lots of men will be inside.

waqt pay pas soosoy sulawtini. Paasat uma nuy tuuvayat pu' nuy saqhönyani. Pu' ang uma kivanawit yuutukye' pu' ang pay pumuy piw saqhönyani. Itam wuwtsimtotokya'yyungqw oovi ima haqawat taataqt, tootim pay songqa angqe' kivanawit tookya. Paasat pu' uma aw yayve' pu' pay uma ang naa'o'yani haqe'yaniqey. Pay uma ang pi aatsavalni," kita yaw amumi. "Pu' uma ang tsiliqekit ömaatotat pu' uma kivats'ova kotqat uwimnaye' pu' uma put aw tsiilit taqtsokyat pu' uma put kivamiq maspayani. Pepeq taataqt wukotangawta. Pu' uma pang kivanawit taataqtuy qöqyani. Pantotit pu' uma momoymuy, mamantuy kwayngyavoq laywisni, pu' tsaatsakwmuy enang. Pu' pep uma kwayngyave pumuy somtotani, maamayamuy aakwayngyavoq somyani. Pay uma pas qa hakiy peetotani." Yan yaw pumuy aw tutapta. Yantotikyaakyangw paasat pu' uma Orayvit pu' mooti imuy momoymuy, mamantuy hiisa'yaniqey, hakimuyyaniqey pumuy ang ayo' o'yani. Paasat pu' ason mimawat tuwatyaniy," kita yaw amumi. "Pay nu' haalayti. Noq oovi nu' it umumi tavini," kitaaqe pu' yaw tiiponiy amumi no'a. "Pay i' yepni. Pay i' pi as pi ihimu. Niikyangw i' hapi yankyangw itim i'i. Noq pay nu' qa pumuyni. Paniqw oovi nu' it umumi maatapni. Noq oovi yep uma it yankyaakyangw haalaykyaakyangw uma talöngni'ywisniy," yaw amumi kitat paasat pu' yaw puma pangqw ahoy nöömay amum wuuwi, kiimi'.

Yanhaqam yaw pumuy aw tutaptaqw pu' yaw oovi puma yan tunatyawkyaakyangw pu' pay pangqe' naat pi oovi yanyungwa. Yankyaakyangw pu' yaw puma pay nuutayyungwa hisatniqw pumuy aa'awnaniqw. Pu' pay yaw puma pankyaakyangw tunipiy ang poptaya. Pu' yaw peetu hoy tsukutotoynaya, pu' yaw piw peetu owavikya'yngway qalatotoynaya, tunipiy yaw huruyukuya. Paasat pu' yaw kipokyuyahiwkyangw pu' yaw piw tayway lewitota, sutat akwa, yaw poosiy angniikyangw yaqay atsva. Pu' yaw yaqay ang nan'ivoq yalahat akw tuuwuuya. Pantotit pu' yaw piw kwavöönakwatota, putakw yaw puma a'niyaniqe oovi. Yaw qa putu'iwkyaakyangw pumuy tuwqamuy ngööngöye' pu' a'ni yuutukni. Nen qa iits yaw maamangu'ani. Panmakyangw pu' yaw taalaw'iwma. Taalaw'iwmakyangw pu' oovi yaw qöyangwnuptuqw paasat pu' yaw puma pay pangsoq pi öki haqami amumi tutaptaqat, pangso tuuwimo qöötsaptsomomi. Pep pu' paasat yaw i' qaleetaqmongwi piw naat amumi yu'a'ata, sinomuy awi. "Uma hapi qa naatusitotani. Uma hapi pas nahongvitotani. Pay hak qa tsawne' nahongvite' ayo' yamakngwu. Uma pantote' uma son hintotini. Pay pi naap yan

Then kill the men who are there. That done, herd the women and girls together at the village dump; include the children also. Tie them there at the dump. Tie up their hands behind them. Be sure you leave no one out. Having accomplished that, you Oraibis can have first choice of the women and girls. Put aside how many you want and which ones. Then let the others have their pick," he said. "I'm content now. Therefore, let me give you this." With that Ta'palo presented them with his chief emblem. "Here, have this. It's supposed to be mine symbolizing my children. But I'm fed up with them. That's why I let you have it. With it in your possession and happy in your hearts I hope you'll make it to the new day." This is what Ta'palo said to them. Thereupon he ascended the mesa with his wife, returning to the village.

Mindful of these instructions, the attackers were encamped there now, waiting for the moment when he would give them the agreed upon signal. The men whiled away the time checking their weapons. Some sharpened the points on their arrows, others the blades of their stone axes. They made sure their gear was tight and strong. Dressing for battle, they painted their faces, putting red ocher along their eyes above the nose. From the nose down across both cheeks they drew lines with black hematite. Next, to be more powerful they tied white eagle plumes in their hair. Now they would be light of weight and would be able to run with great speed in pursuit of the enemy. By the same token, these plumes would assure that they would not tire easily. Finally, the day began to break. By the time the sky showed the first signs of grayish dawn, the attackers had reached the agreed trash piles along the ledge. There the warrior chief once again admonished his men. "Be sure you don't hold back now. Give it all you can. If you're without fear and fight hard, you'll survive, and nothing will happen to you. The Awat'ovi chief wants it this way. Don't show mercy to anyone." This is how he admonished his men.

Just as the sky turned the colors of the yellow dawn, Ta'palo rose to his feet on the kiva roof. He waved his blanket in the air, whereupon the attackers climbed to the top of the mesa and began the assault. There were many of them, so many in fact that they filled the village of Awat'ovi. They exactly followed the orders they had received. Running from kiva to kiva, they found that the men were inside. Immediately, they pulled out the ladders, thereby depriving those inside of any chance to escape. Now, all of them had come to

naawakna. Qa hakiy uma ookwatutwani." Yan pumuy a'ni öqalanta pami'.

Naat yaw pu' sikyangwnuptuqw pay yaw pam kikmongwi kivats'ove wunuptu. Pu' yaw pösaalay wiiwilaqw pu' yaw puma angqw aw yayvaqe pu' yaw aw yuutu. Pas pi yaw puma kyaysiwqw pavan oopo pepeq, Awat'oveq. Pu' yaw hin pumuy amumi tutavo'y-taqw pu' yaw puma put oovi pantsatna. Pu' yaw puma kivanawit. Antsa yaw ang taataqt pay tangawta. Pu' yaw puma pay pumuy tangawtaqamuy saqhönya. Pantotit pu' antsa pi ura puma aqwyaqe soosoyam laaput paas sisngiwtaqat enang hinwisa pu' tepkohot piiw, pay hingsa'. Paasat put hapi kur yaw puma engem put panwisa. Pu' yaw oovi puma kivanawit saaqat ipwatotat paasat pu' yaw puma laapuy uwimnaya. Noq pay pi yaw suuwuwtsimtotokpe puma pepeq pumuy aw ökiqw oovi naat yaw momoyam tumqöpqöva qööhi'yyu-ngwa, pu' yaw pölavikkiy anga'. Noq pangqw yaw puma laapuy akw paalatotaqe put yaw taqtsoktota. Pu' tepkot yaw enang pu' puma put uwimnayat pu' kivamiq put maspaya, pu' yaw nguutayat pu' pay uwimnayat aqw enang maspaya. Pu' puma pangsoq pumuy taataqtuy yaw mumu'yay. Noq puma pi pay yaw qa hin wuuwan-tota, ngasta yaw tunipi'yyungwa, tangawtaqam. Pu' yaw puma kiinawit soosovik yungtiwisa. Pu' yaw pay pi suukwhaqam haqam taaqat, tiyot kiive tutwe' pay pas pep put pay piw niinayangwu. Pu' yaw peetuy ngu'aatotaqe pu' kivamiq maspaya. Qa hakiy yaw puma taaqat, tiyot ayo' yamakni'ywisa.

Noq ephaqam pi yaw Awat'oveq puma a'ni tsiilit aniwnaya-ngwu, Kastiilam. Put hapi Kastilmuy puma put angqw poshumtotaqe pu' yaw a'ni pep paahuuniqw a'ni puma tsili'aniwnayangwuniqw pam ang iikye' yaw haayiwyungwa. Put yaw puma qeq'iwyungqat piingyankyaakyangw tostota. Pay yaw himuwa paysoq mumtsit pu' qööhit aw enang maspangwu, kivamiq. Pay himu uwukniqat pay put puma yaw aqw soosok maspitota, kivamiq. Pantotit pu' yaw kivay-tsiwat ang soosovik utatota. Pantiqw yaw kwiitsingw qa angqw nöngakni. Pu' yaw puma pi epeqyaqam kur hin angqw nöngakni. Pu' yaw pam pepeq kwiitsingwuy enang tsiili uwukkyangw pi is itseni-ngwu, is ananingwu. Pu' hapi yaw tsaykita, töötöqya, öhöhötota. Panmakyangw pu' yaw nawis'ew lestavi uwi. Uwiwitikyaakyangw nuwu yaw aqw sapum'iwma. Pu' yaw pay epehaq sutmakma. Panmakyangw pu' yaw pay so'pumuy aqw soosoy saapu. Paysoq yaw puma aamilti. Qa himu yaw haqam hingqawlawu. Kivanawit pi yaw taataqtuy soosokmuy enang qöqya. Yantoti yaw puma'.

Awat'ovi with finely shredded juniper bark and greasewood kindling. Upon removing the ladders, they lit the bark. The attack took place, of course, on the very eve of the Wuwtsim ceremony. This meant that the women still had their roasting pits going. With fire from those they ignited the juniper bark and the greasewood kindling, which they hurled into the kivas. Next, they set the wood stacks on top of the kivas aflame and threw them down through the hatches. Then they shot their arrows down on the men. The latter had been completely unsuspecting and had no weapons whatsoever. Now the raiders stormed into all the houses. Wherever they came across a man, no matter whether young or old, they killed him. Some they simply grabbed and cast into a kiva. Not a single man or boy did they spare.

At that time the Spaniards used to grow a lot of chili at Awat'ovi. The Hopis had of course obtained seeds from them, and since there was plenty of water there, also harvested great quantities of this spice. Bundles of dry chili were hanging on the walls outside their homes. The attackers pulverized them. They simply grabbed the pods, squeezed them in their hands, and scattered the powder into the kivas, right on top of the flames. Then they closed up the kiva hatches everywhere. As a result, the smoke could not escape. The chili caught fire and, mixed with the smoke, stung most painfully. There was crying, screaming, and coughing. After a while the roof beams caught fire. As they flamed up, they began to collapse, one after the other. Finally, the screams died down and it became still. Eventually, the roofs caved in on the dead, burying them. Then there was just silence. All of the people inside the kivas had perished. This is what happened to them.

To make sure that they had not made a mistake, the raiders now, once more, went from house to house. Wherever they found an old man, they cut him down. Old women they killed too. Younger women and girls they herded together at a place by the dump. Some of the Oraibis, Mishongnovis and Walpis had positioned themselves along the mesa edge and made sure no one was able to descend. Anyone who attempted to escape was killed. Some tried to sneak away secretly. They were shot. Others they simply grabbed and hurled over the mesa edge. They allowed no one to get down. When all the survivors had been rounded up, they attacked the houses

Yantoti yaw pumaniiqe paasat pu' pas qa öwihiniwtotiniqe
paasat pu' puma kiinawit pu' pas piwya, yungtiwisa. Haqam yaw
wuutaqat tutwe' pay niinayangwu. Wuukw, so'wuutit piw yaw
niinayangwu. Pu' puma yaw kwayngyavoqhaqami pepeq kitsokit
epeq pumuy suuvo tsovalantota, momoymuy, mamantuy. Paasat pu'
yaw peetu angqe' tumkyaqe hoongi taataqt, Orayvit, Musangnuvit,
Walpit. Qa hakiy yaw puma pangqw hawnaya. Waayiwmaqat pay
yaw ngu'aye' pay pep niinayangwu. Pu' peetu yaw as nana'uyve
angqw watkitaqw pay put mu'ayangwu. Pu' pay hiitawat ngu'aye'
pu' pay tumpoqhaqami pay tuuvayangwu. Pas yaw puma qa hakiy
pangqw hawnaya. Pantotit paasat pu' yaw puma pumuy soosokmuy
tsovalayaqe paasat pu' puma kiihut aw kiipo. Himu yaw uwikngwu-
qat pu' puma put soosok uwimnaya, kiikihut, kotqayamuy. Qa
soniway yaw Awat'ovi. Pas yaw puma put kiiqötota.

Pu' pay yaw kur piw peetu Awat'oveq taataqt, tootim hin haqe'
na'uytotaqw pumuy qa tutwa. Pay yaw qa wuuhaqniiqam. Niikyangw yaw pumuy hapi qa tutwaqe pumuy oovi qa qöqya. Noq
oovi yaw puma pumuy momoymuy, mamantuy, tsaatsakwmuy
tsovalayaqe pangqaqw pu' yaw puma pumuy tsamkyaakyangw ahoy
ninma. Orayvit pi pas suyan, pu' Musangnuvit. Noq pu' paasat yaw
ima Awat'oveq tootim, taataqt hikiyom akwsingqam puma paasat
pu' yaw pang na'uypiy ang nöngakqe pu' kiinawityaqe pu' hiita
tsovalaya tunipit. Put yaw puma tsovalayaqe pu' puma naamahin qa
wuuhaqyakyaakyangw pu' yaw puma pumuy pangqw amungkya.
Haqam pu' yaw puma amungk ökiiqe pu' pumuy as aw pi kiipo piw
tuwat. Noq pay pi yaw Orayngaqwyaqam pi kyaysiwqe pay puma
pumuy su'angwutota. Paasat pu' yaw puma pumuy pas soosokmuy
qöqya. Qöqyakyangw pu' yaw puma pumuy qötömawya, nit pu'
yaw haqami suuvo puma tsovalaya, qötöyamuy. Pep hapi haqam i'
yan hiniwtiqw pep pu' pam Masqötö yan pam pep maatsiwa puu'.
Naat pan maatsiwa pami'.

Noq antsa yaw pepeq Awat'oveq a'ni yan i' hiniwma, naanaywaqw. A'ni hiniwmaqw pay yaw kur piw peetu Walpit pu' Musangnuvit pay yaw kur puma piw aapiy ang momoymuy mamantuy piw
haqamiwat tsovalantota, neengem. Niiqe oovi pay yaw puma nuutum pangqw aapiyyaqe pay piw nuutum mamantuy, momoymuy
tsamya, Walpit pu' Musangnuvit. Pu' Orayvi pi yaw pas naayawqe
pay qa pas wuuhaq naat ayo' oya ispi qa pan pasiwtaqw oovi'o. Naat
yaw hapi yukiltiqw pep pu' paasat Orayvi hapi mooti pumuy ang
namortani, hiituy, hiisa' tsamniqey mamantuy, momoymuy. Noq

themselves. Whatever would burn, they set aflame, the buildings and their wood stacks. Awat'ovi presented a terrible sight. It had been turned into a ruin.

Evidently, a handful of Awat'ovi men and boys had managed to hide somehow and had not been discovered. However, the number of those who were not found and survived the killing was small. Meanwhile, the Oraibis and Mishongnovis were getting ready to go home, taking the women, girls and children with them. At this point, a few of the Awat'ovi boys and men who had remained alive emerged from their hiding places and, searching the houses, gathered whatever arms they could get hold of. Then, small though their number was, they set out in pursuit of the enemies. At some place they came upon them and attacked. However, those on the Oraibi side far outnumbered them and quickly overpowered them, killing them all. Having killed them, they cut off their heads and gathered them in a pile. The place where this happened came to be known as Masqötö or "Skull." It is still known under this name today.

These are the terrible events that took place during the sacking of Awat'ovi. While the attack was going on, some of the Walpis and Mishongnovis had already begun to round up some of the womenfolk for themselves. As they were leaving with the others now, they took their captured women and girls along. The Oraibis, however, who had concentrated on the fighting, had not been able yet to pick out a lot of women. After all, it had not been planned this way. They were not supposed to make their selection before the end of the battle.

naat yaw puma qa pantotiqw pay kur piw Walpi, Musangnuvi pay aapiy ang peetuy nunukwngwamuy poopongqe pumuy oovi pangqaqw tsamkyangw ahoy kiikiy puma awya. Noq pu' ura amungk kiipokqw pep pu' puma pumuy pi pay pas soosokmuy qöqya Awat'ongaqw taataqtuy, tootimuy. Puma hapi as momoymuy oovi pumuy aw kiipo piwnit pay pö'yya.

Pantotiqw pu' oovi puma pangqaqw pumuy nanap yankyaakyangw pu' pangqaqw nankwusakyaakyangw pu' Walpiy taavangqöyvehaqam pu' puma yaw tsovalti soosoyam, Walpit, Musangnuvit, Orayvit. Nanap momoymuy, mamantuy puma tsamya. Pep pu' Orayvi amumi pangqawu, "Qa yanta ura i'. Qa yan ura mongwi naawakna. Ura Orayvi mooti hiitaniqey ang poopongni, hiisa'niqey pumuy ang poopongni. Paasat pu' ason Musangnuvi angk tuwatni, pu' Walpi pi pay ura tutskwayat oovini. Noq uma qa antoti. Uma oovi itamumi o'yani. Ima itaamumu. Ason itam hiituy akwsingwnayaqw pumuy pu' uma tuwatyaniy," yaw amumi kita.

Pay yaw qa naanakwha. "Qa'ey," yaw kitota, "pay itam nuwu pi imuy neengem tsovalayaqe itam imuy tsamyaqw ima itaamumu. Pay itam oovi son umumi o'yani."

Pu' yaw puma pep yan hingqaqwa, yu'a'atota, hin as aw lomahintiqw panyaniqey. Pay yaw qa hin sunya. Qa naanakwha yaw amumi o'yaniqw. Paasat pu' yaw Orayngaqw pu' haqawa yaw pangqawu, "Pay tur qa hak imuyniy," yaw kita. "Pay itam imuy kur qöqyani. Itam soosokmuy qöqyaqw pay qa hak imuyni."

Kitotaqe paasat pu' puma pumuy momoymuy, mamantuy qöyanvaya. Himuwa yaw sukwat ngu'e' pu' yaw hinwat niinangwu, sen söökwiknangwu, sen mu'angwu. Pu' yaw as okiw peetu momoyam, mamant tsaykikyaakyangw, "Pay nu' umumumni. Pay uma nuy qa niinayani. Nu' umumumni." Haktonsa yaw as yan hingqaqwa momoyam. Pu' pay yaw puma wuukoqöqya pumuy. Pay yaw oovi puma wuukoqöqyaqw paasat pu' piw haqawa pangqawu, "Itam peeti momoyam hiita wiiwimkyamuy," yaw kitota. "Itam yoytuwi'yyungwa. Itam put umuy tutuwnayani itamuy qa qöqyat itamuy tsamyaqw. Pay itam hiita hin sinmuy akw yesniqat itam put tuwi'yyungwa uma itamuy qa qöqyaqw itam umuy put tutuwnayani."

Yuk pu' yaw paasat puma peetuy ookwatutwa panyungqamuy, son pi qa Mamrawtuy, Lalkontuy, pay pumuy hiituy wiiwimkyamuy. Pu' yaw peetuy puma qa qöqyaqamuy a'ni tuuhotota, maayamuy ayo' tutkitota, hokyayamuy. Pu' yaw peetuy taataqtuy, momoymuy amungem lavaytotiqamuy puma kwasiyamuy, löhavuyamuy

They now realized that the Walpis and Mishongnovis had already selected some of the more attractive ones and were returning home with them. While doing so they had been attacked by the pursuing Awat'ovis, who in turn were all killed in the attempt. They had attacked to free the women, but instead all lost their lives.

By now they were all bound for home, each group with the women they had picked. At a place on the southwest side of Walpi the contingents from Walpi, Mishongnovi, and Oraibi came together, all with the women and girls they had gathered. There the Oraibis protested, "Remember, this is not the way it was to be. Ta'palo wanted it otherwise. We were to have first choice and were to pick whatever women and as many as we wanted. Then you Mishongnovis were to have your turn. You Walpis were to be rewarded with the land. So what you did was not right. We therefore demand that you give us back the women. They belong to us. Those that we leave over, you can have."

The Walpis and Mishongnovis, however, did not agree. "No," they cried, "we've already chosen these for us, so we'll take them along. These are ours. We won't give them back to you."

The three groups argued back and forth, urging one another to do what was right. But they could not come to terms. The Walpis and Mishongnovis simply refused to give up their women. Thereupon one of the Oraibis exclaimed, "In that case no one shall have them. Let's get rid of them. If we kill them all, nobody can have them."

No sooner had this been proposed than they started slaughtering the women and girls. They would just grab one and kill her any old way, either by stabbing her or shooting her. Some of the women and girls, poor wretches, were crying, "Let me go with you. Don't kill me. I'd like to go with you." But they were pleading in vain, and a great number of them were killed. As the massacre continued, one of them cried, "Some of us women are initiates of a society. We know how to make rain. We'll teach you the art of rain-making if you spare us and take us along."

At this point they showed mercy to some of the society initiates, such as the members of the Maraw and Lakon society. But others who they did not murder they injured severely by cutting off their arms or legs. Some men who interceded on behalf of the women they mutilated by severing their penises and testicles. In some cases they also cut off the women's breasts. Finally, they showed some mercy to a few who were versed in certain skills and put them aside. Those

ayo' tutkitota. Pu' yaw piw momoymuy piihuyamuy ang tutkitota.
Pantotit pu' yaw puma hikikmuy ang ookwatutwaqe ayo' pumuy
o'ya, hiita tuwi'yyungqamuy. Pu' yaw pumuy tuuhototaqe pay
pumuy pep maatatve. Pu' yaw puma pay okiw pephaqam pankyaakyangw pay himuwa mokngwu. Yanhaqam yaw puma pep pumuy
oovi a'ni hintotiqe wuukoqöqya piw pumuyu, momoymuy, mamantuy. Tsaatsakwmuy pay yaw puma qa hintsatsna.

Pephaqam pu' yaw puma oovi pay sunhaqam pumuy naahuyva,
momoymuy, mamantuy. Noq Orayngaqw yaw puma hakiy taaqat
kur enang wikya. Pam yaw it sipalat tuwat pas tuwi'yta. Paniqw yaw
oovi Orayvi pas a'ni sipalat aniwnangwu. Pu' ayangqw Musangnu-
ngaqw pangqw pu' it tuwat hak yaw tawaktsit kya pi himu'ytaqat
enang wikyaqe yaw oovi tuwat yaw a'ni tawaktsit aniwnayangwu.
Pu' yaw pay Walpit son pi qa tsaqaptatuwi'yyungqamuy tsamyaqe
oovi tuwat tsaqaptat tuwi'yyungwa. Yanhaqam yaw puma pep
hintotiqe pep pumuy wuukoqöqya momoymuy. Noq paniqw yaw
oovi pam pephaqam Mastsomo. Paapiy yan put pep tuwi'yyungwa.

Yantoti yaw puma'a. Pu' yaw puma pumuy sun naahuyvaqw
oovi qa haqawa wuuhaq tsaama. Pu' yaw yantoti hapiniqw oovi yang
it kitsokit ang peetu hapi pangqw Awat'ongaqw sinom yeese.

Noq pu' yaw qavongvaqw pu' Orayngaqw pu' Walngaqw pu'
ima piw aqw ahoyya, epeq kiipokmayaqam. Puma hapi yaw pas
suyanyani, pay qa hak epehaq qatuqw sen hak ayo' yamakqw. Pu'
puma yaw epeq ökiiqe pu' ang piw pootaya. Pay yaw panis angqe'
kwiikwitsi. Pu' yaw himu naat haqam wunuqw pu' put sakwito-
tangwu. Puma yaw ang yaktaqe haqam himu naat tuukwa wunuqw
put yaw saapuknayangwu. Pu' yaw himu tsaqaptaniqw piw yaw
yoohayangwu. Pu' yaw saaqat haqaqw wunuqw piw yaw qöqhito-
tangwu. Pu' yaw mamtat yongoytiwisa. Pu' yaw hiita yawi'oypit,
tuletat, puuvut qöqhitiwisa. Pu' pay yaw hiitasa himu'ytiwqatsa pay
angqw neengem yawmangwu, poyot'ewakw pu' yaw piw tuukwavit'ewakw, maaponat pu' yaw hoohut siptsuku'ytaqat pu' awtat piw.
Pas yaw nukwangw'awtat hak tuwe' pay yaw neengemningwu. Pu'
piw yaw eyokinpit pu' lansat nenge'emtota. Put yaw Aa'altniqw
Kwaakwant Orayve himu'yyungwa. Qa hak yaw haqam. Pay yaw
pas puma naanami yu'a'atinumyaqey putsa nanvotya. Qa hak yaw
haqam. Yaw sutmakiwta. Yan yaw puma put pepeq pas kiiqötota,
tutskwatota. Noq pu' yaw paasat oovi pangqw puma pumuy sinmuy
tsamvayaqamuy pu' pumuy amumi pu' puma pangqaqwa, qa hisat
pansoqhaqami ahoy unangwa'yyungwni, qa hisat aqwhaqami ahoy-

who had been wounded they left where they were. One after the other the poor things perished there miserably. This is how they dealt with their female captives. A large number of them, women and girls, were murdered. The children they did not harm.

Now they distributed the remaining prisoners in equal lots. The group from Oraibi even took one man from Awat'ovi along because he was familiar with peaches. For this reason lots of peaches are now harvested at Oraibi. The contingent from Mishongnovi found someone who owned the sweet corn. That's why they always raise lots of sweet corn. The Walpis must have found some women who had the knowledge of making pottery, for they know how to make pots now. This is what took place there when so many women were massacred. For this reason the location is called Mastsomo, "Death Hill." Ever since that day it's been known that way.

This is what happened there. All the captives had been fairly distributed now, and none of the groups took an excessive number. And because of this distribution descendants of the Awat'ovis live in our villages here.

The next day those Oraibis and Walpis who had participated in the raid returned to Awat'ovi. They wanted to be sure that no soul was living there any more. Upon arrival they checked the village ruins. Only smoke was rising in the air. Where a building still happened to be standing, it was demolished. Freestanding walls were toppled over. Pots were smashed and ladders burned, metates broken into pieces. Looms, beams to hang things on, they set afire as they went along. Once in a while a man would put a precious thing aside for himself, such as a knife or a necklace, a bowguard, metal-tipped arrows or a nice bow. They also appropriated bells and lances. These the members of the Al society still have in Oraibi. There was nobody around any more. As the men walked about they only heard each other talking. Not a soul anywhere. There was only silence. This is how Awat'ovi was destroyed and leveled to the ground. Those villagers who had been led away were warned never to show any longing for the place, never to think of returning to it. The ruin was to stay the way it was. Being that way, they wanted no trace of it to be left. This had been the village leader's express wish. Ta'palo had, of course, lost his life together with the others.

yani, Awat'omiqa. Pay yaw pam pepeq pantani. Pay pam yaw pankyangw pas tuuvoyniqat itsa puma naanawakna. Pu' yaw pay pi
mongwi pi naap yan naawaknaqe pu' hapi oovi nuutum qatsiy
kwahi. Pam pay qa haqam oovi.

   Yantotiqe pu' yaw puma nukusqatsit, qa lomaqatsit, tuskyapqa-
tsit, honaqqatsit, soosok hiita qa lomahintaqat akw hapi put pepeq
kikmongwi naap timuy kuwaatiqw ima yangqw pumuy kikmongwit
pa'angwayaqe put pepeq Awat'ovit kiiqötota. Noq naat oovi yang
aqwhaqami kitsokinawit puma son pi peetu qa pumuy angqwyaqam
naat yeese. Noq Awat'ovi pepeq hapi oovi qa haqam pu' himu. Aw
anti hapi yaw oovi Ta'palo, tunatyay. Paysoq yaw tiyat, maanat
niinayaqw pu' piw yaw nöömayat sokoptotaqw paniqw pam yaw
Awat'ovit tuuvoyniqat naawakna. Niiqe yaw aw antiqe nuutum
qatsiy kwayqe, yan Awat'ovit pam oovi so'tapnaqw oovi qa haqam
pu' Awat'ovi. Pay tuukwasa epehaq pi pay. Pay yuk pölö.

Thus the village leader Ta'palo sacrificed his own children to get rid of this life of evil, craziness and chaos. In this endeavor he was helped by the other villages. Together they laid waste to Awat'ovi. Throughout these villages there must still be living some of their descendants. But Awat'ovi no longer exists. Ta'palo's plan came to pass. Because they killed his daughter and seduced his wife, he wanted the village to disappear from the earth. In getting his wish fulfilled he lost his own life. He succeeded in eradicating Awat'ovi, for the village is no more. Only a few remnants of its walls are left. And here the story ends.

Endnotes in Story Text

1. According to Yava, the bodies of the murdered children "had been rubbed with cornmeal before they were thrown into the fire" as a symbolic gesture "that whatever might be planted in Awatovi would never grow" (1978: 94). In the song, as it is presented here, Sakwyeva, the oldest of Pavayoykyasi's sons, himself smears his body with the germs of maize. I assume that this signifies that he is withdrawing his powers of germination.

2. Pövöngvi, the name of the sorcerer kiva at Awat'ovi, is etymologically obscure. Fewkes, who lists Pü-vyüñ-o-bi as the name (1893: 365), cites an explanation from Stephen, according to whom it is derived from the plural of *powaqa*, "witch." This analysis is not tenable, however, since the plural of *powaqa* is *popwaqt*, which is too far removed from the sound structure of the name.

Appendix I: Glossary

Aa'alt

Hak wuwtsimvakninik Aala'ytaqat na'yte' pu' putwat pakingwu, Alwimit. Noq i' Aala'ytaqa pu' lööq aala'ytangwu. Pu' piw sowi'yngwat uskyangw löövaqw yöngösonkyangw pay ngasta tootsi'ytangwu. Pu' pay mongkoy piw yawtangwu. Pu' pay unangwpa nan'ik piw tsokokotangwu, qöötsat akwa, pu' piw maamaynit pu' piw hokyay anga'. Noq ima Aa'alt pi tuwalan'a'yat. Niiqe puma Astotokpe angqe' hintsatskiwqw pu' puma tuutuwalangwu. Pu' hak haqaqw amumi taytaqw puma put pay laalayyangwu haqami. Pu' kur qa nakwhe' amumi rohomtiqw pu' pay puma put niinayangwu.

Aliksa'i

Tuutuwutsniqa sutsep aliksa'it akw yaynangwu. Noq hakim put aw tuuqayyungqam hu'wanayanik hakim, "Oh," kitotangwu. Pu' pay aapiy pam tuutuwutsqw paapiy pu' hakim put piw pay an hu'wantiwisngwu. Noq pay qa soosoyam Hopiit pan tuuwutsit yaynayangwu. Itam Orayngaqwyaqam pay tuwat pan tuwi'yyungqw pu' imawat kiyavaqsinom peetu, "Haliksa'i, kur yaw ituwutsi," yan tuuwutsiy yaynayangwu.

Pongya

Pongya pi pay himu wiimit epningwu. Himuwa wiimi pongya'ytaqw pu' puma yungye' pu' put hongnayangwu. Pu' put aw puma naawakintotangwu. Ephaqam taawit akw naawakintota, pavasiwyangwu. Wiiwimi pay nanap pongyat makiwa'yyungwa, hin hiituwat pongya'yyungngwu.

Angwusngöntaqa

Angwusngöntaqa, pam pi pay suukya wawarkatsina pan maatsiwngwu. Pam pi put angwusit homasayat ngöna'ytaqe oovi paniqw pam oovi Angwusngöntaqa.

Al Society Members

If a Hopi man intends to be initiated into Wuwtsim and he has an Al or "Horn" member as a godfather, he is initiated into the Al society. The Al society member is distinguished by two horns on his head. In addition, he wears a buckskin mantle. Each leg has a tortoise rattle attached, and he walks barefoot. In his hand he holds the *mongko* or "chief stick." Both sides of his chest are marked with white dots. White dots are also on his arms and legs.

The [Two] Horn society members are considered guards, and when the ceremony takes place on *astotokya*, "hair-washing eve," they guard the kiva. Should an intruder try and peep in, they will first try and chase him away. If he fails to comply and resists their efforts, they kill him.

Aliksa'i

A storyteller usually begins with *aliksa'i*. In reply to this formulaic introduction the listeners utter, "Oh." As the narrator continues with his story, we keep acknowledging his story with this same response. But not all Hopis begin their tales in this manner. We, who trace our ancestry to Oraibi, follow this custom, while some living in the distant villages of the other mesas commence by saying, "*Ituwutsi*," which means, "It is my story."

Altar

For an altar to exist there must be a religious society. Any society that has an altar sets it up as soon as it enters the kiva to hold its ceremony. Praying and sometimes also the singing of prayer songs takes place at the altar. The makeup and paraphernalia of each altar vary from one society to another.

Angwusngöntaqa (kachina)

Angwusngöntaqa is one of the Runner kachinas. He wears a ruff of crow feathers, hence his name Angwusngöntaqa, "the one that has crow around his neck."

Apoonivi

Apoonivi pi pay Orayviy taavangqöyvehaqam pay hihin kwiningya tuukwi. Pay hihinqötsatukwi. Pam pi Apoonivi. Noq pay pi
pam Hopiituy piw pas amumi himu, Apoonivi. Hak yaw mookye'
pangsoq yaw hak mooti wupt pu' aapiy piw aqw kwiningqöymiqwat
hawngwu. Pu' aapiy hak maskimiqningwu. Pep yaw nan'ivaqw aqw
tutuvenga, tatkyaqöyngaqwnit pu' kwiningqöyngaqw. Pu' yaw pepeq ooveq kiihu. Pay hak mookye'sa put kiihut tuwangwu.

Hoohu

Hak it hoohut yukunik hak mooti haqami hoongaptongwu. Niikyangw hak it hiita angqw put yukuniqey put susutskwivut pu' piw
hongvit ooviningwu. Noq i' mongpuwvi yaw lomahootingwuniqw
oovi peetu put ooviye' puma haqami yaavo put ooviyangwu. Pu' pay
peetu piw put it teevetnit pu' hunvit angqw put enang yuykuya.
Paasat pu' hak put hoongaviy sutskwiptangwu. Pu' hak piw put
hoohuy sutsvoqwat tsukutoynat pu' ayoqwat sus'ovaqe hak angqe
hövalangwu. Hak put pang hövawtaqat put awtat awatvosiyat aw
tsokyat pu' put langaknat pu' put pookyangwuniiqe oovi pang put
hövalangwu. Pu' pang hövawtaqat atpik pu' hak put paykomuy
homastsiitsikvut kwaptat pu' tahut akw tootonaqw pam aw huurtingwu. Pu' piw hak put homastsiitsikvut haqami so'taqw pang hak
piw put tahut akw tootonangwu. Pu' hak hovenaninik hak mooti
pantit pu' paasat put pan aw homaskwaptangwu.

Noq pu' it tsaakw awtayat hoo'at paalangput akw atkyamiq
lewiwkyangw pu' ang homaskwap'iwtaqw pang pas naap hoove'y-
tangwu. Pu' it tiposhoyat awtayat hoo'at tsukumiq sakwawsat akw
enang pe'ykyangw pam susmootiniiqa it songohut angqw yukiwtangwu. Pu' put susmooti makiwqat angqw hakim ayo' sukw taviye'
pu' hakim put tiyooyat siihuyat aw somye' pu' put haqam pam tii-
tiwqw hakim pep put kyeevelmoq tsuruknayangwu.

Pu' Hopiit it tsuu'at kyalmokiyat akw put hoy hisat lelwiyangwu.
Pu' himuwa put tuwqat akw mu'aqw pam put aasonmi pakye' pu'
pam put aatsavalqw pu' pam putakw pay sumokngwu. Pu' puma hisat naat putsa pas tunipi'yyungngwuniiqe puma put hoohuy engem
pan piw tsikwanpit himu'yyungngwuniiqe oovi hoo'am kur ngölöwtaqw puma putakw hoohuy sutskwiplalwangwu. Noq pam hiita
hurut angqw yukiwkyangw pam ang paayom sen naalöyömhaqam
porom'iwyungngwu. Niikyangw hin puma put sutskwiptotangwu-
niqw pam pu' pay suutokiwa.

Apoonivi (place name)

Apoonivi is an elevation that lies somewhere southwest of the Oraibi mesa and slightly to the northwest. Of whitish appearance, it is an important place for the Hopi. When someone dies, he first ascends this peak and then, after making his descent to the northwest side, continues his journey to Maski, the "Home of the Dead." There are steps leading up to Apoonivi, two on the southeastern and northwestern flanks of the elevation. At its very top is a house. Only the deceased can see this house.

Arrow

To manufacture an arrow one first needs to collect the necessary wood. Desirable are branches which are both very straight and very strong. Apache plume is said to make beautiful arrows, but men going after this plant generally have to travel far. Others use greasewood or cliff-rose to construct their arrows. As a first step, the wooden shafts are straightened out as much as possible. Next, one end of the arrow receives a point, while on the opposite end a groove is cut across the top. Into this groove the bowstring is inserted which, when drawn, projects the arrow. Directly below this grooved end, three split feathers are attached which are held tightly in place by means of sinew wrappings. The other ends of the feathers are also bound to the shaft with sinew. Should a person intend to decorate his arrow, he does so, of course, prior to mounting the feathers.

The arrow that comes with a child's bow is painted red at the lower end. The portion where the feathers are mounted has its own distinct decoration, and the bottom tip is painted blue-green. The very first arrows a baby boy ever receives are fashioned from a small reed. One arrow from this first bundle is set aside for his umbilical cord which is tied to it and then stuck into the ceiling at the home of his birth.

In former days the Hopi used to coat their arrows with rattlesnake poison. When such an arrow was shot at a foe and penetrated his body, the poison would spread within his system and bring on a quick death. In former times when the arrow was one of the few Hopi weapons, they also used shaft straighteners to align their crooked shafts when necessary. This implement was made from some hard material and had three or four perforations. How exactly it was employed has been forgotten, however.

Atsamali

Atsamali pi pam Orayviy kwiningya. Pangso pi Mosayrutuy ta-
viwisngwu, mosayurtikive'yyungwe'. Pangso pumuy hoonayangwu,
Atsamaliy awi'.

Pep pi piw tuuwuhiwta ahopkye'. Orayve naahonayaqw pam
Yukiwma paapiy nakwsuniqe pu' pang tuuwuha. Paapiy pu' pam
nakwse' put tutskwat pay himu'ykyangwniqey ooviyo.

Awat'ovi

Awat'oveq pi as pas kur wukoyesngwu, pep Pongsikyay tatkya
taavang oove. Aawatngyam pepeq put kitsoktota. Noq pay kur ura
pam kiiqöti. Awat'opsinom aasi'ytaqat panayaqw pay Hopisinom
ang kitsokiva ki'yyungqam itsivutotiqe pumuy amumi kiipokqe pas
pumuy yukuya.

Paaqavi

Paaqavi pi pay nuutungk kitsokti. Puma pi pay Orayve naaho-
niwyaqat ep hooniwyaqe mooti Hotvelpe yesva. Nit pu' peetu ahoy
as oraymiyaqw qa tangatota. Pu' pay pangso Paaqavit aw naakwiipa.
Noq i' Kuwannömtiwa, tuwawungwa, pumuy pep amungem kitsokta.

Tuupevu

Tuupevu pay i' tawaktsi tuupewtaqaningwu. Put hak koysömiq
tuupengwu. Noq pu' hakim put pangqw ipwaye' pu' put hotom-
nayat pu' put taplakni'yyungngwu. Paasat pu' pam pas lakqw pu'
hakim hisat piw tuupevutyanik hakim pay put panis ahoy kwalak-
nayaqw pay pam piw ahoy antingwu. Noq i' katsina pay pas son piw
put enang qa na'mangwu'yvangwu.

Qa Naani

Himuwa hiita ep pay sen kyaahintini sen hiita neengem nukngwat sen lolmat himu'yvaniqw hak put aw qa kwangwatayte' hak
pan qa naaningwu, qa pam hapi pantiqe oovi. Noq pu' himuwa
panhaqam hintiqw mi'wa ayangqw aw qa kwangwataytaqa pay pas
put son hinwat qa sasvingwu. Ephaqam pam put powaqsasvingwu.

Atsamali (place name)

Atsamali is located at a point northwest of Oraibi. This is the place where the Buffalo dancers are taken during the rest periods of their public performance. Here too they are sent home after the last dance.

Northeast of Atsamali a line is drawn. At the time of the schism of Oraibi, Yukiwma intended to start out from this point and therefore drew the line. In starting out from there he was going to claim the land beyond this mark.

Awat'ovi (place name)

Awat'ovi used to be a big settlement, on the mesa southwest of Pongsikya or Keams Canyon. The Bow clan had established its village there, but it fell into ruin, as is well known. When the people of Awat'ovi allowed the Christians into their community, the Hopis of the other villages became so angry that they attacked them and wiped them out.

Bacavi (Third Mesa village)

Bacavi was the last Hopi village to be founded. When during the schism of Oraibi the "hostiles" were driven out, they first settled in Hotevilla. Some of them tried to return to Oraibi, but were not admitted. It was then that they established themselves at Bacavi. Kuwannömtiwa, a member of the Sand clan, was the one who built the village there for his followers.

Baked Sweet Corn

Tuupevu is sweet corn baked in a pit oven. After removal from the underground oven it is strung up and then dried in the sun. Once the *tuupevu* has hardened and people want to eat some, they need only boil it for it to return to its moist state. A kachina always includes *tuupevu* when he comes bearing gifts.

Begrudge/Envy the possession or enjoyment of something

Whenever a Hopi does something spectacular or acquires something valuable or good, another person is bound to be envious. The person will begrudge the former his good fortune because he is not the one who has been blessed with it. In such a case, the person who is jealous will almost always put the other down in some way. He

Pu' ephaqam himuwa pangqawngwu pam mashuyi'ytaqe oovi put hiita nukngwat aw pitu. Pay yanhaqam pam put naap hin sasvingwu.

Pösaala

It Hopivösaalat put pi pay Hopiit naap yuykuya. Noq put pi pay taataqt, tootimsa pööqantotangwu. Pu' puma naap piw put engem tontotangwu put yukuyanik. Pay pi puma son put qa suukw qöötsatnit pan tonyat paasat pu' akw ang peenayaniqey pu' put kuwantotangwu. Nen pu' put pantaqat enang pu' nana'löngöt pööqayangwu. Noq pu' pam ang hingsa' puuvutsi naanangk pöqniwtangwu. Qöötsaniqw pu' haqe'wat piw qömviningwu. Pu' ephaqam piw sakwawsa angqe enangningwu.

Awta

It awtat hak yukunik hak mooti haqami it hiita hongvit, hurut awtangaptongwu. Noq i' kwingvisa pas put aw awiwa. Pu' put awtangaptamaqa put ahoy kwusive' pam put mooti ang hin hintaniqat pan paas tsatsvit pu' paasat hin ngölöwtaniqat pan pam put hiita aw somi'ytaqw pu' pam pan laakiwmangwu. Pu' pam paas lakqw paasat pu' pam put engem awatvostiwngwut yukungwu. Pam it tahut naat mowa'iwtaqat, murukiwtaqat put awatvostoynangwu. Pu' himuwa piw aakwayngyavaqe it tahut enang tsokyaqw pam put enang hongvi'ytangwu. Noq it yantaqat awtat ta'ikwiwtaqa yan tuwi'yyungngwu. Pam pantaqa hakiy naamahin put a'ni langaknaqw pam naamahin a'ni ngölöltikyangw qa qöhikngwu. Pu' hak put pan a'ni langaknaqw pam hoohu a'ni öqalat yamakngwu.

Pu' i' yantaqa awta piw pay qa it tsako'awtat an putsqaningwu. Pam pay hihin sumringpuningwu. Noq pu' i' tsako'awta piw nana'löngöt kuwanat akw pe'ytangwu. Put ngungu'ypi'at qöötsaningwuniikyangw pu' put nan'ivaqw sakwawsat akw pe'ytangwu. Pu' paasat put atsve paalangpuniikyangw pu' paasat sikyangpuningwu. Pu' qalaveq pam pay it kavihintööqökput akw so'tangwu. Noq pu' it sakwawsatnit pu' it sikyangpuyat ang paayom sen naalöyömhaqam qömvit akw tsokom'iwtangwu. Pu' pam aakwayngyavaqe paalangpuningwu. Pu' put awatvosi'at piw soosoy paalangpuningwu. Pu' himuwa piw aakwayngyavaqe sakwawsat akw lölöqangwve'ytangwu, hotsitsve'ytangwu. Niikyangw pamwa paasat it qömvit atsva pan pe'ytangwu. Pu' pam mongaqw ngungu'ypiyat nan'ivoqniikyangw pu' awatvosi'at piw sikyangpuningwu. Noq ima totim-

may label him a sorcerer, or even claim that he sold a corpse to gain his things of value. In these ways Hopis typically slander one another.

Blanket

Hopi blankets are manufactured by the Hopis themselves. As a rule, it is the men and boys who do the weaving. They also carry out the spinning themselves. They definitely spin a white yarn and if a weaver wants to create a blanket with varicolored stripes, he dyes the yarn. Then he weaves it in different colors. Normally a blanket is woven in narrow consecutive bands. These bands are usually black and white, but occasionally a blue-green stripe is also part of the design.

Bow

To make a bow one first sets out to get the necessary wood, which needs to be strong and rigid. Oak is most suited for this purpose. Upon returning from one's collecting trip, one first prepares the wood by hewing it properly. Then it is lashed to something so that it will attain the desired shape in the drying process. Once the wood is thoroughly dried, one fashions the bowstring. Generally, the string attached to the bow is of animal sinew which one twists while it is still moist. Some bow makers also place sinew along the back of the bow in order to give it more strength. Such a bow is referred to as "one which carries sinew on its back." A sinew-backed bow does not break even when drawn with great force and curved in a sharp arc. When the bowstring is drawn hard, the arrow is released with great velocity. The bow described above is not flat like the child's bow. Rather, its wood is slightly rounded.

Unlike the adult bow, a child's bow is decorated with an array of colors. The place where it is held is painted white; this area is flanked on both sides with blue-green. Next comes a red section followed by yellow. The outer ends are painted purple. The blue-green and yellow color zones are spotted with either three or four black dots. The back of the bow is colored red, as is also the entire length of the string. Some bows have blue-green zigzag designs painted on their backs. While the designs are applied on a black background, the rest of the inside from the handle outward is yellow, which is also true for the bowstring. Children's bows are given to the young, uninitiated boys during the Powamuy and Niman ceremonies.

hooyam pantaqat awtat Powamuyvenit pu' Nimantikive makiwya-
ngwu.

Poli'ini

I' maana wuuyoqte' kongtanisaytiqw pu' put yu'at aw poli'inna-
ngwu. Niiqe pam mooti put paas naawusnat pu' pam put angayat
sunasavaqe tsiikyat pu' paasat it ngölat akw pu' sutsvaqw aw
yukunat pu' paasat ayangqwwat piwningwu. Pu' himuwa maana
wupa'anga'ykyangw pu' piw a'ni höömi'yte' pam wokovoli'intangwu. Noq Hopi pan wukovoli'intaqat aw sutsep kwangwa'ytuswa-
ngwu. Noq it maanat poli'ini'at it povolhoyat masayat aw pay hihin
hayawtaqw oovi paniqw pam poli'ini yan maatsiwa.

Atö'ö

I' atö'ö pay it tsaaqatwat oovat aasaqahaqamningwu. Niikyangw
pam nan'ikyaqe sus'atkyaqenit pu' sus'ovaqe qalavaqe pay qa pas
a'ni puutsi qömvit akw pe'ytangwuniikyangw pu' atsva paalangput
it qömvit ep hihin wuuyaqat puutsit akw pe'ytangwu. Niikyangw
pu' ang sunasava pam pay soosoy qöötsat tutskwa'ytangwu. Put pay
pas hiitasa ep himuwa yuwsingwu. Niikyangw pay ima mamant,
momoyamsa pas put yuuyuwsiya. Pu' ima peetu katsinam piw put
usyungkyaakyangw pu' piw put pitkuna'yyungngwu.

Maahu

I' maahu yaw tuwat it hiita mumkiwuy tuwi'ytaqw oovi Hopi
put paniqw pas hiita'yta. Pam yaw leelenqw pu' yaw paasat kwang-
qattingwu. Noq ima Leelent put tuwat aw enang naawakinkyaa-
kyangw wiimiy hintsatskyangwu. Noq pu' ima Leeniwuy himu'y-
yungqam yaw hisat naat qa peqw Hopiikimiq ökikyangw naat angqe'
haqe' nankwusaniqey panyakyangw yaw pas suskwiniwiq ökikyangw pepeq pu' yaw puma as putakw it patusngwat paalalwa-
kyangw put qa angwutota.

Qaa'ö

Hopit qatsiyat ep i' qaa'ö pas qa sulawningwu. Hak tiitiwe' tsots-
mingwut mooti enang yu'ytangwu. Pu' itam put angqw hiita yuykuya, nöösiwqat, hoomat, ngumnit. Himu haqam hintsakqw i' qaa'ö
sen put angqw himu yukiltiqa pam qa hisat pep qa sulaw. Noq oovi

Butterfly Hairdo

When a girl reaches a marriageable age, her mother styles her hair in a way termed *poli'ini*. First she brushes her hair thoroughly before parting it in the center. Then, using a wooden hoop for support, she fashions a whorl on each side of her daughter's head. When the girl's hair is long and luxuriant, she will inevitably have large whorls. A girl wearing her hair in this fashion is most attractive in the eyes of the Hopi. The similarity of the whorls in the girl's hair style to the wings of a butterfly accounts for its appellation *poli'ini*, or "butterfly hairdo."

Pre-adolescent girls, on the other hand, have a hairdo referred to as *naasomi*. The *naasomi* is worn on both sides of the head above the ears and is not as large as the *poli'ini*.

Cape

The *atö'ö*, or "cape," is about the size of the smaller of the two wedding robes woven for a Hopi bride. The bottom and the top portions of the cape are bordered by two stripes: a narrow outer black one and somewhat narrower inner red one. The field in the middle is pure white. This garment is worn only on special occasions, mostly by young girls and women. However, some kachinas also use it, either in the form of a wrap around the shoulders, or in the form of a kilt around the waist.

Cicada

The cicada is supposed to have the knowledge of producing warmth. This is why the Hopi hold it in high regard. It is said that when the cicada plays its flute, warm weather arrives. Members of the Flute society pray to the cicada, among other things, when conducting their ceremony. Long ago when the Hopi had not yet come to their destined land but were still engaged in their migration, the owners of the Flute ritual reached the northernmost spot on earth. They tried in vain to melt the ice there, using their knowledge of producing heat, before they arrived in Hopi country.

Corn

Corn is ever present in the life of a Hopi. At birth, a perfect ear of white corn represents the symbolic mother of a child. From corn a variety of items are made: food, sacred cornmeal, flour. Wherever a special event is going on, corn or its byproduct is never missing. Corn

pam it Hopit aw pas himuniqw oovi antsa hiita taawit'ewakw ep
hiitawat qaa'öt tungwani'yte' pay piw pam put yu'ytangwu. Pu' hak
mokqw pu' pay piw putakw hakiy engem homvöötotaqw pu' hak
paasat haqaminiqey put angningwu.

Pösövi

Pay hisat Orayvi piw it pösövit enang uylawu. Noq oovi pep
Orayviy kwiningya pam pan maatsiwa, Pitsinvastsomo. Pang puma
put uylalwangwu. Pu' put angqw oovat möömö'wituy amungem
yuykuya. Hisat haqam pi as piw pas utuhu'tingwu. Noq oovi puma
pay naap put piw a'aniwnaya. Noq pu' pi pay qa an utuhu'niqw oovi
pay qa hak put uylawu.

Noq pay pi hakimuy pangqaqwangwu, "Uma pösövit qa haqami
maatatvemante' sutsep pösövit mapritote' naap tal'angwuy tsaapto-
tani. Uma qa mukipkiyamantani," pay hakimuy aw kitotangwu,
wuuwuyom. Noq pay kur i' pas qa atsa. Sutsep möömö'wit löqöm'-
iwma, tömölnawitnit tal'angwuy anga'. Paniqw oovi tal'angw pu'
tsaap'iwta.

Iisaw

I' iisaw Hopitniqw pay qa hiita aw awiwaniiqe oovi pam pay put
qa pas hiita'yta. Pay sen hisathaqam as ima hisatsinom put aapiy hin
mongvasyaqw put pay qa hisat hak panhaqam yu'a'ata. Noq pu'
pam tuuwutsit epnen pam hiita suutuptsiwe' pam pay naap hiita qa
lomahintaqat aqw naavitsinaqw hakim put aw tsutsuyngwu. Noq
oovi himuwa piw hiita suutuptsiwngwuniqw hakim put ihu yan
tuwi'yyungngwu. Pu' pam piw hiita pas sonqa naawinngwu. Pu'
pam piw hiitawat tuuwutsit ep nuvöy akw piw hiita nukushiita aqw
naavitsinangwu. Niikyangw pay pam suushaqam hiitawat ep it sinot
engem hiita lolmat hintingwu.

Noq pu' ima pasvayaqam put pas qa atsat qa haalayya. Pam soq
pumuy kawayvatngayamuynit pu' melooniyamuy pasva hovalanti-
numngwuniqw oovi. Niiqe hisat puma pumuy ii'istuy qöqyaninik
puma hisat islalayyangwu. Niikyangw pay as puma pumuy puukyayamuy pu' piw sikwiyamuy as qa hintsatsnangwu.

Pu' ima peetu Hopiit put iisawuy naatoyla'yyungqe oovi is-
ngyamniiqey pangqaqwangwu.

is so precious that whenever it is incorporated into a Hopi's song, it is spoken of as his mother. At death, a path of cornmeal is made along which the deceased travels wherever he is destined to go.

Cotton

Long ago the Oraibis used to grow cotton along with everything else they planted. For this reason there still exists a place northwest of Oraibi which is called Pitsinvastsomo, "cotton field hill." Here cotton was grown. Wedding robes were fashioned from the cotton for all the daughters-in-law. In former times the weather used to get quite hot; that's why people were able to grow this crop. Nowadays the climate is not as hot anymore, so no one is planting cotton.

Once there was a saying which went like this: "If you never let go of the cotton and keep rubbing it (i.e. to weave wedding robes), you will cause the summer to become shorter. You won't have much of a warm season any more." This is what the old people used to say. Evidently it is true. There are always weddings taking place today, one after the other, both in winter and summer. That's why the warm season is short now.

Coyote

A Hopi has no use for the coyote whatsoever; therefore, he does not prize him. It may be that the ancient Hopi benefitted from him somehow, but no one has ever mentioned anything along these lines. In many stories Coyote believes everything he is told. As a result, he gets into all sorts of predicaments, and people laugh at him. Any person therefore, who is equally easily duped is labeled *ihu* by the Hopi, which denotes both "coyote" and "sucker." Coyote also has to imitate everything. In other tales he gets himself into sticky situations because of his lecherousness. Once in a while, however, he will do something beneficial for people.

Farmers certainly do not appreciate the coyote. After all, it roams their fields destroying their watermelons and musk melons. Thus, long ago people used to organize coyote drives to get rid of these pests. However, neither its pelt nor its meat was ever used.

For some Hopi the coyote constitutes a clan totem. Consequently they refer to themselves as belonging to the Coyote clan.

Iswungwa

Iswungwa pi pay pam iisawuy aapiy iswungwa. Pay puma hikiyom piw naat Hotvelpeq yeese. Pu' pep Orayve piw puma pay isngyam. Puma pi pay imuy kookopngyamuy amumumya. Isngyam pi tuwat iisawuy naatoyla'yyungwa. Son pi puma put aw hin qa tuwat lomananaptaqe oovi put wu'yatota. Noq pam pi iisaw piw maktuwi'ykyangw pu' piw hiita hintininik mooti aw paas wuuwat, mooti aw hahaskyelawt put aw hintsanngwu. Paniqw oovi isngyam put tuwat wu'ya'yyungwa.

Tsa'akmongwi

I' tsa'akmongwi hisat imuy tepngyamuy tuwat amungaqwningwu. I' kikmongwi put hiita tsa'law'ayataqw pu' pam put tsa'lawngwu. Pu' hiita hintsakpit engem tokiltotaqw sen Nimantotokyat sen maakiwniqat pay ii'it pam tsa'lawngwu. Noq pu' put aw hin tsa'lawniqat tutaptaqw pam put pas su'an tsa'lawngu. Kur sen haqam natönvastani sen öhömtiniqw pam piw pas put su'antingwu.

Ruupi

Ruupi pi pay owaningwu, suyantal'owa. Put akw poosi'ytaqa hakiy aw taatayngwu. Pu' hakiy ep himu hintaqw tuwangwu. Pu' hakiy aw pangqawngwu.

Tiikive

I' tiikive pay sutsep hakiy sen hiita tokilayat susnuutungk talöngvaqat epeqningwu. Noq pu' kur ep himu wunimaniniqw pam tuwat pep qeni'ytangwu. Noq pay qa suukya himu Hopit hintsakpi'at tiikivet akw so'tingwu. Noq pu' ima hiitu tiitso'nayaqw pam pay paasat pangso yukiltingwu.

Noq ima hiita yungiwtaqam puma suukop taalat aqw put tiikivey wiikiye' pu' puma paasat ep tiivangwu. Ima Tsuutsu't, Leelent, Wuwtsimtniqw pu' ima Mamrawt pantotingwu. Noq pu' imuy Nimankatsinmuy amungem tiingapyaqw pu' puma put angk ökye' pu' puma ep piw tiivangwuniikyangw puma pay qa yungiwtangwu. Pu' ima tsetslet pay piw qa yungiwtakyangw pay puma piw tiikivey angk ökye' puma piw ep tiivangwu.

Coyote Clan Member

A Coyote clan member takes his existence from the coyote. A few affiliates of this clan still live in Hotevilla. There are also some in Oraibi. They are together in one phratry with the Kookop clan. Having the coyote as a clan symbol, they must have found something good in the animal to take him as their clan ancestor. The coyote is, of course, a good hunter. Also, when he plans to do something, he first ponders every aspect of the situation carefully. Next, he makes several attempts, and finally he executes its plan. For this reason the Coyote clan has the animal as a clan totem.

Crier Chief

In the past the person in charge of public announcements came from the Greasewood clan. Whenever the *kikmongwi* commissioned him to make an announcement, he would do his bidding. If a date had been set for a certain event such as the Niman ceremony or if there was to be a hunt, the *tsa'akmongwi* would announce it publicly. After he had been instructed as to the announcement, he would carry it out verbatim. If the *kikmongwi* cleared his voice at a certain spot or coughed, the crier would do likewise.

Crystal

A crystal is a stone that is transparent. The "crystal gazer" or shaman employs it in his diagnosis by looking through it. He can see if something is wrong with a patient. Then he informs the patient about this.

Dance Day

The day called *tiikive* can refer to two things: it either marks the last day of a given time span set by an individual or it constitutes the last day of a ceremony. If the latter is to include a public performance, it occurs on that day. Several activities conclude with *tiikive*.

When those who are congregating in secret rituals have come to their last day, *tiikive* is the day on which they dance. This applies to the initiates of the Snake, Flute, Wuwtsim, and Maraw societies. When the day set for the Niman kachinas arrives they likewise perform their dance on *tiikive*, but on this occasion no secret rites are performed. In a similar way, the social dancers do not engage in any secret rituals, but they also close their public performance as soon as *tiikive* comes. Thus, public dances mark the completion of the ceremonies for all these various groups.

Tuviphayangw

Tuviphayangw pi pay i' himu huukyangw haqaqw qöninitima-
ngwu, hiihiita mömtsikvut e'nang. Pu' ephaqam pay hiisayhoyaniqw
pu' hak haqe' waynumqw hakiy su'aqwniqw pu' hak unangwmi
sutsvaqw may akw ngu'angwu, pu' sutsvaqw piw koopamiq ngu-
'angwu. Pu' hak huur mo'ay uutsi'ytangwu. Yaw pam hakiy
unangwhoroknangwuniqw ooviyo. Paniqw oovi Hopiit put mam-
qasya.
      Pu' hak ephaqam pay malatsiy aw leepeknangwu. Noq pay hakiy
qa awningwu. Pay ephaqam yaw pam hakiy taaha'atningwu, sen pay
tupko'at, himuwa pay hisat mokqa. Pay sen yaw pam powaqanen
putakw waynumngwu. Noq oovi pay hak paniqw put qa naami
nakwhanangwu. Pay pi piw pas sutsep haqam tsaatsayom naataplal-
waqw piw pay haqaqw amumi tuviphayangwhoyaningwu.

Tuwqa

I' tuwqa pay haqawa hakiy hiita akw yuuyuynaqa, hakiy qa aw
yan unangwa'ytaqa, tuwqaningwu. It naaqöyiwuy ep hakiy aw kii-
pokqa pam mitwat tuwqa'atningwu. Pu' hikis himuwa hakiy naap
sino'at hakiy tuwqa'ytangwu. Noq hisat ima himusinom Tasavum,
Payotsim, Yotsi'em, Kumantsim, Kaywam, Tsimwaavam, Kooninam,
puuvuma himusinom hisat yukiq Hopiikimiq kikiipokyangwuniiqe
oovi puma paniqw Hopiituy hisattuwqamat.

Tsögösiw

I' tsöngösiw himu qa lolmaningwuniqw hakim put aw ökye'
hakim kyaananaptangwu. Mooti hakimuy uuyi'am hintaqat akw qa
aniwtingwu. Paapiy pu' pay i' tuu'oyi soosoy sulaw'iwmangwu.
Paasat pu' hakim kur paapu hiita nöönösaniqw pam paasat pu' pep i'
tsöngösiwningwu. Pas ason himu hakimuy ookwatuwe' pu' hakimuy
hiita qa'antipuyamuy ep amungem aw antsanqw paasat pu' hakim
piw angqw ahoytotingwu. Noq pay Hopi put qa suus aw pitu.

Mö'wi

I' hakimuy aangaqwvi'am nöömataqw put nööma'at pamni-
ngwu, mö'wi. Noq oovi hakim himungyamniqw pangqw puma
taataqtuy nöömamat möömö'witningwu. Niiqe hakim soosoyam
ngyam pu' piw hakimuy amumumyaqam pumuy mö'wi'yyungngwu. Pu' piw hakimuy ti'am nöömataqw pam piw mö'winingwu.
Noq paasat pay ima taataqtsa put namat put mö'wi'yyungngwu.

Dust Devil

A dust devil is a wind that comes along in a circulating motion, carrying all sorts of debris with it. Occasionally a small dust devil may directly move towards a person walking about. When this happens, the person lays one hand on his heart, the other on top of his head. In addition, he tightly closes his mouth. For it is said that the dust devil will tear out a person's heart. This is the reason the Hopi are afraid of the dust devil.

Once in a while someone will flip his finger at the wind. This prevents it from approaching the person. People claim that sometimes the dust devil is someone's long deceased uncle or younger brother. He may be a sorcerer walking around in this guise. For this reason people won't let a dust devil close to them. Frequently a tiny dust devil can be seen whirling up to children that are at play.

Enemy

An enemy is someone who causes another person harm or grief or is not friendly toward him. In a war the enemy is the one who raids the other side. Of course, even one's own tribesman can be one's enemy. Long ago such tribal groups as the Navajos, Apaches, Comanches, Kiowas, Chemehuevis, and Yavapais came to raid the Hopi villages and, consequently, were the Hopis' enemies of old.

Famine

A famine is a very tragic event, causing people terrible suffering whenever it occurs. Its initial phase is usually marked by crop failure. As time passes, all the stocked corn reserves are slowly depleted. At the point when nothing is left to consume anymore, the famine is on. And not until a god has compassion with the people, and rights the wrong committed by them, can recovery begin. The Hopi have experienced famines on many occasions.

Female In-Law

Mö'wi is a kinship term reserved for the female who marries a man that is related to you clan-wise. Thus, the wives of the men of a certain clan are *mö'wi* to all members of that clan and the phratry it belongs to. When a son marries, his wife is also a *mö'wi*. But in this case only the father and his male clan relatives consider her as their *mö'wi*.

Noq pu' pam mö'wi pas himuningwuniqw oovi hakim put qa tungwayangwu. Hak put yaw tungwaqw i' taawa yaw hakiy enang pakingwu. Noq pay hintiqw pi pangqaqwangwu.

Qöpqö

I' qöpqö pay sutsep kivaapeq it saaqat su'atpipningwu. Noq put akwniwi hakim hiita hintsatskyangwu. Pu' pam hisatqöpqö hisat pay nevewvutsqaningwuniikyangw pu' pam aqw atkyamiqwat pay hiisavo hötsiningwu. Pu' pam it tusyavut akw angqe ngöyakiwtangwu. Noq pu' puma hiita qööqööyaniqey put saaqat atpik maskya'yyungngwu. Noq pu' i' hak put aw tunatyawtaqa pam tsoylan'aya'amningwu.

Leelent

Orayveq Leelent pi pay piw pas qatsitotangwu. Noq pay pi puma piw as lööpwatyangwu, Masilelentniqw pu' Sakwalelent. Noq Orayve pi pay suukw yaasangwuy ep qe'yat pu' piw ayoqwat yaasangwuy ep pi piwyangwu. Puma pi sumataq Tsuutsu'tuy amumum nana'waqtiwisngwu. Pu' puma leelenyaqam pu' put mit wupalenat ang leelentiwisngwu. Puma pi Leelent peetu leenat heeki'ytaqat ang leelentiwisngwu, nan'ikyaqeyaqam leelentiwisqam pas piw nukwangwyuwsi'ywisngwu. Pitkunkyaakyangw, mötsapngönkwewa'ykyaakyangw pu' piw pavayoykyasit iikwiwyungngwu. Pu' nukwangwsupnaltsöqa'asi'yyungngwu. Pu' pankyaakyangw puma pu' qötöveq lensit kopatsoki'yyungngwu. Noq lööyöm taaqat moopeqniiqamsa put atö'öt ustakyangw nan'ivaqw mooti'ymangwu. Noq pu' puma mima maanat yoywuupaqam oovatsa kwasa'ykyangw pepeq sunasaveq wunimantimangwu.

Paatuwvota

It tuuwutsit ep i' himuwa pay pas a'ni himuniiqa pay pas son it hiita paatuwvotat qa pooko'yte' pam putakw waynumngwu. Noq pam oovi put akw oovi naap haqami suptungwu, pam yaw putakw puuyawnumngwuniiqe oovi. Noq pam yaw it pösövit angqw yukiwkyangw pay it oovat an pöqniwtangwu. Pu' pam put pooko'ytaqa put aqw wuuve' pu' hiita langangaykinat pu' aw pangqawqw pu' pam oomi hölölte' pu' put haqami wikngwu. Pu' pam hawninik pay piw antingwu.

Because a *mö'wi* is generally very revered, we do not address her by name. However, if someone mentions her by her given name, he is said to be taken along by the setting sun. Why this saying exists, no one knows.

Fire Pit

Within a kiva the fire pit is always situated just beneath the entrance ladder. It is in the area northwest of this fire pit that most activities take place. The ancient fire pits were usually square and slightly dug into the floor. Its side walls consisted of flat rocks. The fuel was always kept in stock underneath the ladder. The person who looked after the fire was known as *tsoylan'aya*, or "fire tender."

Flute Society Members

Long ago, the members of the Flute society used to entertain the people in Oraibi with their ceremonies. There were two groups, the Gray Flutes and the Blue-green Flutes. In Oraibi they performed every other year, taking turns with the initiates of the Snake society. Some of the Flute members used to play a flute with a broad rim at the end. They were usually the ones walking along the outer sides of the group as it made its procession into the village. They were beautifully costumed, dressed in kilt and embroidered kachina sash and wore a *pavayoykyasi*, or "moisture tablet," on their back.

Flying Shield

In stories powerful beings, such as gods, are bound to own a *paatuwvota*, or "flying shield," that they employ as a mode of transportation. With it they reach any destination in no time because they can fly about with the shield. The shield is made from cotton and is woven in the manner of a Hopi wedding robe. The owner of such a vehicle needs only to climb aboard, tug on something and utter a command, whereupon the shield rises in the air and takes him wherever he says. When the being wishes to descend, he goes through the same procedure.

Pamösi

Ima hiitu pavamöst pay yokve' ang ayo' aapiyyaqw pu' puma tuwat ökingwu. Pumuy ökiqw pay hakim qa pas haalaytotingwu. Puma pay tutskwat, pu' sipalat, uuyit laknayangwu. Pu' piw pay ang huur hintiqw qa taalaningwu. Noq oovi pumuy ang pan huur hintaqw hakimuy angqw susnuutungkniiqa, sisipi'am, pumuy aw poovoyangwu. Noq pu' puma aapiyyangwu.

Leetayo

It leetayot puukyayat akw i' Hopi pay a'ni mongvasi. Pam put puukyayat suru'ykyangw hiita wunimangwu. Meh, ima tootim, taataqt put suru'ykyaakyangw poliititipkoyangwu. Pu' ima katsinam peep soosoyam piw put suruyat pan aakwayngyavoq haayi'yyungngwu.

Noq pu' it Hopit navoti'atniqw i' taawa put yawkyangw yamakye' pu' put kivay atsve söngnaqw paasat yaw qöyangwnuptungwu. Noq i' wa qöyaletayo yan pas maatsiwa.

Ngumanta

Wuuti, maana ngumantanik pam mooti hiisa'niqey paasa' huumit pu' paasat put wuwhingwu. Pu' pam put pantiqw pu' i' tsiipu'atniqw pu' i' aa'avu'iwyungqa ang ayo' löhökngwu. Paasat pu' pam put hakomtamiq oye' pu' pam put pangqe haakokintangwu. Ephaqam put hakomtat mataaki'at pööngalaningwu. Pu' hak putakw put tuqyaknangwu. Tuqyaknat pu' pam paasat piw ahoy oomiq kweete' paasat pu' pam put angqe piw pan ngumantangwu, angqe haanintakyangw pu' pam hihin tsaatsakwtangwu. Paasat pu' pam put hakwurkwakyangw pu' kur pay pangsayniniqw pu' pam ahoy put intangwu. Inte' pu' pam haqam tulakinsivut qööhe' paasat pu' pam put aqw tulaknangwu. Pangsoq pu' pam put laknat paasat pu' put angqw ahoy tsaame' pu' pam put pingyamtamiqwat oyangwu. Pu' pam put pangqe möyikni'ykyangw put hukyani'ykyangw pu' pam ason hukyaqw paasat pu' pam put angqe piingyantangwu. Pu' pam put paas put piingye' pu' pam paasat put tsaatsayat pu' ang tsiipuyat ayo' maspat paasat pu' hak piw ephaqam angqe haananik pantingwu.

Hehey'a

I' suukya katsina antsa piw Hehey'a yan maatsiwa. Noq peetu ima Kuwanhehey'am puma pay pas suhiituniqw pu' pumuy taa-

Fog

Fog usually comes after the rain has cleared off. People are not happy about the fog because it is said to dry up the land, the peaches, and plants. Also, there is no light when it is thick. Each time the fog is really bad, the last child of a family, the one referred to as *sisipi* or "chamber pot," can blow at the fog. As a result, it generally burns off then.

Fox

The Hopi makes use of fox pelts in many ways. He employs the skin as a pendant in the back from the waist down when he dances. For example, boys and men wear it in this fashion when they dance the Butterfly Dance. Most of the kachinas do likewise. According to Hopi mythology, the sun god emerges from his kiva in the morning carrying a fox skin. He puts the skin up on top of his kiva, at which time gray dawn appears. This particular fox is called Gray Fox.

Grinding Corn

When a woman or girl intends to grind corn, she first shells the amount of corn she wants and then winnows it so that the chaff and worm-eaten kernels can be separated. Next, she puts the corn kernels into the coarse grinding stone and there begins to crush them, coarse-grinding everything. This done, she brings the corn back up in the slanted metate and grinds it repeatedly to make it finer. Finally, the corn becomes cornmeal, and when it is the desired texture, she scoops it from the grinding bin. Next, she builds a fire under a roasting pot, and dry-roasts the cornmeal until no trace of moisture is left. Then she places the corn in a finer metate, spreading it out there to cool off, at which time she fine-grinds it. This accomplished, she sifts the cornmeal to remove any remaining chaff and, if she wishes, grinds it once more.

Hehey'a (kachina)

There is one particular kachina whose name is Hehey'a. One type, known as Kuwanhehey'a, or "Colorful Hehey'a," is very

ha'am pay tuwat okiw hin'ewayniikyangw pu' piw ahoytuqayta.
Noq i' Hehey'amuy Taaha'am mangpukqötö'ykyangw pu' tsiilit
nakwa'ytangwu. Pu' pam qömvit taywa'ykyangw pu' toritsangw-
tangwu. Pu' pam piw sööngöt yaqa'ytaqw put ooveq it koyongot
masa'at aqw tsööqökiwtaqw pu' put poosi'at qa haalayqat an soniwngwu. Panmakyangw pu' pam tumatsöqa'asi'ykyangw pu'
paalangput akw maynit pu' qaspe nan'ip sowi'ingwtanat peeni'y-
tangwu. Pu' pam piw it kapir'aapat torikiwkyangw pu' atsva
sipkwewtangwu. Pankyangw pu' pam it pas pitkunat kurivaqe
pitkuntangwu. Pu' pam piw hokyanavankyangw pu' put angqe
kwewawyat akw namoy ang somi'ytangwu. Pankyangw pu' pam
lomasawkototskyangw pu' honhokyaasomkyangw pu' pam piw it
tsöptanat pi'alhaytangwu. Pu' pam imuy Hehey'amuy amumum
pite' pam pumuy pay amuqle' wunimantinumkyangw pu' paasat
pumuy hiita taawi'yyungqw pam put maasantangwu. Pu' piw pam
imuy manawyatuy ngumantaqw ep puma lööyöm piw pumuy
amumum pite' puma pumuy matayamuy iikwiwnumngwu. Pu'
pumuy manawyatuy wunimaqw puma pumuy nan'ivaq qatuwkyangw pu' piw taawit an maasankyangw pu' pumuy manawyatuy
toosiyamuy aw pingvoptangwu. Pu' puma pay qa suukya imuy
Sooso'yoktuy amumum ökingwu wikpangwa'ykyaakyangw.

Homol'ovi

Homol'ovi pi pay pephaqam Paayut qalave hisathopikitsoki. Nit
pay piw hintaqat akw kiiqöti. Noq pangqw puma Hopisinom pay
piw kya pi ang aatsavala, yang Hopiikiva. Himungyam pi oovi pep
kiiqö'yyungwa. Pay pi pangqaqwangwuniqw yaw Palatkwappeq
kiiqö'yyungqam Homol'ove hiisavo yest pu' pangqw pu' puma
Hopiikiva naakwiipa.

Hopi

Itam Hopiit pay pas kyaahisat yepeq yesvakyangw naat pay itam
yepeqya. Niikyangw i' pay qa itaatutskwa. Itam pay naat yep haa-
kyese. Niikyangw itam yaw pay soosok hiituy sinmuy amumum as
Öngtupqaveq nöngakkyangw pay itam pangqw naanan'i'voq nankwusa.

Noq i' hak mooti yep qatuuqa itamumi hin tutaptaqw pay itamsa
naat pay put tutavoyat hihin anhaqam yeese. Noq itam yaw mooti
angqe' haqe' wuukonankwusat pu' peqw Hopiikimiq öki. Niiqe itam
yaw angqe' a'ni kiiqötotaqw naat pam angqe' hongya. Niiqe itam oo-

handsome. Hehey'amuy Taaha'am, the "Uncle of the Hehey'a," on the other hand, is very homely and speaks backwards. He has hair consisting of lamb's wool and adorns his head with a bunch of red peppers. His face is black with a distorted mouth. For a nose he has a corn cob in whose top is inserted a turkey wing feather. His eyes are sad-looking. Kaolin is used for his body paint, and red deer hoofs are depicted on both sides of his arms and thighs. His whole upper torso is clad with a goat skin, and his waist is girdled with a silver concho belt. In addition, the uncle wears a kilt and footless black stockings that go up to the knee and are tied to the shin by means of narrow woven belts. His brown-colored moccasins are decorated with embroidered ankle bands, and from his hips dangles a rattle made of antelope hoofs. Wherever the uncle arrives in the company of the Kuwanhehey'a, he acts as their side dancer and mimes the words of their chants. During the performance of the Sa'lako puppet drama, a pair of Hehey'a uncles participates who tote on their backs the grinding stones of the little puppets. During the actual dance of these two marionettes, the two uncles act out the words of the song in pantomime and also check the fineness of the sweet cornmeal the puppets are grinding. More than one Hehey'amuy Taaha'am also comes with the So'yoko ogre kachinas. In this role, they carry ropes.

Homol'ovi (place name)

Homol'ovi is an ancient Hopi village on the bank of the Little Colorado. For some reason it fell into ruin, and the people living there became scattered all over Hopi land. I don't know what clans own the ruin. But they say that those who were from the ruined settlement of Palatkwapi stayed in Homol'ovi for a while until they became absorbed in the Hopi villages.

Hopi

We Hopi settled here ages ago and we are still here. But the land is not ours. We are here only as tenants. We made our emergence from the underworld at the Grand Canyon with all sorts of other people and from there migrated into all directions. The being who first inhabited this upper world gave us certain instructions, and we are the only people that still live in some ways by these instructions. Tradition has it that at first we undertook a great migration before arriving here in Hopi country. Along the way we left many ruins which still exist. It is as if we marked the land area that is ours in this way.

vi songyawnen angqe' hiisaq tutskwa'yyungqey put akw itam angqe' tuvoylatota. Noq pu' peetu piw pay as angqe' nankwusaqam pay as piw itamun hopiitniikyaakyangw pay puma haqamiwat ökye' pay puma hiita akw pep pas huruyesva. Noq itam hapi as naat yuk yaw haqami Tuuwanasami mooti ökit pu' paasat pep pas suus yesvaniqat yan as i' itamumi tutavoniqw pay pumawat qa pantoti.

Noq pu' i' Hopi as hiita qa nukpanat himuyat suupan hintsakqe oovi pan natngwani'yta. Noq pay peetu itamungaqw nuunukpant.

Hovi'itstuyqa

Hovi'itstuyqa pay yep Nuvatukya'oviy aatatkyahaqam tuukwi pan maatsiwqa. Noq put atpip pay qa suukya kiiqö. Noq pay ima Hopiit piw put pangso tuwa'yyungqe pay piw pangqaqwangwuniqw yaw pay puma pep hisat yesqam piw Hopiit. Noq itam sinom qa sun yukiwyungqw haqawat peetu wukohovi'yyungqw hiitawat hoovi'at pay pavan ayo' iitsiwtangwu. Noq hak put aw taytaqw pay suupan pam hakiy hoovi'at angqw ayo' iitsiwtangwuniqw oovi pan put Hopi tuwi'yta.

Hömsona

Pam i' pi Hömsona pay piw suukya wawarkatsina pan maatsiwngwu. Pam pi pay hiitawat warikne' amum warikye' wiikye' pu' höömiyat angqw pay hiisa' tukungwu. Niiqe paniqw pam oovi Hömsona. Pam pi pay sutsep poyot pu' pay hiita tsaatsangwsivat yawtangwu. Pu' pam hakiy warikne', wiikye', pu' ang tutskwava tatskweknangwu. Pu' ephaqam pas hömsomayat tukungwu, pu' pay ephaqam hiisakw haqaqw höömiyat tukungwu.

Pay qömvit pukuwtangwu. Pu' pay motsovu'ytangwu. Pu' pay qötöveq homasat nahoyleetsi'ytangwu. Pu' pay letaypukyat ngöntangwu. Pu' pay pitkunat pitkunkyangw mötsapngönkwewa'ykyangw Hopikwewat kwewta.

Huk'ovi

Huk'ovi pi Orayviy taavang tuukwi. Pep pi piw pam kiiqö. Noq pay kya pi sutsep pep huuhukngwu. Noq oovi paniqw pay kya pam put tungwayaqw oovi pam Huk'ovi.

Katsina

I' katsina it Hopit aw pas himu. Noq pam katsina pay as qataymataq qatukyangw pay haqawa Hopiikiveq pumuy wangwayqw pay

Some of those who went through the migration are Hopi just as we, but when they arrived at certain locations, they settled there permanently for some reason. Yet our destination was a place called Tuuwanasavi, or "Earth Center," and only after reaching this place were we to settle for good. These were our instructions though they were not followed by the others.

It seems as though a Hopi does not do any evil, thus the name Hopi. But some of us are evil.

Hovi'itstuyqa (Mount Elden)

Hovi'itstuyqa is a promontory situated southeast of the San Francisco Mountains. Several ruins can be found at its foot. The Hopi are well familiar with this place and claim that the people who lived there in ancient times are some of their forebears. The Hopi remark that people are not all physically built the same, some having more prominent buttocks than others. As one looks at Hovi'itstuyqa, it resembles a person's buttocks jutting out and for this reason the Hopi refer to the mountain feature as "Buttocks-sticking-out Point."

Hömsona (kachina)

Hömsona is one of the Runner kachinas. Whenever he challenges someone to a race and catches up with him while they run, he cuts some of the loser's hair off. That's why the kachina's name is Hömsona, or "hair craver." He always carries a knife or some sort of scissors. Upon catching up with a person, in a race he flings him to the ground and on occasion may cut off his entire hair knot; once in a while, he only snips off a lock from the hair.

The kachina's face is black, and he has a snout. On his head he wears feathers arranged in a crosswise fashion. Around his neck is wound a yellow fox ruff. In addition, Hömsona is clad in kilt, embroidered sash, and Hopi belt.

Huk'ovi (place name)

Huk'ovi is a butte southwest of Oraibi. There is a ruin there. It seems to be windy there all the time. For this reason the location is referred to as Huk'ovi, "Windy High Place."

Kachina

A kachina is something very special to a Hopi. Although the kachinas live unseen, they appear in person when one calls them at

puma pepeq pas naap ökingwu. Noq pay hakim paasat pumuy oovi tuwa'yyungngwu. Nen pu' puma piw hakimuy taawanawit song-yawnen tiitaptotangwu. Niikyangw pay puma soosok hiita lolmatni-qat enang tunatyawkyaakyangw hakimuy pootayangwu. Pu' haki-muy amungem na'mangwuy siwamuy noovayamuy oo'oyayangwu. Noq pu' puma tiitso'nayaqw pu' hakim piw pumuy yuwsinayat pu' pumuy amumi okiwlalwangwu. Puma hapi naanan'i'vo tuu'aw-wisqw pew yooyangw piptuniqat oovi. Niikyangw Hopi pay qa neengemsa it yan naawaknangwu, pay pam sopkyawatuy sinmuy paanaqso'iwyungqamuy amungem enang naawaknangwu, pu' piw imuy popkotuy amungem pu' uuyiy piw engem. Pay pam soosok hiita hiihikwqat engem pumuy amumi yoynawaknangwu.

Pu' puma pay haahaqe' piw ki'yyungwa. Haqam paahu yama-kiwtaqw pay puma pang tuwat yeese. Niikyangw pay puma imuy oo'omawtuy akw yaktaqe oovi puma putakw hakimuy poptaya-ngwu.

Noq Hopi hisat as it katsinawuy qa naap hintsakngwu. Hisat ima pas katsinam pas naap imuy Hopiituy amumi ökiwtangwuniqw pay pi i' Hopi nukpananiiqe oovi pay pumuy haqaapiy qa kyaptsi'ymaqw pu' puma pay son pi put ep haalaytotiqe pu' pay puma pumuy pas suus maatatve. Niikyangw pay puma pumuy piw put tuwiy mooti amumi no'ayat pu' haqamiya. Paapiy pu' pay Hopi nawus naap put katsinawuy hintsakma.

Katsinmuy Na'am

Katsinmuy na'am pi pay pumuy katsinmuy tumala'ytangwu. Taalö' tiikive'yyungqw pam pumuy hoohomnangwu, pu' piw aqw katsinkimiq tsamngwu. Pu' piw ahoy kiisonmi tsamngwu. Pay pam pan pumuy tumala'ytangwu.

Pu' piw tiivaniqw tiivantivaqw pu' angqe homnanikyangw pu' amuukwayngyavaqe aqw kukuynaqat aqw pite' pu' amumi tsa'law-ngwu, pu' öqalangwu. Pantit pu' aapiy nuutungkniiqat aqwnen pu' pangqe pangso homni'ymangwu. Pu' ahoy angqe mookyaqe pu' moopeqniiqat aqw so'tapne' pu' aapiy homvöötapngwu.

Mötsapngönkwewa

Mötsapngönkwewa pay piw suukyawa Hopit yuwsi'atnii-kyangw pam pay qa naaqavo put yuuyuwsi. Pay pam pas hiita ep pu' put yuwsingwu. Noq put pay Hopi naap yuykukyangw pam put naayuyuwsina. Pu' ima katsinam piw put yuuyuwsiya. Pu' pay it

Hopi country. At that time they are visible. Upon their arrival, they entertain us all day long. They visit us with intentions that everything will be good. They bring us gifts which consist of foods prepared by their sisters. At the conclusion of their dances we present them with prayer feathers and pray to them that they will take our messages into every direction so that we may be constantly visited by rain. But a Hopi does not pray solely for himself, he prays for everyone who is thirsty, including animals and plants. He prays to the kachinas for rain for all things.

The kachinas inhabit a variety of places. They reside where springs surface. They travel about by way of clouds and that is the mode they use when they visit us.

Way back in the past the Hopis did not carry out the kachina ceremony on their own. At that time it was the real kachinas who came to the Hopi. Because some Hopis were evil, however, and began to show disrespect for the kachinas, the kachinas abandoned them. But before they departed, they turned over their secrets to the Hopi. From that time forward the Hopi had to carry on the kachina cult on their own. As a result, they endure hardships whenever they do so.

Kachina Father

The kachina father takes care of the kachinas. Whenever they dance during the day, he sprinkles them with sacred cornmeal and takes them to their resting place at the Katsinki or "kachina shrine." He also leads them back to the plaza for the next dance round. In this fashion he takes care of them.

As soon as the kachinas are ready to dance again and start stomping, he sprinkles them with the cornmeal. To do so he comes along the rear of the dance line until he reaches the song starter. Here he calls out to the kachinas, exhorting them. Having done that, he steps up to the last dancer and, scattering his cornmeal as he goes from kachina to kachina, moves along to the front end of the dance line. Stopping in front of the first dancer, he then lays out a cornmeal path on the ground.

Kachina Sash

The *mötsapngönkwewa*, or "kachina sash," is an article of Hopi clothing which is not worn every day. Put on only on special occasions, some kachinas include it as a part of their attire. However, it is also worn by the men in various ceremonies. The Maraw society,

wiimit ang piw ima taataqt put yuwsiyangwu. Pu' i' Maraw pitkunte' pam piw put enang yuwsingwu. Noq pam pi pay lööyöm namitskiwtangwuniiqe oovi wuupaningwu. Noq pu' put yuwsiqa pam put kwewtangwuniikyangw pu' pam hiisavat qa kwewtaqw pam putvoqwat haayiwtangwu.

Noq pu' put atsvaniikyangw pu' atpik it qömvit pay qa pas a'ni puutsit akw tuuwuhiwtangwuniqw pang pam piw qöötsat akw pöqangwkukve'ytangwu. Pu' put mötsapngönkwewat suusunasave pam it mokingput tutskwa'ytaqe pam yaw it tuuwaqatsit tu'awi'ytaqw pu' put piw suusunasave i' paalangput akw pe'ytaqa pam yaw it sihut tu'awi'yta, siitalniqat oovi. Noq pu' put nan'ivaqw i' lööyöm qöötsat akw pe'ytaqa, pam yaw haruve'atningwu. Pamwa it mori-'uyit naat pu' kuyvaqat yaw tu'awi'yta. Pu' pam sus'atkyavaqeniikyangw pu' piw sus'ovaqe pay pas puutsit qömvit akw kwilawtangwuniqw pang pam piw tamave'ytangwu.

Katistsa

Katistsa pi pay haqam Hopoqkivehaq haqamwat epe'.

Kawestima

Kawestima pi Orayviy suukwiningyahaq haqam, wukotuusingaqw kiiqö. Tawakwaptiwa pi Yukiwmat hoonaqw pu' pam Kawestimay as namorta pangsoqniqey. Nit pay qa aqw pitut pay Hotvelpeq qatuptu.

Pitkuna

It pitkunat i' Hopi piw naap yuykukyangw pu' pam put yuuyuwsi. Pu' ima katsinam piw put enang yuuyuwsiyaqw pam pay pas sonqa pe'ytangwu. Pay i'sa Sootukwnangw qa pe'ytaqat pitkuntangwu. Pam qa pe'ytaqa pay paasat kwatskyavu yan maatsiwngwu. Pu' hak put pitkuntaqw pam pay piw putvoqwat hötsiniikyangw pu' pangsoqwat piw pe'atningwu. Noq pu' put atsva hak ephaqam mötsapngönkwewtangwu.

Pu' i' pitkuna pe'ytaqa pam angqe sus'atkyaqe qömvit akw aqwhaqami pay hiisa' puutsit akw tuu'ihiwtangwu. Noq pu' hisat put atsva as pay hihin wuuyaqa piw sakwawsat akw lewiwtangwuniqw pu' pay qa himuwa haqam pantaqa. Pu' put qömvi'ytaqat atsva payp sen naalöphaqam piw naat pöqangwkukve'ytangwu. Noq pu' pam nan'ikyaqe piw tuu'ihiwtangwu. Noq sus'atkyaqeniiqa pam it qöö-

whose members are women, make use of it too. The sash consists of
two identical pieces that are sewn together at the middle, which
accounts for its overall length. The person wearing this sash girds it
around his waist once and lets the remaining portion hang down to
the right side of his body.

Both above and underneath are fairly narrow bands of black color
decorated with paired markings of white generally referred to as
pöqangwkuku or "Pöqangw tracks." Right in the center of the sash is a
blue-green area said to represent the earth. Its middle portion has red
design elements that represent flowers, the idea being a desire for
fields covered with flowers. The designs, flanking each side of the
flower elements, are *haruveni*, or "bean markers," and symbolize a
newly sprouted bean plant. The broad black sections at the very bottom and the very top of the sash, finally, incorporate so-called "tooth
marks."

Katistsa (place name)

Katistsa is a community somewhere at the Eastern Pueblos along
the Rio Grande.

Kawestima (place name)

Kawestima is a ruin situated under an overhang somewhere far
away northwest of Oraibi. When Tawakwaptiwa threw out Yukiwma
during the Oraibi split, the latter chose Kawestima as his destination.
But he never reached the place. Instead, he settled at Hotevilla.

Kilt

The kilt, which is woven by the Hopi men themselves, forms part
of the native apparel. Whenever it is worn by the kachinas, it is nearly
always embroidered. The only exception is Sootukwnangw who
dresses in one that is unadorned. Such a plain kilt is called a *kwatskyavu*. Properly worn, the kilt is open on the right where the decorated side also shows. On certain occasions the embroidered sash
known as a *mötsapngönkwewa* is worn over the kilt.

The embroidered kilt has a narrow black border all along the bottom edge. In the past, above the border there used to be a somewhat
broader band of blue-green, but kilts like this are not made anymore.
Also located right above that black edge are about three or four pairs
of vertical marks which are called *pöqangwkuku* or "Pöqangw tracks."
Each end of the kilt is decorated with embroidery. In the very bottom

tsatnit pu' it paalangput akw ang atkyamiq tuuwuhiwyungngwu. Noq pam pang tuuwuhiwyungqa it oomawuy yoylekiyat tu'awi'ytangwuniqw oovi put atsve i' oomawuy piw tu'awi'ytaqa pe'ytangwu. Pam aasonve soosoy qömviniikyangw tutuvengve'ytangwu. Pu' pam qöötsat akw angqe uutsiwkyangw pu' yoylekiyat aw paasavo paalangput tutskwa'ytangwu. Pu' put paalangput ang atkye' pam it hiisaq puutsit akw tukiwtangwu.

Kiva

Yang kivanawit pay hiihiitu katsinam tiilalwangwu. Niikyangw pay qa pumasa it kivat akw mongvasya. Pay hiituywatuy wiimiyamuy aw pituqw puma piw pang yungiwta. Ima taataqt it Wuwtsimuy ang puma pang hintsatskyangwu. Pu' ima Popwamuyt, Leelent, Tsuutsu't, pay puuvuma haqamwat yungiwtangwu.

Noq ima momoyam piw naap wiimi'yyungqe oovi ima Mamrawt, Lalkont piw haqamwat put aw pituqw pep kivaape yungiwtangwu. Niiqe oovi pay qa taataqtsa pang yesngwu. Pu' ima tsetslet tuwanlalwe' pay puma piw kivanawit pantsatskyangwu. Noq pu' hakim taataqt, tootimnen yangqe' tömölnawit piw hakim kivaapa yesngwu. Pu' hakim pay pang hiihiita pay taqahiita tumala'yyungngwu. Ephaqam himuwa tuulewniy pangso yawme' pam pep put langakni'ytangwu. Pu' hakim piw it hiita tihut, awtat, puuvut hiita Powamuymi pang kivanawit yuykuyangwu. Pay ima tsaatsayomsa qa wiiwimkyam pangso qa yungtangwu. Pas ason Paamuynawit pu' piw angktiwqat ep ima katsinam pang yungiwmaqw pu' pam tsay pangsoq yuy, soy amum tiimaytongwu. Pu' puma pangsoq ep tiimaywise' puma pay tuuwingaqwsa tiitimayyangwu imuy momoymuy amumum. Hikis ima mamant naamahin wiiwimkyamniikyangw hisat qa nanalt pangsoq tiimaywisngwu, pu' piw tsetsletuy tuwantawise'.

Noq ima hisatsinom as soosoyam kivat ang yesngwu. Niiqe oovi i' kiva Hopitniqw pay piw kiihuningwu. Niikyangw pam pay itamuy pu' hinyungqat ki'yyungqw qa pantangwu. Pam hisat pay yaw tutskwat aqw hangwniwkyangw pu' ki'amiwtangwu. Niiqe oovi himuwa pangsoq pakininik pam pay it saaqatsa ang pangsoq pakingwu.

field are alternating white and red stripes in vertical alignment which symbolize the rain falling from the clouds. Hence, above them is a design depicting a cloud. The design, which is entirely black inside and resembles the steps of a staircase, is enclosed by a white border while the background up to the rainfall symbols is red. Below the red is a narrow band which separates the red from the rainfall pattern.

Kiva

Many different kachinas hold their dance performances in the kivas. But they are not the only ones who make use of the kiva. When the initiated members of a secret society are to hold their ceremonies, they also assemble within these underground structures. For example, the men stage their religious activities here during Wuwtsim. In addition, the Powamuy, the Flute and the Snake societies, to mention only a few, congregate here for their secret endeavors.

Since the women, too, have rituals of their own, the Maraw, Lakon, and Owaqöl societies also carry out their ceremonies in a kiva. So these religious chambers are not occupied solely by men. Social dancers, too, use the kivas to practice. In winter men and boys occupy the kivas engaging in whatever activities are assigned to them. Thus, one may bring his weaving to the kiva and set up a loom there. For Powamuya, kachina dolls, bows and arrows, and other items of this nature are manufactured. A kiva is off limits only to uninitiated children. It is not until the month of Paamuya and the night dances following the Powamuy rites, that these children, accompanied by their mothers or grandmothers, are allowed to witness the dances. On these occasions they watch the dances, together with the women, from the raised area to the southeast of the kiva's interior. At one time even young girls who are initiated were not permitted to witness dances unaccompanied. The same was true when they went there to practice for a social dance.

The ancestors of the Hopi all lived in kivas once. Thus, in the eyes of the Hopi, the kiva is also a home. However, it was not like the dwellings we inhabit today; it was simply a hole dug in the ground with a cover on top. Entering the kiva was, therefore, only possible by descending a ladder.

Kooyemsi

I' Kooyemsi itamuy Hopiituyniqw pu' Si'ootuyniqw pay piw katsina. Noq put qötö'at pay it sutat akw lewiwkyangw pu' hak haqam naqvu'ytangwuniqw pam pepnit pu' koopaveqnit pu' qötöy aakwayngyaveq tatsi'ytangwu, niiqe pay ephaqam oovi himuwa put Tatsiqtö kitangwu. Noq pu' pam haqam tatsi'ytaqw put angqw i' koyongvöhö piw enang haayiwtangwu. Niikyangw pu' pay pam naap hintaqat poosi'ykyangw pu' mo'a'ytangwu. Panmakyangw pu' pam pay hiita tsatsakwmötsaput ngöntangwu. Pu' pam tuwat it kanelmötsaput nömökput pitkunkyangw pu' sipkwewtangwu. Pu' pam piw hokyanavankyangw pu' paasat sawkototskyangw pu' epha-qam pay piw qötsatotstangwu. Pu' ephaqam pam pay piw sukuk-vuyawtangwu. Pankyangw pu' pam putngaqw aaya'ykyangw pam pay piw pas naap hintaqat aaya'ykyangw pu' suyngaqw kwaawukit yawtangwuniiqe pu' pam putakw maasankyangw wunimangwu. Pu' aakwayngyangaqw pam piw sukw pitkunay aqw tsurukni'ytangwu.

Pu' pam pay tuwat qa suukw hiita aw awiwa. Noq pam pay as qa tsukuniikyangw pay pam piw tsukut an kunalawngwu. Niikyangw pam hisat as pay piw pas imuy tsutskutuy amun tsukulawngwunii-kyangw pam tuwat imuy pas taqkatsinmuy, imuy Hootemuy, Hooli-muy, Tsaatsa'kwaynamuy, pumuy hiituy amumi tsukulawngwu. Niikyangw pu' pam pay qa hisat haqam Hopiikiveq pumuy amumi tsukulawngwu. Niikyangw pam yepwat Si'ookiveq pay naat pumuy katsinmuyatuy amumi tsukulawngwu. Pu' pam piw pay hiituywatuy pusukintotaqamuy amungem pusukintangwu.

Pu' hisat ima taataqt naat kanelvokmu'yyungngwuniqw epha-qam himuwa nuutumnen naat laalaye' qa qeni'yte' pam pay putsa ang pakit pu' pay hiituywatuy amumumningwu. Noq oovi ephaqam pay suukyawa piw koyemos'angaktsinaningwu, pu' pay sen hooteni-ngwu. Pam pay pumuy amun yuwsi'ykyangw pay qötöveqsa koo-yemsiningwu.

Pu' ephaqam piw puma kyaysiwqam hiituywatuy amungem tawvongya'yyungngwu. Pu' piw katsinmuy amumi tsukulalwaqw ima peetu pay pas kiipokniqey ökingwuniiqe puma oovi kipokko-koyemsimningwu. Pu' piw puma hisat as Ösömuyvahaqe' navö-'ökye' puma kiisonve imuy mamantuy amumum nanavö'yangwu, pay naap hiita akwa'. Pu' puma ephaqam pay piw mihikqwtikive paniqw ökingwu.

Kooyemsi (kachina)

The Kooyemsi is a kachina for both the Hopi and the Zuni people. His head is painted with reddish-brown ocher; small globes are attached in place of his ears and on the top and back of his head. This accounts for the appellation Tatsiqtö, or "Ball Head" occasionally applied to him. From the balls hang turkey feathers. The kachina's mouth and eyes can take on various shapes. Around his neck some sort of cloth is usually tied. For a kilt he wears a folded woman's dress and his waist is adorned by a silver concho belt. On his legs and feet he wears footless black stockings and brown (sometimes white) moccasins. At times he may also go barefooted. In his right hand the Kooyemsi carries a rattle that has its own distinctive style, and in his left hand he holds an eagle wing feather with which he motions while dancing. A second feather is tucked into his kilt on his back.

A Kooyemsi can fulfill more than one function. While not considered a clown, the kachina will perform in funny ways similar to a clown. In the past he acted in this role only during dances performed by kachinas classified as *taqkatsinam*, or "powerful, manly kachinas," such as the Hoote, Hooli, and Tsa'kwayna. Today, he no longer clowns for the *taqkatsinam* in any of the villages. Only at Zuni does he still carry out this function. Whenever a kachina group requires a drummer, the Kooyemsi will also take on this task.

In the days when the Hopi men still herded sheep, a shepherd participating in a kachina dance might once in a while not have the time to prepare an elaborate mask. He would then simply put on a Kooyemsi mask, and join the dance group. A Kooyemsi could therefore appear in conjunction with such diverse costumes as those worn by the Long Hair kachina or the Hoote. The dancer would dress exactly like the other kachinas except for the head, which would represent a Kooyemsi.

There are occasions when a large group of Kooyemsi will sing as a chorus for the other nonchanting kachinas. Also, each time clowns are part of a kachina plaza dance, a few Kooyemsi always act as *kipokkatsinam*, or "Raider kachinas." Hence they are named *kipokkokoyemsim*, or "Raider Kooyemsi." Also in the past they used to arrive in the village during the month of Ösömuyaw (approximately March) to challenge the girls to all sorts of guessing games in the dance court. Occasionally, they would also come during kachina night time performances for this same reason.

Koyaanisqatsi

I' kooyanisqatsi pi pay soosoy himu nukusqatsiningwu. Hakim koyaanisqatsit aw ökiqw i' qatsi soosoy simokiwmangwu. I' naakyaptsi qa haqamningwu. Sinom wuuwukwmuy momngwituy qa amumi tuuqayyungngwu. Pu' puma piw wiimiy, tuptsiwniy qa aw tunatyaltotingwu. Pu' sinom piw soosok hiita akw naanami qa yan unangwa'yyungngwu. Tsaatsayom haqam wuukw aw ökye' pay piw put okiw yuuyuynayangwu. Pu' i' nami'ynangwa qa haqamningwu. Pu' sinom mongqenit oovi naanaqasyangwu. Pu' puma piw tuskyaptote' puma timuy tatamtotangwu, pay pas it kwangwa'ewqatsit oovi. Noq oovi it koyaanisqatsit angqw pas qa himu nukngwaningwu.

Niikyangw i' koyaanisqatsi pay qa pu'haqam yayva. Pay i' Hopi naat atkyavehaqam qatukyangw put mooti aw pitu. Noq pu' puma pas qa unangwtalyaqw pu' oovi paasat pumuy himu powataniqa pu' paasat pumuy peetuy haqami hintsana. Mootiwatniiqe pam it uuwingwuy akw pumuy haqami hintsana. Pu' angkniiqe pu' pam it paatsikiwuy akwa. Noq pu' paasat pam imuy qa hiita akw hinyungqamuy amungem pewwat pumuy amungem qatsituwa. Noq pay puma motisinom angqaqw pan hintsakwiskyaakyangw pu' paasat pewwat nönga. Niikyangw pu' yaw puma piw qa suus yepwat pan qatsitota. Pu' puma aasakis pantotiqw pu' pay himu pumuy pay pas son hinwat qa powatangwu.

Kwaakwant

Pay pi i' himu Kwaani'ytaqa Wuwtsimuy ep pas pumuy angqw moopeqa. Pay pi hisat naat puuvut yungtiwisqw pu' hiihiimu naat aw antaqw Kwankivamiqsa ima Wuwtsimt yewastuvinglalwangwu. Pu' imuy Aa'altuy pu' puma Kwaakwant pumuy aya'yyungngwu. Puma Aa'alt pumuy amungem hiita hintotingwu. Oovi it Wuwtsimuy ep pumuy yungqw pu' pam Aala'ytaqa Wuwtsimtuy amungem qööqöötanik Kwankivamiqsa pam mooti put kwistongwu, töövuyamuy. Pangqw pu' pam ahoy naat pas kivay aqwnen pepeq mooti pumuy amungem qööngwu. Pangqw pu' pam Wuwtsimtuy amuupa amungem qööqöötimakyangw ahoy aqw kivay aqwningwu. Pas pantiqw pu' puma tuwat noovamokwisngwu.

Pay pi i' Kwaani'ytaqa suukw aala'ytangwu. Pu' sowi'yngwat ustangwu. Pu' putngwaqwwat lansat yawtangwu, pu' suyngaqwwat mongkoy yawkyangw eyokinpit enang. Pu' qöötsat pukuwtangwu. Pu' unangwpa nan'ik atkyamiq tsokokotangwu. Maayat ang piw nan'ivaqw pu' hokyava piw ang tsokokotangwu.

Koyaanisqatsi

The concept of *koyaanisqatsi* stands for all states of life that are negative. When people reach the state of *koyaanisqatsi*, life in its entirety breaks down. Respect for others disappears. People do not heed the words of the elders and leaders. Their ceremonial rites and beliefs are forsaken. No opportunity is omitted that people can't use to set themselves against each other. When the youngsters encounter an elderly person, they pester him. Mutual love is nonexistent. People compete for leadership positions. They become so crazed that they abandon their children for a life of amusement. Therefore, no good comes with *koyaanisqatsi*, this "life of turmoil and disorder."

Koyaanisqatsi did not begin at this present time. The Hopis first encountered this sort of life while they were still living in the underworld. When they did not come to their senses, someone who intended to set them right did away with some of them. At first it was with fire that he destroyed them. The second time it was with a flood. For those who were pure of heart he sought a new life on this present world. Hence those first people went along in these ways and then emerged into this world. But here again they experienced *koyaanisqatsi* many times over. And each time they did this, there was always something to correct this situation.

Kwan Society Members

An affiliate of the Kwan, or "Agave," society is thought to hold the highest rank among the four Wuwtsim groups. Long ago when the kivas were still entered for the performance of the Wuwtsim ritual and when the ceremonies were still intact, the various Wuwtsim groups would go to the Kwan kiva first to ask there for permission to dress in ceremonial garb. The Kwan members had the Al, or "Horn," society initiates as helpers. The latter would do things for them. Thus, when the Kwan members were in session during Wuwtsim and an Al member wanted to make fire for all the Wuwtsim groups, he would first go to the Kwan kiva and get glowing embers there. From there he returned to his own kiva and lit a fire for his own group. Then he would visit the remaining societies and build fires for them before reentering his own kiva. Next, all the societies went to get food.

In appearance the Kwan member is distinguished by one horn. He wears a buckskin for a mantle and carries a lance in his right hand. In his left he holds the *mongko*, or "chief stick," and a bell. His face is daubed white, and on both sides of his chest dotted lines run

Kwiptosi

Hak kwiptosit yukuninik qötsaqa'öt huumingwu, pay hiisa'niqey paasa'. Pu' hak put kwipngwu. Pu' aw popte' angqw pay suukw ngarokngwu. Pay qa pas paas mowatiqw pu' hak pay put angqw tsamngwu. Pu' ang kuuyiy tsoykuqw paasat pu' hak naksivut tsokyangwu. Pu' aqw naakit oyangwu. Pu' pam naakit mukiitiqw pu' hak put humitkwiviy angqw aqw hiisa' oyangwu. Pu' hak put ep qöritangwu. Pu' pam patotoykye', kwase', pay hihintaskyaptiqw paasat pu' hak angqw kutuktsayanpit aqw inte' pu' tsaatsayangwu. Pan hak soosok kutukte' pu' hak hiisavo piw put mööyangwu. Pu' pam hihin tsakqw paasat pu' hak put hakomtamiq oyangwu. Pu' hak put soosok piw hakwurkwangwu. Pu' ang tsiipu'at ayo'ningwu. Paasat pu' piw hak put tulaknangwu. Pantit pu' hak paasat put pingyamtavaqe put haanangwu. Paasat pu' hak piw naat put tsaatsayangwu. Paasat pu' hingsayhooya tsiipu'at ang ayo'ningwu. Paasat pu' pam kwiptosiningwu.

Saaqa

Hisat naat qa haqam i' hötsiwaningwuniqw ima hisatsinom kiy aw saaqatsa ang yungta. Noq oovi himuwa pas mooti kits'omiq it saaqat sen tutuvengat ang wupt pu' paasat ang atkyamiq aapami naat pay piw saaqat ang pakingwu. Noq pu' pay it Pahaanat angqw itam it hötsiwat himu'yvayaqe oovi pu' putsa ang kiimi yungta. Hikis kivamiq itam pu' pay pan yungta.

Lalkont

Lokonaw pi pay piw momoywimi. Pay kya pi Lakonaw it Marawuy pay aw hayawta. Pay amun piw nanal taalat aqw tiingapyangwu. Pu' pay put sunasamiq pituqw pu' kivami yungngwu. Pu' pay nanal taalat epeq tiikive'yyungwa. Pu' ep kiisonmiye' pu' angqe qöniwwiskyangw naanangk hongvantangwu. Pu' tawkuynaye' tiivantivangwu. Yungyaput akw maasantotangwu.

Pu' wawhitoqam amungk awningwu. Pu' Lakontaqa pumuy aw wiiki'yme' pu' amungem oomawuy pentimangwu. Pu' pangsoq pu' Lakonmanat ngölay tuuvat pu' angk aqw mötövuy tuuvangwu. Mooti sikyangput akwnit pu' piwnen pu' sakwawsat pu' paalangput pu' qöötsat. Pantit pu' amuminen pu' amuusonmiq pakingwu. Pu'

down his body. Arms and legs are also covered with dots.

Kwiptosi (dish)

To make *kwiptosi* one first shells as much white corn as desired. The corn is then boiled. Checking its softness, a kernel is cracked every so often with one's teeth. Before the corn is completely soft, it is taken out, and the water is allowed to drain. Next, a kettle for parching corn is put on the fire. It is filled with dune sand, and when the latter is hot, some of the boiled corn kernels are put inside. Now everything is stirred. Once the kernels start popping and are done and slightly browned, one places them into a sifting scoop and sifts them. Once all the corn is parched, it is spread out to dry for a while. As soon as it is slightly dry, it is heaped on the coarse grinding metate. Now everything is ground to a coarse flour. This in turn is sifted to eliminate the chaff. Next, the coarsely ground cornmeal is roasted in a vessel over the fire. Then the fine-grinding process is completed on the fine grinding metate. The resulting flour is now sifted once more, thereby removing tiny pieces of chaff. Then it is finally *kwiptosi*.

Ladder

Long ago, when doors in the modern sense did not yet exist, the only way the ancient people entered their homes was by means of ladders. In those days, therefore, one had to ascend to the rooftop first either by way of steps or on a ladder and then climb indoors, again, by using another ladder. But now that the Hopi have acquired doors from the White man, they enter a house only through them. Even for kivas this entrance mode is the preferred one today.

Lakon Society Members

The Lakon ritual is a women's ceremony, quite similar to the one performed by the Maraw society initiates. Like the latter, they announce the ceremony for a length of eight days. At the halfway mark the members enter the kiva and on the eighth day they stage a public performance. Proceeding to the plaza, the Lakon initiates line up in a circle. Upon beginning to sing and dance, they motion with the wicker plaques they hold in their hands.

The two Lakon girls who come to throw gifts into the crowd arrive after the dancers. As the *Lakontaqa*, or "Lakon man," guides them to the plaza, he draws cloud symbols for them on the ground. Onto these the Lakon girls cast their hoops, whereupon they cast darts at

put ngölay, mötövuy enang ayo' oyat put wahiipiy angqw lööqha-
qam kwusungwu. Pu' kwiningyaqw aqw pakiiqa tatkyaq wunuptungwu. Pu' mi'wa tatkyaqw aqw pakiiqa kwiningyaq wunuptungwu. Pu' puma wahiipiy akw naami maamasangwu. Pu' paasat
puma pantit pu' maspitangwu, na'mangwuy. Pu' ima tootim, taataqt
hohomyangwu.

Pu' taawanasami pituqw pu' puma hohongvit tootim hanngwu,
tutskwami. Pu' Lakontaqa aqw haqami tsovaltiqw pu' pam pangsoq-
nen pu' pangqw pumuy yuutuknangwu. Poota tsaavoniiqa pay epeq
qatsngwu. Pu' yaavoqniiqa, pam kiisonve tiivaqamuy amuusonveq
oyingwu. Put oovi puma yuutukqam aasatotangwu.

Lansa

It lansat pi pay Hopi hisat enang tunipi'ytangwu. Noq pam pay
qa sungsavaningwu. Suukyawa pi wuupaningwu pu' suukyawa pay
tsaavaningwu. Noq pam it kwaanit ööqayat angqw yuykiwa. Niikyangw pu' pay piw pam it hiita suwipniiqatnit pu' hiita hongvit
enang angqw yuykiwa. Oovi ephaqam put pay piw kwingvit angqw
yukuyangwu. Pu' put haqamiwat tsuku'ytaniqat pepeq pu' put it
wuuyaqat yoysivat aw tsokyayat pu' paasat it tahut akw angqe too-
tonayaqw pam huurtingwu. Noq put tahut it tsayrisat hot'öqayat ang
qaapuknayangwu. Pu' put piw himuwa it kwasrut aw enang som-
ngwu. Pu' it wuupat lansat himuwa pay pumuy tuwqamuy amuu-
sonmi tuuvangwu. Noq pu' it tsaavatniiqat akw pu' himuwa pas
tuwqamuy amumi pite' paasat pu' himuwa putakw amuupa sökwi-
numngwu.

Leetotovi

I' Leetotovi pi pay piw himu suukya wawarkatsina pan maatsiwngwu. Pam himu qömvit pukuwtangwu, pu' piw pay qömvit tsöqa-
'asi'ytangwu. Niikyangw pep taywave posvaqenit pu' mo'ava nan-
'ivoq paalangput akw tuuwuhiwtangwu. Pu' qötövaqe letaypukya
tsokingwu, aakwayngyavoq haayiwtangwu. Pay pam hakiy warikne', wiikye', pay pi wuvaatangwu, moohot akwa'.

Löhavutsotsmo

Hak yangqw Hopiikingaqw yuk nuvatukya'ominiikyangw pay
naat hak qa pas aw pituqw pang i' naanaqle' tsotsmo. Noq put pang
tsotsmot i' Hopi pan tuwi'yta, Löhavutsotsmo. Pay hak naat pu' kak-
tsintuyqangaqwniikyangw pay hak put tsotsmot aw yorikqw pay

them. First the yellow one, next the blue-green one, then the red one, and finally the white one. In this fashion the two Lakonmanas enter the circle of the dancers. After putting their hoops and darts aside, they pick up a couple of things to throw into the crowd of spectators. The girl who entered from the southwest takes up her position at the southeast, the other who entered from the southeast, places herself at the northwest. Next, both bow to each other with their gifts, whereupon they hurl them to the young men and boys who grab for them.

At noontime all the young men who are strong runners descend from the mesa to the plain below. From their gathering place then the Lakontaqa sends them off in a race. There is a coiled plaque which is a short distance away and others which are far away at the plaza in the midst of the dancers. These plaques the runners earn as prizes.

Lance

One of the Hopi weapons in the past was the lance. Lances come in various lengths. One type is very long; another is quite short. The lance is fashioned from agave stalks, but also from other material that is both straight and sturdy, frequently oak. Its head is tipped with a large piece of flint held tightly in place with sinew wrappings. This particular sinew is peeled off the spine of an elk. Some men also tie an eagle tail feather to the weapon. While the longer lance is simply hurled into the midst of the enemy, the shorter version is used to stab at a foe from close range.

Leetotovi (kachina)

Leetotovi is the name of one of the Runner kachinas. His face and body are painted black. Across the eyes and the mouth of the kachina run bands of red color. On his head the Leetotovi wears a yellow fox pelt which hangs down to the back. When Leetotovi challenges someone for a race and catches up with him, he beats the loser with his yucca whip.

Löhavutsotsmo (Volcanic hills northeast of Flagstaff)

Shortly before reaching Nuvatukya'ovi (the San Francisco Mountains) as one comes from Hopi, there is an area with a series of hills and mounds in close proximity to each other. These elevations are known to the Hopis as Löhavutsotsmo, or "Testicle Hills." When

pam put löhavut anhaqam soniwngwuniqw paniqw oovi pam pang pan maatsiwa.

Söqavungsino

Söqavungsino pi himu o'okiwhoya, pay pas qa hiita himu'ytaqa. Pu' piw qa nuutum sinomatsiwta. Niiqe oovi pay puma söqavungsinom haqe' kwayngyavaqe ki'yyungwa.

Marawwimi

It Marawwimit pi pay ima momoyam tuwat hintsakwisa. Niikyangw pay hikiyom taataqt piw put wiiwimkyamniiqe pay oovi pumuy yungiwtaqw puma as amumumyangwuniikyangw pay qa soosok hiita ang amumum hintsakwisa. Pu' puma Paamuyve yungye' puma ep paahototangwu. Noq pu' ep mihikqw ima katsinam tuwat ökye' pu' kivanawit yungiwmangwu. Pu' it angukmuyawuy ep puma piw pas yungye' puma paasat suukop aqw tiikivey tokiltotakyangw pu' aapiy piw nanal taalat ang yungiwtangwu. Noq pu' tuho'os puma Mamrawt piw yungye' pu' puma paasat timuy, kyekyelhoymuy hoohoynayangwu. Noq ep puma oovi naanangk pivitkunye' puma qaasiy maataknayangwu. Noq pu' pam pitkuntaqa pavan pas oova pitkuntangwuniqw oovi put qaasi'at susmataqningwu. Pu' put pitkunat sus'aatöqe pe'ytaqa put kuritskuyat su'angqe'ningwu. Noq pu' pam pitkuntaniqa yang tamöy atsva kwilawtangwu. Pu' piw hihin oova suukyaningwu. Noq pu' pam naalökye' qömvit akw atkyamiq tuuwuhiwtangwu. Paasat pu' pam putngaqwwat tamöy atkyamiq sakwaapikit akw lewiwtangwuniikyangw pu' ayangqwwat sikyaapikit akwa'. Noq ep puma Mamrawt pan oovahaqe' pitkunyungngwuniqw oovi ima taataqt ep tuwat qastimaywisngwu. Noq peetuyniqw puma ep pan pivitkunyaqw put Qastikive yan tuwi'yyungwa.

Kwaatsi

Pay hak hiita ang pakiwkyangw hiita akw naatupki'ytangwuniqw pam itamuy Hopiituyniqw tuvikuningwu. Pu' pay itam piw put kwaatsi yan tuwi'yyungwa. Niikyangw pay pam naamahin as pamsaniikyangw hak put yuwsinaqw pam taatayngwu. Niiqe pu'

looking at these hills on one's way from Kaktsintuyqa, they closely resemble testicles, hence the name.

Low-class Person

A *söqavungsino*, or "low-class person," is one who is destitute and poor. He has no possessions of his own and is not recognized as a *bona fide* member of the community. People of this status live along the refuse area of the village.

Maraw Ceremony

The Maraw is basically a woman's ceremony, although a few male initiates also belong to it. When the Mamrawt, or "Maraw society members," are in session, these men participate in some but not in all phases of the ceremony. The Mamrawt begin their rites in the month of Paamuya (approximately January), at which time they make prayer feathers. In the course of that night, kachinas arrive and perform their dances within the various kivas. Then, during the month of Angukmuyaw (approximately September) they conduct a second, much longer ceremony. While setting their public dance performance date sixteen days in advance, they spend the last eight days confined within their kiva. During this fall ritual, the Maraw participants make their novices, or ceremonial children, fully initiated members.

It is at this occasion that Maraw members take turns showing their thighs publicly as they don their kilts. The initiated member wears her kilt much higher than is the norm, which accounts for her thighs being exposed. A design which runs along the bottom border of the kilt girds the woman exactly around the high points of her buttocks. Right above her knee is a horizontal stripe, and another circles the thigh a little further up. These two stripes, in turn, are connected by four vertical lines. The leg, right below the knee, is decorated with blue or green body paint, while the one below the left leg is painted yellow. And since at this occasion the Maraw initiates sport their kilts so high, the men all go to ogle their thighs. This public display is also known as *Qastikive*, or "Thigh dance."

Mask

Whatever someone wears over his head to hide his face constitutes a *tuviku*, or "mask," for the Hopi. Another term for such a device is *kwaatsi*, which literally translates as "friend." Although merely a mask, it becomes alive the minute it is put on. And when the living

pam oovi piw hakiy aw hin hiita nukusnavote' pam hakiy put ep songyawnen ahoy aw naa'oyngwu. Noq oovi ephaqam himuwa naat pay tiikive qa tapkinat pay maangu'yngwu. Pu' himuwa oovi piw pangqawngwu put kwaatsi'at tuuholawqat. Naat as pu' talavaynenhaqam qa aw hin nanvotqw pu' pay naat yankyangw pam put pantsanngwu. Pu' kur pam hak put ang pakiwtaqa naa'alöngtaqw pay pam paasat piw put qa tuuholawngwu. Yaniqw oovi hak put qa hinwat yuuyuynangwu. Pu' piw hak oovi as sonqa suyanis'unangwa'ykyangw put katsinawuy hintsakngwu.

Pu' yaw hak it hiihiita nöösiwqat tungla'ykyangw put kwaatsiy aw hiita kwaplawngwu. Niiqe oovi hak unangwngaqw pangqawngwu, "Nam i' naqvu'at sipalaniikyangw yep it aw yantani. Nam i' posvölö'at oovaniikyangw yep it aw somiltini. Nam i' motsovu'at patnganiikyangw aw piw yantini." Yaayan hak wuuwankyangw hak hin hakiy kwaatsi'at nuumi'ytaniqat pan aw hiita kwaplawngwu.

Noq ima pay hakiy kiiyat ep haqaqw qa susmataqpungaqw tangawtangwu. Pu' pay ephaqam piw kivaapeningwu. Noq pu' totokpe hakim pumuy yuwsinaye' pu' hakim piw pumuy it momospalat nopnayangwu. Pu' haqam pam mo'ahötsiniqw pangsoq put hiisakw tsakwayangwu. Put ephaqam hakim pay amuupa pavoyayangwu.

Pu' ima katsinam naat pay pas hisat qa kwatstangawtangwuniiqe puma it salavit akw naatupki'yyungngwuniqw oovi ima tsaatsayom yaw hisat qa tiimaywisngwu. Noq pu' pay ima Tuutukwnangwt piw qa kwatstangawkyaakyangw puma it koyongvöhöt qeq'iwtaqat akw naatupki'yyungngwu. Pu' ima hiituwat sen pi Paavangwt piw ephaqam panyungngwu. Pu' Hopaqkivaqe puma peetu pay naat salavit akw naatupki'yyungngwu. Noq ima hiitu yanyungqam yaw hiitu piniitomningwu. Pu' i' Tsito piw pay naat pan salavitsa akw naatupki'ytangwu.

Matsonpi

Matsonpi pi Hotvelay hoopoqnit kwiniwiq pösöyat epeq kiiqö. Pay hihin tuukwive pam kiiqö. Noq pay pangqaqwangwuniqw puma pep uwikyaqe paniqw pangqw aapiyya.

Tuuhikya

Ima Hopitutuhikt pay piw tuwat qa suupwatya. I' suukyawa öqatuhikyaniiqa pay pas hakiy ööqayatsa haqam hintaqat put aw

mask detects something negative about its wearer, it will take revenge on him. Thus, during a particular ceremony, a dancer may
become weary before the day is over. Another may complain that the
mask is hurting him. He may feel fine in the morning, but then all of a
sudden the mask may turn on him. If the wearer of the mask then
changes his attitude, the mask quickly ceases to cause him pain.
Consequently, a mask must not be upset or toyed with under any
circumstances, and it is imperative to have a pure heart when engaging in a kachina ceremony.

Traditionally, the kachina impersonator wishes for various foods
while adding the various attachments to the bare mask. Typically, he
will say, "Let this ear be a peach as it goes on here. Let this eyeball be
grapes as it gets tied on here. Let this snout become a squash as it is
attached here." Thoughts of this kind cross the impersonator's mind
while he is mounting all the pieces which form part of the mask.

Generally, masks are kept at home and out of sight. Sometimes
they are also stored at a kiva. On *totokya*, the day before a dance
ceremony, the masks are first assembled properly and then fed with
honey. A drop of honey is placed right into the mouth hole. At times
people may put the honey in their mouth, mix it with saliva and then
spray the mixture over the mask.

Long ago, when the kachinas did not wear masks yet, they used
to hide their faces with Douglas fir. As a result, children never at-
tended a dance performance in those days. Today, Tuutukwnangwt,
or "Cumulus Cloud kachinas," still do not don masks but conceal
themselves behind an array of turkey feathers held together with
twine. Others, such as the Paavangwt, or "Mountain Sheep kachinas,"
may do the same at times. In the eastern pueblos along the Rio
Grande, kachinas still disguise their faces with Douglas fir. Such kachinas are termed *piniitom* by the Hopi. To this day, the Hopi kachina
known as Tsito covers his features in this manner with fir branches.

Matsonpi (place name)

Matsonpi is a ruin situated at the northeast corner of Hotevilla.
The ruin, which lies on a small mound, is said to have perished in a
fire. For this reason it was abandoned by its inhabitants.

Medicine Man

There is more than one type of Hopi medicine man. One is the
bone doctor who treats or cures only maladies of a person's bones.

mamkyangwu, put aw yukungwu. Pu' i' suukyawa piw ngatwi'y-
taqa, pam it soosok hinyungqat ngahut tuwi'ytangwuniiqe pam putakw tuwat hakiy tuuyayat qalaptsinangwu. Noq pu' i' piw suukya
povosqa, pam piw pay tuwat pas naap hinwat tuwi'yta. Pam hakiy
hiita aw tuwe' pu' pam hakiy hintaqat put aa'awnat pu' paasat hak
hin put qalaptsinaniqat pam hakiy put piw aa'awnangwu. Pu' pam
piw ephaqam hakiy ep it hiita tuukyaynit horoknangwu. Pay ephaqam it hiita kuutat'ewakw sen sotsavat'ewakw hakiy aw himuwa
panaqw pam put hakiy ep horoknangwu. Pu' sen hak pay hiita ep qa
nanap'unangway qa an hintiqw pu' pam piw put hakiy aw tuwe' pu'
pay put hakiy aa'awnat pu' hak hin put aw ahoy antsanniqat hakiy
aw tutaptangwu. Noq ima povosyaqam pu' pay sulawtiqw oovi qa
hak pu' put tuwi'yta.

Pu' Hopi piw navoti'ytaqw i' honani piw a'ni tuuhikyaningwu.
Noq ima tuutuhikt tuwat piw pay hiita aw yankyaakyangw putakw
sinmuy tumala'yyungwa. Ephaqam himuwa it hoonawuy pan-
'ewakw hiita pay pavanniiqat namaqangwunen pam put na'ykyangw
pu' put pantsakngwu.

Mata

I' Hopiwuuti pay sutsep ngumnit hintsakngwuniiqe oovi pam
hisat pay pas sonqa naap mata'ytangwu. Noq pam mata lööpwani-
ngwu. Suukya hakomtaniqw pu' mi'wa pingyamtaningwu. Noq i'
hakomta ephaqam lööqmuy mataaki'ytangwu. Pam wuuti susmooti
huumit pu' pam put hakomtavaqe hingsakwniqat put qayaknangwu.
Pu' pam piwnen pu' pam put hakwurkwangwu. Paasat pu' pam put
pangqw matangaqw ipwat paasat pu' pam put tulaknat pu' paasat
pam put pingyamtamiqwat tangate' pu' paasat pangqe put löös,
paayishaqam haanangwu.

Noq pam hongni'at naanan'i'vaqw matamiq i' tusyavu ki'iwtangwu. Pu' put matat mookyaqe hiisaq puutsi, pam put matavuva'atningwu. Pu' pam nan'ikyaqe aqw oomiq pay piw an puutsiningwu-
niikyangw pu' angqe oovaqe pay piw an hiisaq puutsit matavuva'y-
tangwu. Noq i' mata ooveqwat pay atkyaqniiqat ep hihin ooveni-
ngwuniqw oovi ngumantaqa put atkyamiqwatsa haanintangwu. Noq
pu' himuwa angqw aakwayngyangaqw möyiqtuwkyangw ngumantangwuniqw pangqw pam put mataptsö'atningwu.

Paasat pu' hak put ngumniy piingyankyangw pangsoq tsaqaptay
aqw inlawngwu. Pu' pam put aqw huur ngungu'ytikyangw put
pangsoq inlawngwu. Pu' pam put pantsakkyangw pay qa soosokinta-

Another one is the herb doctor, knowledgeable in the use of all medicinal plants, who performs his remedies by means of them. The last is the crystal gazer or shaman who has his own method of treatment. Looking through his crystal, he will diagnose the ailment of a person and then instruct him in the appropriate treatment. At other times he will remove the object causing the sickness. For instance, he may draw out a thorn or a shell implanted in the patient by another person. Moreover, if the shaman detects that someone has unknowingly violated a taboo or committed some other wrong act, he will enlighten the person and instruct him in the remedy he should apply. These shamans no longer exist, and with them has died the knowledge of their practice.

The Hopi also perceive the badger as a great healer. Medicine men in general rely on some animal as they serve their patients. Sometimes a medicine man may choose a powerful being such as a bear to be his symbolic father to help him practice his skills.

Metate

A Hopi woman utilizes corn flour on a daily basis. Consequently, in the past it was a must for her to possess her own grinding stone or metate. There are two types of grinding stones. One is a coarse-grained slab, the other is a fine-grained one. Sometimes the coarser metate is equipped with two hand stones or manos, implements with which the grinding is carried out. Generally, the woman first shells her corn, then grinds it down to the proper size in the coarse grinding bin. By repeating this process she produces flour with a coarse texture. After she removes the flour from the bin, she dries it in a hot kettle. Next, she places it on the finer stone slab where she regrinds the entire amount two or three times.

The metate proper forms an enclosure with four sides of thin flat stone slabs. In the front of the grinding stone is a narrow channel referred to as *matavuva*. A similar channel runs along each side. These channels, about equal in width to the front one, are sloped upward. Along the top there is still another channel that is also termed *matavuva*. Overall, the top end of the metate is positioned somewhat higher than the bottom part, so that the person grinding is compelled to make downward strokes only. The place behind the grinding bin where the grinding is carried out in kneeling position is referred to as *mataptsö*, or "metate corner."

As the process of fine grinding the corn goes on, the finished

ngwu. Pu' pam qa soosok intaqw pam angqw hiisa'hoya peetingwu. Pu' pam matawsiy ang lengitsmiqw pu' pam mowatingwu. Nen pu' pam put tutsvalay akw put hiisa'hoyat peetiqat put matawsit akw aw tongongoykinaqw pu' pam put aw huurtiqw pan pam put pangqw soosok ipwangwu.

Pu' yaw hak pangsoq matamiq qa pakingwuqat hakimuy amumi pangqaqwangwu. Hak yaw pangsoq pakye' hak yaw pakoymakngwu.

Musangnuvi

Pam Musangnuvi pi pay susmooti peqw pituuqe pam yep Kwangwup'oviy taavangqöyveq mooti kitsokta. Kitsoktat pu' pam as songoopaviniwtiniqe pu' pam oovi pangso kikmongwit aw maqaptsita. Pu' yaw pam piw a'ni lavayi'yta, a'ni yaw nukpantuqayta kya pi pam Musangnuvi. Noq yaw kikmongwi hingqawqw pay yaw pam piw naap hin put aw sulvaytingwu. Noq pay yaw pam put aw pangqawu, "Pay kur uma hin yep Songoopave itamum yesniy," yaw kita. "Pay itam wuuhaqti yep'e. Pu' uma pas antsa yep itamum Hopiituy amumum yep yesninik uma pep hoop tuukwive naap kitsoktotani. Pep hapi nu' ivoshmiy hiihiita tanga'yta. Kur uma pas antsa yep itamumyaninik uma pangsoye' uma pep kiitote' pu' uma pep ivoshumtangay tuuwalayaniy," yaw amumi kita. Pu' yaw pay Musangnuvi nakwhaqe pu' panti.

Neyangmakiw

Neyangmakiw pi mamant tootimuy amumum maqwisniniqw oovi paniqw pam neyangmakiw. Put pan tsa'lawqw pu' hisatyaniqw mamant noovalalwangwu. Hak amumum maqtoniqey naawine' pu' talavay pay iits novawutngwu, somivikit yukuniqey. Pu' put yukye', kwasine', put mokyaatangwu. Pu' hakiy na'at pu' sen pay paava'at, taaha't engem moorot sen kawayot yuwsinaqw hak putakwningwu. Pay maamaakyat haqami tsovaltiqw pay amumum hakim mamant pangso tsovaltingwu.

Pu' pangqw nankwusaqw mamant amuupa tunatyawnumyangwu. Haqam himuwa taavot, sowit niinaqw pu' mamant aqw naanaqasyangwu. Mooti aqw pituuqa askwaltat pu' nawkingwu. Pu' hak

flour is placed into a pottery vessel where it is firmly packed down. Not all the flour can be removed from the slab, however; a small amount always remains. So the person grinding takes a brush, licks it in order to moisten it, and with spittle removes the small amount remaining by touching it with her brush. In this way all the flour is cleaned off the metate.

People are told not to step inside the grinding bin. Should someone do so, according to a saying, one's colon will protrude from one's anus.

Mishongnovi (Second Mesa village)

When the Mishongnovi people arrived here, they first settled on the southwest side of Kwangwup'ovi. In due course, when they expressed a desire to become integrated members of the village of Shungopavi they approached the *kikmongwi* to ask his permission. Tradition has it that they were very loquacious and that they spoke quite aggressively. Whenever the *kikmongwi* said something they were quick to give a negative reply. But the kikmongwi of Shungopavi spoke to them as follows: "There is no way that you can live with us here in Shungopavi. We have become quite numerous here. If your heart is indeed set on living here with the Hopi, build your own settlement at that butte off to the east. There I have my seeds stored. If you really want to settle here among us go to that place, establish a village, and guard my seeds." The Mishongnovis consented and did exactly that.

Mixed Hunt

The concept of the mixed hunt is based on the fact that on this occasion young men and girls go hunting together. As soon as the event has been announced, the girls prepare food on the day they intend to go. Whoever plans to participate in the hunt, mixes her batter early in the morning to make *somiviki*. As soon as she is done cooling her food, she wraps it up in a bundle. Then a girl's father, older brother or uncle saddles a burro or horse with which she can ride out. The girls then join the hunters at their gathering place.

Upon setting out on the hunt, the girls pay close attention to the hunters. Wherever one of them kills a cottontail or a jackrabbit, the girls race for it, competing with each other. The one who gets there first, thanks the boy for the kill and takes it away from him. The girl also keeps track from whom she acquires rabbits and how many.

pumuy aw piw enang tunatyaltingwu, hiisa'niiqamuy hak nawkye'
pu' hakimuy ökiqw hakiy yu'at tiyot engem piktangwu. Pu' hak put
piikit pumuy amuupa oyaatangwu. Pay pangso pam yukiltingwu.

Naalös

Hopi pay pas sutsep naalössa aqw hiita hintingwu. Pu' pam pay
piw nanalsikisniikyangw pu' piw suukop enang akw hintsakma. Noq
oovi hiituwat sen hiita yungiwte' kur puma pas aqwhaqami pan yu-
ngiwtaninik puma suukop taalat ang aqw yungiwtangwu. Pu' puma
ephaqam pay panis nanalsikis sen naalös yungiwtangwu. Pu' oovi
piw himuwa hiita sen aw maqaptsitaninik pam piw naat naalös
pantit pu' pay paasavoningwu. Ason pepeq pu' pam hinwat put aw
lavaytingwu, kur pay qa aapiy hu'wananinik. Pay oovi qa himu
Hopit hiita himu'at qa naalöq aqw tuwani'yta. Pu' pay i' hak itamuy
it hikwsit maqaaqa pu' pay paayista itamuy powataqw oovi pu' yaw
pam kur piw naat itamuy hiitawat akw powataniniqw paapiy pu'
yaw itam pas hin yesniqey pas pan yesni.

Nuvakwewtaqa

Nuvakwewtaqa pay i' tuukwi pan maatsiwa. Pam Homol'oviy
angqw teevenge pay qa wuuyavo. Noq oovi Hopiit pay pam haqamniqw put tuwa'yyungwa. Noq hisat nuvate' pam it nuvat pay songyawnen kwewtangwuniiqe oovi paniqw pan maatsiwa.

Nuvatukya'ovi

Nuvatukya'ovi pay it Hopiikit aatavang tuukwi pan maatsiwa.
Pangso itam tuwat it itaahintsakpiy Nimaniwuy ep pu' piw ephaqam
Powamuyve uymokwisngwu. Pu' pang piw tuutuskyaniqw pang
piw puma uymokwisqam it paahoy oo'oytiwisngwu. Pu' pam pep
piw itamuyniqw imuy katsinmuy kii'amniqw oovi yaw pepeq ooveq
piw pas kiva. Pu' i' Hopi hiisaq tutskwa makiwa'ytaqw pam piw put
qalalni'at.

Kookyangwso'wuuti

Kookyangwso'wuuti pi pas nawiso'aningwu. Hak oovi hiita pas
tuwi'yvaniqey naawakne' put aw tuuvingtangwu. Pay naap hisat pas
piktuwi'yvaniqey piw sen tsaqaptat nawiso'tiniqey sen yungyaput

Upon her return to the village the girl's mother then makes piki for her daughter. This piki the girl distributes among the hunters. After that the mixed hunt is over.

Number Four

A Hopi always does things four times, or in multiples of four, for example, eight and sixteen times. Thus, when a group of people are engaged in a ceremony which is planned to run its entire length, they will be in session for the full sixteen days. At other times they may go on for only eight or even four days. By the same token, when a Hopi seeks a response to his inquiry, he will ask only four times and then quit. At that point he will be given an answer if he did not receive one right away. Thus, there is not a single thing in Hopi culture that does not require the number four as a determiner. Likewise, the creator has now purified us thrice. If he cares to repeat this purification and cleanses us once more, thereafter we will live as we should.

Nuvakwewtaqa (place name)

A mountain range known by the name of Nuvakwewtaqa lies a short distance southwest of Homol'ovi (Winslow). Therefore, the Hopi know where it is situated. After a snowfall it is as if this elevation had a belt of snow, and for this reason it is called "That-which-wears-a-snow-belt."

Nuvatukya'ovi (San Francisco Mountains)

The mountain range to the southwest of Hopi land is known by the name of Nuvatukya'ovi. We go to that place during our ceremonials such as the Niman and also occasionally on Powamuya to gather evergreens. Since there are shrines at that location, those who go to gather these evergreens deposit paho at these sites. In our belief the San Francisco Mountains are one of the homes of the kachinas; therefore, there is a kiva on top of one of its peaks. Nuvatukya'ovi is also one of the boundary markers of Hopiland.

Old Spider Woman

Old Spider Woman is a personage extremely talented in all creative arts. For this reason, whenever a Hopi girl or woman wishes to acquire a certain skill, she turns to her in prayer. For example, one may want to learn how to make piki, to become skilled in pottery making or wicker plaque weaving. On each occasion one prays to

oovi hak aw naawaknangwu. Pam pi Pöqangwhoyatuy so'am. Pay
oovi piw puma Pöqangwhoyat put su'anta, hiihiita tuhisat. Pay pi
tuuwutsit ang pam hiitawat pa'angwangwu hinwat sen tuwqamuy
engem qenitangwu. Piw hiitawat aw hin tutaptangwu hintiniqat.

Orayvi

Peetuyniqw Hopi yaw Songoopave susmooti kitsokta. Noq pu'
yaw puma hakim pep naatupkom, i' kikmongwiniqw pu' tupko'at,
kya pi hiita ep neepewtiqw pu' i' tupko'atwa yaw pangqw naako-
panqe pu' pam kwiniwiqniiqe pu' Orayve tuwat naap kitsokta. Noq
pay pi qa soosoyam it sun navoti'yyungqw peetuyniqw Hopi pay
Öngtupqaveq yamakkyangw pu' angqe' mooti nakwsukyangw pu'
paasat Orayve mooti kitsokta.

Noq pu' hayphaqam puma pep it Pahanqatsit, tutuqayiwuy ep
piw neepewtotiqw pu' paasat puma pep naahonayaqw pu' ima qa
Pahannanawaknaqam pu' pangqw nöngakqe pu' oovi Hotvelpeq
tuwat kitsoktota. Pu' pay puma piw tuwat hiita ep neepewtotiqe pu'
puma peetu Paaqavitwat ep yesva. Noq pu' ima peetu pay Pahannanawaknaqam Orayve huruutotiqam atkyami hanqe pu' piw pepwat
tuwat yesva. Pay puma pep tumalyesva. Noq pam pepeq pu' Kiqötsmovi yan natngwani'yta. Paasat pu' piw peetu Munqamiqwat hintiqw pi oovi tuwat nönga. Niikyangw pangsoq pay ima Orayvit hisat
sasqaya. Puma pepeq paasa'yyungngwuniiqe oovi pangsoq naap
hisat sasqayangwu. It naatsikiwuy akw pu' oovi Orayviy kwiniwiqwat pu' qa suukya kitsoki.

Ösömuya

Ösömuya pi pay Powamuyat angkningwu. Pay pi kya pi put muuyawuy angqe' sutsep huuhuklawngwuniqw oovi paniqw put pangqaqwangwu, Ösömuya. Pu' pay angqe' angkwaningwu piw.

Paamuya

Paamuya pi pay Kyaamuyat angkningwu. Niikyangw piw pam
pi Hopiituyniqw haalaymuyaw. Put qaatsiptuqw panis muytutwat
pay pususuykinayangwu. Pu' pay ang kivanawit pususutoynaya-
ngwu, taatawlalwangwu. Pu' hiituwat mantangtotaniqey naawinye'
pantotingwu.

her. Since she is the grandmother of the Pöqangw Brothers, Pöqangwhoya and Palöngawhoya are just like her, versed in many
things. In stories Old Spider Woman helps anyone in need. Thus, she
has ways of doing away with a person's enemies. Also she always
gives a person advice on what to do.

Oraibi

According to some, the Hopi first settled at Shungopavi. There
the *kikmongwi* and his younger brother are said to have differed over
some matter. As a result, the younger brother left, headed north and
started his own community at Oraibi. However, not everyone shares
the same version of this event. Some others say that the Hopi, after
their emergence at the Grand Canyon, first embarked on a migration
before they established their first settlement at Oraibi.

Then, in the more recent past, the people there clashed again due
to different views regarding the white man's way of life, in particular,
schooling. This led to the banishment of those who rejected the Anglo
way of life. In turn they established the village of Hotevilla. After renewed differences there, some people settled at Bacavi. Next, several
of those who wanted the way of the whites and had remained at
Oraibi moved below the mesa and founded another village where
they worked for the government. Today that place is known as Kykotsmovi. Yet others for some reason migrated to Moencopi where
the Oraibi people had been going on foot for a long time already
because they owned fields there. Thus, as a result of the banishment,
several villages now exist northwest of Oraibi.

Ösömuya (month)

Ösömuya (approximately March) is the lunar month following
Powamuya (approximately February). Its name, "whistle-month," is
attributed to the fact that the wind blows constantly at this time of the
year. Ösömuya is also the time for night dances.

Paamuya (month)

The lunar month of Paamuya (approximately January) follows
Kyaamuya (approximately December). In the eyes of the Hopi Paamuya is a happy month, for as soon as the moon appears and people
spot it, they start beating their drums. Drumming and singing can be
heard in all of the kivas then. Whenever some of the men decide to
bring girls into the kivas for social dances, they do so.

Paayu

It Homol'oviy aatevenge' muunangwuy mumunqat i' Hopi Paayu yan tuwi'yta. Noq pu' i' Öngtupqavaqeniiqa pavan hihin wukomunangw Pisisvayu yan maatsiwa.

Payotsim

Ima Payotsim pay piw tuwat himusinom, niikyangw puma pay hisat Hopiikimiq ökiwkyangw puma pangsoq kiipokye' pu' pangsoq ökingwu. Puma pay tuwat kwiningyahaqaqw pangsoq ökiwtangwu. Noq pu' hakim tseletikive piw imuy himusinmuy enang yuuyaangwuniiqe oovi hakim imuy Payotsimuy akw tsetselyangwu.

Pavayoykyasi

I' Pavayoykyasi pay tuwat yaw pas su'its talavay imuy Hopiituy uuyiyamuy ang waynume' pam pang maakwannumngwu. Noq oovi pantiqw antsa hak pu' uuyiy aw pituqw put uuyit ang paatsöpölöwyungwa. Noq pay lavaytangwuniqw pam hak himu suhimutiyo. Pu' pay pam piw sutsep lomayuwsi'ynumngwu.

Noq pu' i' piw suukya pavayoykyasi yan maatsiwqa put i' himu Kwaakatsina'eway iikwiwtangwu, pu' i' Leenangw piiwu.

Piiki

I' piiki pas it Hopit hisatnösiwqa'at. Wuuti piktanik pam mooti tumay aqw qööngwu. Qööt pu' pam tuupatangwu. Tuupate' pu' kwalakqw pu' pam put sakwapngumniy aw wuutangwu. Ngumniy aw wuutat paasat pu' pam qötsvit aqw piw kuyqw pu' put paqwri'at put qöösapkuyit akw kuwantingwu. Pu' put tuma'at mukiitiqw pu' pam put sivostosit sumitsovalat paasat pu' pam put ang taqtsokt pu' paasat put akw tumay ang maamapringwu. Pam pantiqw pu' put tuma'at ahoy taviltingwu. Pu' pam paasat pik'oyqw pu' pam paasat kwasingwu. Put pam sukw ang ayo' hölöknat pu' pam piw ep lelwingwu. Pu' pam put mootiniiqat put naat pu' ang lelwiqey atsmi taviqw pu' pam pay söviwangwuy akw mowatingwu. Paasat pu' pam put muupat pu' ayo' tavingwu. Nit paasat pu' pam pay piw antikyangw pu' pay pansa put aapiy yuykungwu, put muupankyangw pu' put naanatsva oo'oyngwu.

Pay it Kookyangwso'wuutit pangqaqwangwuniqw pam yaw tuhisaniikyangw pu' piw nawiso'aniqw oovi himuwa piktuwi'yvanik pam yaw put aw naawaknangwu. Noq ayam Orayviy taavangqöyve pep atkyahaqam pam kur piw ki'yta. Noq oovi hak pan piktuwi'y-

Paayu (Little Colorado River)

The river that flows past the southwest side of the Homol'ovi ruins is called Paayu by the Hopi. The river that flows through the Grand Canyon, however, which is much larger, is referred to as Pisisvayu (Colorado River).

Paiutes

The Paiutes are a native people with a culture quite different from that of the Hopi. For ages they sought out the Hopi country on their raids. Generally, they arrived from a northwesterly direction. Today, during the event of a social dance, the Hopi also disguise themselves to resemble other tribes, including the Paiutes.

Pavayoykyasi (deity)

They say that very early in the morning Pavayoykyasi walks about asperging the crops in the Hopi's fields. And, indeed, just as one arrives at his field, there are drops of dew clinging to the crops. People describe Pavayoykyasi as a handsome youth who is always dressed very nicely.

The term *pavayoykyasi* is also used to mean a "moisture tablet" which is worn for example on the back of an Eagle kachina. A member of the Flute society also carries one.

Piki (dish)

Piki is an ancient food of the Hopi. When a woman plans to make it she begins by heating up her stone griddle. She then boils some water and pours it on the blue flour. That accomplished, she adds wood ashes mixed with water which gives the batter its hue. As soon as her stone griddle is hot enough, she spreads ground melon seeds over it and allows them to burn into the stone. Then she makes her first piki, stacking them next to her. As she continues with the process removing each piki sheet, she spreads a new layer of batter over the griddle. The previously baked piki is next placed on top and becomes moist from the steam of the new batter. The completed piki can then be rolled up for storage. From that point on she continues rolling and stacking one piki on top of another.

It is said that Old Spider Woman is skillful, and talented in many things, so someone eager to learn to make piki prays to her. Old Spider Woman also resides somewhere southwest of Oraibi. Thus, whenever a girl wishes to learn the art of piki making, she takes some

vanik hak pangso put kiiyat aw kohot kimangwu. Pu' hak hoomat enang put aw oyangwu.

Piktotokya

I' piktotokya lööq taalat akw it tiikivet angk qa pitsiwtangwu. Pam it suus qa hiita angkningwu. Noq pu' paasat put angk totokyaningwu. Noq it piktotokyat ep ima momoyam tuwat put piikit pisoq yuykuyangwuniqw oovi pam paniqw piktotokya.

Tsoongo

Pam i' tsoongo pi pay tsöqat angqw yukiwtangwu. Himuwa tsaqaptalawngwunen pi pay put enang kya pi yuykungwu. Himuwa naawakne' put hakiy ayatangwu. Pu' pay ephaqam taataqt pi pay piw put naap yukuyangwu. Put puma tsoongot momoypitoynayangwu. Pam pay momoypi'atniqa pam pay mit paaqavit angqw yukiwtangwu.

Pivanhonkyapi

Pivanhonkyapi Orayviy taavang, Apooniviy hopqöyngaqw kiiqö. Pay tumpoq haykyawput ep kiiqö. Noq angqe tatkyaqe tumkyaqe koro'yungwa. Pang lestavit tsöqömnayangwu, saqtivaninik. Pu' himuwa put ang wupngwu, lestavit tsööqökiwtaqat, pu' pangqw piw sukwwat aw tso'omtingwu. Pay yaw kyaatataypi'ewakw hinta. Haq naayaq koro'ta. Pu' aqw tatkyaqöymiq pay pas piw tuupela'yta.

Kiisonvi

I' kiisonvi pam pay haqamwat kitsokit ep pay sunasavehaqamningwuniqw oovi pam pan natngwani'yta. Noq himu hintsakye' sen katsina pite' pam pep wunimangwu. Pu' pay piw aapiy hiihiimu tiitikive pep hintsakiwa. Meh, pay ima Tsuutsu't, Lalkont, Kwaakwant, pay ii'ima pep tiikive'yyungngwu.

Pu' pay pangqw naanan'i'vaqw kiikihu aqwwat hoongi. Pu' pay angqw piw aw kiskya'yyungngwu. Pu' hisat himuwa hiita huuyaniniqw haqawa put engem pan tsa'lawqw pu' pam paasat piw ephaqam pep huuyangwu.

Powamuya

Powamuyat ep hakimuy powatotangwu, sinmuy. Noq oovi pam Powamuya. Hakimuy pi Powamuymongwi powatangwu soosok

wood to her abode and leaves it there for her along with some sacred cornmeal.

Piktotokya (ceremonial day designation)

Piktotokya occurs two days before *tiikive*, the "day of the public dance performance." *Piktotokya*, in turn, is preceded by the day *suus qa himu*, "once nothing day." On *piktotokya* the women are traditionally busy preparing piki, hence the name *piktotokya*, or "piki totokya."

Pipe

The pipe is made out of clay. Any potter who fashions bowls makes pipes along with other pottery. Whoever needs a pipe, simply places an order with the potter. Sometimes the men also make their own. The mouth piece which is added to the pipe generally consists of a reed.

Pivanhonkyapi (place name)

Pivanhonkyapi is a ruin southwest of Oraibi, on the northeastern side of Apoonivi. The ruined village lies close to the mesa rim. There are holes in the bedrock along the southeastern edge. Into these holes the people of Pivanhonkyapi used to insert poles whenever they wanted to perform the ladder dance. A dancer would climb up the inserted pole and then jump to the next pole over. This spectacle must have been awesome to behold, for the holes are far apart. In addition, the southeastern side has a steep cliff.

Plaza

The plaza is usually situated somewhere near the middle of a village, hence it is used as the dance court if a ceremonial activity is taking place, for example, and kachinas have come. Various other dances are also performed in the plaza. The Snake, Lakon, and Kwan societies, for instance, carry out their dance performances there.

Houses are erected on all four sides of the plaza, and alleys lead into it. In the past, when certain items were to be traded, someone would make a public announcement on behalf of the vendor, who would then sell his things at the plaza.

Powamuy Ceremony

During the Powamuy ceremony people are being purified. That's the reason for its name Powamuya. It is the Powamuy leader who

hiita angqw, qa masasatotani, qa potsatsatotani momoyneyang it muuyawuy ang. Noq it muuyawuy ep katsinam haaruy höqye' put totokpe talavay tsaatsakwmuy amungem kivayangwu. Pu' ep mihikqw pu' kivanawit yungiwmangwu, tiikive'yyungngwu. Qa wimkya pay pumuy qa tiimaytongwu.

Nakwakwusi

Nakwakwusit hak pay piw aw okiwlawkyangw put yukungwu. Pu' hak piw naat put aw tsootsongngwu. I' nakwakwusi pay qa suupwat engem. I' suukya pöötaviningwu; pu' paasat pay hak piw put nakwa'ytangwu. Pu' ephaqam hak hiita put hikwsitoynangwu. I' nakwakwusi pay it kwavöhötnit pu' pösöptonit angqw yukiwta.

Paaho

I' himu paahoniqa pam pay soosok hiita angqw yukiwkyangw pu' piw qa sun yuykiwa. Niikyangw pam pay qa hisat kwavöhöt angqw yukilti. Pu' pay piw it koyongvöhöt angqw enang paaholalwa. Meh, pay kivaapa panyungwa, haqaqw kyeevelngaqw haayiwyungngwu. Pu' pay imuy katsinmuy ninmaniniqw pu' pumuy put huytotangwu. Pu' pay piw ima hiihiitu Kwaakwant, Aa'alt, Wuwtsimt puma piw qa sunyungqat paaholalwa. Pu' piw Soyalangwuy ep qa suukya paaho yukiltingwu. Pay imuy hiituy amungem put yuykuyaqw puma tuwat put ömaatote' yaw tuwat haalaytotingwu. Pu' pay piw pam hakiy unangwvaasiyat, okiwayat enang yawmangwu. Pu' pay himuwa tuuhikya hakiy aw mamkyaqa piw paahot enang hakiy hiita tuuyayat enang hom'oytongwu. Pu' pay Hopi qa hiita qa engem paahotangwu. It taawat, muuyawuy, pu' imuy qataymataq yesqamuy, pu' pay aapiy soosok hiituy amumi enang taqa'nangwqey pumuy amungem pam piw paaholawngwu.

Tsa'lawu

Hisat himuwa sinmuy hiita navotnaninik pam hakiy tsa'law'ayatangwu. Pu' ephaqam i' pas tsa'akmongwi naap put hiita tunvotnangwu. Noq tsa'lawqa pay sutsep haqami oomiq wupt pu' paasat pangqw tsa'lawngwu. Niikyangw pam it mooti akw yaynangwu: "Pangqe' kya uma sinom yeese, kur huvam pew tuqayvastota'a." Itakw pam yaynat pu' paasat pam mitakw so'tapnangwu: "Pay yanhaqam inumi tutaptotaqw oovi nu' yanhaqam umuy aa'awna. Pay

does the purifying. He purifies people from everything, especially not to be dancing in social dances any more. During this month the kachinas harvest bean sprouts and bring them to the children on the morning of *totokya*, "the ceremonial eve." That same night there are kachina dances in the kivas which uninitiated children are not permitted to watch.

Prayer Feather

A *nakwakwusi* is fashioned to the accompaniment of a prayer. Then it is also smoked upon. This type of prayer feather has more than one function. It can be the symbol of a path laid out, but it can equally well be worn on the head. It also serves to represent symbolically the breath of life. A *nakwakwusi* is produced from the downy breast feather of an eagle together with hand-spun cotton twine.

Prayer Stick/Prayer Feather

A paho is not only made from a variety of items, but it is also fashioned in many different ways. While it is never made from the breast feather of the eagle, it can be made from turkey feathers. Paho can be found hanging from the ceilings of kivas. For example, when kachinas are to return to their homes, they are given paho. The members of the Kwan, Al, and Wuwtsim societies each fashion their own unique paho. A great diversity of paho are made at the time of Soyalangw. It is said that those for whom the paho is intended are elated upon receiving it. A paho carries with it a person's most intense wishes and prayers. A medicine man who has treated you takes what ails you along with a paho and goes to deposit that. In fact, there is nothing that the Hopi does not make a paho for. He makes it for the sun, the moon, deities who exist unseen, and all the other beings that he relies upon for his existence.

Public Announcement

In the past when a Hopi wished to inform his fellow villagers of certain things, he would petition someone to make a public announcement on his behalf. At other times, a formal announcement could be made by the *tsa'akmongwi*, or official "village crier." To broadcast his message, the crier always climbed on a rooftop. The opening formula of his announcement usually sounded as follows: "Those of you people out there heed my words." The conclusion was equally formalized: "This is the announcement I was instructed to make known to you. That's about it." Whenever the crier shouted out

yanhaqamo." Pu' tsa'lawqa piw sutsep hiita tsa'lawe' put wiisilanmangwu.

Qa'ötaqtipu
Qa'ötaqtipu pi Paaqaviy hopqöyvehaqam haqam kiiqö. Pep yaw qaa'öt taq'iwyungqat tutwaqw oovi pam pep Qa'ötaqtipu yan maatsiwa.

Qömi
Qömi pi toosit angqw yukiwtangwu. Hakim tuupeptote' pu' put hotomnayangwu. Pantaqat put hak laknangwu. Pu' pam lakqw pu' hak put angqw hiisa' huume' pu' put ngumangwu. Pam pi paasat toosiningwu. Pu' hak put angqw hiisa' tsaqaptat aqw oye' pu' put aqw kuuyit kuyngwu. Pu' put aqw qöritangwu, mutstangwu. Pu' hin hurutniqat pan hak put paavaqwringwu. Pam pi qöminingwu. Pay hak pantit put pan qömt pay pantaqat put angqw tuumoytangwu, suusungwat.

Pu' pay ephaqam piw himuwa maana put angqw aw qöqömiwyat yukye' put ini'ytangwu, Powamuyve mihikqwtikive. Pay hisat kya pi hak piw siwatuwte' yumuyatuy navotnanik hiisa' nömömvut piikit intat pu' atsmiq qömit tsokyat pantaqat tiyot kiiyat aw yawmangwu. Pu' kur pay hakiy qa naanakwhe' pu' hakiy inpiyat aw sikwit intat pantaqat ahoy aw yawmangwu.

Tangaqwunu
Tangaqwunu pam pay pi nukushimu. Yaw pam hin'ur hovaqtu. Yaw pam hin'ur hovaqtungwuniqw oovi ima oo'omawt tuwat put mamqasyangwuniiqe oovi haqami puma tunatyawkyaakyangwyaqw pu' amutpik laholtiqw pu' pay puma ahoyyangwu. Nawus qa pangso put hakiy engem yoknayangwu. Pam pay nukpananiiqat kitotangwu piw oovi pay. Noq oovi pay pam oo'omawtuy uutaqw pay pangqaqwangwu, "Pay pi son pew ökini. Son yokvani. Pay pi ang uuta," kitotaqw pay antsa hakimuy qa aw ökingwu.

Wiimi
Hak hiita wimkyaniikyangw pu' put aw aasi'ytaqw pam hakiy wiimi'atningwu. Niikyangw Hopi as qa suukw wiimi'ykyangw pam pay qa soosok put tuwitangwu. Peehu wiimi pay taataqtuysa amu

his announcement, he typically drew out the last word of each sentence.

Qa'ötaqtipu (place name)

Qa'ötaqtipu is a ruin site somewhere on the northeast side of Bacavi. Burned corn was discovered there, hence the appellation Qa'ötaqtipu, "Burned Corn."

Qömi (dish)

Qömi is made from *toosi*, or "ground, roasted sweet corn." After baking sweet corn in an earth oven, people usually string the cobs up, whereupon they let them dry. When the drying process is complete, people shell some of the baked sweet corn and grind it up. It now becomes *toosi*. The *toosi* is placed in a pottery bowl, into which water is added. Both ingredients are now stirred and kneaded. When the mixture acquires the desired consistency, it is *qömi*, or "sweet corn cake." Having made the *qömi* in this way, it is eaten cold.

Occasionally, a girl will fashion little sweet corn cakes and take them into the kiva on a flat tray during a night dance in the month of Powamuya. Also, in the old days, when a girl had a sweetheart and wanted to let the boy's parents know about this, she would stack a small amount of folded piki on a tray, place some sweet corn cakes on top and take this to the boy's house. If the parents were not in favor of the girl, they simply put some meal on the girl's tray and took it back to her.

Rainbow

The rainbow is an evil force. They say it exudes a terrible stench, which is one of the reasons why the clouds are afraid of it. Thus, if the clouds are on the way to some destination and a rainbow arches under them, they retreat. As a result, they cannot bring rain to the people. That's why one commonly hears that a rainbow is bad. People say that it closes in the clouds. "They can't come to us now. It's not going to rain. The rainbow closes the clouds in." And it's true, they fail to come then.

Ritual Requiring Initiation

Whatever religious practice a Hopi is initiated into, by means of a hair-washing rite, constitutes his *wiimi*. The Hopis engage in many rituals, and no one Hopi is familiar with the esoteric practices for all

ngemniqw pu' peehu pay momoymuysa piw amungem. Niikyangw
hak tsaynen it katsinawuy pay pas son nawus mooti qa tuwitangwu.
Ason pas hak pan wimkyate' paasat pu' hak hiitawat katsinnay sen
katsinyuy pam haqawa hiita wimkyaniqw paasat pu' hak put wiimiyat tuwitangwu.

Noq ayangqaqw pay naat as hiihiita yungtiwisngwuniqw peqwhaqami pu' pay pam peehu wiimi so'ti. I' himu Nakyawiminiqw pu'
i' Tsukuwimi pay pu' qa haqam. Pu' ima Momtsit, puma pay pu' qa
hisat yungya. Pay imasa naat haaqe' kitsokiva pay naat hiita yungngwu, ima Popwamuyt, Wuwtsimt, Sosyalt, Aa'alt, Kwaakwant,
Taatawkyam, Tsuutsu't, Tsöötsöpt, Leelent, Lalkont, O'waqölt pu'
Mamrawt.

Wawarkatsinam

Wawarkatsinam pi tuwat Ösömuyva ökingwu. Pay puma piw
pas qa navotnit akw pay ökingwu. Nen pu' hiihiita na'mangwuy
e'nang ökiwisngwu. Pu' pay haqam tuuyuyutnayaniqey pangsoya-
ngwu. Pu' peetu kivapt pay kya pi navoti'yyungwe' pu' pas yuuyaangwu. Pay naap hin himuwa yuwsi'ytangwu. Pankyaakyangw pu'
puma aw haqami haqam wawarkatsinamyaqw pu' puma amumiye'
pu' hak hiitawat namortangwu amum warikniqey. Pu' pay wawarkatsinam tiitimaytuy haqawatuy langamintotangwu. Hakiy katsina
amum warikniqey put aqwnen pu' langaknangwu. Pu' aw tuuwuhit
aw wikqw ephaqam panis aw wunuusaltit pay warikngwu. Pu' pam
ngöytangwu.

Pay pi puma ökye' pas hiihinyungqam wawarkatsinamningwu.
Hiihin maamatsiwyangwu. Meh, Tatsiipölölö hakiy tatsiy akw taa-
tuvangwu. Tsöqaapölölö piw hakiy tsöqat pölangput akw taatuva-
ngwu. Tsilitosmoktaqa hakiy wiikye', pu' ngu'e', tsiilit tos'iwtaqat
hakiy nopnangwu. Kwitanono'a hakiy kwitat nopnangwu. Pu' Aykatsina pay hakiy moohot akw wuvaatangwu. Nahoyleetsi'ytaqa piw
pay su'antangwu. Hakiy moohot akw wuvaatangwu. Kokopölmana
pay hiitawat ngu'e' tatskweknangwu. Pu' atsva suutsoraltingwu. Pu'
aqw yomimiykungwu.

Hooma

It hoomat akw i' Hopi as hisat pas naaqavo hintsakngwu. Aasakis
talavay pam kuyvate' pam naat piw putakw talpumiq naawaknangwu.

of them. Some rites are exclusively for men; others are only for women. The first exposure to a *wiimi* takes place when a child is initiated into the kachina cult. Thereafter, the Hopi can learn about the ritual of another society. Usually, it is the society which is affiliated with one's kachina god father or god mother.

Long ago people were involved in a great variety of rituals conducted by special societies, some of which have become extinct. For example, the Nakya rites and the clown ritual no longer exist. Also the Momtsit do not carry on their ritual anymore. Only the initiates of the Powamuy, Wuwtsim, Soyal, Al, Kwan, Taw, Snake, Antelope, Flute, Lakon, Owaqöl, and Maraw societies still conduct their esoteric practices in some villages.

Runner Kachinas

Runner kachinas typically come during the month of Ösömuya (approximately March). As a rule, they appear without anyone's prior knowledge. They bring all sorts of gifts with them as they proceed to the location where they plan to challenge people to a race. Some of the kachinas' kiva partners know about their arrival of course, and dress up in fanciful ways. They then go in this guise to where the Runner kachinas are and challenge a Runner kachina to a race. But the kachinas, too, pull in spectators if one of them fancies one to run with him. Taking his victim to a line, the latter usually dashes off as soon as he stops at the line. The kachina then sets out in pursuit of him.

There is a great variety of Runner kachinas. They all have different names. Tatsiipölölö, for instance, throws his ball at the loser, Tsöqaapölölö metes out his punishment with balls of clay. Tsilitosmoktaqa, upon catching up with his victim and grabbing him, force-feeds him chili powder. The Kwitanono'a, on the other hand, feeds his victim excrement. Aykatsina, or "Rattle kachina," whips the loser with yucca strips. Nahoyleetsi'ytaqa does the same. The Kokopölmana, finally, flings her victim on the ground as soon as she catches him. Then she flattens out on top of him and executes several pelvic thrusts into her victim.

Sacred Cornmeal

Sacred cornmeal was once used by the Hopi on an everyday basis. Each morning as he went out to pray toward the rising sun, he made it a habit to pray with *hooma*.

Pu' i' katsinmuy na'am pumuy tumala'yte' pay naat pam piw putakw pumuy tumala'ytangwu. Naalakyaniqw pu' amungem pöötapngwu. Put pumuy nopnaqw pu' puma tiivantivayangwu. Pu' tapkiqw yukuyaqw pay naat pam piw put enang pumuy yuwsinaqw pu' puma ninmangwu.

Pu' mö'öngna'yat yukiltiqw pu' pam mö'wi nimaniniqw paasat pu' piw put engem homvöötotangwu. Pu' hiitu yungiwte', pavasiwye', puma hoomat piw naat enang akw hintsatskyangwu. Pu' i' piw Kwaani'ytaqa Astotokpe putakw hoomat akw haqe' pöhut utatangwu. Pu' himuwa paahoy oyate' pam piw sutsep it hoomat enang kimangwu. Nen pu' pam haqam put oye' pam piw naat hoomay akw put aw naawaknat pu' paasat put oyangwu. Paniqw oovi himuwa hom'oytoqat pangqaqwangwu.

Poosi'ytaqa

Hisat ima peetu tuutuhikt nuutuupa tuukyaynit ipwantota. Puma pumuy pi pangqaqwangwu, poosi'ytaqa. Pam pi hakiy aw ruupit akw taataye' pu' himu haqam hakiy ep hintaqw hakiy aw pas pangqawngwu. Pu' piw tuukyaynit tuwe' put ep horoknangwu. Ephaqam himuwa pay tuuhikyat aw hepte' pay naap naatukyayangwu. Put ep put tuwe' pay aw tavingwu. Pay naap haqami hintsanniqat aw pangqawngwu.

Supawlavi

Supawlavi pi pay yangqw Songoopangaqw pangso kwiipilti. Yaw hisat yep Songoopavi sulawtiqw puma yaw put hiita wiimiyat aapiytotani. Niikyangw pay naat Songoopavi qa haqaminiqw pay ima Supawlavit pu' pew Songoopami hiihiita wiimit tuwitawisngwu, Wuwtsimuy, Marawuy. Pay hiita it puma pep qa tuwilalwa. Pu' puma Tsuutsu't oovi pongyay pep oyi'yyungwa.

Songoopavi

Songoopavi pay Orayviy aatatkyahaqam. Noq peetuy navoti'amniqw pep yaw i' Hopi susmooti kitsokta. Niikyangw pay qa pep

The kachina father, that is, the man who tends the kachinas, also uses it as he takes care of them during their dances. When the kachinas are to change dance positions, the father makes a cornmeal path for them. He ceremonially feeds them with the cornmeal, whereupon they commence dancing. In the evening, at the conclusion of their performance, sacred cornmeal is again an ingredient in ritually preparing the kachinas for their journey home.

On the occasion of a wedding, after the ceremony is completed and the bride is to return home, a cornmeal path once more is marked on the ground for her. Again, when there is a ritual in progress and prayers are being conducted, cornmeal is involved. On *astotokya*, the climactic night of the Wuwtsim initiation, a member of the Kwan society seals off the paths leading into the village with cornmeal. Finally, when one goes to deposit a paho one always takes cornmeal along. Before the paho is deposited, one first prays to it using the cornmeal. This accounts for the expression *hom'oyto*, "he is going to deposit cornmeal."

Shaman

In times past a small group of medicine men were capable of removing foreign objects that had been implanted into a patient by sorcery to cause an ailment. A medicine man of these qualifications was referred to as a crystal gazer or shaman. He would diagnose the patient through a crystal, and if there was a problem, he would point it out to the patient. When he discovered the foreign object responsible for the ailment, he removed it. Once in a while someone would seek out a medicine man to test his powers and insert this foreign object into his body himself. If the medicine man found it, he gave it to the patient telling him to get rid of it.

Supawlavi (Second Mesa village)

The village of Shipaulovi is an offshoot of Shungopavi. It is said that if ever Shungopavi becomes extinct, the people of Shipaulovi are to carry on its ceremonies. But as Shungopavi still exists, the inhabitants of Shipaulovi go there to be initiated into the necessary societies, such as the Wuwtsim and the Maraw. Consequently, the altar pieces of the Snake society are also kept at Shungopavi.

Shungopavi (Second Mesa village)

Shungopavi lies approximately southeast of Oraibi. According to the traditions of some the Hopi established their first settlement there.

oove, pay puma aapiy wuuyavotiqw pu' pangso yayva. Noq pu' piw peetu navoti'yyungqw yaw puma hakim pep naatupkom, i' kikmongwiniqw pu' put tupko'at Matsito yan maatsiwqa, hiita ep pay neepewtiqw pu' pam tupko'atwat oraymiqniiqe pu' pepeq tuwat peetuy sinmuy tsamkyangw pu' qatuptu. Noq pay hintaqat akw pi puma Songoopavitniqw pu' Orayvit qa sun tuuqayyungwa naamahin as puma sun hopiitniikyaakyangw.

Sikyatki

I' Sikyatki pay Walpiy aahoophaqam kiiqö. Noq pep yaw ima isngyam mooti yesva. Nit pu' puma pay pangqw son pi hintaqat akw qa nankwusaqe pu' pay Hopiikivaqe aatsavala.

Tsootsongo

Hisat Hopi yaw pas naaqavo hiita aw okiwlawngwuniikyangw pam it tsoongot pas sonqa akw enangningwu. Pu' i' kikmongwi hisat hakiy kya pi pitsine' pam put piw pas sonqa tsootsongnangwu. Noq pu' haqaqwwat katsinamyaniqw hak nuutumninik hak aqw pakiqw paasat pu' i' pepeq mong'iwtaqa piw hakiy pas mooti tsootsongnaqw pu' hak pumuy amumumningwu. Pu' paasat hakim hiita yungiwte', hakim mooti pu' piw yukuye', pu' hakim piw tsotsongqöniwmangwu. Pu' hakiy tsootsongnaqa aw tsoongoy taviqw pu' paasat hak angqw hiisakishaqam tsootsongnat pu' paasat hak put aw hin yantaqey pangqawngwu. Sen hak na'yte' hak pangqawngwu, "Ina'a." Noq pu' pam hakiy tuwat hu'wane' pu' pangqawngwu, "Iti'i." Pay hak hisat hakiy aw hinwat yantaqey pay hak put tuwi'ytangwu. Niikyangw pay ephaqam hak hakiy qa tuwi'yte' pay pam kur hakiy epniiqe wuuyoqniqw pay hak sen, "Ina'a," aw kitangwu. Pu' pay sen hakiy epniiqe qa pas wuuyoqniqw pay hak son kya qa, "Ipava," kitangwu. Noq pu' paasat pay hak qa pangqawninik pay hak piw ayangqawngwu, "I'unangwsungwa," pay hak piw kitangwu.

Noq hak tsootsongye' hak mooti unangwngaqw hiita nukngwat, hiita lolmat as okiw aw aniwtiniqat yan hak hutunvastat pu' put kwiitsingwuy mo'angaqw nöngaknangwu. Noq pu' i' kwiitsingw yaw hakiy hiita okiwlawqw put yaw pam haqami imuy pas pavanyaqamuy paasat kimangwu. Yan it Hopi navoti'ytaqe oovi pam aasakis hiita hintsakqw i' piivaniqw pu' i' tsoongo pas son pep sulawningwu.

But they did not settle on top of the mesa then. To that location they migrated much later. Tradition also has it that two brothers, the *kikmongwi* and his younger brother Matsito, had differences of opinion which resulted in the latter's moving to Oraibi. He took some people along and founded Oraibi. For some unknown reason the people of Shungopavi and the people of Oraibi do not speak the same dialect, even though they are both Hopi.

Sikyatki (place name)

Sikyatki is a ruin northwest of Walpi. The place was first settled by the Coyote clan. Then, for some reason, the members of this clan moved away, and now they have spread throughout the Hopi villages.

Smoking

Long ago a Hopi prayed every day, and while he did this he always smoked a pipe. Also, whenever the *kikmongwi* had a caller, he had to offer him his pipe. Likewise, when one plans to participate in a kachina dance and goes to the kiva from which the impersonators will come, the person in charge of the ceremony must first offer you a smoke before you can join in. When a ceremony is in progress, there is a round of smoking at the beginning and end of the ritual. As soon as your neighbor has finished, he hands you the pipe. You now take a few puffs and address him in the manner according to which you are related to him. If he is your father, you would say, "My father." When his turn comes to reply he would say, "My child." In the past all people knew how they were related to one another. If one is not familiar with one's neighbor and that person happens to be older than you, you may address him as, "My father." And if he is not much older than you, the proper form of address would be, "My elder brother." If one does not wish to use this expression, an alternative form of address is, "Companion of my heart."

The person smoking first prays fervently from his heart that things will turn out beneficial for him and prosper before he exhales the smoke. This smoke then carries one's prayers to those who are more powerful. This is what ritual smoking means to a Hopi. Thus it is little wonder that whenever he is engaged in a certain endeavor, tobacco and pipe are ever present.

Somiviki

Somiviki pay it sakwapngumnit paqwri'iwtaqat angqw yuykiwa. Pam it angvut ang mookiwkyangw pu' löökye' it moohot akw somiwtangwu. Put pan mokyaatotat pu' paasat put kwalaknayangwu.

Taatawi

Hopi hiita hintsakninik pam hisat taawit akw enang hiita hintsakngwu. Meh, taaqa hisat pasminen tawkyangwningwu. Pam yaw uuyiy navotnaniqe oovi tawkyangw pangso pitutongwu, aasavo yaw puma havivokyalniqat oovi. Pu' pam pang waynumkyangw piw tawkyangwningwu.

Noq pu' wuuti, maana piw ngumante' pam taawit akw enang ngumantangwu. Pam ngumantawiningwu. Taawit akw yaw put tumala'at pay qa pas maqsoniningwuniqw oovi pam tuwat tawkyangw ngumantangwu. Noq pu' wuuti piw tiy puupuwvitsne' pam piw put aw puwvitstawit tawlawngwu. Noq pu' hakim tsaatsayomnen hakim hohonaqye' hakim piw naat pay taawit akw enang hohonaqyangwu. Pu' piw hakim momoryaqw pep pu' piw naat suukya taawiningwu. Pu' hikis piw nukpana it hiita tuskyaptawit piw maskya'yta. Putakw pam yaw hakiy wariknangwu hakiy aw tungla'yte'.

Pu' soosoy himu wiimi taawitsa akw pasiwta. Noq pu' ima Wuwtsimt, Mamrawt, katsinam, tsetslet, tsutskut, ii'ima soosoyam nanap taawi'yyungwa. Pu' i' piw Tsu'tawiniqw pu' Lentawiniqw pu' Kwantawi. Noq pu' sosotukwyaqam piw pas naap taatawi'yyungwa. Puma pantsatsyaqam put tawkyaakyangw nanavö'yangwu. Pu' momoyam piw yungyaplalwe' puma ephaqam pay it Owaqöltatawit tawkyaakyangw pantsatskyangwu.

Noq pu' paasat i' tuutuwutsi as hisat pay sumataq pas sonqa taawi'ytangwu. Niikyangw peehu pay pu' suutokiwa. Pu' Hopi yaw pay yaapaniiqe oovi qa suukw hiituy lavayiyamuy ang enang yeewatima. Niiqe oovi ephaqam himuwa taawi si'olalvayngwu pu' piw tasaplalvayngwu. Pu' pay aapiy piw himusinmuy lavayi'am hiita taawit pay pas son ep qa pakiwtangwu. Pu' pay peehu taatawi pay pas hisattatawiniqw oovi pay peehu kur hiita lalvayya.

Noq iisaw hiita tuuwutsit ep tawme' pam pas sonqa wukotawmangwu. Qa hisat pay pam tsaakw ang tawma, pavan pam umukni'ytangwu.

Somiviki (dish)

Somiviki is made from the batter of blue corn flour. It is wrapped in a corn husk and then tied in two places with yucca strips. After packaging it in this way, it is boiled.

Songs

In the past, when a Hopi was to do something, he usually did this to the accompaniment of a song. For example, long ago a man would go to the fields singing. The reason for the singing was to alert his crops of his approach. He wanted them fully awake before his arrival. And as he walked about his plants, he also sang. Likewise when a woman or a young girl grinds corn, she does it to the tune of a song. That is a grinding song. With the accompaniment of a song her work is not so tedious; therefore, she also sings while grinding. Whenever a woman puts her child to sleep, she also sings it a lullaby. When we were playing as children, we did so while singing a song. Also while we swam, there was still another song.

Even an evil person has a song at hand, a song that makes you go crazy. With it he causes a person to go wild when he desires that person sexually.

All rituals are complete only with song. Thus, the members of the Wuwtsim and Maraw societies, the kachinas, the social dancers, and even the clowns all have their individual songs. There is also the Snake dance song, the Flute ceremonial song, and the Kwan song.

People who played the guessing game *sosotukwpi* also had songs of their own. Players sang as they competed against one another.

At times when women are weaving wicker plaques, they weave while singing the Owaqöl, or "Basket dance" songs.

Finally, it seems that folktales generally included a song, but some of them have been forgotten. It is said that the Hopi is a mockingbird. That is why he composes songs using the languages of many other people. Thus, one song might be in the Zuni language, another in Navajo. As a matter of fact, songs always include words from other Indian groups. Some are so ancient that the meaning of the words are completely obscure.

When coyote sings within a story, he always does so in a very deep voice. He never sings in a high pitched tone. He bellows the song out.

Powaqa

I' powaqa pi pay songyawnen nukpananingwuniqw oovi itam Hopiit as pumuy qa awini'ykyaakyangw pewwat atkyangaqw nöngakniniqw pay puma hin pi nanaptaqe oovi pew antsa itamum nönga. Noq pay puma haqam yaw Palangwuy epeq tuwat tsovaltingwuqat pay yan lavayta. Pu' pay hin pi puma tuwat sinot naanami tuuwiklalwa. Pu' pay puma qa naap yep yeese. Puma yaw naap sinomuy qatsiyamuy akw yaaptotingwu. Pu' pam yaw hakiy akw yaaptinik pam yaw hiita patukyat akw hakiy unangwhoroknangwu. Pu' pay puma tuwat mihikqwsa put hiita tuwiy hintsatskyangwu. Pu' pay puma piw yaw imuy hiituy popkotuy akw enang yakta.

Noq pu' piw himuwa haqam pay as naap maqsoniy akw hiita haqamniqw pay himuwa qa naane', hakiy aw qa kwangwatayte', pam hakiy a'ni powaqsasvingwu. Noq himuwa pam himunen son put nakwhangwu. Pu' yaw hak put panhaqam hintsakqat nu'ansanqw pam yaw hakiy hiita nukngwat akw uunatoynaniqey antingwu, it hiita himu'ytiwngwut sen tokoy, hak yaw put qa lalvayniqat oovi.

Sosotukwpi

Sosotukwpi pam Hopiituy tuwat navö'himu'am. Sosotukwpit akw nanavö'yaqam pay Paamuyve, tamö'vamuyve puma pantsatskyangwu. Niikyangw puma pi kivaapayangwu. Pay puma qöpqöt kwinigya nan'ip tsovawtangwu. Puma nan'ip pusukinpi'yyungngwu. Pu' hiituwat naalöq paksivut hongnayangwu. Pu' hiituwat aw pitsinaye' puma mooti tawkuynayangwu. Pu' maamatslalwaniqam naakwapyangwu. Naakwapyaqw pu' tawlalwaqamuy angqw put soomokit tupkyayangwu, put pakwsivut hiitawat akwa'. Pu' naakwapyungqam ayo' nawlöknayaqw pu' pumuy angqw pu' suukya aw heptongwu. Pu' pam put ang ma'ynumngwu, pakwsivut anga'. Put soomokit hepnumngwu. Pu' pam ang wuuwankyangw hepnumngwu. Sen yepe, sen yepe, sen yepe'. Yaw haqam pakiwtaqw susmataq yaw maayat aqw hukvangwu, pay hin aa'awnangwu. Pu' paasat ep pakwsivut kwusungwu. Ep kwuse' pu' nuutumi maataknangwu. Qa himu epniqw pu' pay put ayo' hoyoknangwu. Pu' kur sakine' pu' paayisni'ymakyangw pu' ephaqam suuput kwusungwu angqw soomoki pakiwtaqw paasat pu' pan puma pumuywatuy pö'ayangwu. Oovi paayistakyangw qa tuwaqw pu' pay puma pö'yyangwu. Hak suustakyangw suuput wa'öknaqw pu' yaw pam supakoymakngwu.

Sorcerer/Sorceress (male or female sorcerer)

A sorcerer is the equivalent of an evildoer. For this reason we, the Hopi, did not inform the sorcerers that we wanted to ascend to this upper world. Somehow, however, the sorcerers found out about it and made the emergence with us. They are reputed to congregate at a place called Palangwu. Sorcerers and witches do not live on their own. They lengthen their life span through the lives of their own relatives. All witchcraft activities are carried out only at night. Whenever one of them seeks to extend his life, he extracts a person's heart with a spindle. Sorcerers are also said to go about in the guise of some animals.

Sometimes when a Hopi acquires something through his own hard work, another person who is envious and looks upon the former with disfavor, will label him a witch. If he is one, he will never admit it of course. A witch who is caught red-handed performing acts of witchery will try to entice his captor to accept some valuable possession (in the case of a sorcerer) or even her own body (in the case of a sorceress). This is to keep the captor from revealing the sorcerer's identity.

Sosotukwpi (game)

Sosotukwpi is a Hopi game. It is generally played in the kivas during the winter month of *Paamuya* (approx. January). The competing players assemble in two groups on the northwest side of the fire place. One group sets up the four *pakwsivu* or "gaming cylinders" which are fashioned from cottonwood. The group that actually begins starts up a chant. Next, the players of the group who will be doing the guessing cover themselves up with blankets. That done, a member of the singing group hides the *soomoki*, "the object to be guessed," under one of the cottonwood cylinders. The other group now takes off its blanket covers, and one of their members steps up to search for the hidden object. He moves his hand back and forth over the cylinders searching for the hidden piece. He is concentrating while he does so. "Maybe it's here or here, or here," he keeps thinking. From the cylinder containing the hidden object a breeze seems to be emanating toward his hand, which may reveal the location. The guesser then picks up the cylinder and shows it to the others. If there is nothing underneath, he puts it aside. If he is lucky and by the third try picks up the right cylinder with the hidden object in it, his group wins. However, if he fails to guess correctly three times in a row, his side

Pu' paasat pö'ayaqam piw hongnayangwu. Pu' mima pö'yyaqam piw aw sukwwat laalayyangwu. Pu' pam paasat tuwat aw pite' pu' paasat ang piw yannumngwu, ma'ynumngwu. Pu' pö'ayaqam taatawlalwangwu piw tuwat pumuy amumi. Pay puma pan pep nanavö'lalwangwu.

Aasakis pö'ayaqw pu' suukya mimuy pö'yyaqamuy awnen put angqw wuusiyamuy hiisa' tsoopangwu. Pu' put kimangwu. Pay puma naanahoy naanami put homtotangwu. Pu' hiituwat mooti soosok wuusiy pö'yye' pu' puma pö'yyangwu. Noq it tuuwutsit ep pay taataqt momoymuy amumum neengawkyaakyangw tookyep sosotukwyangwu. Pu' pas a'nitote' pu' puma pas taalawnayangwu. Taawat yamakqw pu' angqw nöswisngwu. Niikyangw hisat hapi pan qatsi, pay hisato, qa puu'. Pu' pi pay qa haqam himu pam'i.

Soyalangw

Soyalangw pay tömölnawit it Wuwtsimuy panis yukiltiqwningwu. Niikyangw pam suukop taalat ang pan soyalangwningwu. Noq ep ima Sosyalt yungiwtangwunen pu' puma ep soosokmuy pu' piw soosok hiita akw mongvasyaqey soosok hiituy amungem paaholalwangwu. Ep pu' i' taawa piw tuwat tömö'kiy aqw pite' pu' pam paasat paapiy tala'kiwat aqw hoytangwuniqw pu' paapiy i' taawa wup'iwmangwu. Noq ep i' Soyalkatsina susmooti pitungwu. Noq pu' paasat aapiy pantaqw pu' ima Qööqöqlöm ökye' pu' puma paasat it kivat pas soosok ang hötaatotaqw pu' mimawat katsinam ökimantani.

Kookyangw

I' kookyangw pay tuwat peetuy Hopiituy wu'ya'am, pu' pay mimuywatuy put qa wu'ya'yyungqamuy amumi pam pay qa pas himu. Noq oovi himuwa kiy ep put waynumqat pay niinangwu. Pu' pam yaw piw hakiy aw sisiwkuqw hakiy yaw aapa u'ya'yvangwu.

Noq pu' i' so'wuuti pam Hopit a'ni hiita akw pa'angwankyangw pu' piw nu'okso'wuuti. Pu' pam piw a'ni himu. Naat i' himu pooko pu' it hikis tuuwaqatsit naat qa yukiltiqw pay put i' hikwsit himu'ytaqa mootihaq yuku. Noq itam Hopiit put so'wuutit Kookyangwso'wuuti yan tuwi'yyungwa. Noq pay kya qa hak put pas suyan navoti'ytani hintiqw pam tuwat pan maatsiwqw.

loses. When a player knocks over the right cylinder the very first time, they say the hidden object comes out of the cottonwood cylinder at once.

Now the winners set the game up again. The losers in turn send one of their group over. While the guesser moves his hand over the cylinders, the winners start up a song again to distract the others. That's how *sosotukwpi* is played.

In stories the game is always described as one in which men and women play together. They get so involved that they compete until daybreak the following morning. Not before sunrise do they go eat breakfast. Long ago, life was like this, way back in time. Nowadays the game is not played anymore.

Soyalangw (Soyal ceremony)

Soyalangw is a ceremony which takes place during the winter, not long after the Wuwtsim ritual. This entire event lasts sixteen days. During this time the Sosyalt, or "members of the Soyal society," carry out esoteric rites in their kiva, and they fashion prayer feathers of various kinds for everything from which the Hopi benefit. It is also at this time that the sun reaches its winter home. From that point on it journeys towards its summer home, and the days grow increasingly longer. In addition, Soyalangw marks the beginning of the new kachina season with the appearance of the Soyal kachina. Somewhat later, the Qööqöqlö kachinas arrive to ceremonially open all the kivas so that the other kachinas, too, are now able to make their visits.

Spider

For some Hopi the spider constitutes a clan totem. To those who are not of the Spider clan, a spider has no significance whatsoever. Thus, when a person comes across a spider in his home, he will kill it. It is also commonly believed that if a spider urinates on you, you will break out in sores.

There exists an old woman in Hopi mythology who assists the Hopi in many ways. She is very compassionate and very powerful. The giver of all life created her before the animals were created, even before this world was made. This woman is known as Kookyangwso'-wuuti, or "Old Spider Woman," by the Hopi. But it is not known for sure why she is referred to in this way.

Paahu

Hisat Hopi naat angqaqw haqaqw hoytaqe pam it hiita kuywikorot enang yanma. Niiqe pu' pam haqam huruutininik pam pep put tutskwave amqw pu' pam paahu pep yamakqw pangqw pu' puma hiihikwyangwu. Noq pu' puma yukiq Hopiikimiq ökiiqe pu' puma yang pay haqam i' paahu nööngantaqw pang puma pay put ahaykye' yesva. Niiqe pu' puma yang it haqe' paahuniqw puma pang put tuwi'yvayaqe pu' put nanap tungwaatota. Pu' himuwa piw haqam paahut naat pu' yamakqat tuwe' pam put naatoylay aw tungwangwu.

Noq pu' yang it paavahut ang haaqe' piw ima katsinam ki'yyungwa. Niiqe oovi ima Hopiit pangso enang hom'o'oyya, it yooyangwuy oovi. Noq pu' i' paahu it Hopit aw pas himuniqw oovi puma hisat piw aasakis yaasangwvaqw puma pangqw paytsinayangwu.

Noq pu' pep piw it' Paalölöqangw yaw qatungwuniqw oovi hakimuy tsaatsakwmuyniqw ima wuuwuyoqam hakimuy amumi pangqaqwangwuniqw oovi yaw hak qa pangqe paavaqe hintsaknumngwu. Pu' pam yaw piw suutawanasave pepeq yamakngwu. Pu' piw yaw hak haqaqw paangaqw hikwninik hak yaw pangqw piw qa motolhikwngwu. Hak yaw hiita akw kuyt pu' pangqw hikwngwu. Pu' hak ngasta kuyapi'yte' hak yaw pay may akw pangqw kuyt pu' hikwngwu. Pu' i' piw suukyawa maqastutavo, hak yaw qa paahut aqlap piw naatsoptangwu. Hakiy yaw pantiqw yaw pam maana Paalölöqangwuy engem nö'yiltingwu.

Tiikuywuuti

Pay Tiikuywuuti pi pam himu hin'ur himuningwu. Pam hapi tilawkyangw mokqe paapiy pay pam tiikuywuutiningwu. Pam ti'at qa yamakqe ang kuytaqw pam put aw Tiikuywuuti. Pay naap haqam pam ki'ytangwu. Pay yaw pam tuutuvosiptuy yu'am.

Pay yaw pam piw himu pas wuuti, niikyangw tuviku'yta. Pam yaw pas lomawuuti aasonva. Pay yaw oovi pam piw it Qötsamanat, katsinat, an hiita ngöna'ytangwu. Pu' qöötsat pukuwtangwu. Put naami hiita ööqat poshötsit puhikni'ytangwu. Pu' poosiyat atsve tsokokotangwu, suuvu'ytangwu. Pu' söhöt naasomtangwu. Pu' angqw naasomiyat angqw söhöt paapu'at haayiwyungngwu.

Noq himuwa qa maakyanen pay pan put naawaknangwu, pam Tiikuywuuti tsopniqatnen pu' maqsohoptingwu. Noq pay hiitawat aw pam pituqw himuwa qa taqa'nangwanen pay mashuruutingwu. Noq pu' pay hiitawat tsopngwu. Nen pay mashuruute' qa navot

Spring

Ages ago, when the Hopi were still on their migratory route, it was customary for them to take a water vessel along. Each time they intended to settle at a site, they buried the vessel in the ground, whereupon a spring emerged, affording them a source of water supply. When they finally arrived at Hopi country, they established settlements at places situated close by springs. As soon as they became familiar with the springs in the area, they gave them names. Thus, the discoverer of a newly emerged spring would name it according to his clan totem.

Some springs are inhabited by kachinas, so the Hopi go to these sites to deposit prayer feathers to ask for rain. Obviously, water is most precious to the Hopi. For this reason they conduct communal spring-cleaning parties which take place every year.

The elders also remind children that Paalölöqangw, the Water Serpent, inhabits every spring and that one should therefore not play around these locations. The Serpent is said to make his appearance there exactly at noon. When someone wants to drink from a spring, he should not do so by bending over it. Instead, one should ladle the water out. If a ladle is lacking, the cupped hands should be used to take a drink. A third taboo relating to pools of water forbids sexual intercourse in or near the water. A consequence of breaking it is that the girl will be impregnated by the Serpent.

Tiikuywuuti (deity)

Tiikuywuuti is a being with greater than human powers. She died giving birth when her child did not come out. Hence her name "child-sticking-out woman." She makes her home just about anywhere and is the mother of all the game animals.

Tiikuywuuti is a female deity endowed with a mask. Underneath this mask is a beautiful woman. She is said to resemble the Qötsamana. Just like this kachina she wears a ruff and her face is daubed white. Attached to the face are flat bones featuring eyeholes. Above her eyes are a number of dots which represent the brows. Tied to both sides of her head [in *naasomi* hair style] is galleta grass. From the *naasomi* hang the pods of the grass.

A Hopi who is not a good hunter prays that Tiikuywuuti may have intercourse with him so that he can become a good hunter. Whenever the goddess comes to someone and he is not brave, he freezes with fright. As he is petrified with fear, he is not aware of her

ngwu hintsanqw, tsopqw. Pu' pay yan unangwte' pu' kukhepngwu.
Pay yaw sowitsa kukyat ephaqam tuwangwu. Noq pay pam pan
kuuku'ytangwu, i' himu Tiikuywuuti. Tuwapongtumasi as pi piw
suukya pan natngwani'yta, niikyangw pay yaw piw pam pami',
Tiikuywuuti.

Tiiponi

Pay i' soosoy wiiwimi kur hin qa tiiponi'ytangwu, pay kya pi piw
pas himuniqw oovi. Pam pi pay it kwaahut homasayat angqw homasa'ykyangw pu' piw pay soosok hiituy tsirootuy piw angqw enang
homasayamuy angqw yukiwta. Pepeq atkyaveq pösöptonit akw ang
toonaniwyungwa. Pu' aasonveq soosok hiita tuusaqat poosiyat enang
pam mookiwta. Pam pumuy amungem tunösmaskya'iwta. Hak put
himu'ytaqa put yu'ytangwu. Nen pangqawngwu, "I' ingu." Pu' pay
pam haqam put mongwit put tiiponit himu'ytaqat kiiyat ep qatsngwu. Pay pam pongyat ep qatsqw pay wiiwimkyam hoomat akw
tiiponit aw naanawaknangwu.

Toosi

Hak toositninik hak tuupevut huume' pu' hak put ngumangwu.
Pu' piingye' pu' pay tsaatsayat pu' pay intangwu. Pu' pay put pantaqat angqw tuumoytangwu, maptaklawngwu.

Kopitsoki

I' kopitsoki pam pay i' laapu paas sisngiwtaqa pu' pay sen koho
kop'iwtangwu. Niiqe oovi pan paniqw pam maatsiwngwu, kopitsoki.
Noq pu' put hak uwiknanik hak put it pilakinpit akw hiita pösövit-
'ewakw taqtsoknat paasat pu' hak put angqw paalatangwu. Noq pu'
hisat naat qa kohotövu'yyungngwuniqw hiitawat qööhi'at tokqw pu'
pam it kopitsokit akw pangso hakiy kiiyat aw kookoste' pu' paasat
put kopitsokit pangso yawme' pu' pam paasat pep neengem put
qööhiyat angqw kookostangwu.

Totolospi

I' piw himu totolospi pam piw hisattsatsakwmuy nanavö'pi'am
pan maatsiwngwu. Hakim haqam pay hiita tusyavut, wunavutsit
tutwe' pu' tövumsit akw ang peenayangwu. Pu' qalavaqe pay hihin
puutsit akw peenayangwu. Paasat pu' angqe qalavaqe pu' pam pi
uutsiwtangwuniqw pang pu' hakim tuutuwuutotangwu. Tsivotsikik
hak tuutuwuutat pu' hak ep yan pongoknangwu. Pu' aapiy piw

coupling with him. Upon coming to again, the man looks for tracks. Occasionally he will find some, but only the tracks of a jackrabbit. Those are the tracks Tiikuywuuti leaves behind. Tuwapongtumasi, "sand altar clan's woman," is another name for the goddess.

Tiiponi (ceremonial object)

All religious societies must possess a *tiiponi*, which is a very important item. It is made from eagle feathers and the feathers of all the other birds. At its base the resulting feather bundle is wrapped with cotton string. Inside the wrapping are also the seeds of all types of grasses, which are set aside as food for the birds. The owner of a *tiiponi* regards it as a mother. In addressing it he says, "My mother." It is stored in the house of the religious leader who owns it. When it is placed on the altar, the initiates of a given society pray to it with sacred cornmeal.

Toosi (dish)

Whoever wants some *toosi*, or "ground, roasted sweet corn," shells some sweet corn that was baked in an earth oven and then grinds it. After fine-grinding the latter, it is sifted and heaped on a tray. In this form it is eaten by taking pinches from it.

Torch

A torch consists either of finely shredded cedar bark, or of other sticks which are bound together. Hence its Hopi name *kopitsoki*, literally "dry sticks bundled together." To light a torch one uses a flint on a material such as cotton. Once the cotton is ignited, one can take the light from it. In the days when matches were not yet available to the Hopi, and when someone's fire went out, one simply took a torch to somebody else's house and used it to borrow fire there.

Totolospi (game)

Totolospi is a game that the children of long ago used to play. One must first find some sort of rock slab or a wooden board, which is then marked with charcoal. Along the border of the gaming board a not too narrow band is drawn. On this band, which closes in the gaming board, lines are marked. First five lines, then a number of little circles. This intermittent design band leads to an opening from

tsivotsikik tuutuwuutat pep pu' hak piw pongoknangwu. Pan pam angqe aqwhaqami panmakyangw pu' pam aqw hötsiwa'ytangwu. Pangqw pu' pam aasonmiqwat aqw pu' lölöqangwuy an pam pe'ykyangw suru'ytangwu. Suruyat pu' ang hak piw aqwhaqami tsivotsikik tuuwuut pep pu' paasat hak piw pongoknangwu. Pam pang pö'atningwu.

Paasat pu' hak hiita pooko'ytaniqey put hepngwu. Pay hak oovi piw naap hiita pooko'ytangwu. Ephaqam pay owawyat, sen pay sööngöt motsiwngwayat. Pay naap hiita pan'ewakw. Paasat pu' hak paaqavit sunasavaqe kwanaknaqw pantaqat akw nanavö'yangwu. Pu' pam paaqavi piw aakwayngyavaqe pay naap hin pe'ytangwu, ephaqam put ang hotsikve'ytangwu.

Pu' hakim piw paayom, naalöyöm nasungwtotangwu. Noq hakim sunasangaqw yaynayangwu. Pangso hak hiita pookoy akwniqey tavingwu. Paasat pu' hak put paaqavit yan matsvongtangwu. Matsvongtat paasat pu' hak oomiq put iitat pu' put maatapqw pu' pam aw aasonmi hinwat yeevangwu. Hak pantiqw pu' puma naama oomiq hötsitniqw pam tsivot hiikya'ytangwu. Pu' naama paaqavit kuutsiltiqw pam pakwt hiikya'ytangwu. Mit pi totolospit ang pe'ytaqat ang pam tsivotsikik tuuwuhiwyungqw paasat oovi put ang hak hoytangwu. Hakiy paaqavi'at oomiq lööyöm hötsitniqw hak tsivotsikis hoyokngwu. Pu' naama kuutsiltiqw paasat yaw pam tsomakngwu. Paasat hak pakwt ang hoyokngwu. Pu' hak pan hoytimakyangw pu' ason hakiy paaqavi'at suukya kuutsiltiqw pu' suukya oomiq hötsiniqw paasat pu' pay hak pö'yngwu. Pay paasat qe'tiqw pu' hakiy angk mi'wa paaqawni'ytaqa paasat pu' tuwatningwu. Pu' hak sunasangaqw yamakye' paasat pu' pay hak naap haqamiwat wariknangwu, pookoy, putvoq sen suyvoqwat. Pay hak naap haqe'watningwu. Pu' hakim panmakyangw suukya hakiy wiikye', pokyat su'atsmi hoyokye', paasat pu' pam hakiy qeninawkye', pu' pam pay hakiy ahoy piw pas sunasamiq tuuvangwu, suruyat aqw. Paasat pu' hak pas piw pangqw ahoy hoytangwu. Pu' qa haqam hintiqa angqe poniwmakyangw ahoy sunasamiq pakye' pam hakimuy pö'angwu. Pay yanhaqam hakim totolosyangwu.

Kwitavit

Ima Hopiit pay imuy hiituy kwitavituy ayangqaqw yu'a'atotangwu. Puma pay it hiita tuuwutsit pay pas son ep qa nuutumyangwu. Noq himuwa haqam hiita nukngwat hintiqw puma pay put qa hisat ep tsutsuyyaqe oovi puma tuwat pay put lolmat hintsakqat pas

which it moves inward somewhat like the tail of a snake. This tail, too, is marked with segments of five lines and circles all the way to its tip. This band is the path on which the gaming pieces are moved.

Next, one searches for something to be used as gaming pieces. Anything can serve this purpose. Sometimes it is a little pebble or the tip of a corncob. Just anything of this sort will do. Finally, one splits a reed down the middle. The two halves, which serve as dice, may be painted on their back, sometimes with a zigzag design.

To actually play, as a rule three or four people band together. The starting point is in the very center. That's where the gaming pieces are placed. Then one grabs the reeds in such a way that they stick up. When released, they usually fall sort of inward. If both reed halves come to rest with their open side up, it counts five points. When the split reeds land upside down, the throw is worth ten points. Since there are groups of five lines and circles marked on the *totolospi* board, one advances in multiples of five. With both reeds showing the flat, open side, one moves five times. With both the curved sides up, one gets ten points and can advance ten places. However, should one split reed land upside down and the other with the flat side up, one loses one's throw. The player must now quit and the one next in line has his turn. As one leaves the center area of the gaming board, one can move one's gaming piece either to the right or left. Any route is fine. However, if one player catches up with someone else's gaming piece and lands right on top of him, he robs him of his place and sends him all the way back to the starting line at the center, the tip of the snake's tail. Now one has to begin all over. The player who first succeeds in entering back into the center without any problems beats the others. This is how *totolospi* is played.

Turds (derogatory label for sorcerers)

Since the beginning of time the Hopi have been speaking of certain people as "turds" or "feces." They represent sorcerers and witches and are almost a necessary force in a narrative. Sorcerers frown upon benevolent people and, for this reason, conjure up schemes to harm or destroy them. They particularly dislike a man who marries an exceptionally beautiful girl in their village. They then plot how to take his wife away from him. Eventually, however, the man harmed by them overcomes his evil opponents with the help of a more powerful being. Nevertheless, these turds are said to be very

sonqa hinwat haqami hintsatsnaniqey pansa engem pavasiwyangwu. Pu' piw himuwa ephaqam pumuy kitsokiyamuy ep pas hakiy lolmat, nukngwat nöömataqw puma qa naaniye' pay puma piw paasat put hin nömanawkiyaniqey engem yukuyangwu. Niikyangw pay himuwa hin hinmakyangw ephaqam pas pavanniiqat pa'angwniyat akw pay pumuy sonqa pö'angwu. Noq pay yaw puma piw hiitu a'niya. Puma yaw a'ni hiita tuwi'yyungwa.

Tuutsiitsiklawqa

Tuutsiitsiklawqa pi pay piw i' himu suukya wawarkatsina. Pam pay nuutum wawarvite' pu' hiitawat amum warikye', wiikye', pu' ngu'e' napnayat tsiikyangwu. Paniqw oovi pam Tuutsiitsiklawqa.

Tuutukwi

Tuutukwi pi pay Orayviy tatkyahaq pam i' naanaqle' tuukwi. Piw yangsavaniiqe oovi paniqw pan Tuutukwi.

Kwayngyavomoki

It tuuwutsit ang himuwa haqaminen sen himu pay nukpana-'eway haqami hiitawat wikqw i' Kookyangwso'wuuti pay put paas navoti'ytangwuniiqe oovi pam put hakiy aw naamaataknaninik pam piw put hin kwayngyavoniqat unangwtoynangwu. Noq pu' oovi pam hak kwayngyavomokye' pu' pam put wikqat angqw ayo'nen pu' pep haqam kwayngyaptaniniqw paasat pu' pam Kookyangwso'-wuuti put aw mooti hingqawngwu. Niiqe pam pay oovi sutsep hakiy aw pangqawu, "Itse, hak yaavonitningwu." Paasat pu' pam put aw tutaptangwu ason pam kwayngyaptat pu' put kiiyat aqw pakiniqat. Yan pam put aa'awnangwu. Noq hintiqw pi oovi pam hiitawat aw yansa naamaataknangwu.

Poksö

I' hisatki pay pas sutsep haqaqw poksö'ytangwu. Noq hisat pi pay Hopiki qa panaptsa'ytangwuniqw oovi pam kiiki panyungngwu. Pu' taala' utuhu'niqw pangqw i' kosngwaw papkiqw pep kiihut aasonve qa pas utuhu'tingwu. Noq pu' haqam himuwa ngumantaqw pep piw pay pas hisat sonqa poksö'ytangwuniqw pangqw i' tiyo mantuway aw yu'a'ataqw pam pep ngumantangwu.

potent themselves, for they have at their disposal a multitude of ways and means of doing things.

Tuutsiitsiklawqa (kachina)

Tuutsiitsiklawqa is one of the many Runner kachinas in the Hopi kachina pantheon. Whenever he comes to race, competes with someone and catches up with him, he grabs the loser and tears his shirt. This is the reason for his name, "one who keeps tearing the clothes of others."

Tuutukwi (place name)

The place name Tuutukwi refers to the area of free-standing volcanic plugs somewhere southeast of Oraibi. They are quite tall, hence the name Tuutukwi, "Buttes."

Urge to Defecate

Often in a story, when the hero or heroine is either on the way to an unfamiliar destination or is being taken somewhere by an evil being, Old Spider Woman knows about it. If she then intends to show herself to them, she will in some magical way cause in them the urge to defecate. As soon as the urge is felt, the male or female protagonist will step aside, and before they can empty their bowels, Old Spider Woman will speak to them. She typically begins by saying, "Phew! Can't you move farther away and then defecate?" Next she instructs them to enter her abode after they have finished with their business. The reason that Old Spider Woman employs this method to reveal herself to a mortal only at a time like this may be that at that moment one is all alone.

Vent Hole

The ancient dwellings were never without vent holes. Because the Hopi did not have windows in those days, vent holes were there for the same purpose. In summer, when the weather was hot, it was through this opening that a cool breeze entered the house. Then it was not so hot in the interior. The room where a person ground corn was always equipped with this opening. Through it a suitor talked to his girlfriend while courting her.

Kitsoki

I' Hopi haqam kitsokte' pam pay pas pepsa qatungwu. Ason pay pam pas hiita qa antaqat aw pite' pu' pam pangqw kitsokiy angqw haqamiwat qatsiheve' pu' pam piw supwat kitsoktangwu. Niiqe oovi pam qa imuy peetuy himusinmuy amun angqe' nanaalaktinumngwu. Pu' pam piw it owatnit pu' tsöqatsa angqw kiitangwu, niikyangw pay i'sa kii'ami'atsa pay lestavitnit himutskitnit pu' tsöqat akw kii'amiwta. Noq pu' pam haqam kitsokte' pam piw it kiisonvit pas sonqa enangningwu. Noq put kiisonviy akwningyaqw ima honngyam, kiikyam pas sonqa ki'yyungngwu. Pu' aapiy pay naap himuwa haqam kiitaniqey pan wuuwe' pu' pep kiitangwu. Niikyangw pep kitsokive piw qa suukya kiletsiningwu. Pu' Hopi piw qa suup natsve ki'ytangwu. Haqamwat pam hiita qaa'öy pu' hiita natwaniy oyi'ytaniqey put engem piw paas kiitangwu. Pu' Hopiki piw oovi tumtsokki'ykyangw pu' piw yeyespi'ytangwu.

Kikmongwi

I' hisatkikmongwi imuy honngyamuy angqwningwu. Pam yaw pay haqam kitsokive soosokmuy na'amningwu. Pu' pam oovi hisat piw susmooti taytangwu, pu' pam piw nuutungk tuwat puwtongwu. Pu' pam pay qa hisat pas hakiy hiita pas nu'an ayalawu. Pam qa naamisa wuuwankyangw hiita hintsakngwu. Pam imuy timuy amungem nukngwatiniqat put wuuwankyangw hiita hintingwu. Pu' pam oovi piw qa naala hiita aw yukungwu. Pam naat piw imuy mongsungwmuy amumi maqaptsitikyangw hiita aw antsani'ymangwu. Noq oovi it Pahaanat mongwi'atniqw pu' Hopit mongwi'at puma qa sunta.

Walpi

Walpi pay pas hisatkitsoki. Pay puma Walpit son oovi qa imuy Orayvituy pu' piw imuy Songoopavituy amuusaqhaqam pepeq tuwat yesvakyangw haqaqw pi puma tuwat pangsoq öki. Noq pay puma piw imuy Songoopavituy amun as atkya yesngwuniqw pu' pay i' himu tuwqa pas peqw Hopiikimiq kikiipoklawqw pu' pay puma haqam kitsoktotaqey put aa'omi yayvaqe pu' pepwat pay ngas'ewya. Noq pu' Walpiy angqw hoopowat puma peetu naakwiipayat pu' pep piw it sukwat kitsoktotaqw pamwa pep Sitsom'ovi yan natngwani'yta. Pu' pepeq sushopaq it waala'ytaqat aatavang piw ima Hopaqkingaqwyaqam piw hisat peqw ökiiqe pu' pepeq yesva. Pay pam navoti qa sunta. Noq pepeq put kitsokit i' Hopi Hanoki yan tuwi'yta.

Village

Whenever the Hopi established a village, they settled there with the intention of staying permanently. As soon as some sort of disaster struck the community, however, they usually moved on in search of a place with better living conditions where they could found another village. Unlike some other Indian groups, the Hopi, therefore, were not nomads. Homes were built using only stone and mortar, except for the roof, which was constructed from log beams covered with brush and mud. Wherever a village was erected, a village center or plaza had to be part of it. In general, the northwestern end of the plaza was occupied by members of the Bear clan who constituted the Hopi elite. The three remaining sides of the plaza were open for anyone who wished to build there. Within the village were several rows of houses which were often multi-storied. They consisted of rooms especially built to store corn and other crops, a chamber where piki was made, and of course an area which served as living quarters.

Village Leader

The *kikmongwi*, or "village leader," of old came from the Bear clan. In a given village he is supposed to be the father to all. Therefore, in the olden days, he was the first to rise in the morning and the last to retire at night. The *kikmongwi* never gives orders. He does not think of himself only when he does things. On the contrary, his only concern is that as an end result his children will benefit. Therefore, he is not alone when he takes on a task. He seeks advice from his fellow leaders as he works on it. Obviously, a white man's "chief" and the *mongwi* of the Hopi are not synonymous.

Walpi (First Mesa village)

Walpi is an old village. The people of Walpi may have settled at this location approximately during the same period as the people of Oraibi and Shungopavi, but one cannot say for certain where they came from. Just as the Shungopavi residents, they used to live below the mesa. But due to the constant raids of enemy groups they moved to a site above the original settlement where they were better off. In time, some relocated at a place northeast of Walpi and founded another village which is known as Sichomovi. Finally, people from a Rio Grande pueblo arrived and settled at the northeasternmost end of the mesa, just southwest of the Gap. That village is referred to as Hanoki by the Hopi.

Oova

I' oova lööpwatningwuniqw i' suukyawa pay qa mitwat aasaqaningwu. Noq i' oova it mö'wit engem yuykiwa. Noq pam tuwat yaw putakw haqami maskimiqningwu. Niiqe pam oovi it wuutit hahawpi'atningwu. Noq pam oovi as put qa huyangwu. Pu' himuwa hisat put qa huye' pam pay ephaqam put angqw it tukput yukungwu. Pu' pay puma piw put atsvewlalwangwu. Pu' yaw piw hak put as qa peenangwu. Hak yaw put pantiqw pam yaw a'ni pituute' hakiy Öngtupqamiq qa hawnangwu hak Maskimiq hoytaqw.

Pu' pam yaw piw i' paatsayanpiningwu. Putakw yaw ima oo-'omawt paalay tsaayantotangwu. Noq hak yaw mookye', hak yaw oomawniikyangw pan sinmuy ahoy popte', putakw yaw hak put yooyangwuy tsaayantangwu. Pam it yooyangwuy tsaatsayaqw pam qa lemowa yokvangwu, pam i' suvuyoyangw paasat yokvangwu. It lemowat pay Hopi qa naawakna, ispi pam hakiy uuyiyat aw yokve' pam put nukushintsanngwu. Pu' pam it meloonit, kawayvatngat piw soq poromnangwu.

Noq pu' pam oova haqamwat pösöveq nanalsikip paalangput tonit akw angqe tuu'ihiwtangwu. Pam yaw put maanat ungwayat tu'awi'ytangwu. Noq pu' pepeq i' qaa'ö put aw wiwtangwu. I' pay qaa'ö qa pas i' tuu'oyit angningwuqa, pam pay it hiita nana'löngöt tonit angqw yukiwtangwu. Niikyangw pay pi antsa qaa'öt an soniwngwu.

Qötsaqaasi

Hopitaqatniqw i' wuutiniqw pu' piw maana tuwat qötsaqaasi'yte' nukngwaningwu. Noq oovi taataqt, tootim sen hiitawat aw pan navoti'yyungwe' put pan yu'a'atotangwu. Niikyangw pu' pay piw it qötsatotko'ytaqat, sikyavut, i' Hopitaqa tuwat pas naayongni'ytangwu.

Wukoqalvoliit

Wukoqalvoliit pi pay ima hiitu Poliit ngasta pöngi'yyungqam pay susmataq qala'yyungwa. Paniqw oovi puma Wukoqalvoliit. Meh, peetu pi suuvaqw tonsihu'yyungwa, pu' sutsvoq aala'yyungwa. Pu' supwat piw nan'ivaqw koyongtsitoma'yyungwa. Pay piw mimuywatuy su'amun wukoqala'yyungwa. Pu' peetu piw yungyapnasomyungwa.

Wedding Robe

The *oova*, or "wedding robe," comes in two sizes, one being quite a bit larger than the other. The large one is woven for the bride so that she can journey to Maski, the "Home of the Dead." As the robe constituted a married woman's vehicle to make her descent to the underworld, she was not supposed to sell it. In previous times when the oova was never sold, the woman would sometimes fashion a sack from it. People also used the garment as a sitting mat. It was also not supposed to be decorated. Embroidery would have added weight to it, and not permitted the dead woman to ride it down the Grand Canyon on her way to the underworld.

The bridal robe is further said to function as a water sieve. With its help the clouds sift their moisture to produce the very fine rain. In Hopi belief, upon one's demise a mortal is transformed into a cloud personage, and whenever a woman checks on the people she left behind, she employs the *oova* as a sieve. By using the *oova* to sift the rains, a fine drizzle is produced instead of hail. Hail is dreaded by the Hopi because it ruins the corn crops and smashes holes into musk melons and watermelons.

One of the corners of the wedding robe is embroidered with sixteen stitches of red yarn. They symbolize a young woman's menstruation. Also attached at this corner is a corncob. This corncob is not a real cob but is made from varicolored yarn. However, it closely resembles a corncob.

White Thigh

A woman or girl possessing light-complexioned thighs is sexually most desirable to the Hopi male. When men or boys know of a female with this asset, they spread the word. By the same token, men are attracted to a female who is, overall, lighter skinned than average. The term for a woman like that is *sikyavu* which, literally translated, means "yellow person."

Wukoqal Butterfly Dancers

Wukoqalvoliit, literally, "big forehead butterfly dancers," are Butterfly dancers whose foreheads are clearly visible because they are not covered with hair bangs. That's how they got their name. Some of them have a flower made of yarn attached on one side of their head and a horn on the other. Another type is distinguished by bundles of turkey feathers worn at the side of the head. A third group, finally, sports wicker plaques tied to both sides of the hair.

Wupatki

Nuvatukya'oviy hopqöyve pi pam kiiqö Wupatki yan maatsiwa. Pay pi pangqaqwangwuniqw pay pi yaw Hopiit as pep hisathaqam yesngwu.

Wuwtsimtotokya

Wuwtsimt pi pay suukop aqw tokiltotangwu. Put sunasamiq pituqw pu' pay mongwi pakingwu, Wuwtsimmongwi. Pu' pay put su'aasaq pakiniqa pay pakingwu. Pu' puma pay pep kivanawit noonovakyaakyangw pu' aqw tiikivey angk hoyoyotangwu. Pu' nalöstalqw pu' paapiy pu' puma put pas oyiwisngwu. Suus piw nalöstala: suus qa himu, piktotokya, totokya, tiikive. Totokpe mihikqw qa tokngwu, tookyep tiilalwangwu. Noq qavongvaqw pu' tiikive'yyungwa.

Sikyaatayo

Hopiit sikyaatayot maqwisngwu. Puma pumuy pi puukyayamuy oovi pumuy mamaqangwu. Pu' pay put puukyayat hootaknaye' pu' pantaqat laknayaqw pu' put katsinam haayungngwu. Pu' himuwa piw katsina pay put ngöna'ytangwu. Noq Hopiituyniqw taawa kiiy epeq put sikyaataypukyat saaqat ooveq söngnangwu. Paasat pu' sikyangwnuptungwu.

Wupatki (place name)

On the northeastern side of Nuvatukya'ovi, the "San Francisco Mountains," lies a ruin named Wupatki. People say that long ago Hopis used to live there.

Wuwtsim Eve

The members of the Wuwtsim society plan their ceremony for a duration of sixteen days. At mid-point the Wuwtsim leader enters the kiva, and whoever else wants to go in with him, does so. They then live, eat and sleep in the kivas in pursuit of the day on which the public dance takes place. From day four on, the men keep track of the days by marking each day off with a line. There is now one more set of four days. The first is termed *suus qa himu*, "once nothing," the second *piktotokya*, "piki eve," the third *totokya*, "eve," and the last one *tiikive*, "dance day." On *totokya*, or "eve," at night the society members are not allowed to sleep. Instead, they keep dancing all through the night. The following day they stage their public performance.

Yellow Fox

The Hopis make it a habit to hunt the yellow fox. They stalk the animal for its pelt. After stretching the hide out on the ground, they let it dry. The kachinas then wear the pelt dangling from the rear waist. Some kachinas also employ it as a ruff. According to Hopi mythology Taawa, the Sun god, places the yellow fox skin on a ladder pole at his house. At that time it gets to be yellow dawn.

Appendix II: The Hopi Alphabet

Hopi, an American Indian language spoken in northeastern Arizona, is a branch of the large Uto-Aztecan family of languages, that covers vast portions of the western United States and Mexico. It is related to such languages as Papago, Paiute, Shoshone, Tarahumara, Yaqui, and Nahuatl, the language of the Aztecs, to mention only a few. Navajo, Apache, Havasupai, Zuni, Tewa, and many other languages in the American Southwest are completely unrelated to it, however. At least three regional Hopi dialects, whose differences in terms of pronunciation, grammar, and vocabulary are relatively minimal, can be distinguished. No prestige dialect exists.

While traditionally the Hopi, like most American Indian groups, never developed a writing system of their own, there today exists a standardized—yet unofficial—orthography for the Hopi language. Ronald W. Langacker has presented a "simple and linguistically sound writing system" (Milo Kalectaca, *Lessons in Hopi*, edited by Ronald W. Langacker, Tucson, 1978) for the Second Mesa dialect of Shungopavi (Songoopavi). My own generalized Hopi orthography is equally phonemic in nature and is based on the dialect habits of speakers from the Third Mesa communities of Hotevilla (Hotvela), Bacavi (Paaqavi), Oraibi (Orayvi), Kykotsmovi (Kiqötsmovi), and Moencopi (Munqapi), who comprise the majority of Hopis. Speakers from the First Mesa villages of Walpi and Sichomovi (Sitsom'ovi) as well as from the communities of Shungopavi (Songoopavi), Mishongnovi (Musangnuvi), and Shipaulovi (Supawlavi) simply need to impose their idiosyncratic pronunciation on the written "image" of the preponderant dialect, much as a member of the Brooklyn speech community applies his brand of pronunciation to such words as "bird" or "work."

Hopi standardized orthography is thus truly pan-Hopi; it is characterized by a close fit between phonemically functional sound and corresponding symbol. Unusual graphemes are avoided. For example, the digraph *ng* stands for the same phoneme that *ng* represents in English si*ng*. Symbols like *ñ*, as the translator of the New Testament into Hopi elected to do, or ŋ which is suggested in the symbol inventory of the International Phonetic Alphabet, are not employed. In all, twenty-one letters are sufficient to write Hopi, of which only the umlauted *ö* is not part of the English alphabet. For the glottal stop, one of the Hopi consonants, the apostrophe is used.

Hopi distinguishes the six vowels *a, e, i, o, ö,* and *u,* the last of which represents the international phonetic symbol *i*. Their long counterparts are written by doubling the letter for the corresponding short vowel: *aa, ee, ii, oo, öö,* and *uu.* The short vowels are found in combination with both the *y*- and *w*-glide to form the following diphthongs: *ay, ey, iy, oy, öy, uy,* and *aw, ew, iw, öw, uw.* Only the diphthong *ow* does not occur. The inventory of consonants contains a number of sounds which have to be represented as digraphs or trigraphs (two- or three-letter combinations): *p, t, ky, k, kw, q, qw, ', 'y, m, n, ngy, ng, ngw, ts, v, r, s,* and *l.* The two semi-vowels are the glides *w* and *y.* Notably absent are the sounds *b, d,* and *g,* to mention only one prominent difference between the Hopi and English sound inventories. Because Hopi *p, t,* and *k* are pronounced without aspiration, speakers of English tend to hear them as *b, d,* and *g.* This accounts for many wrong spellings of Hopi words in the past.

The following table lists all the functional Hopi sounds, with the exception of those characterized by a falling tone—a phonetic feature not shared by First and Second Mesa speakers. Each phoneme is illustrated by a Hopi example and accompanied by phonetic approximations drawn from various Indo-European languages.

Phoneme	Sample Word	Sound Approximations English (E), French (F) German (G), Russian (R)			

1. Vowels:

(a) short vowels

a	p*a*s	very	E	c*u*t	F	p*a*tte
e	p*e*p	there	E	m*e*t	F	h*e*rbe
i	s*i*hu	flower	E	h*i*t	G	m*i*t
o	m*o*mi	forward	F	c*o*l	G	s*o*ll
ö	q*ö*tö	head	F	n*eu*f	G	L*ö*ffel
u	t*u*wa	he found it	R б*ы*ть		E	j*u*st (when unstressed)

(b) long vowels

aa	p*aa*s	carefully	F	p*â*te	G	St*aa*t
ee	p*ee*p	almost	F	*ê*tre	G	M*äh*ne
ii	s*ii*hu	intestines	F	r*i*re	G	w*ie*
oo	m*oo*mi	he is pigeon-toed	F	r*o*se	G	B*oo*t
öö	q*öö*tö	suds	F	f*eu*	G	T*ö*ne
uu	t*uu*wa	sand	G	B*ü*hne (but lips spread without producing an [i] sound)		

2. Diphthongs:

(a) with y-glide

ay	ts*ay*	small/young	E	fl*y*	G	Kl*ei*der
ey	*ey*kita	he groans	E	m*ay*		
iy	yaap*iy*	from here on	E	fl*ea*		
oy	ah*oy*	back to	E	t*oy*	G	h*eu*te
öy	h*öy*kita	he growls	F	*oei*l		
uy	*uy*to	he goes planting	G	pf*ui* (but with lips spread instead of rounded)		

(b) with w-glide

aw	*aw*ta	bow	E	f*ow*l	G M*au*s	
ew	p*ew*	here (to me)	E	m*e*t + E *w*et		
iw	p*iw*	again	E	h*i*t + E *w*et		
ow		nonexisting				
öw	ngöl*öw*ta	it is crooked	G L*ö*ffel + E *w*et			
uw	p*uw*moki	he got sleepy	R б*ы*ть + E *w*et			

3. Consonants:

(a) stops

p	paahu	water/spring	F	pain
t	tupko	younger brother	F	table
ky	kyaaro	parrot	E	cure
k	koho	wood/stick	F	car
kw	kwala	it boiled	E	quit
q	qööha	he built a fire	G	Kraut (but k articulated further back in mouth)
qw	yangqw	from here	E	wet, added to pronunciation of q
'	pu'	now/today	G	Ver'ein
'y	ki'yta	he has a house		glottal stop followed by a very brief [i]-sound

(b) nasals

m	malatsi	finger	E	me
n	naama	both/together	E	nut
ngy	ngyam	clan members	E	king + E yes E singular (casually pronounced)
ng	ngöla	wheel	E	king G fangen
ngw	kookyangw spider		E	king + E wet E penguin (casually pronounced)

(c) affricate

ts	tsuku	point/clown	E	hits G Zunge

(d) fricatives

v	votoona	coin/button	E	veal G Winter
r	roya	it turned		syllable initial position: E leisure (with tongue tip curled toward palate)

r	hin'u*r*	very (female speaking)	syllable final position: E *sh*ip F *ch*arme
s	*s*akuna	squirrel	E *s*ong
h	*h*o'apu	carrying basket	E *h*elp

(e) lateral

| l | *l*aho | bucket | E *l*ot |

4. Glides:

(a) preceding a vowel

| w | *w*aala | gap/notch | E *w*et |
| y | *y*uutu | they ran | E *y*es |

(b) succeeding a vowel: see diphthongs

Bibliography

Bandelier, Adolph F.
  1892 "Final Report of Investigations among the Indians of the Southwestern United States, Carried on Mainly in the Years from 1880 to 1885." *Papers of the Archaeological Institute of America. American Series*, vol. 4 (part 2). Cambridge, England: University Press. Reprint New York: AMS Press, 1976.

Bascom, William R.
  1955 "Verbal Art." *Journal of American Folklore* 68:245-252.

Bartlett, Katharine
  1934 "Spanish Contact with the Hopi: 1540-1823." *Museum of Northern Arizona Notes* 6,12:55-60.

Beaglehole, Ernest and Pearl Beaglehole
  1935 "Hopi of the Second Mesa." *American Anthropological Association Memoirs* 44:1-65.

Bourke, John G.
  1884 *The Snake-Dance of the Moquis of Arizona*. Tucson: University of Arizona Press, 1984.

Brew, John Otis
  1941 "Preliminary Report of the Peabody Museum Awatovi Expedition of 1939." *Plateau* 13,3:37-48.

  1979 "Hopi Prehistory and History to 1850." In *Handbook of North American Indians*, vol. 9. *Southwest*, edited by Alfonso Ortiz, 514-523. Washington, D.C.: Smithsonian Institution.

Colton, Harold S.
  1959 *Hopi Kachina Dolls with a Key to their Identification*. Albuquerque: University of New Mexico Press.

Colton, Harold S. and Edmund Nequatewa
  1932 "The Ladder Dance. Two Traditions of an Extinct Hopi Ceremonial." *Museum of Northern Arizona Notes* 5,2:5-12.

Colton, Mary-Russel Farrell, Edmund Nequatewa, and Harold S.
Colton
  1933   "Hopi Legends of the Sunset Crater Region." *Museum of
         Northern Arizona Notes* 5,4:17-23.

Courlander, Harold
  1970   *People of the Short Blue Corn: Tales and Legends of the Hopi
         Indians*. New York: Harcourt Brace Jovanovich.

  1971   *The Fourth World of the Hopis*. Greenwich, Conn.: Fawcett
         Publications.

  1982   *Hopi Voices: Recollections, Traditions, and Narratives of the
         Hopi Indians*. Albuquerque: University of New Mexico
         Press.

Curtin, L.S.M.
  1971   "Spanish and Indian Witchcraft in New Mexico." *Master-
         key* 45,3:89-101.

Curtis, Edward S.
  1922   *The Hopi*. Vol. 12 of *The North American Indian*, reprint New
         York and London: Johnson Reprint Corporation, 1970.

Dittert, Alfred E., Jr. and Fred Plog
  1980   *Generations in Clay*. Flagstaff: Northland Press.

Ediger, Donald
  1971   *The Well of Sacrifice*. Garden City, New York: Doubleday
         and Company.

Eliade, Mircea
  1964   *Shamanism: Archaic Techniques of Ecstasy*, trans. Willard R.
         Trask. Bollingen Series LXXVI. Princeton: Princeton Uni-
         versity Press.

Farmer, Malcom F.
  1955   "The Identification of Ho-vi-itsi-tu-qua Pueblo." *Plateau*
         28,2:44-45.

Fewkes, Jesse W.
   1893   "A-wa'-to Bi: An Archeological Verification of a Tusayan
           Legend." *American Anthropologist* 6,4:363-375.

   1895   "Preliminary Account of an Expedition to the Cliff Villages
           of the Red Rock Country, and the Tusayan Ruins of
           Sikyatki and Awatobi, Arizona, in 1895." *Smithsonian
           Institution Annual Report*, 557-588.

   1896   "Preliminary Account of an Expedition to the Pueblo
           Ruins Near Winslow, Arizona, in 1896." *Smithsonian
           Institution Annual Report*, 517-540.

   1898   "Archaeological Expedition to Arizona in 1895." *Bureau of
           American Ethnology, 17th Annual Report for the Years 1895-
           1896*, Part 2:519-742. Washington, D.C.: Smithsonian
           Institution.

   1896   "The Prehistoric Culture of Tusayan." *American Anthro-
           pologist* 9,5:151-73.

   1903   "Hopi Katcinas, Drawn by Native Artists." *Bureau of
           American Ethnology, 21st Annual Report for the Years 1899-
           1901*, 3-126. Washington, D.C.: Smithsonian Institution.

Fewkes, Jesse W. and A.M. Stephen
   1893   "The Pá-lü-lü-kon-ti: A Tusayan Ceremony." *Journal of
           American Folklore* 6:269-284.

Geertz, Armin W. and Michael Lomatuway'ma
   1987   *Children of Cottonwood: Piety and Ceremonialism in Hopi
           Indian Puppetry*. American Tribal Religions, vol. 12, edited
           by Karl Luckert. Lincoln and London: University of
           Nebraska Press.

Gimbutas, Marija
   1989   *The Language of the Goddess*. San Francisco: Harper.

González Torres, Yolotl
1985   *El Sacrificio Humano Entre Los Mexicas*. México: Instituto
Nacional de Antropología e Historia. Fondo de Cultura
Económica.

Hammond, George P. and Agapito Rey
1929   *Expedition into New Mexico Made by Antonio de Espejo, 1582-
1583, as Revealed in the Journal of Diego Perez de Luxan, a
Member of the Party*. Los Angeles: The Quivira Society
Publications.

Hargrave, Lyndon L.
1930   "Shungopovi." *Museum of Northern Arizona Notes* 2,10:1-4.

1931   "First Mesa." *Museum of Northern Arizona Notes* 3,8:1-6.

1935   "The Jeddito Valley and the First Pueblo Towns in Arizona
to be Visited by Europeans." *Museum of Northern Arizona
Notes* 8,4:17-23.

1937   "Sikyatki: Were the Inhabitants Hopi?" *Museum of
Northern Arizona Notes* 9,12:61-66.

Hartmann, Horst
1975   "Alosaka und Muyingwa." *Baessler-Archiv* 23:293-346.

Haury, Emil W.
1986   "Tree Rings. The Archaeologist's Time-Piece." In *Emil W.
Haury's Prehistory of the Southwest*, edited by J. Jefferson
Reid and David E. Doyel, 61-72. Tucson: University of
Arizona Press.

Hodge, Frederick Webb
1910   *Handbook of American Indians North of Mexico*. Smithsonian
Institution, Bureau of American Ethnology, Bulletin 30. 2v.
First Greenwood Reprinting 1969. New York: Greenwood
Press.

Holterman, Jack
　1955　"Mission San Bartolomé de Xongopavi: One of Arizona's
　　　　Forgotten Missions." *Plateau* 28,2:29-36.

Hooper, Mildred and C.R.
　1975　"Awatobi: High Place of the Bow." *Outdoor Arizona* 47:18-
　　　　19.

James, George Wharton
　1901　"The Storming of Awatobi." *Chautauquan* 33,5:497-500.

　1917　*Arizona the Wonderland*. Boston: Page.

James, Harry C.
　1974　*Hopi History*. Tucson: University of Arizona Press.

Kabotie, Fred
　1982　*Designs from the Ancient Mimbreños with a Hopi Inter-
　　　　pretation by Fred Kabotie*. Flagstaff: Northland Press.

Langley, Dama Margaret (Mrs. White Mountain Smith)
　1939　"When the Hopi Deserted Their Ancient Gods." *Desert
　　　　Magazine* 3,1:16-18.

Leonard, Jonathan Norton
　1967　*Ancient America*. New York: Time.

Luckert, Karl
　1975　*The Navajo Hunter Tradition*. Tucson: University of Arizona
　　　　Press.

　1976　*Olmec Religion: A Key to Middle America and Beyond*.
　　　　Norman: University of Oklahoma Press.

Malotki, Ekkehart
　1983　*Hopi Time: A Linguistic Analysis of the Temporal Concepts in
　　　　the Hopi Language*. Trends in Linguistics. Studies and
　　　　Monographs, vol. 20. Edited by Werner Winter. Berlin,
　　　　New York, Amsterdam: Mouton Publishers.

1991 "Language as a Key to Cultural Understanding: New Interpretations of Central Hopi Concepts." *Baessler-Archiv,* Neue Folge 39:43-75.

Malotki, Ekkehart and Michael Lomatuway'ma
1987 *Earth Fire: A Hopi Legend of the Sunset Crater Eruption.* Flagstaff: Northland Press.

1987 *Maasaw: Profile of a Hopi God.* American Tribal Religions, vol. 11, edited by Karl Luckert. Lincoln and London: University of Nebraska Press.

Mindeleff, Cosmos
1891 "Traditional History of Tusayan." In "A Study of Pueblo Architecture: Tusayan and Cibola," edited by Victor Mindeleff. *Bureau of American Ethnology, 8th Annual Report for the Years 1886-87,* 16-41. Washington, D.C.: Smithsonian Institution.

Mindeleff, Victor
1891 "A Study of Pueblo Architecture: Tusayan and Cibola." *Bureau of American Ethnology, 8th Annual Report for the Years 1886-87,* 3-228. Washington, D.C.: Smithsonian Institution.

Montgomery, R.G., Watson Smith, and J.O.Brew
1949 "Franciscan Awatovi." *Papers of the Peabody Museum of American Archaeology and Ethnology 36,* Cambridge: Harvard University Press.

Nequatewa, Edmund
1936 *Truth of a Hopi: Stories Relating to Origin, Myths, and Clan Histories of the Hopi.* Edited by Mary-Russel F. Colton. Bulletin of the Museum of Northern Arizona 8. Second printing 1967.

1938 "The Destruction of Elden Pueblo: A Hopi Story." *Plateau* 28,2:37-44.

Parsons, Elsie Clews
    1926   *Tewa Tales*. New York: American Folk-Lore Society.

    1939   *Pueblo Indian Religion*. 2 vols. Chicago: University of
            Chicago Press.

Pilles, Peter
    1991   "Elden Pueblo: The Frustration of Following Fewkes."
            Paper read at 56th Annual Meeting of the Society for
            American Archaeology, 26 April 1991, at New Orleans,
            Louisiana. Mimeographed.

Rawson, Philip, ed.
    1973   *Primitive Erotic Art*. New York: G.P. Putnam's Sons.

Renaud, E.B.
    1938   "Petroglyphs of North Central New Mexico."
            Archaeological Survey Series, Eleventh Report. Denver:
            University of Denver, Department of Anthropology.

Ross, Anne
    1973   "Celtic and Northern Art." In *Primitive Erotic Art*, edited
            by Philip Rawson. New York: G.P. Putnam's Sons, 77-106.

Shannon, Elaine
    1983   "Lost Idols of Shungopavi." *Newsweek*, January 31:32-3.

Shorris, Earl
    1971   *The Death of the Great Spirit*. New York: Simon and
            Schuster.

Simmons, Marc
    1974   *Witchcraft in the Southwest*. Flagstaff: Northland Press.

Smith, Watson
    1952   "Kiva Mural Decorations at Awatovi and Kawaika-a."
            *Papers of the Peabody Museum of American Archaeology and
            Ethnology*, vol. 37. Cambridge: Harvard University Press.

Stephen, Alexander M.
    1894   "The Po-boc-tu among the Hopi." *American Antiquarian and Oriental Journal* 16,4:212-214.

    1929   "Hopi Tales." *Journal of American Folk-Lore* 42,163:1-75.

    1936   "Hopi Journal." Edited by Elsie Clews Parsons, 2 vols. *Columbia University Contributions to Anthropology* 23.

    1940   "Hopi Indians of Arizona-III." *Masterkey* 14:102-09.

Titiev, Mischa
    1942   "Notes on Hopi Witchcraft." *Papers of the Michigan Academy of Science, Arts and Letters* 28:549-557.

    1944   "Two Hopi Tales from Oraibi." *Papers of the Michigan Academy of Science, Arts, and Letters* 29:425-437.

    1948   "Two Hopi Myths and Rites." *Journal of American Folklore* 61:31-43.

    1956   "Shamans, Witches and Chiefs among the Hopi." *Tomorrow* 4,3:51-56.

Tozzer, Alfred M.
    1957   "Chichen Itzá and Its Cenote of Sacrifice: A Comparative Study of Contemporaneous Maya and Toltec." *Memoirs of the Peabody Museum of Archaeology and Ethnology* 11-12. Cambridge: Harvard University Press.

Turner, Christy G. and Nancy T. Morris
    1970   "A Massacre at Hopi." *American Antiquity* 35,3:320-331.

Tyler, Hamilton A.
    1964   *Pueblo Gods and Myths*. Norman: University of Oklahoma Press.

Underhill, Ruth. M. et al.
    1979   *Rainhouse and Ocean: Speeches for the Papago Year.* American
            Tribal Religions, vol. 4. Edited by Karl Luckert. Flagstaff:
            Museum of Northern Arizona Press.

Vecsey, Christopher
    1988   *Imagine Ourselves Richly: Mythic Narratives of North
            American Indians.* New York: Crossroad.

Voth, Henry R.
    1905   *The Traditions of the Hopi.* Field Columbian Museum 96,
            Anthropological Series 8.

Wallis, Wilson D.
    1936   "Folk Tales from Shumopovi, Second Mesa." *Journal of
            American Folk-Lore* 49,191-92:1-68.

Waters, Frank
    1963   *Book of the Hopi.* New York: Viking Press.

Whiting, Alfred F.
    1939   *Ethnobotany of the Hopi.* Bulletin of the Museum of
            Northern Arizona, 15. Flagstaff: Northland Press, 1966.

Willard, Theodore A.
    1926   *The City of the Sacred Well.* New York: Grosset and Dunlap.

Wilson, John P.
    1972   "Awatovi—More Light on a Legend." *Plateau* 44,3:125-130.

Yava, Albert
    1978   *Big Falling Snow: A Tewa-Hopi Indian's Life and Times and the
            History and Traditions of His People.* Edited and annotated
            by Harold Courlander. New York: Crown Publishers.

DATE DUE

DEC 10 1995	
DEC 06 2004	
DEC 11 2007	
MAY 01 2008	